Mani

University of Nebraska Press

Lincoln and London

Edited by Mary Ann Caws

festo

A Century of Isms

Publication of this volume was
assisted by The Virginia
Faulkner Fund, established in
memory of Virginia Faulkner,
editor-in-chief of the University
of Nebraska Press.

Library of Congress Cataloging-
in-Publication Data
Manifesto: a century of isms /
edited by Mary Ann Caws.
p. cm. Includes bibliographical
references. ISBN 0-8032-6407-0
(paperback: alkaline paper)
1. Civilization, Modern – 20th
century – Sources.
2. Intellectual life – History –
20th century – Sources. 3. Arts,
Modern – 20th century – Sources.
4. Social movements – History –
20th century – Sources.
5. Europe – Civilization – 20th
century – Sources.
6. America – Civilization – 20th
century – Sources.
I. Caws, Mary Ann.
CB427.M287 2001 909.82–dc21
00-033783

To proclaim a manifesto you have to want: A.B.C.,
thunder against 1,2,3, lose your patience and sharpen
your wings to conquer and spread a's, b's, c's little and big,
sign, scream, swear, arrange the prose in a form of absolute
and irrefutable evidence, prove your non-plus-ultra and
maintain that novelty resembles life just as the latest
appearance of a whore proves the essence of God. . . .

 °
° °

I am writing a manifesto and I don't want anything,
I say however certain things and I am on principle against
manifestoes, as I am also against principles. . . . I am writing
this manifesto to show that you can do contrary actions together,
in one single fresh breath; I am against action; for continual
contradiction, for affirmation also, I am neither for nor
against and I don't explain because I hate common sense.

Tristan Tzara, "Dada Manifesto," 1918

N.B.: Modernism is often in movement, between regions and thoughts. In the table of contents, if two regions are listed, it means either that the founder(s) moved, and thus that the movement moved with them, or that the movement has two similar manifestations. If the movements are separated by a slash (e.g., Nowism/Presentism/Simultaneism) it means they are simply different names for more or less the same phenomenon. If they are separated by commas (e.g., De Stijl, Plasticism, and Neoplasticism), such similar manifestations have been grouped together for convenience.

Contents

Part 3. Cubism

France

Part 4. Nowism/Presentism/Simultaneism

France

Germany

United States

Part 5. Futurisms

The Poetics of the Manifesto

Nowness and Newness

Knock hard. Life is deaf.
MIMI PARENT

POWER PLAY AND MANIPULATIONS

Originally a "manifesto" was a piece of evidence in a court of law, put on show to catch the eye, "A public declaration by a sovereign prince or state, or by an individual or body of individuals whose proceedings are of public importance, making known past actions and explaining the motives for actions announced as forthcoming." Since the "manus" (hand) was already present in the word, the presentation was a handcrafted marker for an important event.[1]

The manifesto was from the beginning, and has remained, a deliberate manipulation of the public view. Setting out the terms of the faith toward which the listening public is to be swayed, it is a document of an ideology, crafted to convince and convert. The stance taken may be institutional or individual and independent. The *Communist Manifesto* of Friedrich Engels and Karl Marx in 1848 is the original model, of immense influence and historical importance for later aesthetic proclamations and political statements.[2] Recently Steven Marcus has described its "transpersonal force and sweep" as marking "the accession of social and intellectual consciousness to a new stage of inclusiveness. It has become part of an integral modern sensibility. . . . It emerges ever more distinctly as an unsurpassed dramatic representation, diagnosis and prophetic array of visionary judgment on the modern world." It is "incandescent" action writing, says Marcus.[3] Yet even in lesser documents the actual efficacy of the political or theological manifesto depends on its power of declamation and persuasion. That of the artistic manifesto, whose work will be carried on in another world altogether—aesthetic battles having different consequences—depends on its context as well as its cleverness, and on the talents of its producer. In the aesthetic field the Italian showman Filippo Tommaso Marinetti wins the all-time Oscar for producing and presenting the ur-manifesto, that of Futurism in 1909.

At its most endearing, a manifesto has a madness about it. It is peculiar and angry, quirky, or downright crazed. Always opposed to something, particular or general, it has not only to be striking but to stand up straight. We stand "erect on the summit of the world," says "The Founding and Manifesto of Futurism" (5.5), deliberately macho-male.

The manifest proclamation itself marks a moment, whose trace it leaves as a post-event commemoration. Often the event is exactly its own announcement and nothing more, in this Modernist/Postmodernist genre. *What it announces is itself.* At its height, it is the deictic genre par excellence: LOOK! it says. NOW! HERE!

The manifesto is by nature a loud genre, unlike the essay.[4] What I would call the "high manifesto," on the model of "high Modernism," is often noisy in its appearance, like a typographical alarm or an implicit rebel yell. It calls for capital letters, loves bigness, demands attention. Rem Koolhaas's "Bigness: Or the Problem of Large" begins, "Beyond a certain scale, architecture acquires the properties of Bigness. The best reason to broach Bigness is the one given by climbers of Mount Everest: 'because it is there.' Bigness is ultimate architecture," and ends, "Bigness surrenders the field to after-architecture."[5] The violent typography of Wyndham Lewis's *BLAST* Vorticist manifestos is the model of the shout. The manifesto makes an art of excess. This is how it differs from the standard and sometimes self-congratulatory ars poetica, rational and measured. The manifesto is an act of *démesure*, going past what is thought of as proper, sane, and literary. Its outreach demands an extravagant self-assurance. At its peak of performance, its form creates its meaning.

The occasional coincidence of form and function—like Stéphane Mallarmé's "A Throw of Dice Not Ever Will Abolish Chance" ("Un coup de Dés jamais n'abolira le Hasard"; 1.7) in its defeat of the linear—*demonstrates* or makes a *manifestation,* a *manif* in French parlance: and the French know something about revolution.

WE-SPEAK

Generally posing some "we," explicit or implicit, against some other "they," with the terms constructed in a deliberate dichotomy, the manifesto can be set up like a battlefield. It can start out as a credo, but then it wants to make a persuasive move from the "I believe" of the speaker toward the "you" of the listener or reader, who should be sufficiently convinced to join in.[6] "We shall henceforward put the spectator in the centre of the picture" (Umberto Boccioni and others, "Futurist Painting: Technical Manifesto," [5.2]).

In their preface to the second volume of *Poems for the Millennium,* Jerome Rothenberg and Pierre Joris, writing about "the push by poets to self-define their workings," say that the manifesto is both a "personal accounting & a prescription/directive for future acts," nonpolitical as it is nonarchitectural. They quote Marinetti's demand for both "violence & precision . . . to stand on the rock of the word 'We' amidst the sea of boos & outrage."[7] We are right, in the terms of the manifesto: "We are continuing the evolution of art," begins a typical manifesto.[8] The tone is hortatory, contrarian, bullying, rapid-paced. Marinetti insists, in the Futurist manifestos, on the elimination of all adjectives or useless words that would slow down the others. Tristan Tzara, in his "Dada Manifesto 1918," celebrates the intense speed of his new movement hurtling down the mountain, as opposed to the slowness of the past: "Morality is the infusion of chocolate in the veins of all men."[9] Stripped to its bare bones, clean as a whistle and as piercing, the manifesto is immodest and forceful, exuberant and vivid, attention-grabbing. Immediate and urgent, it never mumbles, is always in overdose and overdrive.

THE MANIFESTO PRESENCE

High on its own presence, the manifesto is Modernist rather than ironically Postmodernist. It takes itself and its own spoof seriously. The manifesto moment positions itself between what has been done and what will be done, between the accomplished and the potential, in a radical and energizing division. The moment may be marked by an epitaph for what has gone: for Maurice Denis, "Gauguin is dead," for Pierre Boulez, "Schoenberg is dead."[10] The prototypical view is that stated by Barnett Newman, in his 1948 statement "The Sublime Is Now" (30.9), declaring the nowness and newness of American art, in credo form: "I believe that here in America, some of us, free from the weight of European culture . . . are reasserting man's natural desire for the exalted, for our relationship to the absolute emotions . . . without the nostalgic glasses of history." In this the manifesto differs from the *defense*, such as Joachim Du Bellay's sixteenth-century "Deffense et illustration de la langue françoise."[11] It does not defend the status quo but states its own agenda in its collective concern.

As opposed to the standard ars poetica, the outlandish 1885 declamation of James Abbott McNeill Whistler in his celebrated "Ten O'Clock" lecture (1.1) marks a new moment. It was delivered in London at ten, deliberately after the fashionable audience would have dined, so that they could concentrate on it alone. As it inaugurated the Symbolist excitement at the end of the nineteenth century, it inaugurates also this anthology. If the First World War put an end to that poetic shout of the Great Age of the Manifesto, the form is still extant, but changed. Manifestos will be written subsequently but scarcely in the same high spirit.

THE GREAT MANIFESTO MOMENT

After the Fauve moment of 1905, Modernist excitement broke out all at once, in a ten-year period of glorious madness that I am calling the Manifesto Moment. It stretched from 1909, with Marinetti's first Futurist manifesto, the grandfather of the rest, to the glory days of 1912 and the Cubist Section d'Or and Collage in Paris, through 1913 and Wassily Kandinsky's influential *On the Spiritual in Art*, the Armory show in New York, the Simultaneist movement in Paris, and the Cubo-Futurist and Rayonist movements in Russia. Nineteen thirteen is the year that Kasimir Malevich placed his black square on a white ground and founded Suprematism, the year that Ilya Zdanevich lectured on "everythingism," with the intense 1912–14 dizziness we can see extending to Vorticism in London of 1916 and 1917, then Imagism there and in America, Dada in Switzerland and Berlin, and De Stijl in Holland. In 1919 Lyubov Popova wrote her "statement" for the Nonobjective Creation and Suprematism exhibition ("Statement in Catalogue of Tenth State Exhibition," 15.4), in graphically arresting form. The largest number of selections here celebrate this heyday and then its aftermath, from Surrealism to phonetic poetry, Lettrism, and the erotics of Spatialism.

And yet even some Modernist manifestos give off an odd aura of looking back, to some moment they missed. Haunted by nostalgia, they have the feeling of longing rather than constructing, like a post-manifesto moment in a too-lateness. If the Postmodernist manifesto shrugs off this nostalgia, it has often a kind of dryness that undoes its energy. The attraction of those initial or founding manifestos of violence was and is their energy and their potential for energizing.

You are walking along a street, and on the wall of some building, right where it says "Défense d'afficher" (Forbidden to post anything here), you see posted some call to mental war, some exhortation to leave where you are ("Leave Dada, Leave your parents, Leave your wife") and go somewhere else. Or then, as in Venice in the early part of the century, leaflets rain upon your head. The manifesto gets you right in your smugness, like the Belgian Pie Philosopher Noël Godin of 1998, practicing a pie-in-your-face attack on those too self-satisfied, like Bill Gates of Microsoft fame and fortune and Bernard-Henri Levy, the French political philosopher of unbuttoned shirt and untold charm.[12]

As if defining a moment of crisis, the manifesto generally proclaims what it wants to oppose, to leave, to defend, to change. Its oppositional tone is constructed of *againstness* and generally in a spirit of a one time only moment. When it is thought of, like the Surrealist moment of love André Breton calls upon so eloquently—"Always for the first time"—the accent falls on the *first* more than the *always*.[13] An un-new manifesto is an oxymoron.

BUILDING THE SPACE

The manifesto builds into its surroundings its own conditions for reception, instructs the audience how to respond to what is heard or read or seen. So its form and function often profit from some strong central image, like the volcano, holding the rest together. Yet even a less magnetic image, like the tree Paul Klee uses to give root and shelter to his aphorisms in "On Modern Art," can work as an organizing principle.

So Malevich's black square makes a statement strong enough to daunt the weak-hearted:

> When, in the year 1913, in my desperate attempt to free art from the ballast of objectivity, I took refuge in the square form and exhibited a picture which consisted of nothing more than a black square on a white field, the critics and, along with them, the public sighed, "Everything which we loved is lost. We are in a desert. . . . Before us is nothing but a black square on a white background!"
>
> . . .
>
> The square seemed incomprehensible and dangerous to the critics and the public . . . and this, of course, was to be expected.
>
> The ascent to the heights of non-objective art is arduous and painful.[14]

This tone sets a forward-looking "we" against a predictable camp of the cowardly "them," implicitly inviting the reader/listener to the side of the brave.[15]

Ever since Plato voted for God as the architect of everything, the architectural spirit has swelled, until the manifesto became a natural form to the architect. Charles Jencks's preface to the anthology *Theories and Manifestoes of Contemporary Architecture*, entitled "The Volcano and the Tablet," discusses "this curious art form, like the haiku, with its own rules of brevity, wit, and *le mot juste*. . . . The good manifesto mixes a bit of terror, runaway emotion and charisma with a lot of common sense. . . . The genre demands blood."[16]

But there is a positive curiosity built into the modernism of the manifesto. John Cage, in an aside before his "Lecture on Nothing," declares: "If you hear that Rauschenberg has painted a new painting, the wisest thing to do is to drop everything and manage one way or another to see it."[17]

LABELS

The manifesto itself may declare in its title its new stance, such as the Futurist "Against Past-Loving Venice!" or it may be as blank as a tabula rasa: "Manifesto of Surrealism," waiting for the theory to fill it in and the audience to give its support to the movement it advocates.[18]

The labels under which the texts here are grouped are meant to be loosely attached. Many appellations of recent date do not refer to established schools or movements, sometimes simply to the determining elements that seem to permit the coherence of the rest around them. "Concretism," for example, is both an art term—as in the Constructivists' emphasis on materials, for example in the Ferroconcrete poems of Vasilii Kamensky—and a term for a kind of shaped poetry. "Expressionism," originally designating the opposite pole from Impressionism, includes so many differing national forms—German, Polish, and so on—that it should require the plural: "Expressionisms." The same is true for "Futurisms," "Realisms," and so on. The plural is more fitting in some movements than others. Although there can be seen to be various Dadas, for example, referring both to the artists and writers and to the movements Dada comprises, for Surrealism—given Breton's desire for cohesion—the singular is more appropriate.[19]

Such overlappings abound. So the widespread urge to "Primitivism," characteristic of the 1890s through the 1940s in art and literature, permeates writings in many fields, to the point where its label stretches and loses its original shape. The two leaders of the movement called Rayonism, Mikhail Larionov and Natalya Goncharova, were doing Neoprimitivist art in 1909 and were explaining why they painted their faces not long after. As Wyndham Lewis, Ur-Vorticist, puts it bluntly: "The Art-Instinct is permanently primitive."[20]

So too with sound: the Noisism of the Italian Futurists leads to Sound Art, the Rayonists play with sonorities and include bars of music in their paintings, and Kandinsky's *Yellow Sound* is discussed in *The Blaue Reiter Almanac*. In fact, the deliberate repetitions and emphasis of painterly painting can be seen as analogous to the L=A=N=G=U=A=G=E writings. Compactism, tongue in cheek from its birth, fathered by the mathematician-novelist-poet of Oulipo Jacques Roubaud, and thinking minimally, can be seen by the American reader as casting a headlong glance at the American poet Marianne Moore's "compacity"—her term for the poetic condensation she aimed at, and found.

Such eclecticism is one of the characteristics of Modernism itself and rules against neat divisions. It is the dizzying quality so famously displayed in the years from 1912 to just before World War I, for instance, at Roger Fry's Second Post-Impressionist Exhibition of 1912, with its Cubist paintings by Georges Braque, Pablo Picasso, and Robert Delaunay, with its Futurist works by David and Vladimir Burlyuk and by the Rayonists Larionov and Goncharova.[21] In the best of moments avant-garde currents meet, converge, and converse—often in manifesto-speak.

THE MANIFESTO STYLE

Generally the manifesto stands alone, does not need to lean on anything else, demands no other text than itself. Its rules are self-contained, included in its own body. If we use Robert Venturi's celebrated distinction, the manifesto is on the side of the duck and not of the decorated shed.[22] What is meant to sell duck, he says, wants to look like duck. But what shelters as shed can be ornamented: decoration is appendage. Manifesto is duck. What it wants to sell is itself.

It is not, generally, a prefatory pre-appendage to something else— although such texts as Wordsworth's preface to the *Lyrical Ballads* or Victor Hugo's preface to *Cromwell* had the effect of manifestos and their certainty of tone. Oscar Wilde's preface to *The Picture of Dorian Gray*, the aphoristic declaration about the inutility of art, is included here, alongside his declaration about the use of the poet among the people.

The initial shock of an unusual form is as appealing as the beginning anecdote, like the ur-case of Marinetti's "The Founding and Manifesto of Futurism" of 1909 (5.5): "We had stayed up all night, my friends and I, under hanging mosque lamps with domes of filigreed brass, domes starred like our spirits, shining like them with the prisoned radiance of electric hearts." Interior and exterior, image and person, the starry heavens of nature and the exotic Eastern lamps of culture, heart and soul, all converge in the excitement of the Futurist happening.

A manifesto can take a dialogue mode, as in Pierre Albert-Birot's "Nunic Dialogue" (4.5) or Samuel Beckett's *Three Dialogues* with Georges Duthuit (written by Beckett). The two points of view should work against each other in interesting articulation, or there can be a straight man and an elucidator/ creator, as in Piet Mondrian's "Dialogue on the New Plastic":

A. A Singer

B. A Painter

A. I admire your earlier work. Because it means so much to me, I would like better to understand your present way of painting. I see nothing in these rectangles. What are you aiming at?

B. My new paintings have the same aim as the previous ones. Both have the *same* aim, but my latest work brings it out more clearly.

This kind of binarism is particularly suited to the genre: take Pierre Boulez's "Demythologizing the Conductor" of 1960 (30.3), where, from the opening throughout the text, a refrain in triplet characterizes the conductor by indirection or negative definition echoes—"neither . . . nor . . . !":

neither dictator nor artisan!

.   .   .

neither messiah nor sacristan!

.   .   .

neither angel nor animal!

The present tense suits the manifesto, as does the rapid enumeration of elements in a list or bullet form, as in "Manifesto I of De Stijl" (16.1) or "The Initiative Individual Artist in the Creativity of the Collective" of Vladimir Tatlin (14.2):

1. The initiative individual is the collector of the *energy* of the collective, directed towards knowledge and invention.
2. The initiative individual serves as a contact between the invention and the creativity of the collective.

The most graphic manifestos, such as Marinetti's "Zum Tumb" or his "words in freedom" cover of 1919, Guillaume Apollinaire's semi-calligram "L'Antitradition futuriste" of 1913 (5.11), Wyndham Lewis's loud "Our Vortex" (10.3) and the Blasts and Blesses in his *BLAST* and Gaudier-Brzeska's "Vortex (Written from the Trenches)" of 1914–15, and Lyubov Popova's "Statement in Catalogue of Tenth State Exhibition" scheme of 1919 (15.4), make the most arresting visual poetics.[23]

The manifesto has to draw the audience into the belief of the speaker, by some hook or crook. The Symbolist Odilon Redon begins his "Suggestive Art" of 1909 (1.9) with a question: "What was it that at the beginning made

my work difficult?" as does Paul Klee in his 1924 lecture "On Modern Art":
"May I use a simile, the simile of a tree?"[24] Since we are invited to answer,
we feel included. A manifesto is generally, by mode and form, an exhortation to a whole way of thinking and being rather than a simple command
or a definition. As so often, however, Marcel Duchamp makes a brilliant
exception in his imperative about what a non-picture might be:

> Use "delay" instead of "picture" or
> "painting"; . . .
>   It's merely a way
> of succeeding in no longer thinking
> that the thing in question is
> a picture . . .
> . . .—a "delay in glass"
>   as you would say a "poem in prose"
>   or a spittoon in silver[25]

So a definition can be also a poem, and a title can be the entire work.
The threshold is important in setting the manifesto apart from the "real
world." So Naum Gabo and Antoine Pevsner start their "Realistic Manifesto" of 1920 (14.1) with a three-line verse prelude, marking it temporally
as of the moment, of "today," and address it to those involved in the artistic
enterprise, couched in the poetry of an epic setting:

> Above the tempests of our weekdays,
> Across the ashes and cindered homes of the past,
> Before the gates of the vacant future,
> We proclaim today to you artists, painters, sculptors, musicians,
>   actors, poets . . .

The manifesto, at its height, is a poem in heightened prose.
The manifesto profits from many other modes of discourse: the brief
forcefulness of the prose poem, as in the passage just cited, or the high
drama of such gnomic utterances of the absolute, both negative and positive, as John Cage's *Silence* in their extreme and attention-getting interrupted and interruptive modes:

> There is no
> such thing as silence. Something is al-
> ways happening that makes a sound.
> .   .   .

It is very simply but extra-urgent
The Lord knows whether or not
the next

(Bang fist) [26]

Or the rhetorical question of self-conscious musing: "If I were teaching, would I say *Caution Watch Your Step* or Throw yourself in where the fish are thickest?" [27]

Like a mirror of the personality of the author, single or collective, the manifesto takes on as many styles as there are writers and speakers. But it has to grab us.

MANIFESTO CONFUSION

Adding to the impossibility of neat and linear presentation of a diachronic kind, given the combination of so many various artistic and philosophic fields, is the complication of the time frame. The frequent extension of movements beyond their originating moment often produces texts more interesting than those dating from the moment itself. For example, the movement of Symbolism, dating from Whistler's celebrated "Ten O'Clock" lecture of 1885 (1.1), was translated by Mallarmé in his original revolutionary text of 1897, "Un coup de Dés jamais n'abolira le Hasard" ("A Throw of Dice Not Ever Will Abolish Chance," 1.7) and continued in the post-Symbolist phase of the two Pauls, Claudel and Valéry.[28] Cubism itself, which would ordinarily be dated with Picasso and Braque, say, from 1907 to 1914, has reverberations in literature that extend through Blaise Cendrars and Apollinaire and Pierre Reverdy, say to 1917, and later.

The manifestos and statements here do not include those of an umbrella-like nature, for example, Roger Fry's description of the Second Post-Impressionism Exhibition in London. They are each written by a practitioner of the particular art movement, so that they speak from the inside and not from outside: I have preferred the manifesto or statement of the believer to the explanatory talk of the aftercoming critic. Thus the tone of passion that pervades many of these texts, from the Modernist Moment.[29] The spirit of modernism is characterized in good part by its refusal of description, for what it conceives of as its own form of reality: art, representing often simply itself.

Being an alternative genre, the manifesto can *always* be redefined; it makes its own definition each time. It is context dependent and shows its colors: so R. B. Kitaj's "Manifesto" or *First Diasporist Manifesto* begins, "Diasporist painting, which I just made up, is enacted under peculiar historical and personal freedoms, stresses, dislocations, rupture and momentum."[30] A case can be made for the poem-manifesto, the painting-manifesto, the aphorism-manifesto, the essay-manifesto. In its extreme case of self-definition, the manifesto consists of reflections on the manifesto itself: these become *meta-manifestos*. There will always be other manifesto styles, even in what seems a post-manifesto moment. Someone will come along, alone or in a group, to invite us, loudly, to some new way of thinking.

NOTES

1. "Festus," said the authorities in that far-off ancient land, had sprung up from the root "fendere," as in "offendere": see the *Oxford Universal Dictionary on Historical Principles* (Oxford: Clarendon Press, 1955).

2. Take, for instance, among manifestos written in French, Emile Zola's "J'accuse," the "Manifesto of the 121" (about Algeria), Michèle Lalonde's "SPEAK WHITE," and Aimé Césaire's "In the Guise of a Manifesto." These examples are given in Jeanne Demers, "Le Manifeste, crise—ou caution?—du système," in the special manifesto issue of *L'Esprit créateur* 23:4 (winter 1983): 5. Other articles, by Micheline Tison-Braun and Alice Kaplan, in this journal are equally helpful in defining the genre, as is Claude Abastado's "Introduction à l'analyse des manifestes," in *Littérature*, the special issue on "L'Écriture manifestaire," no. 39 (October 1980).

3. "Marx's Masterpiece at 150," *New York Times Book Review*, April 26, 1998, 39.

4. So much so that Robert Venturi's "Non-Straightforward Architecture: A Gentle Manifesto" is a deliberate surprise. It is included in his *Complexity and Contradiction in Architecture* of 1966, quoted in *Theories and Manifestoes of Contemporary Architecture*, ed. Charles Jencks and Karl Kropf (Chichester, West Sussex: Academy Editions, 1997), 52–56.

5. Rem Koolhaas, *Delirious New York: A Retroactive Manifesto for Manhattan* (New York: Oxford University Press, 1978), 307, 310.

6. As in John Cage's *Silence: Lectures and Writings* (Middletown CT: Wesleyan University Press, 1961; reprint, Cambridge: MIT Press, 1966).

7. *Poems for the Millennium*, vol. 2, *From Postwar to Millennium*, ed. Jerome Rothenberg and Pierre Joris (Berkeley: University of California Press, 1997), 405.

8. Lucio Fontana's "White Manifesto," written with his students in Buenos Aires, 1946, in *Art in Theory, 1900–1990: An Anthology of Changing Ideas*, ed. Charles Harrison and Paul Wood (Oxford: Blackwell, 1993).

9. Tristan Tzara, *Approximate Man and Other Writings*, ed. and tr. Mary Ann Caws (Detroit: Wayne State University Press, 1973), 156.

10. Maurice Denis, "The Influence of Paul Gauguin," in Herschell Chipp, ed., *Theories of Modern Art: A Source Book by Artists and Critics* (Berkeley: University of California Press, 1968), 100; Pierre Boulez, *Notes of an Apprenticeship*, texts collected and presented by Paule Thévenin, trans. Herbert Weinstock (New York: Knopf, 1968) (originally published in a different version in *Score* [London], May 1952).

11. Du Bellay, 1549; see Morris Bishop, *A Survey of French Literature* (New York: Harcourt Brace, 1955), 96, for a summary.

12. My thanks to Frank Duba for bringing me this pie-in-your-face bit of information from the *New York Times*, international edition, of Monday, April 20, 1998, and *Harper's Magazine* of May 1998.

13. Breton, "L'Air de l'eau" (1934), in *Poems of André Breton*, tr. and ed. Jean-Pierre Cauvin and Mary Ann Caws (Austin: University of Texas Press, 1982), 108–9.

14. Malevich, "Suprematism" (item 15.1, this volume).

15. It has been pointed out that a great way to write one of these things is when you are, like Trotsky, on the run: "They have an hysterical, telegraphic quality [or today an Internet truncation] as if the sender did not want to pay for extra syllables" (Jencks, ed., "The Volcano and the Tablet," introduction to *Theories and Manifestoes*, 11). A typical manifesto-on-the-run is Rem Koolhaas's famous 1978 "Delirious New York: A Retroactive Manifesto for Manhattan," the preface for his book about Manhattanism and the modern, late modern, new modern, postmodern form that this particular -*ism* takes (Koolhaas, *Delirious New York*).

16. He refers back to Ulrich Conrads's *Programmes and Manifestoes on Twentieth-Century Architecture* of 1964; quote in *Theories and Manifestoes*, 6.

17. Cage, *Silence*, 108.

18. "Against Past-Loving Venice!" in *Marinetti: Selected Writings*, ed. R. W. Flint (New York: Farrar Straus, 1971); "Manifesto of Surrealism," in André Breton, *Manifestos of Surrealism*, tr. Richard Seaver and Helen R. Lane (Ann Arbor: University of Michigan Press, 1969), 1–48.

19. Then, too, the term "Magic Realism," the Latin American equivalent of Surrealism, allies the movement to the originally French movement, itself based on the Dada movement of Swiss-German-Austrian-Rumanian origin.

20. R. Aldington and others, "Beyond Action and Reaction" (item 10.2, this volume).

21. Larionov was exhibited at *Der Sturm*'s Autumn Salon in Berlin from September to December of 1913, where there were represented also the Cubists of Paris: Robert and Sonia Delaunay, Albert Gleizes, Piet Mondrian, and Francis Picabia, as well as Marc Chagall and Aleksander Archipenko, and even the naive painter Henri Rousseau; Kandinsky and the artists of the *Blaue Reiter* in Munich; and the Futurist Giacomo Balla's celebrated *Dynamism of a Dog on a Leash* of 1912. When Larionov and Goncharova went to Paris, their exhibition was attended by the entire avant-garde world: Coco Chanel (the sometimes lover of Pierre Reverdy, the Cubist poet) and Anna Pavlova, Jacques-Emile Blanche and Misia Sert, Guillaume Apollinaire and André Salmon, Ricciotto Canudo and Max Jacob, Robert Delaunay and Jean Cocteau, Blaise Cendrars and Constantin Brancusi, Braque and Picasso.

22. In Venturi's "Leaving Las Vegas," included in *Theories and Manifestoes*, 53.

23. For Marinetti, see Chipp, ed., *Theories of Modern Art*, 291; for Lewis and Gaudier-Brzeska, see Charles Harrison, Paul Wood, and Jason Gaiger, eds., *Art in Theory, 1815–1900* (Oxford: Blackwell, 1997), 160–61 and *BLAST* (1914) and *BLAST 2* (autumn 1915), reprinted in *BLAST: Review of the Great English Vortex* (New York: Kraus Reprints, 1967).

24. The Redon quote can be found in Chipp, ed., *Theories of Modern Art*, 116, and Redon, *A soi-même: Journal, 1867–1915* (Paris: Corti, 1961). Paul Klee's quote can be

found in "On Modern Art," in *Paul Klee: On Modern Art*, trans. Paul Findlay (London: Faber and Faber, 1948), 343.

25. Duchamp, "Kind of Sub-Title" (item 9.20, this volume).

26. Cage, *Silence*, 80.

27. Cage, *Silence*, 108.

28. Mallarmé insisted on the small letter *c* and the large *D* in his title. The central themes of risk and nothingness in Mallarmé's text are more quietly questioned by André Gide at the end of the nineteenth century and the beginning of the twentieth. Its influence reverberates right through its rediscovery in the Cubist epoch, made clear in a Picasso collage of 1911 ("Un Coup de thé," short for *théâtre*, about the Balkan war)—see the works by Christine Pioggi and others, summed up in Rosalind E. Krauss's *The Picasso Papers* (New York: Farrar Straus Giroux, 1998)—and extends into the post-post-Symbolist twenties, when it is rediscovered.

29. And the many others I might have included, in particular Carolee Schneemann from "Meat Joy"; the manifesto of the Russian Link group in 1908 and the Russian SOTS; Guy Debord's "Society of the Spectacle"; Robert Venturi's "Complexity and Contradiction"; the "Redstockings Manifesto"; R. B. Kitaj's "Diasporist Manifesto"; the Guerrilla Girls's proclamations and performances; and so on.

30. Kitaj, *First Diasporist Manifesto* (London: Thames and Hudson, 1989), 10.

Very Rough Chronology

1880s–90s	Symbolism
1908–12	Primitivism and Neoprimitivism
1907–12	Cubism
1907–25	Orphism
1916–18	Nowism/Nunism, Simultaneism/Presentism

Futurisms:

    Italian Futurisms

        1909–29   Noisism/Bruitism, Cerebrism, Tactilism

    Russian Futurisms

        1910–21   Acmeism

        1912–14   Ego-Futurism

        1913–14   Hylea Group: Cubo-Futurism

        1912–16   Zaoum

        1912–14   Rayonism

1910–17	Spanish Avant-Gardes
1910–18	Expressionisms
1911–14	*Der Blaue Reiter*
1910–19	Scuola Metaphysica
1914–25	Creationism
1917–21	Dada

    Zurich Dada

    Berlin Dada

    New York Dada and Surrealism

1914–15	Vorticism
1914–18	Imagism
1913–29	Constructivism
1915–23	Suprematism
1917–31	De Stijl and Neoplasticism
1919–33	Bauhaus/Elementalism
1918–25	Purism
1919–23	Ultraism

Brazilian Avant-Gardes:

        1922   Klaxonism, Hallucinism

        1928   Cannibalism

1924–45	Surrealism
1928–30	Dynamism

Manifesto

And afterwards.

Now that is all.

Gertrude Stein, "Composition as Explanation"

PART 1

Symbolism

Among the first of a long list of "isms" to have its own manifesto, this long-lasting movement had its moment in the fourth quarter of the nineteenth century. Stéphane Mallarmé, its most influential figure, insisted on the "disappearance of the poet as speaker, yielding his initiative to words," self-mirroring and nonreferential, whose "reciprocal reflections" are themselves their meaning. At the heart of Symbolism is the power of suggestion as opposed to statement, the image of the flower more present for being "absent from every bouquet" ("Crisis in Poetry," 1.6). Mallarmé's prose/poem/play *Igitur*, with its Hamlet figure poised on the edge of a tomb, a stair, and a roll of dice, leads, almost thirty years later, to his great antilinear manifesto with its remarkable typographic experimentation: *Un coup de Dés jamais n'abolira le Hasard* " ("A Throw of Dice Not Ever Will Abolish Chance," 1.7) of 1897, whose reverberations were felt in the worlds of art as well as poetics.

Jean Moréas's 1886 "Symbolist Manifesto" (1.8) is a pale thing, particularly in juxtaposition with James Abbott McNeill Whistler's "Ten o'Clock" lecture (1.1) of the year previous, making Moréas's own classicist tendencies all too visible. Whistler's celebrated lecture, given at ten o'clock so that the elegant Londoners would have had time to dine first, is a pronouncement, lyrical and mocking, of art for the artist and for art's sake. Using the rhythms of the King James Bible to rail against narrative as against usefulness, this orientalizing statement calls attention to itself in proper manifesto style. It was Mallarmé, Whistler's close friend, who, with the poets Francis Viélé-Griffin and George Moore, translated this singular outpouring into French and helped to spread its renown. "Put my name as translator small under Whistler's," Mallarmé said to the publisher, "so as not to take away anything from his glory."

The art for art's sake tradition of Symbolism permeates the writings of Oscar Wilde, he too frequenting Mallarmé's "Mardis," his Tuesday night gatherings, and continues in the Irish tradition through William Butler Yeats, with his mythological musings and his own art of suggestion. Much of the poetry of France in the early twentieth century was Neosymbolist, and the original suggestion of Symbolism made its way, often through the translations of Mallarmé by Arthur Symons and Roger Fry, into English Symbolism.

Symbolism as a movement reached far beyond France. The futurist Filippo Tommaso Marinetti would translate Mallarmé into Italian, the Spaniard Ruben Darío would call a collection of his poems *Azul* after Mallarmé's celebrated poem about the heavens that begins "L'Azur! l'Azur! l'Azur! l'Azur!" and in Switzerland, Fernand Hodler's theory of parallel equivalences was appropriately illustrated in the formal balance of his scenes of mountain and sky. If Whistler took to yellow walls for the exhibitions of his paintings, the Russian Symbolists of the Blue Rose group in 1907 preferred Mallarmé's azure blue. Symbolist exhibitions abounded in Russia as everywhere else. At the Salon of the Golden Fleece, in Moscow in April and May of 1908, the French Symbolist artists were exhibited along with the Russians, making the first dialogue between the Russians and French Modernism, which was to be all-important. In this time of ferment, ideas were on the move like their perpetrators.

1.1 JAMES ABBOTT MCNEILL WHISTLER

The Ten O'Clock

1885

LADIES AND GENTLEMEN:

It is with great hesitation and much misgiving that I appear before you, in the character of The Preacher.

If timidity be at all allied to the virtue modesty, and can find favour in your eyes, I pray you, for the sake of that virtue, accord me your utmost indulgence.

I would plead for my want of habit, did it not seem preposterous, judging from precedent, that aught save the most efficient effrontery could be ever expected in connection with my subject—for I will not conceal from you that I mean to talk about Art. Yes, Art—that has of late become, as far as much discussion and writing can make it, a sort of common topic for the tea-table.

Art is upon the Town!—to be chucked under the chin by the passing gallant—to be enticed within the gates of the householder—to be coaxed into company, as a proof of culture and refinement.

If familiarity can breed contempt, certainly Art—or what is currently taken for it—has been brought to its lowest stage of intimacy.

The people have been harassed with Art in every guise, and vexed with many methods as to its endurance. They have been told how they shall love Art, and live with it. Their homes have been invaded, their walls covered with paper, their very dress taken to task—until, roused at last, bewildered and filled with the doubts and discomforts of senseless suggestion, they re-sent such intrusion, and cast forth the false prophets, who have brought the very name of the beautiful into disrepute, and derision upon themselves.

Alas! ladies and gentlemen, Art has been maligned. She has naught in common with such practices. She is a goddess of dainty thought—reticent of habit, abjuring all obtrusiveness, purposing in no way to better others.

She is, withal, selfishly occupied with her own perfection only—having no desire to teach—seeking and finding the beautiful in all conditions and in all times, as did her high priest Rembrandt, when he saw picturesque grandeur and noble dignity in the Jews' quarter of Amsterdam, and lamented not that its inhabitants were not Greeks.

As did Tintoret and Paul Veronese, among the Venetians, while not halting to change the brocaded silks for the classic draperies of Athens.

As did, at the Court of Philip, Velasquez, whose Infantas, clad in inæsthetic hoops, are, as works of Art, of the same quality as the Elgin marbles.

No reformers were these great men—no improvers of the way of others! Their productions alone were their occupation, and, filled with the poetry of their science, they required not to alter their surroundings—for, as the laws of their Art were revealed to them they saw, in the development of their work, that real beauty which, to them, was as much a matter of certainty and triumph as is to the astronomer the verification of the result, foreseen with the light given to him alone. In all this, their world was completely severed from that of their fellow-creatures with whom sentiment is mistaken for poetry; and for whom there is no perfect work that shall not be explained by the benefit conferred upon themselves.

Humanity takes the place of Art, and God's creations are excused by their usefulness. Beauty is confounded with virtue, and, before a work of Art, it is asked: "What good shall it do?"

Hence it is that nobility of action, in this life, is hopelessly linked with the merit of the work that portrays it; and thus the people have acquired the habit of looking, as who should say, not *at* a picture, but *through* it, at some human fact, that shall, or shall not, from a social point of view, better their mental or moral state. So we have come to hear of the painting that elevates, and of the duty of the painter—of the picture that is full of thought, and of the panel that merely decorates.

A favourite faith, dear to those who teach, is that certain periods were especially artistic, and that nations, readily named, were notably lovers of Art.

So we are told that the Greeks were, as a people, worshippers of the beautiful, and that in the fifteenth century Art was engrained in the multitude.

That the great masters lived in common understanding with their patrons—that the early Italians were artists—all—and that the demand for the lovely thing produced it.

That we, of to-day, in gross contrast to this Arcadian purity, call for the ungainly, and obtain the ugly.

That, could we but change our habits and climate—were we willing to wander in groves—could we be roasted out of broadcloth—were we to do without haste, and journey without speed, we should again *require* the spoon of Queen Anne, and pick at our peas with the fork of two prongs. And so, for the flock, little hamlets grow near Hammersmith, and the steam horse is scorned.

Useless! quite hopeless and false is the effort!—built upon fable, and all because "a wise man has uttered a vain thing and filled his belly with the East wind."

Listen! There never was an artistic period.

There never was an Art-loving nation.

In the beginning, man went forth each day—some to do battle, some to the chase; others, again, to dig and to delve in the field—all that they might gain and live, or lose and die. Until there was found among them one, differing from the rest, whose pursuits attracted him not, and so he stayed by the tents with the women, and traced strange devices with a burnt stick upon a gourd.

This man, who took no joy in the ways of his brethren—who cared not for conquest, and fretted in the field—this designer of quaint patterns—this deviser of the beautiful—who perceived in Nature about him curious curvings, as faces are seen in the fire—this dreamer apart, was the first artist.

And when, from the field and from afar, there came back the people, they took the gourd—and drank from out of it.

And presently there came to this man another—and, in time, others—of like nature, chosen by the Gods—and so they worked together; and soon they fashioned, from the moistened earth, forms resembling the gourd. And with the power of creation, the heirloom of the artist, presently they went beyond the slovenly suggestion of Nature, and the first vase was born, in beautiful proportion.

And the toilers tilled, and were athirst; and the heroes returned from fresh victories, to rejoice and to feast; and all drank alike from the artists' goblets, fashioned cunningly, taking no note the while of the craftsman's pride, and understanding not his glory in his work; drinking at the cup, not from choice, not from a consciousness that it was beautiful, but because, forsooth, there was none other!

And time, with more state, brought more capacity for luxury, and it became well that men should dwell in large houses, and rest upon couches, and eat at tables; whereupon the artist, with his artificers, built palaces, and filled them with furniture, beautiful in proportion and lovely to look upon.

And the people lived in marvels of art—and ate and drank out of masterpieces—for there was nothing else to eat and to drink out of, and no bad building to live in; no article of daily life, of luxury, or of necessity, that had not been handed down from the design of the master, and made by his workmen.

And the people questioned not, *and had nothing to say in the matter.*

So Greece was in its splendour, and Art reigned supreme—by force of fact, not by election—and there was no meddling from the outsider. The mighty warrior would no more have ventured to offer a design for the temple of Pallas Athene than would the sacred poet have proffered a plan for constructing the catapult.

And the Amateur was unknown—and the Dilettante undreamed of!

And history wrote on, and conquest accompanied civilisation, and Art spread, or rather its products were carried by the victors among the vanquished from one country to another. And the customs of cultivation covered the face of the earth, so that all peoples continued to use what *the artist alone produced.*

And centuries passed in this using, and the world was flooded with all that was beautiful, until there arose a new class, who discovered the cheap, and foresaw fortune in the facture of the sham.

Then sprang into existence the tawdry, the common, the gewgaw.

The taste of the tradesman supplanted the science of the artist, and what was born of the million went back to them, and charmed them, for it was after their own heart; and the great and the small, the statesman and the slave, took to themselves the abomination that was tendered, and preferred it—and have lived with it ever since!

And the artist's occupation was gone, and the manufacturer and the huckster took his place.

And now the heroes filled from the jugs and drank from the bowls—with understanding—noting the glare of their new bravery, and taking pride in its worth.

And the people—this time—had much to say in the matter—and all were satisfied. And Birmingham and Manchester arose in their might—and Art was relegated to the curiosity shop.

Nature contains the elements, in colour and form, of all pictures, as the keyboard contains the notes of all music.

But the artist is born to pick, and choose, and group with science, these elements, that the result may be beautiful—as the musician gathers his notes, and forms his chords, until he bring forth from chaos glorious harmony.

To say to the painter, that Nature is to be taken as she is, is to say to the player, that he may sit on the piano.

That Nature is always right, is an assertion, artistically, as untrue, as it is one whose truth is universally taken for granted. Nature is very rarely right, to such an extent even, that it might almost be said that Nature is usually wrong: that is to say, the condition of things that shall bring about the perfection of harmony worthy a picture is rare, and not common at all.

This would seem, to even the most intelligent, a doctrine almost blasphemous. So incorporated with our education has the supposed aphorism become, that its belief is held to be part of our moral being, and the words themselves have, in our ear, the ring of religion. Still, seldom does Nature succeed in producing a picture.

The sun blares, the wind blows from the east, the sky is bereft of cloud, and without, all is of iron. The windows of the Crystal Palace are seen from all points of London. The holiday-maker rejoices in the glorious day, and the painter turns aside to shut his eyes.

How little this is understood, and how dutifully the casual in Nature is accepted as sublime, may be gathered from the unlimited admiration daily produced by a very foolish sunset.

The dignity of the snow-capped mountain is lost in distinctness, but the joy of the tourist is to recognise the traveller on the top. The desire to see, for the sake of seeing, is, with the mass, alone the one to be gratified, hence the delight in detail.

And when the evening mist clothes the riverside with poetry, as with a veil, and the poor buildings lose themselves in the dim sky, and the tall chimneys become campanili, and the warehouses are palaces in the night, and the whole city hangs in the heavens, and fairy-land is before us—then the wayfarer hastens home; the working man and the cultured one, the wise man and the one of pleasure, cease to understand, as they have ceased to see, and Nature, who, for once, has sung in tune, sings her exquisite song to the artist alone, her son and her master—her son in that he loves her, her master in that he knows her.

To him her secrets are unfolded, to him her lessons have become gradually clear. He looks at her flower, not with the enlarging lens, that he may gather facts for the botanist, but with the light of the one who sees in her choice selection of brilliant tones and delicate tints, suggestions of future harmonies.

He does not confine himself to purposeless copying, without thought, each blade of grass, as commended by the inconsequent, but, in the long curve of the narrow leaf, corrected by the straight tall stem, he learns how grace is wedded to dignity, how strength enhances sweetness, that elegance shall be the result.

In the citron wing of the pale butterfly, with its dainty spots of orange, he sees before him the stately halls of fair gold, with their slender saffron pillars, and is taught how the delicate drawing high upon the walls shall be traced in tender tones of orpiment, and repeated by the base in notes of graver hue.

In all that is dainty and lovable he finds hints for his own combinations, and *thus* is Nature ever his resource and always at his service, and to him is naught refused.

Through his brain, as through the last alembic, is distilled the refined essence of that thought which began with the Gods, and which they left him to carry out.

Set apart by them to complete their works, he produces that wondrous thing called the masterpiece, which surpasses in perfection all that they have contrived in what is called Nature; and the Gods stand by and marvel, and perceive how far away more beautiful is the Venus of Melos than was their own Eve.

For some time past, the unattached writer has become the middleman in this matter of Art, and his influence, while it has widened the gulf between the people and the painter, has brought about the most complete misunderstanding as to the aim of the picture.

For him a picture is more or less a hieroglyph or symbol of story. Apart from a few technical terms, for the display of which he finds an occasion, the work is considered absolutely from a literary point of view; indeed, from what other can he consider it? And in his essays he deals with it as with a novel—a history—or an anecdote. He fails entirely and most naturally to see its excellences, or demerits—artistic—and so degrades Art, by supposing it a method of bringing about a literary climax.

It thus, in his hands, becomes merely a means of perpetrating something further, and its mission is made a secondary one, even as a means is second to an end.

The thoughts emphasised, noble or other, are inevitably attached to the incident, and become more or less noble, according to the eloquence or mental quality of the writer, who looks the while, with disdain, upon what he holds as "mere execution"—a matter belonging, he believes, to the training of the schools, and the reward of assiduity. So that, as he goes on with his translation from canvas to paper, the work becomes his own. He finds poetry where he would feel it were he himself transcribing the event, invention in the intricacy of the *mise en scène,* and noble philosophy in some detail of philanthropy, courage, modesty, or virtue, suggested to him by the occurrence.

All this might be brought before him, and his imagination be appealed to, by a very poor picture—indeed, I might safely say that it generally is.

Meanwhile, the *painter's* poetry is quite lost to him—the amazing invention that shall have put form and colour into such perfect harmony, that exquisiteness is the result, he is without understanding—the nobility of thought, that shall have given the artist's dignity to the whole, says to him absolutely nothing.

So that his praises are published, for virtues we would blush to possess—while the great qualities, that distinguish the one work from the thousand, that make of the masterpiece the thing of beauty that it is—have never been seen at all.

That this is so, we can make sure of, by looking back at old reviews upon past exhibitions, and reading the flatteries lavished upon men who have since been forgotten altogether—but, upon whose works, the language has been exhausted, in rhapsodies—that left nothing for the National Gallery.

A curious matter, in its effect upon the judgment of these gentlemen, is the accepted vocabulary of poetic symbolism, that helps them, by habit, in dealing with Nature: a mountain, to them, is synonymous with height—a lake, with depth—the ocean, with vastness—the sun, with glory.

So that a picture with a mountain, a lake, and an ocean—however poor in paint—is inevitably "lofty," "vast," "infinite," and "glorious"—on paper.

There are those also, sombre of mien, and wise with the wisdom of books, who frequent museums and burrow in crypts; collecting—comparing—compiling—classifying—contradicting.

Experts these—for whom a date is an accomplishment—a hall mark, success!

Careful in scrutiny are they, and conscientious of judgment—establishing, with due weight, unimportant reputations—discovering the picture, by the stain on the back—testing the torso, by the leg that is missing—filling folios with doubts on the way of that limb—disputatious and dictatorial, concerning the birthplace of inferior persons—speculating, in much writing, upon the great worth of bad work.

True clerks of the collection, they mix memoranda with ambition, and, reducing Art to statistics, they "file" the fifteenth century, and "pigeon-hole" the antique!

Then the Preacher "appointed"!

He stands in high places—harangues and holds forth.

Sage of the Universities—learned in many matters, and of much experience in all, save his subject.

Exhorting—denouncing—directing.

Filled with wrath and earnestness.

Bringing powers of persuasion, and polish of language, to prove—nothing.

Torn with much teaching—having naught to impart.

Impressive—important—shallow.

Defiant—distressed—desperate.

Crying out, and cutting himself—while the gods hear not.

Gentle priest of the Philistine withal, again he ambles pleasantly from all point, and through many volumes, escaping scientific assertion—"babbles of green fields."

So Art has become foolishly confounded with education—that all should be equally qualified.

Whereas, while polish, refinement, culture, and breeding, are in no way arguments for artistic result, it is also no reproach to the most finished scholar or greatest gentleman in the land that he be absolutely without eye for painting or ear for music—that in his heart he prefer the popular print to the scratch of Rembrandt's needle, or the songs of the hall to Beethoven's "C minor Symphony."

Let him have but the wit to say so, and not feel the admission a proof of inferiority.

Art happens—no hovel is safe from it, no Prince may depend upon it, the vastest intelligence cannot bring it about, and puny efforts to make it universal and in quaint comedy, and coarse farce.

This is as it should be—and all attempts to make it otherwise are due to the eloquence of the ignorant, the zeal of the conceited.

The boundary line is clear. Far from me to propose to bridge it over—that the pestered people be pushed across. No! I would save them from further fatigue. I would come to their relief, and would lift from their shoulders this incubus of Art.

Why, after centuries of freedom from it, and indifference to it, should it now be thrust upon them by the blind—until wearied and puzzled, they know no longer how they shall eat or drink—how they shall sit or stand—or wherewithal they shall clothe themselves—without afflicting Art.

But, lo! there is much talk without!

Triumphantly they cry, "Beware! This matter does indeed concern us. We also have our part in all true Art!—for, remember the 'one touch of Nature' that 'makes the whole world kin.' "

True, indeed. But let not the unwary jauntily suppose that Shakespeare herewith hands him his passport to Paradise, and thus permits him speech among the chosen. Rather, learn that, in this very sentence, he is condemned to remain without—to continue with the common.

This one chord that vibrates with all—this "one touch of Nature" that calls aloud to the response of each—that explains the popularity of the "Bull" of Paul Potter—that excuses the price of Murillo's "Conception"—this one unspoken sympathy that pervades humanity, is—Vulgarity!

Vulgarity—under whose fascinating influence "the many" have elbowed "the few," and the gentle circle of Art swarms with the intoxicated mob of mediocrity, whose leaders prate and counsel, and call aloud, where the Gods once spoke in whisper!

And now from their midst the Dilettante stalks abroad. The amateur is loosed. The voice of the æsthete is heard in the land, and catastrophe is upon us.

The meddler beckons the vengeance of the Gods, and ridicule threatens the fair daughters of the land.

And there are curious converts to a weird *culte,* in which all instinct for attractiveness—all freshness and sparkle—all woman's winsomeness—is to give way to a strange vocation for the unlovely—and this desecration in the name of the Graces!

Shall this gaunt, ill-at-ease, distressed, abashed mixture of *mauvaise honte* and desperate assertion call itself artistic, and claim cousinship with the artist—who delights in the dainty, the sharp, bright gaiety of beauty?

No!—a thousand times no! Here are no connections of ours.

We will have nothing to do with them.

Forced to seriousness, that emptiness may be hidden, they dare not smile—

While the artist, in fulness of heart and head, is glad, and laughs aloud, and is happy in his strength, and is merry at the pompous pretension—the solemn silliness that surrounds him.

For Art and Joy go together, with bold openness, and high head, and ready hand—fearing naught, and dreading no exposure.

Know, then, all beautiful women, that we are with you. Pay no heed, we pray you, to this outcry of the unbecoming—this last plea for the plain.

It concerns you not.

Your own instinct is near the truth—your own wit far surer guide than the untaught ventures of thick heeled Apollos.

What! will you up and follow the first piper that leads you down Petticoat Lane, there, on a Sabbath, to gather, for the week, from the dull rags of ages wherewith to bedeck yourselves? that, beneath your travestied awkwardness, we have trouble to find your own dainty selves? Oh, fie! Is the world, then, exhausted? and must we go back because the thumb of the mounte bank jerks the other way?

Costume is not dress.

And the wearers of wardrobes may not be doctors of taste!

For by what authority shall these be pretty masters? Look well, and nothing have they invented—nothing put together for comeliness' sake.

Haphazard from their shoulders hang the garments of the hawker—combining in their person the motley of many manners with the medley of the mummers' closet.

Set up as a warning, and a finger-post of danger, they point to the disastrous effect of Art upon the middle classes.

Why this lifting of the brow in deprecation of the present—this pathos in reference to the past?

If Art be rare to-day, it was seldom heretofore.

It is false, this teaching of decay.

The master stands in no relation to the moment at which he occurs—a monument of isolation—hinting at sadness—having no part in the progress of his fellow men.

He is also no more the product of civilisation than is the scientific truth asserted dependent upon the wisdom of a period. The assertion itself requires the *man* to make it. The truth was from the beginning.

So Art is limited to the infinite, and beginning there cannot progress.

A silent indication of its wayward independence from all extraneous advance, is in the absolutely unchanged condition and form of implement since the beginning of things.

The painter has but the same pencil—the sculptor the chisel of centuries.

Colours are not more since the heavy hangings of night were first drawn aside, and the loveliness of light revealed.

Neither chemist nor engineer can offer new elements of the masterpiece.

False again, the fabled link between the grandeur of Art and the glories and virtues of the State, for Art feeds not upon nations, and peoples may be wiped from the face of the earth, but Art *is*.

It is indeed high time that we cast aside the weary weight of responsibility and co-partnership, and know that, in no way, do our virtues minister to its worth, in no way do our vices impede its triumph!

How irksome! how hopeless! how superhuman the self-imposed task of the nation! How sublimely vain the belief that it shall live nobly or art perish.

Let us reassure ourselves, at our own option is our virtue. Art we in no way affect.

A whimsical goddess, and a capricious, her strong sense of joy tolerates no dulness, and, live we never so spotlessly, still may she turn her back upon us.

As, from time immemorial, she has done upon the Swiss in their mountains.

What more worthy people! Whose every Alpine gap yawns with tradition, and is stocked with noble story; yet, the perverse and scornful one will none of it, and the sons of patriots are left with the clock that turns the mill, and the sudden cuckoo, with difficulty restrained in its box!

For this was Tell a hero! For this did Gessler die!

Art, the cruel jade, cares not, and hardens her heart, and hies her off to the East, to find, among the opium-eaters of Nankin, a favourite with whom she lingers fondly—caressing his blue porcelain, and painting his coy maidens, and marking his plates with her six marks of choice—indifferent in her companionship with him, to all save the virtue of his refinement!

He it is who calls her—he who holds her!

And again to the West, that her next lover may bring together the Gallery at Madrid, and show to the world how the Master towers above all; and in their intimacy they revel, he and she, in this knowledge; and he knows the happiness untasted by other mortal.

She is proud of her comrade, and promises that in after-years, others shall pass that way, and understand.

So in all time does this superb one cast about for the man worthy her love—and Art seeks the Artist alone.

Where he is, there she appears, and remains with him—loving and fruitful—turning never aside in moments of hope deferred—of insult—and of ribald misunderstanding; and when he dies she sadly takes her flight, though loitering yet in the land, from fond association, but refusing to be consoled.*

With the man, then, and not with the multitude, are her intimacies; and in the book of her life the names inscribed are few—scant, indeed, the list of those who have helped to write her story of love and beauty.

From the sunny morning, when, with her glorious Greek relenting, she yielded up the secret of repeated line, as, with his hand in hers, together they marked in marble, the measured rhyme of lovely limb and draperies flowing in unison, to the day when she dipped the Spaniard's brush in light and air, and made his people live within their frames, and *stand upon their legs*, that all nobility and sweetness, and tenderness, and magnificence should be theirs by right, ages had gone by, and few had been her choice.

Countless, indeed, the horde of pretenders! But she knew them not.

A teeming, seething, busy mass, whose virtue was industry, and whose industry was vice!

Their names go to fill the catalogue of the collection at home, of the gallery abroad, for the delectation of the bagman and the critic.

Therefore have we cause to be merry!—and to cast away all care—resolved that all is well—as it ever was—and that it is not meet that we should be cried at, and urged to take measures!

Enough have we endured of dulness! Surely are we weary of weeping, and our tears have been cozened from us falsely, for they have called out woe! when there was no grief—and, alas! where all is fair!

We have then but to wait—until, with the mark of the Gods upon him—there come among us again the chosen—who shall continue what has gone before. Satisfied that, even were he never to appear, the story of the beautiful is already complete—hewn in the marbles of the Parthenon—and broidered, with the birds, upon the fan of Hokusai—at the foot of Fusiyama.

* And so have we the ephemeral influence of the Master's memory—the afterglow, in which are warmed, for a while, the worker and disciple.

The Poets and the People

By One of the Latter

1887

Never was there a time in our national history when there was more need than there is now for the creation of a spirit of enthusiasm among all classes of society, inspiring men and women with that social zeal and the spirit of self-sacrifice which alone can save a great people in the throes of national misfortune. Tirades of pessimism require but little intellectual effort, and the world is not much the better for them; but to inspire a people with hope and courage, to fill them with a desire after righteousness and duty, this is work that requires the combination of intelligence and feeling of the highest order. Who, in the midst of all our poverty and distress, that threatens to become intensified, will step into the breach and rouse us to the almost superhuman effort that is necessary to alter the existing state of things?

There is one class of men to whom we have a right to look for assistance, to whom the task of stirring the national conscience should be accepted with delight. When the poor are suffering from inherent faults of their own, and the greediness of capitalists, and both are in danger of suffering still more from causes over which they have but partial control, surely the hour has come when the poets should exercise their influence for good, and set fairer ideals before all than the mere love of wealth and ostentatious display on one side and the desire to appropriate wealth on the other. But we listen in vain for any inspiring ode or ballad that shall reach the hearts of the people or touch the consciences of capitalists. What do those who are designated in the columns of our newspapers as great poets bring to us in this hour of national trial, when we are so much in need of the service of a truly great poet? One gives us a string of melancholy pessimism that has achieved no higher results than increasing the poet's fortune and drawing a magazine article from Mr. Gladstone. Another who has hitherto posed as the poet of freedom, and even licence — some would say licentiousness — when he does turn his attention to practical affairs does his best to abuse and dishearten a nation that is heroically struggling against the injustice of centuries and panting for national freedom. These things are bad enough, but what shall be said of the conduct of one who in the eyes of many is esteemed the greatest of living poets? He, at the hour when his country requires inspiration and encouragement, prostitutes his intelligence to the production of a number of unwieldy lines that to the vast majority of Englishmen are unintelligible jargon. What right has a man to the title of poet when he fails to produce music in his lines, who cannot express his thoughts in simple language that the people can understand; but, on the contrary, has so imperfect a command of his mother tongue that all the efforts of a society of intellectual pickaxes cannot discover what his words really mean? Above all, what right has a man to the title of poet who has so little sense of his duty to his fellow men as to indulge in composition of word puzzles and ear-torturing sentences when a whole people needs the assistance of every man and woman who is capable of thinking and acting? The Roman despot who played the fiddle while his city was burning might plead the ignorance of himself and his time, but Mr. Browning is living in the nineteenth century, and has no such excuses for banging his intellectual tin kettle while a fourth part of his fellow-countrymen are struggling against poverty, and are weighed down by the gloomy outlook towards the future. We are assured by his admirers that he is a great thinker—yes, more, a philosopher as well as a poet. Now, England was never in greater need of such a man, and it is Mr. Browning's duty, if he has the ability, to write plain English and act the poet's true part. Let any sensible man outside the Browning Society dip into the mysterious volume of literary hocus-pocus that has recently been so solemnly reviewed, and see whether he can find a single passage likely to stir the pulses of any man or woman, create a desire to lead a higher, a holier, and a more useful life in the breast of the indifferent average citizen. The struggle to live in all parts of Western Europe, and perhaps especially England, is so fierce that we are in danger of having all that is idealistic and beautiful crushed out of us by the steam engine and the manipulations of the Stock Exchanges. We were never in greater need of good poets, and never better able than in this practical age to do without literary medicine men and mystery mongers. Is it possible that Mr. Browning can see nothing in the world around him to induce him to make an earnest endeavour to help the people out of their difficulties and to make their duty plain? He may be a man of genius so sublime that the language of the common people is inadequate to clothe his thoughts, but his right to the title of poet is not so clear as that of the humblest writer of doggerel lines in the poets' corner of a provincial newspaper, who is aiming in his own honest way to set his followers straight. The people are suffering, and are likely to suffer more; where is the poet who is the one man needful to rouse the nation to a sense of duty and inspire the people with hope?

1.3 OSCAR WILDE

Preface to *The Picture of Dorian Gray*

1891

The artist is the creator of beautiful things.

> To reveal art and conceal the artist is art's aim.

The critic is he who can translate into another manner or a new material his impression of beautiful things.

> The highest as the lowest form of criticism is a mode of autobiography.

Those who find ugly meanings in beautiful things are corrupt without being charming.

This is a fault.

> Those who find beautiful meanings in beautiful things are the cultivated. For these there is hope.

They are the elect to whom beautiful things mean only Beauty.

> There is no such thing as a moral or an immoral book. Books are well written, or badly written. That is all.

The nineteenth century dislike of Realism is the rage of Caliban seeing his own face in a glass.

> The nineteenth century dislike of Romanticism is the rage of Caliban not seeing his own face in a glass.

> The moral life of man forms part of the subject-matter of the artist, but the morality of art consists in the perfect use of an imperfect medium.

No artist desires to prove anything. Even things that are true can be proved.

> No artist has ethical sympathies. An ethical sympathy in an artist is an unpardonable mannerism of style.

> No artist is ever morbid. The artist can express everything.

Thought and language are to the artist instruments of an art.

Vice and virtue are to the artist materials for an art.

From the point of view of form, the type of all the arts is the art of the musician. From the point of view of feeling, the actor's craft is the type.

> All art is at once surface and symbol.

Those who go beneath the surface do so at their peril.

Those who read the symbol do so at their peril.

It is the spectator, and not life, that art really mirrors.

Diversity of opinion about a work of art shows that the work is new, complex, and vital.

When critics disagree the artist is in accord with himself.

We can forgive a man for making a useful thing as long as he does not admire it. The only excuse for making a useless thing is that one admires it intensely.

All art is quite useless.

France

1.4 PIERRE-LOUIS [MAURICE DENIS]
Definition of Neo-Traditionism (*excerpt*)
1890

I

We should remember that a picture — before being a war horse, a nude woman, or telling some other story — is essentially a flat surface covered with colours arranged in a particular pattern.

.   .   .

III

Let us go to the Museum, and consider each canvas on its own, detaching it from all the others: each one will give you if not a complete illusion of nature then at least some allegedly real aspect of nature. You will see in each picture what you would expect.

Now, if it is possible, through an effort of the will, to see "nature" in these pictures, it is equally possible not to. There is an inevitable tendency among painters to relate aspects of perceived reality to aspects of paintings that they have already seen.

It is impossible to determine all the factors that may modify our modern vision, but there is no doubt that the whirlwind of intellectual activity through which most young artists pass, causes them to create genuine optical anomalies. After searching for ages to decide whether certain greys are violet or not, we now see them quite clearly as violet.

That irrational admiration for old pictures which makes us seek out their faithful renderings of "nature," since we feel obliged to admire them, has certainly distorted the eyes of the teachers of art.

Admiring modern pictures, if we study them with the same degree of dedication, generates other disturbances. Have we noticed how that elusive "nature" is always changing, that it is not the same in the 1890 Salon as in the Salons of thirty years ago, and that there is always one kind of "nature" in fashion—a whim that changes like frocks and hats?

IV

Thus the modern artist, through choice and synthesis, adopts the at once eclectic and exclusive habit of interpreting optical sensation, and this becomes the criterion of naturalism, the painter's sense of self, which the literati were later to call "temperament." It is a kind of hallucination which has nothing to do with Aesthetics, since our reason has to take it on trust but cannot control it.

.   .   .

VII

Moreover, everything to do with our sensations, whether as subject or as object, is constantly changing. You would have to be an exceptionally diligent pupil to recreate the same composition on your table for two successive days. Here are life, intensity of colour, light, movement, atmosphere— a dozen things which you can't render. Here I am dealing with familiar themes, which are none the less true and obvious!

.   .   .

IX

"Be sincere: you need only be sincere in order to paint well. Be naive. Paint quite simply what you see."

What infallible, rigorously precise machines we have tried to produce in the academies!

.   .   .

XIII

One of the young Neo-Traditionists, while at the Ecole des Beaux-Arts, having painted a woman, whose very white body shimmered with iridescent light—and it was the colour which interested him, he had taken a week to get it right—heard a modern master say: "She's not natural, you would never go to bed with a woman like that!"

How much there would be to say, if we adopted that viewpoint, about the morality of a work of art! We could compare the symbols of the Phoenicians and the Hindus, pornographic photographs, Chavannes's or Michelangelo's nudes, Rodin's amorous compositions—but with what? with analytic works, with their trompe-l'oeil, their licence pleasing both to callow youths and aged libertines: all those Roman baths, all those Temptations, all those Andromedas, all those Models, all those Studies by our young Academicians of the last fifteen Salons!

.   .   .

XVIII

Our times are literary through and through: refining even minutiae, eager for complexity. Do you really believe that Botticelli had planned all the unhealthy sensitivity and sentimental preciosity that we now perceive in his *Primavera?* This is the kind of formulae that you are bound to come up with, if you work to such a clever hidden agenda!

In all periods of decadence, the plastic arts dwindle into literary affectation or naturalistic negation.

XIX

It would be too much to ask of us to settle our spirits. The Renaissance artists just let their infinitely profound and aesthetic work pour forth from the very fullness of their nature. A Michelangelo did not have to struggle to appear great, unlike a Bernini or an Annibale Carracci. His sensations, channelled through his perfect understanding of art, automatically turned into art. It is trying too hard which has ruined the Romantics.

.   .   .

XXII

And such is the only true form of Art. When we have eliminated unjustifiable bias and illogical prejudice, the field remains open to painters of imagination and to aesthetic thinkers who appreciate the beauty of appearances.

Neo-Traditionism must not become trapped in extravagantly learned psychological theories, or in literary sentimentality, dressed up as legend, all things which do not belong to its emotional realm.

Neo-Traditionism has reached the moment of definitive synthesis. All is contained within the beauty of the work of art.

.   .   .

XXIV

Art is the sanctification of nature, that mundane nature which is content merely to be alive. What is great art—the art we call decorative—the art of the Indians, the Assyrians, the Egyptians and the Greeks, the art of the Middle Ages and the Renaissance, and the decidedly superior works of Modern Art, but the disguising of vulgar feelings — of natural objects — as sacred, hermetic and impressive icons?

What lies behind the hieratic simplicity of figures of the Buddha? Mere monks, transformed by the aesthetic sense of a pious people. Again, compare the natural lion with the lions of Khorsabad: which forces us to kneel? The Doryphorus, the Diadumenus, the Achilles, the Venus de Milo, the Winged Victory, these are, in truth, a redemption of the human form. Should we mention the Saints of the Middle Ages, both men and women? Should we add Michelangelo's Prophets and Leonardo da Vinci's Women?

I have seen the work by the Italian artist, Pignatelli, which inspired Rodin's John the Baptist, and instead of some banal model, I saw a venerable bronze, the embodiment of the Word in motion. And what kind of man was it that Puvis de Chavannes selected to be his *Poor Fisherman*, expressing eternal sorrow?

Everywhere those with aesthetic imagination triumph over those who attempt crude imitation, the emotions of Beauty triumph over the lies of Naturalism.

1.5 STÉPHANE MALLARMÉ
Action Restricted
1886

Several times a Colleague came to me, the same one, this other, to confide in me his need to act: what was he aiming at — since his approaching me announced on his part also, young as he was, the concern with creation, seemingly supreme, and success with words; I repeat, what did he mean exactly?

Unclenching your fists, breaking off with some sedentary dream, for a violent tête-à-tête with the idea, as when a fancy strikes one, or moving: but this generation seems not very concerned — even beyond its lack of interest in politics — with the desire for physical exertion. Except of course, with the monotony of winding along the pavement between one's shin bones, according to the machine at present in favor, the fiction of continuous dazzling speedway.

Acting, leaving this aside, and for the one who only smokes as a beginning, meant, oh visitor I understand you, philosophically to effect motion on many, which yields in return the happy thought that you, being the cause of it, therefore exist: no one is sure of that in advance. This can be accomplished in two ways: either in a lifetime of willing and ignoring it, until the explosion—that is thinking, or in the outpourings now in reach of the prudent grasp, the daily newspapers and their whirlwind, determining in them, in one sense, some strength—which several will dispute, whatever it is— with the immunity of no result.

As you like, according to disposition, plenitude, haste.

Your act is always applied to paper; for meditating without leaving any traces becomes evanescent, nor should instinct be exalted in some vehement and lost gesture that you sought.

To write—

The inkstand, crystal as a conscience, within its depths its drop of shadow relative to having something be: then take away the lamp.

You noticed, one does not write luminously on a dark field; the alphabet of stars alone, is thus indicated, sketched out or interrupted; man pursues black on white.

This pleat of somber lace which retains the infinite woven by a thousand, each according to the thread or the prolongation, its secret unknown, assembles distant interlacings where there sleeps some luxury to take account of—a ghoul, a knot, some foliage—and to present.

With the indispensable nothing of mystery, which remains, expressed little.

I do not know if the Host circumscribes perspicaciously his domain: it will please me to mark it out, and also certain conditions. The right to accomplish nothing exceptional, or lacking in vulgar bustle: anyone must pay for it by being omitted and, you might say, by death as a person. His exploits are committed while dreaming, so as to bother no one; but still their program is displayed for those who care nothing about it.

The writer must make himself, in the text, the spiritual actor either of his sufferings, those dragons he has nurtured, or of some happiness.

Floor, lamp, clouding of cloths and melting of mirrors, real even down to the exaggerated jerking of our gauzy form around the virile stature stopped upon one foot; a Place comes forth, a stage, the public enhancement of the spectacle of Self; there, through the mediation of light, flesh, and laughter, the sacrifice of personality made by the inspirer is complete; or else in some foreign resurrection, he is finished: his word from then on, reverberating and useless, is exhaled by the orchestral chimera.

A theater hall: he celebrates himself, anonymous, in the hero.

Everything as the playing out of festivals: a people bears witness to its transfiguration into truth.

Honor.

Be on the lookout for something similar—

Will it be recognized in these suspicious buildings detached by some banal excess from the common alignment, claiming to synthesize the miscellaneous bits of the neighborhood? If some facade in the forward-looking French taste makes an isolated apparition on some square, I salute it. Indifferent to what is uttered, in this place and that, as the flame with lowered tongues runs along the pipes.

Thus Action of the kind agreed upon, literary, does not transgress the Theater, limiting itself to representation—the immediate disappearance of the written. Let it end; in the street, somewhere else, the mask falls; I have nothing to do with the poet: perjure your verse, it is gifted with only a feeble outer power. You preferred to feed the remainder of intrigues entrusted to the individual. Why should I make it clear for you, child, you know it just as I do, retaining no notion of it except by some quality or lack which is childhood's alone; this point, that everything, whether vehicle or investment, now offered to the ideal, is contrary to it—almost a speculation on your modesty, for your silence—or it is defective, not direct and legitimate in the sense that impulse required just now, and it is tainted. Since uneasiness was never enough, I shall certainly clarify, however many future digressions it may take, this reciprocal contamination of work and means: but first was it not good to express myself spaciously, as with a cigar in convolutions whose vagueness, at the very least, traced its outline on the raw electric daylight?

A delicate being has, or so I hope, suffered—

Outside, like the cry of space, the traveler perceives the whistle's distress. "Probably," he persuades himself, "we are going through a tunnel—*the epoch*—the last long one, snaking under the city to the all-powerful train station of the virginal central palace, like a crown." The underground passage will last (how impatient you are), as long as your thoughtful preparation of the tall glass edifice wiped clean by Justice in flight.

Suicide or abstention, doing nothing, why?—Time unique in the world, since because of an event I have still to explain, there is no Present, no—a present does not exist . . . Lack the Crowd declares in itself, lack—of everything. Ill-informed anyone who would announce himself his own contemporary, deserting, usurping with equal impudence, when the past ceased and when a future is slow to come, or when both are mingled perplexedly to cover up the gap. Except for the first Paris editions supposed to divulge some faith in daily nothingness, inept if the malady measures its duration by a fragment, important or not, of a century.

So watch out and be there.

Poetry, consecration; trying out, lonely in its chaste crises, during the other gestation as it continues.

Publish.

The Book, where the satisfied spirit dwells, in case of misunderstanding, is obligated, by some struggle, to shake off the bulk of the moment. Not personalized, the volume, from which one is separated as the author, does not demand that any reader approach it. You should know that as such, without any human accessories, it happens all alone; made, being. The hidden meaning stirs, and lays out a choir of pages.

No more arrogant denial of the moment, even in the celebrations: it is to be noticed that some chance forbids to dreams the materials to fight with, or favors a certain attitude.

You, Friend, must not be deprived of years because you parallel the deaf drudgery of the many, the case is strange: I ask you, without judging, for lack of sudden preamble, to treat my information as a madness, I admit it, rare. However, it is already modified by this wisdom, or this understanding, if that's all it is—risking on some surrounding condition, incomplete at the very least, certain extreme conclusions about art which can explode, diamontinely, in this forever time, in the integrity of the Book—to play them, but and by a triumphant reversal, with the tacit injunction that nothing, pulsing in the unknown womb of the hour, shown in the pages as clear and evident, is to find this readily or perhaps another which this may illuminate.

1.6 STÉPHANE MALLARMÉ

Crisis in Poetry (*excerpt*)

1886

. . . Each soul is a melody which must be picked up again, and the flute or the viola of everyone exists for that.

Late in coming, it seems to me, is the true condition or the possibility not just of expressing oneself but of modulating oneself as one chooses.

Languages are imperfect in that although there are many, the supreme one is lacking: thinking is to write without accessories, or whispering, but since the immortal word is still tacit, the diversity of tongues on the earth keeps everyone from uttering the word which would be otherwise in one unique rendering, truth itself in its substance . . . *Only,* we must realize, *poetry would not exist;* philosophically, verse makes up for what languages lack, completely superior as it is.

.   .   .

The pure work implies the disappearance of the poet as speaker, yielding his initiative to words, which are mobilized by the shock of their difference; they light up with reciprocal reflections like a virtual stream of fireworks over jewels, restoring perceptible breath to the former lyric impulse, or the enthusiastic personal directing of the sentence.

.   .   .

One desire of my epoch which cannot be dismissed is to separate so as to attribute them differently the double state of the immediate or unrefined word on one hand, the essential one on the other.

.   .   .

What good is the marvel of transposing a fact of nature into its almost complete and vibratory disappearance with the play of the word, however, unless there comes forth from it, without the bother of a nearby or concrete reminder, the pure notion.

I say: a flower! and outside the oblivion to which my voice relegates any shape, insofar as it is something other than the calyx, there arises musically, as the very idea and delicate, the one absent from every bouquet.

A Throw of Dice Not Ever Will Abolish Chance

1897

A THROW OF DICE

NOT EVER

EVEN   WHEN   FLUNG   IN   ETERNAL

CIRCUMSTANCES

AT THE BOTTOM OF A SHIPWRECK

THAT IS
　　　　either

　　　　　　　　　the Abyss

　　　　　bleached white
　　　　　　　　　slackened
　　　　　　　　　　　　raging

　　　　　　　　　　　　under　an　incline
　　　　　　　　　　　　　by its own sail

　　　　　　　　　　　　　　　　desperately

　　　　　　　　　　　　　　　hovers
　　　　　　　　　　　　　　　　　before

fallen   back   from   a   misdirected   flight
                              and covering over the splashes
                                          cutting back its soaring

                from the deep interior recounts

          the   shadow   folded   in   the   depth   by   this   alternative   canvas

                                    until adjusted
                                        to the spread

                      its   depth   yawning   as   much   as   the   hull

                              of   a   ship

                        pitched from one side to the other

THE MASTER

arisen
    inferring

         of this conflagration

               which

           as one threatens

     the unique Number which can not

                  hesitates
             corpse by the arm

rather
   than to play
     as the old madman
       the contest
     in the name of the waves
                 one

          that direct shipwreck

beyond ancient calculations
where manipulations are forgotten with age

              once he grasped the helm

at his feet
         from the unanimous horizon

prepares itself
    is tossed and merges
        with the fist which would grip it
destiny and the wind

be another

        Spirit
           to hurl it
                into the tempest
            to seal the division and to go proudly

kept apart from the secret that it holds

overcomes the man in charge
flows through his compliant beard

of the man

    without a boat
        in   vain
            no matter where

ancestrally   not   to   open   his   hand
                              clenched
                       above a useless head

        legacy in dissipation

                      to someone
                              ambiguous

               the ulterior immemorial demon

having
        from nonexistent regions
                       led
the old man toward this supreme conjunction with probability

                              this
                                 his juvenile shadow
caressed and polished and returned and washed
                       suppled by the wave and removed
               from the hard bones lost among the planks

                              born
                                 of a frolic
the sea attempting through the ancestor or the ancestor against the sea
                       a useless luck

                                                        Betrothal

whose
        veil of illusion aroused their obsession
        as the phantom of a gesture

                       will   stagger
                       will collapse

                              madness

WILL ABOLISH

AS   IF

A   mere

in silence

into   some   nearby

flutters

insinuation

rolled up with irony
                    or
                        the mystery
                                hurled down
                                        bellowed

whirlwind of hilarity and horror

around the chasm

                neither to strew it
                                nor to flee

        and from there soothes the untouched landmark

                                                AS   IF

solitary plume lost

except

that it meets or it brushes a midnight toque
                    and immobilizes
          in the velvet crumpled by a burst of dark laughter

                    this rigid whiteness

ridiculous

                    in opposition to the heavens
          too much
                    not to make its mark
                              however small
                                        for whomever

                    bitter prince of the reef

                    puts it on his head as if heroically
                    irresistible but contained
                    by his little virile reason

                                        in a flash of lightning

anxious

     atoning and pubescent

                                             silent

                             The lucid and seignoral vertiginous
                                    invisible on the brow
                         sparkles
                               then overshadows
               a   delicate   darkened   upright
                     in the twisting of a mermaid

               with   eager   scales   terminally

laughter

which

IF

aigrette

stature

for the time
it takes to slap
forked

a rock

a false cottage
suddenly
evaporated in mists

that assigned
a   limit   to   infinity

THIS WAS
stellar born

THIS WOULD BE

worse

not

more   nor   less

but indifferently as much

THE NUMBER

WERE IT TO EXIST
other than as scattered hallucinations of agony

WERE IT TO BEGIN AND WERE IT TO STOP
emergent but denied and enclosed when apparent
finally
in rarity by some abundance poured out
WERE IT TO SUM UP

evidence of the total though as small as one
WERE IT TO ILLUMINATE

CHANCE

Thus falls
the plume
rhythmic suspense of the disaster
to be enshrouded
in the primordial foam
from where lately his frenzy surged into a peak
blunted
by the equivalent neutrality of the chasm

NOTHING

of the memorable crisis
or what was
the   event

fulfilled   itself   in   every   voided   result
                                                    of   humanity

WILL HAVE TAKEN PLACE
an   ordinary   elevation   sheds   absence

BUT THE PLACE
lower   down   splashing   quotidian   as   if   to   disperse   the   empty   act
                                    abruptly which otherwise
                                    by its falsehood
                                    had formed
                                    perdition

in these latitudes
                        of   waves
                                in which all reality dissolves

EXCEPT
            at the height
                        PERHAPS

                                    as   distant   as   a   site

that merges with the beyond

outside of interests
that have signaled to it
in general
according to such obliqueness by such declivity
of flames

toward
what must be
the Septentrion as North

A CONSTELLATION

cold from neglect and disuse
not so much
that it does not enumerate
on   some   vacant   and   higher   surface
the   next   stroke
sidereally
of a total count in the making

watching
doubting
revolving
shining and meditating

before stopping
at some last point which sanctifies it

All Thought emits a Throw of Dice

The Symbolist Manifesto (*excerpt*)

1886

Like all the arts, literature evolves: in a cycle with its returns strictly determined, complicated by various shifts over time and in the changing climates. It is clear how each new phase in artistic evolution corresponds precisely with the senile decrepitude, the ineluctable end of the school just before it. . . .

So we have been expecting the inevitable manifestation of a new art; it has been hatching for a long time. And all the silly jokes that have so delighted the press, all the concern of the serious critics, all the ill temper of the public surprised in its sheeplike torpor: more and more this all affirms how vital is the present evolution in French writing, so mistakenly called decadence by those always in a rush to judge. But notice how decadent literatures are always ambitious and lengthy, timorous and even servile: all Voltaire's tragedies, for instance, are marked with such patches of decadence. And for what could anyone reproach the new school? For its refusal of pompousness; for its strangeness of metaphors, its new vocabulary, where harmonies meld with colors and lines: these are characteristics of every renaissance.

We have already proposed the name *Symbolism* as the only reasonable designation of the present tendency of the creative spirit in art. . . .

Inimical to pedantry, to declamation, to false sensitivity, to objective description, Symbolist poetry tries to house the Idea in a meaningful form not its own end, but subject to the Idea. The latter in its turn will never appear without the sumptuous clothing of analogy; for the essential character of Symbolist art consists in never going so far as to conceive of the Idea in itself. So this art will never show details of nature, actions of humans, concrete phenomena: for they are only the appearances destined to represent to the senses their esoteric affinities with primordial Ideas.

Readers will accuse this aesthetics of obscurity: we aren't surprised. What can you do? Weren't Pindar's *Odes*, Shakespeare's *Hamlet*, Dante's *Vita Nuova*, Goethe's *Faust Part II*, Flaubert's *Temptation of Saint Anthony* said to be ambiguous?

To translate its synthesis exactly, Symbolism needs an archetypal complex style: untainted words, sentences with a central high point alternating with those with highs and lows, meaningful pleonasms, mysterious ellipses, the hanging anacoluthon, and every daring and multiform trope imaginable: the good old language set on a sure footing and modernized—the rich and joyous French language from before writers like Vaugelas and Boileaux-Despréaux, the tongue of François Rabelais and Philippe de Commynes, of Villon, of Rutebeuf and so many other free writers sending out their sharp-tongued darts, as the archers of Thrace sent out their flexible arrows.

As for the rhythm, let's have a rejuvenation of the old metrics; a cleverly ordered disorder; with gleaming rhyme hammered like a shield of gold and bronze next to a rhyme fluid and abstruse; the alexandrine with its multiple and mobile caesuras; the use of uneven numbers. . . .

Prose—novels, novellas, stories, fantasies—is evolving in a direction analagous to that of poetry. Heterogeneous elements concur here: Stendhal's translucid psychology, Balzac's extravagant vision, Flaubert's great swirling cadences, Edmond de Goncourt's suggestive modern impressionism.

The conception of the Symbolist novel is polymorphous: a single character may move about in an atmosphere deformed by his own hallucinations, his temperament: the only *reality* resides in this deformation. Beings with mechanical gestures, with shadowy silhouettes, surround this single character: they are only pretexts for his feelings and conjectures. He himself is a tragic or comic masque of a humanity rational and perfected. —Or then crowds, superficially affected by all the ambient representations, move by jolts and spurts toward actions that remain incomplete. Sometimes, individual determinations appear, attracting each other, clustering together, heading toward an end that, whether it is attained or missed, disperses them into their original elements. . . .

So, disdaining the puerile method of Naturalism—Zola was saved through his marvelous writer's instinct,—the Symbolist novel will build its work of *subjective deformation,* strong in this axiom: that art can find in *objectivity* only a simple and succinct point of departure.

Suggestive Art (*excerpt*)

1922

Suggestive art is like an illumination of things for dreams, toward which thought also is directed. Decadence or not, it is so. Let us say rather that it is growth, the evolution of art for the supreme elevation and expansion of our personal life through a necessary exaltation—our highest point of strength or moral support.

This suggestive art lies completely within the exciting realm of the art of music, and more freely and radiantly. It is also my own art through a combination of various elements brought together, of forms that are transposed and transformed without any relation to the contingencies at hand, but which nevertheless possess a logic all their own. All the errors made by critics concerning my first works were the result of their inability to see that it was not at all necessary to define, to understand, to limit, to be precise, because everything that is sincerely and humbly new—such as the beautiful from elsewhere—carries its meaning within itself.

The designation of my drawings by titles is often redundant, so to speak. A title is justified only when it is vague, indeterminate and when it aims even confusedly at the equivocal. My drawings *inspire* and do not offer explanations. They resolve nothing. They place us, just as music does, in the ambiguous world of the indeterminate.

They are a sort of *metaphor*, explained Remy de Gourmont in setting them apart, far from any sort of geometric art. He sees in them an imaginative logic. I believe that this writer has said more in a few lines than anything else formerly written about my first works.

Imagine arabesques or various types of linear involutions unwinding themselves not on a flat surface but in space, with all that which the deep and indeterminate limits of the sky can offer the spirit; imagine the play of their lines projecting upon and combining with the most diverse elements imaginable, including that of the human face. If this face possesses the particularities of him whom we encounter daily in the street, along with its very real, immediate but unexpected truth, you will have then the usual combinations that appear in many of my drawings.

Further explanation could hardly make the fact any clearer that they are the reverberations of a human expression, that, by means of the license of fantasy, they have been embodied in a play of arabesques. I believe that this action will originate in the mind of the beholder and will arouse in his imagination any number of fantasies whose meaning will be broad or limited according to his sensitivity and imaginative aptitude to enlarge or diminish.

Moreover, everything derives from universal life; a painter who neglects to draw a wall vertically draws poorly because he diverts the spirit from the idea of stability. The same is true of the painter who fails to render his water with consideration for the horizontal (to cite only the very simplest of phenomena). But in the vegetal world, for example, there are certain secret and inherent life tendencies that a sensitive landscape painter could not possibly misinterpret: the trunk of a tree forcefully thrusts out its branches according to the laws of growth and the flow of sap. A true artist must feel this and must represent it accordingly.

The same is true with animal or human life. We cannot move a hand without our entire body being displaced in obedience to the laws of gravity. A draftsman knows that. In creating certain fantastic creatures I believe that I have complied with these intuitive suggestions of the instincts. Contrary to the insinuations of Huysmans, they do not owe their conception to that terrifying world of the infinitely minute as revealed by the microscope. Not at all. While creating them I took the greatest care to organize their structure.

There is a method of drawing which the imagination has liberated from those bothersome worries presented by the details of the exterior world in order to represent only imaginary objects. I have created various fantasies based on the stem of a flower, the human face, or even on certain skeletal elements, which, I believe, were drawn, constructed and formed as they had to be. They are thus formed because they possess an organism. Any time a human figure cannot give the illusion that it is about to leave the picture frame, so to speak, to walk, act or think, the drawing is not truly modern. They cannot take away from me the merit of giving the illusion of life to my most fantastic creations. All my originality consists, therefore, in endowing completely improbable beings with human life, according to the laws of the probable and in placing, as much as possible, the logic of the visible at the service of the invisible.

This method proceeds naturally and easily from the vision of the mysterious world of shadows for which Rembrandt, in revealing it to us, supplied the key.

But, on the other hand, as I have often said, the method that has been the most fruitful and the most necessary to my development is the copying of real things, carefully reproducing the objects of the exterior world in their most minute, individual and accidental details. After attempting to copy minutely a pebble, a sprout of a plant, a hand, a human profile or any other example of living or inorganic life, I experience the onset of a mental excitement; at that point I need to create, to give myself over to representations of the imaginary. Thus blended and infused, nature becomes my source, my yeast and my leaven. I believe that this is the origin of my true inventions. I believe that this is true of my drawings; and it is likely that, even with the weakness, unevenness, and imperfection inherent in all that man recreates, one could not for an instant stand the sight of them (because they are humanly expressive), if they were not, as I have just said, created, formed, and built according to the law of life and the moral transmission necessary to all existence.

Switzerland

1.10 FERDINAND HODLER

Parallelism

C. 1900

I call parallelism any kind of repetition.

When I feel most strongly the charm of things in nature, there is always an impression of unity.

If my way leads into a pine wood where the trees reach high into heaven, I see the trunks that stand to the right and to the left of me as countless columns. One and the same vertical line, repeated many times, surrounds me. Now, if these trunks should be clearly outlined on an unbroken dark background, if they should stand out against the deep blue of the sky, the reason for this impression of unity is parallelism. The many upright lines have the effect of a single grand vertical or of a plane surface. . . .

A tree always produces the same form of leaf and fruit. When Tolstoy, in *What Is Art?* says that two leaves of the same tree are never exactly alike, one might more correctly answer that nothing looks more like a maple leaf than the leaf of the maple. . . .

I must also point out that in nearly all the examples I have just given, the repetition of color enhances that of form. The petals of a flower, as well as the leaves of a tree, are generally of the same color.

Now we also recognize the same principle of order in the structure of animal and human bodies in the symmetry of the right and left halves. . . .

Let us then sum up: Parallelism can be pointed out in the different parts of a single object, looked at alone; it is even more obvious when one puts several objects of the same kind next to each other.

Now if we compare our own lives and customs with these appearances in nature, we shall be astonished to find the same principle repeated. . . .

When an important event is being celebrated, the people face and move in the same direction. These are parallels following each other. . . .

If a few people who have come together for the same purpose sit around a table, we can understand them as parallels making up a unity, like the petals of a flower.

When we are happy we do not like to hear a discordant voice that disturbs our joy.

Proverbially, it is said: Birds of a feather flock together.

In all these examples parallelism, or the principle of repetition, can be pointed out. And this parallelism of experience is, in expression, translated into the formal parallelism which we have already discussed. . . .

If an object is pleasant, repetition will increase its charm; if it expresses sorrow or pain, then repetition will intensify its melancholy. On the contrary, any subject that is peculiar or unpleasant will be made unbearable by repetition. So repetition always acts to increase intensity. . . .

Since the time that this principle of harmony was employed by the primitives, it has been visually lost, and so forgotten. One strove for the charm of variety, and so achieved the destruction of unity. . . .

Variety is just as much an element of beauty as parallelism, provided that one does not exaggerate it. For the structure of our eye itself demands that we introduce some variety into any absolutely unified object. . . .

To be simple is not always as easy as it seems. . . .

The work of art will bring to light a new order inherent in things, and this will be: the idea of unity.

1.11 V. BRYUSOV

Keys to the Mysteries (*parts I and II*)

1904

I

When unsophisticated people are confronted with the question "What is art?" they do not try to comprehend where it came from, what place it holds in the universe, but accept it as a fact, and only want to find some application for it to their lives. Thus arise the theories of useful art, the most primitive stage in the relationship between man's thought and art. It seems natural to people that art, if it exists, should be suitable for their dearest small needs and necessities. They forget there are many things in the world that are completely useless in terms of human life, like beauty, for example, and that they themselves constantly commit acts that are totally useless—they love and they dream.

It seems ridiculous to us now, of course, when Tasso assures us that poetic inventions are similar to the "sweets" that are used to coat the edge of a dish with bitter medicine; we read, with a smile, Derzhavin's poems to Catherine the Great, in which he compares poetry to sweet lemonade. But did not Pushkin, partially under the influence of echoes of Schelling's philosophy and partially arriving at the same opinions independently, reproach the dark masses for seeking "usefulness" and say that they were worth less than a "cooking pot," and didn't his tongue slip in "Monument" when he wrote these verses:

> And I will long be the favorite of the people,
> Because I aroused good feelings with my lyre.

And didn't Zhukovsky, adapting Pushkin's poems for print, furnish the following line in a more direct way: "That I was useful because of the vital charm of my verses. . . ," which gave Pisarev cause for rejoicing.

In the greater public, the public that knows art in terms of serialized novels, operatic productions, symphonic concerts, and exhibits of paintings, the conviction that art's function is to provide noble diversion prevails, indivisibly, to this day. Dancing at balls, skating, playing cards—these are also diversions, but less noble ones; and people who belong to the intelligentsia, meanwhile, read Korolenko, or even Maeterlinck, listen to Chaliapin, go to the Peredvizhnaya, and to decadents' exhibits. A novel helps to pass the time in a train or in bed, before falling asleep, you meet acquaintances at the opera, and find diversion at art exhibits. And these people attain their goals, they really relax, laugh, are entertained and fall asleep.

None other than Ruskin, an "apostle of beauty," speaks out in his books as a defender of "utilitarian art." He advised his pupils to draw olive leaves and rose petals, in order to discover for themselves and to give others more information than we have had up to now about Grecian olives and England's wild roses. He advised them to reproduce cliffs, mountains, and individual rocks, in order to obtain a more complete understanding of the character- istics of mountainous structure. He advised them rather to depict ancient, disappearing ruins, so that their images could be preserved, at least on can- vas, for the curiosity of future ages. "Art," says Ruskin, "gives Form to knowl- edge, and Grace to utility; that is to say, it makes permanently visible to us things which otherwise could neither be described by our science, nor re- tained by our memory." And more: "the entire vitality of art depends upon its being either full of truth or full of use. Great masters could permit them- selves in awkwardness, but they will never permit themselves in uselessness or in unveracity."

A very widespread, if not prevailing, school of literary historians treats poetry in the same way that Ruskin does the plastic arts. They see in poetry only the exact reproduction of life, from which it is possible to learn the customs and mores of that time and country where the poetic work was cre- ated. They carefully study descriptions of the poet, the psychology of the characters he has created, his own psychology, passing on then to the psy- chologies of his contemporaries and the characteristics of his times. They are totally convinced that the whole sense of literature is to help in the study of life in this or that century, and that readers and poets themselves fail to realize this, as uneducated people, and simply remain in error.

Thus the theory of "useful art" has rather eminent supporters, even in our time. It is more than obvious, however, that it is impossible to stretch this theory to cover all the manifestations of art, that it is ridiculously small for it, as a dwarf's caftan would be for the Spirit of the Earth. It is impossible to limit all art to Suderman and Bourget, just to please the good bourgeois, who want "noble diversions" from art. Much in art does not come under the concept of "pleasure," if one considers this word only in its natural sense, and does not pu the term "aesthetic pleasure" under it, because it does not say anything and itself demands an explanation. Art terrifies, it shakes us, it makes us cry. In art there is an Aeschylus, an Edgar Allan Poe, a Dosto- evsky. Just recently L. Tolstoy, with his customary accuracy of expression, compared those who seek only pleasures in art to people who would try to convince us that the only goal of eating is the pleasure of taste.

It is also just as impossible to please science and knowledge by seeing only reflections of life in art. Although the most divine Leonardo wrote essays about *come lo specchio è maestro de' pittori,* and although until recently in literature and the plastic arts, "realism" seemed to be the final word (that is what is written in today's textbooks)—art has never reproduced but has always changed reality: even in da Vinci's pictures, even among the most ardent realist authors, like Balzac, our Gogol, and Zola. There is no art that can repeat reality. In the external world, nothing exists that corresponds to architecture and music. Neither the Cologne cathedral nor Beethoven's symphonies can reproduce what surrounds us. In sculpture there is only a form without any paint, in a painting there are only colors without form, but in life, however, the one and the other are inseparable. Sculpture and painting give immobile moments, but in life everything flows in time. Sculpture and painting repeat only the exterior of objects: neither marble nor bronze is able to render the texture of skin; a statue has no heart, lungs, or internal organs; there are no hidden minerals in a drawing of a mountain ridge. Poetry is deprived of any embodiment in space; it snatches up only separate moments and scenes from countless feelings, from the uninterrupted flow of events. Drama unites the means of painting and sculpture with the means of poetry, but beyond the decoration of the room there are no other parts of the apartment, no streets, no city; the actor who goes off into the wings stops being Prince Hamlet; what in actuality lasted twenty years can be seen on the stage in two hours.

Art never deceives people, with the exception of anecdotal cases, like the foolish birds pecking at fruits painted by Zeuxis. No one believes a picture is a view through an open window, no one greets the bust of his acquaintance, and not one author has been sentenced to prison for an imaginary crime in a story. Besides, we refuse to call artistic precisely those works which reproduce reality with a singular resemblance. We recognize neither panoramas nor wax statues as art. And what has been accomplished if art succeeds in mimicking nature? Of what use can the doubling of reality be? "The advantage of a painted tree over a real one," says August Schlegel, "is only that there won't be any caterpillars on it." Botanists will never study a plant according to drawings. The most expertly depicted marina will never replace a view of the ocean for the traveler, if only because a salty breeze will not blow in his face and the sounds of waves crashing against the beach rocks will not be heard. We will leave the reproduction of reality to photography and the phonograph—technicians' inventions. "Art belongs to reality as wine does to grapes," Grillparzer said.

The defenders of "utilitarian art" have, it's true, one refuge. Art does not serve the goals of science. But it can serve society, the social order. The use of art could be that it unites separate personalities, transfusing one person's feelings into another, so that it welds the classes of society into one whole and helps their historic struggle among themselves. Art from this point of view is only one means of communication for people among a number of different means, which are, first of all, the word, then writing, the press, the telegraph, the telephone. The common word and prose speech render thoughts, art renders feelings. . . . Guyau defended such a sphere of thought with force and wit. Here in Russia, L. Tolstoy has recently preached the same ideas, in a slightly altered form.

But does this theory really explain why artists create and why audiences, readers, and viewers seek artistic impressions? When sculptors knead clay, when painters cover canvases with paints, when poets seek the right word in order to express what they have to—not one of them sets his mind on transmitting his feelings to others. We know of artists who have scorned humanity, who have created only for themselves, without a goal, without the intention of making their works public. Is there really no self-satisfaction in creation? Did not Pushkin say to the artist: "Your work is your reward?" And why don't the readers cut this telegraph line between themselves and the soul of the artist? What is there for them in the feelings of someone they don't know, who may have lived many years ago, in another country? The task of scholarship about art is to solve the riddle of what consolidates the artist's dark cravings and the corresponding cravings of his listeners and viewers. And there is no solution in the scholastic answer: "art is useful because it facilitates the intercourse of feelings; and we want intercourse by feelings because we have a special instinct for communication."

The stubbornness of the advocates of "utilitarian art," despite all attacks on them by European thinkers of the last century, has not weakened yet and will probably not run dry as long as arguments about art continue to exist. There is always the possibility of pointing to its usefulness in one way or another. But how easy it is to use this object, that force! Archeologists learn about ancient life from the remains of buildings, but we don't build houses so that their ruins can help archeologists in the twenty-fifth century. Graphologists affirm that it is possible to learn about the character of a person from his handwriting. But the Phoenicians (according to the myth) invented writing for an entirely different purpose. The peasant in Krylov's fable condemned the ax to cut chips. The ax noted with justification that it was not guilty of being dull. In Mark Twain's book about the prince and pauper, poor Tom, once he is in the palace, uses the state seal to crack nuts. Perhaps Tom cracked nuts very successfully, but the state seal was meant to be used for other things.

II

People who think differently, who put aside the question of what art is needed for, what use it is, have asked themselves another metaphysical question: What is art? Separating art from life, they examine its creations as something self-important, self-contained. Thus arose the theories of "pure art"—the second stage in the relationship between man's thought and art. Carried away by the struggle with the defenders of applied, utilitarian art, these people have gone to the other extreme and have affirmed that art need never have any kind of utility, that art is diametrically opposed to all profit, all purpose: art is purposeless. Our Turgenev has expressed these thoughts with merciless frankness: "Art has no purpose other than art itself." And in a letter to Fet he is even more explicit "It's not that useless art is rubbish; uselessness is precisely the diamond in its crown." When the supporters of these views asked: what unites into one class the creations that people recognize as artistic, the pictures of Raphael, and Byron's verses, and Mozart's melodies—why is all of this art?—what do they have in common? They answered—Beauty!

This word, first uttered in the same sense in antiquity, then seized upon and repeated thousands of times by German aestheticians, has become an incantation *sui generis*. They have satiated themselves, made themselves drunk with it, not even wanting to fathom its sense.

A genius should admire
Only youth and beauty . . .

Pushkin said. Maykov repeated his precept almost word for word when he said that art:

Is like revelations
From the heights above the stars,
From the kingdom of eternal youth
And eternal beauty.

Baudelaire, who it would seem would be foreign to them, created a stunning image of Beauty, destructive and attractive:

Je suis belle, ô mortels! comme un rêve de pierre,
Et mon sein, où chacun s'est meurtri tour à tour,

Est fait pour inspirer au poète un amour
Eternel et muet ainsi que la matière

. . . .

Et jamais je ne pleure et jamais je ne ris.

When the theory of pure art had just been created, it was possible to understand that beauty meant exactly what it means in the language. It was possible to apply the word "beautiful" to almost every work of ancient art and to art of the time of pseudoclassicism. The nude bodies of statues, the images of gods and heroes were beautiful; tragedies' myths were sublimely beautiful. There were, however, hanged slaves, incest, and a Thersites in Greek sculpture and poetry—which did not fit too well with the concept of beauty. Aristotle and his later imitator Boileau had to advise artists to depict ugliness in such a way that it seemed, nevertheless, attractive. But the Romantics and their successors, the realists, rejected this embellishment of reality. All the world's ugliness invaded artistic works. Deformed faces, rags, the pitiful conditions of reality stepped out into pictures; novels and poems changed their place of action from regal castles to dank cellars and smoky attics. Poetry took on the hustle and bustle of everyday life, with the vices, horrors, and vanity of the petty, commonplace, little people of today. When the talk turned to Plyushkin, there was not any possibility of referring even to spiritual beauty. Beauty, like the virgin Astrae of mythology, the *ultima coelestum*, evidently abandoned art once and for all, and after Gogol, after Dickens, after Balzac, one was able to praise revelations only with an eye completely blind to the surroundings:

From the heights above the stars,
From the kingdom of eternal youth
And eternal beauty.

In addition, even the very concept of beauty is not immutable. There is no special, universal measure of beauty. Beauty is no more than an abstraction, a common notion, similar to the notions of truth, good, and many other widespread generalizations of human thought. Beauty varies with the centuries. Beauty is different for different centuries. What was beautiful to the Assyrians seems ugly to us; fashionable clothes, which captivated Pushkin by their beauty, arouse laughter in us; what the Chinese now consider beautiful is foreign to us. But in the meantime, works of art from all ages and all nations conquer us equally. History was recently a witness to how Japanese art subjugated all of Europe, even though beauty in these two worlds is completely different. There is inalterability and immortality in art, which beauty doesn't have. And the marble statues of the Pergamon altar are eternal not because they are beautiful, but because art has inspired its own life in them, independent of beauty.

In order to reconcile the theory of "pure art" with the facts somewhat, its defenders have had to violate the notion of beauty in every possible way. Since ancient times, when speaking about art, they began to give the concept of "beauty" different, often rather unexpected meanings. Beauty was identified with perfection, with unity in diversity, it was sought in undulating lines, in softness, in moderateness of dimensions. "The unfortunate notion of beauty," says a German critic, "has been stretched in all directions, as if it were made of rubber. . . . they say that, in relation to art, the word 'beauty' should be understood in a broader sense, but it would be better to say too broad a sense. To affirm that Ugolino is beautiful in a broader sense is the same as avowing that evil is good in a broader sense and that a slave is a master in a broader sense."

The substitution of the word "typicality" for "beauty" has enjoyed particular success. People have assured us that works of art are beautiful because they represent types. But if you lay these two concepts one on top the other, they are far from congruent. Beauty is not always typical, and not everything typical is beautiful. *Le beau c'est rare,* says one whole school of art. Emerald green eyes seem beautiful to too many people, although they are rarely encountered. Winged human figures in Eastern pictures are striking because of their beauty, but they are the fruit of fantasy and themselves create their own types. On the other hand, are there not animals that are ugly by their very distinguishing marks, which are impossible to depict typically in any other way than ugly? Such as cuttle-fish, skates, spiders, and caterpillars? And the types of all inner ugliness, all vices, all that is base in a man, or stupid, or trite—how could they become beauty? And isn't the new art, more and more boldly entering into the world of individual, personal feelings, sensations of the moment and of just this moment, breaking absolutely and forever with the specter of typicality?

In one place Pushkin speaks about the "Science of love," about "love for love," and notes:

> this important amusement,
> Praised in our forefathers' time,
> Is worthy of old apes.

These same words can be repeated about "art for art's sake." It separates art from life, i.e., from the only soil on which something can grow into humanity. Art for the sake of aimles Beauty (with a capital letter) is dead art. No matter how irreproachable the sonnet's form, no matter how beautiful the marble face of a bust, if there is nothing beyond these sounds, beyond the marble, what will attract me to it? Man's spirit cannot be reconciled with peace. "*Je hais le mouvement qui déplace les lignes*" — I hate any movement that displaces lines, says Baudelaire's Beauty. But art is always seeking, always an outburst, and Baudelaire himself poured not deathly immobility, but whirl-pools of grief, despair, and damnation into his chiseled sonnets. The same state seal that Tom used to crack nuts in the palace probably sparkled very prettily in the sun. But even its beautiful shine was not its purpose. It was created for something greater.

. . . Our personal benefit is tied to the benefit of mankind. All of us live in eternity. Those questions of existence that art can answer will never stop being topical. Art is perhaps the greatest power that mankind possesses. At the same time when all the crowbars of science, all the axes of public life, are not able to break down the walls and doors that enclose us — art con-ceals within itself awesome dynamite, which can shatter those walls, and moreover it is the *sesame* that makes doors open by themselves. Let con-temporary artists consciously forge their works in the shape of keys to the mysteries, in the shape of mystical keys that will unlock for mankind the doors of its "blue prison" to eternal freedom.

1.12 VYACHESLAV IVANOV

Thoughts about Symbolism

1912

I met a shepherd mid deserted mountains
Who trumpeted on an Alpine horn.
His song was pleasing; but his sonorous horn
Was only used to rouse a hidden echo in the mountains.
Each time the shepherd waited for its coming,
Having rung out his own brief melody,
Such an indescribably sweet harmony
Came amid the gorges that it seemed
An unseen chorus of spirits,
On instruments not of this world,

Was translating the languages of earth
Into the language of heaven.
And I thought: "O genius! like this horn
You sing earth's song to rouse in our hearts
Another song. Blessed is he who hears!"
From beyond the mountains a voice responded:
"Nature is a symbol, like this horn,
It sounds for the echo—the echo is God!
Blessed is he who hears both song and echo!"

If, as a poet, I know how to *paint* with the word (poetry is similar to paint-ing—"*Ut pictura poësis*"—classical poetics stated, through Horace, after an-cient Simonides), to *paint* so that the imagination of the listener repro-duces what I depict with the clear visual quality of what is seen, and things which I name present themselves to his soul prominent in their tangibility and graphic in their picturesqueness, darkened or illuminated, moving or frozen, according to the nature of their visual manifestation;

if as a poet, I know how to *sing* with a magical power (for "it is not suffi-cient that verses be beautiful: let them also be delightful and willfully lead the soul of the listener"—"*non satis est pulchra esse poëmata, dulcia sunto et quocumque volent animum auditoris agunto*"—as classical poetry stated, through Horace, concerning this tender constraint), if I know how to *sing* so powerfully and sweetly that the soul, entranced by the sounds, follows submissively after my pipes, longs with my desires, grieves with my grief, is enflamed with my ecstasy, and the listener replies with a harmonious beat-ing of his heart to all the tremblings of the musical wave bearing the melo-dious poem;

if, as a poet and sage, I possess the knowledge of things, and delighting the heart of the listener, I edify his intellect and educate his will;

but, if crowned with the triple crown of melodious power, I, as a poet, do not know how, with all this threefold enchantment, to force the soul of the listener to sing together with me in another voice than mine, not in unison with its psychological superficiality, but in the counterpoint of its hidden depth—to sing about that which is deeper than the depths revealed by me, and higher than the heights revealed by me—if my listener is only a mirror, only an echo, only one who receives, only one who absorbs—if the ray of my *word* does not betroth my *silence* to his silence through the *rainbow* of a mysterious precept:

then I am not a *Symbolist* poet.

II

If art is in general one of the mightiest means of uniting humanity, one could say of Symbolist art that the principle of its activity is, above all, union, union in the direct and most profound sense of this word. In truth, not only does it unite, it also combines. Two are combined by a third, the highest. The symbol, this third, resembles a rainbow that has burst into flames between the ray of the word and the moisture of the soul which reflected the ray. . . . And in every work of genuinely symbolic art is the beginning of Jacob's ladder.

Symbolism combines consciousnesses in such a way that they jointly give birth "in beauty." The purpose of love, according to Plato, is "birth in beauty." Plato's depiction of the paths of love is a definition of Symbolism. From enamorment of the beautiful body, the soul, growing forth, aspires to the love of God. When the aesthetic is experienced erotically, artistic creation becomes symbolic. The enjoyment of beauty is similar to enamorment of beautiful flesh and proves to be the initial step in erotic ascent. The meaning of artistic creation as that which has been experienced is itself inexhaustible. The symbol is the creative principle of love, Eros the leader. Between the two lives—that one incarnated in creation and the other creatively joined to it (*creatively* because Symbolism is that art which transforms whoever accepts it into a *co-participant* in creation)—is accomplished what is spoken of in the ancient, naive profundity of an Italian song, where two lovers arrange a rendezvous on the condition that a third person will also appear together with them at the appointed hour—the god of love himself:

Pur che il terzo sia presente,
E quel terzo sia l'Amor.

III

L'Amór / che muove il Sóle / e l'altre Stélle—"The Love that moves the Sun and the other Stars . . ." In this concluding verse of Dante's *Paradiso,* images are composed into myth and music teaches it wisdom.

Let us examine the musical structure of this melodic line of verse. In it there are three rhythmic waves, brought forth by the caesuras, pushing forward the words: *Amór, Sóle, Stelle*—for on them rests the *ictus.* The radiant images of the god of Love, the Sun and the Stars seem blinding as a consequence of this word arrangement. They are separated by the low points in the rhythm, the obscure and dark *muove* (moves) and *altre* (others). Night gapes in the intervals between the radiant outlines of those three ideas.

Music is embodied in a visual manifestation: the Apollonian vision emerges above the gloom of the Dionysian frenzy: indivisible and yet not combined is the Pythian dyad, the soul. But the soul, as the beholder (epopt) of the mysteries, is not abandoned without some instructive direction clarifying that which is perceived by consciousness. Some hierophant standing over it intones: "Wisdom! you see the movement of the radiant heavenly vault, you hear its harmony: know then that it is Love. Love moves the Sun and other Stars." This sacred word of the hierophant *ieros logos* is the word as *logos*.

Thus Dante is crowned with that triple crown of melodious power. But this is not yet all that he achieves. The shaken soul not only accepts, not only echoes the prophetic word: it discovers within itself and out of the mysterious depths painlessly gives birth to its fulfilling inner word. The mighty magnet has magnetized it: it too becomes a magnet. The universe is revealed within itself. What it espies in the heights above gapes in it here below. And within it is Love; for after all it already loves. *"Amór"*. . . at this sound which affirms the magnetism of the living universe its molecules arrange themselves magnetically. And within it are the sun and the stars and the harmonious tumult of the spheres moved by the might of the divine Mover. It sings in harmony with the cosmos its own melody of love that it sang in the soul of the poet when he prophesied his cosmic words—Beatrice's melody. The line of verse under discussion (which is examined not merely as the object of pure aesthetics, but in relation to the subject, as the perpetrator of spiritual experience and inner experience) proves to be not only filled with an external musical sweetness and an inner musical energy, but is polyphonic as well, the consequence of the fulfilling musical vibrations summoned forth by it and the awakening of overtones clearly perceived by us. This is why it is not only an artistically perfect verse, but a *symbolic* verse as well. This is why it is divinely poetic. Being composed, moreover, of symbolic elements insofar as its separate words are pronounced so powerfully in the given connection and the given combinations that they appear as symbols in themselves, it represents in itself a synthetic judgment in which for the subjective symbol (Love) the poet's mytho-creating intuition finds the effective word (moves the Sun and the Stars). And thus before us is the *mytho-creating* crowning of Symbolism. For the myth is the synthetic judgment where the predicate verb is joined to the symbol-subject. The sacred word, *ieros logos,* is transformed into the word as *mythos.*

If we dared to give an evaluation of the above-mentioned effect of the concluding words of the Divine Comedy from the point of view of the hierarchy of values of a religio-metaphysical order, we would have to recognize this effect as *theurgic*. And with this example we could test the already frequently pronounced identification of the genuine and exalted Symbolism (in the above-mentioned category of examination, by no means, incidentally, unnecessary for the aesthetics of Symbolist art)—with theurgy.

IV

And thus I am not a Symbolist if I do not arouse in the heart of the listener a subtle hint or influence those incommunicable sensations which at times resemble some primeval rememberance ("and for a long time on earth the soul languished, filled with a wondrous desire, and the monotonous songs of earth could not replace for it the heavenly sounds"), at times a distant, vague premonition, at times a trembling at someone's familiar and long-desired approach—whereby this remembrance and this premonition or presence we experience as the incomprehensible expansion of our individual personality and empirically restricted self-consciousness.

I am not a Symbolist if my words do not evoke in the listener feelings of the connection between that which is his "ego" and that which he calls his "*non*-ego,"—the connection of things which are empirically separated; if my words do not convince him immediately of the existence of a hidden life where his intellect had not suspected life; if my words do not move in him the energy of love towards that which he was previously unable to love because his love did not know of the many abodes it possessed.

I am not a Symbolist if my words are not equal to themselves, if they are not the echo of other sounds about which you know nothing, as about the Spirit, where they come from and where they go—and if they do not arouse the echo in the labyrinths of souls.

V

I am not a Symbolist, then, for my listener. For Symbolism signifies a relationship, and the Symbolist work in itself, as an object removed from the subject, cannot exist.

Abstract aesthetic theory and formal poetics examine an artistic work in itself; in this regard they have no knowledge of Symbolism. One can speak about Symbolism only by studying the work in relationship to the perceiving subject and to the creating subject as undivided personalities. Hence the following conclusions:

1) Symbolism lies outside all aesthetic categories.
2) Every artistic work is subordinated to evaluation from the point of view of Symbolism.

3) Symbolism is connected with the wholeness of both the individual as
   the artist himself, as well as the one who experiences the artistic
   revelation.

Obviously the Symbolist-artisan is inconceivable; just as inconceivable
is the Symbolist-aesthete. Symbolism deals with man. Thus it resurrects the
word "poet" in the old meaning—of the poet as a person (*poëtae nascuntur*)
—in contrast to the everyday use of the word in our time which strives to
lower the value of this elevated name to the meaning of "a recognized artist-
versifier, gifted and clever in his technical area."

VI

Is the symbolic element required in the organic composition of a perfect creation? Must a work of art be symbolically effective in order for us to consider
it perfect?

The demand of symbolic effectiveness is just as non-obligatory as the demands of "*ut pictura*" or "*dulcia sunto . . .*" What formal characteristic is at
all unconditionally necessary in order that a work be considered artistic?
Since this characteristic has not been named, even in our day, there is no
formal aesthetic in our time.

To make up for it there are schools. And the one is distinguished from
the other by those particular seemingly super-obligatory demands which it
voluntarily imposes on itself as the rules and vows of its artistic order. And
thus the Symbolist school demands more of itself than of others.

It is clear that these very same demands can be realized unconsciously,
outside of all rules and vows. Each work of art can be tested from the point
of view of Symbolism.

Since Symbolism designates the relationship of the artistic object to the
two-fold subject, creating and receiving, then whether the given work appears for us to be symbolic or not essentially depends on our reception. We
can, for instance, accept in a symbolic sense the words of Lermontov: "From
beneath the mysterious, cold demi-mask I heard your voice. . . ." Although
in all probability, for the author of these verses, the foregoing words were
equivalent to themselves in their logical extent and content and he had in
mind simply an encounter at a masquerade.

On the other hand, examining the relationship of the work to the integral personality of its creator we can, independent of the actual reception
itself, establish the symbolic character of the work. In any case Lermontov's
confession appears this way to us:

You will not meet the answer
Amid the noise of this world.
Out of flame and light
The word is born.

The effort of the poet to express in the external word the inner word is clear, as is his despairing of the accessibility of this latter word to reception by listeners, which nonetheless is necessary lest the flaming word, the radiant word be enveloped by darkness.

Symbolism is magnetism. The magnet attracts only iron. The normal state of molecules of iron is potentially magnetic. And that which is attracted by the magnet becomes magnetized. . . .

And thus we Symbolists do not exist if there are no Symbolist listeners. For Symbolism is not merely the creative act alone, but the creative reciprocal action, not merely the artistic objectivization of the creative subject, but also the creative subjectivization of the artistic object.

"Is Symbolism dead?" contemporaries ask. "Of course it's dead!" others reply. It's better for them to know whether Symbolism has perished for them. But we who have perished bear witness, whispering in the ears of those celebrating at our funeral feast, that there is no death.

VII

But if Symbolism has not died, then how it has grown! It is not the might of its standard bearers that has waxed strong and grown—I wish to say—but the sacred branch of laurel in their hands, the gift of the Muses of Helikon that commanded Hesiod to prophesy only the truth—their living banner.

Not long ago many took Symbolism as a device of poetic depiction, related to Impressionism, formally capable of being carried over into the category of stylistics concernin tropes and figures. After the definition of the metaphor (it seems that I am reading a fully realizable but not realized fashionable textbook on the theory of philology)—under the paragraph concerning the metaphor I envisage an example for grammar school pupils: "If the metaphor consists not of a single part of speech but is developed into an entire poem, then it is acceptable to call such a poem symbolic."

We have come a long way from the Symbolism of poetic rebuses, of that literary device (again only a device!) that consisted in the art of evoking a series of notions capable of arousing associations, the sum total of which forces one to guess and, with a special power, to perceive the subject or experience, purposely obscured, not expressed by direct meaning, but having to be deciphered. This kind, beloved in the period after Baudelaire by the

French Symbolists (with whom we have neither a historical nor ideological reason for joining forces), does not belong in the circle of Symbolism outlined by us. Not only because this is merely device; the reason lies deeper. The goal of the poet becomes in this case—to give the lyrical ideal an illusion of a great compass, in order, little by little, to decrease the compass, to condense and give substance to its content. We were about to abandon ourselves to dreams about "dentelle" and "jeu suprême" and so on,—but Mallarmé only wants our thought, having described wide circles, to alight on a single point designated by him. For us Symbolism is, on the contrary, energy liberating us from the bounds of the given, lending the soul the movement of a broadening spiral.

We want, in opposition to those who call themselves "Symbolists," to be true to the purpose of art, which takes something small and makes it great, and not vice-versa. For such is the humility of an art that loves the small. It is more characteristic for genuine Symbolism to depict the earthly than the heavenly: the power of the sound is not important to it, but rather the might of the echo. *A realibus ad realiora. Per realia ad realiora.* Genuine Symbolism does not tear itself away from the earth; it wants to combine roots and stars and grow like a starry flower out of the nearby, native roots. It does not replace things, and when speaking of the sea, means the earthly sea, and snowy heights ("and what age gleams whitely there, on the snowy heights, but the dawn, and now sows fresh roses on them,"—Tyutchev) are understood as the peaks of earthly mountains. It strives, like art, towards one thing: the elasticity of the image, its inner vitality and extensiveness in the soul, where it falls like seed and must give rise to a seed-pod. Symbolism in this sense is the affirmation of the extensiveness of the word and of art. This extensive energy does not seek or avoid intersection with spheres that are heteronomous to art, for example with religious systems. Symbolism, as we affirm it, does not fear a Babylonian Captivity in any of these spheres; it alone realizes the real freedom of art; it alone believes in its real might.

Those who have called themselves Symbolists, but did not know (as at one time Goethe, the distant father of our Symbolism, knew) that Symbolism speaks of the universal and the collective—they led us by the path of symbols through the radiant valleys in order to return to our prison, to the cramped cell of the insignificant "ego." Illusionists, they did not believe in the divine expanse and knew only the expanse of fantasy and the enchantment of slumberous daydream out of which we awoke to find ourselves in a prison. Genuine Symbolism sets a completely different goal for itself: the liberation of the soul (*katharsis*) as a development of inner experience.

The Theater of One Will

1908

On the vessel there is a seal—
on the seal, a name—
only the one who has sealed it
and the initiated know
what is hidden in the vessel.

E. C. WIESNER, *The First Bride's Silence,* a novel

You're philosophizing like a poet.

DOSTOEVSKY, *Letters*

Out of all the things that have at any time been created by the genius of man, perhaps the lightest creation on the visible surface and the most terrifying, in the depths it can reach, is theater. The fatal steps—a game—a spectacle—mystery . . . High tragedy to the same degree as light comedy and coarse farce.

Tragic horror and a fool's laughter shake the dilapidated but still seductive curtains of our world before us with equally unconquerable force. The world that seems so usual and suddenly, in the vacillation of the game, so unexpected, so wierd, astounding or repulsive. Neither the tragic nor the comic mask deceives the attentive viewer in equal measure—as they did not deceive the participants in the game, enchanting him, as they will not deceive the participant in the mystery, giving him access to the secret.

Beyond the rotting masks and beyond the rouged mugs of the carnival jester, and the pale mask of the tragic actor—the one Face shines through. Terrifying, indomitably calling . . .

The fatal steps. We played when we were children, and we've already lost heart for the simple games, now we're curious, we come to look at the spectacles and the hour is approaching when, in the transformation of mind and body, we will come to true unity in liturgical action, in a rite of mystery. . . .

When we were children, when we were alive—

Only the children are alive
We're dead, long dead.

—we played. We divided up the roles among ourselves and played them—until they called us to go to bed. Our theater was partly like everyday life—

we were very imitative and observant—partly symbolic with an undoubted tendency toward decadence—we loved fairy tales so much and words of strange, old incantations, and all the amusing and useless—useless from the practical point of view—rites of the game. The conventionalities, the naivities, and the absurdities were so dear in our games. We were well aware that it was pretending, that it was all for fun. We didn't need a decorator or a propman. We saddled a chair and agreed:

"This will be a horse."

But if we really wanted to run a little bit more, we said:

"I'll be the horse."

We weren't exclusive or one-sided in the character of our games. There was a game for the greater public, with lots of people, noise, and uproar, in the corridors of large halls, in the garden or a field:—"a fight isn't a fight, a game isn't a game"—and there were intimate games in secluded corners, where grownups and strangers never looked. There things were merry and tiring. Here it was eerie and also merry, and our cheeks reddened more deeply than when we were running wildly and dull fires were lit in our eyes.

We played and didn't know that our games were only grownups' hand-me-downs. We replayed something old that seemed new for us. And in this replaying of someone else's game, we were infected by the heavy poison of the obsolete.

The significance of a game was not in its contents, however. The drops of burning poison mixed in with the vernal nectar of a young life. The riotousness of a new life made us dizzy with light, sweet intoxication, our legs were inspired by swift racing—the heavy burdens of a difficult earthly time burned up in the ecstasy of bright oblivion. And sharp, fleeting moments burned up, and from their ashes a new world, our world, was built. A world blazing in young ecstasy . . .

And if later we wanted something else from a game, which became only a spectacle for us—and from tragedy, from comedy? We go so willingly to the theater, especially to the premieres of famous plays—but what do we want from theater? Do we want to learn the art of living or purge ourselves of obscure experiences? To decide a moral, social, aesthetic, or still another kind of problem? To see a "reed, shaken by the wind? a person dressed in soft clothes, a prophet?"

Of course all this and lots of other things can be dragged into the theater, not without foundation and even without utility—but all of this must burn up in the true theater, as old rags burn in a fire. And no matter how different the external contents of a drama are, we always want from it—if

we have still remained somewhat alive from the peaceful days of our childhood—what we wanted before from our children's games—fiery ecstasy
that abducts our soul from the tight chains of a boring and meager life. Enchantment and ecstasy—this is what attracts each of us into the theater.
These are the means by which the genius of tragedy draws us into participating in its mysterious intentions. But what makes up these intentions?

Either I absolutely don't know what drama is to a person, or it is only
for drawing a person to Me. To carry him from the kingdom of the whimsical Aisa, from the world of strange and ridiculous accidents, from the area
of comedy into the kingdom of the stern and comforting Ananke, into the
world of necessity and freedom, into the area of high tragedy. To abolish
the temptations of life and crown the eternal comforter, not the false one,
but the one who doesn't deceive.

A theatrical spectacle, to which people come for amusement or diversion, will not long remain only a spectacle for us. And soon the viewer, tired
of the alternations of spectacles alien to him will want to become a participant in a mystery play, as he was at one time a participant in a game. The
person banished from Eden will soon knock on the door with a brave hand;
behind the door the bridegroom is feasting with the wise virgins. He was a
participant in an innocent game when he still lived in paradise, in My beautiful garden between the two rivers. And now his only way to resurrection
is to become a participant in a mystery play, to join his hand with that of
his brother, with the hand of his sister in a liturgical rite, to press his lips,
eternally parched with thirst, to the mystery-filled cup, where I "mix blood
with water." To do in the bright and public temple what is now only done
in the catacombs.

But a theatrical spectacle is a necessary transitory condition and in our
time theater, unfortunately, still cannot be anything other than only a spectacle and is often an idle spectacle. Mere spectacle—that is, unless we are
speaking of the intimate theater that must be brought into being, but to
speak of which—indeed, how can one speak of it? After all this is a temptation for the uniniated . . . really only hints and outlines.

Contemporary theater wants to be primarily a spectacle. Everything in
it is set up only for spectacle. For a spectacle, there are professional actors,
footlights and a curtain, cleverly painted decorations that aspire to give the
illusion of reality, intelligent contrivances of the theater of everyday life, and
the wise fictions of conventional theater.

If a path has already begun to show in our consciousness, however, a
path along which the development of the theater must pass so that theater

answers to its high calling, then the task of the theater worker—author of drama, director, actor—consists of bringing it nearer to ecumenical activity, to mystery play and liturgy, by raising theatrical spectacle to all the perfections that are only attainable for a spectacle.

It seems to me that the first obstacle that must be surmounted on this way is the actor. The actor attracts too much of the viewer's attention to himself, and by this he overshadows both the drama and the author. The more talented the actor is, the more intolerable his tyranny is for the author, and the more harmful for the tragedy. To depose this seductive, but nevertheless harmful, tyranny, there are two methods: either transfer the center of the theatrical presentation to the viewer in the audience or transfer it to the author offstage.

The first thought that might follow upon the recognition of theater as a field of ecumenical activity would be, evidently, that the footlights must be destroyed, the curtain, perhaps, removed, and the viewer made a participant in or even a creator of the presentation. Instead of two-dimensional decorations leave four adorned walls or the external space of a street, square or field. To turn the spectacle into a masquerade, which is a combination of game and spectacle. But then why get together? Only so that the "folks get their extreme unction," as one of the contemporary ditties has it? Not a bad occupation, but where does it lead?

It's true that elements of mystery are admixed to game and spectacle in masquerade. Hints about it, secrets. But this is still not sacrament. Just as the most eerie fears come at noon, when, risen to his zenith and hidden behind violet shields, the evil Dragon weaves his spells, so the deepest secret also appears only when the masks are removed.

All the meridians meet at one pole (or two, if you wish—but by the law of the identity of polar opposites, it's always sufficient to speak of only one pole)—all earthly roads invariably lead to the one eternal Rome—"always and in everything, there is only *I*, there is no Other, nor was, nor shall be." Every unity of people has significance in so far as it leads to Me—from the vain-seductive disunity to genuine unity. The pathos of a mystery play is nourished by the accidental multitude of My and only My possibilities, the totality of which creates laws but itself moves with freedom.

And thus there is only one who wills and acts in tragedy, which adds to the unities of action, place, and time the unity of the will's aspiration in the drama.

(Perhaps the transitions in thoughts here will seem rather unexpected to some—but I don't argue, and not because I can't do it, I'm only stating one thought. "I'm philosophizing, like a poet.")

The one who wills and acts in a tragedy should always be alone, not in the sense that he leads the action of the chorus, but in the sense that he is the one who expresses the inevitable, not the tragic hero, but his fate.

Contemporary theater presents a sad spectacle of a splintered will, and for this reason, disunited action. "It takes all kinds," the simple-minded playwright thinks, "to each his own." He goes to different places, notes down the conditions, mores, and everyday life, observes various people, and depicts all of it with great verisimilitude. Kozmodemyansky and Nalimov and Vaksel recognize themselves and their neckties, and are very happy if the author—for friendship's sake—has flattered them, or they become angry if the author has made it understood that he doesn't like their looks or their behavior. The director is happy that he has enough material for an entertaining staging of a play. The actor is happy that he can get himself made up in a good and interesting way, and can mimic the looks and mannerisms of painter X, or poet Y, engineer A, advocate B. . . . The public is in ecstasy— it recognizes its acquaintances and nonacquaintances, and feels at an undoubted advantage: no matter how widespread the sins dragged out onto the stage are, every viewer, except for the small number of people on display, clearly sees, nonetheless, that he is not being depicted, but someone else.

And none of this is necessary. No mores, no customs, no everyday life, only an eternal mystery is being played out. No plots or denouements; all the plots were begun long ago, and all the denouements long ago predicted—only an eternal liturgy is being performed. What are words and dialogue? There is only one eternal dialogue; the questioner answers himself and craves an answer. And what themes? Only Love, only Death.

There are no different people, there is only one person, only one *I* in the whole universe, willing, acting, suffering, burning in an unquenchable fire, and from the fury of a horrible and ugly life saved in the good and joyful embrace of the universal comforter—Death.

I put on many masks, of My own free will, but I am always and remain in everything myself—like some Chaliapin who is always the same in all his roles. And beneath the terrifying mask of the tragic hero, and beneath the ridiculous disguise of the jester, whom the comedy makes a jest of, and in the bright coveralls of multi-colored rags that dress the body of a puppet-show clown who grimaces for the amusement of the peanut gallery—beneath all these coverings, the viewer should discover Me. The theatrical spectacle must appear before him like a problem with one unknown.

If a viewer comes to the theater, as a simple-minded gawker comes to the world, "to see the sun," then I, a poet, create a drama in order to recreate the world according to My intentions. As My will alone rules in the wide world, so only one will—the will of the poet—should rule in the small circle of the theatrical spectacle.

Drama—like the universe, also a work of one design—is a work of one creative thought. Only the author presents the fate of the tragedy, the accident of comedy. Isn't his powerful will in everything? As he wishes, so it will be. By his whim, he can unite lovers or sadly separate them, exalt the hero or cast him into a gloomy abyss of despair and ruination. He can crown beauty, youth, loyalty, bravery, insane daring, selflessness—but nothing prevents him from glorifying ugliness and debauchery, and from placing the betrayer Judas above all the apostles.

> As a rebuke to the unjust day I will raise abuse
> over the world and tempting, will tempt.

But the actor is vainglorious. He has overshadowed the author by his arbitrary interpretation, by his unsuitable and disjointed social and psychological observations, and he has turned the drama itself into a collection of roles for different parts. Then the director comes and abolishes the author's directions. Then the nemisis of the dramatic action, the hollow voice of the commanding Moira, is hidden by the theater manager's order in the narrow prompter's box. And when there have been few rehearsals, then everyone on stage focuses on one point, from which an annoying voice is heard by those in the first rows. And they mercilessly garble the poet's words.

But do I really want to have my voice heard from a narrow cellar? to have windows I thought up turned into unnecessary (for my purposes) columns on the stage by the whim of a director? to have my words and stage directions realized only in the painted sets?

No, my words should sound loudly and clearly. The visitor at a theatrical spectacle should hear the poet before the actor.

This is how I imagine a theatrical spectacle: the author, or a reader who replaces him—and even better a reader, passionless and calm, and not agitated by the author's shyness before the viewers who will shout praise or approbation at him (both are equally unpleasant), and perhaps they have brought with them some latchkeys for whistling merrily—the reader will sit near the stage, somewhere to the side. On the table in front of him will be the play that is to be presented. The reader will begin, in order, at the beginning:

He reads the title of the drama. The name of the author.

If there is an epigraph, he reads it. There are interesting and useful ones.

For instance, the epigraph of *The Inspector General:* "It's no use scolding the mirror if your mug's crooked. A folk saying." A coarse epigraph, as was the author—but fair and suitable for the establishment of the appropriate connection between the viewer and the action on stage.

Then the list of the dramatis personae.

The preface or the stage directions, if there are any.

The first act. The setting. The names of the people on stage.

The actors' entrances and exits, as they are noted in the text of the drama.

All the stage directions, not omitting even the slightest, even if it's just one word.

As the reader is near the stage reading, the curtain moves, is raised. The stage is revealed. The setting requested by the author is lit. The actors come out on stage, and do what is spelled out for them in the author's stage directions, just read, and they say what is stated by the text of the drama. If the actor forgets a word—and when doesn't he forget them!—the reader reads it, just as calmly, also aloud, like all the rest.

And the action unfolds before the viewer, as it unfolds before us in life itself; we go and speak according to our own wills (or so we imagine); we do what we have to do, or what comes into our heads, and try to realize our own desires (or so it seems), in so far as the laws of nature or the desires of other people do not hinder us; we see, listen, smell, touch, taste. We use all our senses and mental efforts to find out what there is in the real world, what has its own existence and laws, partly understandable to us, partly miraculous for us; we feel love for one person and hate for another, and we are aroused by still other passions, in conformity with them establish our relationships with the world and with people. And we usually don't know that we have no independent will, that our every movement and our every word are dictated and even long ago predicted in the demonic creative plan of the universal game once and for all, so that we have neither choice nor freedom, nor even ad-libbing, so dear to the actor, because it has been included in the text of the universal mystery by some unknown censor: and that world we are cognizant of is nothing other than a marvelous decoration, and beyond it there is backstage untidiness and dirt. We play the role dictated to us the best we know how, actors and at the same time viewers, alternately applauding or booing each other, sacrificing and at the same time being sacrificed.

Can the theater give us any spectacle other than that of a world too wide for our strengths and too narrow for our will? And should it? Play as you live, transfer your life to the stage, isn't that what the theater of everyday life wants?

But what will remain of the actor's playing then? After all, the actor will turn into a speaking marionette, and an actor can't like this, especially if he likes strong roles and the audience's attention turned toward him and the cries of the simple-minded in the peanut gallery, and the newspapers' clamor around his name. Such theater is unacceptable for the contemporary actor. He will say scornfully:

"That won't be a theatrical presentation, but simply a literary reading, accompanied by conversations and movements. Then it would be better to organize a marionette theater, a child's amusement. Let painted dolls move, let one person offstage speak with seven voices—speak and jerk the strings."

And why shouldn't an actor be like a marionette, however? It's not insulting for a person. Such is the unshakable law of the universal game. That a person is like a marvelously made marionette. And it's impossible for him to leave this behind, and even impossible for him to forget it.

Everyone's appointed hour will come, and everyone will turn into an immobile and lifeless doll, no longer able to play any roles. . . .

Here it is, a worn-out doll that no one needs, lying on the canvas for the last ablution, its arms are crossed as they crossed them, its legs are extended, as they pulled them, its eyes are closed, as they closed them—a poor marionette fit for tragic play alone! Back there, in the wings, someone indifferently pulled your invisible strings, some cruel person tortured you with the fiery torment of suffering, some evil person frightened you with the pale horrors of a hateful life, you turned your grieving gaze toward some merciless person in pre-death langor. But here, in the main floor seats, your clumsy movements—caused by the jerking of the terrible strings—your confused words—the hidden prompter spoke so softly—and your useless tears and your pitiful laughter, as useless as the tears, have amused someone. Enough, all the words of your role are somehow spoken, all the author's directions have been followed fairly closely—the strings are rolled up—and your dried lips now want to say some new word in vain—they open and close mechanically—and fall silent forever. They'll hide you and dig a place for you, and forget you. . . .

An actor, even one with great genius, is no more than a person. His role, even the strongest, is less than life and easier than it. And it is of course better for him to be a speaking marionette and to move in accordance with the intelligible and passionless voice of the reader than desperately mix up his lines, to the accompaniment of the hoarse whispering of the prompter hidden in his box.

The single, even, and passionless voice of the "man in black" leads the entire theatrical action—and in correspondence with this, everything on stage should aspire to the unity that is necessary so that the viewer's unsteady attention is not dispersed, so that nothing is distracted from what is singularly substantive in a theatrical spectacle—the exposure, by dramatic action, of My single, changeless Image, beneath the many and varied masks.

The person performing the action is never onstage by himself. Even when there are no other actors on the visible stage, the person who remains before the viewers' eyes carries on a constant dialogue with someone. The aspiration toward unity, toward Me, can originate only in that which is My polar opposite—the many, the not-I. But all streams must flow together into one sea and not be lost in the quicksand of the divided multitude. The single Image, hidden under masks, should show through to the viewers in the course of the theatrical action. From this comes the demand that there be only one hero, essentially one dramatis persona, only one point on which the viewers' attention is focused. And the rays of stage action should come together in one focus, so that the bright flame of ecstasy suddenly flares up.

The other personae in the drama should be only necessary steps in the progression toward the single Image. Their significance in the drama depends entirely on the degree of their proximity to the center of the will's aspiration in the drama, as it is revealed in the hero. Only in this kind of arrangement, on the descending scale of ranks of one and the same staircase of dramatic action, lies the basis of their individual differences, their separate characteristics, which otherwise would in no way be needed in the drama. Desdemona is significant in the tragic situation not because she has a great and touching role, not because Othello loved and destroyed her, but because she was that fatal person whose hand removed his mask and revealed only to him the fatal falsehood and ambivalence of the world.

It follows, from the fact that an actor in a tragedy should essentially be alone, that theater should be freed from play-acting. A game, with all its variety of faithfully observed and accurately reproduced gestures and intonations, with all that has entered into theatrical tradition, that is acquired by diligent training, or that is discovered again by the gifted actor's guessing and inventing, this is the game that seems normal to us, inspired or serenely deliberate, that presents a depiction of conflict and struggle of totally separate people, each of which is sufficient unto himself. But there are no such autonomous personalities on earth. Thus there are no struggles between them. There is only the appearance of a struggle, the fatal dialectics on their faces. And a struggle with fate is unthinkable, there is only a demonic game, fate's amusement with its marionettes.

The better the actor plays the role of Man, the more pathetically he cries: "We'll bang our shields, we'll cross our swords," the more ridiculous is his irrelevant game, the more clear his incomprehension of the role. "Someone in gray" has never accepted a challenge to a duel from anyone. A little girl doesn't fight with her dolls—she tears them up and breaks them, and she laughs or cries, depending on her mood.

It becomes funny for us to see an actor being too zealous, and a grandiose declamation, and a majestic gesture, and extreme conscientiousness in transmitting particulars of everyday life—all these charming things make us feel a little uncomfortable. Uncomfortable, as when someone suddenly begins speaking loudly and excitedly and begins to gesticulate in front of a sedate gathering. It's not worth it to act very zealously. Only the people in the peanut gallery will laugh or cry at what is presented on stage—the people on the main floor smile slightly, sometimes sadly, sometimes almost gaily, always ironically. It's not worth acting for them.

Tragedy tears away the world's enchanting mask, and where it seemed to us there was harmony, predetermined or created, it opens up before us the world's eternal contradictino, the eternal identification of good and evil and other polar opposites. It affirms every contradiction and to every one of life's pretensions, correct or not, it equally and ironically says *Yes!* To neither good nor evil will it say the lyrical *No!* Tragedy is always irony; it is never lyrical. We must stage it that way.

And so there should be no acting on the stage. Only the even transmission, word by word, the calm reproduction of situations, scene by scene. And the fewer scenes there are, the slower they change, the clearer the tragic intentions emerge before the enchanted viewer. Let the tragic actor stop straining and grimacing—extreme gestures and bombastic declamation should be left to the clowns and the buffoons. The actor should be cool and calm, his every word should resound smoothly and deeply, his every movement should be slow and beautiful. The presentation of tragedy should not remind us of the flickering of pictures at a cinema. And the attentive viewer must pass along the very long path to comprehending tragedy without this annoying and useless flickering.

Furthest of all from the viewer stands the hero of the tragedy, the chief manifestation of My will—the path to understanding him is the longest of all, the viewer has to ascend a steep staircase to him, to overcome and conquer much within and without himself. And the further from the hero, the nearer to the viewer, the more comprehensible it is for him, and finally the characters come so close to the viewer that they more or less coincide with him. They begin to resemble the chorus in an ancient tragedy, saying what the people seated on the steps of the ampitheater would have said.

And so the peaceful and content bourgeois comes to the theater. How is he to accept the plot and the denouement of the drama, and what will he understand in it, if these speeches, all foreign to his notions, will ring out from the stage? Just as you do not have a Shakespearean tragedy without a jester, so contemporary drama cannot get along without these cliched mannequins, whose faces are obliterated, whose mechanisms are slightly damaged and squeak, and whose words are dull and commonplace. And if the bourgeois himself were to shudder at their intolerable flatness, then that would be good, there would be a comforting sign in this, a sign that he is nearing the comprehension of the single Image, who hides under various masks, injured but not killed by the flatness of earthly speech. In this lies the true justification of light comedy and farce, and even puppet show buffoonery.

There is also another meaning in this—because until now this has been the only means in the public theater—again I am not speaking of intimate theater, most desired and dear for us, but about which it is so difficult to speak—the only means of involving the viewer in the action. It is the only way and in many cases it is perhaps enough.

And even mystery itself, being action that is ecumenical to a great degree, still demands one performer, priest and victim, for the sacrament of self-sacrifice. Not only the highest kind of social activity, the mystery, but social accomplishment in general is at the same time completely individual. Every common deed is performed according to the thought and plan of one person, every parliament listens to one orator and doesn't raise a hubbub together, gathering together in a common, merry din. "On the vessel there is a seal, on the seal a name; only the one who sealed it and the initiated know what is hidden in the vessel." The temple is open to everyone, but the name of the builder is chiselled in stone. The person coming to the altar must leave his spite at the threshold. And so the crowd—viewers—cannot be mixed into the tragedy, except by means of burning their old and trivial words in themselves. Only passively. The person performing the action is always alone.

What can the interest for the stage be in flooding it with a multitude of people, each of whom pretends to have his own character and his separate role in the drama? Their flickering is annoying to one who understands drama, it's difficult to keep them all straight, and there's no point. It's even hard, for this reason, to read a drama—you always have to look at the dramatis personae. That's why drama isn't in favor in the book business.

Isn't it all the same to me who is fussing and bustling about on stage, Shuysky or Vorotynsky—if I know that before me a tragedy of imposture is going on, so brilliantly plotted by the genius of Russian history (and yet so insipidly outlined by the geniuses of Russian literature)! One person speaks, or another, aren't these your words, simple-minded viewer? Aren't those your dull, long ago effaced and still dear, nickels rolling on the floor of the stage, next to the ruddy gold of poetry?

It is a naive accounting—but wise and true—that as the theatergoer greedily picks up his nickels, he will take even My heavy gold with them and sell Me in exchange his soul, which, though it be of little weight, is still dear to me. But it's better, nonetheless, if less of this change is on the floor of the stage: a plea addressed to the authors of drama.

As only one in a drama has a will—the author, and only one performs the action—the actor, so should there be only one viewer. In this respect, that insane king who saw the play of his actors alone in his magnificent theater, hiding behind the thick damask in the silence and darkness of his royal loge, was right. In tragic theater every viewer should feel like this insane king who hid from everyone. And no one should see his face and no one be surprised that

> he veiled the game of
> his passions with a secret,
> at times happy at the grave
> and sad at the feast.

And if he dozes or falls deeply asleep—art is a golden dream—and why couldn't the dream be a rhythmic dream vision—no one will laugh at him, and no one will be disturbed or shocked by his sudden snoring in the most pathetic part.

And he himself should neither see nor hear anyone—neither the people artlessly reflecting on their faces all the feelings, moods, distresses, and sympathies, nor those who pretend to understand and be intelligent. Not see a handkerchief by reddened eyes, a nervously wadded glove in restless hands. Not hear those who sniff and sob, or those who laugh when they're supposed to laugh and even when they're supposed to cry. The viewer of a tragic spectacle should be in darkness, silence and solitude. Like the prompter in his narrow box. Like a theater mouse.

Not distracted by anything peripheral, a viewer should not be distracted by anything on stage that is not strictly necessary for the drama. Whether the excellently painted sets should be on the stage or only drapes hanging over or lying on it—in any case the stage should be arranged in two dimensions. This spectacle should be like a painting, so that the viewer doesn't have to look for an actor in the depths of a multidimensional stage, in that area where something can be externally hidden, at the same time when his attention should be concentrated on him who acts and wills and contemplates.

Scenery on stage is pleasant—it sets the desired mood straightaway, gives the viewer all the external hints—and why shouldn't it be there? If, in the wide, external world also:

> And suddenly it all seemed like
> flat decorations to me then—
> the dawn stretched out like a paper strip,
> a star twinkled like spangles.

But a person lost in the world of external decorations comes to the theater to find himself—to come to Me. And it's impossible to distract his gaze by an unnecessarily splendid variety of scenery. By the way, it's better, for this reason, for the drama to be performed with only one set of scenery. In any case at every given moment the viewer should know what he is supposed to be looking at, what he should be seeing and listening to on the stage. The author's directions, loudly pronounced by the reader, will of course help in this, and all the art of mechanical contrivances will help him in this too. Everything that appears to the viewer on stage should be significant, each detail of the setting should be strictly thought out, so that there is nothing superfluous, nothing beyond what is most necessary, in front of the viewer.

The lighting arrangements are perhaps appropriate and advisable along these same lines: perhaps the viewer should only be shown what he must see at a given moment, and all the rest should disappear in darkness, as everything we pay no attention to falls under the threshold of our consciousness. It exists, but at the same time it seems like it doesn't. Because for Me, only what is in Me and for Me exists—all the rest, despite its possible reality for someone else, lies only in the world of possibilities, only awaits its turn to be.

Such is the outline of the form for a theatrical spectacle. And the contents put into this form can be the tragic play of Fate with its marionettes, a spectacle of the fatal melting of all earthly masks, or a mystery of complete self-affirmation. Playing, I play with dolls and masks—and the masks and covers, visible to the world, fall away—and My single image is mysteriously revealed, and rejoicing. My single will triumphs. My fatal error ties all knots

and I struggle with the constricting fetters of irresolvable, earthly contradiction—until a sharp stiletto, piercing My heart, cuts the fatal knots. I have
raised worlds with a merry game—and I am victim and I am priest. Burning love is comforting, and consuming, it burns—and the final comforter
is—Death.

Of course theater gravitates toward tragedy. And it should become tragic.

Every farce in our time becomes a tragedy, our laughter sounds more
terrifying than our lament to the sensitive ear, and hysterics precede our
ecstasy. In the old days, happy, healthy people laughed. The victors laughed
and the defeated cried. Among us, the grieving and the insane laugh, Gogol
laughs. . . . My insanity has happy eyes.

Our comedy, to put it simply, is nothing more than funny and amusing
tragedy. But tragedy is also funny for us.

The sorrows of young Werther? No. They're the sorrows of a conscientious high school student. It's very funny but also very serious. He could
have been birched—but he shot himself. Little girls crowd around the grave
dug for him, roses fall on his coffin—parents cry and sniff. They wanted to
birch him, but they didn't make it in time. It's not their fault.

Around us rippling laughter pours forth like music. It is rhythmic perhaps. It calls for dances. And does only Death dance on the fresh graves?
We also know how to dance. We're a terrible merry people—we dance like
a family of gravediggers during a cholera epidemic. . . .

No matter what the contents of future tragedy are it cannot manage without dance. It's not surprising that quick-witted authors of drama are now
putting the cakewalk, maxixe and other kinds of nonsense in their plays.

But the dance, I hope, will be choral. And for this we must take away the
footlights in the theater.

If the contemporary viewer can only participate in the theatrical spectacle in such a way that he will recognize himself in the more or less distorted
mirrors placed on the stage for him, then the next step of his participation
in tragic action should be his participation in tragic dance.

It's good that Isadora Duncan dances with her legs bare, inspired by
the dance. . . .

> How nice it is to know that there is
> another life with us!
> VALERY BRYUSOV

But soon we will all become infected with this "other life," and like religious zealots, will gush onto the stage and whirl in violent zeal.

The action of the tragedy will be accompanied by and alternate with dance. Merry dancing? Perhaps. In any case more or less violent. Because dance is no more than rhythmic violence of body and soul, submerging in the tragic element of music.

If you look at a person dancing and think that as he is turning he is being bathed in sweat, and thus loves to be bathed in a tender aroma of scents, then you are mistaken, of course. He is not turning before you—the world around him revolves ever faster and faster, dying, decaying, melting in swift, free, and light movement. But you don't see this universal whirling, because you're shy and sensible, and don't dare to give yourself up to the violent rhythm of dance that dissolves the chains of everyday life. You see only the humorous—the faces too red, an arm awkwardly put out to the side or un-flatteringly bent, damp locks of hair, and those disgusting little drops on young skin. You don't know that it is the world's whirling that fans sweet fire onto the frenzied body which has surrendered to the universal dance, and Eden's dew combined in itself joyous coolness and joyous heat.

A black lock beats against a white neck, the tip of a white slipper flickers from under a white dress, a happy smile on vermillion lips sparkles and is carried away, the train sweeps and brushes. Put on your gloves, invite whichever lady you want, don't be afraid—this is only a ballroom dance, and you're not at Brocken but in the dance hall of Baronness Jourfixe. The floor is waxed—"the gift of the wise bees"—but is not dangerous at all. "The Maiden Snandulia dances only with those who are worthy of being her partner" (Wedekind: *The Awakening of Spring*)—she is a well-bred maiden, although "her dress is low-cut in front and back—in back to her waist, in front to drive a man mad. She has, of course, no shift."

This ballroom dance is only a hint at what should be a tragic dance. It's true that the dancing lady's corset, gloves, and slippers partly, although only to a slight degree, correspond to the mask of the ancient tragic actor. But after all we know that we need no mask made by a theatrical propman, no matter how good it is. We always wear our own masks, and they fulfill their purposes so well that we often deceive ourselves and others with the game of the expressions.

The entire world is only scenery, behind which the creative soul hides. My soul. Every earthly face and every earthly body is only a mask, only a marionette for a single performance of the earthly tragicomedy—a mario-nette made for words, gestures, laughter and tears. But tragedy comes, re-fines the decorations and appearances, and through the decorations the world transformed by Me, the world of My soul, the fulfillment of My will, shows through — and through the masks and appearances, My single image and transformed flesh show through. Beautiful and liberated flesh.

The rhythm of liberation is the rhythm of the dance. The pathos of liberation is the joy of the beautiful, naked body.

The dancing viewers, male and female, will come to the theater, and at the threshold, they will leave their coarse, petty bourgeois clothes. And they will dart about in light dancing.

And so the crowd that came to watch will be transformed into a group dancing in a ring that has come to participate in the tragic drama.

Ireland

1.14 WILLIAM BUTLER YEATS

Anima Hominis (excerpt)

1917

I

When I come home after meeting men who are strange to me, and sometimes even after talking to women, I go over all I have said in gloom and disappointment. Perhaps I have overstated everything from a desire to vex or startle, from hostility that is but fear; or all my natural thoughts have been drowned by an undisciplined sympathy. My fellow-diners have hardly seemed of mixed humanity, and how should I keep my head among images of good and evil, crude allegories.

But when I shut my door and light the candle, I invite a Marmorean Muse, an art, where no thought or emotion has come to mind because another man has thought or felt something different, for now there must be no reaction, action only, and the world must move my heart but to the heart's discovery of itself, and I begin to dream of eyelids that do not quiver before the bayonet: all my thoughts have ease and joy, I am all virtue and confidence. When I come to put in rhyme what I have found it will be a hard toil, but for a moment I believe I have found myself and not my anti-self. It is only the shrinking from toil perhaps that convinces me that I have been no more myself than is the cat the medicinal grass it is eating in the garden.

How could I have mistaken for myself an heroic condition that from early boyhood has made me superstitious? That which comes as complete, as minutely organised, as are those elaborate, brightly lighted buildings and sceneries appearing in a moment, as I lie between sleeping and waking, must come from above me and beyond me. At times I remember that place in Dante where he sees in his chamber the "Lord of Terrible Aspect," and how, seeming "to rejoice inwardly that it was a marvel to see, speaking, he said, many things among the which I could understand but few, and of these this: ego dominus tuus"; or should the conditions come, not as it were in a gesture—as the image of a man—but in some fine landscape, it is of Boehme, maybe, that I think, and of that country where we "eternally solace ourselves in the excellent beautiful flourishing of all manner of flowers and forms, both trees and plants, and all kinds of fruit."

II

When I consider the minds of my friends, among artists and emotional writers, I discover a like contrast. I have sometimes told one close friend that her only fault is a habit of harsh judgment with those who have not her sympathy, and she has written comedies where the wickedest people seem but bold children. She does not know why she has created that world where no one is ever judged, a high celebration of indulgence, but to me it seems that her ideal of beauty is the compensating dream of a nature wearied out by over-much judgment. I know a famous actress who in private life is like the captain of some buccaneer ship holding his crew to good behaviour at the mouth of a blunderbuss, and upon the stage she excels in the representation of women who stir to pity and to desire because they need our protection, and is most adorable as one of those young queens imagined by Maeterlinck who have so little will, so little self, that they are like shadows sighing at the edge of the world. When I last saw her in her own house she lived in a torrent of words and movements, she could not listen, and all about her upon the walls were women drawn by Burne-Jones in his latest period. She had invited me in the hope that I would defend those women, who were always listening, and are as necessary to her as a contemplative Buddha to a Japanese Samurai, against a French critic who would persuade her to take into her heart in their stead a Post-Impressionist picture of a fat, ruddy, nude woman lying upon a Turkey carpet.

There are indeed certain men whose art is less an opposing virtue than a compensation for some accident of health or circumstance. During the riots over the first production of the *Playboy of the Western World* Synge was confused, without clear thought, and was soon ill—indeed the strain of that week may perhaps have hastened his death—and he was, as is usual with gentle and silent men, scrupulously accurate in all his statements. In his art he made, to delight his ear and his mind's eye, voluble dare-devils who "go romancing through a romping lifetime . . . to the dawning of the Judgment Day." At other moments this man, condemned to the life of a monk by bad health, takes an amused pleasure in "great queens . . . making themselves matches from the start to the end." Indeed, in all his imagination he delights in fine physical life, in life when the moon pulls up the tide. The last act of *Deirdre of the Sorrows,* where his art is at its noblest, was written upon his death-bed. He was not sure of any world to come, he was leaving his betrothed and his unwritten play—"Oh, what a waste of time," he said to me; he hated to die, and in the last speeches of Deirdre and in the middle act he accepted death and dismissed life with a gracious gesture. He gave to Dierdre the emotion that seemed to him most desirable, most difficult, most fitting, and maybe saw in those delighted seven years, now dwindling from her, the fulfilment of his own life.

III

When I think of any great poetical writer of the past (a realist is an historian and obscures the cleavage by the record of his eyes) I comprehend, if I know the lineaments of his life, that the work is the man's flight from his entire horoscope, his blind struggle in the network of the stars. William Morris, a happy, busy, most irascible man, described dim colour and pensive emotion, following, beyond any man of his time, an indolent muse; while Savage Landor topped us all in calm nobility when the pen was in his hand, as in the daily violence of his passion when he had laid it down. He had in his *Imaginary Conversations* reminded us, as it were, that the Venus de Milo is a stone, and yet he wrote when the copies did not come from the printer as soon as he expected: "I have . . . had the resolution to tear in pieces all my sketches and projects and to forswear all future undertakings. I have tried to sleep away my time and pass two-thirds of the twenty-four hours in bed. I may speak of myself as a dead man." I imagine Keats to have been born with that thirst for luxury common to many at the outsetting of the Romantic Movement, and not able, like wealthy Beckford, to slake it with beautiful and strange objects. It drove him to imaginary delights; ignorant, poor, and in poor health, and not perfectly well-bred, he knew himself driven from tangible luxury; meeting Shelley, he was resentful and suspicious because he, as Leigh Hunt recalls, "being a little too sensitive on the score of his origin, felt inclined to see in every man of birth his natural enemy."

IV

Some thirty years ago I read a prose allegory by Simeon Solomon, long out of print and unprocurable, and remember or seem to remember a sentence, "a hollow image of fulfilled desire." All happy art seems to me that hollow image, but when its lineaments express also the poverty or the exasperation that set its maker to the work, we call it tragic art. Keats but gave us his dream of luxury; but while reading Dante we never long escape the conflict, partly because the verses are at moments a mirror of his history, and yet more because that history is so clear and simple that it has the quality of art. I am no Dante scholar, and I but read him in Shadwell or in Dante Rossetti, but I am always persuaded that he celebrated the most pure lady poet ever sung and the Divine Justice, not merely because death took that lady and Florence banished her singer, but because he had to struggle in his own heart with his unjust anger and his lust; while unlike those of the great poets, who are at peace with the world and at war with themselves, he fought a double war. "Always," says Boccaccio, "both in youth and maturity he found room among his virtues for lechery"; or as Matthew Arnold preferred to change the phrase, "his conduct was exceeding irregular." Guido Cavalcanti, as Rossetti translates him, finds "too much baseness" in his friend:

And still thy speech of me, heartfelt and kind,
Hath made me treasure up thy poetry;
But now I dare not, for thy abject life,
Make manifest that I approve thy rhymes.

And when Dante meets Beatrice in Eden, does she not reproach him because, when she had taken her presence away, he followed in spite of warning dreams, false images, and now, to save him in his own despite, she has "visited . . . the Portals of the Dead," and chosen Virgil for his courier? While Gino da Pistoia complains that in his *Commedia* his "lovely heresies . . . beat the right down and let the wrong go free":

Therefore his vain decrees, wherein he lied,
Must be like empty nutshells flung aside;
Yet through the rash false witness set to grow,
French and Italian vengeance on such pride
May fall like Anthony on Cicero.

Dante himself sings to Giovanni Guirino "at the approach of death":

The King, by whose rich grave his servants be
With plenty beyond measure set to dwell,

Ordains that I my bitter wrath dispel,
And lift mine eyes to the great Consistory.

V

We make out of the quarrel with others, rhetoric, but of the quarrel with
ourselves, poetry. Unlike the rhetoricians, who get a confident voice from
remembering the crowd they have won or may win, we sing amid our uncertainty; and, smitten even in the presence of the most high beauty by
the knowledge of our solitude, our rhythm shudders. I think, too, that no
fine poet, no matter how disordered his life, has ever, even in his mere life,
had pleasure for his end. Johnson and Dowson, friends of my youth, were
dissipated men, the one a drunkard, the other a drunkard and mad about
women, and yet they had the gravity of men who had found life out and
were awakening from the dream; and both, one in life and art and one in
art and less in life, had a continual preoccupation with religion. Nor has
any poet I have read of or heard of or met with been a sentimentalist. The
other self, the anti-self or the antithetical self, as one may choose to name
it, comes but to those who are no longer deceived, whose passion is reality.
The sentimentalists are practical men who believe in money, in position,
in a marriage bell, and whose understanding of happiness is to be so busy
whether at work or at play, that all is forgotten but the momentary aim.
They find their pleasure in a cup that is filled from Lethe's wharf, and for
the awakening, for the vision, for the revelation of reality, tradition offers
us a different word—ecstasy. An old artist wrote to me of his wanderings
by the quays of New York, and how he found there a woman nursing a sick
child, and drew her story from her. She spoke, too, of other children who
had died: a long tragic story. "I wanted to paint her," he wrote, "if I denied
myself any of the pain I could not believe in my own ecstasy." We must not
make a false faith by hiding from our thoughts the causes of doubt, for faith
is the highest achievement of the human intellect, the only gift man can
make to God, and therefore it must be offered in sincerity. Neither must we
create, by hiding ugliness, a false beauty as our offering to the world. He
only can create the greatest imaginable beauty who has endured all imaginable pangs, for only when we have seen and foreseen what we dread shall we
be rewarded by that dazzling unforeseen wing-footed wanderer. We could
not find him if he were not in some sense of our being and yet of our being
but as water with fire, a noise with silence. He is of all things not impossible
the most difficult, for that only which comes easily can never be a portion of
our being, "Soon got, soon gone," as the proverb says. I shall find the dark

grow luminous, the void fruitful when I understand I have nothing, that the ringers in the tower have appointed for the hymen of the soul a passing bell.

The last knowledge has often come most quickly to turbulent men, and for a season brought new turbulence. When life puts away her conjuring tricks one by one, those that deceive us longest may well be the wine-cup and the sensual kiss, for our Chambers of Commerce and of Commons have not the divine architecture of the body, nor has their frenzy been ripened by the sun. The poet, because he may not stand within the sacred house but lives amid the whirlwinds that beset its threshold, may find his pardon.

VI

I think the Christian saint and hero, instead of being merely dissatisfied, make deliberate sacrifice. I remember reading once an autobiography of a man who had made a daring journey in disguise to Russian exiles in Siberia, and his telling how, very timid as a child, he schooled himself by wandering at night through dangerous streets. Saint and hero cannot be content to pass at moments to that hollow image and after become their heterogeneous selves, but would always, if they could, resemble the antithetical self. There is a shadow of type on type, for in all great poetical styles there is saint or hero, but when it is all over Dante can return to his chambering and Shakespeare to his "pottle pot." They sought no impossible perfection but when they handled paper or parchment. So too will saint or hero, because he works in his own flesh and blood and not in paper or parchment, have more deliberate understanding of that other flesh and blood.

Some years ago I began to believe that our culture, with its doctrine of sincerity and self-realisation, made us gentle and passive, and that the Middle Ages and the Renaissance were right to found theirs upon the imitation of Christ or of some classic hero. St. Francis and Caesar Borgia made themselves over-mastering, creative persons by turning from the mirror to meditation upon a mask. When I had this thought I could see nothing else in life. I could not write the play I had planned, for all became allegorical, and though I tore up hundreds of pages in my endeavour to escape from allegory, my imagination became sterile for nearly five years and I only escaped at last when I had mocked in a comedy my own thought. I was always thinking of the element of imitation in style and in life, and of the life beyond heroic imitation. I find in an old diary: "I think all happiness depends on the energy to assume the mask of some other life, on a re-birth as something not one's self, something created in a moment and perpetually renewed; in playing a game like that of a child where one loses the infinite pain of self-realisation, in a grotesque or solemn painted face put on that one may hide from the terror of judgment. . . . Perhaps all the sins and energies of the world are but the world's flight from an infinite blinding beam"; and again at an earlier date: "If we cannot imagine ourselves as different from what we are, and try to assume that second self, we cannot impose a discipline upon ourselves though we may accept one from others. Active virtue, as distinguished from the passive acceptance of a code, is therefore theatrical, consciously dramatic, the wearing of a mask. . . . Wordsworth, great poet though he be, is so often flat and heavy partly because his moral sense, being a discipline he had not created, a mere obedience, has no theatrical element. This increases his popularity with the better kind of journalists and politicians who have written books."

VII

I thought the hero found hanging upon some oak of Dodona an ancient mask, where perhaps there lingered something of Egypt, and that he changed it to his fancy, touching it a little here and there, gilding the eyebrows or putting a gilt line where the cheek-bone comes; that when at last he looked out of its eyes he knew another's breath came and went within his breath upon the carven lips, and that his eyes were upon the instant fixed upon a visionary world: how else could the god have come to us in the forest? The good, unlearned books say that He who keeps the distant stars within His fold comes without intermediary, but Plutarch's precepts and the experience of old women in Soho, ministering their witchcraft to servant girls at a shilling a piece, will have it that a strange living man may win for Daemon an illustrious dead man; but now I add another thought: the Daemon comes not as like to like but seeking its own opposite, for man and Daemon feed the hunger in one another's hearts. Because the ghost is simple, the man heterogeneous and confused, they are but knit together when the man has found a mask whose lineaments permit the expression of all the man most lacks, and it may be dreads, and of that only.

The more insatiable in all desire, the more resolute to refuse deception or an easy victory, the more close will be the bond, the more violent and definite the antipathy.

VIII

I think that all religious men have believed that there is a hand not ours in the events of life, and that, as somebody says in *Wilhelm Meister*, accident is destiny; and I think it was Heraclitus who said: the Daemon is our destiny.

When I think of life as a struggle with Daemon who would ever set us to the hardest work among those not impossible, I understand why there is a deep enmity between a man and his destiny, and why a man loves nothing but his destiny. In an Anglo-Saxon poem a certain man is called, as though to call him something that summed up all heroism, "Doom eager." I am persuaded that the Daemon delivers and deceives us, and that he wove that netting from the stars and threw the net from his shoulder. Then my imagination runs from Daemon to sweetheart, and I divine an analogy that evades the intellect. I remember that Greek antiquity has bid us look for the principal stars, that govern enemy and sweetheart alike, among those that are about to set, in the Seventh House as the astrologers say; and that it may be "sexual love," which is "founded upon spiritual hate," is an image of the warfare of man and Daemon; and I even wonder if there may not be some secret communion, some whispering in the dark between Daemon and sweetheart. I remember how often women when in love, grow superstitious, and believe that they can bring their lovers good luck; and I remember an old Irish story of three young men who went seeking for help in battle into the house of the gods at Slieve-na-mon. "You must first be married," some god told them, "because a man's good or evil luck comes to him through a woman."

I sometimes fence for half-an-hour at the day's end, and when I close my eyes upon the pillow I see a foil playing before me the button to my face. We meet always in the deep of the mind, whatever our work, wherever our reverie carries us, that other Will.

IX

The poet finds and makes his mask in disappointment, the hero in defeat. The desire that is satisfied is not a great desire, nor has the shoulder used all its might that an unbreakable gate has never strained. The saint alone is not deceived, neither thrusting with his shoulder nor holding out unsatisfied hands. He would climb without wandering to the antithetical self of the world, the Indian narrowing his thought in meditation or driving it away in contemplation, the Christian copying Christ, the antithetical self of the classic world. For a hero loves the world till it breaks him, and the poet till it has broken faith; but while the world was yet debonair, the saint has turned away, and because he renounced Experience itself, he will wear his mask as he finds it. The poet or the hero, no matter upon what bark they found their mask, so teeming their fancy, somewhat change its lineaments, but the saint, whose life is but a round of customary duty, needs nothing the whole world does not need, and day by day he scourges in his body the Roman

and Christian conquerors: Alexander and Caesar are famished in his cell.
His nativity is neither in disappointment nor in defeat, but in a temptation
like that of Christ in the Wilderness, a contemplation in a single instant perpetually renewed of the Kingdoms of the World; all, because all renounced,
continually present showing their empty thrones. Edwin Ellis, remembering that Christ also measured the sacrifice, imagined himself in a fine poem
as meeting at Golgotha the phantom of "Christ the Less," the Christ who
might have lived a prosperous life without the knowledge of sin, and who
now wanders

> "companionless a weary spectre day and night."
> "I saw him go and cried to him
>> 'Eli, thou hast forsaken me.'
>> The nails were burning through each limb,
>> He fled to find felicity."

And yet is the saint spared, despite his martyr's crown and his vigil of
desire, defeat, disappointed love, and the sorrow of parting.

> O Night, that did'st lead thus,
> O Night, more lovely than the dawn of light,
> O Night, that broughtest us
> Lover to lover's sight,
> Lover with loved in marriage of delight!

> Upon my flowery breast,
> Wholly for him, and save himself for none,
> There did I give sweet rest

> To my beloved one;
> The fanning of the cedars breathed thereon.

> When the first morning air
> Blew from the tower, and waved his locks aside,
> His hand, with gentle care,
> Did wound me in the side,
> And in my body all my senses died.

> All things I then forgot,
> My cheek on him who for my coming came;
> All ceased and I was not,
> Leaving my cares and shame
> Among the lilies, and forgetting them.

X

It is not permitted to a man, who takes up pen or chisel, to seek originality, for passion is his only business, and he cannot but mould or sing after a new fashion because no disaster is like another. He is like those phantom lovers in the Japanese play who, compelled to wander side by side and never mingle, cry: "We neither wake nor sleep and passing our nights in a sorrow which is in the end a vision, what are these scenes of spring to us?" If when we have found a mask we fancy that it will not match our mood till we have touched with gold the cheek, we do it furtively, and only where the oaks of Dodona cast their deepest shadow, for could he see our handiwork the Daemon would fling himself out, being our enemy.

XI

Many years ago I saw, between sleeping and waking, a woman of incredible beauty shooting an arrow into the sky, and from the moment when I made my first guess at her meaning I have thought much of the difference between the winding movement of nature and the straight line, which is called in Balzac's *Seraphita* the "Mark of Man," but comes closer to my meaning as the mark of saint or sage. I think that we who are poets and artists, not being permitted to shoot beyond the tangible, must go from desire to weariness and so to desire again, and live but for the moment when vision comes to our weariness like terrible lightning, in the humility of the brutes. I do not doubt those heaving circles, those winding arcs, whether in one man's life or in that of an age, are mathematical, and that some in the world, or beyond the world, have foreknown the event and pricked upon the calendar the life-span of a Christ, a Buddha, a Napoleon: that every movement, in feeling or in thought, prepares in the dark by its own increasing clarity and confidence its own executioner. We seek reality with the slow toil of our weakness and are smitten from the boundless and the unforeseen. Only when we are saint or sage, and renounce Experience itself, can we, in the language of the Christian Caballa, leave the sudden lightning and the path of the serpent and become the bowman who aims his arrow at the centre of the sun.

XII

The doctors of medicine have discovered that certain dreams of the night, for I do not grant them all, are the day's unfulfilled desire, and that our terror of desires condemned by the conscience has distorted and disturbed our dreams. They have only studied the breaking into dream of elements that have remained unsatisfied without purifying discouragement. We can satisfy in life a few of our passions and each passion but a little, and our characters indeed but differ because no two men bargain alike. The bargain, the compromise, is always threatened, and when it is broken we become mad or hysterical or are in some way deluded; and so when a starved or banished passion shows in a dream we, before awaking, break the logic that had given it the capacity of action and throw it into chaos again. But the passions, when we know that they cannot find fulfilment, become vision; and a vision, whether we wake or sleep, prolongs its power by rhythm and pattern, the wheel where the world is butterfly. We need no protection but it does, for if we become interested in ourselves, in our own lives, we pass out of the vision. Whether it is we or the vision that create the pattern, who set the wheel turning, it is hard to say, but certainly we have a hundred ways of keeping it near us: we select our images from past times, we turn from our own age and try to feel Chaucer nearer than the daily paper. It compels us to cover all it cannot incorporate, and would carry us when it comes in sleep to that moment when even sleep closes her eyes and dreams begin to dream; and we are taken up into a clear light and are forgetful even of our own names and actions and yet in perfect possession of ourselves murmur like Faust, "Stay, moment," and murmur in vain.

XIII

A poet, when he is growing old, will ask himself if he cannot keep his mask and his vision without new bitterness, new disappointment. Could he if he would, knowing how frail his vigour from youth up, copy Landor who lived loving and hating, ridiculous and unconquered, into extreme old age, all lost but the favour of his muses.

> The mother of the muses we are taught
> Is memory; she has left me; they remain
> And shake my shoulder urging me to sing.

Surely, he may think, now that I have found vision and mask I need not suffer any longer. He will buy perhaps some small old house where like Ariosto he can dig his garden, and think that in the return of birds and leaves, or moon and sun, and in the evening flight of the rooks he may discover rhythm and pattern like those in sleep and so never awake out of vision. Then he will remember Wordsworth withering into eighty years, honoured and empty-witted, and climb to some waste room and find, forgotten there by youth, some bitter crust.

PART 2

Primitivism and Neoprimitivism

The widespread Primitivist impulse of Modernist and avant-garde art can be allied with Expressionism. In the avant-garde movements of the early part of the century, there were frequent infusions of what was thought of as the Other. Tristan Tzara, the Dadaist, and André Breton, the Surrealist, were noted collectors of African art objects, and Tzara used snippets of African tongues in his early poems. On the one hand, old, tired Europe was to regain new force through this other way of seeing, being, and creating; and then again, it was discovering the sources of its own national popular tradition.

There is a strong connection between Russian Futurism and several forms of Expressionism, such as that found in Poland, with its universalist declarations. The "Young Poland" artists were in contact also with French, German, and Scandinavian circles, as was the Italian Futurist Filippo Tommaso Marinetti with the French and international communities. Marinetti's "Founding and Manifesto of Futurism" (5.5) appeared in Poland soon after its publication in *Le Figaro* in 1909.

Stanislaw Przybyszewski's manifesto "Primitivists to the Nations of the World and to Poland" (2.2) first appeared in *GGa: The First Polish Almanac of Futurist Poetry: A Primitivist Bimonthly.* He was the leader of the Polish "Moderna" and of Expressionism in Poland; as the editor of the periodical *Zycie* (Life), he was closely connected with the international community.

Russian Neofuturism, like French Fauvism and German Expressionism, went against "civilized" or effete art forms and turned to naive painters, to folk art and its woodcuts or *lubok,* and to the art of children. There was a particular revival of religious icons, initiated by their rediscovery in 1904, when Andrei Rublev's *Old Testament Trinity* was cleaned, its original bright colors restored, and the contrast perfectly appreciated in the film devoted to him: the first part is black and white and suddenly the color emerges at the end, its shock value immense.

From these manifestations of the "noble savages" art was to draw its strength. The *Blaue Reiter Almanac* printed an influential article by the Russian Futurist David Burliuk on "The 'Savages' of Russia." If the French Fauves took on many colors, so did the Russian artists, like the Rayonists Michael Larionov and Ilya Zdanevich, who felt themselves closely allied to Neoprimitivism. They not only painted their bodies, and had themselves portrayed doing so, but also wrote manifestos on the topic, like their celebrated "Why We Paint Ourselves: A Futurist Manifesto" (5.26). This gesture was at once primitivizing and symbolical: like Kasimir Malevich's "Art of the Savages," it was to add strength.

The myth of the wild man, the predecessor of Outsider Art, is as important for Russian avant-garde art as Breton's myth of the madman, the wild man, and the child would prove to be for Surrealism in the 1930s. As Picasso and his friends had fêted the "Douanier Rousseau" at a banquet in 1908, so Wassily Kandinsky printed seven of his paintings in *Der Blaue Reiter Almanac* of 1912, as the author of a "new, greater reality." Naive expressionism, childlike perception, and the art of madmen are linked, as in Surrealism's appreciation of all three.

The colorful force seen in all the varieties of primitive strength: "neo" and "tectonic," "Negro" and "Redskin," celebrated by the Pole Stanislaw Przybyszewski, the Russian Alexander Shevchenko, the Rumanian Tristan Tzara, and the American Gary Snyder, makes a welcome dynamic opposition to all the pale academic cerebrations of traditional art. As Frank O'Hara says in his manifesto "Personism" (26.4): "What can we expect of Personism? . . . It, like Africa, is on the way." True enough. The Primitivisms of Modernist and avant-garde art run deep.

2.1 TRISTAN TZARA

Note 6 on Negro Art

1917

The new art is right on the line: concentration-angles of the pryamid toward the summit, a cross; with this purity we have first deformed, decomposed the object, we have approached its surface, penetrated it. We want clarity, which is direct. Art is grouped into its camps, with its special crafts, within its borders. The foreign influences mixing in are shreds of a Renaissance lining, still stuck to the soul of our neighbors, for my brother's soul has the sharp black branches of autumn.

My other brother is naive and good and laughs. He eats in Africa and in the bracelet of oceanic islands: he concentrates his view on the head, the waist in ironwood, patiently, and loses the conventional relation between the head and the rest of the body. He thinks like this: man walks straight up, everything in nature is symmetrical. In working, new relations arrange themselves necessarily: from this purity expressio is born.

From black we dip out light. Simplerich. Luminous naivete. Diverse materials equilibrium of form. Construct in balanced hierarchy.

Eye: button open up, broad round pointed to penetrate my bones and my belief. Transform my country in joyful prayer of anguish. Cotton eye run in my blood.

Art was a prayer in the infancy of time. Wood and stone were truth. In man I see moon, plants, blackness, metal, star, fish. Let the cosmic elements slide by symmetrically. Deform, boil. The hand is very large. The mouth holds the power of the obscure, an invisible substance, goodness, fear, wisdom, creation, fire.

No one has seen as clearly as I have tonight, whiteness being milled.

Poland

2.2 ANATOL STERN AND ALEKSANDER WAT

primitivists to the nations of the world and to poland

1920

the great rainbow monkey named dionysis expired long ago. we announce that we are throwing out his rotten legacy

I. CIVILIZATION, CULTURE, WITH THEIR ILLNESSES — TO THE TRASH.

we choose simplicity ordinariness, happiness health, triviality, laughter. from laughter the spirit fattens and grows strong stout calves. we complain to each other gratuitously of propriety, importance, pietism. we use the laurel leaves that crown us as a seasoning for food.

II. WE CROSS OUT HISTORY AND POSTERITY.

just as tolstoy's rome, the india hats of critique, bavaria and cracow. poland ought to cast itself out from tradition, from the mummy of prince joseph and the theater. we are storming the city. every mechanism — airplanes, tramways, telephonic devices. only folding and mobile homes. speech shouted and rhymed.

III. social order we understand as the authority of essential idiots and capitalists. this is the most fertile ground in laughter and in revolution.

IV. those guilty of war will be rolled over by the fist. murder is unhygienic. women should be exchanged frequently. the value of a woman depends on her fertility.

V. THE PRIMITIVE.

VI. art is only that which yields health and laughter. THE ESSENCE OF

ART—IN ITS CIRCUS CHARACTER SPECTACLES FOR GREAT MOBS. its features of externality and universality, pornography unmasked.

art is science.

from the muddled pot-house of squalid infinity we sweep out the hysterical creators called poets, crushed by the insatiable pain of life's joy. aesthetic ecstasy, inspiration, eternity. instead of aesthetics anti-grace. instead of ecstasy—intellect. intelligible and purposeful creation.

VII. whirling objects as the material of art. theaters to change into circus buildings.

music is two bodies beaten together. everything else is noise. we will battle the antifuturistic violin and every voice of nature. streetfights with the beethovenists.

it is necessary to tear from the walls the scraps of canvas called pictures. paint faces dressed in linen. people, houses sidewalks. sculpture does not exist.

VIII. poetry. we leave rhyme and rhythm behind wherever they are first even being conceived. the destruction of limiting rules of creation a virtue of awkwardness. freedom of grammatic form. spelling and punctuation. in accordance with the creators. mickiewicz is limited słowacki is an incomprehensible sputter.

THE WORD has its own weight, sound, color, outline. TAKING ITS PLACE IN SPACE. these are the deciding values of the word. the shortest word (the sound) and the longest word (the book). the meaning of the word is a subordinate thing and not dependent on the ascribed concept proper to it to be treated as auditory material for NONONOMATOPOETIC USES.

IX. the chief values of books—format and printing closely alongside them—is content. therefore the poet together with the typesetter and the binder of his books should well be screaming them everwhere. not declaiming. for publication use the gramophone and film, newspapers. gramophones spinning, the canvas screen, or the wall as the collective paper for books read out loud. newspapers edited only by poets.

X. we praise understanding and therefore throw out logic, that limitation and cowardice of the mind. nonsense is wonderful by virtue of its untranslatable content, which brings our creation into relief with breadth and strength.
likewise art manifests our love toward people and toward everything. we breathe love.

let's open our eyes. then swine will seem more enchanting to us than a nightingale, and the gga of a gander dazzles us more than swansong.

gga. gga, ladies and gentlemen, has fallen into the world arena. brandishing like a knight its double g, and crying, a—this is the mouth of that wonderful and ordinary beast. murder's proper muzzle, or snout.

United States

2.3 GARY SNYDER

Poetry and the Primitive

Notes on Poetry as an Ecological Survival Technique

1967

BILATERAL SYMMETRY

"Poetry" as the skilled and inspired use of the voice and language to embody rare and powerful states of mind that are in immediate origin personal to the singer, but at deep levels common to all who listen. "Primitive" as those societies which have remained non-literate and non-political while necessarily exploring and developing in directions that civilized societies have tended to ignore. Having fewer tools, no concern with history, a living oral tradition rather than an accumulated library, no overriding social goals, and considerable freedom of sexual and inner life, such people live vastly in the present. Their daily reality is a fabric of friends and family, the field of feeling and energy that one's own body is, the earth they stand on and the wind that wraps around it; and various areas of consciousness.

At this point some might be tempted to say that the primitive's real life is no different from anybody else's. I think this is not so. To live in the "mythological present" in close relation to nature and in basic but disciplined body/mind states suggests a wider-ranging imagination and a closer subjective knowledge of one's own physical properties than is usually available to men living (as they themselves describe it) impotently and inadequately in "history"—their mind-content programmed, and their caressing of nature complicated by the extensions and abstractions which elaborate tools are. A hand pushing a button may wield great power, but that hand will never learn what a hand can do. Unused capacities go sour.

Poetry must sing or speak from authentic experience. Of all the streams of civilized tradition with roots in the paleolithic, poetry is one of the few that can realistically claim an unchanged function and a relevance which will outlast most of the activities that surround us today. Poets, as few others, must live close to the world that primitive men are in: the world, in its nakedness, which is fundamental for all of us—birth, love, death; the sheer fact of being alive.

Music, dance, religion, and philosophy of course have archaic roots—a shared origin with poetry. Religion has tended to become the social justifier, a lackey to power, instead of the vehicle of hair-raising liberating and healing realizations. Dance has mostly lost its connection with ritual drama, the miming of animals, or tracing the maze of the spiritual journey. Most music takes too many tools. The poet can make it on his own voice and mother tongue, while steering a course between crystal clouds of utterly incommunicable non-verbal states—and the gleaming daggers and glittering nets of language.

In one school of Mahayana Buddhism, they talk about the "Three Mysteries." These are Body, Voice, and Mind. The things that are what living *is* for us, in life. Poetry is the vehicle of the mystery of voice. The universe, as they sometimes say, is a vast breathing body.

With artists, certain kinds of scientists, yogins, and poets, a kind of mindsense is not only surviving but modestly flourishing in the twentieth century. Claude Lévi-Strauss (*The Savage Mind*) sees no problem in the continuity: ". . . it is neither the mind of savages nor that of primitive or archaic humanity, but rather mind in its untamed state as distinct from mind cultivated or domesticated for yielding a return. . . . We are better able to understand today that it is possible for the two to coexist and interpenetrate in the same way that (in theory at least) it is possible for natural species, of which some are in their savage state and others transformed by agriculture and domestication, to coexist and cross . . . whether one deplores or rejoices in the fact, there are still zones in which savage thought, like savage species, is relatively protected. This is the case of art, to which our civilization accords the status of a national park."

MAKING LOVE WITH ANIMALS

By civilized times, hunting was a sport of kings. The early Chinese emperors had vast fenced hunting reserves; peasants were not allowed to shoot deer. Millennia of experience, the proud knowledges of hunting magic—animal habits—and the skills of wild plant and herb gathering were all but scrubbed away. Much has been said about the frontier in American history, but overlooking perhaps some key points: the American confrontation with a vast wild ecology, an earthly paradise of grass, water, and game

—was mind-shaking. Americans lived next to vigorous primitives whom they could not help but respect and even envy, for three hundred years. Finally, as ordinary men supporting their families, they often hunted for food. Although marginal peasants in Europe and Asia did remain part-time hunters at the bottom of the social scale, these Americans were the vanguard of an expanding culture. For Americans, "nature" means wilderness, the untamed realm of total freedom—not brutish and nasty, but beautiful and terrible. Something is always eating at the American heart like acid: it is the knowledge of what we have done to our continent, and to the American Indian.

Other civilizations have done the same, but at a pace too slow to be remembered. One finds evidence in T'ang and Sung poetry that the barren hills of central and northern China were once richly forested. The Far Eastern love of nature has become fear of nature: gardens and pine trees are tormented and controlled. Chinese nature poets were too often retired bureaucrats living on two or three acres of trees trimmed by hired gardeners. The professional nature-aesthetes of modern Japan, tea-teachers and flower-arrangers, are amazed to hear that only a century ago dozens of species of birds passed through Kyoto where today only swallows and sparrows can be seen; and the aesthetes can scarcely distinguish those. "Wild" in the Far East means uncontrollable, objectionable, crude, sexually unrestrained, violent; actually ritually polluting. China cast off mythology, which means its own dreams, with hairy cocks and gaping pudenda, millennia ago; and modern Japanese families participating in an "economic miracle" can have daughters in college who are not sure which hole babies come out of. One of the most remarkable intuitions in Western thought was Rousseau's Noble Savage: the idea that perhaps civilization has something to learn from the primitive.

Man is a beautiful animal. We know this because other animals admire us and love us. Almost all animals are beautiful and paleolithic hunters were deeply moved by it. To hunt means to use your body and senses to the fullest: to strain your consciousness to feel what the deer are thinking today, this moment; to sit still and let your self go into the birds and wind while waiting by a game trail. Hunting magic is designed to bring the game to you—the creature who has heard your song, witnessed your sincerity, and out of compassion comes within your range. Hunting magic is not only aimed at bringing beasts to their death, but to assist in their birth—to promote their fertility. Thus the great Iberian cave paintings are not of hunting alone—but of animals mating and giving birth. A Spanish farmer who saw some reproductions from Altamira is reported to have said, "How beautifully this cow gives birth to a calf!" Breuil has said, "The religion of those days did *not* elevate the animal to the position of a god . . . but it was *humbly entreated* to be fertile." A Haida incantation goes:

> The Great One coming up against the current
> > begins thinking of it.
> The Great One coming putting gravel in his mouth
> > thinks of it
> You look at it with white stone eyes—
> > Great Eater begins thinking of it.

People of primitive cultures appreciate animals as other people off on various trips. Snakes move without limbs, and are like free penises. Birds fly, sing, and dance; they gather food for their babies; they disappear for months and then come back. Fish can breathe water and are brilliant colors. Mammals are like us, they fuck and give birth to babies while panting and purring; their young suck their mothers' breasts; they know terror and delight, they play.

Lévi-Strauss quotes Swanton's report on the Chickasaw, the tribe's own amusing game of seeing the different clans as acting out the lives of their totemic emblems: "The Raccoon people were said to live on fish and wild fruit, those of the Puma lived in the mountains, avoided water of which they were very frightened and lived principally on game. The Wild Cat clan slept in the daytime and hunted at night, for they had keen eyes; they were indifferent to women. Members of the Bird clan were up before daybreak: 'They were like real birds in that they would not bother anybody . . . the people of this clan have different sorts of minds, just as there are different species of birds.' They were said to live well, to be polygamous, disinclined to work, and prolific . . . the inhabitants of the 'bending-post-oak' house group lived in the woods . . . the High Corncrib house people were respected in spite of their arrogance: they were good gardeners, very industrious but poor hunters; they bartered their maize for game. They were said to be truthful and stubborn, and skilled at forecasting the weather. As for the Redskunk house group: they lived in dugouts underground."

We all know what primitive cultures don't have. What they *do* have is this knowledge of connection and responsibility which amounts to a spiritual ascesis for the whole community. Monks of Christianity or Buddhism, "leaving the world" (which means the games of society) are trying, in a decadent way, to achieve what whole primitive communities—men, women, and children—live by daily; and with more wholeness. The Shaman-poet is simply the man whose mind reaches easily out into all manners of shapes and other lives, and gives song to dreams. Poets have carried this function forward all through civilized times: poets don't sing about society, they sing about nature—even if the closest they ever get to nature is their lady's queynt. Class-structured civilized society is a kind of mass ego. To transcend the ego is to go beyond society as well. "Beyond" there lies, inwardly, the unconscious. Outwardly, the equivalent of the unconscious is the wilderness: both of these terms meet, one step even farther on, as *one.*

One religious tradition of this communion with nature which has survived into historic Western times is what has been called Witchcraft. The antlered and pelted figure painted on the cave wall of Trois Frères, a shaman-dancer-poet, is a prototype of both Shiva and the Devil.

Animal marriages (and supernatural marriages) are a common motif of folklore the world around. A recent article by Lynn White puts the blame for the present ecological crisis on the Judaeo-Christian tradition—animals don't have souls and can't be saved; nature is merely a ground for us to exploit while working out our drama of free will and salvation under the watch of Jehovah. The Devil? "The Deivill apeired vnto her in the liknes of ane prettie boy in grein clothes . . . and at that tyme the Deivil gaive hir his markis; and went away from her in the liknes of ane blak dowg." "He wold haw carnall dealling with ws in the shap of a deir, or in any vther shap, now and then, somtyme he vold be lyk a stirk, a bull, a deir, a rae, or a dowg, etc, and haw dealling with us."

The archaic and primitive ritual dramas, which acknowledged all the sides of human nature, including the destructive, demonic, and ambivalent, were liberating and harmonizing. Freud said *he* didn't discover the unconscious, poets had centuries before. The purpose of California Shamanism was "to heal disease and resist death, with a power acquired from dreams." An Arapaho dancer of the Ghost Dance came back from his trance to sing:

I circle around, I circle around

The boundaries of the earth,
The boundaries of the earth

Wearing the long wing feathers as I fly
Wearing the long wing feathers as I fly.

THE VOICE AS A GIRL

"Everything was alive—the trees, grasses, and winds were dancing with me, talking with me; I could understand the songs of the birds." This ancient experience is not so much—in spite of later commentators—"religious" as it is a pure perception of beauty. The phenomenal world experienced at certain pitches is totally living, exciting, mysterious, filling one with a trembling awe, leaving one grateful and humble. The wonder of the mystery returns direct to one's own senses and consciousness: inside and outside; the voice breathes, "Ah!"

Breath is the outer world coming into one's body. With pulse—the two always harmonizing—the source of our inward sense of rhythm. Breath is spirit, "inspiration." Expiration, "voiced," makes the signals by which the species connects. Certain emotions and states occasionally seize the body, one becomes a whole tube of air vibrating; all voice. In mantra chanting, the magic utterances, built of seed-syllables such as OM and AYNG and AH, repeated over and over, fold and curl on the breath until—when most weary and bored—a new voice enters, a voice speaks through you clearer and stronger than what you know of yourself; with a sureness and melody of its own, singing out the inner song of the self, and of the planet.

Poetry, it should not have to be said, is not writing or books. Non-literate cultures with their traditional training methods of hearing and reciting, carry thousands of poems—death, war, love, dream, work, and spirit-power songs—through time. The voice of inspiration as an "other" has long been known in the West as The Muse. Widely speaking, the muse is anything other that touches you and moves you. Be it a mountain range, a band of people, the morning star, or a diesel generator. Breaks through the ego-barrier. But this touching-deep is as a mirror, and man in his sexual nature has found the clearest mirror to be his human lover. As the West moved into increasing complexities and hierarchies with civilization, Woman as nature, beauty, and The Other came to be an all-dominating symbol; secretly striving through the last three millennia with the Jehovah or Imperator God-figure, a projection of the gathered power of anti-nature social forces. Thus in the Western tradition the Muse and Romantic Love became part of the same energy, and woman as nature the field for experiencing the universe as sacramental. The lovers' bed was the sole place to enact the dances and ritual dramas that link primitive people to their geology and the Milky Way. The contemporary decline of the cult of romance is linked to the rise of the sense of the primitive, and the knowledge of the variety of spiritual practices and paths to beauty that cultural anthropology has brought us. We begin to move away now, in this interesting historical spiral, from monogamy and monotheism.

Yet the muse remains a woman. Poetry is voice, and according to Indian tradition, voice, vāk (vox)—is a Goddess. Vāk is also called Sarasvati, she is the lover of Brahma and his actual creative energy; she rides a peacock, wears white, carries a book-scroll and a vīna. The name Sarasvati means "the flowing one." "She is again the Divine in the aspect of wisdom and learning, for she is the Mother of Veda; that is of all knowledge touching Brahman and the universe. She is the Word of which it was born and She is that which is the issue of her great womb, Mahāyoni. Not therefore idly have men worshipped Vāk, or Sarasvati, as the Supreme Power."

As Vāk is wife to Brahma ("wife" means "wave" means "vibrator" in Indo-European etymology) so the voice, in everyone, is a mirror of his own deepest self. The voice rises to answer an inner need; or as BusTon says, "The voice of the Buddha arises, being called forth by the thought of the living beings." In esoteric Buddhism this becomes the basis of a mandala meditation practice: "In their midst is Nayika, the essence of *Ali,* the vowel series— she possesses the true nature of Vajrasattva, and is Queen of the Vajra-realm. She is known as the Lady, as Suchness, as Void, as Perfection of Wisdom, as limit of Reality, as Absence of Self."

The conch shell is an ancient symbol of the sense of hearing, and of the female; the vulva and the fruitful womb. At Koptos there is a bas-relief of a four-point buck, on the statue of the god Min, licking his tongue out toward two conches. There are many Magdalenian bone and horn engravings of bear, bison, and deer licking abstract penises and vulvas. At this point (and from our most archaic past transmitted) the mystery of voice becomes one with the mystery of body.

How does this work among primitive peoples in practice? James Mooney, discussing the Ghost Dance religion, says "There is no limit to the number of these [Ghost Dance] songs, as every trance at every dance produces a new one, the trance subject after regaining consciousness embodying his experience in the spirit world in the form of a song, which is sung at the next dance and succeeding performances until superseded by other songs originating in the same way. Thus a single dance may easily result in twenty or thirty new songs. While songs are thus born and die, certain ones which appeal especially to the Indian heart, on account of their mythology, pathos, or peculiar sweetness, live and are perpetuated."

Modern poets in America, Europe, and Japan are discovering the breath, the voice, and trance. It is also for some a discovery to realize that the universe is not a dead thing but a continual creation, the song of Sarasvati springing from the trance of Brahma. "Reverence to Her who is eternal, Raudri, Gaurī, Dhātri, reverence and again reverence, to Her who is the Consciousness in all beings, reverence and again reverence. . . . Candī says."

HOPSCOTCH AND CATS' CRADLES

The clouds are "Shining Heaven" with his different bird-blankets on
HAIDA

The human race, as it immediately concerns us, has a vertical axis of about 40,000 years and as of 1900 AD a horizonal spread of roughly 3000 different languages and 1000 different cultures. Every living culture and language is the result of countless cross-fertilizations—not a "rise and fall" of civilizations, but more like a flowerlike periodic absorbing—blooming—bursting and scattering of seed. Today we are aware as never before of the plurality of human life-styles and possibilities, while at the same time being tied, like in an old silent movie, to a runaway locomotive rushing headlong toward a very singular catastrophe. Science, as far as it is capable of looking "on beauty bare" is on our side. Part of our being modern is the very fact of our awareness that we are one with our beginnings—contemporary with all periods—members of all cultures. The seeds of every social structure or custom are in the mind.

The anthropologist Stanley Diamond has said "The sickness of civilization consists in its failure to incorporate (and only then) to move beyond the limits of the primitive." Civilization is so to speak a lack of faith, a human laziness, a willingness to accept the perceptions and decisions of others in place of your own—to be less than a full man. Plus, perhaps, a primate inheritance of excessive socializing; and surviving submission/dominance traits (as can be observed in monkey or baboon bands) closely related to exploitative sexuality. If evolution has any meaning at all we must hope to slowly move away from such biological limitations, just as it is within our power to move away from the self-imposed limitations of small-minded social systems. We all live within skin, ego, society, and species boundaries. Consciousness has boundaries of a different order, "the mind is free." College students trying something different because "they do it in New Guinea" is part of the real work of modern man: to uncover the inner structure and actual boundaries of the mind. The third Mystery. The charts and maps of this realm are called mandalas in Sanskrit. (A poem by the Sixth Dalai Lama runs "Drawing diagrams I measured / Movement of the stars / Though her

tender flesh is near / Her mind I cannot measure.") Buddhist and Hindu philosophers have gone deeper into this than almost anyone else but the work
is just beginning. We are now gathering all the threads of history together
and linking modern science to the primitive and archaic sources.

The stability of certain folklore motifs and themes—evidences of linguistic borrowing—the deeper meaning of linguistic drift—the laws by which
styles and structures, art-forms and grammars, songs and ways of courting,
relate and reflect each other are all mirrors of the self. Even the uses of the
word "nature," as in the seventeenth-century witch Isobel Gowdie's testi-
mony about what it was like to make love to the Devil—"I found his nature
cold within me as spring-well-water"—throw light on human nature.

Thus nature leads into nature—the wilderness—and the reciprocities
and balances by which man lives on earth. Ecology: "eco" (*oikos*) meaning
"house" (cf. "ecumenical"): Housekeeping on Earth. Economics, which is
merely the housekeeping of various social orders—taking out more than it
puts back—must learn the rules of the greater realm. Ancient and primitive cultures had this knowledge more surely and with almost as much empirical precision (see H. C. Conklin's work on Hanunoo plant-knowledge,
for example) as the most concerned biologist today. Inner and outer: the
Brihadāranyaka Upanishad says, "Now this Self is the state of being of all
contingent beings. In so far as man pours libations and offers sacrifice, he is
in the sphere of the gods; in so far as he recites the Veda he is in the sphere
of the seers; in so far as he offers cakes and water to the ancestors, in so
far as he gives food and lodging to men, he is of the sphere of men. In so
far as he finds grass and water for domestic animals, he is in the sphere of
domestic animals; in so far as wild beasts and birds, even down to ants, find
something to live on in his house, he is of their sphere."

The primitive world view, far-out scientific knowledge and the poetic
imagination are related forces which may help if not to save the world or
humanity, at least to save the Redwoods. The goal of Revolution is Transformation. Mystical traditions within the great religions of civilized times have
taught a doctrine of Great Effort for the achievement of Transcendence. This
must have been their necessary compromise with civilization, which needed
for its period to turn man's vision away from nature, to nourish the growth
of the social energy. The archaic, the esoteric, and the primitive traditions
alike all teach that beyond transcendence is Great Play, and Transformation. After the mind-breaking Void, the emptiness of a million universes
appearing and disappearing, all created things rushing into Krishna's devouring mouth; beyond the enlightenment that can say "these beings are

dead already; go ahead and kill them, Arjuna" is a loving, simple awareness
of the absolute beauty and preciousness of mice and weeds.

Tsong-kha-pa tells us of a transformed universe:

1. This is a Buddha-realm of infinite beauty
2. All men are divine, are subjects
3. Whatever we use or own are vehicles of worship
4. All acts are authentic, not escapes.

Such authenticity is at the heart of many a primitive world view. For the
Anaguta of the Jos plateau, Northern Nigeria, North is called "up"; South is
called "down." East is called "morning" and West is called "evening." Hence
(according to Dr. Stanley Diamond in his *Anaguta Cosmography*), "Time
flows past the permanent central position . . . they live at a place called noon,
at the center of the world, the only place where space and time intersect."
The Australian aborigines live in a world of ongoing recurrence—comrade-
ship with the landscape and continual exchanges of being and form and
position; every person, animals, forces, all are related via a web of reincar-
nation—or rather, they are "interborn." It may well be that rebirth (or inter-
birth, for we are actually mutually creating each other and all things while
living) is the objective fact of existence which we have not yet brought into
conscious knowledge and practice.

It is clear that the empirically observable interconnectedness of nature is
but a corner of the vast "jewelled net" which moves from without to within.
The spiral (think of nebulae) and spiral conch (vulva/womb) is a symbol
of the Great Goddess. It is charming to note that physical properties of
spiral conches approximate the Indian notion of the world-creating dance,
"expanding form"—"We see that the successive chambers of a spiral Nau-
tilus or of a straight Orthoceras, each whorl or part of a whorl of a peri-
winkle or other gastropod, each additional increment of an elephant's tusk,
or each new chamber of a spiral foraminifer, has its leading characteristic at
once described and its form so far described by the simple statement that
it constitutes a *gnomon* to the whole previously existing structure." (D'Arcy
Thompson)

The maze dances, spiral processions, cats' cradles, Micronesian string
star-charts, mandalas and symbolic journeys of the old wild world are with
us still in the universally distributed children's game. Let poetry and Bushmen lead the way in a great hop forward:

> In the following game of long hopscotch, the part
> marked H is for Heaven: it is played in the usual way

except that when you are finishing the first part, on the
way up, you throw your tor into Heaven. Then you hop
to 11, pick up your tor, jump to the very spot where your
tor landed in Heaven,
and say, as fast as you can,
the alphabet forwards and backwards,
your name, address and telephone number (if you have
one), your age,
and the name of your boyfriend or girlfriend (if you have
one of those).
PATRICIA EVANS, *Hopscotch*

PART 3

Cubism

The main poets of Cubism refused the term: nevertheless, Blaise Cendrars, Pierre Reverdy, Max Jacob, and Guillaume Apollinaire are generally counted as Cubists, although Apollinaire advocated also a tendency he called "Orphic": "the Orphic explanation of the earth." These poets were allied by friendship and aesthetic tendency to the Cubist painters such as Pablo Picasso and Georges Braque.

The latecoming theoreticians of Cubism, Albert Gleizes and Jean Metzinger, joined with Fernand Léger and Robert Delaunay and the Puteaux group of Marchel Duchamp, Jacques Villon, and Rayond Duchamp-Villon and shared the outlook of Braque and Picasso in the Section d'Or exhibition of October 1912. Apollinaire's essay "Cubism Differs" (3.4) defines the movement as "the art of painting new structures out of elements borrowed not from the reality of sight, but from the reality of insight." He contrasts Futurism, which he finds confusing, disorganized, scattered, and scattering, with Cubism, which is lucid, pure, and organized, assembling many ideas about an object in order to "elicit a single emotion."

Apollinaire's real manifesto about the art he loves is found in his "Esthetic Meditations," where his original typography speaks loudly of his love:

> J'AIME L'ART d'aujourd'hui parce que J'AIME
>   avant tout la LUMIÈRE et tous les hommes
>   AIMENT avant tout la LUMIÈRE
>   ils ont inventé le FEU
> [I LOVE THE ART of today because I LOVE
>   above all LIGHT and everyone
>   LOVES above all LIGHT
>   they invented FIRE]

This is the truest voice of the poet whom we associate with Cubism.

3.1 PIERRE ALBERT-BIROT
The Sun Is in the Staircase
1916–1924

PLACARD-POEM.

THE SUN
IS IN THE STAIRCASE

FOR INFORMATION
CONTACT THE WINE MERCHANT
DOWN THE ROAD

3.2 GUILLAUME APOLLINAIRE
Picasso
1905

If we were alert, all the gods would awaken. Born of the profound self-knowledge which humanity has kept of itself, the adored pantheisms resembling it have drowsed. But despite the eternal sleep, there are eyes reflecting humanities akin to these divine and joyous phantoms.

Such eyes are as attentive as the flowers whose desire it is always to behold the sun. O inventive joy, there are men who see with these eyes!

Picasso had been observing the human images which float in the azure of our memories, and partake of divinity, in order to damn the metaphysicians. How pious are his skies, alive with flights, and his heavy sombre lights, like those of grottoes!

There are children who have strayed off without having learned the catechism. They stop, and the rain stops falling. "Look, in those buildings there are people whose clothes are shabby." These children, whom one does not caress, know so much. "Mama, love me to death!" They can take things in their stride, and their successful dodges are mental evolutions.

The women one no longer loves come back to mind. By this time they have repeated their brittle ideas too often. They do not pray; they worship memories. Like an old church, they crouch in the twilight. These women renounce everything, and their fingers are itching to plait crowns of straw. At daybreak they disappear; they console themselves in silence. They cross many a threshold; mothers guard the cradles, so that the newborn may not inherit some taint; when they bend over the cradles, the little babes smile, sensing their goodness.

They often give thanks, and their forearms tremble like their eyelids.

Enveloped in frozen mist, old men wait unthinkingly, for it is only children who meditate. Inspired by far countries, animal struggles, locks of hardened hair, these old men beg without humility.

Other beggars have been used up by life. These are the infirm, the cripples, the bums. They are amazed to have come to the goal, which is still blue, but no longer the horizon. Old, they have become as foolish as kings who have too many troops of elephants bearing citadels. They are travelers who confound the flowers with the stars.

Grown old like oxen at twenty-five, the young have conducted nurslings to the moon.

On a clear day, certain women hold their peace; their bodies are angelic, and their glances tremble.

In the face of danger they smile an inner smile. They have to be frightened into confessing their little sins.

For a year, Picasso lived this type of damp painting, blue as the humid depth of an abyss, and full of pity.

Pity made Picasso harsher. The public squares held up one who had been hanged; he was stretched against the houses above the oblique passerby. The condemned awaited a savior. Miraculously the gallows hung athwart the roofs; the window panes flamed with flowers.

In rooms penniless painters drew fleecy nudes by lamplight. Women's shoes left by the bed were expressive of tender haste.

Calm followed this frenzy.

The harlequins go in splendid rags while the painting is gathering, warming or whitening its colors to express the strength and duration of the passions, while the lines delimited by the tights are bending, breaking off, or darting out.

In a square room, paternity transfigures the harlequin, whose wife bathes with cold water and admires her figure, as frail and slim as her husband, the puppet. Charming lilts mingle, and somewhere passing soldiers curse the day.

Love is good when one dresses it up, and the habit of spending one's time at home redoubles paternal feeling. The child brings the woman Picasso wanted glorious and immaculate closer to the father.

Primiparous mothers no longer expect the baby to arrive, because of certain ill-omened, raven-like chatterers. Christmas! They bring forth acrobats in the midst of pet monkeys, white horses, and dogs like bears.

The adolescent sisters, treading in perfect balance the heavy balls of the saltimbanques, impose on these spheres the radiant motion of worlds. These still adolescent youngsters have the anxieties of innocence; animals instruct them in the religious mystery. Some harlequins match the splendor of the women, whom they resemble, being neither male nor female.

The color has the flatness of frescoes; the lines are firm. But, placed at the frontiers of life, the animals are human, and the sexes are indistinct.

Hybrid beasts have the consciousness of Egyptian demigods; taciturn harlequins have their cheeks and foreheads paled by morbid sensuality.

These saltimbanques should not be confounded with actors. They should be observed with piety, for they celebrate mute rites with difficult dexterity. It is this which distinguishes Picasso from the Greek pottery painters whose designs he sometimes approaches. There, on the painted earthenware, bearded, garrulous priests offered in sacrifice animals, resigned and powerless. Here, virility is beardless, and shows itself in the sinews of thin arms; the flat part of the face and the animals are mysterious.

Picasso's taste for a running, changing, penetrating line has produced some probably unique examples of linear dry-point, in which he has not altered the general traits of things.

This Malagueño bruised us like a brief frost. His meditations bared themselves silently. He came from far away, from the rich composition and the brutal decoration of the seventeenth-century Spaniards.

And those who had known him before could recall swift insolences, which were already beyond the experimental stage.

His insistence on the pursuit of beauty has since changed everything in art.

* * *

Then he sharply questioned the universe. He accustomed himself to the immense light of depths. And sometimes he did not scorn to make use of actual objects, a two-penny song, a real postage stamp, a piece of oil-cloth furrowed by the fluting of a chair. The painter would not try to add a single picturesque element to the truth of these objects.

Surprise laughs savagely in the purity of light, and it is perfectly legitimate to use numbers and printed letters as pictorial elements; new in art, they are already soaked with humanity.

It is impossible to envisage all the consequences and possibilities of an art so profound and so meticulous.

The object, real or illusory, is doubtless called upon to play a more and more important role. The object is the inner frame of the picture, and marks the limits of its profundity, just as the actual frame marks its external limits.

Representing planes to denote volumes, Picasso gives an enumeration so complete and so decisive of the various elements which make up the object, that these do not take the shape of the object, thanks to the effort of the spectator, who is forced to see all the elements simultaneously just because of the way they have been arranged.

Is this art profound rather than noble? It does not dispense with the observation of nature, and acts upon us as intimately as nature herself.

There is the poet to whom the muse dictates his chants, there is the artist whose hand is guided by an unknown being using him as an instrument. Such artists never feel fatigue, for they never labor, and can produce abundantly day in and day out, no matter what country they are in, no matter what the season: they are not men, but poetic or artistic machines. Their reason cannot impede them, they never struggle, and their works show no signs of strain. They are not divine and can do without their selves. They are like prolongations of nature, and their works do not pass through the intellect. They can move one without humanizing the harmonies they call forth. On the other hand, there are the poets and artists who exert themselves constantly, who turn to nature, but have no direct contact with her; they must draw everything from within themselves, for no demon, no muse inspires them. They live in solitude, and express nothing but what they have babbled and stammered time and again, making effort after effort, attempt after attempt just to formulate what they wish to express. Men created in the image of God, a time comes when they are able to rest to admire their work. But what fatigue, what imperfections, what crudenesses!

*   *   *

Picasso was the first type of artist. Never has there been so fantastic a spectacle as the metamorphosis he underwent in becoming an artist of the second type.

The resolve to die came to Picasso as he watched the crooked eyebrows of his best friend anxiously riding his eyes. Another of his friends brought him one day to the border of a mystical country whose inhabitants were at once so simple and so grotesque that one could easily remake them.

And then after all, since anatomy, for instance, no longer existed in art, he had to reinvent it, and carry out his own assassination with the practiced and methodical hand of a great surgeon.

The great revolution of the arts, which he achieved almost unaided, was to make the world his new representation of it.

Enormous conflagration.

A new man, the world is his new representation. He enumerates the elements, the details, with a brutality which is also able to be gracious. Newborn, he orders the universe in accordance with his personal requirements, and so as to facilitate his relations with his fellows. The enumeration has epic grandeur, and, when ordered, will burst into drama. One may disagree about a system, an idea, a date, a resemblance, but I do not see how anyone could fail to accept the simple act of enumerating.

From the plastic point of view, it might be argued that we can do without so much truth, but, having once appeared, this truth became necessary. And then there are countries. A grotto in a forest where one cuts capers, a ride on a mule to the edge of a precipice, and the arrival in a village where everything smells of warm oil and spoiled wine. Or again, a walk to a cemetry, the purchase of a faience crown (the crown of immortals), the mention of the Mille Regrets, which is inimitable. I have also heard of clay candelabra, which were so applied to a canvas that they seemed to protrude from it. Pendants of crystal, and that famous return from Le Havre.

As for me, I am not afraid of art, and I have not one prejudice with regard to the painter's materials.

Mosaicists paint with marble or colored wood. There is mention of an Italian artist who painted with excrement; during the French revolution blood served somebody as paint. You may paint with whatever material you please, with pipes, postage stamps, postcards or playing cards, candelabra, pieces of oil cloth, collars, painted paper, newspapers.

For me it is enough to see the work; this has to be seen, for it is in terms of the quantity of an artist's production that one estimates the worth of a single work.

Delicate contrasts, parallel lines, a workman's craft, sometimes the object itself, sometimes an indication of it, sometimes an individualized enumeration, less sweetness than plainness. In modern art one does not choose, just as one accepts the fashion without discussion.

Painting . . . an astonishing art whose light is illimitable.

3.3 GUILLAUME APOLLINAIRE

The New Painting

Art Notes

1912

The new painters have been sharply criticized for their preoccupation with geometry. And yet, geometric figures are the essence of draftsmanship. Geometry, the science that deals with space, its measurement and relationships, has always been the most basic rule of painting.

Until now, the three dimensions of Euclidean geometry sufficed to still the anxiety provoked in the souls of great artists by a sense of the infinite — anxiety that cannot be called scientific, since art and science are two separate domains.

The new painters do not intend to become geometricians, any more than their predecessors did. But it may be said that geometry is to the plastic arts what grammar is to the art of writing. Now today's scientists have gone beyond the three dimensions of Euclidean geometry. Painters have, therefore, very naturally been led to a preoccupation with those new dimensions of space that are collectively designated, in the language of modern studios, by the term *fourth dimension.*

Without entering into mathematical explanations pertaining to another field, and confining myself to plastic representation as I see it, I would say that in the plastic arts the fourth dimension is generated by the three known dimensions: it represents the immensity of space eternalized in all directions at a given moment. It is space itself, or the dimension of infinity; it is what gives objects plasticity. It gives them their just proportion in a given work, whereas in Greek art, for example, a kind of mechanical rhythm is constantly destroying proportion.

Greek art had a purely human conception of beauty. It took man as the measure of perfection. The art of the new painters takes the infinite universe as its ideal, and it is to the fourth dimension alone that we owe this new measure of perfection that allows the artist to give objects the proportions appropriate to the degree of plasticity he wishes them to attain.

Nietzsche foresaw the possibility of such an art:

"O divine Dionysus, why are you pulling my ears?" Ariadne asks her philosophical lover in one of the famous dialogues on the Isle of Naxos.

"I find something very pleasant, very agreeable about your ears, Ariadne. Why aren't they even longer?"

In this anecdote, Nietzsche put an indictment of Greek art into Dionysus's mouth.

Wishing to attain the proportions of the ideal and not limiting themselves to humanity, the young painters offer us works that are more cerebral than sensual. They are moving further and further away from the old art of optical illusions and literal proportions, in order to express the grandeur of metaphysical forms. That is why today's art, although it does not emanate directly from specific religious beliefs, nevertheless possesses several of the characteristics of great art, that is to say, of religious Art.

One could give the following definition of art: creation of new illusions. Indeed, everything we feel is only illusion, and the function of the artist is to modify the illusions of the public in accordance with his own creation. Thus, the general structure of an Egyptian mummy conforms to the figures drawn by Egyptian artists, even though the ancient Egyptians were very different from one another. They simply conformed to the art of their time. It is the function of Art, its social role, to create this illusion: the type. God knows that the paintings of Manet and Renoir were ridiculed in their time! Yet one has only to glance at some photographs of the period to see how exactly people and objects conformed to Manet's and Renoir's paintings of them.

This illusion seems quite natural to me, since works of art are the most dynamic products of a period from a plastic point of view. This dynamism imposes itself on human beings and becomes, through them, the plastic standard of a period. Thus, those who ridicule the new painters are ridiculing their own faces, for the humanity of the future will form its image of the humanity of today on the basis of the representations that the most vital, that is, the newest, artists will have left of it. Do not tell me that there are other painters today who paint in such a way that humanity can recognize its own image in their works. All the works of art of a period end up resembling the most dynamic, most expressive, and most typical works of their time. Dolls, which are popular or folk art, always seem to be inspired by the great art of their period. This is a fact one can easily verify. Yet, who would dare assert that the dolls that were sold in any emporium around 1880 had been fashioned with a feeling analogous to Renoir's when he painted his portraits? No one noticed it at the time. What it means, however, is that Renoir's art was dynamic enough, and alive enough to impose itself on our senses, while to the public that first saw his early works, Renoir's conceptions seemed to be so many absurdities and follies.

Today's public resists the works of the young painters, just as the public of 1880 resisted Renoir's works. It goes so far as to accuse them of being cheap tricksters, and at most, it will condescend sometimes to say simply that they are wrong.

Now, in the whole history of art, there is not a single case known of a collective hoax, or of a collective artistic error. There are isolated cases of hoax and error, but there cannot possibly be collective ones. If the new school of painting were one such case, that would constitute an event so extraordinary as to be called a miracle. To imagine a case of this kind would be to imagine that suddenly all the children in a given country were born without a head or a leg or an arm—clearly an absurd idea. There are no collective errors or hoaxes in art, there are only diverse periods and diverse schools of art. All are equally respectable, and according to the changing notions of beauty, every school is, in turn, admired, scorned, and admired again.

I personally am a great admirer of the modern school of painting, because it seems to me the most audacious school that ever existed. It has raised the question of what beauty is in itself.

The modern painters want to represent beauty detached from the pleasure that man finds in man—and that is something that no European artist, from the beginning of recorded time, had ever dared to do. The new artists are searching for an ideal beauty that will no longer be merely the prideful expression of the species.

Today's art invests its creations with a grandiose, monumental appearance that exceeds anything the artists of previous periods had conceived in that respect; at the same time, today's art contains not a trace of exoticism. It is true that our young artists are familiar with Chinese works of art, with African and Australian effigies, and with the minutiae of Islamic art, but their works reflect none of these influences, nor that of the Italian or German primitives. Today's French art was born spontaneously on French soil. That proves the vitality of the French nation; it is far from decadence. One could easily establish a parallel between contemporary French art and Gothic art, which planted admirable monuments in the soil of France and of all Europe. Gone are the Greek and Italian influences. Here is the rebirth of French art, that is to say, of Gothic art—a rebirth wholly spontaneous and free of pastiche. Today's art is linked with Gothic art through all the genuinely French characteristics of the intervening schools, from Poussin to Ingres, from Delacroix to Manet, from Cézanne to Seurat, and from Renoir to the Douanier Rousseau, that humble but so very expressive and poetic expression of French art.

The vitality of this dynamic and infinite art that springs from the soil of France offers us a marvelous spectacle. But no man is a prophet in his own country, and that is why this art encounters more resistance here than anywhere else.

3.4 GUILLAUME APOLLINAIRE

Cubism Differs

1913

Cubism differs from the old schools of painting in that it aims, not at an art of imitation, but at an art of conception, which tends to rise to the height of creation.

In representing conceptualized reality or creative reality, the painter can give the effect of three dimensions. He can to a certain extent cube. But not by simply rendering reality as seen, unless he indulges in *trompe-l'oeil*, in foreshortening, or in perspective, thus distorting the quality of the forms conceived or created.

I can discriminate four trends in cubism. Of these, two are pure, and along parallel lines.

Scientific cubism is one of the pure tendencies. It is the art of painting new structures out of elements borrowed not from the reality of sight, but from the reality of insight. All men have a sense of this interior reality. A man does not have to be cultivated in order to conceive, for example, of a round form.

The geometrical aspect, which made such an impression on those who saw the first canvases of the scientific cubists, came from the fact that the essential reality was rendered with great purity, while visual accidents and anecdotes had been eliminated. The painters who follow this tendency are: Picasso, whose luminous art also belongs to the other pure tendency of cubism, Georges Braque, Albert Gleizes, Marie Laurencin, and Juan Gris.

Physical cubism is the art of painting new structures with elements borrowed, for the most part, from visual reality. This art, however, belongs in the cubist movement because of its constructive discipline. It has a great future as historical painting. Its social role is very clear, but it is not a pure art. It confuses what is properly the subject with images. The painter-physicist who created this trend is Le Fauconnier.

Orphic cubism is the other important trend of the new art school. It is the art of painting new structures out of elements which have not been borrowed from the visual sphere, but have been created entirely by the artist himself, and been endowed by him with fullness of reality. The works of the orphic artist must simultanously give a pure aesthetic pleasure, a structure which is self-evident, and a sublime meaning, that is, a subject. This is pure art. The light in Picasso's paintings is based on this conception, to which Robert Delaunay's inventions have contributed much, and towards which Fernand Léger, Francis Picabia, and Marcel Duchamp are also addressing themselves.

Instinctive cubism, the art of painting new structures of elements which are not borrowed from visual reality, but are suggested to the artist by instinct and intuition, has long tended towards orphism. The instinctive artist lacks lucidity and an aesthetic doctrine; instinctive cubism includes a large number of artists. Born of French impressionism, this movement has now spread all over Europe.

Cézanne's last paintings and his water-colors belong to cubism, but Courbet is the father of the new painters; and André Derain, whom I propose to discuss some other time, was the eldest of his beloved sons, for we find him at the beginning of the fauvist movement, which was a kind of introduction to cubism, and also at the beginnings of this great subjective movement; but it would be too difficult today to write discerningly of a man who so willfully stands apart from everyone and everything.

*   *   *

The modern school of painting seems to me the most audacious that has ever appeared. It has posed the question of what is beautiful in itself.

It wants to visualize beauty disengaged from whatever charm man has for man, and until now, no European artist has dared attempt this. The new artists demand an ideal beauty, which will be, not merely the proud expression of the species, but the expression of the universe, to the degree that it has been humanized by light.

The new art clothes its creations with a grandiose and monumental appearance which surpasses anything else conceived by the artists of our time. Ardent in its search for beauty, it is noble and energetic, and the reality it brings us is marvelously clear. I love the art of today because above all else I love the light, for man loves light more than anything; it was he who invented fire.

Horse Calligram

1913–1916

  Man you will find here
a new representation of the universe
at its most poetic and most modern
Man man man man man man
Give yourself up to this art where the sublime
does not exclude charm
and brilliancy does not blur the nuance
it is now or never the moment
to be sensitive to poetry for it dominates
all dreadfully

Vase

1913–1916

Why weep
Come back tomorrow
There are also poisonous flowers
and flowers always open in the evening
she loves the cinema
she has been in Russia
Love married with disdain
Pearl-studded watch
a trip to Montrouge
Maisons-Lafitte
and everything finishes in perfumes
remember
Let the flower bloom and let the fruit rot
and let the grain sprout
while the storms rage

Bleuet

1917

BLEUET

Jeune homme
de vingt ans
Qui as vu des choses si affreuses
Que penses-tu des hommes de ton enfance

Tu   *Tu*
  as
    vu   *connais*
      la
        mort   *la bravoure et la ruse*
            en
              face
                plus
                  de
                    cent
                      fois
                        tu
                          ne
                            sais
Transmets ton intrépidité   *pas*
                                                ce
A ceux qui viendront   *que*
                                                      c'est
      Après toi   *que*
                                                            la
                                                              vie

            Jeune homme
        Tu es joyeux ta mémoire est ensanglantée
            Ton âme est rouge aussi
          De joie
    Tu as absorbé la vie de ceux qui sont morts près de toi
            Tu as de la décision
          Il est 17 heures et tu saurais
                mourir
      Sinon mieux que tes aînés
            Du moins plus pieusement
              car tu connais mieux la mort que la vie
          O douceur d'autrefois
                lenteur immémoriale

            GUILLAUME APOLLINAIRE

The Little Car

1918

The 31st day of August 1914
I left Deauville a little before midnight
In Rouveyre's little car

With his driver there were three of us

We said goodbye to an entire epoch
Furious giants were rising over Europe
The eagles were leaving their aeries expecting the sun
The voracious fish were rising from the depths
The masses were rushing toward some deeper understanding
The dead were trembling with fear in their dark dwellings

The dogs were barking towards over there where the frontiers are
I went bearing within me all those armies fighting
I felt them rise up in me and spread out over the countries they wound
    through
With the forests the happy villages of Belgium
Francorchamps with l'Eau Rouge and the mineral springs
Region where the invasions always take place
Railway arteries where those who were going to die
Saluted one last time this colorful life
Deep oceans where monsters were moving
In old shipwrecked hulks
Unimaginable heights where man fights
Higher than the eagle soars
There man fights man
And falls like a shooting star
I felt in myself new and totally capable beings
Build and organize a new universe
A merchant of amazing opulence and astounding size
Was laying out an extraordinary display
And gigantic shepherds were leading
Great silent flocks that were browsing on words
With every dog along the road barking at them

I'll never forget that night when none of us said a single word

O
dark   O
departure   ten
when our   der
three head   pre-   O
lights were   w a r   vil
d y i n g   night   lages   with   the rushing

BLACKSMITHS CALLED UP

between midnight and one o'clock in the morning

   to   sil
   v e r   v e r
  y b l u e   or else   y V e r
   L i s i   s a i l
   eux   les

and 3 times we stopped to change a tire that had blown out

And when having passed that afternoon
Through Fontainebleau
We arrived in Paris
Just as the mobilization posters were going up
We understood my buddy and I
That the little car had taken us into a New epoch
And although we were both grown men
We had just been born

Reflections on Painting

1917

In art, progress does not consist in extension, but in the knowledge of limits.

Limitation of means determines style, engenders new form, and gives impulse to creation.

Limited means often constitute the charm and force of primitive painting. Extension, on the contrary, leads the arts to decadence.

New means, new subjects.

The subject is not the object, it is a new unity, a lyricism which grows completely from the means.

The painter thinks in terms of form and color.

The goal is not to be concerned with the *reconstitution* of an anecdotal fact, but with *constitution* of a pictorial fact.

Painting is a method of representation.

One must not imitate what one wants to create.

One does not imitate appearances; the appearance is the result.

To be pure imitation, painting must forget appearance.

To work from nature is to improvise.

One must beware of a formula *good for everything*, that will serve to interpret the other arts as well as reality, and that instead of creating will only produce a style, or rather a stylization.

The arts which achieve their effect through purity have never been arts that were good for everything. Greek sculpture (among others), with its decadence, teaches us this.

The senses deform, the mind forms. Work to perfect the mind. There is no certitude but in what the mind conceives.

The painter who wished to make a circle would only draw a curve. Its appearance might satisfy him, but he would doubt it. The compass would give him certitude. The pasted papers [*papiers collés*] in my drawings also gave me a certitude.

Trompe l'œil is due to an *anecdotal chance* which succeeds because of the simplicity of the facts.

The pasted papers, the imitation woods—and other elements of a similar kind—which I used in some of my drawings, also succeed through the simplicity of the facts; this has caused them to be confused with *trompe l'œil*, of which they are the exact opposite. They are also simple facts, but are *created by the mind*, and are one of the justifications for a new form in space.

Nobility grows out of contained emotion.

Emotion should not be rendered by an excited trembling; it can neither be added on nor be imitated. It is the seed, the work is the flower.

I like the rule that corrects the emotion.

3.10 BLAISE CENDRARS

On Projection Powder

1917

The engine is rocking us like a cradle. We are entering the zone of attractions, gravitation, conjugations, calculations of Melancholy, and monograms of the Heart. The network of nerves and veins stands out against the unleavened wafer of night like a microscopic preparation.

Parabolas. Caroms.

Everything cools. Graphic beauty is muddled. This is old age which touches us unexpectedly, sudden and terrible like a comet. Is this 7? Is this 4? We cannot count on our fingers any more. My companions turn white from head to toe and fall into dust.

'Everyone to his post!'

There isn't even a skull to snicker. We will be agglomerated, digested, annihilated, thrown to the moray eels behind the sky. I cannot battle against the decomposition, but I can still control our direction. We must return to our home port. I believe I still have the force to return among men. I employ a small vaporizer. The projection powder transmutes our engine into pure solar matter. Nothing can stop us now; we are returning to our origin.

Already we are rising, we are falling vertiginously. We leave the picturesque tableau of the sky behind us—the chieftains, the slaves, the bazaar, the tattoos made for export—to greet in passing the most familiar astronomies, flying by in pairs.

Constellations in flocks like birds announce that we are nearing home. Here already is the great waterfall. I am fainting. I no longer have the strength to land. We speed through the human atmosphere like a meteorite. Golden scarab. Zigzagging like a question mark. Explosion.

PARIS, COURCELLES, NICE, & LA PIERRE

Profound Today

1917

I no longer know if I'm looking with my naked eye at a starry sky or at a drop of water through a microscope. Since the origin of the species, the horse moves, supple and mathematical. Machines are already catching up, moving ahead. Locomotives rear and steamships whinny on the water. Never will a typewriter commit an etymological spelling error, but the man of intellect stammers, chews his words, and breaks his teeth on antique consonants. When I think all my senses burst into flame and I'd like to violate all beings, and when I give rein to my destructive instincts I find the triangle of a metaphysical solution. Inexhaustible coal mines! Cosmogonies find a new life in trademarks. Extravagant signboards over the multicolored city, with the ribbon of trams climbing the avenue, screaming monkeys hanging on to each other's tails, and the incendiary orchids of architectures collapsing on top of them and killing them. In the air, the virgin cry of trolleys! The material world is as well trained as an Indian chief's stallion. It obeys the faintest signal. Pressure of a finger. A jet of steam sets the piston going. A copper wire makes the frog's leg jerk. Everything is sensitized. It is all within range of the eye. You can almost touch it. Where is man? The gesturings of protozoa are more tragic than the history of a woman's heart. The lives of plants more stirring than a detective story. The musculature of the back in motion dances a ballet. This piece of fabric should be set to music and that jar of preserves is a poem of ingenuity. The proportion, angle, appearance of everything is changing. Everything moves away, comes closer, cumulates, misses the point, laughs, asserts itself, and gets aggravated. Products from the five corners of the world turn up in the same dish, on the same dress. We feed on the sweat of gold at every meal, every kiss. Everything is artificial and very real. Eyes. Hands. The immense fleece of numbers on which I lay out the bank. The sexual furor of factories. The turning wheel. The hovering wing. The voice traveling along a wire. Your ear in a trumpet. Your sense of direction. Your rhythm. You melt the world into the mold of your skull. Your brain hollows out. Unsuspected depths, in which you pluck the potent flower of explosives. Like a religion, a mysterious pill activates your digestion. You get lost in the labyrinth of stores where you renounce yourself to become everyone. With Mr. Book you smoke the twenty-five-cent Havana featured in the advertisement. You are part of the great anonymous body of a café. I no longer recognize myself in the mirror, alcohol has blurred my features. He espouses the novelty shop as he would the first passerby. Every one of us is the hour sounding on the clock. To control the beast of your impatience you rush into the menagerie of railway stations. They leave. They scatter. Fireworks. In all directions. The capitals of Europe are on the trajectory of their inertia. The terrible blast of a whistle furrows the continent. Overseas countries lie still within the net. Here is Egypt on camelback. Choose Engadine for winter sports. Read Golf's *Hotels* under the palm trees. Think of four hundred windows flashing in the sun. You unfold the horizon of a timetable and dream of southern islands. Romanticism. Flags of countryside float at the windows while flowers fall from the garlands of the train and take root and names, forgotten villages! On the move, kneeling in the accordion of the sky through the telescoped voices. The most blasé go furthest. Motionless. For entire days. Like Socrates. With an activity in the mind. The Eiffel Tower sways on the horizon. The sun, a cloud, anything is enough to stretch it or shrink it. The metal bridges are just as mysterious and sensitive. Watches set themselves. From every direction ocean liners move toward their connections. Then the semaphore signals. A blue eye opens. The red one closes. Soon there is nothing but color. Interpenetration. Disk. Rhythm. Dance. Orange and violet hues devour each other. Checkerboard of the port. Every crate is heaped with what you earned by inventing that game, Dr. Alamede. Steam-driven cranes empty thunder from their hampers. Pell-mell. East. West. South. North. Everything turns cartwheels along the docks while the lion of the sky strangles the cows of twilight. There are shiploads of fruit on the ground and on the rooftops. Barrels of fire. Cinnamon. European women are like subaqueous flowers confronting the stern laboring of longshoremen and the dark red apotheosis of machines. A tram slams into your back. A trap door opens under your feet. There's a tunnel in your eye. You're pulled by the hair to the fifteenth floor. Smoking a pipe, your hands at the faucets—cold water, hot water—you think of the captain's wife, whose knee you will soon surreptitiously caress. The golden denture of her smile, her charming accent. And you let yourself slip down to dinner. The tongues are stuffed. Everyone must grimace to be understood. Gesticulate and laugh loudly. Madame wipes her mouth with her loincloth of a napkin. Boeuf Zephir. Café Euréka. Pimodan or Pamodan. Seated in my rocking chair I'm like a Negro fetish, angular beneath the heraldic electricity. The orchestra plays *Louise*. To amuse myself, I riddle the fat body of an old windbag that is floating at the level of my eyes with pinpricks. A deep-sea diver, submerged in the smoke from my cigar, alone, I listen to the dying music of sentimentality that resonates in my helmet. The lead soles of my boots keep me upright and I move forward, slow, grotesque, stiff-necked, and bend with difficulty over the swamp life of the women. Your eye, sea horse, vibrates, marks a comma, and passes. Between two waters, the sex, bushy, complicated, rare. This cuttlefish discharges its ink cloud at me and I disappear into it like a pilot. I hear the engine of the waters, the steel forge of leeches. A thousand suction pores function, secreting iodine. The skin turns gelatinous, transparent, incandesces like the flesh of an anemone. Nerve centers are polarized. All functions are independent. Eyes reach to touch; backs eat; fingers see. Tufts of grassy arms undulate. Sponges of the depths, brains gently breathe. Thighs remember and move like fins. The storm rips out your tonsils. A scream passes over you like the shadow of an iceberg. It freezes and sunders. The being reassembles itself with difficulty. Hunger draws the limbs together and gathers them around the vacuum of the stomach. The body dons the uniform of weight. The spirit, scattered everywhere, concentrates in the rosette of consciousness. I am man. You are woman. Good-bye. Everyone returns to his room. There are shoes in front of the door. Don't confuse them. Mine are yellow. The valet is waiting for his tip. I give him the shield from my coat of arms. I've forgotten to sleep. My glottis moves. This attempt at suicide is regicide. I'm impaled on my sensibility. The dogs of night come to lick the blood running down my legs. They turn it into light. The silence is such that you can hear the mechanism of the universe straining. A click. Suddenly everything is one notch larger. It is today. A great foaming horse. Diseases rise to the sky like stars on the horizon. And here is Betelgeuse, mistress of the seventh house. Believe me, everything is clear, ordered, simple, and natural. Minerals breathe, vegetables eat, animals emote, man crystallizes. Prodigious today. Probe. Antenna. Door-face-whirlwind. You live. Eccentric. In integral solitude. In anonymous communion. With everything that is root and summit and that throbs, revels, jubilates. Phenomena of this congenital hallucination which is life in all its manifestations and the continual activity of consciousness. The motor spirals. The rhythm speaks. Chemistry. You are.

Words in Freedom

1917

The goal of art is artistic emotion, brought about in a certain way. Everything not that way in all its ups and downs and its limitations only weighs down and weakens. The best effect is reached by exercising the freest choice of artistic ideas, not at all those of philosophers. To delight in useless beauties is to spoil a child by too much love. Weakness when faced with inspiration leads to weakness when faced with the reader. Art's obligations are the ones imposed on the artist by himself, in his own logic. Will is the essence of art, the form it takes is the way of it: even "words in freedom" can be that way. The partisans of romantic disorder aren't going to keep us back with all that glorious naming: the way they got it was through the classics. Style is a French tradition forcefully represented by Victor Hugo. Two qualities that guarantee eternity to a work guarantee it for Musset's comedies: creation and context or situation.

A work is created when each of its parts works for the whole, whether or not the words appear free. It is situated when all its movements, resembling the others or not, take place elsewhere. So the poems of Mallarmé are situated, those of Guillaume Apollinaire so magnificently inspired are always situated, but not those of the imitators. You can recognize what is created from the necessity of the parts, what is situated, by its liveliness within its generality, and, for the people who know, by the aura you can detect around the work. The usefulness of the components is characteristic of living or lasting organisms, whereas the lastingness is characteristic of a work of art. Mere charms pass with passing fashions and only return with them. Jules Laforgue's neological babble, so exquisite in 1880, is completely unbearable today. The compositions of the poet Heinrich Heine have admirers that are now lacking to various travelers' tales. Verlaine's words, "so specious and so sweet," are no longer like that, whereas the spirit of La Fontaine, who never gave in to that sweetness, is still vital. "Written works will live," it is sometimes said; style is the necessity of words. Perhaps the partisans of words in freedom will take advantage of their own authority in this matter. Let's be free in regard to the reader, not ourselves. Let's chastise ourselves if we don't want to be chastised by others. Let's sacrify our own talents if we don't want our words to be sacrificed.

Aesthetics is the philosophy of the beautiful; in a discourse that treats of the former, let's not be surprised by the terms of the latter. To go with one's mind to the geographical and supernatural place that a creator desires, and to return from it is a mental joy and just exactly the movement that bestows artistic pleasure. Such is not the case for the realistic comparisons that only satisfy an amour propre that longs to be equal with the author. Pathos draws tears, reality does it better. Art is indispensable to man, as is proven by all the games of the child and the savage; it would not be so if tears were its goal. Thought itself is not art, although it can get there by going around; it is rather a lesson, filling in for the lacks of our own thought. Art is not in the expectation of some unknown end, for it exists in itself and would no longer exist for someone aware of its ins and outs. Art remains therefore the appeal to a sensitivity by a will, and the constructor's appeal suffices to provide emotion. So why should we ask of art some spatial precision?

We ask of a book its power of liberation. The self is a prison whose key is the book. Fairy queens and Balzacian countesses wipe out the real storms of our own life by their imaginary ones. Workers look for great ladies in Zevacco and great ladies look for workers elsewhere. The naturalists have misunderstood this truth by offering to the bourgeois their own particular truths. Such is, *grosso modo,* the principle of transplantation; there is another, strictly artistic. The human spirit does not call for generalizations only because they offer a means of transplanting all readers, but rather because they constitute a false atmosphere realized through the strength of the poet. The greatest generalization in a work lets it address everyone, certainly, but above all it transplants the mind of each one: that's the beauty of religious books that the seventeenth century used to study. No school speaks of this ideal localisation, and yet it preoccupies them all: the seventeenth century tends that way through the generalization of character types, the eighteenth century through style, the romantics on the stilts of frenzy (and vainly at that), the Parnassians through Mallarmean impersonality, the symbolists through the word and the dream that gave Apollinaire his first manner. The theory of words in freedom no more produces it than romantic frenzy. One of its partisans, perhaps ignorant of the fact that art is indispensable to life, cannot, alas, overlap with it, answers the question of the localization of works by that of the milieux within the work. NO! the return trip of the mind is artistic emotion; that of the imagination is only a voyage "around my room" and does not produce it.

On Cubism

1917

The painting movement which, born some ten years ago, has been called Cubism, is perhaps not the one which surprised the World the most, nor the one which, after getting the greatest number of enemies, recollected the most of adepts; but it is undoubtedly the artistic *Effort* which, being the most important of our time, brought in it the most of confusion.

This confusion, in which at first people seemed to delight, itself, lasted long enough. The efforts attempted by each artist to make it cease is a proof of it. The need of understanding and of better understanding is felt everywhere. I am speaking of artists, as it is not only amongst people but also amongst artists that the ambiguity existed and, unfortunately, exists still with persistence.

The matter is not only the divergencies of taste which existed always amongst them and will happily never cease, but there are several essential points which it would be perhaps useful to reach and to admit in common, in order to establish a base for an art which many claim for absolutely different and even opposed reasons. The matter is yet an art which by its persistence and its development has proved enough its reasons and its rights to exist.

The opinion of a single man could certainly not make everybody agree; but it is perhaps not useless to attempt to some explanations of general order, some precisions of particular order, useful in any case to resolve a clear difference. The serious efforts of several would certainly gain by not being confounded with the more or less justified, more or less honest (artistically spoken) fancies of painters which, having nothing to bring to the movement, are only attracted by the beyond-measure modernism when it is not by other less avowable reasons.

Some pretended to go beyond Cubism, which is the art in evolution of our time, and in order to get out of it, they went backward. Back again to the art of imitation in choosing only between the most modern objects to be represented, they believed, in avoiding the difficulty, to solve an arduous problem. With the titles under which they were obliged to complete their works, they left the plastic domain for a literary symbolism, the fantasmagoria of which is, in the domain of painting, absolutely worthless. Also, if it is difficult to find *new means* in an art, it is only worthy *to find them proper to this art* and not in another one. This is to say that the literary means used for the art of painting (and vice versa) can only give us an easy and dangerous appearance of novelty.

Cubism is an eminently plastic art; but *an art of creation* and not of reproduction or interpretation.

Now, what can a man create in painting, if not a picture, and this creation with new adapted means? The first cubist painters found proper means and those who followed their traces did not pay enough attention to them. The latter took the appearance of works yet realised and worked "in the manner" with the pretention to start on their account, a new art. It is time to notice it, otherwise people would make of this deep art — of which only the superficial side was seen — a superficial art. By this disastrous way of judging, people saw only incoherence where there was, even at start, *research of discipline.* To-day, for few rare elected, *the discipline is established,* and as no one has ever dreamed of a cold, mathematic and antiplastic, solely cerebral art, the works which the cubist artists produce, appeal direct to the eye and to the sense of the lovers of painting. But to love this painting it must be first understood why its appearance is so much different from the one our eye is accustomed to.

The purpose is different: the means must also be so, and *the result equally:* to please the public, which will be the consequence of the result, is only a question of education of the latter.

Since the creation of perspective as pictural means, nothing more important has been found in art.

Our period is the time when the equivalent of these marvellous means has been found. As perspective is *the means to represent* objects after *their visual appearance,* there exist in cubism *the means to construct the picture* in paying attention to the objects only as *elements* and not on behalf of the anecdotic point of view.

It now becomes necessary to ascertain the difference which exists between the *object* and the *subject.* The latter is *the result of the gained means of creation;* it is *the picture itself.* Objects being taken only as elements, it will be understood *that the question is* not to express their appearance but *to clear, for the use of the picture, all what is eternal and constant* (for instance — the round form of a glass, etc.) and *to exclude the rest.*

The explanation of the deformation of objects, explanation which was never made known before to people, is there! *The deformation is a consequence* and ought not to be considered as an arbitrary fancy of the painter. Otherwise we would never get rid of the caricatural deformations excused by this out-of-date expression "the way of seeing." After this, it will be understood that *we do not admit that a cubist painter makes a portrait.* No confusion ought to be made here. *The matter is to create a work, a picture* as a matter of fact, and *not a head* or *an object,* constructed according to new rules which would not justify enough the appearance by which they end.

It is this creation [. . .] which will mark out our time. *We live in a period of artistic creation* in the course of which *no more stories are told,* more or less agreeably, but *during which works are created* which, *breaking off with life, come in again* because *they have their own existence, outside evocation or reproduction of things of life.* After this, the art of to-day is an art of great reality. But it must be understood: *artistic reality* and *not realism;* the latter is the genre which is the most opposed to us.

It can then be said that *cubism is painting itself* as well as [that] *to-day's poetry is poetry itself. Never mind,* after this, *the objects which are used, never mind their novelty if they are used with means not born with them* or *for them. There only,* in this entire appropriation of means, *is the birth of the "style"* which characterises a period.

In the domain of art it is never the creations of another kind which served as stepping-stones, and when we speak of period we mean *artistic period*—as I am not a motor-car driver.

PART 4

Nowism / Presentism / Simultaneism

Although Pierre Albert-Birot's journal called *SIC* (Sons Idées Couleurs Formes; Sounds Ideas Colors Forms) dates from 1916–18, and thus later than the Cubist movement in painting, the avant-garde writers associated with it are called "Cubists" because of their association with the Cubist theories and poets—Max Jacob, Guillaume Apollinaire, and Pierre Reverdy (in spite of Reverdy's frequent declarations that "Cubist poetry does not exist"). Albert-Birot contributed most of the entries in the journal, including all the brief manifestos, typographically experimental and generally comic, even witty.

Reverdy went on to found *Nord-Sud*, with its original illustration by Georges Braque on the cover (itself figuring the journal *Nord-Sud*, under a lamp), and it is there that his celebrated article on "The Image" is found. Strictly speaking, therefore, his "imagism" could be placed in parallel with the Imagist movement of England (associated with T. E. Hulme and, later, Ezra Pound) and the United States (Amy Lowell's "amygism"). In fact, his theory of the image would be picked up by André Breton (one of whose earliest articles is also found in *SIC*), when Breton developed the theory of the Surrealist image, taken from two different realms to make its explosive contact.

With their varying forms—Nowism or Nunism, from the Latin (see Albert-Birot's manifesto "Nunism," 4.6), or Presentism, as in the writings of Blaise Cendrars or Henri Barzum—these movements all had the same initial impulse: things happening together. They are of course allied with Simultaneism.

Nowism insists on the *hic and nunc*, the actual here and now, as the name indicates, letting the heavens take care of themselves. Its title allies it also to Raoul Hausmann's Presentism of 1921, whereas its synthesizing efforts ally it to Syncretism and other attempts at bridging different disciplines.

One of the more interesting points about Nunism, apart from its ardent good humor, is the way in which Albert-Birot combined words to make new ones, quite like the Futurist synthetic merging of the moving bus with the cheek of the spectator or the wall of a building. Here is an example of one of his Nunist poems from *SIC* (no. 5, May 1916; my translation), aimed, as are all the Nunist declamations—and most manifestos, of course—at liveliness and newness:

A Poem: Youth

        Youth curveproud
        Greengreengreen

Imperialascensional strength

Autocracyearthrightangled

Yellowredgreen	Shocksblowsreversals
Freneticmotor	Tearscriessongs
Wavesofeternity	Center of gravity
Smell of life	Waveofeternity

But the apparently easygoing demeanor of the Nunist was no match for the other journals of the time. Francis Picabia's jesting "Newspaper of Instantaneism" as a special issue of the journal *391* reflects this epoch. And it is hard to overlook the particular if unconscious and traditional chauvinism, even xenophobia, of such inward-turning manifestos as Albert-Birot's "Banality" (4.1), with its insistence on France for the French.

The writings of Blaise Cendrars concretize the sense of presentness. His ars poetica "The ABCs of Cinema" (4.8), like all his work, manifests the adventure—both aesthetic and physical—that Simultaneism stressed. His epic poem *The Prose of the Transsiberian and of Little Jeanne of France* (Paris, 1913), illustrated by Sonia Delaunay in a long and colorful scroll, puts that adventure into poetry.

4.1 PIERRE ALBERT-BIROT

Banality

1916

Do we worship Isis, Jupiter, Janus, Jehovah, Christ, Boudha, Moloch? No. Do we wear tunics, peplums, or armor? No. Do we speak Egyptian, Greek, Roumanian, Hebrew . . . Roman or Chinese? No. So why should our arts be Egyptian, Greek, Rumanian, Gothic, Chinese, or Japanese?

Our idea, our costume, our language, is it the same as in the time of Louis XIV, Louis XV, Louis XVI? No. Why should our arts be the same? Is our ideal, our way of dressing or of speaking, the same as last century's? Does our time resemble that of our parents? No. So let's do as each people has done in each period of time, LET'S BE MODERN; let our works be the expression of the time in which they were born, these works alone are living, ALL THE OTHERS ARE ARTIFICIAL

TO EACH TIME ITS ART.

Ça ne se fait pas (It isn't done)

1916

ÇA NE SE FAIT PAS

AVANT, en France,
vous demandiez un vêtement pas comme les
autres:

ÇA NE SE FAIT PAS.

Un instrument pas comme les autres:

ÇA NE SE FAIT PAS.

Un papier, une étoffe pas comme les autres:

ÇA NE SE FAIT PAS.

Une machine pas comme les autres:

ÇA NE SE FAIT PAS.

Un artiste présentait une œuvre pas comme
les autres:

ÇA NE SE FAIT PAS.

Or maintenant la France réveillée

S A I T

que tout "CE QUI NE SE FAIT PAS"

PEUT SE FAIRE

et se FERA

IT ISN'T DONE

BEFORE, in France,
you asked for some clothes not like the rest:
> IT ISN'T DONE.
Some instrument not like the rest:
> IT ISN'T DONE.
Some paper, some material not like the rest:
> IT ISN'T DONE.
Some machine not like the rest:
> IT ISN'T DONE.
An artist presented a work not like the rest:
> IT ISN'T DONE.
But now France awakened
> KNOWS
that everything "THAT ISN'T DONE"
CAN BE DONE
and will *BE DONE*

L'ESPRIT MODERNE

RETARDATAIRES!
ÊTES-VOUS CONVAINCUS?

Qu'est-ce qui nous a vaincus
à Charleroi ?

L'ESPRIT MODERNE

Qu'est-ce qui les a vaincus dans la Somme
et à Verdun?

L'ESPRIT MODERNE

Allons cachez-vous
néfastes troglodytes!

et

merci Guillaume

THE MODERN SPIRIT
SLUGGARDS!
Are you convinced?
What defeated us at Charleroi?
THE MODERN SPIRIT
What defeated them in la Somme and Verdun?
THE MODERN SPIRIT
Go on get lost you hateful old troglodytes!
and
thank you Guillaume

La Loi (The law)

1916

LA LOI

A bas la rouille
A bas le moisi
A bas la ruine

A BAS LE VIEUX

C'est sale
Ça pue

ÇA SENT LA MORT

Aimons la maison neuve
Aimons la maison blanche
Aimons le rouge, le bleu, le vert
et l'or
C'est chaud, c'est jeune
C'est propre

Aimons le neuf
ÇA SENT LA VIE

THE LAW

Down with rust

Down with mold

Down with ruins

DOWN WITH THE OLD

It's dirty

It stinks

IT SMELLS LIKE DEATH

Let's love the new house

Let's love the white house

Let's love red, blue, green, and gold

It's warm, it's young

It's clean

LET'S LOVE THE NEW

IT SMELLS LIKE LIFE

4.5 PIERRE ALBERT-BIROT

Nunic Dialogue

Z and A in Front of Modern Paintings

1916

A. No, no, what to do? I just don't get it.

Z. What's the problem?

A. Everything! I don't see anything I recognize. So that's a woman, right? Ok, well why is her head square, her neck thick, and her legs short? With those proportions she doesn't look like any woman I ever met. Nature doesn't look like that, you know.

Z. It never crossed my mind to think about it. If this woman was made like what you call "nature," this painting wouldn't be a work of art.

A. Yes, you all answer like that, but we have the example of the past, you can't deny that all those great masters . . .

Z. Ah, I was just going to mention that. Have you really looked at them?

A. How can you ask? I spend all my free moments in a museum.

Z. Now tell me, is "nature" like Egyptian granite?

A. Ah no, but it's something else, and . . .

Z. Is "nature" like Phidias marble?

A. Obviously not.

Z. Like one of Giotto's saints?

A. No, but . . .

Z. Like a figure of Michelangelo?

A. No, it's more . . .

Z. Like a Rubens?

A. No, he's Flemish!

Z. Like a Velázquez?

A. No, less . . .

Z. Like a Rembrandt?

A. No, obviously it's more violent, but how you choose them, or talk about a Leonardo, a Raphael, that's nature for you!

Z. Tell me if you find in all sincerity that "nature" is like a St. Jean of Leonardo or a Virgin of Raphael?

A. Those figures are far lovelier than in nature.

Z. That's one opinion, but since you find them lovelier than "nature" they aren't like "nature."

A. In that sense you're right.

Z. So you just yourself observed that the masters of the great epochs never gave in their works a complete "nature," in other terms none of the works of the past is a purely objective representation.

A. That's true, I didn't realize it clearly until now.

4.6 PIERRE ALBERT-BIROT

Nunism

1916

An "ism" to outlast the others.

Nunism was born with man and will only disappear with him.

All the great philosophers, the great artists, the great poets, the great scientists, all the flamebearers, the creators of all ages have been, are, will be nunists.

All of us who are seeking something, let's be nunists first.

No life outside of nunism.

To be a nunist or not be.

Pas de corset! (No girdle!)

1917

PAS DE CORSET!

« Allons donc Messieurs les nunistes vous nous conduisez à l'anarchie avec tous vos renversements des lois existantes, vous oubliez qu'il faut un corset pour contenir les affaissements et les débordements! »

« Voyons, Monsieur, vous savez bien que ce qui a le plus de valeur en ce monde est justement ce qui se tient tout seul. »

NO GIRDLE!

"Really you Nunists, you are taking us straight to anarchy, the way you keep upsetting our rules: you forget it takes a girdle to stop everything sliding and spilling over!"

"Look here, Sir, you know perfectly well that what is most valuable in this world of ours is just what holds up by itself."

4.8 BLAISE CENDRARS
The ABCs of Cinema
1917–1921

Cinema. Whirlwind of movement in space. Everything falls. The sun falls. We fall in its wake. Like a chameleon, the human mind camouflages itself, camouflaging the universe. The world. The globe. The two hemispheres. Leibniz's monads and Schopenhauer's representation. My will. The cardinal hypotheses of science end in a sharp point and the four calculators cumulate. Fusion. Everything opens up, tumbles down, blends in today, caves in, rises up, blossoms. Honor and money. Everything changes. Change. Morality and political economy. New civilization. New humanity. The digits have created an abstract, mathematical organism, useful gadgets intended to serve the senses' most vulgar needs and that are the brain's most beautiful projection. Automatism. Psychism. New commodities. Machines. And it is the machine which recreates and displaces the sense of direction, and which finally discovers the sources of sensibility like the explorers Livingston, Burton, Speke, Grant, Baker, and Stanley, who located the sources of the Nile. But it is an anonymous discovery to which no name can be attached. What a lesson! And what do the celebrities and the stars matter to us! A hundred worlds, a thousand movements, a million dramas simultaneously enter the range of the eye with which cinema has endowed man. And, though arbitrary, this eye is more marvelous than the multifaceted eye of a fly. The brain is overwhelmed by it. An uproar of images. Tragic unity is displaced. We learn. We drink. Intoxication. Reality no longer makes any sense. It has no significance. Everything is rhythm, word, life. No longer any need to demonstrate. We are in communion. Focus the lens on the hand, the corner of the mouth, the ear, and drama emerges, expands on a background of luminous mystery. Already there is no need for dialogue, soon characters will be judged useless. At high speed the life of flowers is Shakespearean; all of classicism is present in the slow-motion flexing of a biceps. On screen the slightest effort becomes painful, musical, and insects and microbes look like our most illustrious contemporaries. Eternity in the ephemeral. Gigantism. It is granted an aesthetic value which it has never had before. Utilitarianism. Theatrical drama, its situation, its devices, becomes useless. Attention is focused on the sinister lowering of the eyebrows. On the hand covered with criminal calluses. On a bit of fabric that bleeds continually. On a watch fob that stretches and swells like the veins at the temples. Millions of hearts stop beating at the same instant in all the capitals of the world and gales of laughter rack the countryside in far-flung villages. What is going to happen? And why is the material world impregnated with humanity? To such a point! What potential! Is it an explosion or a Hindu poem? Chemistries knot into complex plots and unravel toward conclusions. The least pulsation germinates and bears fruit. Crystallizations come to life. Ecstasy. Animals, plants, and minerals are ideas, emotions, digits. A number. As in the Middle Ages, the rhinoceros is Christ; the bear, the devil; jasper, vivacity; chrysoprase, pure humility. 6 and 9. We see our brother the wind, and the ocean is an abyss of men. And this is not some abstract, obscure, and complicated symbolism, it is part of a living organism that we startle, flush out, pursue, and which had never before been seen. Barbaric evidence. Sensitive depths in an Alexandre Dumas drama, a detective novel, or a banal Hollywood film. Over the audience's heads, the luminous cone quivers like a cetacean. Characters, beings and things, subjects and objects, stretch out from the screen in the hearth of the magic lantern. They plunge, turn, chase each other, encounter each other with fatal, astronomical precision. A beam. Rays. The prodigious thread of a screw from which everything is whirled in a spiral. Projection of the fall of the sky. Space. Captured life. Life of the depths. Alphabet. Letter. ABC. Sequence and close-up. *What is ever seen is never seen.* What an interview! "When I began to take an interest in cinematography, film was a commercial and industrial novelty. I've put all my energies into expanding it and raising it to the level of a human language. My only merit consists in having been able to find the first two letters of this new alphabet, which is still far from complete: the *cut-back* and the *close-up*," David Wark Griffith, the world's foremost director declares to me. "Art at the movies? Great Art?" responds Abel Gance, France's foremost director, to a journalist who came to watch him at work in Nice. "Perhaps we could have made it that from the beginning. But first we had to learn the visual alphabet ourselves, before speaking and believing in our power; then we had to teach this elementary language." Carlyle wanted to trace the origin of the modern world back to the legendary founder of the city of Thebes, to Cadmus. As he imported the Phoenician alphabet into Greece, Cadmus invented writing and the book. Before him, writing, mnemonic, ideographic, or phonetic, was always pictorial—from prehistoric man to the Egyptians, from the drawings that grace the walls of stone-age caves to hieroglyphics, the hieratic, traced on stone tablets, or the demotic, painted on ceramics, by way of the pictographs used by Eskimos and Australian aborigines, the Red Skins' colorful tattoos and the embroidery on Canadian wampum, the ancient Mayans' decorative quipus and the burls of the forest tribes of central Africa, the Tibetan, Chinese, and Korean calligrams — writing, even cuneiform writing, was above all else an aid to memory, a memorial to a sacred initiation: autocratic, individual. Then comes the black marketeer Cadmus, the magus, the magician, and immediately writing becomes an active, living thing, the ideal democratic nourishment, and the common language of the spirit. FIRST WORLD REVOLUTION. Human activity redoubles, intensifies. Greek civilization spreads. It embraces the Mediterranean. Commercial conquest and the literary life go hand in hand. The Romans engrave their history on copper or pewter plates. There's a library in Alexandria. The Apostles and the Holy Fathers write on parchment. Propaganda. Finally, painting interpenetrates the Christian world and, during the fourteenth century, Jan van Eyck of Bruges invents oil painting. Adam and Eve, naked. SECOND WORLD REVOLUTION. In 1438, Korster prints with wood blocks in Harlem. Six years later, Jean Gensfleisch, known as Gutenberg, invents the mobile letter, and thirteen years later Schoeffer casts that letter in metal. With Caxton, printing intensifies. There is a deluge of books. Everything is reprinted and translated, the monastic missals and the writings of the ancients. Sculpture, drama, and architecture are reborn. Universities and libraries proliferate. Christopher Columbus discovers a new world. Religion splits in two. There is much general progress in commerce. Industry constructs boats. Fleets open up faraway markets. The antipodes exist. Nations are formed. People emigrate. New governments are founded on new principles of liberty and equality. Education becomes democratic and culture refined. Newspapers appear. The whole globe is caught in a network of tracks, of cables, of lines — overland lines, maritime lines, air lines. All the world's peoples are in contact. The wireless sings. Work becomes specialized, above and below. THIRD WORLD REVOLUTION. And here's Daguerre, a Frenchman, who invents photography. Fifty years later, cinema was born. Renewal! Renewal! Eternal Revolution. The latest advancements of the precise sciences, world war, the concept of relativity, political convulsions, everything foretells that we are on our way toward a new synthesis of the human spirit, toward a new humanity and that a race of new men is going to appear. Their language will be the cinema. Look! The pyrotechnists of Silence are ready. The image is at the primitive sources of emotion. Attempts have been made to capture it behind outmoded artistic formulas. Finally the good fight of white and black is going to begin on all the screens in the world. The floodgates of the new language are open. The letters of the new primer jostle each other, innumerable. Everything becomes possible!

The Gospel of Tomorrow, the Spirit of Future Laws, the Scientific Epic, the Anticipatory Legend, the Vision of the Fourth Dimension of Existence, all the Interferences. Look! The revolution.

A *On location*

The camera which moves, which is no longer immobile, which records all levels simultaneously, which reverberates, which sets itself in motion.

B *In the theaters*

The spectator who is no longer immobile in his chair, who is wrenched out, assaulted, who participates in the action, who recognizes himself on the screen among the convulsions of the crowd, who shouts and cries out, protests and struggles.

C *On earth*

At the same time, in all the cities of the world, the crowd which leaves the theaters, which runs out into the streets like black blood, which extends its thousand tentacles like a powerful animal and with a tiny effort crushes the palaces, the prisons.

Z *Deep in the heart*

Watch the new generations growing up suddenly like flowers. Revolution. Youth of the world. Today.

4.9 BLAISE CENDRARS

Simultaneous Contrast

1919

Our eyes reach out to the sun.

A color is not color itself. It is only color in contrast with one or several other colors. A blue is only blue in contrast with a red, a green, an orange, a gray, and all the other colors.

Contrast is not black against white, an opposition, a dissimilarity. Contrast is a similarity. We travel so that we can collect, recollect men, things, and animals. To live with them. We come near them, we do not go away from them. Men differ most in what they have most in common. The two sexes contrast. Contrast is love. Contrast propels stars and hearts. Contrast creates their depth. Contrast is depth. Form.

Today's art is the art of depth.

The word "simultaneous" is a term of professional jargon, like "reinforced concrete" in construction, or "sublimation" in medicine. Delaunay uses it when he works with tower, port, house, man, woman, toy, eye, window, book, when he is in Paris, New York, Moscow, in bed or in the sky. The "simultaneous" is a technique. The technique shapes primary matter, universal matter, the world.

Poetry is mind into matter.

Sounds, colors, voices, dances, passions, mineral, vegetable, animal, textiles, butchery, chemistry, physics, civilization, offspring, father, mother, paintings, dresses, posters, books, poems, this lamp, this whistle, are the technique, the craft. Simultaneous contrast is the newest improvement in this craft, this technique. Simultaneous contrast is depth perceived. Reality. Form. Construction. Representation.

Depth is the new inspiration. All we see is seen in depth. We live in depth. We travel in depth. I am there. The senses are there. And the spirit.

4.10 ROBERT DELAUNAY

Light

1912

Impressionism is the birth of Light in painting.
Light reaches us through our perception.
Without visual perception, there is no light, no movement.
Light in Nature creates color-movement.
Movement is provided by relationships of *uneven measures*,
of color contrasts among themselves that make up *Reality*.
This reality is endowed with *Depth* (we see as far as the stars) and thus
becomes *rhythmic simultaneity*.
Simultaneity in light is the *harmony*, the *color rhythms* which
give birth to *Man's sight*.
Human sight is endowed with the greatest Reality since it comes to us
directly from the contemplation of the Universe.
The Eye is our highest sense, the one which communicates most closely

with our *brain and consciousness,* the idea of the living movement of
the world, and its movement *is simultaneity.*

Our understanding is *correlative* with our *perception.*

Let us seek to see.

Auditory perception is insufficient for our knowledge of the Universe.
It lacks depth.

Its movement is *successive.* It is a species of mechanism; its
principle is the *time of mechanical* clocks which, like them, has
no relation to our perception of the visual movement in the Universe.
This is the evenness of things in geometry.

Its character makes it resemble *the Object conceived geometrically.*

The *Object* is not endowed with *Life or movement.*

When it has the *appearance of movement,* it becomes *successive, dynamic.*

Its greatest limitation is of a *practical order.* Vehicles.

The railroad is the image of this successiveness which resembles
parallels: *the track's evenness.*

So with Architecture, so with Sculpture.

The most powerful object on Earth is bound by these same laws.

It will become the illusion of height:

The Eiffel Tower

of breadth:

Cities

length:

Tracks.

Art in nature *is rhythmic and abhors constraint.*

If Art is attached *to the Object,* it becomes *descriptive, divisive, literary.*

It stoops to imperfect modes of expression, it condemns itself of
its own free will, it is its own negation, *it does not liberate
itself from mimesis.*

If in the same way it represents *the visual relationships*
of an object or *between objects* without *light playing the role
of governing the representation.*

It is conventional. It does not achieve *plastic purity.* It is
a weakness. It is life's negation and the negation of *the
sublimity of the art of painting.*

For art to attain the limits of sublimity, it must approach our
harmonic vision: clarity.

Clarity will be color, proportions; these proportions are composed
of various simultaneous measures within an action.

This action must be representative harmony, *the synchromatic movement (simultaneity) of light,* which is the *only reality.*
This synchromatic action will thus be the Subject which is the representative harmony.

Auditory perception is insufficient for our knowledge of the Universe since it lacks duration.
Its successiveness fatally commands evenness;
it is a kind of mechanism where depth, and therefore rhythm, become impossible.
It is a mathematics where there is no space.
Its law is the time of mechanical clocks. where there is no relationship at all to the movement of the Universe.
It is the evenness of things of this kind that condemns them to nothingness.
Its quality resembles the Object.
The object is not endowed with life.
When the object is . . . there is the successive dynamic, but no rhythm. It becomes a similitude of movement.
Its greatest limitation is of a practical order. Vehicles.
The railroad track is the image of the successive approaching the parallel: the tracks.
Thus Architecture.
These are only appearances.
The greatest object on Earth is subject to the very same laws:
it will become a record appearance of height or breadth or length, etc.
Art is rhythmic as Nature, that is to say, eternal.
If it begins with an object, Art is descriptive, stooping to assume weak functions.
It condemns itself freely—it is its own negation. Its most representative mode is wax sculpture.
If Art is the visual relations of an object or between objects themselves, without light playing the role of *governing the representation,* it is conventional, and turns out to be a language like any other, and by consequence, successive. Thus literature, which has no plastic purity.
It is a weakness of Plastic Art. It is the negation of life, a negation of the sublimity of art.
Art comes from the most perfect organ of Man

The Eye. The eyes are the windows of our soul.
It can become the living harmony of Nature
and it is then a fundamental element of our judgment toward
purity. To see becomes the comprehension [of the] good.

The idea of the living movement of the world which
passes judgment upon our soul.
Our understanding is thus adequate to our sight. It is necessary
to look in order to see.
An auditory perception is not sufficient in our judgment to
know the universe, because it does not abide within duration.
Its successiveness leads fatally to its death.
It is a species of mechanism where there is no depth, and
therefore no rhythm. It is a mathematics that lacks space.
It is evenness of this sort that is condemned to death
Its quality resembles the Object. The Object is eternally
committed to death and its greatest limitation is of a practical order.
So with Architecture. These are only appearances.
The greatest object on earth is obliged by the same law.

4.11 ROBERT DELAUNAY

Historical Notes on Painting

Color and the Simultaneous

1913

First Collective Manifestation, 1910.
Room 41 at the *Indépendants* surprised everybody. The painters understood
nothing about the tempest that they had unreflectively released. They were
not provocative other than hanging some already completed pictures, with
much conviction and anxiety, on the wooden partitions of the *Indépendants*.
The designation "cubist" dates from this exhibition (Albert Gleizes, *Arts
Plastiques*, No. 1).

A photographic image, but not an image in the pure sense of the word—
that is to say, the *plastic, organic element, the plastic organization*, etc. . . .

Image in the pure sense of the word means the plastic, organic element,
plastic organization in the vital sense of rhythm. It is human and it is *natu-*

ral. It is the childhood of all art. Robert Delaunay and Sonia Delaunay after the break with cubism—the beginning of all modern anxiety—search for a plastic image through the most sensual element: color. Breaking with everything that had been done in art in means and in form, they made the first simultaneous pictures. And concerning this, G. Apollinaire in his famous article in *Le Temps* 1912—"The Beginning of Cubism"—said in substance and literally that Robert Delaunay had silently invented an art of pure color. This was an allusion to the first *Fenêtres,* windows that open to new plastic horizons.

It was the inspired Chevreul who observed *the laws of simultaneous colors in his theoretical studies.* Seurat was aware of them, but Seurat did not have the audacity to push composition to the point of breaking with all the conventional methods of painting. In his work there is the *retinal* image, the image in the popular sense of imagery. Line and chiaroscuro are still the plastic basis of his art.

4.12 ROBERT DELAUNAY

Simultaneism in Contemporary Modern Art, Painting, Poetry

1913

Our simultaneous craft in painting (not the simultaneous vision that has always existed in art). These investigations date from the *Manèges* [Carousels], the *Saint-Séverin,* from the *Villes,* the *Tours,* the *Fenêtres,* and the *Soleils.*
[There follows a list of Delaunay's paintings from 1907 to 1911 which illustrate the origins of the simultaneist crafts.]

Art and image in contrast to the descriptive or the illustrative. Art is not conventional serial writing (note on "Light," which appeared in *Der Sturm* in 1913).

The sequential in design, in geometry, etc. . . . . Example: the railway train is the image of the sequential that approaches the parallel: the evenness of railroad tracks.

But an art of simultaneous contrasts consists in *the forms of color.* (*Aesthetic Meditations* by Guillaume Apollinaire, October 1912. "The works of the orphic artists must simultaneously present a pure aesthetic agreement, a construction that makes sense and a sublime significance, which is to say the subject. It is pure art.")

Orphism is a designation given by Apollinaire to one of the four tendencies of cubism as he has quartered it, but the *simultaneism* under discussion here is actually universal. It does not link up with cubism. In fact it is sufficient in itself and originates earlier than he has discerned. In impressionism there already were symphonies of construction through color that are not yet formal, but complementary.

Simultaneism in color creates a total formal construction, an aesthetic of all the crafts: furnishings, dresses, books, posters, sculpture, etc. . . . The simultaneous: my eyes see up to the stars.

The line is the limit. Color gives depth (not perspective, *nonsequential,* but *simultaneous*) *and form and movement.*

The simultaneous vision of the futurists is of a completely different kind. Consider, for example, a title of one of their pictures: *Simultaneity.* This word is etymological in literature, thus classical, and passé. Sequential dynamism is the mechanical in painting and that is the scope of their manifestos. Futurism is a machinist movement. It is not vital. The first simultaneous representation: The *Fenêtres simultanées sur la Ville* [Simultaneous Windows on the City] (April 1912, exhibited in Zurich, June 1912, article by Paul Klee in *Die Alpen,* exhibited in 1912 in New York).

Color-construction, discovered in 1911, December to January 1912, is the key to these images.

And regarding this, a Smirnoff-Delaunay conversation during the summer of 1912 at La Madeleine.

Beginnings of synchromism.

Notes published in *Soirées de Paris* and *Der Sturm.*

Birth of an art of color (article in *Le Temps,* October 14, 1913, by Apollinaire).

Delaunay quietly invented an Art of color or synchromist image.

The necessity for a new subject has inspired poets to set off on a new road and their poetry about *La Tour,* which communicates with the whole world, shows it. Rays of light, symphonic auditory waves.

The factories, the bridges, the ironworks, dirigibles, the incalculable movement of airplanes, windows simultaneously seen by crowds.

These modern sensibilities converge simultaneously.

Cendrars (April 1912), "Easter," written in New York—while walking one Easter night through the districts of New York, under the suspension bridges, in the Chinese section, among the skyscrapers, in the subway (appeared in October 1912). On his return to Paris he went to see Apollinaire in all sincerity of art. This meeting inspired Apollinaire who published "Zone" (November 1912 in *Soirées de Paris,* republished in *Der Sturm* and then in *Alcools*).

At this time Cendrars met Delaunay. He was impressed by the beauty of the *Tour* and *Saint-Séverin* and by Madame Delaunay's colors and book bindings.

This is what gave birth to the *Premier Livre Simultané* [First Simultaneous Book] (February 1913). The movement was established. In December 1912 the beautiful poem "Windows" by Guillaume Apollinaire appeared (December 1912, on the first page of the Delaunay album where there was a very beautiful play of colors. The window opened like an orange, that beautiful fruit of light), a poem inspired by the *Fenêtres simultanées* of Robert Delaunay, 1911.

This is one of the first documents of the simultaneous poem and the first poem without punctuation.

Apollinaire's and Cendrars's art are completely different. Apollinaire, a sensitive man, was always curious about any new contribution. . . . Cendrars belongs to a younger generation that is new. Other young men like Arthur Cravan, nephew of Oscar Wilde, published "Sifflet" [Whistle] in *Maintenant.*

Barzun, [with his] sound and song, appeared during the month of June 1912, perhaps it was May. Attracted by Delaunay's paintings, Barzun came one Sunday evening to his house. Cendrars, Smirnoff, and Minsky were there, and Barzun spoke enthusiastically about the *Tour* which he connected with dramaturgy. He spoke to us about his *Poème et Drame* [Poem and Drama], a work on which he had been working for ten years, which was to be for the modern world what tragedy had been for the Greeks (he cited Euripides and Aeschylus). He told us about the imminent publication of a theoretical tract on modern art which defined his theory of dramaturgy.

The latter book appeared six weeks later under an unexpected title. The awaited *Dramatisme* [Dramatism] was entitled: *Voix, Chant et Rythme simultané* [Simultaneous Voice, Song, and Rhythm], which provoked in some informed circles a clear reaction. The book was not "simultaneous" at all. M. Barzun had enlisted and exploited a word that he had not understood and that he developed only in its etymological dimension.

Now, in October 1913, he announces the impending appearance of his first simultaneous poem.

This announcement is made at a time when a fortnight earlier the newspapers had been talking about the *Premier Livre Simultané* that had been exhibited at Berlin and about which the world press had been informed through a color prospectus of simultaneous contrasts, and about which the French, English, American, and German press had commented.

Article by Cendrars on the *Premier Livre Simultané* in *Der Sturm.*

Poem by Cendrars called "Contrastes."

Article by Rubiner on the *Premier Livre Simultané, Der Aktion,* Berlin.

Simultaneism in literature only expresses itself, as conceived by Barzun and his imitators, through the voice (of the masses) parallel or divergent, harmonized or discordant, speaking together at the same time. This conception is not new. It is practiced in all operas, and above all in Greek tragedy. This is no longer simultaneism, but literary counterpoint.

Literary simultaneism is perhaps achieved by contrasts of words.

[*La Prose du*] *Transsibérien* [*et de la petite*] *Jehanne de France* is a simple contrast (a continuous contrast which is the only one that can reveal the profundity of living form).

[*La Prose du*] *Transsibérien* [*et da la petite*] *Jehanne de France* permits a latitude to sensibility to substitute one or more words, a movement of words, which forms the form, the life of the poem, the simultaneity.

In the same way visuality is achieved through colors in simultaneous contrast.

In a movement a new depth.

The simultaneous word . . . through simultaneous color and through contrast of simultaneous words there comes forth . . . a new aesthetic, an aesthetic representative of the times.

4.13 ROBERT DELAUNAY

Simultaneism

An Ism of Art

1925

Simultaneity of color, simultaneous contrasts and every uneven proportion that results from color, as they are expressed in their representative movement: this is the only reality with which to construct a picture.

Germany

4.14 RAOUL HAUSMANN

Manifesto of PREsentism

1920

And now here is the

Manifesto of
PREsentism
against the Dupontism of the Teutonic soul
— — — — — — — — — —

To live means: to compress all the possibilities, all the givens of every second into a tangible energy—Wisdom.

Eternity is nothing, it is neither older or better than the Middle Ages, it comes from yesterday, it is in the moon or the toothless mouth of the old man, reinforced by a ridiculous bourgeois intelligence just like an air brake!

Let's get rid of all the old prejudices, the prejudice that yesterday something was good or that tomorrow it will be better still. No! Let's seize each second today! Time is an onion: under its first skin there appears, in the light, another and still another. But we want the light!

Man has two essential tendencies: one toward the impossible and the other toward all the innumerable possibilities. He won't succeed in the impossible instantly, in our time, today—whether it is God or the Creative Principle or Living Dynamism that, like a vacuum cleaner compresses the world, life, and events in making them form a possible world. Through a ridiculous naivete, man needs to show his nostalgia for the unrealizable ideal, and this unrealizable impossibility is to transform himself into a monstrous ball animated by a perpetual motion, that would hover in space like the sun! Down with this nostalgia, down with the impossible, the unrealizable! Leave it to heroes and heroines!

. . .

The individual, considered as an atom, has only one duty: to find his law through no matter what form of work imposed on his own hardened ego—against this ego. In this newly present world we should realize the voluntary abandon of all the forces inherent in the atom! ! !

Berlin, February 1920
All hail to the Comrades!

The Sublime Is Now

1948

Michelangelo knew that the meaning of the Greek humanities for his time involved making Christ—the man, into Christ—who is God; that his plastic problem was neither the mediaeval one, to make a cathedral, nor the Greek one, to make a man like a god, but to make a cathedral out of man. In doing so he set a standard for sublimity that the painting of his time could not reach. Instead, painting continued on its merry quest for a voluptuous art until in modern times, the Impressionists, disgusted with its inadequacy, began the movement to destroy the established rhetoric of beauty by the Impressionist insistence on a surface of ugly strokes.

The impulse of modern art was this desire to destroy beauty. However, in discarding Renaissance notions of beauty, and without an adequate substitute for a sublime message, the Impressionists were compelled to preoccupy themselves, in their struggle, with the cultural values of their plastic history so that instead of evoking a new way of experiencing life they were able only to make a transfer of values. By glorifying their own way of living, they were caught in the problem of what is really beautiful and could only make a restatement of their position on the general question of beauty; just as later the Cubists, by their Dada gestures of substituting a sheet of newspaper and sandpaper for both the velvet surfaces of the Renaissance and the Impressionists, made a similar transfer of values instead of creating a new vision, and succeeded only in elevating the sheet of paper. So strong is the grip of the *rhetoric* of exaltation as an attitude in the large context of the European culture pattern that the elements of sublimity in the revolution we know as modern art, exist in its effort and energy to escape the pattern rather than in the realization of a new experience. Picasso's effort may be sublime but there is no doubt that his work is a preoccupation with the question of what is the nature of beauty. Even Mondrian, in his attempt to destroy the Renaissance picture by his insistence on pure subject matter, succeeded only in raising the white plane and the right angle into a realm of sublimity, where the sublime paradoxically becomes an absolute of perfect sensations. The geometry (perfection) swallowed up his metaphysics (his exaltation).

The failure of European art to achieve the sublime is due to this blind desire to exist inside the reality of sensation (the object world, whether distorted or pure) and to build an art within the framework of pure plasticity (the Greek ideal of beauty, whether that plasticity be a romantic active surface, or a classic stable one). In other words, modern art, caught without a sublime content, was incapable of creating a new sublime image, and unable to move away from the Renaissance imagery of figures and objects except by distortion or by denying it completely for an empty world of geometric formalisms—a *pure* rhetoric of abstract mathematical relationships, became enmeshed in a struggle over the nature of beauty; whether beauty was in nature or could be found without nature.

I believe that here in America, some of us, free from the weight of European culture, are finding the answer, by completely denying that art has any concern with the problem of beauty and where to find it. The question that now arises is how, if we are living in a time without a legend or mythos that can be called sublime, if we refuse to admit any exaltation in pure relations, if we refuse to live in the abstract, how can we be creating a sublime art?

We are reasserting man's natural desire for the exalted, for a concern with our relationship to the absolute emotions. We do not need the obsolete props of an outmoded and antiquated legend. We are creating images whose reality is self-evident and which are deviod of the props and crutches that evoke associations with outmoded images, both sublime and beautiful. We are freeing ourselves of the impediments of memory, association, nostalgia, legend, myth, or what have you, that have been the devices of Western European painting. Instead of making *cathedrals* out of Christ, man, or "life," we are making it out of ourselves, out of our own feelings. The image we produce is the self-evident one of revelation, real and concrete, that can be understood by anyone who will look at it without the nostalgic glasses of history.

PART 5

Futurisms

All the branches of the Futurist movement—in Italy, Russia, Spain, and England—claim to find a new beauty: "power under control, speed, intense light, simultaneous concurrence of diverse rhythms" (Marinetti, *Marinetti*). Their experiments are different, but all are linked to a feeling of joyousness and rapidity, associated with the power of the machine, the delights of technology, and scientific enumeration of what had been sensitivity to aesthetic beauties (thus the manifesto "Against Past-Loving Venice" of 1910). They share an interest in the interrelations of objects (a speeding vehicle cutting across the cheek of a passerby), and above all, the positive revolutionary banner raised high against "pastisms."

Filippo Tommaso Marinetti's "Founding and Manifesto of Futurism" (5.5) of 1909 is the ur-manifesto. Its shape, style, and substance make the perfect loud noise, unmistakable in its public intentions and monumental. "We had stayed up all night," it begins, and its drama continues. This is a case of the manifesto making the movement. Marinetti lectured around Europe in 1912–14 on Vitalism and against the "effeminate" pastness, or "passéism," which he identifies with the horizontal or supine position, claiming for the Futurist the dynamic of the male vertical. He claims for written and painted works the presence of an industrial product, metallic and dynamic. Responding to his ur-manifesto with its sense of the proclamatory is the gigantic poster he had placed in the streets of Milan, with the letters spelling FUTURISM in red and in gigantic proportion.

Marinetti's most important manifesto of Italian Futurism, the "Technical Manifesto of Futurist Literature," was published directly in French in June 1912. Its "Supplement" continues its theorizing about the "words in futurist liberty," doing away with conventions and permitting the aural stage of emotivity, with its bodily sensation. Noise brings forth direct reaction, corporeal more than intellectual. Marinetti declaimed parts of his book *Zang Tumb Tumb* in various art galleries and theaters in the capitals of Europe. In fact, at the time of the founding of Dada, Marinetti had just declared his 1916 manifesto, "The Dynamic and Synoptic Declamation," and futurist compositions were being exhibited in the Cabaret Voltaire.

Futurisms abound in Italy (Aeropoetry and Aeromusic, Bruitism or Noisism, Mechanical Art) and in Russia, with the linguistic Zaoum experiments of Victor Khlebnikov and Alexey Kruchonykh in 1913 (founding documents for the later European verbo- and opto-phonetic theoreticians), Cubo-Futurism (the object seen from many directions at once), and the "Pictorial Rayonism" of Mikhail Larionov and Natalya Goncharova, with its notion of electric rays emanating from objects, analogous to the "force lines" described by the Italian futurist Carlo Carrá and to the reflection, refraction, and interpenetration of light rays in the paintings of Giacomo Balla. Larionov and Goncharova were to become central figures in Modernist circles in Paris.

Italian Futurism

There are, of course, many Futurisms even in Italy. The Futurism of Noise, Tactile Futurism, and even a Futurism of Woman, including her Futurist Theater. Marinetti made such a noise that it reverberated around Europe and became a legend even as it was still sounding. *Against everything past and passéist, the Future.* If Marinetti preferred the noise of a honking automobile to the Victory of Samothrace, it is because he had his own myth, that of Pegasus or Icarus, visible in his novel of 1907–10, *Mafarka the Futurist.*

Although some of the experiments in Futurism had no prolongation beyond themselves, such as Aeropoetry (speaking of Icarus) and Aeromusic, both of whose manifestos were translated into French and published in Paris, many of them found a resonance in movements outside Italy, such as Dada in Switzerland and Germany, Vorticism in England, Rayonism in Russia. Futurism invented the evening of insults, the punitive expedition in which you assault your enemies verbally and physically. Francesco Cangiullo takes a stick to the "bourgeois passéistes" at the theater, as will Richard Hülsenbeck in the Cabaret Voltaire and André Breton in the street.

After working for six years at his international journal *Poesia,* said Marinetti, hoping to free Italian poetry from its traditional chains, "I felt, all of a sudden, that articles, poetries, and polemics no longer sufficed. You had to change methods, go down in the street, seize power in all the theatres, and introduce the fisticuff into the war of art" ("The Caffeine of Europe," Marinetti, *Marinetti,* 6). His manifestos, which he traveled all over Europe to read, sound and look like that fisticuff. They are intended to show maleness and deliberately exercise their power over what Marinetti considered the passivity of the mass audience. "I have had enough experience of the femininity of crowds and the weakness of their collective virginity in the course of forcing Futurist free verse upon them" ("Caffeine of Europe," 6).

But Marinetti did not always find success. When he went in January of 1914 to Moscow, his brand of Italian Futurism did not take. The Asian soul with its deep attachment to archaistic language and its native primitivism was at odds with the urban technologies lauded by Italian Futurism. Marinetti went home, angrily exclaiming that the "pseudofuturists live in *plusquamperfectum* rather than in *futurum*" ("Caffeine of Europe," 6). So much for universal Futurism.

5.1

Futurist Synthesis of the War

1914

FUTURIST SYNTH

We glorify war, which for us is the only hygiene of the world.
(First Futurist Manifesto), whereas for the Germans it serves as
a fat feast for crows and hyenas. The old cathedrals do not interest; but we deny medieval, plagiarist, clumsy Germany, un-

ELASTICITY
INTUITIVE SYNTHESIS
INVENTION
MULTIPLICATION
OF FORCES
INVISIBLE ORDER
CREATIVE GENIUS

AGAINST

SERBIA
{ INDEPENDENCE
AMBITION
TEMERITY

ENGLAND
{ PRACTICAL SPIRIT
SENSE OF DUTY
COMMERCIAL HONESTY
RESPECT FOR
INDIVIDUALITY

BELGIUM
{ ENERGY
WILL
INITIATIVE
INDUSTRIAL
PERFECTION

MONTENEGRO
{ INDEPENDENCE
AMBITION
TEMERITY

FRANCE
{ INTELLIGENCE
COURAGE
SPEED
ELEGANCE
SPONTANEITY
EXPLOSIVENESS
EASE

JAPAN
{ AGILITY
PROGRESS
RESOLUTENESS

ITALY
{ ALL THE STRENGTHS
ALL THE WEAKNESSES
OF **GENIUS**

AGAINST

RUSSIA
{ POWER
SOLIDITY
IMPREGNABILITY
QUANTITY

MARINETTI
BOCCIONI
CARRÀ
RUSSOLO
PIATTI

ESIS OF THE WAR

endowed with creative genius, the Futuristic right to destroy works of art. This right belongs solely to the Italian creative Genius, capable of creating a new and greater beauty on the ruins of the old.

RIGIDITY
ANALYSIS
METHODICAL IMITATION
ADDITION
   OF IDIOCIES
NUMISMATIC ORDER
GERMAN CULTURE

GERMANY {
SHEEPISHNESS
  — AWKWARDNESS
  — PHILOSOPHICAL FUMES
  — HEAVINESS
  — CRUDENESS
  — BRUTALITY
  — ESPIONAGE
  — PROFESSIONAL PEDANTRY
  — ARCHAEOLOGY
  — CONSTIPATION OF
       INDUSTRIAL CAMELOTS
  — BOTCHERS AND GAFFEURS

FUTURISM AGAINST PASSÉISM

8 PEOPLE-POETS AGAINST THEIR PEDANTIC CRITICS

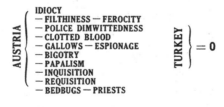

AUSTRIA {
IDIOCY
  — FILTHINESS — FEROCITY
  — POLICE DIMWITTEDNESS
  — CLOTTED BLOOD
  — GALLOWS — ESPIONAGE
  — BIGOTRY
  — PAPALISM
  — INQUISITION
  — REQUISITION
  — BEDBUGS — PRIESTS

TURKEY } = 0

From the Milanese Cell, *September 20, 1914*
Directory of the Futurist Movement: Corso Venezia, 61—MILAN

Technical Manifesto of Futurist Sculpture

1912

All the sculpture on monuments and in exhibitions to be seen in all European cities presents such a pathetic spectacle of barbarism, ineptitude and tedious imitation that my Futurist eyes turn away from it with the deepest loathing!

Sculpture in every country is dominated by the moronic mimicry of old, inherited formulas; this blind imitation is encouraged by the ghastly facility with which it can be done. Latin countries are bowed down under the opprobrious burden of the Greeks and Michelangelo, which is borne in Belgium and France with a certain seriousness and talent, and in Italy with grotesque imbecility. In the Teutonic countries we find nothing but a kind of gothicky, Hellenophilic fatuity which is being turned out in Berlin or feebly reproduced with effeminate fuss by the German academics of Munich. In Slav countries, on the other hand, we have a discordant clash between an Archaic Greek style and Nordic and Oriental prodigies. There is an unformed mass of accumulated influences, from the excesses of complicated Asiatic detail to the infantile and grotesque over-simplification of the Lapps and Eskimos.

In all these sculptures, even in those which have a breath of bold innovation, we see the perpetuation of the same old kind of misapprehension: an artist copies a nude or studies classical statues with the naive conviction that here he will find a style that equates to modern sensibility without stepping outside the traditional concepts of sculptural form. These concepts, along with such famous catchwords as "ideals of beauty," which everyone speaks of in hushed tones, are never separated from the glorious periods of ancient Greece and its later decadence.

It is almost inexplicable that thousands of sculptors can go on, generation after generation, constructing puppet figures without bothering to ask themselves why the sculpture halls arouse boredom or horror, or are left absolutely deserted; or why monuments are unveiled in squares all over the world to the accompaniment of general mirth or incomprehension. The same situation does not exist in painting, since painting is continually undergoing renewal. Though this process of modernization is very slow, it still provides the best and clearest condemnation of all the plagiaristic and sterile work being turned out by all the sculptors of our own days.

Sculpture must learn one absolute truth: to construct and try to create, now, with elements which have been stolen from the Egyptians, the Greeks or Michelangelo is like trying to draw water from a dry well with a bottomless bucket.

There can be no renewal in art unless its whole essence is brought up to date. This essence lies in the vision and the conception of the lines and masses which form the internal arabesque. Art does not become an expression of our own times merely by reproducing the external aspects of contemporary life; and hence sculpture as it has been understood by artists of the last and present centuries is a monstrous anachronism.

Sculpture has not progressed because of the limits inherent within the accepted field of the academic concept of the nude. An art that must take all the clothes off a man or woman in order to produce any emotive effect is a dead art! Painting has given itself a shot in the arm, has broadened and deepened its scope, using the facts of landscape and the environment which act simultaneously on the human figure and on objects, thereby achieving our Futurist INTERPENETRATION OF PLANES (Futurist Painting: Technical Manifesto, 11 April 1910). Sculpture may also be able to find new sources of inspiration along these lines and hence renew its style and extend its plastic capacities to the kind of objects, which up till now a kind of barbaric idiocy has persuaded us to believe were divided up or intangible—and, therefore, inexpressible in plastic form.

We must take the object which we wish to create and begin with its central core. In this way we shall uncover new laws and new forms which link it invisibly but mathematically to an EXTERNAL PLASTIC INFINITY and to an INTERNAL PLASTIC INFINITY. This new plastic art will then be a translation, in plaster, bronze, glass, wood or any other material, of those atmospheric planes which bind and intersect things. This vision, which I have called PHYSICAL TRANSCENDENTALISM (Lecture on Futurist Painting, May 1911), could provide for the plastic arts those sympathetic effects and mysterious affinities which create formal and reciprocal influences between the different planes of an object.

Sculpture must, therefore, make objects live by showing their extensions in space as sensitive, systematic and plastic; no one still believes that an object finishes off where another begins or that there is anything around us—a bottle, a car, a house, a hotel, a street—which cannot be cut up and sectionalized by an arabesque of straight curves.

Two attempts have been made to bring sculpture into the twentieth century: one was concerned with the decorative side of style; the other merely with the plastic side—materials. The former was a nameless and disorganized movement lacking any coordinating technical genius, and since it was too much tied up with the economic necessities of the building trade, it produced only pieces of traditional sculpture, which were more or less decoratively synthesized and framed by architectural, decorative motifs or mouldings. All houses and blocks of flats with a claim to modernity incorporate essays of this kind in marble, cement or beaten metal.

The second attempt was more attractive, more detached and more poetic; but it was too isolated and fragmentary. It lacked any synthesis of thought which might have resulted in the formulation of a law. To make new art it is not enough to believe in it fervently. You must be prepared to champion your cause and set up certain rules as a guideline towards progress. Here I am referring to the genius of Medardo Rosso, an Italian, the only great modern sculptor who has tried to open up a whole new field of sculpture, by his representation in plastic art of the influences of the environment and the atmospheric links which bind it to his subject.

Of the other three great contemporary sculptors, Constantin Meunier has contributed nothing in the way of fresh sensibilities to sculpture. His statues are nearly always a clever fusion of Greek heroism and the humble athleticism of the docker, the sailor or the miner. His plastic concepts and his construction of statues and bas-reliefs still belong to the world of the Parthenon and the classical hero, in spite of the fact that he was the first artist who tried to create and deify subjects which before his time were held of little account, or were only given mediocre or realistic interpretations.

Bourdelle's sculpture—a mass of abstract architectonic forms—shows a severity which is almost pure fury. His temperament is that of the grimly passionate and sincere experimenter, but unfortunately he does not know how to free himself from certain archaic influences and the example of all those unnamed masons who made our Gothic cathedrals.

Rodin's mental agility is much greater than the others, and this allows him to move on from the Impressionism of his Balzac portrait to the uncertainty of his *Burghers of Calais* and all his other Michelangelo-type sins. He brings to his sculpture an unquiet inspiration, a grandiose lyrical impetus, which would have been well and truly modern if Michelangelo and Donatello had not already possessed them in almost the identical form four hundred years ago, or if he himself had used these gifts to show a completely new sort of reality.

So, in the works of these three great geniuses we find influences from different periods: Greek for Meunier; Gothic for Bourdelle; and the Italian Renaissance for Rodin.

The work of Medardo Rosso, on the other hand, is revolutionary, modern, profound, and necessarily contained. In his sculptures there are no heroes and no symbols, but the planes in the forehead of a woman, or child, which betray a hint of spatial liberation, will have far greater importance in the history of the spirit than that with which he has been credited in our times. Unfortunately the Impressionists' need for experiment has limited the researches of Medardo Rosso to a species of both high and low relief. This shows that he is still conceiving the figure as something of a world to itself, with a traditional foundation, imbued with descriptive aims.

Medardo Rosso's revolution, then, although very important, springs from extrinsic, pictorial concepts, and ignores the problem of constructing planes. The sensitive touch of the thumb, imitating the lightness of Impressionist brushwork, gives a sense of vibrant immediacy to his works, but necessitates a rapid execution from life which deprives a work of art of any elements of universality. Consequently he has fallen prey to the same qualities and defects as the Impressionist painters; although it is from their experiments that our own aesthetic revolution springs, we shall move away to a diametrically opposed position.

In sculpture as in painting, renewal is impossible without looking for the STYLE OF MOVEMENT, that is, making a systematic and definitive synthesis of the fragmentary, accidental and hence analytical approach of the Impressionists. And this systematization of the vibrations of lights and the interpretations of planes will produce a Futurist sculpture, whose basis will be architectural, not only as a construction of masses, but in such a way that the sculptural block itself will contain the architectural elements of the *sculptural environment* in which the object exists.

In this way we shall be producing a sculpture of the ENVIRONMENT.

A piece of Futurist sculpture will contain all those wonderful mathematical and geometrical elements of which objects are composed in our own times. And these objects will not be juxtaposed with a statue, like explanatory attributes or detached decorative elements, but, following the laws of a new concept of harmony they will be encapsulated inside the muscular lines of a body. In this way, the cogs of a machine might easily appear out of the armpits of a mechanic, or the lines of a table could cut a reader's head in two, or a book with its fanned-out pages could intersect the reader's stomach.

Traditionally, a statue cuts into, and stands out from, the atmosphere of the place where it is on view; Futurist painting has gone beyond all these antiquated concepts of the rhythmic continuities of lines in a figure, of its

isolation from its background, and of the INVISIBLE ENVELOPING SPACE.
"Futurist poetry," according to the poet Marinetti, "now that it has destroyed
traditional rhythms and created free verse, now destroys Latin syntax and
phrasing. Futurist poetry is a spontaneous and uninterrupted current of
analogies, all intuitively bound by their essential substance. So that we have
imagination without strings, and words-in-freedom." The Futurist music
of Balilla Pratella is also breaking away from the chronometric tyranny of
rhythm.

Why should sculpture be the one to lag behind, loaded down with laws
which no one has the right to impose? Let's turn everything upside down
and proclaim the ABSOLUTE AND COMPLETE ABOLITION OF FINITE LINES
AND THE CONTAINED STATUE. LET'S SPLIT OPEN OUR FIGURES AND PLACE
THE ENVIRONMENT INSIDE THEM. We declare that the environment must
form part of the plastic whole, a world of its own, with its own laws: so that
the pavement can jump up on to your table, or your head can cross a street,
while your lamp twines a web of plaster rays from one house to the next.

We want the entire visible world to tumble down on top of us, merging and creating a harmony on purely intuitive grounds; a leg, an arm or
an object has no importance except as an element in the plastic rhythm of
the whole, and can be eliminated, not because we are trying to imitate a
Greek or Roman fragment, but in order to conform with the general harmony the artist is trying to create. A sculptural whole, like a painting, should
not resemble anything but itself, since figures and objects in art should exist
without regard to their logical aspect.

Thus a figure may have one arm clothed and the other unclothed, while
the different lines of a vase of flowers may run around with complete abandon between the lines of a hat and those of a neck.

Thus transparent planes, glass, strips of metal sheeting, wire, streetlamps
or house-lights may all indicate planes—the shapes, tones and semitones
of a new reality.

In the same way a new intuitive shading of white, grey, black, can add to
the emotive power of surfaces, while the hue of a coloured plane should be
used to accentuate the abstract meaning of a plastic fact.

What we said when we talked about force-lines in painting (Preface-
Manifesto, Catalogue of First Futurist Exhibition, Paris, February 1912) is
also applicable to sculpture—bringing the static muscular line to life in the
dynamic force-line. In the muscular line the straight line must be given pride
of place since it is the only one which corresponds to the internal simplicity
of the synthesis by which we oppose external, baroque exhibitionism.

However the straight line will not lead us to imitate the Egyptians, the primitives or the savages, as it has some sculptors desperately trying to free themselves from the hold of the Greeks. Our straight lines will be living and palpitating. This will show everyone the necessities inherent in the limitless expressive potentialities of matter, and its severe and fundamental bareness will be the symbol of the severity of steel in the lines of modern machinery.

We should finally like to state that in sculpture the artist must not be afraid of any new method of achieving REALITY. There is no fear more stupid than one which makes the artist nervous of departing from the art in which he works. There is neither painting nor sculpture, neither music nor poetry: there is only creation! Hence if a composition seems to demand a particular rhythmic movement which will add to or contrast with the circumscribed rhythms of the SCULPTURAL WHOLE (the basic requirement of any work of art), you may use any kind of contraption to give an adequate sense of rhythmic movement to planes or lines.

We cannot forget that the swing of a pendulum or the moving hands of a clock, the in-and-out motion of a piston inside a cylinder, the engaging and disengaging of two cog-wheels, the fury of a fly-wheel or the whirling of a propeller, are all plastic and pictorial elements, which any Futurist work of sculpture should take advantage of. The opening and closing of a valve creates a rhythm which is just as beautiful to look at as the movements of an eyelid, and infinitely more modern.

CONCLUSIONS

1. Achieve an abstract reconstruction of planes and volumes in order to determine form of sculpture and not figurative value.
2. Abolish in sculpture as in all other art the TRADITIONAL "SUBLIME" IN SUBJECT-MATTER.
3. Deny in sculpture any attempt at realistic, episodic structures; affirm the absolute necessity of using all elements of reality in order to rediscover the basic elements of plastic sensitivity. By considering bodies and their parts as PLASTIC ZONES, any Futurist sculptural composition will contain planes of wood or metal, either motionless or in mechanical motion, in creating an object; spherical fibrous forms for hair, semicircles of glass for a vase, wire and netting for atmospheric planes, etc.
4. Destroy the literary and traditional "dignity" of marble and bronze statues. Refuse to accept the exclusive nature of a single material in the construction of a sculptural whole. Insist that even twenty different types of

materials can be used in a single work of art in order to achieve plastic movement. To mention a few examples: glass, wood, cardboard, iron, cement, hair, leather, cloth, mirrors, electric lights, etc.

5. Maintain that, in the intersecting planes of a book and a corner of a table, in the straight lines of a match, in a blind drawn across a window, there is more truth than in all the knotted muscles, all the breasts and buttocks of heroes and Venuses, which are still the main inspiration of our demented modern sculptors.

6. Only use very modern and up-to-date subjects in order to arrive at the discovery of NEW PLASTIC IDEAS.

7. A straight line is the only way to discover the primitive purity of a new architectural structure of masses and sculptural zones.

8. There can be no renewal unless it is through ENVIRONMENTAL SCULPTURE, since only by this means can plastic art develop and come to MODEL THE ATMOSPHERE which surrounds our objects.

9. The things we are creating are only a bridge between an outer plastic infinity and an inner plastic infinity, hence objects can never be finite, but intersect each other through an infinite combination of powers which attract and repel.

10. Destroy the systematic nude and the traditional concept behind statuary and monuments.

11. Courageously refuse to accept any work, whatever the reward, which does not, in itself, involve a pure construction of plastic elements which have been completely renewed.

5.3 UMBERTO BOCCIONI *and others*

Futurist Painting

Technical Manifesto

1910

On the 18th of March, 1910, in the limelight of the Chiarella Theatre of Turin, we launched our first manifesto to a public of three thousand people — artists, men of letters, students and others; it was a violent and cynical cry which displayed our sense of rebellion, our deep-rooted disgust, our haughty contempt for vulgarity, for academic and pedantic mediocrity, for the fanatical worship of all that is old and worm-eaten.

We bound ourselves there and then to the movement of Futurist Poetry which was initiated a year earlier by F. T. Marinetti in the columns of the *Figaro*.

The battle of Turin has remained legendary. We exchanged almost as many knocks as we did ideas, in order to protect from certain death the genius of Italian Art.

And now during a temporary pause in this formidable struggle we come out of the crowd in order to expound with technical precision our programme for the renovation of painting, of which our Futurist Salon at Milan was a dazzling manifestation.

Our growing need of truth is no longer satisfied with Form and Colour as they have been understood hitherto.

The gesture which we would reproduce on canvas shall no longer be a fixed *moment* in universal dynamism. It shall simply be the *dynamic sensation* itself.

Indeed, all things move, all things run, all things are rapidly changing. A profile is never motionless before our eyes, but it constantly appears and disappears. On account of the persistency of an image upon the retina, moving objects constantly multiply themselves; their form changes like rapid vibrations, in their mad career. Thus a running horse has not four legs, but twenty, and their movements are triangular.

All is conventional in art. Nothing is absolute in painting. What was truth for the painters of yesterday is but a falsehood today. We declare, for instance, that a portrait must not be like the sitter, and that the painter carries in himself the landscapes which he would fix upon his canvas.

To paint a human figure you must not paint it; you must render the whole of its surrounding atmosphere.

Space no longer exists: the street pavement, soaked by rain beneath the glare of electric lamps, becomes immensely deep and gapes to the very centre of the earth. Thousands of miles divide us from the sun; yet the house in front of us fits into the solar disk.

Who can still believe in the opacity of bodies, since our sharpened and multiplied sensitiveness has already penetrated the obscure manifestations of the medium? Why should we forget in our creations the doubled power of our sight, capable of giving results analogous to those of the X-rays?

It will be sufficient to cite a few examples, chosen amongst thousands, to prove the truth of our arguments.

The sixteen people around you in a rolling motor bus are in turn and at the same time one, ten, four, three; they are motionless and they change places; they come and go, bound into the street, are suddenly swallowed up by the sunshine, then come back and sit before you, like persistent symbols of universal vibration.

How often have we not seen upon the cheek of the person with whom we are talking the horse which passes at the end of the street.

Our bodies penetrate the sofas upon which we sit, and the sofas penetrate our bodies. The motor bus rushes into the houses which it passes, and in their turn the houses throw themselves upon the motor bus and are blended with it.

The construction of pictures has hitherto been foolishly traditional. Painters have shown us the objects and the people placed before us. We shall henceforward put the spectator in the centre of the picture.

As in every realm of the human mind, clear-sighted individual research has swept away the unchanging obscurities of dogma, so must the vivifying current of science soon deliver painting from academism.

We would at any price re-enter into life. Victorious science has nowadays disowned its past in order the better to serve the material needs of our time; we would that art, disowning its past, were able to serve at last the intellectual needs which are within us.

Our renovated consciousness does not permit us to look upon man as the centre of universal life. The suffering of a man is of the same interest to us as the suffering of an electric lamp, which, with spasmodic starts, shrieks out the most heartending expressions of colour. The harmony of the lines and folds of modern dress works upon our sensitiveness with the same emotional and symbolical power as did the nude upon the sensitiveness of the old masters.

In order to conceive and understand the novel beauties of a Futurist picture, the soul must be purified; the eye must be freed from its veil of atavism and culture, so that it may at last look upon Nature and not upon the museum as the one and only standard.

As soon as ever this result has been obtained, it will be readily admitted that brown tints have never coursed beneath our skin; it will be discovered that yellow shines forth in our flesh, that red blazes, and that green, blue and violet dance upon it with untold charms, voluptuous and caressing.

How is it possible still to see the human face pink, now that our life, redoubled by noctambulism, has multiplied our perceptions as colourists? The human face is yellow, red, green, blue, violet. The pallor of a woman gazing in a jeweller's window is more intensely iridescent than the prismatic fires of the jewels that fascinate her like a lark.

The time has passed for our sensations in painting to be whispered. We wish them in future to sing and re-echo upon our canvases in deafening and triumphant flourishes.

Your eyes, accustomed to semi-darkness, will soon open to more radiant visions of light. The shadows which we shall paint shall be more luminous than the high-lights of our predecessors, and our pictures, next to those of the museums, will shine like blinding daylight compared with deepest night.

We conclude that painting cannot exist today without Divisionism. This is no process that can be learned and applied at will. Divisionism, for the modern painter, must be an *innate complementariness* which we declare to be essential and necessary.

Our art will probably be accused of tormented and decadent cerebralism. But we shall merely answer that we are, on the contrary, the primitives of a new sensitiveness, multiplied hundredfold, and that our art is intoxicated with spontaneity and power.

WE DECLARE:

1. That all forms of imitation must be despised, all forms of originality glorified.
2. That it is essential to rebel against the tyranny of the terms "harmony" and "good taste" as being too elastic expressions, by the help of which it is easy to demolish the works of Rembrandt, of Goya and of Rodin.
3. That the art critics are useless or harmful.
4. That all subjects previously used must be swept aside in order to express our whirling life of steel, of pride, of fever and of speed.
5. That the name of "madman" with which it is attempted to gag all innovators should be looked upon as a title of honour.
6. That innate complementariness is an absolute necessity in painting, just as free metre in poetry or polyphony in music.
7. That universal dynamism must be rendered in painting as a dynamic sensation.
8. That in the manner of rendering Nature the first essential is sincerity and purity.
9. That movement and light destroy the materiality of bodies.

WE FIGHT:

1. Against the bituminous tints by which it is attempted to obtain the patina of time upon modern pictures.
2. Against the superficial and elementary archaism founded upon flat

tints, and which, by imitating the linear technique of the Egyptians, reduces painting to a powerless synthesis, both childish and grotesque.

3. Against the false claims to belong to the future put forward by the secessionists and the independents, who have installed new academies no less trite and attached to routine than the preceding ones.

4. Against the nude in painting, as nauseous and as tedious as adultery in literature.

We wish to explain this last point. Nothing is *immoral* in our eyes; it is the monotony of the nude against which we fight. We are told that the subject is nothing and that everything lies in the manner of treating it. That is agreed; we too, admit that. But this truism, unimpeachable and absolute fifty years ago, is no longer so today with regard to the nude, since artists obsessed with the desire to expose the bodies of their mistresses have transformed the Salons into arrays of unwholesome flesh!

We demand, for ten years, the total suppression of the nude in painting.

UMBERTO BOCCIONI, CARLO CARRÀ, LUIGI RUSSOLO,
GIACOMO BALLA, GINO SEVERINI

5.4 UMBERTO BOCCIONI *and others*

Manifesto of the Futurist Painters

1910

TO THE YOUNG ARTISTS OF ITALY!

The cry of rebellion which we utter associates our ideals with those of the Futurist poets. These ideals were not invented by some aesthetic clique. They are the expression of a violent desire which boils in the veins of every creative artist today.

We will fight with all our might the fanatical, senseless and snobbish religion of the past, a religion encouraged by the vicious existence of museums. We rebel against that spineless worshipping of old canvases, old statues and old bric-a-brac, against everything which is filthy and worm-ridden and corroded by time. We consider the habitual contempt for everything which is young, new and burning with life to be unjust and even criminal.

Comrades, we tell you now that the triumphant progress of science makes profound changes in humanity inevitable, changes which are hacking an abyss between those docile slaves of past tradition and us free moderns, who are confident in the radiant splendour of our future.

We are sickened by the foul laziness of artists who, ever since the sixteenth century, have endlessly exploited the glories of the ancient Romans.

In the eyes of other countries, Italy is still a land of the dead, a vast Pompeii, white with sepulchres. But Italy is being reborn. Its political resurgence will be followed by a cultural resurgence. In the land inhabited by the illiterate peasant, schools will be set up; in the land where doing nothing in the sun was the only available profession, millions of machines are already roaring; in the land where traditional aesthetics reigned supreme, new flights of artistic inspiration are emerging and dazzling the world with their brilliance.

Living art draws its life from the surrounding environment. Our forebears drew their artistic inspiration from a religious atmosphere which fed their souls; in the same way we must breathe in the tangible miracles of contemporary life — the iron network of speedy communications which envelops the earth, the transatlantic liners, the dreadnoughts, those marvellous flights which furrow our skies, the profound courage of our submarine navigators and the spasmodic struggle to conquer the unknown. How can we remain insensible to the frenetic life of our great cities and to the exciting new psychology of night-life; the feverish figures of the bon viveur, the cocotte, the apache and the absinthe drinker?

We will also play our part in this crucial revival of aesthetic expression: we declare war on all artists and all institutions which insist on hiding behind a façade of false modernity, while they are actually ensnared by tradition, academicism and, above all, a nauseating cerebral laziness.

We condemn as insulting to youth the acclamations of a revolting rabble for the sickening reflowering of a pathetic kind of classicism in Rome; the neurasthenic cultivation of hermaphroditic archaism which they rave about in Florence; the pedestrian, half-blind handiwork of '48 which they are buying in Milan; the work of pensioned-off government clerks which they think the world of in Turin; the hotchpotch of encrusted rubbish of a group of fossilized alchemists which they are worshipping in Venice. We are going to rise up against all superficiality and banality — all the slovenly and facile commercialism which makes the work of most of our highly respected artists throughout Italy worthy of our deepest contempt.

Away then with hired restorers of antiquated incrustations. Away with affected archaeologists with their chronic necrophilia! Down with the critics, those complacent pimps! Down with gouty academics and drunken, ignorant professors!

Ask these priests of a veritable religious cult, these guardians of old aesthetic laws, where we can go and see the works of Giovanni Segantini today. Ask them why the officials of the Commission have never heard of the existence of Gaetano Previati. Ask them where they can see Medardo Rosso's sculpture, or who takes the slightest interest in artists who have not yet had twenty years of struggle and suffering behind them, but are still producing works destined to honour their fatherland?

These paid critics have other interests to defend. Exhibitions, competitions, superficial and never disinterested criticism, condemn Italian art to the ignominy of true prostitution.

And what about our esteemed "specialists"? Throw them all out. Finish them off! The Portraitists, the Genre Painters, the Lake Painters, the Mountain Painters. We have put up with enough from these impotent painters of country holidays.

Down with all marble-chippers who are cluttering up our squares and profaning our cemeteries! Down with the speculators and their reinforced-concrete buildings! Down with laborious decorators, phoney ceramicists, sold-out poster painters and shoddy, idiotic illustrators!

These are our final CONCLUSIONS:

With our enthusiastic adherence to Futurism, we will:

1. Destroy the cult of the past, the obsession with the ancients, pedantry and academic formalism.
2. Totally invalidate all kinds of imitation.
3. Elevate all attempts at originality, however daring, however violent.
4. Bear bravely and proudly the smear of "madness" with which they try to gag all innovators.
5. Regard art critics as useless and dangerous.
6. Rebel against the tyranny of words: "Harmony" and "good taste" and other loose expressions which can be used to destroy the works of Rembrandt, Goya, Rodin. . . .
7. Sweep the whole field of art clean of all themes and subjects which have been used in the past.
8. Support and glory in our day-to-day world, a world which is going to be continually and splendidly transformed by victorious Science.

The dead shall be buried in the earth's deepest bowels! The threshold of the future will be swept free of mummies! Make room for youth, for violence, for daring!

UMBERTO BOCCIONI, CARLO CARRÀ, LUIGI RUSSOLO,
GIACOMO BALLA, GINO SEVERINI

The Founding and Manifesto of Futurism

1909

We had stayed up all night, my friends and I, under hanging mosque lamps with domes of filigreed brass, domes starred like our spirits, shining like them with the prisoned radiance of electric hearts. For hours we had trampled our atavistic ennui into rich oriental rugs, arguing up to the last confines of logic and blackening many reams of paper with our frenzied scribbling.

An immense pride was buoying us up, because we felt ourselves alone at that hour, alone, awake, and on our feet, like proud beacons or forward sentries against an army of hostile stars glaring down at us from their celestial encampments. Alone with stokers feeding the hellish fires of great ships, alone with the black specters who grope in the red-hot bellies of locomotives launched down their crazy courses, alone with drunkards reeling like wounded birds along the city walls.

Suddenly we jumped, hearing the mighty noise of the huge double-decker trams that rumbled by outside, ablaze with colored lights, like villages on holiday suddenly struck and uprooted by the flooding Po and dragged over falls and through gorges to the sea.

Then the silence deepened. But, as we listened to the old canal muttering its feeble prayers and the creaking bones of sickly palaces above their damp green beards, under the windows we suddenly heard the famished roar of automobiles.

"Let's go!" I said. "Friends, away! Let's go! Mythology and the Mystic Ideal are defeated at last. We're about to see the Centaur's birth and, soon after, the first flight of Angels! . . . We must shake the gates of life, test the bolts and hinges. Let's go! Look there, on the earth, the very first dawn! There's nothing to match the splendor of the sun's red sword, slashing for the first time through our millennial gloom!"

We went up to the three snorting beasts, to lay amorous hands on their torrid breasts. I stretched out on my car like a corpse on its bier, but revived at once under the steering wheel, a guillotine blade that threatened my stomach.

The raging broom of madness swept us out of ourselves and drove us through streets as rough and deep as the beds of torrents. Here and there, sick lamplight through window glass taught us to distrust the deceitful mathematics of our perishing eyes.

I cried, "The scent, the scent alone is enough for our beasts."

And like young lions we ran after Death, its dark pelt blotched with pale crosses as it escaped down the vast violet living and throbbing sky.

But we had no ideal Mistress raising her divine form to the clouds, nor any cruel Queen to whom to offer our bodies, twisted like Byzantine rings! There was nothing to make us wish for death, unless the wish to be free at last from the weight of our courage!

And on we raced, hurling watchdogs against doorsteps, curling them under our burning tires like collars under a flatiron. Death, domesticated, met me at every turn, gracefully holding out a paw, or once in a while hunkering down, making velvety caressing eyes at me from every puddle.

"Let's break out of the horrible shell of wisdom and throw ourselves like pride-ripened fruit into the wide, contorted mouth of the wind! Let's give ourselves utterly to the Unknown, not in desperation but only to replenish the deep wells of the Absurd!!"

The words were scarcely out of my mouth when I spun my car around with the frenzy of a dog trying to bite its tail, and there, suddenly, were two cyclists coming toward me, shaking their fists, wobbling like two equally convincing but nevertheless contradictory arguments. Their stupid dilemma was blocking my way—damn! Ouch! . . . I stopped short and to my disgust rolled over into a ditch with my wheels in the air. . . .

Oh! Maternal ditch, almost full of muddy water! Fair factory drain! I gulped down your nourishing sludge; and I remembered the blessed black breast of my Sudanese nurse. . . . When I came up—torn, filthy, and stinking—from under the capsized car, I felt the white-hot iron of joy deliciously pass through my heart!

A crowd of fishermen with handlines and gouty naturalists were already swarming around the prodigy. With patient, loving care those people rigged a tall derrick and iron grapnels to fish out my car, like a big beached shark. Up it came from the ditch, slowly, leaving in the bottom like scales its heavy framework of good sense and its soft upholstery of comfort.

They thought it was dead, my beautiful shark, but a caress from me was enough to revive it; and there it was, alive again, running on its powerful fins!

And so, faces smeared with good factory muck—plastered with metallic waste, with senseless sweat, with celestial soot—we, bruised, our arms in slings, but unafraid, declared our high intentions to all the *living* of the earth:

MANIFESTO OF FUTURISM

1. We intend to sing the love of danger, the habit of energy and fearlessness.

2. Courage, audacity, and revolt will be essential elements of our poetry.

3. Up to now literature has exalted a pensive immobility, ecstasy, and sleep. We intend to exalt aggressive action, a feverish insomnia, the racer's stride, the mortal leap, the punch and the slap.

4. We say that the world's magnificence has been enriched by a new beauty; the beauty of speed. A racing car whose hood is adorned with great pipes, like serpents of explosive breath—a roaring car that seems to ride on grapeshot—is more beautiful than the *Victory of Samothrace*.

5. We want to hymn the man at the wheel, who hurls the lance of his spirit across the Earth, along the circle of its orbit.

6. The poet must spend himself with ardor, splendor, and generosity, to swell the enthusiastic fervor of the primordial elements.

7. Except in struggle, there is no more beauty. No work without an aggressive character can be a masterpiece. Poetry must be conceived as a violent attack on unknown forces, to reduce and prostrate them before man.

8. We stand on the last promontory of the centuries! . . . Why should we look back, when what we want is to break down the mysterious doors of the Impossible? Time and Space died yesterday. We already live in the absolute, because we have created eternal, omnipresent speed.

9. We will glorify war—the world's only hygiene—militarism, patriotism, the destructive gesture of freedom-bringers, beautiful ideas worth dying for, and scorn for woman.

10. We will destroy the museums, libraries, academies of every kind, will fight moralism, feminism, every opportunistic or utilitarian cowardice.

11. We will sing of great crowds excited by work, by pleasure, and by riot; we will sing of the multicolored, polyphonic tides of revolution in the modern capitals; we will sing of the vibrant nightly fervor of arsenals and shipyards blazing with violent electric moons; greedy railway stations that devour smoke-plumed serpents; factories hung on clouds by the crooked lines of their smoke; bridges that stride the rivers like giant gymnasts, flashing in the sun with a glitter of knives; adventurous steamers that sniff the horizon; deep-chested locomotives whose wheels paw the tracks like the hooves of enormous steel horses bridled by tubing; and the sleek flight of planes whose propellers chatter in the wind like banners and seem to cheer like an enthusiastic crowd.

It is from Italy that we launch through the world this violently upsetting, incendiary manifesto of ours. With it, today, we establish *Futurism* because we want to free this land from its smelly gangrene of professors, archaeologists, ciceroni, and antiquarians. For too long has Italy been a dealer in secondhand clothes. We mean to free her from the numberless museums that cover her like so many graveyards.

Museums: cemeteries! . . . Identical, surely, in the sinister promiscuity of so many bodies unknown to one another. Museums: public dormitories where one lies forever beside hated or unknown beings. Museums; absurd abattoirs of painters and sculptors ferociously macerating each other with color-blows and line-blows, the length of the fought-over walls!

That one should make an annual pilgrimage, just as one goes to the graveyard on All Souls' Day—that I grant. That once a year one should leave a floral tribute beneath the *Gioconda*, I grant you that. . . . But I don't admit that our sorrows, our fragile courage, our morbid restlessness should be given a daily conducted tour through the museums. Why poison ourselves? Why rot?

And what is there to see in an old picture except the laborious contortions of an artist throwing himself against the barriers that thwart his desire to express his dream completely? . . . Admiring an old picture is the same as pouring our sensibility into a funerary urn instead of hurling it far off, in violent spasms of action and creation.

Do you, then, wish to waste all your best powers in this eternal and futile worship of the past, from which you emerge fatally exhausted, shrunken, beaten down?

In truth I tell you that daily visits to museums, libraries, and academies (cemeteries of empty exertion, calvaries of crucified dreams, registries of aborted beginnings!) is, for artists, as damaging as the prolonged supervision by parents of certain young people drunk with their talent and their ambitious wills. When the future is barred to them, the admirable past may be a solace for the ills of the moribund, the sickly, the prisoner. . . . But we want no part of it, the past, we the young and strong *Futurists!*

So let them come, the gay incendiaries with charred fingers! Here they are! Here they are! . . . Come on! set fire to the library shelves! Turn aside the canals to flood the museums! . . . Oh, the joy of seeing the glorious old canvases bobbing adrift on those waters, discolored and shredded! . . . Take up your pickaxes, your axes and hammers, and wreck, wreck the venerable cities, pitilessly!

*   *   *

The oldest of us is thirty: so we have at least a decade for finishing our work. When we are forty, other younger and stronger men will probably throw us in the wastebasket like useless manuscripts—we want it to happen!

They will come against us, our successors, will come from far away, from every quarter, dancing to the winged cadence of their first songs, flexing the hooked claws of predators, sniffing doglike at the academy doors the strong odor of our decaying minds, which already will have been promised to the literary catacombs.

But we won't be there.... At last they'll find us—one winter's night—in open country, beneath a sad roof drummed by a monotonous rain. They'll see us crouched beside our trembling airplanes in the act of warming our hands at the poor little blaze that our books of today will give out when they take fire from the flight of our images.

They'll storm around us, panting with scorn and anguish, and all of them, exasperated by our proud daring, will hurtle to kill us, driven by hatred: the more implacable it is, the more their hearts will be drunk with love and admiration for us.

Injustice, strong and sane, will break out radiantly in their eyes.

Art, in fact, can be nothing but violence, cruelty, and injustice.

The oldest of us is thirty: even so we have already scattered treasures, a thousand treasures of force, love, courage, astuteness, and raw will power; have thrown them impatiently away, with fury, carelessly, unhesitatingly, breathless and unresting.... Look at us! We are still untired! Our hearts know no weariness because they are fed with fire, hatred, and speed! ... Does that amaze you? It should, because you can never remember having lived! Erect on the summit of the world, once again we hurl our defiance at the stars!

You have objections?—Enough! Enough! We know them ... we've understood! ... Our fine deceitful intelligence tells us that we are the revival and extension of our ancestors—perhaps! ... If only it were so!—But who cares? We don't want to understand! ... Woe to anyone who says those infamous words to us again!

Lift up your heads!

Erect on the summit of the world, once again we hurl defiance to the stars!

5.6 Filippo Tommaso Marinetti
After the Marne, Joffre Visited the Front in an Automobile
1915

5.7 FILIPPO TOMASSO MARINETTI, EMILIO SETTIMELLI, AND BRUNO CORRA

The Futurist Synthetic Theatre

1915

As we await our much prayed-for great war, we Futurists carry our violent antineutralist action from city square to university and back again, using our art to prepare the Italian sensibility for the great hour of maximum danger. Italy must be fearless, eager, as swift and elastic as a fencer, as indifferent to blows as a boxer, as impassive at the news of a victory that may have cost fifty thousand dead as at the news of a defeat.

For Italy to learn to make up its mind with lightning speed, to hurl itself into battle, to sustain every undertaking and every possible calamity, books and reviews are unnecessary. They interest and concern only a minority, are more or less tedious, obstructive, and relaxing. They cannot help chilling enthusiasm, aborting impulses, and poisoning with doubt a people at war. War—Futurism intensified—obliges us to march and not to rot [*marciare, non marcire*] in libraries and reading rooms. THEREFORE WE THINK THAT THE ONLY WAY TO INSPIRE ITALY WITH THE WARLIKE SPIRIT TODAY IS THROUGH THE THEATRE. In fact ninety percent of Italians go to the theatre, whereas only ten percent read books and reviews. But what is needed is a FUTURIST THEATRE, completely opposed to the passéist theatre that drags its monotonous, depressing processions around the sleepy Italian stages.

Not to dwell on this historical theatre, a sickening genre already abandoned by the passéist public, we condemn the whole contemporary theatre because it is too prolix, analytic, pedantically psychological, explanatory, diluted, finicking, static, as full of prohibitions as a police station, as cut up into cells as a monastery, as moss-grown as an old abandoned house. In other words it is a pacifistic, neutralist theatre, the antithesis of the fierce, overwhelming, synthesizing velocity of the war.

Our Futurist Theatre will be:

Synthetic
That is, very brief. To compress into a few minutes, into a few words and gestures, innumerable situations, sensibilities, ideas, sensations, facts, and symbols.

The writers who wanted to renew the theatre (Ibsen, Maeterlinck, An-

dreyev, Claudel, Shaw) never thought of arriving at a true synthesis, of freeing themselves from a technique that involves prolixity, meticulous analysis, drawn-out preparation. Before the works of these authors, the audience
is in the indignant attitude of a circle of bystanders who swallow their anguish and pity as they watch the slow agony of a horse who has collapsed
on the pavement. The sigh of applause that finally breaks out frees the audience's stomach from all the indigestible time it has swallowed. Each act is
as painful as having to wait patiently in an antechamber for the minister
(*coup de théâtre:* kiss, pistol shot, verbal revelation, etc.) to receive you. All
this passéist or semi-Futurist theatre, instead of synthesizing fact and idea
in the smallest number of words and gestures, savagely destroys the variety
of place (source of dynamism and amazement), stuffs many city squares,
landscapes, streets, into the sausage of a single room. For this reason this
theatre is entirely static.

We are convinced that mechanically, by force of brevity, we can achieve
an entirely new theatre perfectly in tune with our swift and laconic Futurist
sensibility. Our acts can also be moments [*atti — attimi*] only a few seconds
long. With this essential and synthetic brevity the theatre can bear and even
overcome competition from the *cinema.*

Atechnical

The passéist theatre is the literary form that most distorts and diminishes
an author's talent. This form, much more than lyric poetry or the novel,
is subject to *the demands of technique:* (1) to omit every notion that doesn't
conform to public taste; (2) once a theatrical idea has been found (expres-
sible in a few pages), to stretch it out over two, three or four acts; (3) to
surround an interesting character with many pointless types: coat-holders,
door-openers, all sorts of bizarre comic turns; (4) to make the length of each
act vary between half and three-quarters of an hour; (5) to construct each
act taking care to (*a*) begin with seven or eight absolutely useless pages, (*b*)
introduce a tenth of your idea in the first act, five-tenths in the second, four-
tenths in the third, (*c*) shape your acts for rising excitement, each act being
no more than a preparation for the finale, (*d*) always make the first act *a
little boring* so that the second can be *amusing* and the third *devouring;* (6) to
set off every *essential* line with a hundred or more insignificant *preparatory*
lines; (7) never to devote less than a page to explaining an entrance or an exit
minutely; (8) to apply systematically to the whole play *the rule of a superficial
variety,* to the acts, scenes, and lines. For instance, to make one act a day,
another an evening, another deep night; to make one act pathetic, another

anguished, another sublime; when you have to prolong a dialogue between two actors, make something happen to interrupt it, a falling vase, a passing mandolin player. . . . Or else have the actors constantly move around from sitting to standing, from right to left, and meanwhile vary the dialogue to make it seem as if a bomb might explode outside at any moment (e.g., the betrayed husband might catch his wife red-handed) when actually nothing is going to explode until the end of the act; (9) to be enormously careful about *the verisimilitude of the plot;* (10) to write your play in such a manner that *the audience understands in the finest detail the how and why of everything that takes place on the stage, above all that it knows by the last act how the protagonists will end up.*

With our synthetist movement in the theatre, we want to destroy the Technique that from the Greeks until now, instead of simplifying itself, has become more and more dogmatic, stupid, logical, meticulous, pedantic, strangling. THEREFORE:

1. *It's stupid to write one hundred pages where one would do,* only because the audience through habit and infantile instinct wants to see character in a play result from a series of events, wants to fool itself into thinking that the character really exists in order to admire the beauties of Art, meanwhile refusing to acknowledge any art if the author limits himself to sketching out a few of the character's traits.

2. *It's stupid* not to rebel against the prejudice of theatricality when life itself (which consists *of actions vastly more awkward, uniform, and predictable* than those that unfold in the world of art) is for the most part *antitheatrical* and even in this offers *innumerable possibilities for the stage.* EVERYTHING OF ANY VALUE IS THEATRICAL.

3. *It's stupid* to pander to the primitivism of the crowd, which, in the last analysis, wants to see the bad guy lose and the good guy win.

4. *It's stupid* to worry about verisimilitude (absurd because talent and worth have little to do with it).

5. *It's stupid* to want to explain with logical minuteness everything taking place on the stage, when even in life one never grasps an event entirely, in all its causes and consequences, because reality throbs around us, bombards us *with squalls of fragments of inter-connected events, mortised and tenoned together, confused, mixed up, chaotic.* E.g., it's stupid to act out a contest between two persons *always* in an orderly, clear, and logical way, since in daily life we nearly always encounter mere *flashes of argument* made *momentary* by our modern experience, in a tram, a café, a railway station, which remain cinematic in our minds like

fragmentary dynamic symphonies of gestures, words, lights, and
sounds.

6. *It's stupid* to submit to obligatory *crescendi, prepared effects,* and
postponed climaxes.

7. *It's stupid* to allow one's talent to be burdened with the weight of a
technique that *anyone* (even imbeciles) *can acquire by study, practice,
and patience.*

8. IT'S STUPID TO RENOUNCE THE DYNAMIC LEAP IN THE VOID OF
TOTAL CREATION, BEYOND THE RANGE OF TERRITORY PREVIOUSLY
EXPLORED.

Dynamic, simultaneous

That is, born of improvisation, lightning-like intuition, from suggestive and
revealing actuality. We believe that a thing is valuable to the extent that it is
improvised (hours, minutes, seconds), not extensively prepared (months,
years, centuries).

We feel an unconquerable repugnance for desk work, *a priori,* that fails to
respect the ambience of the theatre itself. THE GREATER NUMBER OF OUR
WORKS HAVE BEEN WRITTEN IN THE THEATRE. The theatrical ambience
is our inexhaustible reservoir of inspirations: the magnetic circular sensation invading our tired brains during morning rehearsal in an empty gilded
theatre; an actor's intonation that suggests the possibility of constructing
a cluster of paradoxical thoughts on top of it; a movement of scenery that
hints at a symphony of lights; an actress's fleshiness that fills our minds with
genially full-bodied notions.

We overran Italy at the head of a heroic battalion of comedians who imposed on audiences *Elettricità* and other Futurist syntheses (alive yesterday,
today surpassed and condemned by us) that were revolutions imprisoned in
auditoriums. — From the Politeama Garibaldi of Palermo to the Dal Verme
of Milan. The Italian theatres smoothed the wrinkles in the raging massage
of the crowd and rocked with bursts of volcanic laughter. We fraternized
with the actors. Then, on sleepless nights in trains, we argued, goading each
other to heights of genius to the rhythm of tunnels and stations. Our Futurist theatre jeers at Shakespeare but pays attention to the gossip of actors,
is put to sleep by a line from Ibsen but is inspired by red or green reflections from the stalls. WE ACHIEVE AN ABSOLUTE DYNAMISM THROUGH
THE INTERPENETRATION OF DIFFERENT ATMOSPHERES AND TIMES. E.g.,
whereas in a drama like *Più che L'Amore* [D'Annunzio], the important events
(for instance, the murder of the gambling-house keeper) don't take place

on the stage but are narrated with a complete lack of dynamism; and in the first act of *La Figlia di Jorio* [D'Annunzio] the events take place against a simple background with no jumps in space or time; in the Futurist synthesis, *Simultaneità*, there are two ambiences that interpenetrate and many different times put into action simultaneously.

Autonomous, alogical, unreal
The Futurist theatrical synthesis will not be subject to logic, will pay no attention to photography; it will be *autonomous*, will resemble nothing but itself, although it will take elements from reality and combine them as its whim dictates. Above all, just as the painter and composer discover, scattered through the outside world, a narrower but more intense life, made up of colours, forms, sounds, and noises, the same is true *for the man gifted with theatrical sensibility, for whom a specialized reality exists that violently assaults his nerves:* it consists of what is called THE THEATRICAL WORLD.

THE FUTURIST THEATRE IS BORN OF THE TWO MOST VITAL CURRENTS in the Futurist sensibility, defined in the two manifestos "The Variety Theatre" and "Weights, Measures, and Prices of Artistic Genius," which are: (1) our frenzied passion for real, swift, elegant, complicated, cynical, muscular, fugitive, Futurist life; (2) our very modern cerebral definition of art according to which no logic, no tradition, no aesthetic, no technique, no opportunity can be imposed on the artist's natural talent; he must be preoccupied only with creating synthetic expressions of cerebral energy that have THE ABSOLUTE VALUE OF NOVELTY.

The *Futurist theatre* will be able to excite its audience, that is make it forget the monotony of daily life, by sweeping it through *a labyrinth of sensations imprinted on the most exacerbated originality and combined in unpredictable ways.*

Every night the *Futurist theatre* will be a gymnasium to train our race's spirit to the swift, dangerous enthusiasms made necessary by this Futurist year.

CONCLUSIONS

1. TOTALLY ABOLISH THE TECHNIQUE THAT IS KILLING THE PASSÉIST THEATRE.
2. DRAMATIZE ALL THE DISCOVERIES (no matter how unlikely, weird, and antitheatrical) THAT OUR TALENT IS DISCOVERING IN THE SUBCONSCIOUS, IN ILL-DEFINED FORCES, IN PURE ABSTRACTION,

IN THE PURELY CEREBRAL, THE PURELY FANTASTIC, IN RECORD-
SETTING AND BODY-MADNESS. (E.g., *Vengono,* F. T. Marinetti's first
drama of objects, a new vein of theatrical sensibility discovered by
Futurism.)

3. SYMPHONIZE THE AUDIENCE'S SENSIBILITY BY EXPLORING IT,
   STIRRING UP ITS LAZIEST LAYERS WITH EVERY MEANS POSSIBLE;
   ELIMINATE THE PRECONCEPTION OF THE FOOTLIGHTS BY
   THROWING NETS OF SENSATION BETWEEN STAGE AND AUDIENCE;
   THE STAGE ACTION WILL INVADE THE ORCHESTRA SEATS, THE
   AUDIENCE.

4. FRATERNIZE WARMLY WITH THE ACTORS WHO ARE AMONG THE
   FEW THINKERS WHO FLEE FROM EVERY DEFORMING CULTURAL
   ENTERPRISE.

5. ABOLISH THE FARCE, THE VAUDEVILLE, THE SKETCH, THE COMEDY,
   THE SERIOUS DRAMA, AND TRAGEDY, AND CREATE IN THEIR PLACE
   THE MANY FORMS OF FUTURIST THEATRE, SUCH AS: LINES
   WRITTEN IN FREE WORDS, SIMULTANEITY, INTERPENETRATION,
   THE SHORT, ACTED-OUT POEM, THE DRAMATIZED SENSATION,
   COMIC DIALOGUE, THE NEGATIVE ACT, THE REECHOING LINE,
   "EXTRA-LOGICAL" DISCUSSION, SYNTHETIC DEFORMATION, THE
   SCIENTIFIC OUTBURST THAT CLEARS THE AIR.

6. THROUGH UNBROKEN CONTACT, CREATE BETWEEN US AND THE
   CROWD A CURRENT OF CONFIDENCE RATHER THAN
   RESPECTFULNESS, IN ORDER TO INSTILL IN OUR AUDIENCES THE
   DYNAMIC VIVACITY OF A NEW FUTURIST THEATRICALITY.

These are the *first* words on the theatre. Our first eleven theatrical syntheses
(by Marinetti, Settimelli, Bruno Corra, R. Chiti, Balilla Pratella) were victo-
riously imposed on crowded theatres in Ancona, Bologna, Padua, Naples,
Venice, Verona, Florence, and Rome, by Ettore Berti, Zoncada, and Petro-
lini. In Milan we soon shall have the great metal building, enlivened by all
the electro-mechanical inventions, that alone will permit us to realize our
freest conceptions on the stage.

Tactilism

Marinetti, having experimented with so many diverse forms of Futurism
since 1909, had one final blast with yet another category. Having tried Noisism or Bruitism, and having experimented with Futurist cooking (in a way

that could be called Tastism), he then moved, late, to the -ism of touch, or Tactilism.

If the manifesto does not have the raging enthusiasm of the earlier ones, or the kooky delights of Aeropoetry, it is nonetheless the last gasp of a manifesto creator like no other.

5.8 FILIPPO TOMMASO MARINETTI
Tactilism
1924

In January of 1921 I presented to the Parisian intellectual public gathered in the auditorium of the *Théâtre de L'Oeuvre* my tactile tables, the first account of a tactile art that I had thought out, based on the harmonious combination of tactile values. My investigations have intensified between that famous lecture and today.

Before expounding them to my readers, I think it proper to tell them about the origins of this invention of mine.

A tactile sensibility has existed for a long time in literature and plastic art. My great friend Boccioni, the Futurist painter and sculptor, already in 1911 was feeling tactilistically when he created his plastic ensemble *Fusion of a Head and Window*, with materials entirely contrary to each other in weight and tactile value: iron, porcelain, clay, and woman's hair. This plastic complex, he told me, was made to be not only seen, but also touched. One night during the winter of 1917 I was crawling on hands and knees down to my pallet in the darkness of an artillery battery's dugout. Hard as I tried not to, I keep hitting bayonets, mess tins, and the heads of sleeping soldiers. I lay down, but didn't sleep, obsessed with the tactile sensations I'd felt and classified. For the first time that night I thought of a tactile art.

During the summer of 1911, at Antignano, where the Amerigo Vespucci Road curves around as it follows the seacoast, I created the first tactile table.

Red banners were snapping over factories manned by workers.

I was naked in the silky water that was being torn by rocks, by foaming scissors, knives, and razors, among beds of iodine-soaked algae. I was naked in a sea of flexible steel that breathed with a virile, fecund breath. I was drinking from a sea-chalice brimming with genius as far as the rim. With its long searing flames, the sun was vulcanizing my body and welding the keel of my forehead rich in sails.

A peasant girl, who smelt of salt and warm stone, smiled as she looked at my first tactile table. "You're having fun making little boats!" I answered her, "Yes, I'm making a launch that will carry the human spirit to unknown shores."

Still, the difficulties were enormous. I had to begin to educate my tactile sense. By sheer will power I localized the confused phenomena of thought and imagination on the different parts of my body. I observed that healthy bodies can use this education to give precise and surprising results.

On the other hand, diseased sensibilities, which derive their excitability and their apparent perfection from their bodies' very weakness, achieve the great tactile faculty less easily, more haphazardly and unreliably.

Among the different experiences, I found the following three preferable:

1. to wear gloves for several days, during which time the brain will force the condensation into your hands of a desire for different tactile sensations;
2. to swim underwater in the sea, trying to distinguish interwoven currents and different temperatures tactilistically;
3. every night, in complete darkness, to recognize and enumerate every object in your bedroom.

In this way I created the first educational scale of touch, which at the same time is a scale of tactile values for Tactilism, or the Art of Touch.

First scale, flat, with four categories of different touches — First category: certain, abstract, cold touch. Sandpaper. Emery paper.

Second category: colorless, persuasive, reasoning touch. Smooth silk. Shot silk.

Third category: exciting, lukewarm, nostalgic. Velvet. Wool from the Pyrenees. Plain wool. Silk-wool crepe.

Fourth category: almost irritating, warm, willful. Grainy silk. Plaited silk. Spongy material.

Second scale of values — Fifth category: soft, warm, human. Chamois leather. Skin of horse or dog. Human hair and skin. Marabou.

Sixth category: warm, sensual, witty, affectionate. This category has two branches: Rough iron. Light brush bristles. Sponge. Wire bristles. Animal or peach down. Bird down.

After long concentration of my attention on the sensations felt by my hands in stroking these scales of tactile values, I put them brutally aside. Rapidly, in bursts of intuition, I created the first abstract suggestive tactile table, the name of which is *Sudan-Paris*. In its *Sudan* part this table has spongy material, sandpaper, wool, pig's bristle, and wire bristle. (*Crude, greasy, rough, sharp, burning tactile values, that evoke African visions in the mind of the toucher.*)

In the *sea* part, the table has different grades of emery paper. (*Slippery, metallic, cool, elastic, marine tactile values.*)

In the *Paris* part, the table has silk, watered silk, velvet, and large and small feathers. (*Soft, very delicate, warm and cool at once, artificial, civilized.*)

This still-embryonic tactile art is cleanly distinct from the plastic arts. It has nothing in common with painting or sculpture.

As much as possible one must avoid variety of colors in the tactile tables, which would lend itself to plastic impressions. Painters and sculptors, who naturally tend to subordinate tactile values to visual values, would have trouble creating significant tactile tables. Tactilism seems to me especially reserved to young poets, pianists, stenographers, and to every erotic, re-fined, and powerful temperament.

Tactilism, on the other hand, must avoid not only collaboration with the plastic arts, but also morbid erotomania. Its purpose must be, simply, to achieve tactile harmonies and to contribute indirectly toward the perfection of spiritual communication between human beings, through the epidermis.

The distinction between the five senses is arbitrary. Today one can un-cover and catalog many other senses.

Tactilism promotes this discovery.

TOWARD THE DISCOVERY OF NEW SENSES

Imagine the Sun leaving its orbit and forgetting the Earth! Darkness. Men stumbling around. Terror. Then, the birth of a vague sense of security and adjustment. Precautions of the skin. Life on hands and knees. After having tried to make new artificial lights, men adapt themselves to the shadows. They admire the night-seeing animals. Dilatation of human pupils, which perceive the thin gleams of light mixed in the shadows. Attention accumu-lates in the optic nerve.

A visual sense is born in the fingertips.

X-ray vision develops, and some people can already see inside their bodies. Others dimly explore the inside of their neighbors' bodies. They all realize that sight, smell, hearing, touch, and taste are modifications of a single keen sense: touch, divided in different ways and localized in different points.

Other localizations take place. For instance: the epigastrium sees. The knees see. The elbows see. All admire the variations in velocity that differentiate light from sound.

I am convinced that Tactilism will render great practical services, by preparing good surgeons with seeing hands and by offering new ways to educate the handicapped.

The Futurist Balla declares that Tactilism will enable everyone to recover the sensations of his past life with freshness and complete surprise, more than he ever could through either music or painting.

Exactly. But I go beyond that.

We are aware of the hypothesis of material essence. This provisional hypothesis considers matter to be a harmony of electronic systems, and through it we have come to deny the distinction between matter and spirit.

When we feel a piece of iron, we say: This is iron; we satisfy ourselves with a word and nothing more. Between iron and hand a conflict of preconscious force-thought-sentiment takes place. Perhaps there is more thought in the fingertips and the iron than in the brain that prides itself on observing the phenomenon.

With Tactilism we propose to penetrate deeper and outside normal scientific method into the true essence of matter.

Noisism/Bruitism

Allied to syncretism and synesthesia, in that it wanted to join experiences and senses to each other, the Bruitist or Noisist part of Futurism was one of the most joyous. Luigi Russolo's "Art of Noises" (5.10) of 1913, published by the Direction of the Futurist Movement in Milan, like his experimental futurist paintings, joins together all the elements as they run interference with each other. (*House + Light + Sky*, in the Kunstmuseum of Basel, and *Dynamism of an Automobile* of 1911–12 show the rapidity with which the conjunction of noise and light is to be experienced.)

Carlo Carrà's "Painting of Sounds, Noises, and Smells" (5.9) of 1913 combines an impulse toward synthesia with a sense of the clang and rapidity of the contemporary universe, on the move. More radical still, Fortunato Depero's "Manifesto of Moto-Noisism" of 1915 brings in the sound of the motor, the car as well as the mechanism, for the physical object is bolted together with screws. "Depero Futurista," he signed himself, for good reason.

5.9 CARLO CARRÀ

The Painting of Sounds, Noises, and Smells

1913

Before the nineteenth century, painting was a silent art. Painters of antiquity, of the Renaissance, of the seventeenth and the eighteenth centuries, never envisaged the possibility of rendering sounds, noises and smells in painting, even when they chose flowers, stormy seas or wild skies as their themes.

The Impressionists in their bold revolution made some confused and hesitant attempts at sounds and noises in their pictures. Before them — nothing, absolutely nothing!

Nevertheless, we should point out at once, that between the Impressionist mumblings and our Futurist paintings of sounds, noises and smells there is an enormous difference, as great as that between a misty winter morning and a scorching summer afternoon, or — even better — between the first breath of life and an adult man in full development of his powers. In their canvases, sounds and noises are expressed in such a thin and faded way that they seem to have been perceived by the eardrum of a deaf man. Here we do not wish to present a detailed account of the principles and experiments of the Impressionists. There is no need to enquire minutely into all the reasons why the Impressionists never succeeded in painting sounds, noises and smells. We shall only mention here the kind of thing they would have had to destroy if they had wanted to obtain results:

1. The extremely vulgar perspectives of *trompe-l'oeil,* a game worthy of an academic of the Leonardo da Vinci sort or an idiot designer of *verismo* operas.
2. The concept of colour harmonies, a characteristic defect of the French which inevitably forced them into the elegant ways of Watteau and his like, and, as a result, led to the abuse of light blues, pale greens, violets and pinks. We have already said very many times how we regret this tendency towards the soft, the effeminate, the gentle.
3. Contemplative idealism, which I have defined as a *sentimental mimicry of apparent nature.* This contemplative idealism is contaminating the pictorial construction of the Expressionists, just as it contaminated those of their predecessors Corot and Delacroix.
4. All anecdote and detail, which (although it is a reaction, an antidote, to

false academical construction) almost always demeans painting to the level of photography.

As for the Post- and Neo-Impressionists, such as Matisse, Signac and Seurat, we maintain that, far from perceiving the problem and facing up to the difficulties of sounds, noises and smells in their paintings, they have preferred to withdraw into static representations in order to obtain a greater synthesis of form and colour (Matisse) and a systematic application of light (Signac, Seurat).

We Futurists state, therefore, that in bringing the elements of sound, noise and smell to painting we are opening fresh paths.

We have already evolved, as artists, a love of modern life in its essential dynamism—its sounds, noises and smells—thereby destroying the stupid pattern for the solemn, the bombastic, the serene, the hieratic and the mummified: everything purely intellectual, in fact. IMAGINATION WITHOUT STRINGS, WORDS-IN-FREEDOM, THE SYSTEMATIC USE OF ONOMATO-POEIA, ANTIGRACEFUL MUSIC WITHOUT RHYTHMIC QUADRATURE, AND THE ART OF NOISES. These have derived from the same sensibility which has generated the painting of sounds, noises and smells.

It is indisputably true that (1) silence is static and sounds, noises and smells are dynamic, (2) sounds, noises and smells are none other than different forms and intensities of vibration, and (3) any continued series of sounds, noises and smells imprints on the mind an arabesque of form and colour.

We should therefore measure this intensity and perceive these arabesques.

THE PAINTING OF SOUNDS, NOISES AND SMELLS REJECTS:
1. All subdued colours, even those obtained directly and without the help of tricks such as patinas and glazes.
2. The banality of velvets, silks, flesh tints which are too human, too fine, too soft, along with flowers which are excessively pale and drooping.
3. Greys, browns and all mud colours.
4. The use of pure horizontal and vertical lines and all other dead lines.
5. The right angle which we consider passionless.
6. The cube, the pyramid and all other static shapes.
7. The unities of time and place.

THE PAINTING OF SOUNDS, NOISES AND SMELLS DESIRES:
1. Reds, rrrrreds, the rrrrrreddest rrrrrrreds that shouuuuuuut.
2. Greens, that can never be greener, greeeeeeeeeeeeens, that screeeeeeam,

yellows, as violent as can be; polenta yellows, saffron yellows, brass yellows.

3. All the colours of speed, of joy, of carousings and fantastic carnivals, fireworks, cafés and singing, of music-halls; all colours which are seen in movement, colours experienced in time and not in space.

4. The dynamic arabesque as the sole reality created by the artist from the depths of his sensibilities.

5. The clash of all acute angles, which we have already called the angles of will.

6. Oblique lines which affect the soul of the observer like so many bolts from the blue, along with lines of depth.

7. The sphere, ellipses which spin, upside-down cones, spirals and all those dynamic forms which the infinite powers of an artists' genius are able to uncover.

8. Perspectives obtained not as the objectivity of distances but as a subjective interpenetration of hard and soft, sharp and dull forms.

9. As a universal subject and as the sole reason for a painting's existence; the significance of its dynamic construction (polyphonic architectural whole).

When we talk of architecture, people usually think of something static; this is wrong. What we are thinking of is an architecture similar to the dynamic and musical architecture achieved by the Futurist musician Pratella. Architecture is found in the movement of colours, of smoke from a chimney, and in metallic structures, when they are expressed in states of mind which are violent and chaotic.

10. The inverted cone (the natural shape of an explosion), the slanting cylinder and cone.

11. The collision of two cones at their apexes (the natural shape of a water spout) with floating and curving lines (a clown jumping, dancers).

12. The zig-zag and the wavy line.

13. Ellipsoidal curves seen like nets in movement.

14. Lines and volumes as part of a plastic transcendentalism, that is according to their special kind of curving or obliqueness, determined by the painter's state of mind.

15. Echoes of lines and volumes in movement.

16. Plastic complementarism (for both forms and colours), based on the law of equivalent contrast and on the clash of the most contrasting colours of the rainbow.

This complementarism derives from a disequilibrium of form (therefore they are forced to keep moving). The consequent destruction of the *pendants* of volumes. We must reject these *pendants* since they are no more than a pair of crutches, allowing only a single movement, forward and then backward, that is, not a total movement, which we call the spherical expansion of space.

17. The continuity and simultaneity of the plastic transcendency of the animal, mineral, vegetable and mechanical kingdoms.
18. Abstract plastic wholes, that is those which correspond not to the artist's vision but to sensations which derive from sounds, noises and smells, and all the unknown forces involved in these. These plastic polyphonic, polyrhythmic and abstract wholes correspond to the necessity for an internal disharmony which we Futurist painters believe to be indispensable for pictorial sensibility.

These plastic wholes are, because of their mysterious fascination, much more suggestive than those created by our visual and tactile senses, because they are so much closer to our pure plastic spirit.

We Futurist painters maintain that sounds, noises and smells are incorporated in the expression of lines, volumes and colours just as lines, volumes and colours are incorporated in the architecture of a musical work.

Our canvases therefore express the plastic equivalent of the sounds, noises and smells found in theatres, music-halls, cinemas, brothels, railway stations, ports, garages, hospitals, workshops, etc., etc.

From the form point of view: there are sounds, noises and smells which are concave, convex, triangular, ellipsoidal, oblong, conical, spherical, spiral, etc.

From the colour point of view: there are sounds, noises and smells which are yellow, green, dark blue, light blue, violet.

In railway stations and garages, and throughout the mechanical or sporting world, sounds, noises and smells are predominantly red; in restaurants and cafés they are silver, yellow and violet. While the sounds, noises and smells of animals are yellow and blue, those of a woman are green, blue and violet.

We shall not exaggerate and claim that smell alone is enough to determine in our minds arabesques of form and colour which could be said to constitute the motive and justify the necessity of a painting.

But it is true in the sense that if we are shut up in a dark room (so that our sense of sight no longer works) with flowers, petrol or other things with a strong smell, our plastic spirit will gradually eliminate the memory sensation and construct a very special plastic whole which corresponds perfectly, in its quality of weight and movement, with the smells found in the room.

These smells, through some kind of obscure process, have become environment-force, determining that state of mind which for us Futurist painters constitutes a pure plastic whole.

This bubbling and whirling of forms and light, composed of sounds, noises and smells, has been partly achieved by me in my *Anarchical Funeral* and in my *Jolts of a Taxi-cab,* by Boccioni in *States of Mind* and *Forces of a Street,* by Russolo in *Revolt* and Severini in *Bang Bang,* paintings which were violently discussed at our first Paris Exhibition in 1912. This kind of bubbling over requires a great emotive effort, even delirium, on the part of the artist, who in order to achieve a vortex, must be a vortex of sensation himself, a pictorial force and not a cold multiple intellect.

Know therefore! In order to achieve this *total painting,* which requires the active cooperation of all the senses, *a painting which is a plastic state of mind of the universal,* you must paint, as drunkards sing and vomit, sounds, noises and smells!

5.10 LUIGI RUSSOLO

The Art of Noises (*excerpt*)

1913

Dear Balilla Pratella, great Futurist composer,
In Rome, in the Costanzi Theatre, packed to capacity, while I was listening to the orchestral performance of your overwhelming FUTURIST MUSIC, with my Futurist friends, Marinetti, Boccioni, Carrà, Balla, Soffici, Papini and Cavacchioli, a new art came into my mind which only you can create, the Art of Noises, the logical consequence of your marvellous innovations.

Ancient life was all silence. In the nineteenth century, with the invention of the machine, Noise was born. Today, Noise triumphs and reigns supreme over the sensibility of men. For many centuries life went by in silence, or at most in muted tones. The strongest noises which interrupted this silence were not intense or prolonged or varied. If we overlook such exceptional movements as earthquakes, hurricanes, storms, avalanches and waterfalls, nature is silent.

Amidst this dearth of *noises,* the first *sounds* that man drew from a pierced reed or stretched string were regarded with amazement as new and marvellous things. Primitive races attributed *sound* to the gods; it was considered sacred and reserved for priests, who used it to enrich the mystery of their rites.

And so was born the concept of sound as a thing in itself, distinct and independent of life, and the result was music, a fantastic world superimposed on the real one, an inviolable and sacred world. It is easy to understand how such a concept of music resulted inevitably in the hindering of its progress by comparison with the other arts. The Greeks themselves, with their musical theories calculated mathematically by Pythagoras and according to which only a few consonant intervals could be used, limited the field of music considerably, rendering harmony, of which they were unaware, impossible.

The Middle Ages, with the development and modification of the Greek tetrachordal system, with the Gregorian chant and popular songs, enriched the art of music, but continued to consider sound *in its development in time,* a restricted notion, but one which lasted many centuries, and which can still be found in the Flemish contrapuntalists' most complicated polyphonies.

The chord did not exist, the development of the various parts was not subordinated to the chord that these parts put together could produce; the conception of the parts was horizontal not vertical. The desire, search and taste for a simultaneous union of different sounds, that is for the chord (complex sound), were gradually made manifest, passing from the consonant perfect chord with a few passing dissonances, to the complicated and persistent dissonances that characterize contemporary music.

At first the art of music sought and achieved purity, limpidity and sweetness of sound. Then different sounds were amalgamated, care being taken, however, to caress the ear with gentle harmonies. Today music, as it becomes continually more complicated, strives to amalgamate the most dissonant, strange and harsh sounds. In this way we come ever closer to *noise-sound.*

THIS MUSICAL EVOLUTION IS PARALLELED BY THE MULTIPLICATION OF MACHINES, which collaborate with man on every front. Not only in the roaring atmosphere of major cities, but in the country too, which until yesterday was normally silent, the machine today has created such a variety and rivalry of noises that pure sound, in its exiguity and monotony, no longer arouses any feeling.

To excite and exalt our sensibilities, music developed towards the most complex polyphony and the maximum variety, seeking the most complicated successions of dissonant chords and vaguely preparing the creation of MUSICAL NOISE. This evolution towards "noise sound" was not possible before now. The ear of an eighteenth-century man could never have endured the discordant intensity of certain chords produced by our orchestras (whose members have trebled in number since then). To our ears, on the other hand, they sound pleasant, since our hearing has already been educated by modern life, so teeming with variegated noises. But our ears are not satisfied merely with this, and demand an abundance of acoustic emotions.

On the other hand, musical sound is too limited in its qualitative variety of tones. The most complex orchestras boil down to four or five types of instrument, varying in timbre: instruments played by bow or plucking, by blowing into metal or wood, and by percussion. And so modern music goes round in this small circle, struggling in vain to create new ranges of tones.

THIS LIMITED CIRCLE OF PURE SOUNDS MUST BE BROKEN, AND THE INFINITE VARIETY OF "NOISE-SOUND" CONQUERED.

Besides, everyone will acknowledge that all [musical] sound carries with it a development of sensations that are already familiar and exhausted, and which predispose the listener to boredom in spite of the efforts of all the innovatory musicians. We Futurists have deeply loved and enjoyed the harmonies of the great masters. For many years Beethoven and Wagner shook our nerves and hearts. Now we are satiated and WE FIND FAR MORE ENJOYMENT IN THE COMBINATION OF THE NOISES OF TRAMS, BACKFIRING MOTORS, CARRIAGES AND BAWLING CROWDS THAN IN REHEARING, for example, THE "EROICA" OR THE "PASTORAL."

We cannot see that enormous apparatus of force that the modern orchestra represents without feeling the most profound and total disillusion at the paltry acoustic results. Do you know of any sight more ridiculous than that of twenty men furiously bent on redoubling the mewing of a violin? All this will naturally make the music-lovers scream, and will perhaps enliven the sleepy atmosphere of concert halls. Let us now, as Futurists, enter one of these hospitals for anaemic sounds. There: the first bar brings the boredom of familiarity to your ear and anticipates the boredom of the bar to follow. Let us relish, from bar to bar, two or three varieties of genuine boredom, waiting all the while for the extraordinary sensation that never comes.

Meanwhile a repugnant mixture is concocted from monotonous sensations and the idiotic religious emotion of listeners buddhistically drunk with repeating for the nth time their more or less snobbish or second-hand ecstasy.

Away! Let us break out since we cannot much longer restrain our desire to create finally a new musical reality, with a generous distribution of resonant slaps in the face, discarding violins, pianos, double-basses and plaintive organs. Let us break out!

It's no good objecting that noises are exclusively loud and disagreeable to the ear.

It seems pointless to enumerate all the graceful and delicate noises that afford pleasant sensations.

To convince ourselves of the amazing variety of noises, it is enough to think of the rumble of thunder, the whistle of the wind, the roar of a waterfall, the gurgling of a brook, the rustling of leaves, the clatter of a trotting horse as it draws into the distance, the lurching jolts of a cart on pavings, and of the generous, solemn, white breathing of a nocturnal city; of all the noises made by wild and domestic animals, and of all those that can be made by the mouth of man without resorting to speaking or singing.

Let us cross a great modern capital with our ears more alert than our eyes, and we will get enjoyment from distinguishing the eddying of water, air and gas in metal pipes, the grumbling of noises that breathe and pulse with indisputable animality, the palpitation of valves, the coming and going of pistons, the howl of mechanical saws, the jolting of a tram on its rails, the cracking of whips, the flapping of curtains and flags. We enjoy creating mental orchestrations of the crashing down of metal shop blinds, slamming doors, the hubbub and shuffling of crowds, the variety of din, from stations, railways, iron foundries, spinning mills, printing works, electric power stations and underground railways. . . .

WE WANT TO ATTUNE AND REGULATE THIS TREMENDOUS VARIETY OF NOISES HARMONICALLY AND RHYTHMICALLY.

To attune noises does not mean to detract from all their irregular movements and vibrations in time and intensity, but rather to give gradation and tone to the most strongly predominant of these vibrations.

Noise in fact can be differentiated from sound only in so far as the vibrations which produce it are confused and irregular, both in time and intensity.

EVERY NOISE HAS A TONE, AND SOMETIMES ALSO A HARMONY THAT PREDOMINATES OVER THE BODY OF ITS IRREGULAR VIBRATIONS.

Now, it is from this dominating characteristic tone that a practical possibility can be derived for attuning it, that is to give to a certain noise not merely one tone, but a variety of tones, without losing its characteristic tone, by which I mean the one which distinguishes it. In this way any noise obtained by a rotating movement can offer an entire ascending or descending chromatic scale, if the speed of the movement is increased or decreased.

Every manifestation of our life is accompanied by noise. The noise, therefore, is familiar to our ear, and has the power to conjure up life itself. Sound, alien to our life, always musical and a thing unto itself, an occasional but unnecessary element, has become to our ears what an overfamiliar face is to our eyes. Noise, however, reaching us in a confused and irregular way from the irregular confusion of our life, never entirely reveals itself to us, and keeps innumerable surprises in reserve. We are therefore certain that by selecting, coordinating and dominating all noises we will enrich men with a new and unexpected sensual pleasure.

Although it is characteristic of noise to recall us brutally to real life, THE ART OF NOISE MUST NOT LIMIT ITSELF TO IMITATIVE REPRODUCTION. It will achieve its most emotive power in the acoustic enjoyment, in its own right, that the artist's inspiration will extract from combined noises.

Here are the *6 families of noises* of the Futurist orchestra which we will soon set in motion mechanically:

1	2	3	4	5	6
Rumbles	Whistles	Whispers	Screeches	Noises	Voices of
Roars	Hisses	Murmurs	Creaks	obtained	animals
Explosions	Snorts	Mumbles	Rustles	by	and men:
Crashes		Grumbles	Buzzes	percussion	Shouts
Splashes		Gurgles	Crackles	on metal,	Screams
Booms			Scrapes	wood,	Groans
				skin,	Shrieks
				stone,	Howls
				terracotta,	Laughs
				etc.	Wheezes
					Sobs

In this inventory we have encapsulated the most characteristic of the fundamental noises; the others are merely the associations and combinations of these. THE RHYTHMIC MOVEMENTS OF A NOISE ARE INFINITE: JUST AS WITH TONE THERE IS ALWAYS A PREDOMINANT RHYTHM, but around this numerous other secondary rhythms can be felt.

CONCLUSIONS

1. Futurist musicians must continually enlarge and enrich the field of sounds. This corresponds to a need in our sensibility. We note, in fact, in the composers of genius, a tendency towards the most complicated

dissonances. As these move further and further away from pure sound, they almost achieve *noise-sound*. This need and this tendency cannot be satisfied except by the *adding* and the *substitution of noises for sounds.*

2. Futurist musicians must substitute for the limited variety of tones possessed by orchestral instruments today the infinite variety of tones of noises, reproduced with appropriate mechanisms.

3. The musician's sensibility, liberated from facile and traditional Rhythm, must find in noises the means of extension and renewal, given that every noise offers the union of the most diverse rhythms apart from the predominant one.

4. Since every noise contains a PREDOMINANT GENERAL TONE in its irregular vibrations it will be easy to obtain in the construction of instruments which imitate them a sufficiently extended variety of tones, semitones, and quarter-tones. This variety of tones will not remove the characteristic tone from each noise, but will amplify only its texture or extension.

5. The practical difficulties in constructing these instruments are not serious. Once the mechanical principle which produces the noise has been found, its tone can be changed by following the same general laws of acoustics. If the instrument is to have a rotating movement, for instance, we will increase or decrease the speed, whereas if it is not to have rotating movement the noise-producing parts will vary in size and tautness.

6. The new orchestra will achieve the most complex and novel aural emotions not by incorporating a succession of life-imitating noises, but by manipulating fantastic juxtapositions of these varied tones and rhythms. Therefore an instrument will have to offer the possibility of tone changes and varying degrees of amplification.

7. The variety of noises is infinite. If today, when we have perhaps a thousand different machines, we can distinguish a thousand different noises, tomorrow, as new machines multiply, we will be able to distinguish ten, twenty or THIRTY THOUSAND DIFFERENT NOISES, NOT MERELY IN A SIMPLY IMITATIVE WAY, BUT TO COMBINE THEM ACCORDING TO OUR IMAGINATION.

8. We therefore invite young musicians of talent to conduct a sustained observation of all noises, in order to understand the various rhythms of which they are composed, their principal and secondary tones. By comparing the various tones of noises with those of sounds, they will be convinced of the extent to which the former exceed the latter. This will afford not only an understanding, but also a taste and passion for noises. After

being conquered by Futurist eyes our multiplied sensibilities will at last hear with Futurist ears. In this way the motors and machines of our industrial cities will one day be consciously attuned, so that every factory will be transformed into an intoxicating orchestra of noises.

Dear Pratella, I submit these my statements to your Futurist genius, inviting your discussion. I am not a musician, I have therefore no acoustical predilections, nor any works to defend. I am a Futurist painter using a much loved art to project my determination to renew everything. And so, bolder than a professional musician could be, unconcerned by my apparent incompetence and convinced that all rights and all possibilities open up to daring, I have been able to initiate the great renewal of music by means of the Art of Noises.

5.11 GUILLAUME APOLLINAIRE

L'Antitradition futuriste

1913

L'ANTITRADITION FUTURISTE

Manifeste-synthèse

ABAS LEP*ominir* A*liminé* SS*korsusu*
otalo EIS*cramir* ME*nigme*

ce moteur à toutes tendances impressionnisme fauvisme cubisme expressionnisme pathétisme dramatisme orphisme paroxysme DYNAMISME PLASTIQUE MOTS EN LIBERTÉ INVENTION DE MOTS

DESTRUCTION

Pas de regrets

SUPPRESSION DE L'HISTOIRE | **Suppression** de la douleur poétique
des exotismes snobs
de la copie en art
des syntaxes *déjà condamnées par l'usage dans toutes les langues*
de l'adjectif
de la ponctuation
de l'harmonie typographique
des temps et personnes des verbes
de l'orchestre
de la forme théâtrale
du sublime artiste
du vers et de la strophe
des maisons
de la critique et de la satire
de l'intrigue dans les récits
de l'ennui

INFINITIF

CONSTRUCTION

1 Techniques sans cesse renouvelées ou rythmes

Continuité simultanéité en opposition au particularisme et à la division

LA PURETÉ

Littérature pure **Mots en liberté Invention de mots**
Plastique pure (5 sens)
Création invention prophétie
Description onomato-poétique
Musique totale et **Art des bruits**
Mimique universelle et Art des lumières
Machinisme Tour Eiffel Brooklyn et gratte-ciels
Polyglottisme
Civilisation pure
Nomadisme épique exploratorisme urbain **Art des voyages et des promenades**
Antigrâce
Frémissements directs à grands spectacles libres cirques music-halls etc.

LA VARIÉTÉ

2 Intuition vitesse ubiquité

Coups et blessures

Livre ou vie captivée ou phonocinematographie ou **Imagination sans fils**
Trémolisme continu ou onomalopées plus inventées qu'imitées
Danse travail ou chorégraphie pure
Langage véloce caractéristique impressionnant chanté sifflé mimé dansé marché couru
Droit des gens et guerre continuelle
Féminisme intégral ou différenciation innombrable des sexes
Humanité et appel à l'outr'homme
Matière ou **transcendantalisme physique**
Analogies et calembours tremplin lyrique et seule science des langues caīcot Caīcot Calcutta Iaīla Sophia la Sophī suffisant Uffisī officier officiel ô fossiles Aficionado Dona-Sol Donatello Donateur donne à tort torpilleur

ou ou ou flûte crapaud naissance des perles spremine

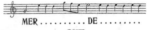

MER . . . . DE . . . .

aux

Critiques
Pédagogues
Professeurs
Musées
Quattrocentistes
Dixseptièmesiècllistes
Ruines
Patines
Historiens
Venise Versailles Pompeī Bruges Oxford Nuremberg Tolède Bénarès etc.
Défenseurs de paysages
Philologues

Essayistes
Néo et post
Bayreuth Florence Montmartre et Munich
Lexiques
Bongiottismes
Orientalismes
Dandysmes
Spiritualistes ou réalistes (sans sentiment de la réalité et de l'esprit)
Académismes

Les frères siamois
D'Annunzio et Rostand
Dante Shakespeare Tolstoī Goethe
Dilettantismes merdoyants
Eschyle et théâtre d'Orange
Inde Égypte Fiesole et la théosophie
Scientisme
Montaigne Wagner Beethoven Edgard Poe Walt Whitman et Baudelaire

ROSE

aux

Marinetti Picasso Boccioni Apollinaire Paul Fort Mercereau Max Jacob Carrà Delaunay Henri-Matisse Braque Depaquit Séverine Severini Derain Russolo Archipenko Pratella Balla F. Divoire N. Beauduin T. Varlet Buzzi Palazzeschi Maquaire Papini Soffici Folgore Govoni Montfort R. Fry Cavacchioli D'Alba Altomare Tridon Metzinger Gleizes Jastrebzoff Royère Canudo Salmon Castiaux Laurencin Aurel Agero Léger Valentine de Saint-Point Delmarie Kandinsky Strawinsky Herbin A. Billy G. Sauvebois Picabia Marcel Duchamp B. Cendrars Jouve H. M. Barzun G. Polti Mac Orlan F. Fleuret Jaudon Mandin R. Dalize M. Brésil F. Carco Rubiner Bétuda Manzella-Frontini A. Mazza T. Derème Giannattasio Tavolato De Gonzagues-Frick C. Larronde etc.

PARIS, le 29 Juin 1913, jour du Grand Prix, à 65 mètres au-dessus du Boul. S.-Germain

GUILLAUME APOLLINAIRE.
(202, BOULEVARD SAINT-GERMAIN - PARIS)

DIRECTION DU MOUVEMENT FUTURISTE
Corso Venezia, 61 - MILAN

Manifesto of Futurist Woman

(Response to F. T. Marinetti)

1912

> We will glorify war—the world's only hygiene—militarism, patriotism,
> the destructive gesture of freedom-bringers, beautiful ideas worth dying for,
> and scorn for woman.
>
> MARINETTI, "The Founding and Manifesto of Futurism"

Humanity is mediocre. The majority of women are neither superior nor inferior to the majority of men. They are all equal. They all merit the same scorn.

The whole of humanity has never been anything but the terrain of culture, source of the geniuses and heroes of both sexes. But in humanity as in nature there are some moments more propitious for such a flowering. In the summers of humanity, when the terrain is burned by the sun, geniuses and heroes abound.

We are at the beginning of a springtime; we are lacking in solar profusion, that is, a great deal of spilled blood.

Women are no more responsible than men for the way the really young, rich in sap and blood, are getting mired down.

It is absurd to divide humanity into men and women. It is composed only of *femininity* and *masculinity*. Every superman, every hero, no matter how epic, how much of a genius, or how powerful, is the prodigious expression of a race and an epoch only because he is composed at once of feminine and masculine elements, of femininity and masculinity: that is, a complete being.

Any exclusively virile individual is just a brute animal; any exclusively feminine individual is only a female.

It is the same way with any collectivity and any moment in humanity, just as it is with individuals. The fecund periods, when the most heroes and geniuses come forth from the terrain of culture in all its ebullience, are rich in masculinity and femininity.

Those periods that had only wars, with few representative heroes because the epic breath flattened them out, were exclusively virile periods; those that denied the heroic instinct and, turning toward the past, annihi-

lated themselves in dreams of peace, were periods in which femininity was
dominant.

We are living at the end of one of these periods. *What is most lacking in
women as in men is virility.*

That is why Futurism, even with all its exaggerations, is right.

To restore some virility to our races so benumbed in femininity, we have
to train them in virility even to the point of brute animality. But we have to
impose on everyone, men and women who are equally weak, a new dogma
of energy in order to arrive at a period of superior humanity.

Every woman ought to possess not only feminine virtues but virile ones,
without which she is just a female. Any man who has only male strength
without intuition is only a brute animal. But in the period of femininity in
which we are living, only the contrary exaggeration is healthy: *we have to
take the brute animal for a model.*

Enough of those women whose "arms with twining flowers resting on their
laps on the morning of departure" should be feared by soldiers; women as
nurses perpetuating weakness and age, domesticating men for their personal pleasures or their material needs! . . . Enough women who create children just for themselves, keeping them from any danger or adventure, that
is, any joy; keeping their daughter from love and their son from war! . . .
Enough of those women, the octopuses of the hearth, whose tentacles ex-
haust men's blood and make children anemic, *women in carnal love who wear
out every desire so it cannot be renewed!*

Women are Furies, Amazons, Semiramis, Joans of Arc, Jeanne Hachettes,
Judith and Charlotte Cordays, Cleopatras, and Messalinas: combative
women who fight more ferociously than males, lovers who arouse, destroy-
ers who break down the weakest and help select through pride or despair,
"despair through which the heart yields its fullest return."

Let the next wars bring forth heroines like that magnificent Catherine
Sforza, who, during the sack of her city, watching from the ramparts as her
enemy threatened the life of her son to force her surrender, heroically pointing to her sexual organ, cried loudly: "Kill him, I still have the mold to make
some more!"

Yes, "the world is rotting with wisdom," but by instinct, woman is not wise,
is not a pacifist, is not good. Because she is totally lacking in measure, she is
bound to become too wise, too pacifist, too good during a sleepy period of

humanity. Her intuition, her imagination are at once her strength and her weakness.

She is the individuality of the crowd: she parades the heroes, or if there are none, the imbeciles.

According to the apostle, the spiritual inspirer, woman, the carnal inspirer, immolates or takes care, causes blood to run or staunches it, is a warrior or a nurse. It's the same woman who, in the same period, according to the ambient ideas grouped around the day's event, lies down on the tracks to keep the soldiers from leaving for the war or then rushes to embrace the victorious champion.

So that is why no revolution should be without her. That is why, instead of scorning her, we should address her. She's the most fruitful conquest of all, the most enthusiastic, who, in her turn, will increase our followers.

But no feminism. Feminism is a political error. Feminism is a cerebral error of woman, an error that her instinct will recognize.

We must not give woman any of the rights claimed by feminists. To grant them to her would bring about not any of the disorders the Futurists desire but on the contrary an excess of order.

To give duties to woman is to have her lose all her fecundating power. Feminist reasonings and deductions will not destroy her primordial fatality: they can only falsify it, forcing it to make itself manifest through detours leading to the worst errors.

For centuries the feminine instinct has been insulted, only her charm and tenderness have been appreciated. Anemic man, stingy with his own blood, asks only that she be a nurse. She has let herself be tamed. But shout a new message at her, or some war cry, and then, joyously riding her instinct again, she will go in front of you toward unsuspected conquests.

When you have to use your weapons, she will polish them.

She will help you choose them. In fact, if she doesn't know how to discern genius because she relies on passing renown, she has always known how to rewarm the strongest, the victor, the one triumphant by his muscles and his courage. She can't be mistaken about this superiority imposing itself so brutally.

Let woman find once more her cruelty and her violence that make her attack the vanquished because they are vanquished, to the point of mutilating them. Stop preaching spiritual justice to her of the sort she has tried in vain. *Woman, become sublimely injust once more, like all the forces of nature!*

Delivered from all control, with your instinct retrieved, you will take your place among the Elements, opposite fatality to the conscious human will. Be the egoistic and ferocious mother, *jealously watching over her children*, have what are called all the rights over and duties toward them, *as long as they physically need your protection*.

Let man, freed from his family, lead his life of audacity and conquest, as soon as he has the physical strength for it, and in spite of his being a son and a father. The man who sows doesn't stop on the first row he fecunds.

In my *Poems of Pride* and in *Thirst and Mirages*, I have renounced Sentimentalism as a weakness to be scorned because it knots up the strength and makes it static.

Lust is a strength, because it destroys the weak, excites the strong to exert their energies, thus to renew themselves. Every heroic people is sensual. Woman is, for them, the most exalted trophy.

Woman should be mother or lover. Real mothers will always be mediocre lovers, and lovers, insufficient mothers, through their excess. Equal in front of life, these two women complete each other. The mother who receives the child makes the future with the past; the lover gives off desire, which leads toward the future.

LET'S CONCLUDE:

Woman who retains man through her tears and her sentimentality is inferior to the prostitute who incites her man, through braggery, to retain his domination over the lower depths of the cities with his revolver at the ready: at least she cultivates an energy that could serve better causes.

Woman, for too long diverted into morals and prejudices, go back to your sublime instinct, to violence, to cruelty.

For the fatal sacrifice of blood, while men are in charge of wars and battles, procreate, and among your children, as a sacrifice to heroism, take Fate's part. Don't raise them for yourself, that is, for their diminishment, but rather, in a wide freedom, for a complete expansion.

Instead of reducing man to the slavery of those *execrable sentimental needs*, incite your sons and your men to surpass themselves.

You are the ones who make them. You have all power over them.

You owe humanity its heroes. Make them!

5.13 Valentine de Saint-Point
Futurist Manifesto of Lust

1913

A reply to those dishonest journalists who twist phrases to make the Idea seem ridiculous;
to those women who only think what I have dared to say;
to those for whom Lust is still nothing but a sin;
to all those who in Lust can only see Vice, just as in Pride they see only vanity.

Lust, when viewed without moral preconceptions and as an essential part of life's dynamism, is a force.

Lust is not, any more than pride, a mortal sin for the race that is strong. Lust, like pride, is a virtue that urges one on, a powerful source of energy.

Lust is the expression of a being projected beyond itself. It is the painful joy of wounded flesh, the joyous pain of a flowering. And whatever secrets unite these beings, it is a union of flesh. It is the sensory and sensual synthesis that leads to the greatest liberation of spirit. It is the communion of a particle of humanity with all the sensuality of the earth. It is the panic shudder of a particle of the earth.

LUST IS THE QUEST OF THE FLESH FOR THE UNKNOWN, just as Cerebration is the spirit's quest for the unknown. Lust is the act of creating, it is Creation.

Flesh creates in the way that the spirit creates. In the eyes of the Universe their creation is equal. One is not superior to the other and creation of the spirit depends on that of the flesh.

We possess body and spirit. To curb one and develop the other shows weakness and is wrong. A strong man must realize his full carnal and spiritual potentiality. The satisfaction of their lust is the conquerors' due. After a battle in which men have died, IT IS NORMAL FOR THE VICTORS, PROVEN IN WAR, TO TURN TO RAPE IN THE CONQUERED LAND, SO THAT LIFE MAY BE RE-CREATED.

When they have fought their battles, soldiers seek sensual pleasures, in which their constantly battling energies can be unwound and renewed. The modern hero, the hero in any field, experiences the same desire and the same pleasure. The artist, that great universal medium, has the same need. And the exaltation of the initiates of those religions still sufficiently new to contain a tempting element of the unknown, is no more than sensuality diverted spiritually towards a sacred female image.

*   *   *

ART AND WAR ARE THE GREAT MANIFESTATIONS OF SENSUALITY; LUST
IS THEIR FLOWER. A people exclusively spiritual or a people exclusively carnal would be condemned to the same decadence—sterility.

LUST EXCITES ENERGY AND RELEASES STRENGTH. Pitilessly it drove
primitive man to victory, for the pride of bearing back to a woman the spoils
of the defeated. Today it drives the great men of business who direct the
banks, the press and international trade to increase their wealth by creating
centres, harnessing energies and exalting the crowds, to worship and glorify
with it the object of their lust. These men, tired but strong, find time for
lust, the principal motive force of their action and of the reactions caused
by their actions affecting multitudes and worlds.

Even among the new peoples where sensuality has not yet been released
or acknowledged, and who are neither primitive brutes nor the sophisticated representatives of the old civilizations, woman is equally the great gal-
vanizing principle to which all is offered. The secret cult that man has for her
is only the unconscious drive of a lust as yet barely woken. Amongst these
peoples as amongst the peoples of the north, but for different reasons, lust
is almost exclusively concerned with procreation. But lust, under whatever
aspects it shows itself, whether they are considered normal or abnormal, is
always the supreme spur.

The animal life, the life of energy, the life of the spirit, sometimes demand a respite. And effort for effort's sake calls inevitably for effort for pleasure's sake. These efforts are not mutually harmful but complementary, and
realize fully the total being.

For heroes, for those who create with the spirit, for dominators of all
fields, lust is the magnificent exaltation of their strength. For every being it
is a motive to surpass oneself with the simple aim of self-selection, of being
noticed, chosen, picked out.

Christian morality alone, following on from pagan morality, was fatally
drawn to consider lust as a weakness. Out of the healthy joy which is the
flowering of the flesh in all its power it has made something shameful and
to be hidden, a vice to be denied. It has covered it with hypocrisy, and this
has made a sin of it.

WE MUST STOP DESPISING DESIRE, this attraction at once delicate and
brutal between two bodies, of whatever sex, two bodies that want each
other, striving for unity. We must stop despising Desire, disguising it in the
pitiful clothes of old and sterile sentimentality.

It is not lust that disunites, dissolves and annihilates. It is rather the mes-
merizing complications of sentimentality, artificial jealousies, words that

inebriate and deceive, the rhetoric of parting and eternal fidelities, literary nostalgia—all the histrionics of love.

WE MUST GET RID OF THE ILL-OMENED DEBRIS OF ROMANTICISM, counting daisy petals, moonlight duets, heavy endearments, false hypocritical modesty. When beings are drawn together by a physical attraction, let them—instead of talking only of the fragility of their hearts—dare to express their desires, the inclinations of their bodies, and to anticipate the possibilities of joy and disappointment in their future carnal union.

Physical modesty, which varies according to time and place, has only the ephemeral value of a social virtue.

WE MUST FACE UP TO LUST IN FULL CONSCIOUSNESS. We must make of it what a sophisticated and intelligent being makes of himself and of his life; WE MUST MAKE LUST INTO A WORK OF ART. To allege unwariness or bewilderment in order to explain an act of love is hypocrisy, weakness and stupidity.

We should desire a body consciously, like any other thing.

Love at first sight, passion or failure to think, must not prompt us to be constantly giving ourselves, nor to take beings, as we are usually inclined to do due to our inability to see into the future. We must choose intelligently. Directed by our intuition and will, we should compare the feelings and desires of the two partners and avoid uniting and satisfying any that are unable to complement and exalt each other.

Equally consciously and with the same guiding will, the joys of this coupling should lead to the climax, should develop its full potential, and should permit to flower all the seeds sown by the merging of two bodies. Lust should be made into a work of art, formed like every work of art, both instinctively and consciously.

WE MUST STRIP LUST OF ALL THE SENTIMENTAL VEILS THAT DISFIGURE IT. These veils were thrown over it out of mere cowardice, because smug sentimentality is so satisfying. Sentimentality is comfortable and therefore demeaning.

In one who is young and healthy, when lust clashes with sentimentality, lust is victorious. Sentiment is a creature of fashion, lust is eternal. Lust triumphs, because it is the joyous exaltation that drives one beyond oneself, the delight in possession and domination, the perpetual victory from which the perpetual battle is born anew, the headiest and surest intoxication of conquest. And as this certain conquest is temporary, it must be constantly won anew.

Lust is a force, in that it refines the spirit by bringing to white heat the excitement of the flesh. The spirit burns bright and clear from a healthy, strong flesh, purified in the embrace. Only the weak and the sick sink into the mire and are diminished. And lust is a force in that it kills the weak and exalts the strong, aiding natural selection.

Lust is a force, finally, in that it never leads to the insipidity of the definite and the secure, doled out by soothing sentimentality. Lust is the eternal battle, never finally won. After the fleeting triumph, even during the ephemeral triumph itself, reawakening dissatisfaction spurs a human being, driven by an orgiastic will, to expand and surpass himself.

Lust is for the body what an ideal is for the spirit—the magnificent Chimaera, that one ever clutches at but never captures, and which the young and the avid, intoxicated with the vision, pursue without rest.

LUST IS A FORCE.

Acmeism

Together with Anna Akhmatova, Nicolay Gumilev, and others grouped around the magazine *Apollon*, Ossip Mandelstam aimed at an Apollonian sharpness and clarity. Their sense of craft led them to form the Guild of Poets, opposing what they found too vague about the soulful musicality of the often esoteric symbolism that had previously penetrated the art and literary scenes in Russia as in the rest of Europe. The Modernist compactness of imagery that is characteristic of their writing and its phonic density has some connection with neoclassicizing theories and classical themes and can be allied to Marianne Moore's "compacity," that dense texture and nonwastefulness much desired in much modern poetics and poetry.

5.14 OSSIP MANDELSTAM

The Morning of Acmeism (*parts I–IV*)

1913

I

Amidst the immense emotional excitement surrounding works of art, it is desirable that talk about art be marked by the greatest restraint. For the immense majority, a work of art is enticing only insofar as it illuminates the artist's perception of the world. For the artist, however, his perception of the world is a tool and an instrument, like a hammer in the hands of a stonemason, and the only thing that is real is the work itself.

To live is the artist's highest self-esteem. He wants no other paradise than being, and when he's told about reality, he only smiles bitterly, because he knows the infinitely more convincing reality of art. The spectacle of a mathematician proclaiming the square of a ten-digit number without stopping to think about it fills us with a certain astonishment. Too often, however, we overlook the fact that the poet raises a phenomenon to its tenth power, and the modest exterior of a work of art often deceives us concerning the prodigiously condensed reality that it possesses. In poetry this reality is the word as such. Just now, for example, while expressing my thought as accurately as possible, yet not at all in poetic form, I am speaking essentially with the consciousness, not with the word. Deaf-mutes understand one another very well, and railroad signals perform their quite complicated assignments without recourse to help from the word. Thus, if one is to regard the sense as the content, one must regard everything else in the word as mechanical ballast that only impedes the swift transmission of the thought. The "word as such" was slow to be born. Gradually, one after the other, all the elements of the word were drawn into the concept of form; only the conscious sense, the Logos, is regarded even to this day erroneously and arbitrarily as the content. From this needless honor, Logos only loses; Logos requires only an equal footing with the other elements of the word. Our Futurist, who could not cope with the conscious sense as creative material, frivolously threw it overboard and in essence repeated the same crude error as his predecessors.

For the Acmeists the conscious sense of the word, the Logos, is just as splendid a form as music for the Symbolists.

And if, among the Futurists, the word as such still crawls on all fours, in Acmeism it has for the first time assumed the more dignified upright position and entered upon the Stone Age of its existence.

II

The cutting edge of Acmeism is not the stiletto and not the pinprick of Decadence. Acmeism is for those who, seized by the spirit of building, do not meekly renounce their gravity, but joyfully accept it in order to arouse and make use of the forces architecturally dormant in it. The architect says: I build. That means, I am right. The consciousness of our own rightness is what we value most in poetry, and scornfully discarding the pick-up-sticks of the Futurists, for whom there is no higher pleasure than to hook a tough word with a crochet hook, we are introducing the Gothic into the relationships of words, just as Sebastian Bach established it in music.

What kind of idiot would agree to build if he did not believe in the reality of his material, the resistance of which he must overcome? A cobblestone in the hands of an architect is transformed into substance, and the man for whom the sound of a chisel splitting stone is not a metaphysical proof was not born to build. Vladimir Soloviev used to experience a special kind of prophetic horror before gray Finnish boulders. The mute eloquence of the granite block disturbed him like an evil enchantment. But Tiutchev's stone that "rolled down from the mountain to the valley floor, torn loose itself, or flung by a sentient hand," is the word. The voice of matter sounds in this unexpected fall like articulate speech. To this call one can answer only with architecture. Reverently the Acmeists pick up the mysterious Tiutchevan stone and lay it in the foundation of their building.

The stone thirsted as it were for another being. It was itself the discoverer of the dynamic potential concealed within it, as if it were asking to be let into the "groined arch" to participate in the joyous cooperative action of its fellows.

III

The Symbolists were bad stay-at-homes. They loved voyages; yet they felt bad, ill at ease, in the cage of their own organisms and in that universal cage which Kant constructed with the help of his categories.

The first condition for building successfully is a genuine piety before the three dimensions of space—to look on the world not as a burden or as an unfortunate accident, but as a God-given palace. Really, what is one to say about an ungrateful guest who lives off his host, takes advantage of his hospitality, yet all the while despises him in his soul and thinks only of how to put something over on him. One can build only in the name of the "three dimensions," because they are the conditions for all architecture. That is why an architect has to be a good stay-at-home, and the Symbolists were bad architects. To build means to fight against emptiness, to hypnotize space. The fine arrow of the Gothic belltower is angry, because the whole idea of it is to stab the sky, to reproach it for being empty.

IV

We tacitly understand a man's individuality, that which makes him a person, and that which forms part of the far more significant concept of the organism. Acmeists share a love for the organism and for organization with the Middle Ages, a period of physiological genius. In its pursuit of refinement the nineteenth century lost the secret of genuine complexity. That which in the thirteenth century seemed a logical development of the concept of the organism—the Gothic cathedral—now has the esthetic effect of something monstrous; Notre Dame is a celebration of physiology, its Dionysian orgy. We do not wish to divert ourselves with a stroll in a "forest of symbols," because we have a more virgin, a denser forest—divine physiology, the infinite complexity of our own dark organism.

The Middle Ages, while defining man's specific gravity in its own way, felt and acknowledged it for each individual quite independently of his merits. The title *maître* was used readily and without hesitation. The most humble artisan, the very least clerk, possessed the secret of down-to-earth respect, of the devout dignity so characteristic of that epoch. Yes, Europe passed through the labyrinth of a fine tracery-work culture, when abstract being, unadorned personal existence, was valued as a heroic feat. Hence the aristocratic intimacy that links all people, so alien in spirit to the "equality and fraternity" of the Great Revolution. There is no equality, no competition— there is the complicity of those united in a conspiracy against emptiness and nonbeing.

Love the existence of the thing more than the thing itself and your own being more than yourself—that is the highest commandment of Acmeism.

The Mezzanine of Poetry

Short-lived, the Mezzanine of Poetry began with the "Overture" (5.17), a witty invitation issued by Lev Zak, writing anonymously for all of them (he had three personalities and two pen names: Krhisanf for poetry, M. M. Rossiianskii[!] for the theory of the "word-image," and himself as an artist). Among the other members were Konstantin Bol'shakov and Riurik Ivnev, as well as Vadim Shershenevich (translator of Marinetti himself).

5.15 GRAAL-ARELSKY [Stepan Stepanovich Petrov]
Egopoetry in Poetry

1912

Life was born out of a primeval mist. Bright stars flared up in the overturned chalice of the universe. Dark planets began to close the circle of their invisible orbits. Motion was born, time was born, man was born. In his conception, nature was reflected vividly and figuratively, incomprehensibly and divinely. Fear of death, which so unexpectedly breaks the thread of life, and the desire to somehow prolong his short existence, compelled man to create religion and art. Death created poetry. Poetry and religion have been inseparably linked throughout the ages, and indeed they will be until heaven finally descends to earth. But, from the very earliest period in man's life, the idea of a universal synthesis arose in his consciousness. He strove to find that invisible thread which could join the credos of all peoples. A whole series of philosophical teachings pass before us—those of Egypt, Greece, and Rome: of the North, still silently sleeping in the azure snows; and of the brightly colored and ecstatically bursting East. Egypt recognizes its powerlessness. The deserts fill with pyramids. All is ashes. Everything passes, and everything repeats itself once more. The East creates Nirvana; Greece, Beauty. Three poles. They cannot come together and unite. And then, in the shady gardens of Galilee, amidst azure lakes and a quiet bright happiness, Christ is born. He says that love is that very thread which all have sought in vain.

Centuries pass, as before; the orbits close and, as before, the question remains unresolved. Science comes upon the stage. It collects facts and erects upon them a temple of Reason. The building grows. The bricks are put in place carefully and quickly. Absolute reality. Cogito ergo sum. But again centuries pass. Science turns out to be relative, like everything else. It doesn't have what it takes to pass through the centuries without changing. Reason is only a camera. We can recognize only that world which is formed in our consciousness, apprehended by our five senses. The world which rules in our intellect is not real, but imaginary. If we survey all of man's searchings we notice the following fact: man strives to transform his ideals into the "unearthly," into a universal mystery. Thinking that apprehension of the "ineffable" requires the death of nature, he tries to rise above that egoism which nature has put within him. He tries to graft into himself an altruism which is alien. It is called Culture. All of history lies before us. Nature created us. Only She should rule us in our actions and efforts. She placed egoism inside of us; we should develop it. Egoism unites all of us, because we are all egoists. There are differences only in stages of biologic evolution. One man requires happiness for himself, another for those around him, a third for all of humanity. The essence always remains the same. We cannot feel ourselves to be happy if there is suffering around us. Thus, for our own personal happiness we require the happiness of others. In the universe there is nothing moral or immoral, there is only Beauty, world harmony, and the force of dissonance which is opposed to it. In its searchings, poetry need be guided only by these two forces. The aim of Egopoetry is the glorification of egoism as the only true and vital intuition.

God is eternity. Man, in being born, is separated from it. But in him there remain those very laws which lead life on earth toward perfect Beauty. The soul is life. Tossing reason aside, we must strive to fuse ourselves with nature, dissolving into her transparently and infinitely. That feeling of clear enlightenment and understanding outside of Reason, that universal harmony, is intuition. All roads lead to true happiness, to fusion with eternity. Every new dawn speaks to people of his happiness and, like a bright road, calls them to the Sun.

5.16 GRAAL-ARELSKY [Stepan Stepanovich Petrov]

The Tables

1912

I. The Glorification of Egoism:
   1. The Unit is Egoism.
   2. The Deity is the Unit.
   3. Human is a fraction of God.
   4. Birth is a fractioning from Eternity.
   5. Life is the fraction outside of Eternity.
   6. Death is reintegration of the fraction.
   7. Human is Egoist.
II. Intuition. Theosophy.
III. Thought until madness: madness is individual.
IV. The prism of style—restoration of the spectrum of thought.
V. The Soul is Truth.

       The Rectorate:

           Igor-Severyanin
           Constantine Olimpov (C. C. Fofanov)
           George Ivanov
           Graal-Arelsky

5.17 LEV ZACK

Overture

1913

Darling! Please, come to the vernissage of our Mezzanine!

Both our landlady and we, the tenants, eagerly request your presence. We are all ready for the reception—the rooms are lit up, the table is set, the fireplaces are glimmering—and we are waiting for you. Of course, to come or not to come depends on you. We would be very happy if you came and liked it here, at our place; and perhaps we would be sad for a few days, and would be angry at each other if you did not feel at ease in the rooms of our mezzanine; but, in any case, please do not be too haughty, and most of all do not tease us: we all have a terribly vulnerable sense of self-esteem. By this invitation to our Mezzanine, we want to do something pleasant for you and for ourselves—wouldn't it be a pleasure for you to meet our wonderful, charming landlady, and spend some time in her company? Our rooms look so cozy to us, and our landlady so divine, that we simply cannot keep from showing them, and her, to you: we need to share our delight with someone, otherwise our souls will burst like bottles of champagne which have been kept at an excessively warm temperature. I have to confess that in general we are all a little crazy; in other words, I want to say that all the tenants of the Mezzanine are terrible eccentrics, but this is of no importance whatsoever. One of them, for example, fancied himself a Pierrot with an unpowdered face, and so he stuck a beauty spot in the shape of a heart to his right cheek and tried to convince everyone that all misfortune comes from the fact that people do not tell enough lies. Another is convinced that he conquered a big nation with the stroke of a pen, and I could tell you about the oddities of all the others if I thought it important. But the fact is that this is not the most important thing. The most important thing is that all the tenants of our Mezzanine are hopelessly in love with their landlady, and this love fills their souls to the brim. In the morning, when the Most Charming One is still asleep, all of them keep a vigil by the door of her bedroom, in order not to be late in greeting her: "Good morning," and to have the chance, as soon as she comes out, to present her with a large rose. During the day, when she is busy with domestic chores, they all run after her around the Mezzanine, pick up the handkerchief she has dropped, stealthily kiss the edge of her dress, loudly pay her the wittiest compliments, help her in the kitchen, look her in the eyes, shiver at every movement she makes, gain hope, lose hope, feel cheerful, feel sad, feel their hearts sinking, feel they are dying of tenderness, of a very sad tenderness, forever. And even if this tenderness is very sad, we are all happy because we know it, and because thanks to our almost hopeless love we proudly look at things from the top of a very high mountain. It's true, our love is almost completely hopeless: the Most Charming One is unattainable, and when we accompany her in the evening to her bedroom door, she answers our "good night" with a gracious smile and enters her bedroom alone, a bedroom which none of the tenants of the Mezzanine has as yet seen, and they all tiptoe away in different directions, and each one, loving and yearning, retires to his room, to worship her in his own way. And yet, our love is not completely hopeless, only almost hopeless: we know that there were some that our landlady loved, and therefore each one of us still has the very smallest of hopes. Of course, we don't dare—we absolutely don't dare—think that one evening the Most Charming One might invite one of us into her bedroom, but everyone nurses the thought of being worthy of her kiss. She has allowed some of us to kiss her hand—today, at the vernissage, you will be able to tell those happy ones: probably, they will be talking a lot of nonsense, but in such a tone that you will feel like covering them with kisses. By the way, if you, darling, come today to the vernissage, you will see those friends of the Mezzanine who are said to be in especially high favor with the landlady. I assure you that we are not jealous in the least, on the contrary, we have for them the greatest esteem—completely unlike our neighbors, who at times wave a handkerchief from their window to our landlady, trying to entice her to their place, and who at all costs want to dispel the rumor that these friends of the Mezzanine have won the attention of the Most Charming One. And indeed, why shouldn't you come to the vernissage, anyway? After all, you have not seen our landlady for such a long time, and since then she has changed considerably, although she has not aged a bit, on the contrary, she looks younger. And that last time, did you take a good look at her face? You know, you walk around all the time arm in arm with "superficialness," darling. As for us, the tenants of the Mezzanine, it will be more intriguing than frightening to meet us: it won't be frightening because we are very nice people, and we never treat our guests worse than they treat us; it will be intriguing because we are somehow different from everybody else. We love what is near, and not what is far away. We talk about what we know, and not about what we have only heard of from others. From the windows of our Mezzanine we see the baker's house, and, darling, we won't tell you a story about an ancient castle with magnificent towers, and if we are sad we would rather compare our sadness to a penknife than to the stormy ocean—where is that ocean? We have not seen it, and even if we had, we couldn't fall in love with it, which is to say we couldn't understand it as well as we do the rooms of our Mezzanine. We would rather compare the ocean to a tureen full of seething broth than a tureen to the ocean. I can see, darling, that these words have already scared you, and you are saying: "*Fi donc,* how prosaic this all is," but we, the tenants of the Mezzanine, are convinced that the baker's house is in no way less poetic than an ancient castle, and that the broth is by no means worse than the ocean. The image of the Most Charming One, which each one of us has locked in his soul, makes all things, all thoughts, and all passions equally poetic. We experience the same things as all lovers do. A man in love walks along the street and everything he sees, in some way or other, reminds him of his beloved; the same happens to us: in everything we see the face of our charming Poetry. Yes, darling, we are greater romantics than others, we are romantics from head to toe. Therefore, don't be afraid, and come to the vernissage of our Mezzanine. All the outside, all the street noise, all the trivial human actions, the feelings, the thoughts trickle through the glass window panes and turn into lofty music. We will treat you to a dinner which, while not copious, will be refined in its simplicity; and, in refined and simple dress, the Most Charming One will come out to meet you.

> Stop the foolish
>> Pranks and spleen.
> Get candles, please,
>> and light them quick.
> Meet on the stairs
>> The vernissage guests!
> If you're too lazy,
>> We'll tell our lady.
> Hello! Here are our rooms —
>> Dining and living.
> Be our guest and don't forget
>> The vernissage of the Mezzanine!

Cubo-Futurism (The Hylea Group)

This Russian variety of Futurism is unlike the Italian variety, known for its emphasis on the interpenetration of "force lines" and objects animate and inanimate: so a house is penetrated by a street, a woman's cheek by a passing bus. Cubo-Futurism adopts, rather, the Cubist technique made famous by Pablo Picasso, Georges Braque, and Juan Gris, that of seeing one object from many different perspectives at once.

Cubo-Futurism, with its distinctive attitude, should not be confused with other Russian Futurisms. Kasimir Malevich's setting and lighting for the 1913 play *Victory over the Sun*, Cubo-Futurist in its inspiration, was, for instance, the contrary of the kind of Neoprimitivism exemplified by the Rayonists Natalya Goncharova and Mikhail Larionov in their opera-ballet *Le Coq d'or* of 1914, choreographed by Michel Fokine. Futurisms may have proliferated in Russia, as in Italy, but they were diverse in nature and should be celebrated as such.

5.18 DAVID BURLIUK *and others*

Slap in the Face of Public Taste

1912

To the readers of our New First Unexpected.

We alone are the *face* of *our* Time. Through us the horn of time blows in the art of the word.

The past is too tight. The Academy and Pushkin are less intelligible than hieroglyphics.

Throw Pushkin, Dostoevsky, Tolstoy, etc., etc. overboard from the Ship of Modernity.

He who does not forget his *first* love will not recognize his last.

Who, trustingly, would turn his last love toward Balmont's perfumed lechery? Is this the reflection of today's virile soul?

Who, faintheartedly, would fear tearing from warrior Bryusov's black tuxedo the paper armorplate? Or does the dawn of unknown beauties shine from it?

Wash Your hands which have touched the filthy slime of the books written by those countless Leonid Andreyevs.

All those Maxim Gorkys, Kuprins, Bloks, Sologubs, Remizovs, Averchenkos, Chornys, Kuzmins, Bunins, etc. need only a dacha on the river. Such is the reward fate gives tailors.

From the heights of skyscrapers we gaze at their insignificance! . . .

We *order* that the poets' *rights* be revered:

1. To enlarge the *scope* of the poet's vocabulary with arbitrary and derivative words (Word-novelty).
2. To feel an insurmountable hatred for the language existing before their time.
3. To push with horror off their proud brow the Wreath of cheap fame that You have made from bathhouse switches.
4. To stand on the rock of the word "we" amidst the sea of boos and outrage.

And if *for the time being* the filthy stigmas of Your "Common sense" and "good taste" are still present in our lines, these same lines *for the first time* already glimmer with the Summer Lightening of the New Coming Beauty of the Self-sufficient (self-centered) Word.

DAVID BURLIUK, ALEXEY KRUCHENYKH,

VLADIMIR MAYAKOVSKY, VELIMIR KHLEBNIKOV

We, Too, Want Meat!

1914

Soldiers, I envy you!
You have it good!

Here on the chipped wall is the five-fingered shrapnel imprint made of bits of human brain. How clever to attach to the stupid battlefield hundreds of severed human heads.

Yes, yes, yes, life's more interesting for you!

You do not have to think about the twenty kopeks you owe Pushkin and about why Yablonovsky writes his articles.

Anyway, this is not the point!

Verses, verses, a billion verses (this was yesterday).

Two billion poets' feet started shuffling happily in the entrance hall, but. . . .

In came Mayakovsky—

And why do many fearfully conceal the sexless children of the cachetic muses?

Let's get it straight.

People say that I am a Futurist?

What's a Futurist? I don't know. I never heard of such a thing. There have never been any.

You heard this tale from Mademoiselle Criticism. I'll show "her"!

You know, there are good galoshes, the brand's "Triangle."

And yet, not a single critic would wear them.

The name scares them.

Galoshes, they would say, must be of an elongated-oval shape, but here it says "Triangle." They'll pinch the feet.

What's a Futurist—it's a brand name like "Triangle."

Under this label performed even the one who embroidered these verses:

Yesterday I was reading, Turgenev
once again fascinated me,

as well as those who shouted, like flagellants in a state of ecstasy,

Dyr bul shchyl . . .

And moreover, the brand "Futurist" is not of our making. We called our first books—*A Trap for Judges, Slap in the Face of Public Taste, The Missal of the Three*—simply collections by the Literary Company.

It was the newspapers that gave us the name "Futurists." Anyway, why get all worked up. It's funny! If Vavila had shouted: "Why am I not Eugene?" what difference would it make?

Futurism for us young poets is a toreador's red *muleta*, we need it only for the bulls (poor bulls!—I compared them to the critics).

I have never been to Spain, but I think that it would not occur to a toreador to wave his red *muleta* in front of a friend who is wishing him good morning. We, too, have no reason to nail a sign to the goodnatured face of some village bard.

In all our demonstrations, this is what came first on our banner:

"Every creative work is free."

Come!

We will meet everyone fairly. But only if the fat figure of Apukhtin does not loom between their eyes and reality, only if their tongue is clean and not corroded by the phrases of the "venerable ones."

Today's poetry is the poetry of struggle.

Every word must be, like the soldier in an army, made of healthy meat, of red meat!

Those who have it—come to us!

So what if we were unfair.

When you are speeding through hundreds of pursuing enemies, you cannot be sentimental: "Oh, we ran over a chicken."

Our cruelty gave us the strength never to surrender to life, to carry on our banner.

Freedom to create words and from words.

Hatred for the language that existed before us.

To reject with indignation the wreath of cheap fame made of bathhouse switches.

To stand on the rock of the word "we" amidst the sea of boos and outrage.

5.20 Vladimir Mayakovsky

A Drop of Tar

1915

A SPEECH TO BE DELIVERED
AT THE FIRST CONVENIENT OCCASION

Ladies and Gentlemen!

This year is a year of deaths: almost every day the newspapers sob loudly in grief about somebody who has passed away before his time. Every day, with syrupy weeping the brevier wails over the huge number of names slaughtered by Mars. How noble and monastically severe today's newspapers look. They are dressed in the black mourning garb of the obituaries, with the crystal-like tear of a necrology in their glittering eyes. That's why it has been particularly upsetting to see these same newspapers, usually ennobled by grief, note with indecent merriment one death that involved me very closely.

When the critics, harnessed in tandem, carried along the dirty road—the road of the printed word—the coffin of Futurism, the newspapers trumpeted for weeks: "ho, ho, ho! serves it right! take it away! finally!" (Concerned alarm in the audience: "What do you mean, died? Futurism died? You're kidding.")

Yes, it died.

For one year now instead of Futurism, verbally flaming, barely maneuvering between truth, beauty, and the police station, the most boring octogenarians of the Kogan-Aikhenvald type creep up on the stage of auditoriums. For one year now, the auditoriums present only the most boring logic, demonstrations of trivial truths, instead of the cheerful sound of glass pitchers against empty heads.

Gentlemen! Do you really feel no sorrow for that extravagant young fellow with shaggy red hair, a little silly, a bit ill-mannered, but always, oh! always, daring and fiery? On the other hand, how can you understand youth? The young people to whom we are dear will not soon return from the battlefield; but you, who have remained here with quiet jobs in newspaper offices or other similar businesses; you, who are too rickety to carry a weapon, you, old bags crammed with wrinkles and gray hair, you are preoccupied with figuring out the smoothest possible way to pass on to the next world and not with the destiny of Russian art.

But, you know, I myself do not feel too sorry about the deceased, although for different reasons.

Bring back to mind the first gala publication of Russian Futurism, titled with that resounding "slap in the face of public taste." What remained particularly memorable of that fierce scuffle were three blows, in the form of three vociferous statements from our manifesto.

1. Destroy the all-canons freezer which turns inspiration into ice.
2. Destroy the old language, powerless to keep up with life's leaps and bounds.
3. Throw the old masters overboard from the ship of modernity.

As you see, there isn't a single building here, not a single comfortably designed corner, only destruction, anarchy. This made philistines laugh, as if it were the extravagant idea of some insane individuals, but in fact it turned out to be "a devilish intuition" which is realized in the stormy today. The war, by expanding the borders of nations and of the brain, forces one to break through the frontiers of what yesterday was unknown.

Artist! is it for you to catch the onrushing cavalry with a fine net of contour lines? Repin! Samokish! Get your pails out of the way—the paint will spill all over!

Poet! don't place the mighty conflict of iambs and trochees in a rocking chair—the chair will flip over!

Fragmentation of words, word renewal! So many new words, and first among them Petrograd, and conductress! die, Severyanin! Is it really for the Futurists to shout that old literature is forgotten? Who would still hear behind the Cossack whoop the trill of Bryusov's mandolin! Today, everyone is a Futurist. The entire nation is Futurist.

FUTURISM HAS *SEIZED* RUSSIA IN A DEATH GRIP.

Not being able to see Futurism in front of you and to look into yourselves, you started shouting about its death. Yes! Futurism, as a specific group, died, but like a flood it overflows into all of you.

But once Futurism has died as the idea of select individuals, we do not need it any more. We consider the first part of our program of destruction to be completed. So don't be surprised if today you see in our hands architectural sketches instead of clownish rattles, and if the voice of Futurism, which yesterday was still soft from sentimental reverie, today is forged in the copper of preaching.

Zaoum

A transnational language, starting from "zero," Zaoum was invented by Victor Khlebnikov and Alexey Kruchenykh in Russia and subsequently gained some notoriety with Iliazd (Ilia Zdanevitch) in Paris. In its radical departure from sense as well as sentiment, it can be considered an originating move of concrete poetry in all its forms, as much of a break with ordinary language as was Stéphane Mallarmé's "Un coup de Dés" (A Throw of Dice) and his desire to "give a purer sense to the words of the tribe."

Kruchenykh emphasizes the importance of African art and the "primitive coarseness" that eliminates the traditional distance between the world and the human being. Futurist poetry, according to him, should be joyous — the opposite of the vague gloom of Symbolism. He aimed at "subjective objectivity," loving every contradiction. Words newly disposed, read backward, all the techniques of newness showed the Zaoumist delight in innovation.

The documents of Zaoum have a style and a zing to them that Paul Schmidt's brilliant translations capture for a lasting language, even in English.

5.21 ANONYMOUS

Bald Mountain Zaum-Poem

1836

1

Kumara
Nich, nich, pasalam, bada.
Eschochomo, lawassa, schibboda.
Kumara
A.a.o. — o.o.o. — i.i.i. — e.e.e. — u.u.u. — ye.ye.ye.
Aa, la ssob, li li ssob lu lu ssob.
Schunschan
Wichoda, kssara, gujatun, gujatun, etc.

2

io, ia, — o — io, ia, zok, io, ia,
pazzo! io, ia, pipazzo!

Sookatjema, soossuoma, nikam, nissam, scholda.
Paz, paz, paz, paz, paz, paz, paz, paz!
Pinzo, pinzo, pinzo, dynsa.
Schono, tschikodam, wikgasa, mejda.
Bouopo, chondyryamo, bouopo, galpi.
Ruachado, rassado, ryssado, zalyemo.
io, ia, o, io, ia, zolk. io nye zolk, io ia zolk.

5.22 VICTOR KHLEBNIKOV AND ALEXEY KRUCHENYKH

The Letter as Such

1913

No one argues any more about the word as such, they even agree with us. But their agreement does no good at all, because all those who are so busy talking after the fact about the word say nothing about the letter. They were all born blind!

The word is still not valued, the word is still merely tolerated.

Why don't they just go ahead and dress it up in gray prison clothes? You've seen the letters of their words—strung out in straight lines with shaved heads, resentful, each one just like all the others—gray, colorless—not letters at all, just stamped-out marks. And yet if you ask a write-wright, a real writer, he'll tell you that a word written in one particular handwriting or set in a particular typeface is totally distinct from the same word in different lettering.

You certainly wouldn't dress up all your lady friends in standard issue overalls! Damn right you wouldn't, they'd spit in your face if you did. But not the word—the word can't say a thing. Because it is dead—martyred like Boris and Gleb. Your words are all born dead.

You're worse than Sviatopolk the martyr-maker!

Two circumstances obtain:

1. Our mood alters our handwriting as we write.
2. Our handwriting, distinctively altered by our mood, conveys that mood to the reader independently of the words. We must therefore consider the question of written signs—visible, or simply palpable, that a blind

man could touch. It's clearly not necessary that the author himself should be the one who writes a handwritten book; indeed, it would probably be better for him to entrust the task to an artist. But until today there have been no such books. The first ones have now been issued by the Futurians, for example: *Old-Time Love,* copied over for printing by Mikhail Larionov; *Blow-Up,* by Nikolai Kulbin and others; *A Duck's Nest,* by Olga Rozanova. About these books it is finally possible to say: every letter is letter perfect.

It's strange that neither Balmont nor Blok—to say nothing of those who would seem to be the most up to date of our contemporaries—has ever thought of giving his offspring to an artist instead of a typesetter.

When a piece is copied over, by someone else or even by the author himself, that person must reexperience himself during the act of recopying, otherwise the piece loses all the rightful magic that was conferred upon it by handwriting at the moment of its creation, in the "wild storm of inspiration."

5.23 VICTOR KHLEBNIKOV AND
ALEXEY KRUCHENYKH
The Word as Such

1913

In 1908 we were preparing materials for *A Jam for Judges I;* some of it wound up in that book, some of it in *The Impressionists' Studio.* In both books V. Khlebnikov, the Burliuks, S. Miasoedov, and others indicated a new path for art: the word was developed as itself alone.

Henceforth a work of art could consist of a *single word,* and simply by a skillful alteration of that word the fullness and expressivity of artistic form might be attained.

But this is an expressivity of another kind. The work of art was both perceived and criticized (at least they had some premonition of this) merely as a word.

A work of art is the art of the word.

From which it followed automatically that tendentiousness and literary pretensions of any kind were to be expelled from works of art.

Our approximation was the machine—impassive, passionate.

The Italians caught a whiff of these Russian ideas and began to copy from us like schoolboys, making imitation art.

They had absolutely no sense of verbal matters before 1912 (when their big collection came out), and none after.

But of course the Italians had started with tendentiousness. Like Pushkin's little devil, they sang their own praises and claimed responsibility for everything contemporary, when what was called for was not sermonizing about it but to leap onto the back of the contemporary age and ride off full speed, to offer it as the grand summation of all their work.

After all, a sermon that doesn't derive from the art itself is nothing but wood painted to look like metal. And who would trust a weapon like that? These Italians have turned out to be noisy self-promotors, but inarticulate pipsqueaks as artists.

They ask us about our ideal, about emotional content? We rule out both destructiveness and accomplishment, we are neither fanatics nor monks—all Talmuds are equally destructive for the word-worker; he remains face to face, always and ultimately, with the word (itself) alone.

5.24 Victor Khlebnikov *and others*
The Trumpet of the Martians
1916

People of Earth, hear this!

The human brain until now has been hopping around on three legs (the three axes of location)! We intend to refurrow the human brain and to give this puppy dog a fourth leg—namely, the axis of TIME.

Poor lame puppy! Your obscene barking will no longer grate on our ears!

People from the past were no smarter than us; they thought the sails of government could be constructed only for the axes of space.

But now we appear, wrapped in a cloak of nothing but victories, and begin to build a union of youth with its sail tied to the axis of TIME, and we warn you in advance that we work on a scale bigger than Cheops, and our task is bold, majestic, and uncompromising.

We are uncompromising carpenters, and once again we throw ourselves and our names into the boiling kettles of unprecedented projects.

We believe in ourselves, we reject with indignation the vicious whispers of people from the past who still delude themselves that they can bite at our heels. Are we not gods? And are we not unprecedented in this: *our steadfast betrayal of our own past,* just as it barely reaches the age of victory, and our steadfast rage, raised above the planet like a hammer whose time has come? Planet Earth begins to shake already at the heavy tread of our feet!

Boom, you black sails of time!

VICTOR KHLEBNIKOV, MARIA SINIAKOVA,
BOZHIDAR, GRIGORY PETNIKOV, NIKOLAI ASEEV

Rayonism

There was a close connection between the Neoprimitive style and Rayonism. For those interested in thematic anecdotes, there is an interesting sidelight cast on the frequent images of hairdressers in Louis Aragon's *Anicet, ou, Le Panorama* (Anicet, or, the panorama), that great early Surrealist novel, by Mikhail Larionov's concentration on the theme of hairdressing. For a period in 1913 Larionov and Natalya Goncharova collaborated with Alexey Kruchenykh and Victor Khlebnikov, founders of Zaoum, illustrating their books such as *The World Backwards.* Larionov illustrated Kruchenykh's book *Pomade* with a Neoprimitive putto rubbing haircream into the primitive goddess of *Spring 1912.*

The Donkey's Tail exhibition of 1912, arranged by Larionov and Goncharova, was a deliberate effort to move the new art forward; the Target exhibition of 1913 advocated Rayonism, in both figurative and abstract forms. These "electric" and "Rayonist" constructions emphasized electric rays emanating from objects, analogous to the Futurist force lines as they are described by Carlo Carrà: "If we paint the phases of a riot, the crowd bustling with uplifted fists and the noisy onslaughts of cavalry are translated upon the canvas in sheaves of lines corresponding with all the conflicting forces. . . . These force lines must encircle and involve the spectator so that he will . . . be forced to struggle himself with the persons in the picture" ("The Exhibitors to the Public," in Taylor, *Futurism,* 127). The reflection and refraction of light rays in the paintings of Giacomo Balla, for example, and those of the Rayonists are similar both in their concept and in their interpenetration, although Larionov's are noisier and more flagrant, Balla's more precise and quieter.

But there was to be a complication in Rayonism's relation to the Ital-

ian Futurism of Filippo Tommaso Marinetti. Upon Marinetti's arrival in
Russia in 1914, Larionov published a reply to a critic who had accused him
of turning away from the Italian. Larionov said that contemporary Futurists should shower the Italian with rotten eggs, as someone whose ideas are
out of date, and that Rayonism was far more attuned to the future. In any
case, Marinetti was attacked by Khlebnikov, David and Vladimir Burlyuk,
and Vladimir Mayakovsky, as well as Larionov, but the audience adored his
theatricalism, including his shouts about burning museums and despising
women. He would have liked them to whistle, to express their displeasure,
a sentiment that Mayakovsky was to pick up.

On the other hand, Larionov's "space sense" that lay at the heart of his
development guaranteed a close connection between Constructivism and
Rayonism, each of them dependent on the sophistication of a spatial sensitivity and its rendering, along with the "radiation" of tangible forms, to
which Larionov refers in his manifesto of 1914, "Pictural Rayonism."

Russia

5.25 MIKHAIL LARIONOV AND
NATALYA GONCHAROVA
Rayonists and Futurists
A Manifesto
1913

We, rayonists and futurists, do not wish to speak about new or old art, and
even less about modern Western art.

We leave the old art to die and leave the "new" art to do battle with it; and
incidentally, apart from a battle and a very easy one, the "new" art cannot
advance anything of its own. It is useful to put manure on barren ground,
but this dirty work does not interest us.

People shout about enemies closing in on them, but in fact, these enemies are, in any case, their closest friends. Their argument with old art long
since departed is nothing but a resurrection of the dead, a boring, decadent
love of paltriness and a stupid desire to march at the head of contemporary,
philistine interests.

We are not declaring any war, for where can we find an opponent our
equal?

The future is behind us.

All the same we will crush in our advance all those who undermine us and all those who stand aside.

We don't need popularization—our art will, in any case, take its full place in life—that's a matter of time.

We don't need debates and lectures, and if we sometimes organize them, then that's by way of a gesture to public impatience.

While the artistic throne is empty, and narrow-mindedness, deprived of its privileges, is running around calling for battle with departed ghosts, we push it out of the way, sit up on the throne, and reign until a regal deputy comes and replaces us.

We, artists of art's future paths, stretch out our hand to the futurists, in spite of all their mistakes, but express our utmost scorn for the so-called ego-futurists and neofuturists, talentless, banal people, the same as the members of the Knave of Diamonds, Slap in the Face of Public Taste, and Union of Youth groups.

We let sleeping dogs lie, we don't bring fools to their senses, we call trivial people trivial to their faces, and we are ever ready to defend our interests actively.

We despise and brand as artistic lackeys all those who move against a background of old or new art and go about their trivial business. Simple, uncorrupted people are closer to us than this artistic husk that clings to modern art, like flies to honey.

To our way of thinking, mediocrity that proclaims new ideas of art is as unnecessary and vulgar as if it were proclaiming old ideas.

This is a sharp stab in the heart for all who cling to so-called modern art, making their names in speeches against renowned little old men—despite the fact that between them and the latter there is essentially not much difference. These are true brothers in spirit—the wretched rags of contemporaneity, for who needs the peaceful renovating enterprises of those people who make a hubbub about modern art, who haven't advanced a single thesis of their own, and who express long-familiar artistic truths in their own words!

We've had enough Knaves of Diamonds whose miserable art is screened by this title, enough slaps in the face given by the hand of a baby suffering from wretched old age, enough unions of old and young! We don't need to square vulgar accounts with public taste—let those indulge in this who on paper give a slap in the face, but who, in fact, stretch out their hands for alms.

We've had enough of this manure; now we need to sow.

We have no modesty—we declare this bluntly and frankly—we consider ourselves to be the creators of modern art.

We have our own artistic honor, which we are prepared to defend to the last with all the means at our disposal. We laugh at the words "old art" and "new art"—that's nonsense invented by idle philistines.

We spare no strength to make the sacred tree of art grow to great heights, and what does it matter to us that little parasites swarm in its shadow—let them, they know of the tree's existence from its shadow.

Art for life and even more—life for art!

We exclaim: the whole brilliant style of modern times—our trousers, jackets, shoes, trolleys, cars, airplanes, railways, grandiose steamships—is fascinating, is a great epoch, one that has known no equal in the entire history of the world.

We reject individuality as having no meaning for the examination of a work of art. One has to appeal only to a work of art, and one can examine it only by proceeding from the laws according to which it was created.

The tenets we advance are as follows:

Long live the beautiful East! We are joining forces with contemporary Eastern artists to work together.

Long live nationality! We march hand in hand with our ordinary house painters.

Long live the style of rayonist painting that we created—free from concrete forms, existing and developing according to painterly laws!

We declare that there has never been such a thing as a copy and recommend painting from pictures painted before the present day. We maintain that art cannot be examined from the point of view of time.

We acknowledge all styles as suitable for the expression of our art, styles existing both yesterday and today—for example, cubism, futurism, orphism, and their synthesis, rayonism, for which the art of the past, like life, is an object of observation.

We are against the West, which is vulgarizing our forms and Eastern forms, and which is bringing down the level of everything.

We demand a knowledge of painterly craftsmanship.

More than anything else, we value intensity of feeling and its great sense of uplifting.

We believe that the whole world can be expressed fully in painterly forms:

Life, poetry, music, philosophy.

We aspire to the glorification of our art and work for its sake and for the sake of our future creations.

We wish to leave deep footprints behind us, and this is an honorable wish.

We advance our works and principles to the fore; we ceaselessly change them and put them into practice.

We are against art societies, for they lead to stagnation.

We do not demand public attention and ask that it should not be demanded from us.

The style of rayonist painting that we advance signifies spatial forms arising from the intersection of the reflected rays of various objects, forms chosen by the artist's will.

The ray is depicted provisionally on the surface by a colored line.

That which is valuable for the lover of painting finds its maximum expression in a rayonist picture. The objects that we see in life play no role here, but that which is the essence of painting itself can be shown here best of all—the combination of color, its saturation, the relation of colored masses, depth, texture; anyone who is interested in painting can give his full attention to all these things.

The picture appears to be slippery; it imparts a sensation of the extra-temporal, of the spatial. In it arises the sensation of what could be called the fourth dimension, because its length, breadth, and density of the layer of paint are the only signs of the outside world—all the sensations that arise from the picture are of a different order; in this way painting becomes equal to music while remaining itself. At this juncture a kind of painting emerges that can be mastered by following precisely the laws of color and its transference onto the canvas.

Hence the creation of new forms whose meaning and expressiveness depend exclusively on the degree of intensity of tone and the position that it occupies in relation to other tones. Hence the natural downfall of all existing styles and forms in all the art of the past—since they, like life, are merely objects for better perception and pictorial construction.

With this begins the true liberation of painting and its life in accordance only with its own laws, a self-sufficient painting, with its own forms, color, and timbre.

5.26 Ilya Zdanevich and Mikhail Larionov

Why We Paint Ourselves

A Futurist Manifesto

1913

To the frenzied city of arc lamps, to the streets bespattered with bodies, to the houses huddled together, we have brought our painted faces; we're off and the track awaits the runners.

Creators, we have not come to destroy construction, but to glorify and to affirm it. The painting of our faces is neither an absurd piece of fiction, nor a relapse—it is indissolubly linked to the character of our life and of our trade.

The dawn's hymn to man, like a bugler before the battle, calls to victories over the earth, hiding itself beneath the wheels until the hour of vengeance; the slumbering weapons have awoken and spit on the enemy.

The new life requires a new community and a new way of propagation.

Our self-painting is the first speech to have found unknown truths. And the conflagrations caused by it show that the menials of the earth have not lost hope of saving the old nests, have gathered all forces to the defense of the gates, have crowded together knowing that with the first goal scored we are the victors.

The course of art and a love of life have been our guides. Faithfulness to our trade inspires us, the fighters. The steadfastness of the few presents forces that cannot be overcome.

We have joined art to life. After the long isolation of artists, we have loudly summoned life and life has invaded art, it is time for art to invade life. The painting of our faces is the beginning of the invasion. That is why our hearts are beating so.

We do not aspire to a single form of aesthetics. Art is not only a monarch, but also a newsman and a decorator. We value both print and news. The synthesis of decoration and illustration is the basis of our self-painting. We decorate life and preach—that's why we paint ourselves.

Self-painting is one of the new valuables that belong to the people as they all do in our day and age. The old ones were incoherent and squashed flat by money. Gold was valued as an ornament and became expensive. We throw down gold and precious stones from their pedestal and declare them valueless. Beware, you who collect them and horde them—you will soon be beggars.

It began in '05. Mikhail Larionov painted a nude standing against a background of a carpet and extended the design onto her. But there was no proclamation. Now Parisians are doing the same by painting the legs of their dancing girls, and ladies powder themselves with brown powder and like Egyptians elongate their eyes. But that's old age. We, however, join contemplation with action and fling ourselves into the crowd.

To the frenzied city of arc lamps, to the streets bespattered with bodies, to the houses huddled together, we have not brought the past: unexpected flowers have bloomed in the hothouse and they excite us.

City dwellers have for a long time been varnishing their nails, using eyeshadow, rouging their lips, cheeks, hair—but all they are doing is to imitate the earth.

We, creators, have nothing to do with the earth; our lines and colors appeared with us. If we were given the plumage of parrots, we would pluck out their feathers to use as brushes and crayons.

If we were given immortal beauty, we would daub over it and kill it—we who know no half measures.

Tattooing doesn't interest us. People tattoo themselves once and for always. We paint ourselves for an hour, and a change of experience calls for a change of painting, just as picture devours picture, when on the other side of a car windshield shop windows flash by running into each other: that's our faces. Tattooing is beautiful but it says little—only about one's tribe and exploits. Our painting is the newsman.

Facial expressions don't interest us. That's because people have grown accustomed to understanding them, too timid and ugly as they are. Our faces are like the screech of the trolley warning the hurrying passers-by, like the drunken sounds of the great tango. Mimicry is expressive but colorless. Our painting is the decorator.

Mutiny against the earth and transformation of faces into a projector of experiences.

The telescope discerned constellations lost in space, painting will tell of lost ideas.

We paint ourselves because a clean face is offensive, because we want to herald the unknown, to rearrange life, and to bear man's multiple soul to the upper reaches of reality.

PART 6

Expressionism and Fauvism

At the end of the nineteenth century certain artists, like Edvard Munch in Norway, James Ensor in Belgium, and Vincent van Gogh in France, so simplified their lines that the intensity of feeling takes over, with a dark pessimism and a gloomy view of human destiny. This is the Expressionist mode, typified by Emil Nolde in Germany, the "bridge" or *Brucke* group in Dresden from 1905 to 1913, and the *Blaue Reiter* group in Munich, 1911–14. The COBRA group, from Belgium, Holland, and Denmark, continued the intensity with its bright colors. The dramatic gestures of the Abstract Expressionists have a predecessor in this Expressionist mode.

6.1 EDVARD MUNCH

The St. Cloud Manifesto

[Impressions from a ballroom, New Year's Eve in St. Cloud]
1889

Danseuse espagnole — 1 fr. — Let me enter. —

It was a long hall with balconies on both sides — under the balconies people were sitting and drinking at round tables — In the middle they stood top hat by top hat — amongst them the ladies' hats!

At the far end above the top hats a small woman in a purple tricot was walking a tightrope — in the middle of the blue-grey tobacco-filled air. —

I strolled through those who were standing.

I searched for a beautiful girl's face — no — yes — there was one who was not too bad. —

When she discovered I was looking at her her face became stiff and mask-like and stared emptily into the air.

I found a chair — and let myself fall into it tired and slack.

There was clapping — the purple-coloured dancer bowed smiling and disappeared. —

The Romanian singers performed. — It was love and hate, yearning and reconciliation — and beautiful dreams — and the gentle music melted into the colours. All these colours — the scenery with green palms and blue-grey water — the strong colours of the Romanian costumes — in the blue-grey haze.

The music and the colours captured my thoughts. They followed the soft clouds and were carried by the gentle tunes into a world of light joyful dreams.—

I should do something—I felt it would be so easy—it should be formed under my hands as if it were magic.—

Then they should see.—

A strong naked arm—a sunburned muscular neck—a young woman places her head against the arched breast.—

She closes her eyes and listens with an open quivering mouth to the words he whispers into her long hair hanging loose.

I must give form to this as I saw it just now, but in the blue haze.—

These two in the moment when they are not themselves but only a part of the chain of the thousand generations that connect generations to generations.—

People must understand the sacredness and power of this moment and remove their hats as if they were in church.

I must produce a number of such pictures. Interiors should no longer be painted, people who read and women who knit.

There must be living people who breathe and feel, suffer and love.

I felt I must do this—it should be so easy. The flesh would take on form and the colours come to life.

There was an interval—the music stopped.

I felt a sadness.

I recalled on how many previous occasions I had felt something similar—and when I had finished the painting—people shook their heads and smiled.

Once again I was out on the Boulevard des Italiens—with the white electric lamps and the yellow gas jets—with the thousands of strange faces that looked so ghostly in the electric light.

6.2 EDVARD MUNCH

The Violet Diary (*excerpt*)

1891–1892

NICE, 2 JANUARY 1891

It would be great fun to preach a bit to all those people who for so many years have looked at our paintings—and have either laughed or shaken their heads in suspicion. They do not understand how it is that these impressions can make very little sense at all—these impressions of a particular moment—that a tree can be red or blue—that a face can be blue or green— they know that this is wrong. Ever since childhood they have known that leaves and grass are green and that the colour of skin is a delicate pink.— They cannot understand that it is meant seriously—it must be a hoax or the result of carelessness—or mental derangement—preferably the latter.

They cannot get it into their heads that these paintings are made in all earnestness—in pain—and that they are the product of sleepless nights— that they have cost blood—and nerves.

And these painters carry on and get worse and worse—Everything turns more and more in what, for them, is the same insane direction.

Yes—because—it is the road to the painting of the future—to the promised land of art.

Because in these images the painter gives what is most valuable to him— he gives his soul—his sorrow—his joy—he gives his own heart's blood.

He presents the human being—not the object. These images will—must —move the spectator all the more powerfully—first a few—then many more, then everyone. Just as when many violins are in a room—one strikes the note to which they are all attuned, they all sound.

I shall try to give an example of this incomprehension about colour—

A billiard table—Go into a billiard hall—After you have stared for some time at the intense green cloth, look up. How strangely red is everything around you. Those gentlemen who a moment ago were dressed in black, now wear costumes of crimson red—and the hall is reddish, its walls and ceiling—

After a while the costumes are black once again—

If you want to paint such an atmosphere—with a billiard table—then I suppose you must paint these things crimson red—

If one is going to paint the immediate impression of a moment, the atmosphere, that which is human—then this is what one must do.

NICE, 22 JANUARY 1892

I was walking along the road with two friends—the sun went down—I felt a gust of melancholy—suddenly the sky turned a bloody red.

I stopped, leaned against the railing, tired to death—as the flaming skies hung like blood and sword over the blue-black fjord and the city—My friends went on—I stood there trembling with anxiety—and I felt a vast, infinite scream [tear] through nature.

6.3 EDVARD MUNCH
Art and Nature
1907–1929

Art is the opposite of nature.

A work of art can come only from the interior of man.

Art is the form of the image formed from the nerves, heart, brain and eye of man.

Art is the compulsion of man towards crystallization.

Nature is the unique great realm upon which art feeds.

Nature is not only what is visible to the eye—it also shows the inner images of the soul—the images on the back side of the eyes.

A work of art is like a crystal—like the crystal it must also possess a soul and the power to shine forth.

It is not enough for a work of art to have ordered planes and lines.

If a stone is tossed at a group of children, they hasten to scatter.

A regrouping, an action, has been accomplished. This is composition. This regrouping, presented by means of color, lines, and planes is an artistic and painterly motif.

It [painting] doesn't have to be "literary"—an invective which many people use in regard to paintings that do not depict apples on a tablecloth or a broken violin.

One good picture with ten holes in it is better than ten bad pictures with no holes. A charcoal mark on the wall can be greater art than ten pictures on a solid background and in costly gold frames.

Leonardo da Vinci's best pictures are destroyed. But they do not die. An ingenious thought lives forever.

6.4 OSKAR KOKOSCHKA

On the Nature of Visions

1912

The state of awareness of visions is not one in which we are either remembering or perceiving. It is rather a level of consciousness at which we experience visions within ourselves.

This experience cannot be fixed; for the vision is moving, an impression growing and becoming visual, imparting a power to the mind. It can be evoked but never defined.

Yet the awareness of such imagery is a part of living. It is life selecting from the forms which flow towards it or refraining, at will.

A life which derives its power from within itself will focus the perception of such images. And yet this free visualising in itself—whether it is complete or hardly yet perceptible, or undefined in either space or time—this has its own power running through. The effect is such that the visions seem actually to modify one's consciousness, at least in respect of everything which their own form proposes as their pattern and significance. This change in oneself, which follows on the vision's penetration of one's very soul, produces the state of awareness, of expectancy. At the same time there is an outpouring of feeling into the image which becomes, as it were, the soul's plastic embodiment. This state of alertness of the mind or consciousness has, then, a waiting, receptive quality. It is like an unborn child, as yet unfelt even by the mother, to whom nothing of the outside world slips through. And yet whatever affects his mother, all that impresses her down to the slightest birthmark on the skin, all is implanted in him. As though he could use her eyes, the unborn receives through her his visual impressions, even while he is himself unseen.

The life of the consciousness is boundless. It interpenetrates the world and is woven through all its imagery. Thus it shares those characteristics of living which our human existence can show. One tree left living in an arid land would carry in its seed the potency from whose roots all the forests of the earth might spring. So with ourselves; when we no longer inhabit our perceptions they do not go out of existence; they continue as though with a power of their own, awaiting the focus of another consciousness. There is no more room for death; for though the vision disintegrates and scatters, it does so only to reform in another mode.

Therefore we must harken closely to our inner voice. We must strive through the penumbra of words to the core within. "The Word became flesh and dwelt among us." And then the inner core breaks free — now feebly and now violently — from the words within which it dwells like a charm. "It happened to me according to the Word."

If we will surrender our closed personalities, so full of tension, we are in a position to accept this magical principle of living, whether in thought, intuition, or in our relationships. For in fact we see every day beings who are absorbed in one another, whether in living or in teaching, aimless or with direction. So it is with every created thing, everything we can communicate, every constant in the flux of living; each one has its own principle which shapes it, keeps life in it, and maintains it in our consciousness. Thus it is preserved, like a rare species, from extinction. We may identify it with "me" or "you" according to our estimate of its scale or its infinity. For we set aside the self and personal existence as being fused into a larger experience. All that is required of us is to RELEASE CONTROL. Some part of ourselves will bring us into the unison. The inquiring spirit rises from stage to stage, until it encompasses the whole of Nature. All laws are left behind. One's soul is a reverberation of the universe. Then too, as I believe, one's perception reaches out towards the Word, towards awareness of the vision.

As I said at first, this awareness of visions can never fully be described, its history can never be delimited, for it is a part of life itself. Its essence is a flowing and a taking form. It is love, delighting to lodge itself in the mind. This adding of something to ourselves — we may accept it or let it pass; but as soon as we are ready it will come to us by impulse, from the very breathing of our life. An image will take shape for us suddenly, at the first look, as the first cry of a newborn child emerging from its mother's womb.

Whatever the orientation of a life, its significance will depend on this ability to conceive the vision. Whether the image has a material or an immaterial character depends simply on the angle from which the flow of psychic energy is viewed, whether at ebb or flood.

It is true that the consciousness is not exhaustively defined by these images moving, these impressions which grow and become visual, imparting a power to the mind which we can evoke at will. For of the forms which come into the consciousness some are chosen while others are excluded arbitrarily.

But this awareness of visions which I endeavor to describe is the viewpoint of all life as though it were seen from some high place; it is like a ship which was plunged into the seas and flashes again as a winged thing in the air.

Consciousness is the source of all things and of all conceptions. It is a sea ringed about with visions.

My mind is the tomb of all those things which have ceased to be the true Hereafter into which they enter. So that at last nothing remains; all that is essential of them is their image within myself. The life goes out of them into that image as in the lamp the oil is drawn up through the wick for nourishing the flame.

So each thing, as it communicates itself to me, loses its substance and passes into the HEREAFTER WHICH IS MY MIND. I incorporate its image which I can evoke without the intermediacy of dreams. "Whenever two or three are gathered together in My name, I am in their midst" [Matt. 18:20]. And, as though it could go out to men, my vision is maintained, fed, as the lamp is by its oil, from the abundance of their living. If I am asked to make all this plain and natural the things themselves must answer for me, as it were, bearing their own witness. For I have represented them, I have taken their place and put on their semblance through my visions. It is the psyche which speaks.

I search, inquire, and guess. And with what sudden eagerness must the lamp wick seek its nourishment, for the flame leaps before my eyes as the oil feeds it. It is all my imagination, certainly, what I see there in the blaze. But if I have drawn something from the fire and you have missed it, well, I should like to hear from those whose eyes are still untouched. For is this not my vision? Without intent I draw from the outside world the semblance of things; but in this way I myself become part of the world's imaginings. Thus in everything imagination is simply that which is natural. It is nature, vision, life.

6.5 PAUL KLEE

Creative Credo

1920

I

Art does not reproduce the visible; rather, it makes visible. A tendency toward the abstract is inherent in linear expression: graphic imagery being confined to outlines has a fairy-like quality and at the same time can achieve great precision. The purer the graphic work—that is, the more the formal elements underlying linear expression are emphasized—the less adequate it is for the realistic representation of visible things.

The formal elements of graphic art are dot, line, plane, and space—the last three charged with energy of various kinds. A simple plane, for instance—that is, a plane not made up for more elementary units—would result if I were to draw a blunt crayon across the paper, thus transferring an energy-charge with or without modulations. An example of a spatial element would be a cloudlike vaporous spot, usually of varying intensity, made with a full brush.

II

Let us develop this idea, let us take a little trip into the land of deeper insight, following a topographic plan. The dead center being the point, our first dynamic act will be the line. After a short time, we shall stop to catch our breath (the broken line, or the line articulated by several stops). I look back to see how far we have come (counter-movement). Ponder the distance thus far traveled (sheaf of lines). A river may obstruct our progress: we use a boat (wavy line). Further on there might be a bridge (series of curves). On the other bank we encounter someone who, like us, wishes to deepen his insight. At first we joyfully travel together (convergence), but gradually differences arise (two lines drawn independently of each other). Each party shows some excitement (expression, dynamism, emotional quality of the line).

We cross an unplowed field (a plane traversed by lines), then thick woods. One of us loses his way, explores, and on one occasion even goes through the motions of a hound following a scent. Nor am I entirely sure of myself: there is another river, and fog rises above it (spatial element). But then the view is clear again. Basket-weavers return home with their cart (the wheel). Among them is a child with bright curls (corkscrew movement). Later it becomes sultry and dark (spatial element). There is a flash of lightning on the horizon (zigzag line), though we can still see stars over-head (scattered dots). Soon we reach our first quarters. Before falling asleep, we recall a number of things, for even so little a trip has left many impressions—lines of the most various kinds, spots, dabs, smooth planes, dotted planes, lined planes, wavy lines, obstructed and articulated movement, counter-movement, plaitings, weavings, bricklike elements, scalelike elements, simple and polyphonic motifs, lines that fade and lines that gain strength (dynamism), the joyful harmony of the first stretch, followed by inhibitions, nervousness! Repressed anxieties, alternating with moments of optimism caused by a breath of air. Before the storm, sudden assault by horseflies! The fury, the killing. The happy ending serves as a guiding thread even in the dark woods. The flashes of lightning made us think of a fever chart, of a sick child long ago.

III

I have mentioned the elements of linear expression which are among the visual components of the picture. This does not mean that a given work must consist of nothing but such elements. Rather, the elements must produce forms, but without being sacrificed in the process. They should be preserved. In most cases, a combination of several elements will be required to produce forms or objects or other compounds—planes related to each other (for instance, the view of a moving stream of water) or spatial structures arising from energy-charges involving the three dimensions (fish swimming in all directions).

Through such enrichment of the formal symphony the possibilities of variation, and by the same token, the possibilities for expressing ideas, are endlessly multiplied.

It may be true that "in the beginning there was the deed," yet the idea comes first. Since infinity has no definite beginning, but like a circle may start anywhere, the idea may be regarded as primary. "In the beginning was the word."

IV

Movement is the source of all change. In Lessing's *Laocoön*, on which we squandered study time when we were young, much fuss is made about the difference between temporal and spatial art. Yet looking into the matter more closely, we find that all this is but a scholastic delusion. For space, too, is a temporal concept.

When a dot begins to move and becomes a line, this requires time. Likewise, when a moving line produces a plane, and when moving planes produce spaces.

Does a pictorial work come into being at one stroke? No, it is constructed bit by bit, just like a house.

And the beholder, is he through with the work at one glance? (Unfortunately he often is.) Does not Feuerbach say somewhere that in order to understand a picture one must have a chair? Why the chair? So that your tired legs won't distract your mind. Legs tire after prolonged standing. Hence, time is needed. Character, too, is movement. Only the dead point as such is timeless. In the universe, too, movement is the basic datum. (What causes movement? This is an idle question, rooted in error.) On this earth, repose is caused by an accidental obstruction in the movement of matter. It is an error to regard such a stoppage as primary.

The Biblical story of the creation is an excellent parable of movement. The work of art, too, is above all a process of creation, it is never experienced as a mere product.

A certain fire, an impulse to create, is kindled, is transmitted through the hand, leaps to the canvas, and in the form of a spark leaps back to its starting place, completing the circle—back to the eye and further (back to the source of the movement, the will, the idea). The beholder's activity, too, is essentially temporal. The eye is made in such a way that it focuses on each part of the picture in turn; and to view a new section, it must leave the one just seen. Occasionally the beholder stops looking and goes away—the artist often does the same thing. If he thinks it worthwhile, he comes back—again like the artist.

The beholder's eye, which moves about like an animal grazing, follows paths prepared for it in the picture (in music, as everyone knows, there are conduits leading to the ear; the drama has both visual and auditive trails). The pictorial work was born of movement, is itself recorded movement, and is assimilated through movement (eye muscles).

A man asleep, the circulation of his blood, the regular breathing of his lungs, the intricate functioning of his kidneys, and in his head a world of dreams, in contact with the powers of fate. An organization of functions, which taken together produce rest.

V

Formerly we used to represent things visible on earth, things we either liked to look at or would have liked to see. Today we reveal the reality that is behind visible things, thus expressing the belief that the visible world is merely an isolated case in relation to the universe and that there are many more other, latent realities. Things appear to assume a broader and more diversified meaning, often seemingly contradicting the rational experience of yesterday. There is a striving to emphasize the essential character of the accidental.

By including the concepts of good and evil a moral sphere is created. Evil is not conceived as the enemy whose victories disgrace us, but as a force within the whole, a force that contributes to creation and evolution. The simultaneous existence of the masculine principle (evil, stimulating, passionate) and the feminine principle (good, growing, calm) result in a condition of ethical stability.

To this corresponds the simultaneous unification of forms, movement and counter-movement, or, to put it more naïvely, the unification of visual oppositions (in terms of colorism: use of contrasts of divided color, as in Delaunay). Each energy calls for its complementary energy to achieve self-contained stability based on the play of energies. Out of abstract elements a formal cosmos is ultimately created independent of their groupings as concrete objects or abstract things such as numbers of letters, which we discover to be so closely similar to the Creation that a breath is sufficient to turn an expression of religious feelings, or religion, into reality.

VI

A few examples: A sailor of antiquity in his boat, enjoying himself and appreciating the comfortable accommodations. Ancient art represents the subject accordingly. And now: the experiences of a modern man, walking across the deck of a steamer: 1. His own movement, 2. the movement of the ship which could be in the opposite direction, 3. the direction and the speed of the current, 4. the rotation of the earth, 5. its orbit, and 6. the orbits of the stars and satellites around it.

The result: an organization of movements within the cosmos centered on the man on the steamer.

An apple tree in bloom, its roots and rising saps, its trunk, the cross section with the annual rings, the blossom, its structure, its sexual functions, the fruit, the core with its seeds.

An organization of states of growth.

VII

Art is a simile of the Creation. Each work of art is an example, just as the terrestrial is an example of the cosmic.

The release of the elements, their grouping into complex subdivisions, the dismemberment of the object and its reconstruction into a whole, the pictorial polyphony, the achievement of stability through an equilibrium of movement, all these are difficult questions of form, crucial for formal wisdom, but not yet art in the highest circle. In the highest circle an ultimate mystery lurks behind the mystery, and the wretched light of the intellect is of no avail. One may still speak reasonably of the salutary effects of art. We may say that fantasy, inspired by instinctual stimuli, creates illusory states which somehow encourage or stimulate us more than the familiar natural or known supernatural states, that its symbols bring comfort to the mind, by making it realize that it is not confined to earthly potentialities, however great they may become in the future; that ethical gravity holds sway side by side with impish laughter at doctors and parsons.

But, in the long run, even enhanced reality proves inadequate.

Art plays an *unknowing* game with ultimate things, and yet achieves them!

Cheer up! Value such country outings, which let you have a new point of view for once as well as a change of air, and transport you to a world which, by diverting you, strengthens you for the inevitable return to the greyness of the working day. More than that, they help you to slough off your earthly skin, to fancy for a moment that you are God; to look forward to new holidays, when the soul goes to a banquet in order to nourish its starved nerves, and to fill its languishing blood vessels with new sap.

Let yourself be carried on the invigorating sea, on a broad river or an enchanting brook, such as that of the richly diversified, aphoristic graphic art.

6.6 PAUL KLEE

We Construct and Construct

1929

We construct and construct, and yet intuition still has its uses. Without it we can do a lot, but not everything. One may work for a long time, do different things, many things, important things, but not everything.

When intuition is joined to exact research it speeds the progress of exact research. . . .

Art, too, has been given sufficient room for exact investigation, and for some time the gates leading to it have been open. What had already been done for music by the end of the eighteenth century has at last been begun for the pictorial arts. Mathematics and physics furnished the means in the form of rules to be followed and to be broken. In the beginning it is wholesome to be concerned with the functions and to disregard the finished form. Studies in algebra, in geometry, in mechanics characterize teaching directed towards the essential and the functional, in contrast to the apparent. One learns to look behind the façade, to grasp the root of things. One learns to recognize the undercurrents, the antecedents of the visible. One learns to dig down, to uncover, to find the cause, to analyze.

Belgium

6.7 JAMES ENSOR
Preface to His *Collected Writings* (*excerpt*)
1921

Let us present our claims fully and philosophically, and if they seem to have the dangerous odor of pride, so much the better.

Definite and proven results:

My unceasing investigations, today crowned with glory, aroused the enmity of my snail-like followers, continually passed on the road. [How can one explain the appreciations of a Semmonier, Mauclair, etc., since] thirty years ago, long before Vuillard, Bonnard, Van Gogh and the luminists, I pointed the way to all the modern discoveries, all the influence of light and freeing of vision[?]

A vision that was sensitive and clear, not understood by the French Impressionists, who remained superficial daubers suffused with traditional recipes. Manet and Monet certainly reveal some sensations—and how obtuse! But their uniform effort hardly foreshadows decisive discoveries.

Let us condemn the dry and repugnant attempts of the Pointillists, already lost both to light and to art. They apply their Pointillism coldly, methodically, and without feeling; and in their correct and frigid lines they achieve only one of the aspects of light, that of vibration, without arriving at its form. Their too-limited method prohibits further investigation. An art of cold calculation and narrow observation, already far surpassed in vibration.

O Victory! the field of observation grows infinite, and sight, freed and sensitive to beauty, always changes; and perceives with the same acuity the effects or lines dominated by form or light.

[Extensive researches will seem contrary.] Narrow minds demand old beginnings, identical continuations. The painter must repeat his little works, and all else is condemned. [That is the advice of certain classifying censors, who segregate our artists like oysters in an oyster bed. O, the odious meannesses that favor the conformists of art! For the shabby in spirit, the outdoor painter may not attempt a decorative composition; the portraitist must remain one for life!] These poor creatures demand that adorable fantasy, roseate flower of heaven, the inspirer of the creative painter, be severely banished from the artistic program. . . .

Yes, before me the painter did not heed his vision.

6.8 JAMES ENSOR

Speech Delivered at a Banquet Given for Him
by La Flandre Littéraire, Ostende (*excerpt*)

1923

Ever since 1882 I've known what I am talking about. Observation modifies vision. The first vulgar vision is simple line, dry and without attempt at color. The second phase is when the more practiced eye discerns the values and delicacy of tones. This vision is already less commonplace.

The last phase of vision is when the artist sees the subtlety and the shifting play of light, its planes and its attractions. These progressive discoveries modify the primitive vision; line weakens and becomes secondary. This vision will be poorly understood; it requires long observation and attentive study. The vulgar will see in it only disorder and error. Thus has art evolved from the line of the Gothic through the color and movement of the Renaissance, finally to culminate in the light of modern times. Again I'll say it: Reason is the enemy of art. Artists dominated by reason lose all feeling, powerful instinct is enfeebled, inspiration becomes impoverished and the heart lacks its rapture. At the end of the chain of reason is suspended the greatest folly, or the nose of a pawn.

All the rules, all the canons of art vomit death exactly like their bronze-mouthed brothers of the battlefield. The learned and reasoned investigation of the Pointillists, researches pointed out and extolled by scientists and eminent professors, are dead, stone dead.

Impressionism is dead, luminism is dead — all meaningless labels. I have seen born, pass and die many schools and promoters of ephemera. Cubists, Futurists [etc., etc.]. . . .

And so, I have cried with all my lungs: the louder these bullfrogs croak the closer they are to bursting.

My friends, works of a personal vision alone will live. One must create a personal pictorial science, and be excited before beauty as before a woman one loves. Let us work with love and without fear of our faults, those inevitable and habitual companions of the great qualities. Yes, faults are qualities; and fault is superior to quality. Quality stands for uniformity in the effort to achieve certain common perfections accessible to anyone. Fault eludes conventional and banal perfections. Therefore fault is multiple, it is life, it reflects the personality of the artist and his character; it is human, it is everything, it will redeem the work.

6.9 JAMES ENSOR
Speech Delivered at His Exhibition at the Jeu de Paume, Paris (*excerpt*)
1932

The Flemish sea gives me all its nacreous fires, and I embrace it every morning, noon, and night. Ah, the wonderful kisses of my beloved sea, sublimated kisses, sandy, perfumed with foam, refreshingly pungent.

I salute you, Paris, and all your hills where people work and have fun. Paris, powerful magnet, all the big stars of Belgium cling to your sides. Paris, fetish, I have brought you my own little star, show me your best profile.

Dear friends, I recall 1929, the year of my most retrospective show at the Palais des Beaux-Arts in Brussels. Your generous critics vied with each other showering me with praise, and now your great men are interested in my labors.

Dear brothers-in-law of France, you will see close-up some of my interiors, my kitchen with curly cabbages, my barbate and striped fishes, my modern animalized goddesses, my lady friends with pursed lips rouged with adorable affectation, my rebellious angels glimpsed in the clouds, and I will be well represented.

All my paintings have come I don't know where from, mostly from the sea.

And my suffering, scandalized, insolent, cruel, malicious masks, and a long time ago I could say and write, "trailed by followers I have joyfully shut myself in the solitary milieu ruled by the mask with a face of violence and brilliance."

And the mask cried to me: Freshness of tone, sharp expression, sumptuous decor, great unexpected gestures, unplanned movements, exquisite turbulence.

O the animal masks of the Ostend Carnival: bloated vicuna faces, misshapen birds with the tails of birds of paradise, cranes with sky-blue bills gabbling nonsense, clay-footed architects, obtuse sciolists, with moldy skulls, heartless vivisectionists, odd insects, hard shells giving shelter to soft beasts. Witness *The Entry of Christ into Brussels,* which teems with all the hard and soft creatures spewed out by the sea. Won over by irony, touched by splendors, my vision becomes more refined, I purify my colors, they are whole and personal.

I see no heavy ochers in our country. Sterile ochers come from the earth, they shall return to earth without drums or trumpets. Ah, the tender flowers of painting were submerged by a wave of mud.

Tarnished, rancid, crackled under the smoky varnishes, or excessively washed and scrubbed, embellished and retouched, the masterpieces of the great old painters have nothing valuable to say.

Iris is no longer there. Restorers, varnishers, listen to my ever-young motto:

Frogs that croak the loudest come closest to bursting. Let us brighten our colors that they may sing, laugh, shout all their joys.

From the heights of the sacred hills of Paris, all lighthouses lit up, shine, green lights of youth, golds and silvers of maturity, pinks of maidenhood.

Roar Fauves, wild beasts, Dodos, Dadas, dance Expressionists, Futurists, Cubists, Surrealists, Orphists. Yours is a great art. Paris is great.

Let us encourage the painter's art and its diverse canons. Fire salvos upon salvos, cannoneers of art, for the salvation of color.

Color, color, life of things living and inanimate, enchantment of painting. Colors of our dreams, colors of our loved ones. . . .

Cannoneers, to your guns, and you too, lady-cannoneers. Fire your salvos to glorify the genius of your artists, fire blanks at painters too fond of comforts.

Painters and lady painters, my friends, your holy cannons do not spew death but light and life.

6.10 Willem de Kooning

What Abstract Art Means to Me

1951

The first man who began to speak, whoever he was, must have intended it. For surely it is talking that has put "Art" into painting. Nothing is positive about art except that it is a word. Right from there to here all art became literary. We are not yet living in a world where everything is self-evident. It is very interesting to notice that a lot of people who want to take the talking out of painting, for instance, do nothing else but talk about it. That is no contradiction, however. The art in it is the forever mute part you can talk about forever.

For me, only one point comes into my field of vision. This narrow, biased point gets very clear sometimes. I didn't invent it. It was already here. Everything that passes me I can see only a little of, but I am always looking. And I see an awful lot sometimes.

The word "abstract" comes from the light-tower of the philosophers, and it seems to be one of their spotlights that they have particularly focused on "Art." So the artist is always lighted up by it. As soon as it—I mean the "abstract"—comes into painting, it ceases to be what it is as it is written. It changes into a feeling which could be explained by some other words, probably. But one day, some painter used "Abstraction" as a title for one of his paintings. It was a still life. And it was a very tricky title. And it wasn't really a very good one. From then on the idea of abstraction became something extra. Immediately it gave some people the idea that they could free art from itself. Until then, Art meant everything that was in it—not what you could take out of it. There was only one thing you could take out of it sometime when you were in the right mood—that abstract and indefinable sensation, the aesthetic part—and still leave it where it was. For the painter to come to the "abstract" or the "nothing" he needed many things. Those things were always things in life—a horse, a flower, a milkmaid, the light in a room through a window made of diamond shapes maybe, tables, chairs, and so forth. The painter, it is true, was not always completely free. The things were not always of his own choice, but because of that he often got some new idea. Some painters liked to paint things already chosen by others, and after being abstract about them, were called Classicists. Others wanted to select the things themselves and, after being abstract about them, were called Romanticists. Of course, they got mixed up with one another a lot too. Anyhow, at that time, they were not abstract about something which was already abstract. They freed the shapes, the light, the color, the space, by putting them into concrete things in a given situation. They *did* think about the possibility that the things—the horse, the chair, the man— were abstractions, but they let that go, because if they kept thinking about it, they would have been led to give up painting altogether, and would probably have ended up in the philosopher's tower. When they got those strange, deep ideas, they got rid of them by painting a particular smile on one of the faces in the picture they were working on.

The aesthetics of painting were always in a state of development parallel to the development of painting itself. They influenced each other and vice versa. But all of a sudden, in that famous turn of the century, a few people thought they could take the bull by the horns and invent an aesthetic before-hand. After immediately disagreeing with each other, they began to form all kinds of groups, each with the idea of freeing art, and each demanding that you should obey them. Most of these theories have finally dwindled away into politics or strange forms of spiritualism. The question, as they saw it, was not so much what you *could* paint but rather what you could *not* paint. You could *not* paint a house or a tree or a mountain. It was then that subject matter came into existence as something you ought *not* to have.

In the old days, when artists were very much wanted, if they got to think-ing about their usefulness in the world, it could only lead them to believe that painting was too worldly an occupation and some of them went to church instead or stood in front of it and begged. So what was considered too worldly from a spiritual point of view then, became later—for those who were inventing the new aesthetics—a spiritual smoke-screen and not worldly enough. These latter-day artists were bothered by their apparent uselessness. Nobody really seemed to pay any attention to them. And they did not trust that freedom of indifference. They knew that they were rela-tively freer than ever before *because* of that indifference, but in spite of all their talking about freeing art, they really didn't mean it that way. Freedom to them meant to be useful in society. And that is really a wonderful idea. To achieve that, they didn't need *things* like tables and chairs or a horse. They needed ideas instead, social ideas, to make their objects with, their con-structions—the "pure plastic phenomena"—which were used to illustrate their convictions. Their point was that until they came along with their theo-ries, Man's own form in space—his body—was a private prison; and that it was because of this imprisoning misery—because he was hungry and over-worked and went to a horrid place called home late at night in the rain, and

his bones ached and his head was heavy—because of this very consciousness of his own body, this sense of pathos, they suggest, he was overcome by
the drama of a crucifixion in a painting or the lyricism of a group of people
sitting quietly around a table drinking wine. In other words, these aestheticians proposed that people had up to now understood painting in terms
of their own private misery. Their own sentiment of form instead was one
of comfort. The beauty of comfort. The great curve of a bridge was beautiful because people could go across the river in comfort. To compose with
curves like that, and angles, and make works of art with them could only
make people happy, they maintained, for the only association was one of
comfort. That millions of people have died in war since then, because of
that idea of comfort, is something else.

This pure form of comfort became the comfort of "pure form." The
"nothing" part in a painting until then—the part that was not painted but
that was there because of the things in the picture which were painted—
had a lot of descriptive labels attached to it like "beauty," "lyric," "form,"
"profound," "space," "expression," "classic," "feeling," "epic," "romantic,"
"pure," "balance," etc. Anyhow that "nothing" which was always recognized
as a particular something—and as something particular—they generalized,
with their book-keeping minds, into circles and squares. They had the innocent idea that the "something" existed "in spite of" and not "because of"
and that this something was the only thing that truly mattered. They had
hold of it, they thought, once and for all. But this idea made them go backward in spite of the fact that they wanted to go forward. That "something"
which was not measurable, they lost by trying to make it measurable; and
thus all the old words which, according to their ideas, ought to be done away
with got into art again: pure, supreme, balance, sensitivity, etc.

Kandinsky understood "Form" as *a* form, like an object in the real world;
and an object, he said, was a narrative—and so, of course, he disapproved
of it. He wanted his "music without words." He wanted to be "simple as a
child." He intended, with his "inner-self," to rid himself of "philosophical
barricades" (he sat down and wrote something about all this). But in turn
his own writing has become a philosophical barricade, even if it is a barricade full of holes. It offers a kind of Middle-European idea of Buddhism or,
anyhow, something too theosophic for me.

The sentiment of the Futurists was simpler. No space. Everything ought
to keep on going! That's probably the reason they went themselves. Either
a man was a machine or else a sacrifice to make machines with.

The moral attitude of Neo-Plasticism is very much like that of Constructivism, except that the Constructivists wanted to bring things out in the open and the Neo-Plasticists didn't want anything left over.

I have learned a lot from all of them and they have confused me plenty too. One thing is certain, they didn't give me my natural aptitude for drawing. I am completely weary of their ideas now.

The only way I still think of these ideas is in terms of the individual artists who came from them or invented them. I still think that Boccioni was a great artist and a passionate man. I like Lissitzky, Rodchenko, Tatlin, and Gabo; and I admire some of Kandinsky's painting very much. But Mondrian, that great merciless artist, is the only one who had nothing left over.

The point they all had in common was to be both inside and outside at the same time. A new kind of likeness! The likeness of the group instinct. All that it has produced is more glass and a hysteria for new materials which you can look through. A symptom of love-sickness, I guess. For me, to be inside and outside is to be in an unheated studio with broken windows in the winter, or taking a nap on somebody's porch in the summer.

Spiritually I am wherever my spirit allows me to be, and that is not necessarily in the future. I have no nostalgia, however. If I am confronted with one of those small Mesopotamian figures, I have no nostalgia for it but, instead, I may get into a state of anxiety. Art never seems to make me peaceful or pure. I always seem to be wrapped in the melodrama of vulgarity. I do not think of inside or outside—or of art in general—as a situation of comfort. I know there is a terrific idea there somewhere, but whenever I want to get into it, I get a feeling of apathy and want to lie down and go to sleep. Some painters, including myself, do not care what chair they are sitting on. It does not even have to be a comfortable one. They are too nervous to find out where they ought to sit. They do not want to "sit in style." Rather, they have found that painting—any kind of painting, any style of painting—to be painting at all, in fact—is a way of living today, a style of living, so to speak. That is where the form of it lies. It is exactly in its uselessness that it is free. Those artists do not want to conform. They only want to be inspired.

The group instinct could be a good idea, but there is always some little dictator who wants to make his instinct the group instinct. There *is* no style of painting now. There are as many naturalists among the abstract painters as there are abstract painters in the so-called subject-matter school.

The argument often used that science is really abstract, and that painting could be like music and, for this reason, that you cannot paint a man leaning against a lamp-post, is utterly ridiculous. That space of science—the space of the physicists—I am truly bored with by now. Their lenses are so thick that seen through them, the space gets more and more melancholy. There seems to be no end to the misery of the scientists' space. All that it contains is billions and billions of hunks of matter, hot or cold, floating around in darkness according to a great design of aimlessness. The stars I think about, if I could fly, I could reach in a few old-fashioned days. But physicists' stars I use as buttons, buttoning up curtains of emptiness. If I stretch my arms next to the rest of myself and wonder where my fingers are—that is all the space I need as a painter.

Today, some people think that the light of the atom bomb will change the concept of painting once and for all. The eyes that actually saw the light melted out of sheer ecstasy. For one instant, everybody was the same color. It made angels out of everybody. A truly Christian light, painful but forgiving.

Personally, I do not need a movement. What was given to me, I take for granted. Of all movements, I like Cubism most. It had that wonderful unsure atmosphere of reflection—a poetic frame where something could be possible, where an artist could practice his intuition. It didn't want to get rid of what went before. Instead it added something to it. The parts that I can appreciate in other movements came out of Cubism. Cubism *became* a movement, it didn't set out to be one. It has force in it, but it was no "force-movement." And then there is that one-man movement; Marcel Duchamp—for me a truly modern movement because it implies that each artist can do what he thinks he ought to—a movement for each person and open for everybody.

If I *do* paint abstract art, that's what abstract art means to me. I frankly do not understand the question. About twenty-four years ago, I knew a man in Hoboken, a German who used to visit us in the Dutch Seamen's Home. As far as he could remember, he was always hungry in Europe. He found a place in Hoboken where bread was sold a few days old—all kinds of bread: French bread, German bread, Italian bread, Dutch bread, Greek bread, American bread and particularly Russian black bread. He bought big stacks of it for very little money, and let it get good and hard and then he crumpled it and spread it on the floor in his flat and walked on it as on a soft carpet. I lost sight of him, but found out many years later that one of the other fellows met him again around 86th Street. He had become some kind of a Jugend Bund leader and took boys and girls to Bear Mountain on Sundays. He is still alive but quite old and is now a Communist. I could never figure him out, but now when I think of him, all that I can remember is that he had a very abstract look on his face.

PART 7

Der Blaue Reiter

Der Blaue Reiter (The blue rider) was the title of a painting created by Wassily Kandinsky in 1903. When he, Gabrielle Munter, and Franz Marc broke with the New Artists' Association in Munich in 1911, when they had their first exhibition, they took this name for their group and its Expressionist movement, which with Kandinsky veered toward abstraction. The *Blaue Reiter Almanac*, put together by Kandinsky and Marc, includes seven of Henri Rousseau's paintings, showing their attachment to naive painting. There are also reproductions of children's drawings. Kandinsky asks: "Are not children, who conceive directly and from their secret feelings, more creative than those who imitate Greek Art?" (*The Blaue Reiter Almanac,* 92). Kandinsky was versed in ethnography, had studied primitive tribes, and so was close to the ideas of Neoprimitivism, with which the *Blaue Reiter* group was imbued.

Kandinsky, Paul Klee, and Lyonel Feininger went to the Bauhaus, and with Alexei Jawlensky, founded Die Blauen Vier (the Blue Four, the name recalling *Der Blaue Reiter*), which toured, lecturing and exhibiting, in Germany, Mexico, and the United States between 1925 and 1934, under the patronage of Galka Scheyer.

7.1 WASSILY KANDINSKY

Seeing

1912

Blue, Blue got up, got up and fell.
Sharp, Thin whistled and shoved, but didn't get through.
From every corner came a humming.
FatBrown got stuck—it seemed for all eternity.
                        It seemed. It seemed.
You must open your arms wider.
                        Wider. Wider.
And you must cover your face with red cloth.
And maybe it hasn't shifted yet at all: it's just that you've shifted.
White leap after white leap.
And after this white leap another white leap.
And in this white leap a white leap. In every white leap a white leap.
But that's not good at all, that you don't see the gloom: in the gloom is
    where it is.
That's where everything begins . . . .
With a . . . . .Crash . . . .

7.2 WASSILY KANDINSKY

Sounds

1912

Face.
Far.
Cloud.
. . . .

. . . .

There stands a man with a long sword. The sword is long and also broad.
Very broad.
. . . .

. . . .

He tried to trick me many times and I admit it: He succeeded too—at
tricking. And maybe too many times.

. . . .

. . . . .

Eyes, eyes, eyes . . . eyes.

. . . . .

. . . . .

A woman, who is thin and not young, who has a cloth on her head, which is like a shield over her face and leaves her face in shadows.

With a rope the woman leads the calf, which is still small and unsteady on its crooked legs. Sometimes the calf walks behind her very obediently. And sometimes it doesn't. Then the woman pulls the calf by the rope. It lowers its head and shakes it and braces its legs. But its legs are weak and the rope doesn't break.

The rope doesn't break.

. . . . .

. . . . .

Eyes look out from afar.

The cloud rises.

. . . . .

. . . . . .

The face.

Afar.

The cloud.

The sword.

The rope.

7.3 WASSILY KANDINSKY

Line and Fish

1935

Approaching it in one way I see no essential difference between a line one calls "abstract" and a fish.

But an essential likeness.

This isolated line and the isolated fish alike are living beings with forces peculiar to them, though latent. They are forces of expression for these beings and of impression on human beings. Because each being has an impressive "look" which manifests itself by its expression.

But the voice of these latent forces is faint and limited. It is the environ-ment of the line and the fish that brings about a miracle: the latent forces awaken, the expression becomes radiant, the impression profound. Instead of a low voice one hears a choir. The latent forces have become dynamic.

The environment is the composition.

The composition is the *organized* sum of the *interior* functions (expres-sions) of every part of the work.

But approaching it in another way there is an essential difference between a line and a fish.

And that is that the fish can swim, eat and be eaten. It has then capacities of which the line is deprived.

These capacities of the fish are necessary extras for the fish itself and for the kitchen, but not for painting. And so not being necessary, they are superfluous.

That is why I like the line better than the fish—at least in my painting.

7.4 WASSILY KANDINSKY AND FRANZ MARC

Preface to *Der Blaue Reiter Almanac*

1912

A great era has begun: the spiritual "awakening," the increasing tendency to regain "lost balance," the inevitable necessity of spiritual plantings, the unfolding of the first blossom.

We are standing at the threshold of one of the greatest epochs that man-kind has ever experienced, the epoch of great spirituality.

In the nineteenth century just ended, when there appeared to be the most thoroughgoing flourishing—the "great victory"—of the material, the first "new" elements of a spiritual atmosphere were formed almost unnoticed. They will give and have given the necessary nourishment for the flourishing of the spiritual.

Art, literature, even "exact" science are in various stages of change in this "new" era; they will all be overcome by it.

Our [first and] most important aim is to reflect phenomena in the field of art that are directly connected with this change and the essential facts that shed light on these phenomena in other fields of spiritual life.

Therefore, the reader will find works in our volumes that in this respect show an *inner* relationship although they may appear unrelated on the surface. We are considering or making note not of work that has a certain established, orthodox external form (which usually is all there is), but of work that has an *inner* life connected with the great change. It is only natural that we want not death but life. The echo of a living voice is only a hollow form, which has not arisen out of a distinct *inner necessity;* in the same way, there have always been created and will increasingly be created, works of art that are nothing but hollow reverberations of works rooted in this inner necessity. They are hollow, loitering lies that pollute the spiritual air and lead wavering spirits astray. Their deception leads the spirit not to life but to death. [With all available means we want to try to unmask the hollowness of this deception. This is our second goal.]

It is only natural that in questions of art the artist is called upon to speak first. Therefore the contributors to our volumes will be primarily artists. Now they have the opportunity to say openly what previously they had to hide. We are therefore asking those artists who feel inwardly related to our goals to turn to us as *brethren.* We take the liberty of using this great word because we are convinced that in our case the establishment automatically ceases to exist.

The artist essentially works for people who are called laymen or the public and who as such have hardly any opportunity to speak. It is natural that their feelings about art and their ideas should be expressed as well. So we are ready to provide space for any serious remarks from this quarter. Even short and unsolicited contributions will be published in the "opinions" column.

[In the present situation of the arts we cannot leave the link between the artist and the public in the hands of others. Reviews are mostly sickening. Because of the growth of the daily press, many unqualified art critics have stolen in among the serious ones; with their empty words they are building a wall in front of the public instead of a bridge. We will devote one special column to this unfortunate, harmful power so that not only the artist but also the public can be enabled to see the distorted face of contemporary art criticism in a clear light.]

Works like ours do not happen at fixed intervals, nor can living creations be ordered by man. Our volumes will therefore not appear at fixed times but rather spontaneously, whenever there is enough important material.

It should be almost superfluous to emphasize specifically that in our case the principle of internationalism is the only one possible. However, in these times we must say that an individual nation is only one of the creators of all art; one alone can never be a whole. As with a personality, the national element is automatically reflected in each great work. But in the last resort this national coloration is merely incidental. The whole work, called art, knows no borders or nations, only humanity.

7.5 FRANZ MARC
Aphorisms
1911–1912

LET THE WORLD SPEAK FOR ITSELF

Is there any more mysterious idea for an artist than the conception of how nature is mirrored in the eyes of an animal? How does a horse see the world, or an eagle, or a doe, or a dog? . . .

What relation has a doe to our picture of the world? Does it make any logical, or even artistic, sense, to paint the doe as it appears to our perspective vision, or in cubistic form because we feel the world cubistically? It feels it as a doe, and its landscape must also be "doe." . . . I can paint a picture: the roe; Pisanello has painted such. I can, however, also wish to paint a picture: "the roe feels." How infinitely sharper an intellect must the painter have, in order to paint this! The Egyptians have done it. The rose; Manet has painted that. Who has painted the flowering rose? The Indians . . .

There is little abstract art today, and what there is is stammering and imperfect. It is an attempt to let the world speak for itself, instead of reporting the speech of minds excited by their picture of the world. The Greek, the Gothic, and the Renaissance artist set forth the world the way he saw it, felt it, and wished to have it; man wished above all to be nourished by art; he achieved his desire but sacrificed everything else to this one aim: to construct homunculus, to substitute knowledge for strength and skill for spirit. The ape aped his creator. He learned to put art itself to the ends of trade. . . .

Only today can art be metaphysical, and it will continue to be so. Art will free itself from the needs and desires of men. We will no longer paint a forest or a horse as we please or as they seem to us, but *as they really are.*

FOLK ART

The people itself (and I do not mean the "masses") has always given art its essential style. The artist merely clarifies and fulfills the will of the people. But when the people does not know what it wants, or, worst of all, wants

nothing, . . . then its artists, driven to seeking their own forms, remain isolated, and become martyrs. . . .

Folk art—that is, the feeling of people for artistic form—can arise again
only when the whole jumble of worn-out art concepts of the nineteenth century has been wiped from the memory of generations.

ART OF THE FUTURE

[*At the front, near Verdun*], *1915*
The day is not far distant on which Europeans—the few Europeans who will
still remain—will suddenly become painfully aware of their lack of formal
concepts. Then will these unhappy people bewail their wretched state and
become seekers after form. They will not seek the new form in the past, in
the outward world, or in the stylized appearances of nature, but they will
build up their form from within themselves, in the light of their new knowledge that turned the old world fable into a world form, and the old world
view into a world insight.

The art of the future will give form to our scientific convictions; this is
our religion and our truth, and it is profound and weighty enough to produce the greatest style and the greatest revaluation of form that the world
has ever seen.

Today, instead of using the laws of nature as a means of artistic expression, we pose the religious problems of a new content. The art of our time
will surely have profound analogies with the art of primitive periods long
past, without, of course, the formalistic similarities now senselessly sought
by many archaistic artists. And our time will just as surely be followed in
some distant, ripe, late European future by another period of cool maturity,
which in its turn will again set up its own formal laws and traditions.

7.6 FRANZ MARC

Der Blaue Reiter

1912

Today art is moving in a direction of which our fathers would never even have dreamed. We stand before the new pictures as in a dream and we hear the apocalyptic horsemen in the air. There is an artistic tension all over Europe. Everywhere new artists are greeting each other; a look, a handshake is enough for them to understand each other!

We know that the basic ideas of what we feel and create today have existed before us, and we are emphasizing that in *essence* they are not new. But we must proclaim the fact that everywhere in Europe new forces are sprouting like a beautiful unexpected seed, and we must point out all the places where new things are originating.

Out of the awareness of this secret connection of all new artistic production, we developed the idea of the *Blaue Reiter*. It will be the call that summons all artists of the new era and rouses the laymen to hear. The volumes of the *Blaue Reiter* are written and edited exclusively by artists. The first volume herewith announced, which will be followed at irregular intervals by others, includes the latest movements in French, German, and Russian painting. It reveals subtle connections with Gothic and primitive art, with Africa and the vast Orient, with the highly expressive, spontaneous folk and children's art, and especially with the most recent musical movements in Europe and the new ideas for the theater of our time.

PART 8

Scuola Metafisica

In Ferrara, Italy, Giorgio de Chirico defined his painting as an attempt at "a new metaphysical psychology of objects" (On Metaphysical Art, 8.2). The work of the Scuola Metafisica, or Metaphysical School, with its dream settings full of melancholy—fittingly called by such titles as "The Melancholy of the Street" and "The Dream of a Poet" and full of designations and symbols of anguish and mystery—was particularly appealing to the Surrealists, who found in them just the unrational elements capable of arousing the imagination. Alas, de Chirico's later paintings, some predated so as to sell, feel like false repetitions of these early ones.

Carlo Carrà, whose 1917 meeting with de Chirico was decisive for his switch from Futurism to the Scuola Metafisica of Italian painting, insisted on the enduring monuments of classical antiquity. Calling "the spasmodic passions" of his previous incarnation as a Bruitist simply one of the craters flowering under the bridges of art—ready to explode, one imagines—he turned to a concept of internal discipline, calling for creation rather than the imitation of phenomena, as had been the goal of the Futurists. Both he and de Chirico would declare themselves attached to the idea of a link with the spiritual—the savage gods, if not the wild Futurist behavior, remain in the Scuola Metafisica, as a part of a lasting atmosphere beyond the human.

8.1 CARLO CARRÀ

Declaration

1918

Looked at for a long time substance grows grey
The ephemeral force of words is lost in idle conjecture
Remote rules and measures and the extinct phantoms of the will are un-
    aware that the sun has long since risen again
We are little suited to public administration and in commerce with men we
    use too much irony
These men swooped down to attack us but unperturbed we ventured into
    the language of secret sweetness
Then we became aware that a vague moisture was dulling our souls and that
    the mentalities which arose possessed abandoned inflections
But now our agitation assumes predominance with new direct needs
From the new planes which are not chimeric we see the first lines of our
    ideal parabola

Clear amazements rediscovered

The precise forms of harmonic proportion have pleasant union with things and destinies

A flash of beauty and we will forget whether our life will be secure

We make contact with new myths

The approaches to reality are always unexpected

We oppose the artifice that supports itself with implications of fantasy

We justify our perverse adventures and this love of vain dreams

Devilry of a bizarre race resolved in a fleeting singing pleasure

The great interrogatives

The obscure pretexts

Ah the scale of values

The wicked happiness of things that give themselves

Having entered a delirious geometry we now emerge not indifferent

They say that the will of prophets can dissolve the dark enigmas and hush the cosmic voices of the free and impure sea

Hence our invitations made us haughty

But in good time we realized that these things were done in mockery

The new needs have changed the terms in our hands

We feel a returning taste for calm and agreeable postures even if they present us with food for sadness

We are caught up in the web of fatality but prefer to absent ourselves from surprising things and light heartedly

To live in the indifferent breath of a piercing light could signify a self-surrender of the so loving defences

And I say that if there is something that cannot be hurt there is also something innocent that could be lost

Time which is right has imposed on us a limit which we do not intend to respect

To sustain the solitude we feel as men out of our epoch, a vague smile from the stars is sufficient

Let us not forget that we are passing through this very life fleeting and ignorant of its destined end

But neither let us forget that this depends upon the law of God who will give us the necessary light to bear the catastrophes that weigh upon us

At the beginning of our day time without limit cannot bar its door on us

Carrà è cheto:
la meta smarrita
vuol per sé la vita

Carrà è lieto:
cavalca senza freni
ponti d'arcobaleni

Carrà is tranquil;
The lost aim
Wants life for itself
Carrà is joyful:
Unbridled he rides astride
Bridges of rainbows

8.2 GIORGIO DE CHIRICO
On Metaphysical Art (*excerpt*)
1919

GEOGRAPHICAL FATALITY

From the geographical point of view it was inevitable that the initial conscious manifestation of the metaphysical movement should have been born
in Italy. In France this could not have happened. The facile talent and carefully cultivated artistic taste, mingled with the dose of *esprit* (not only in
their exaggerated use of the pun) sprinkled on ninety-nine per cent of the
inhabitants of Paris suffocates and impedes the development of a prophetic
spirit. Our soil, on the other hand, is more propitious to the birth and development of such animals. Our inveterate *gaucherie,* and the continual effort
we have to make to get used to a concept of spiritual lightness, bring with
them as a direct consequence the weight of our chronic sadness. And yet
the result would be that great shepherds can only appear among very similar flocks, just as the most monumental prophets throughout history have
sprung from the tribes and races whose destinies are the most miserable.
Hellas, aesthetic in art and nature, could not have given birth to a prophet,
and Heraclitus, the most profound Greek philosopher I know, meditated on
other shores, less happy because closer to the hell of the desert.

MADNESS AND ART

That madness is a phenomenon inherent in every profound manifestation
of art is self-evident.

Schopenhauer defines as mad the man who has lost his memory. A definition full of acumen since that which forms the logic of our normal acts and of our normal life is indeed a continuous string of memories of relationships between objects and ourselves and vice versa.

Let us take an example: I enter a room and see a man seated on a chair, hanging from the ceiling I see a cage with a canary in it, on a wall I notice pictures, and on the shelves, books. All this strikes me, but does not amaze me, since the chain of memories that links one thing to another explains the logic of what I see. But let us suppose that for a moment and for reasons that are inexplicable and independent of my will, the thread of this chain is broken, who knows how I would see the seated man, the cage, the pictures, the bookshelves; who knows what terror and perhaps what sweetness and consolation I would feel when contemplating that scene.

But the scene would not have changed, it would be I who would see it from a different angle. And here we have arrived at the metaphysical aspect of things. One can deduce and conclude that every object has two aspects: one current one which we see nearly always and which is seen by men in general, and the other which is spectral and metaphysical and seen only by rare individuals in moments of clairvoyance and metaphysical abstraction, just as certain hidden bodies formed of materials that are impenetrable to the sun's rays only appear under the power of artificial lights, which could, for example, be X-rays.

For some time, however, I have been inclined to believe that objects can possess other aspects apart from the two cited above: these are the third, fourth and fifth aspects, all different from the first, but closely related to the second, or metaphysical aspect.

THE ETERNAL SIGNS

I remember the strange and profound impression made upon me as a child by a plate in an old book that bore the title "The World before the Flood."

The plate represented a landscape of the Tertiary period. Man was not yet present. I have often meditated upon the strange phenomenon of this absence of human beings in its metaphysical aspect. Every profound work of art contains two solitudes: one could be called "plastic solitude," and is that contemplative beatitude offered to us by genius in construction and formal combination (materials and elements that are dead/alive or alive/dead; the second is the life of the *nature morte*, still-life captured not in the sense of pictorial subject, but of the spectral aspect which could just as well belong

to a supposedly living figure). The second solitude is that of signs, an eminently metaphysical solitude and one which excludes a priori every logical
possibility of visual or psychic education.

There are paintings by Böcklin, Claude Lorrain and Poussin which are
inhabited by human figures, but which, in spite of this, bear a close relationship with the landscape of the Tertiary. Absence of humanity in man. Some
of Ingres's portraits achieve this too. It should, however, be observed that
in the works cited above (except perhaps in a few paintings by Böcklin),
only the first solitude exists: plastic solitude. Only in the new Italian metaphysical painting does the second solitude appear: solitude of signs, or the
metaphysical.

The appearance of a metaphysical work of art is serene; it gives the impression, however, that something new must happen amidst this same serenity, and that other signs apart from those already apparent are about
to enter the rectangle of the canvas. Such is the revealing symptom of the
inhabited depth. For this reason the flat surface of a perfectly calm ocean
disturbs us, not so much because of the idea of the measurable distance
between us and the sea bed, but more because of all the elements of the unknown hidden in that depth. Otherwise we would feel only a vertiginous
sensation similar to that experienced at a great height.

METAPHYSICAL AESTHETIC

In the construction of cities, in the architectural forms of houses, in squares
and gardens and public walks, in gateways and railway stations etc., are contained the initial foundations of a great metaphysical aesthetic. The Greeks
possessed certain scruples in such constructions, guided as they were by
their philosophical aesthetic; porticoes, shadowed walks, and terraces were
erected like theatre seats in front of the great spectacles of nature (Homer,
Aeschylus): the tragedy of serenity. In Italy we have modern and admirable
examples of such constructions. Where Italy is concerned, for me the psychological origins remain obscure. I have meditated at length upon this
problem of the metaphysics of Italian architecture and all my painting of
the years 1910, 1911, 1912, 1913 and 1914 is concerned with this problem. Perhaps the day will come when such an aesthetic, which up to now has been
left to the whims of chance, will become a law and a necessity for the upper
classes and the directors of public concerns. Then perhaps we will be able
to avoid the horror of finding ourselves placed in front of certain monstrous
apotheoses of bad taste and pervading imbecility, like the gleaming white

monument to the Great King [Victor Emmanuel] in Rome, otherwise known as the Altar of the Fatherland, which is to architectural sense as the odes and orations of Tirteo Calvo are to poetic sense.

Schopenhauer, who knew a great deal about such matters, advised his countrymen not to place statues of their famous men on columns and pedestals of excessive height, but to place them on low platforms "like those they use in Italy" he said, "where every marble man seems to be on a level with the passers by and to walk with them."

The imbecilic man, that is, the a-metaphysical man, inclines by instinct towards an appearance of mass and height, towards a sort of architectural Wagnerianism. This is a matter of innocence; they are men who are unacquainted with the terribleness of lines and angles, they are drawn towards the infinite, and in this they reveal their limited psyche enclosed as it is within the same sphere as the feminine and infantile psyche. But we who know the signs of the metaphysical alphabet are aware of the joy and the solitude enclosed by a portico, the corner of a street, or even in a room, on the surface of a table, between the sides of a box.

The limits of these signs constitute for us a sort of moral and aesthetic code of representation, and more than this, with clairvoyance we construct in painting a new metaphysical psychology of objects.

The absolute consciousness of the space that an object in a painting must occupy, and the awareness of the space that divides objects, establishes a new astronomy of objects attached to the planet by the fatal law of gravity. The minutely accurate and prudently weighed use of surfaces and volumes constitutes the canon of the metaphysical aesthetic. At this point one should remember some of Otto Weininger's profound reflections on metaphysical geometry: "As an ornament the arc of the circle can be beautiful: this does not signify the perfect completion which no longer lends itself to criticism, like the snake of Midgard that encircles the world. In the arc there is still an element of incompletion that needs to be and is capable of being fulfilled — *it can still be anticipated.* For this reason the ring too is always the symbol of something non-moral or anti-moral." (This thought clarified for me the eminently metaphysical impression that porticoes and arched openings in general have always made upon me.) Symbols of a superior reality are often to be seen in geometric forms. For example the triangle has served from antiquity, as indeed it still does today in the theosophists' doctrine, as a mystical and magical symbol, and it certainly often awakens a sense of uneasiness and even of fear in the onlooker, even if he is ignorant of this tradition. (In like manner the square has always obsessed my mind. I always saw squares rising like mysterious stars behind every one of my pictorial representations.)

Starting from such principles we can cast our eyes upon the world around us without falling back into the sins of our predecessors.

We can still attempt all aesthetics, including the appearance of the human figure, since through working and meditating upon such problems, facile and deceitful illusions are no longer possible. Friends of a new knowledge, of new *philosophies*, we can at last smile with sweetness upon the charms of our art.

Dada

Dada is a joyful undoing of seriousness, a brilliant sendup of the sober. As Jean (also known as Hans) Arp says, "we were all dada before the existence of Dada" ("Declarations," Lippard, *Dadas on Art*, 22), and certainly, if we listen to the founder and Papa-Dada Tristan Tzara, we are all presidents of Dada, in Cologne or Berlin or Hanover or Zurich or Paris or wherever. Whether it is the name a child babbles first of all things, a hobbyhorse, or just the first word Tzara pointed to in the dictionary, and thus a chance name, Dada has gone far since its 1916 beginning in the Café Voltaire in Zurich. Dada is as much an attitude as a movement, but it is always in motion. It picks up the collage aesthetic, yells out its insults as it shrieks its way down the side of the volcano, sweeping away both cobwebs and rationality.

Tzara was at the origin of Dada, along with Arp, Max Ernst, Hugo Ball, and Sophie Tauber, and then became, for a while, a Surrealist in Paris. As his *25 Poems*, with their African sounds and their rapid-fire intensity, are Dada, his epic lyric poem, *Approximate Man*, is Surrealist. If the Surrealist act *par excellence* is to go down into the street to fire on the first passerby, the Dada act is rather to cut out words from a newspaper, shake them around in a hat, and select pieces at random to throw upon a piece of paper to make a self-portrait. Look! says Tzara. It will resemble you.

Zurich Dada

In the beginning was Zurich Dada. It flourished in 1916 at the Cabaret Voltaire with the Romanian Tzara, Arp, Tauber, Ernst, Richard Huelsenbeck, and Ball (who later was to give himself over to mysticism). At the first Dada evening, on July 14, Huelsenbeck read a poem with "real sounds"—its "objective reality," as the Cubists had introduced reality into their art, Tzara explains. The poem becomes a static object that can be read from all sides at once and, in fact, in several languages at once, like "The Admiral is looking for a house to rent," read simultaneously in German, French, and English. Readings were accompanied by what Ball called "stupendous negro music (with the big drum: BOUM BOUM BOUM)," a Dada prelude to John Cage's *Lecture on the Weather*, in which twelve readers read from different Thoreau texts at the same time. Simultaneous readings had been performed by the Russian Futurists, that of Victor Khlebnikov and Alexey Kruchenykh and their theory of pure sound and that of Wassily Kandinsky, of the *Blaue Reiter* group, all of whose work Ball knew. He would declaim his sound poetry wrapped in a cardboard column and immense cardboard collar: "Gadji beri bimba," his celebrated "Caravan" poem begins, later set to music by the Talking Heads. The poet "crows, curses, sighs, stammers, yodels," freeing the word into its own "innermost alchemy," as the Surrealists would later free thought by their automatic writing (Lippard, *Dadas on Art,* 26). "We have changed the word with forces and energies," said Arp (MacMillan, *Transition,* 104). Dada presentations were to be childlike and symbolical; the grownup audience, as was intended, would generally be in an uproar, and the Dadas would be ecstatic.

Among the Russian sound poets of Zaoum, Euy (Khlebnikov) had also published a book called *Ryav!* (Roar!), like the end of Tzara's great "Manifesto on Feeble Love and Bitter Love," which concludes with a long series of roars. Tzara makes a distinction between Futurist sound poetry and that of Dada, maintaining that the Dada "concert of vowels" uses only the essence of the word or the primitive sounds, and here again he underlines Dada's relation to the Cubists. The accent falls on the word and concept of the primitive. "Art is a procession of continual differences." The Dada poem-in-motion uses "primitive movements," already a kind of body art (Tzara, *Approximate Man,* 167–69). Tzara's *Twenty-five Poems* of 1918 use African syllables and words (some taken from the journal *Anthropos:*)—like Dada performance, they are aimed against the audience, and their beauty is, like that of the Surrealists, convulsive:

> the reader wants to die perhaps or dance and begins to yell
> he is thin stupid dirty he doesn't understand my verses he yells
> he is one-eyed
> there are zigzags on his soul and lots of rrrrrr
> nbaze baze baze look at the submarine tiara which unravels in golden
>   seaweed
> hozondrac trac
> nfounda nbababa nfounda tata
> nbababa

In Zurich or Berlin or Hanover or Paris, Dada is primitive, noisy, passionate.

9.1

Dada Excites Everything

1921

DADA EXCITES EVERYTHING

(The signatories of this manifesto live in France, America, Spain, Germany, Italy, Switzerland, Belgium, etc., but have no nationality.)

DADA knows everything. DADA spits everything out.

BUT.......

HAS DADA EVER SPOKEN TO YOU:

YES – NO

YES – NO

YES – NO

about Italy
about accordions
about women's pants
about the fatherland
about sardines
about Fiume
about Art (you exaggerate my friend)
about gentleness
about D'Annunzio
what a horror
about heroism
about mustaches
about lewdness
about sleeping with Verlaine
about the ideal (it's nice)
about Massachusetts
about the past
about odors
about salads
about genius. about genius. about genius
about the eight-hour day
and about Parma violets

NEVER   NEVER   NEVER

DADA doesn't speak. DADA has no fixed idea. DADA doesn't catch flies.

THE MINISTRY IS OVERTURNED. BY WHOM?

BY DADA

The Futurist is dead. Of What? Of DADA

A young girl commits suicide. Because of What? DADA
The spirits are telephoned. Who invented it? DADA
Someone walks on your feet. It's DADA

YES – NO

If you have serious ideas about life,
If you make artistic discoveries
and if all of a sudden your head begins to crackle with
laughter,
if you find all your ideas useless and ridiculous, know that

IT IS DADA BEGINNING TO SPEAK TO YOU

cubism constructs a cathedral of *artistic* liver paste

WHAT DOES DADA DO?

expressionism poisons *artistic* sardines

WHAT DOES DADA DO?

simultaneism is still at its first *artistic* communion

WHAT DOES DADA DO?

futurism wants to mount in an *artistic* lyricism-elevator

WHAT DOES DADA DO?

unanism embraces allism and fishes with an *artistic* line

WHAT DOES DADA DO?

neo-classicism discovers the good deeds of *artistic* art

WHAT DOES DADA DO?

paroxysm makes a trust of all *artistic* cheeses

WHAT DOES DADA DO?

ultraism recommends the mixture of these seven *artistic* things

WHAT DOES DADA DO?

creationism vorticism imagism also propose some *artistic* recipes

WHAT DOES DADA DO?

WHAT DOES DADA DO?

50 francs reward to the person who finds the best way to explain DADA to us

Dada passes everything through a new net.
Dada is the bitterness which opens its laugh on all that which has been *made consecrated forgotten* in our language in our brain in our habits.
It says to you: There is Humanity and the lovely idiocies which have made it happy to this advanced age

DADA HAS ALWAYS EXISTED

THE HOLY VIRGIN WAS ALREADY A DADAIST

DADA IS NEVER RIGHT

Citizens, comrades, ladies, gentlemen
Beware of forgeries!

Imitators of DADA want to present DADA in an *artistic* form which it has never had

CITIZENS,

You are presented today in a pornographic form, a vulgar and baroque spirit which is not the PURE IDIOCY claimed by DADA

BUT DOGMATISM AND PRETENTIOUS IMBECILITY

Paris   January 12, 1921

For all information
write "AU SANS PAREIL"
37, Avenue Kléber.
Tel. PASSY 25-22

E. Varèse, Tr. Tzara, Ph. Soupault, Soubeyran, J. Rigaut, G. Ribemont-Dessaignes, M. Ray, F. Picabia, B. Péret, C. Pansaers, R. Hülsenbeck, J. Evola, M. Ernst, P. Eluard, Suz. Duchamp, M. Duchamp, Crotti, G. Cantarelli, Marg. Buffet, Gab. Buffet, A. Breton, Baargeld, Arp., W. C. Arensberg, L. Aragon.

9.2 Jean (Hans) Arp
Manifesto of the Dada Crocodarium
1920

The statue lamps come from the bottom of the sea and shout long live DADA to greet the passing ocean liners and the presidents dada a dada the dada the dadas I dada you dada he dadas and three rabbits in india ink by arp dadaist in porcelain of striped bicycle we will leave for london in the royal aquarium ask in any pharmacy for the dadaists of rasputin the tzar and the pope who are valid only for two thirty.

9.3 Jean (Hans) Arp
The Elephant Style versus the Bidet Style
1934

Rational architecture was repressed aesthetics.
Shattered, the porcelain bidets, the glass tables, the nickel chairs cover the
    rude floor of reality.
The fog that is man refuses to be put in a corner.
Reason, that ugly wart, has fallen off man.
Logical non-sense has once again had to yield to illogical non-sense.
On the ruins of rational architure, elephant-style architecture rises,
    peacock-style, bell-style, egg-style, et cetera.
The last architects are sitting on pedestals with mummy faces.
Vigorous ornamentalists benevolently feed them pills of nourishing,
    fortifying, and irrational art.
The detectives of the ornamentalists conscientiously survey the world,
    rigidly making sure that even the tiniest spot does not remain
    unpainted or unsculpted.
Even shoe soles have to be painted or sculpted.
Logical non-sense has once again had to yield to illogical non-sense.
Lightning and thunder are transformed into loud and luminous
    epigraphs.
The winds are colored and follow artificial and decorative currents.
The long-trunked towers with lobworm clouds on their heads stroll about
    on their clawed paws.

The bronze houses without windows or doors but with shutters ring so
loud that the obelisks have babies.
Grass-greenhorns drift across the sky. Horns hang from long tufts.
The immense marble breasts make their entrances through the arches of
triumph, go up on the roller coasters, and vanish in the labyrinths.
The shapes of continents are changed into floral shapes. Europe is shaped
like a lily.

9.4 JEAN (HANS) ARP

Infinite Millimeter Manifesto

1938

we have to first let forms, colors, words, sounds grow
and then explain them.
We have to first let legs, wings, hands grow and then let them fly sing form
manifest themselves.
I for one don't draw up a plan first as if I were dealing with a timetable a
calculation or a war.
The art of stars, flowers, forms, colors is part of the infinite.

9.5 Richard Huelsenbeck, Marcel Janko, and Tristan Tzara

L'Amiral cherche une maison à louer

1916

L'amiral cherche

Poème simultan par R. Huelsenbeck, M. Janko, Tr. Tzara

HUELSENBECK	Ahoi	ahoi	Des	Admirals	gwirktes	Beinkleid	schnell
JANKO, chant			Where	the honny	suckle	wine twines	ilself
TZARA	Boum	boum boum	Il	déshabilla	sa chair	quand les	grenouilles

HUELSENBECK	und	der	Conciergenbäuche	Klapperschlangengrün	sind	milde	ach
JANKO, chant	can	hear	the weopour	will arround	arround	the	hill
TZARA	serpent	à	Bucarest	on dépendra	mes	amis	dorénavant et

HUELSENBECK	prrrza	chrrrza	prrrza		Wer	suchet	dem	wird
JANKO, chant	mine	admirabily		confortabily	Grandmother		said	
TZARA					Dimanche:		deux	éléphants

Intermède rythmique

HUELSENBECK	hihi *ff*	Yabomm	hihi *p*	Yabomm *cresc ff*	hihi	hihi *cresc*	hihiiiii *ff f*
TZARA	rouge bleu *p*	rouge bleu	rouge bleu *f cresc*	rouge bleu *ff*	rouge bleu *cresc fff*
SIFFLET (Janko)	— *p*	·	*cresc*	— *f*	·	— *ff*	·	*fff*
CLIQUETTE (TZ)	rrrrrrrrr *f decrsc*	rrrrrrrrr *f*	rrrrrrrrr *cresc*	rrrrrrrrr *fff*	rrrrrrrrr *uniform*	rrrrrrrrr
GROSSE CAISE (Huels.)	o o o *p*	o o o o o *f*	o o o o o	o o o o *fff*	o o *f*

HUELSENBECK	im	Kloset	zumeistens	was	er nötig	hätt	ahoi iuché ahoi iuché
JANKO (chant)	I	love the	ladies	I love	to be	among	the girls
TZARA	la	concièrge	qui m'a	trompé elle a	vendu	l'appartement	que j'avais loué

HUELSENBECK	hätt'	O süss	gequollnes Stelldichein	des Admirals	im Abendschein	uru uru
JANKO (chant)	o'clock and tea is set	I like	to have	my tea with	some brunet	shai shai
TZARA	Le train	traîne	la fumée	comme	la fuite de	l'animal blessé aux

HUELSENBECK	Der Affe	brüllt	die Seekuh	belit im Lindenbaum	der Schräg	zerschellt tara-
JANKO (chant)	doing it	doing it	see	that ragtime	coupple over there	see
TZARA	Autour du	phare	tourne l'auréole	des oiseaux bleuillis	en moitiés de lumière	vis-

HUELSENBECK		Peitschen um die Lenden	Im Schlafsack gröhlt der
JANKO (chant)		oh yes yes yes yes yes yes yes	yes yes
TZARA	cher c'est si difficile	La rue s'enfuit avec mon bagage à traves la ville	Un métro mêle

NOTE POUR LES BOURGEOIS Les essays sur la transmutation des objets et des couleurs des premiers peintres cubistes (19J7) Picasso, Braque, Picabia, Duchamp-Villon, Delaunay, suscitaient l'envie d'appliquer en poésie les mêmes principes simultans.

Villiers de l'Isle Adam eût des intentions pareilles dans le théâtre, où l'on remarque les tendances vers un simultanéisme schématique; Mallarmé essaya une reforme typographique dans son poème: Un coup de dés n'abolira jamais le hazard; Marinetti qui popularisa cette subordination par ses „Paroles en liberté"; les intentions de Blaise Cendrars et de Jules Romains, dernièrement, ammenèrent Mr Apollinaire aux idées qu'il développa en 1912 au „Sturm" dans une conférence.

Mais l'idée première, en son essence, fut exteriorisée par Mr H. Barzun dans un livre théoretique „Voix, Rythmes et chants Simultanés" où il cherchait une rélation plus étroite entre la symphonie polirythmique et le poème. Il opposait aux principes successifs de la poésie lyrique une idée vaste et parallèle. Mais les intentions de compliquer en profondeur cette t e c h n i q u e (avec le Drame Universel) en éxagerant sa valeur au point de lui donner une idéologie nouvelle et de la cloîtrer dans l'exclusivisme d'une école, — echouèrent.

une maison à louer

```
zerfällt                                          Teerpappe   macht  Rawagen              in    der  Nacht
arround          the    door    a    swetheart    mine     is      waiting    patiently    for    me    1
humides          çommancèrent   à    bruler       j'ai     mis     le         cheval       dans   l'âme  du


verzerrt   in    der    Natur                                    chrza       prrrza        chrrrza
                                                             my   great       room    is
c'est   très     intéressant   les    griffes   des   morsures   équatoriales


aufgetan   Der    Ceylonlöve    ist    kein    Schwan      Wer    Wasser      braucht       find
                                                           I      love        the       ladies
          Journal    de    Genève    au    restaurant     Le     télégraphiste     assassine
```

```
                                                         Find    was     er   nötig
                                                         And     when    it's five
Dans  l'église  après  la  messe  le  pêcheur  dit  à  la  comtesse :  Adieu  Mathilde

uro      uru     uru      uro     uru     uru     uru     uro   pataclan    patablan    pataplan    uri    uri    uro
shai     shai    shai     shai    shai    shai    shai    Every  body is doing it   doing it    doing it    Every  body  is
intestins ecrasés

tata      tarataia   tatatata    In  Joschiwara   dröhnt  der  Brand    und   knallt  mit   schnellen
that    throw there shoulders in the air She said the raising her heart    oh    dwelling                          oh
sant    la distance des batteaux  Tandis que les archanges chient et  les   oiseaux     tombent      Oh!   mon

alte     Oberpriester    und    zeigt    der    Schenkel    volle    Tastatur      L'Amiral   n'a   rien   trouvé
yes    oh yes oh yes  oh yes  oh yes  yes  oh yes         sir                       L'Amiral   n'a   rien   trouvé
       son cinéma la prore de  je vous adore était au casino du sycomore           L'Amiral   n'a   rien   trouvé
```

En même temps Mr Apollinaire essayait un nouveau genre de poème visuel, qui est plus intéressant encore par son manque de système et par sa fantaisie tourmentée. Il accentue les images centrales, typographiquement, et donne la possibilité de commancer à lire un poème de tous les côtés à la fois. Les poèmes de Mrs Barzun et Divoire sont purement formels. Ils cherchent un éffort musical, qu'on peut imaginer en faisant les mêmes abstractions que sur une partiture d'orchestre.

* * *

Je voulais réaliser un poème basé sur d'autres principes. Qui consistent dans la possibilité que je donne à chaque écoutant de lier les associations convenables. Il retient les éléments caractéristiques pour sa personalité, les entremêle, les fragmente etc, restant tout-de-même dans la direction que l'auteur a canalisé.

Le poème que j'ai arrangé (avec Huelsenbeck et Janko) ne donne pas une description musicale. mais tente à individualiser l'impression du poème simultan auquel nous donnons par là une nouvelle portée.

La lecture parallèle que nous avons fait le 31 mars 1916, Huelsenbeck, Janko et moi, était la première réalisation scénique de cette estéthique moderne.

TRISTAN TZARA

9.6 Tristan Tzara

Note on Art

1917

Art is at present the only construction complete unto itself, about which nothing more can be said, it is such richness, vitality, sense, wisdom. Understanding, seeing. Describing a flower: relative poetry more or less paper flower. Seeing.

Until the intimate vibrations of the last cell of a brain-god-mathematics are discovered along with the explanation of primary astronomies, that is the essence, impossibility will always be described with the logical elements of continual contradiction, that swamp of stars and of useless bells. Toads of cold lanterns, squashed flat against the descriptive sense of a red belly. What is written on art is an educational work and in that sense it can be justified. We want to make men realize afresh that the one unique fraternity exists in the moment of intensity when the beautiful and life itself are concentrated on the height of a wire rising toward a burst of light, a blue trembling linked to the earth by our magnetic gazes covering the peaks with snow. The miracle. I open my heart to creation.

Many are the artists who no longer seek solutions in the object and in its relations with the external; they are cosmic or primary, decided, simple, wise, serious.

The diversity of today's artists gathers the fountain's spray into a great crystal freedom. And their efforts create new clear organisms, in a world of purity, with the help of tansparencies and the constructive materiality of a simple image as it forms. They continue the tradition: the past and its evolution push them slowly snakelike toward the interior, direct consequences far beyond surfaces and reality.

Dada Manifesto

1918

The magic of a word—DADA—which has set the journalists at the door
of an unexpected world, has not the slightest importance for us.

To proclaim a manifesto you have to want: A.B.C., thunder against 1,2,3,

lose your patience and sharpen your wings to conquer and spread a's, b's, c's little and big, sign, scream, swear, arrange the prose in a form of absolute and irrefutable evidence, prove your non-plus-ultra and maintain that novelty resembles life just as the latest appearance of a whore proves the essence of God. His existence was already proved by accordions, landscapes, and gentle words. ∘°∘ To impose your A.B.C. is a natural thing—therefore regrettable. Everyone does it in a form of crystalbluff-madonna, a monetary system, a pharmaceutical product, a bare leg beckoning to an ardent and sterile spring. The love of novelty is the agreeable cross, proves a naive Idon'tgiveadamnism, sign with no cause, fleeting and positive. But this need has aged also. By giving to art the impulse of supreme simplicity: novelty, desire to win, a ridiculous knowledge of life, which they have classified, divided, channeled; they insist on seeing categories dance in time to their measure. Their readers snicker and keep going: what is the use?

There is a literature which doesn't reach voracious masses. A work of creators, the result of a real need of the author, and done for himself. Knowledge of a supreme egoism, where laws fade away. ∘°∘ Each page ought to explode, either from deep and weighty seriousness, a whirlwind, dizziness, the new, or the eternal, from its crushing humor, the enthusiasm of principles or its typographical appearance. Here is a tottering world fleeing, future spouse of the bells of the infernal scale, and here on the other side: new men. Harsh, leaping, riders of hiccups. Here are a mutilated world and the literary medicine men with passion for improvement.

I say: there is no beginning and we are not trembling, we are not sentimental. We shred the linen of clouds and prayers like a furious wind, preparing the great spectacle of disaster, fire, decomposition. Let's get ready to cast off mourning and to replace tears with mermaids stretched out from one continent to the next. Pavilions of intense joy, empty of the sadness of poison.

。°。 DADA is the signboard of abstraction; advertising and business are also poetic elements.

I destroy the drawers of the brain and of social institutions: demoralizing everything and hurling the celestial hand to hell, the hellish eyes to heaven, setting up once more the fecund wheel of a universal circus in the actual power and the fantasy of each individual.

Philosophy is the question: from what side to start looking at life, god, the idea, or anything else. Everything you look at is false. I don't believe the relative result to be any more important than the choice between cake and cherries after dinner. The approach of looking quickly at the other side of a thing in order to impose your opinion indirectly is called dialectic, that is, haggling over the spirit of french fries while dancing the method around. If I shout:

IDEAL, IDEAL, IDEAL,

KNOWLEDGE, KNOWLEDGE, KNOWLEDGE,

BOOMBOOM, BOOMBOOM, BOOMBOOM,

I have put down rather exactly the progress, the laws, morality, and all the other lovely qualities that various very intelligent people have discussed in so many books, just in order to say finally that each man has danced anyway according to his own personal boomboom, and that he is right in his boomboom, as a satisfaction of unhealthy curiosity; private ringing for inexplicable needs; bath; monetary difficulties; stomach with repercussions in real life; authority of the mystical wand expressed as a bouquet of orchestraghost with mute bows, greased with potions based on animal manure. With the blue lorgnon of an angel they dug out the inside for a nickel of unanimous gratitude. 。°。 If they are all right and if all pills are just Pink pills, let's try for once to be wrong. 。°。 You think you can explain rationally, by thinking, what is written. But it's quite relative. Thought is a nice thing for philosophy but it's relative. Psychoanalysis is a dangerous sickness, lulls the antirealistic tendencies of man and codifies the bourgeoisie. There is no final Truth. Dialectic is an amusing machine which leads us

in a banal manner

to opinions we would have had anyway.

Do you think that by the scrupulous refinements of logic you have demonstrated truth and established the exactness of your opinions? Logic restricted by the senses is an organic sickness. Philosophers like to add to that element: the power of observation. But precisely this magnificient quality of the mind is the proof of its impotence. You observe, you look at things from one or many points of view, you choose them among the existing millions. Experience is also a result of chance and of individual faculties. .°. Science repulses me as soon as it becomes speculative-system, losing its useful character—so very useless—but at least individual. I hate complacent objectivity and harmony, that science that finds everything in order. Carry on, children, humanity. . . . Science says that we are the servants of nature: everything is in order, make love and die. Carry on children, humanity, nice bourgeois people and virgin journalists . . . .°.

I am against systems, the most acceptable system is the one of not having any system, on principle. .°. Making yourself complete, growing perfect in your own littleness until you have filled up the vase of your self, the courage to fight for and against thought, the mystery of bread sudden unleashing of an infernal helix into economic lilies:

DADAIST SPONTANEITY
I call Idon'tgiveadamnism the state of a life where each person keeps his own conditions, although knowing how to respect other individuals, if not defending himself, the two-step becoming a national hymn, a whatnot store, a radio playing Bach fugues, neon lights and signs for brothels, the organ diffusing carnations for God, all that together and actually replacing photography and unilateral catechism.

Active simplicity
The inability to discern degrees of brightness: licking the penumbra and floating in the great mouth full of honey and excrement. Measured by the scale of Eternity, all action is vain—(if we let thought undertake an adventure whose result would be infinitely grotesque—an important fact for the knowledge of human impotence). But if life is a bad farce, with neither goal nor initial labor pains, and because we think we should withdraw as fresh as washed chrysanthemums from the whole business, we have proclaimed as the single basis of understanding: art. It does not have the importance that we, as mercenaries of the mind, have attributed to it for centuries. Art afflicts no one and those who can get interested in it will earn the right to be caressed and the wonderful occasion to blanket the country with their conversation. Art is a private thing, the artist does it for himself; a comprehensible work is the product of a journalist, and because right now I feel like dabbing this monster in oil paints: a paper tube imitating the metal you squeeze and out come hatred, cowardice, meanness automatically. The artist, the poet are delighted with the venom of the mass concentrated into a section manager of this industry; they love to be insulted: a proof of their

unchanging nature. The author and the artist praised in the papers notice how their work is understood: as the miserable lining of a cloak for public use, rags covering brutality, piss coalescing with the heat of an animal hatching the basest instincts. Flabby insipid flesh multiplying by means of typographic microbes.

We have discarded the sniveling tendency in ourselves. Every filtration of that kind is candied diarrhea. Encouraging this art means directing it. We must have strong, upright works, precise, and forever unintelligible. Logic is a complication. Logic is always false. It draws the strings of ideas, words, along their formal exterior, toward illusory extremes and centers. Its chains kill, like an enormous centipede stifling independence. Married to logic, art would live in incest, swallowing, devouring its own tail still attached, fornicating with itself and the personality would become a nightmare tarred with protestantism, a monument, a heap of heavy gray intestines.

But suppleness, enthusiasm, and even the joy of injustice, that little truth which we practice innocently and which gives us our good looks: we are delicate and our fingers are adjustable and glide like the branches of that insinuating, almost liquid plant; it gives our soul precision, the cynics say. That is a point of view too; but fortunately all flowers aren't saintly, and what is divine in us is the awakening of antihuman action. We're talking about a paper flower for the buttonhole of the gentlemen who customarily frequent the ball of masked life, kitchen of grace, white cousins supple or fat. They do business with whatever we have chosen. Contradiction and unity of polarities in one single stream can be truth. If you are going to pronounce that banality anyway, evil-smelling appendix to a libidinous morality. Morality atrophies like any scourge that intelligence produces. The rigidity of morality and logic have made us impassive in the presence of policemen—the cause of slavery—putrid rats filling middle-class stomachs and infecting the only bright and clean glass corridors which remained open to artists.

Let every man shout: there is a great destructive, negative work to be accomplished. Sweeping, cleaning. The cleanliness of the individual affirms itself after the state of madness, the aggressive, you are human and true about being amused, impulsive and vibrant in order to crucify boredom. At the crossroads of lights, alert, attentive, on the watch for passing years, in the forest. ₒ°ₒ

I am writing a manifesto and I don't want anything, I say however certain things and I am on principle against manifestoes, as I am also against principles (half-pints for judging the moral value of each sentence—too easy; approximation was invested by the impressionists). ₒ°ₒ I am writing this manifesto to show that you can do contrary actions together, in one single fresh breath; I am against action; for continual contradiction, for affirmation also, I am neither for nor against and I don't explain because I hate common sense.

DADA—now there's a word that sets off ideas; each bourgeois is a little playwright, inventing different dialogs, instead of setting characters suitable to the level of his intelligence, like pupae on chairs, seeking causes or purposes (according to the psychoanalytic method he practices) to cement his plot, a story which defines itself in talking. ₒ°ₒ Each spectator is a plotter, if he tries to explain a word (knowledge!). From the cotton-padded refuge of serpentine complications, he has his instincts manipulated. Thence the misfortunes of conjugal life.

Explaining: Amusement of redbellies on the mills of empty skulls.

DADA MEANS NOTHING

If you find it futile and if you don't waste your time for a word that doesn't mean anything. . . . The first thought revolving in these heads is bacteriological: at least find its etymological, historical, or psychological origin. You learn from the papers that the Krou blacks call the tail of a holy cow: DADA. In a certain part of Italy, the cube and the mother: DADA. A hobby-horse, a nurse, double affirmation in Russian and in Rumanian: DADA. Certain learned journalists see in it an art for babies, other holy jesusescallinglittlechildren, a return to a dry and noisy, noisy and monotonous primitivism. You don't build a sensitivity on one word; every construction converges in a boring perfection, the stagnant idea of a gilded swamp, a relative human product. The work of art should not be beauty itself, because that is dead; neither gay nor sad, neither clear nor obscure, simply making individuals happy or sad in serving them cakes of sacred haloes or the sweatings of an arched course across the atmospheres. A work of art is never beautiful by decree, objectively, for everybody. Criticism is therefore useless, it only exists subjectively for each person and without the slightest generality. Do you think you have found the psychic basis common to all humanity? The experience of Jesus and the Bible cover under their broad and benevolent wings: excrement, animals, days. How do you mean to put order in the chaos constituting this infinite and formless variation: man? The principle: "love your neighbor" is an hypocrisy. "Know thyself" is a utopia but more acceptable because it contains nastiness within it. No pity. After the carnage we still have the hope of a purified humanity. I always speak of myself because I don't want to convince anyone, I don't have the right to drag others along in my current, I am not obliging anyone to follow me and everyone does his art in his own way, if he knows the joy ascending like arrows toward the stars, or that burrowing in the mines to the flowers of corpses and their fertile spasms. Stalactites: look for them everywhere, in the cribs pain has widened, their eyes white like angels' hares. So DADA was born of a desire for independence, of a distrust of the community.* Those who belong to us keep their freedom. We don't recognize any theory. We have had enough of cubist and futurist academies: laboratories of formal ideas. Do you practice art to earn money and fondle the middle class? Rhymes ring the assonance of coins and inflection slides along the line of the tummy in profile. All the groupings of artists have ended at this bank even while they rode high along on diverse comets. A door open to the possibilities of luxuriating in cushions and food.

Here we cast anchor in rich earth.

Here we have the right to proclaim for we have known the shivers and the waking. Returning drunken with energy we stab the trident in the unsuspecting flesh. We are the flowing of maledictions in a tropical abundance of vertiginous vegetation, rubber and rain are our sweat, we bleed and burn thirst, our blood is vigor.

Cubism was born from the simple way of looking at the object: Cézanne painted a cup twenty centimeters lower than his eyes, the cubists look at it from above, others complicate its appearance by making one part perpendicular and in putting it nicely on one side. (I am not forgetting the creators, nor the great motives of the matter they make definitive.) ˳°˳ The futurist sees the same cup in movement, a succession of objects one alongside the other embellished maliciously by some lines of force. Which doesn't keep the canvas from being a good or bad painting destined to be an investment for intellectual capital. The new painter creates a world whose elements are also the means of creating it, a sober and definite work, against which there can be no argument. The new artist protests: he no longer paints (symbolic and illusionistic reproduction) but rather creates directly in stone, wood, iron, tin, rocks, and locomotive organisms that can be turned about on any side by the limpid wind of momentary sensation. ˳°˳ Any pictorial or plas-

* In 1916, at the CABARET VOLTAIRE in Zurich.

tic work is useless; let it be a monster frightening to servile minds, and not sickly-sweet in order to decorate the refectories of animals dressed like men, illustrations of this sad fable of humanity. — A painting is the art of making two geometrically parallel lines meet on a canvas, in front of our eyes, in the reality of a world transposed according to new conditions and possibilities. This world is not specified or defined in the work; it belongs in its innumerable variations to the spectator. For its creator, it is without cause and without theory. *Order = disorder; I = not-I; affirmation = negation:* supreme radiations from an absolute art. Absolute in its purity of ordered cosmic chaos, eternal in the globule a second without duration, breathing, light, or control. 。°。 I like an old work for its novelty. Only contrast links us to the past. 。°。 Writers who teach morality and discuss or ameliorate the psychological basis have, in addition to a hidden complete madness of a world left in the hands of bandits who vandalize and destroy centuries. Without goal or plan, disorganized, unconquerable folly, decomposition. Those strong in words or in strength will survive, for they are quick to defend themselves, the agility of body and feeling flames up on their faceted flesh.

Morality has determined charity and pity, two suet balls grown like elephants, like planets, that people call good. They have nothing good about them. Goodness is lucid, bright and determined, pitiless towards compromise and politics. Morality is the infusion of chocolate in the veins of all men. No supernatural force ordains such comportment, rather the monopoly of the idea sellers and the university profiteers. Sentimentality: seeing a group of men arguing and being bored, they invented the calendar and the medicine prudence. The philosophers' battle started by labeling (mercantilism, balance, meticulous and paltry measures) and it was once more understood that pity is a feeling just like diarrhea in its relation to the sickly disgust, the revolting task of corpses to compromise the sun.

I proclaim the opposition of all cosmic faculties to this gonorrhea of a putrid sun coming out of the factories of philosophic thought, the fierce battle with all the possible means of

DADAIST DISGUST

Every product of disgust capable of becoming a negation of the family is *dada;* the whole being protesting in its destructive force with clenched fists: DADA; knowledge of all the means rejected up to this point by the timid sex of easy compromise and sociability: DADA; abolition of logic, dance of all those impotent to create: DADA; of all hierarchy and social equation installed for the preservation of values by our valets: DADA; each and every object, feelings and obscurities, apparitions and the precise shock of parallel lines, can be means for the combat: DADA; abolition of memory; DADA; abolition of archeology: *DADA;* abolition of the prophets: *DADA;* abolition of the future: DADA; an absolute indisputable belief in each god immediate product of spontaneity: DADA; elegant and unprejudicial leap from one harmony to the other sphere; trajectory of a word tossed like a sonorous cry of phonograph record; respecting all individualities in their momentary madness: serious, fearful, timid, ardent, vigorous, determined, enthusiastic; stripping its chapel of every useless awkward accessory; spitting out like a luminous waterfall any unpleasant or amorous thought, or coddling it — with the lively satisfaction of knowing that it doesn't matter — with the same intensity in the bush of his soul, free of insects for the aristocrats, and gilded with archangels' bodies. Freedom: *DADA DADA DADA*, shrieking of contracted colors, intertwining of contraries and of all contradictions, grotesqueries, nonsequiturs: LIFE.

9.8 TRISTAN TZARA

Mr. Antipyrine's Manifesto

1918

DADA is our intensity: which stands the inconsequential bayonets erect the sumatral head of the German baby; Dada is life with neither slippers nor parallels; which is against and for unity and certainly against the future; we know in our wisdom that our brains will become downy cushions, that our antidogmatism is as exclusionist as the civil servant and that we are not free although we shout freedom; severe necessity without discipline or morals and we spit on humanity.

DADA remains in the European framework of weaknesses, still it is a bunch of excrement, but we want to shit in different colors to ornament the zoo of art of all the consulate flags. We are circus masters and we whistle in carnival winds, among the convents, prostitutes, theaters, realities, feelings, restaurants, ohi, hoho, bang, bang.

We declare that the car is a feeling which has spoiled us enough in the slowness of its abstractions like transatlantic steamers, sounds, and ideas. However, we put the facility on the outside, we seek the central essence, and we are happy if we can hide it; we do not want to count the windows of the marvelous elite, for DADA exists for no one and we want everyone to understand that. Over there is Dada's balcony, I assure you. From there you can hear military marches and go down slicing the air like a seraphin in a people's bath to piss and understand the parabola.

DADA is not madness, nor wisdom, nor irony, look at me, there's a good man.

Art was a hazelnut game, children put together words that ring at the end, then they wept and shouted the stanza and put doll shoes on it, and the stanza became a queen so as to die a little and the queen became a whale, the children ran until they were panting.

Then came the great ambassadors of feeling who cried historically in a chorus:
Psychology Psychology hihi
Science Science Science
Long live France
We are not naive
We are successive
We are exclusive
We are not simple
and we know perfectly well how to discuss intelligence. But we, DADA, we do not agree with them, for art is not serious, I assure you, and if we display crime in order to say ventilator in a learned way, it is to make you happy, good audience, I love you so much, I assure you and adore you.

9.9 TRISTAN TZARA

Note on Poetry

1919

The poet of the last station no longer weeps in vain; lamenting would slow down his gait. Humidity of ages past. Those who feed on tears are happy and heavy; they slip them on to deceive the snakes behind the necklaces of their souls. The poet can devote himself to calisthenics. But to obtain abundance and explosion, he knows how to set hope afire TODAY. Tranquil, ardent, furious, intimate, pathetic, slow, impetuous, his desire boils for enthusiasm, that fecund form of intensity.

Knowing how to recognize and follow the traces of the strength we are waiting for, tracks which are everywhere, in an essential language of numbers, engraved on crystals, on seashells, on rail tracks, in clouds, in glass, inside snow, light, on coal, on the hand, in the radiations grouped around magnetic poles, on wings.

Persistence sharpens and shoots joy up like an arrow toward the astral bells, distillation of the waves of impassive food, creator of a new life. Streaming in all colors and bleeding among the leaves of all trees. Vigor and thirst, emotion before the formation unseen and unexplained: poetry.

Let's not look for analogies among the forms in which art finds outer shape; each has its freedom and its limits. There is no equivalent in art; each branch of the star develops independently, extends and absorbs the world appropriate to it. But the parallel sensed between the lines of a new life, free of any theory, will characterize the age.

Giving to each element its integrity, its autonomy, a necessary condition for the creation of new constellations each has its place in the group. A will to the word: a being upright, an image, a unique, fervent construction, of a dense color and intensity, communion with life.

Art is a procession of continual differences. For there is no measurable distance between the "how are you," the level where worlds are expanded, and human actions seen from this angle of submarine purity. The strength to formulate in *the instant* this varying succession is the work itself. Globe of duration, volume born under a fortuitous pressure.

The mind carries in it new rays of possibilities: centralize them, capture them on the lens which is neither physical nor defined—popularly—the soul. The ways of expressing them, transforming them: the means. Clear golden brilliance—a faster beating of spreading wings.

Without pretensions to a romantic absolute, I present some banal negations.

The poem is no longer subject, rhythm, rhyme, sonority: formal action. Projected on the commonplace, these become means whose use is neither regulated nor registered to which I assign the same importance as to the crocodile, burning ore, grass. Eye, water, scales, sun, kilometer, and everything I can conceive at one time as representing a value which can be humanized:

sensitivity. The elements grow fond of each other when they are so tightly joined, really entwined like the hemispheres of the brain and the cabins of an ocean liner.

Rhythm is the pace of intonations you hear; there is a rhythm unseen and unheard: radiation of an interior grouping toward a constellation of order. Rhythm was until now only the beatings of a dried-up heart: tinklings in rotten and muffled wood. I don't want to treat with a rigid exclusiveness of principle a subject where only liberty matters. But the poet will be severe toward his work in order to find true necessity: from this asceticism will flower order, essential and pure. (Goodness without sentimental echo, its material side.)

To be severe and cruel, pure and honest toward your work which you prepare to place among men new organisms, creations living in bones of light and in fabulous forms of action. (REALITY.)

The rest, called *literature,* is a notebook of human imbecility to aid future professors.

The poem pushes or digs a crater, is silent, murders, or shrieks along accelerated degrees of speed. It will no longer be a product of optics, sense or intelligence, but an impression or a means of transforming the tracks left by feelings.

Simile is a literary tool which no longer satisfies us. There are ways of formulating an image or integrating it but the elements will be taken from differing and distant spheres.

Logic guides us no longer and its commerce, easy, impotent, a deceptive glimmer scattering the coins of a sterile relativism, is extinguished for us forever. Other productive forces shout their freedom, flamboyant, indefinable and gigantic, on the mountains of crystal and of prayer.

Freedom, freedom: not being a vegetarian I'm not giving any recipes.

Darkness is productive if it is a light so white and pure that our neighbors are blinded by it. From their light, ahead, begins our own. Their light is for us, in the mist, the miniscule microscopic dance of the shadowy elements in an imprecise fermentation. Isn't matter in its purity dense and sure?

Under the bark of the fallen trees, I seek the painting of things to come, strength, and in the canals perhaps life is swelling already, the darkness of iron and coal.

Mr. AA the Antiphilosopher
Has Sent Us This Manifesto

1920

Here's to the undertakers of combination!

Every act is a mental gunshot—the insignificant gesture or the decisive movement are just so many agressions (I unfold the fan of knockouts to distill the air separating us)—and with words set down on paper, I enter, with great solemnity, toward myself.

I thrust my sixty fingers into the thick hair of ideas and brutally convulse the draperies, the teeth, the articulating hinges.

I close, I open, I spit. Watch out! This is the moment for me to tell you that I was lying. If there is any system in the lack of system—that of my proportions—I never apply it.

That is to say: I am lying. I lie when I apply it, I lie by not applying it, I lie when I am writing that I am lying because I am not lying—for I have lived the mirror of my father—chosen among all the advantages of baccarat—from town to town—for myself was never myself—for the saxophone wears like a rose the murder of the visceral chauffeur—he is made of sexual copper and running leaves. So does the corn drum it out, the alarm and the pellagra where all those matches are growing.

Extermination. Yes, naturally.

But does not exist. Me: mixture kitchen theater. Long live the stretcher-bearers in the convocations of extasy!

Lying is an extasy—which lasts longer than a second—nothing lasts longer. The idiots sit on the century to hatch it—they start all over a few centuries later—the idiots stay in that circle for ten years—the idiots swing on the clockface of a year—myself (idiot) I stay there for five minutes.

How pretentious, all that blood spreading around in my body and my event, the chance color of the first woman I touched with my eyes in these tentacular times. No banditry more bitter than finishing the sentence you've thought out. Banditry of a gramophone, a little antinhuman mirage that I love in myself—because I find it ridiculous and dishonest. But the bankers of language will always take their little percentage of the discussion. The presence of (at least) one boxer is indispensable for the match—the affiliates of a band of dadaist assassins have signed the self-protection contract for that kind of operation. Their number was greatly reduced—the presence of (at least) one singer for the duet, of (at least) one signer for the receipt, of (at least) one eye for the view,—being absolutely indispensable.

Put the photographic plate of the face in the acid bath.

The commotions that have sensitized it will become visible and will astonish you.

Stick your damned fist in your own damned face and drop dead, all of you.

Proclamation without Pretention

1920

Art goes to sleep for the birth of a new world
"ART"—a *parrot word*—replaced by **DADA**
PLESIAUSAURUS, or handkerchief
The talent WHICH YOU CAN LEARN *makes the poet a*
            druggist
TODAY *criticism balances no longer launches resemblances*
Hypertrophic painters hyperestheticized and hypnotized by
            the
hyancinths of muezzins of hypocritical appearance
CONSOLIDATE THE EXACT HARVEST OF
            CALCULATIONS
HYPERDROME OF IMMORTAL GUARANTEES: *There is no importance*
            there
is no transparency or apparency
MUSICIANS BREAK YOUR BLIND INSTRUMENTS on the
            stage
The **SYRINGE** *is only for my understanding.* **I am writing**
            because
it is as natural as pissing as being sick
Art needs an operation
Art is a ***PRETENTION*** heated in the TIMIDITY of the urinary
basin, **Hysteria** born in the **Studio**

We are seeking **upright pure sober unique** strength we are
seeking **NOTHING** we affirm the **VITALITY** of
            each instant
the anti-philosophy of **Spontaneous** acrobatics
In this moment I hate the man who whispers before
            intermission—
eau de cologne—bitter theater. CHEERY WIND.
IF EVERYBODY SAYS THE OPPOSITE IT IS BECAUSE THEY ARE RIGHT.
Prepare the geyser actions of our blood—submarine formation
of transchromatic airplanes, cellular metals numbered in the
leap of images
            above the regulations of the
BEAUTIFUL and its control
It is not for the runts who are still worshipping
their navel

Berlin Dada

Zurich Dada had flourished, in 1917, in exile. Richard Huelsenbeck, who had been a part of Zurich Dada and who was to end up in New York as an analyst under the name Hulbeck, brought the term to Berlin. There, in 1918, he founded the Club Dada (excluding Kurt Schwitters), while the Dadas opposed the Expressionists and Wilhelm Worringer, the popularizer of the term *Expressionism,* lamented the crisis in artistic beliefs of this period before the Great War.

Raoul Hausmann, the knowitall and most versatile of all the Dadas, developed what he called Dada tactics, that is, satire and the "concrete," with the pseudomechanistic applications of automatic processes, both in photomontage and in typography, which he developed under the influence of the theories of Ernst Mach and others. On his calling card, as well as in the Dada Almanac, he was certified by Huelsenbeck as the Dadasoph. He was the first to encourage automatic writing and believed in a common universal new language for the New Man.

Wanting a neutral stance toward his working materials, Hausmann assumed a mechanistic attitude. The title of his "Manifesto of PREsentism" (4.14) of 1920 makes it seem akin to the Nunism or Nowism of Pierre Albert-Birot and the Simultaneism of Blaise Cendrars, but its general effect is that of a Machinism. Hausmann declares: "Naive anthropomorphism has played out its role. The beauty of our daily life is defined by the mannikins, the wig-making skills of the hairdressers, the exactness of a technical construction! We strive anew towards conformity with the mechanical work process: we will have to get used to the idea of seeing art originating in the factories" (Benson, *Raoul Hausmann,* 205). Hausmann's Presentist works diagram the turns of consciousness, as do some of Francis Picabia's works we usually associate with Dada.

Pig's Bladder

1920

Pig's bladder kettle drum cinnobar cru cru cru
Theosophia pneumatica
the great spiritual art = performance of poème bruitiste
for the first time thanks to Richard Huelsenbeck DaDa
or or birribum birribum the ox whizzes round in a circle or
Drill contracts for light rough forged bits 7.6 cm Chauceur
Portion of Soda cal. 98/100%
Setter damo birridamo holla di funga qualla di mango damai da dai
    umbala damo
brrs pffi commencer Abrr Kpppi commence start start
is nowadayz in dermand fer 'omes
Work
Work
breh breh breh breh breh breh breh breh breh
sokobauno sokobauno sokobauno
Shikaneder Shikaneder Shikaneder
the trash cans are growing fat sokobauno sokobauno
the dead step out of them with wreathes of flaming torches about
    their heads
behold the way the horses are bent over the water butts
behold the way the rivers of paraffin descend from the crests of the moon
behold the way Lake Orizunde reads the newspaper and eats its beafsteak
behold the caries sokobauno sokobauno
behold the way the placenta screams in the high-school boys'
    butterfly nets
sokobauno sokobauno
the vicar closeth his trou-serfly rataplan rataplan his trou-serfly and his
    hair juts ou-out of his ears
the buckcatapult the buckcatapult fa-alls from the sky and the
    grandmother hoiks up her breasts
we blow the flour from our tongues and yell and the head wanders about
    on the gable
the vicar closeth his trou-serfly rataplan rataplan his trou-serfly and his
    hair juts ou-out of his ears

the buckcatapult the buckcatapult fa-alls from the sky and the
    grandmother hoiks up her breasts
we blow the flour from our tongues and yell and the head wanders about
    on the gable
wireheadgametot ibn ben zakalupp vauvoi zakalupp
tailbone oxy-hydro-blow-piping
o shaveling-giblet has stained heavenseverin with sweat
tumour in the joint
belu belu ever blue bloompoet yellows the antlers
Beer bar obibor
birchabor botshon ortitshell seviglia o ca sa ca ca sa ca ca sa ca ca sa ca ca
    sa ca ca sa
hemlock in skin purpulation swells on little wormy and monkey has hand
    and backside
O cha chipulala o ta Mpota Masses
Massgulala massgulala kulilibulala
Bambosha bambosh
the vicar closeth his trou-serfly rataplan rataplan his trou-serfly and his
    hair juts ou-out of his ears
Chupuravanta burruh pupaganda burruh
Ischarimunga vurruh his trou-serfly his trou-serfly
kampampa kamo his trou-serfly his trou-serfly
katapena kamo katapena kara
Chuvuparanta da umba da umba da do
da umba da umba da umba da he he
his trou-serfly his trou-serfly
Mpala the glass the eyetooth trara
katapena kara the poet the poet katapena tafoo
Mfunga Mpala Mfunga Koel
Dytiramba toro and the ox and the ox and the toe covered in verdigis next
    to the stove
Mpala tano mpala tano mpala tano mpala tano oyoho mpala tano mpala
    tano ja tano ja tano ja tano o his trou-serfly
Mpala Zufanga Mfisha Dabosha Karamba jubosha daba eloe

Dutch Dada

Theo van Doesburg (sometimes known as I. K. Bonset) addressed himself to Dadaists and non-Dadaists alike. Here is an address for a non-Dadaiast evening in the winter of 1923. As a Constructivist and a De Stijl theorist, van Doesburg was never to lose his Dada spirit; when the parties meet, as it were, and the personas, it is often in and because of him.

9.13 THEO VAN DOESBURG [I. K. BONSET]

Characteristics of Dadaism (*excerpt*)

1923

No one has as yet worn the Sun in his buttonhole.
—Peter Rohl

Dada is the serious morality of our Time.
—Kurt Schwitters

DADA—and for one instant everyone awakens from his daily somnambulism which he calls living.
DADA—and the sick are healed, move about, and sing "The Watch on the Rhine" or dance a Shimmy.
DADA—and the blind see; they see that the world is dada and laugh ceaselessly at the weighty hair-splitting of our moralists and politicians.
DADA—and the bourgeois sweats rubber, makes a camp bed out of his most beautiful Rembrandt, and dances a one-step to choir music. Each bourgeois is a miniature Landru; behind the mask of culture, humanism, esthetics, and philosophy he gives his instincts free rein.
Culture—what is it but the degree of refinement with which our true instincts are expressed?

＊　　＊　　＊

Dada has discovered the world such as it is and the world has recognised itself in Dada. Dada is a mirror in which the world sees itself. The dadaists do not wish the world to be different than the way they see it, namely, dada: at once orderly and disorderly, yes and no, me and not me.

Jesus Christ was the first Dada.

Holland

Paris—New York Dada and Surrealism

The Dadas who arrived in New York were associated with the *Little Review*, especially Francis Picabia (Pipicabia), who codirected it starting in 1921, with Ezra Pound. They brought over the ideas of French poetry and arts. *Secession*, a New York journal of 1922–23, published the work of Tristan Tzara, Louis Aragon, and Jean Arp, as well as William Carlos Williams, and the single issue of *Rong Wrong* (1917) and the two issues of *The Blind Man* (April and May 1917), that of Marcel Duchamp, the meta-ironist.

The Surrealists who came over from France in the early 1940s were associated with *vvv*, the journal of 1942–44 directed by David Hare: André Breton, Max Ernst, and Marcel Duchamp are to be found in its pages. Breton was never to learn English, and he broadcast in French from New York for the Voice of America. *vvv* was far more French in leaning than Charles Henri Ford's avant-garde *View*, equally devoted to the interrelations of the arts. (Breton had asked Ford to take over *vvv* and leave *View*, but Ford preferred his independence.)

Upon Breton's return to France, he was attacked by Tzara in the Sorbonne for having accepted exile during the war. The members of the Surrealist group were now younger, and the spirit had changed. After Breton's death in 1966, the group survived three years as such. While many consider Surrealism defunct, Breton's 1964 statement "Surrealism Continues" sums up the feelings of an ongoing international movement in its various manifestations; "Magic Realism" in Spanish-speaking countries is among its more vivid survivors. The Surrealist spirit is far from dead.

9.14 MARCEL DUCHAMP

Possible

1913

The representation of a possible
(not as the contrary of impossible
nor as relative to the probable
nor as subordinated to the likely)
The *possible* is only
a *physical* "mordant" [vitriolic type]
burning every aesthetics or callistics

9.15 FRANCIS PICABIA

Dada Cannibalistic Manifesto

1920

You are all accused; stand up. The orator will speak to you only if you are standing.
Standing as for the Marseillaise,
standing as for the Russian hymn,
standing as for God save the king,
standing as before the flag.
Finally standing before DADA, which represents life and accuses you of
loving everything out of snobism from the moment that it becomes
    expensive.
Are you completely settled? So much the better, that way you are going to listen to me with greater attention.
What are you doing here, parked like serious oysters—for you are serious, right?
Serious, serious, serious to death.
Death is a serious thing, huh?
One dies as a hero, or as an idiot, which is the same thing. The only word which is not ephemeral is the word death. You love death for others.
To death, death, death.
Only money which doesn't die, it just leaves on trips.

It is God, one respects it, the serious person—money respect of families.

Honor, honor to money; the man who has money is an honorable man.

Honor is bought and sold like ass. Ass, ass represents life like fried
    potatoes,

and all of you who are serious, you will smell worse than cow shit.

DADA doesn't smell anything, it is nothing, nothing, nothing.

It is like your hopes: nothing.

like your paradise: nothing

like your idols: nothing

like your political men: nothing

like your heroes: nothing

like your artists: nothing

like your religions: nothing

Whistle, cry, smash my mouth and then, and then? I will tell you again
    that

you are all pears. In three months we, my friends and I, are going to sell
    you

our paintings for several francs.

9.16 FRANCIS PICABIA

DADA Manifesto

1920

The Cubists want to cover Dada with snow; that may surprise you, but it is so, they want to empty the snow from their pipe to bury Dada.

Are you sure?

Perfectly sure, the facts are revealed by grotesque mouths. They think that Dada can prevent them from practising this odious trade: Selling art expensively.

Art costs more than sausages, more than women, more than everything.

Art is visible like God! (see Saint-Sulpice.)

Art is a pharmaceutical product for imbeciles.

The tables turn thanks to spirit; the paintings and other works of art are like strong-box *tables,* the spirit is inside and becomes more and more inspired according to the auction prices.

Farce, farce, farce, farce, farce, my dear friends.

Dealers do not like painting, they recognize the mystery of spirit . . .

Buy copies of autographs.

Don't be snobs, you will never be less intelligent because your neighbor possesses something exactly like yours.

No more fly specks on the walls.

There will be some anyway, that's clear, but a few less.

Dada is certainly going to become less and less detested, its police-pass will permit it to bypass processions chanting "Come, Ducky," what a sacrilege!

Cubism represents the dearth of ideas.

They have cubed paintings of the primitives, cubed Negro sculptures, cubed violins, cubed guitars, cubed the illustrated newspapers, cubed shit, and the profiles of young girls, how they must cube money!!!

Dada itself wants nothing, nothing, nothing, it's doing something so that the public can say: "We understand nothing, nothing, nothing."

The Dadaists are nothing, nothing, nothing—certainly they will come to nothing, nothing, nothing.

> FRANCIS PICABIA
> who knows nothing, nothing, nothing.

Is an Imbecile, an Idiot, a Pickpocket!!!

1921

FRANCIS PICABIA

Is an imbecile, an idiot, a pickpocket!!!

BUT

he saved Arp from constipation!

THE FIRST MECHANICAL WORK WAS CREATED
BY MADAME TZARA THE DAY SHE PUT LITTLE
TRISTAN INTO THE WORLD, HOWEVER SHE
DIDN'T KNOW IT

FUNNY-GUY

FRANCIS PICABIA

is an imbecilic spanish professor
who has never been dada
FRANCIS PICABIA IS NOTHING!

FRANCIS PICABIA *likes the morality of*
idiots

Arp's binocle is Tristan's testicle

FRANCIS PICABIA IS NOTHING!!!!!!!!!!!

BUT: ARP WAS DADA BEFORE DADA

FRANCIS·PICABIA

IS poor
IS rich
NOT serious
a professor
an imbecile
a Spaniard
NOT a literary man
NOT a painter
a clown
an idiot
a wag

Binet-Valmer too
Ribemont-Dessaignes too
Philippe Soupault too
Tristan Tzara too
Marcel Duchamp too
Theodore Fraenkel too
Louis Vauxcelles too
Frantz Jourdain too
Louis Aragon too
Picasso too
Derain too
Matisse too
Max Jacob too
etc. . . . etc. . . . etc. . . .

EXCEPTING FRANCIS PICABIA
The only complete artist!

advises you to go see his
FRANCIS PICABIA *paintings at the Salon*
d'Automne
and gives you his fingers to kiss FUNNY-GUY

MEN COVERED WITH CROSSES RECALL CEMETERIES

IF YOU WANT TO HAVE CLEAN IDEAS, CHANGE THEM LIKE SHIRTS

9.18 MAN RAY

Statement

1916

Who made Dada? Nobody and everybody. I made Dada when I was a baby and I was roundly spanked by my mother. Now, everyone claims to be the author of Dada. For the past thirty years.

In Zurich, in Cologne, in Paris, in London, in Tokyo, in San Francisco, in New York. I might claim to be the author of Dada in New York. In 1912 before Dada.

In 1919, with the permission and with the approval of other Dadaists I legalized Dada in New York. Just once. That was enough. The times did not deserve more. That was a Dadadate. The one issue of *New York Dada* did not even bear the names of its authors. How unusual for Dada! Of course, there were a certain number of collaborators. Both willing and unwilling. Both trusting and suspicious. What did it matter? Only one issue. Forgotten—not even seen by most Dadaists or antidadaists. Now, we are trying to revive Dada. Why? Who cares? Who doesn't care? Dada is dead. Or is Dada still alive? We cannot revive something that is alive just as we cannot revive anything that is dead.

Is Dadadead?
Is Dadalive?
Dada is.
Dadaism.

9.19 HANS RICHTER

Against Without For Dada

1919

?!Dada!!—Nobody belongs to it!?—
We nevertheless belong to it, . . .

Belief in belonging to anything is missing, and we thank your form of "society" (oh state) for this, your "community"; (which forces us to distinguish ourselves from it by all means) was the detergent that led to the birth of this moonstone colored Dada—

The obligation which we took upon ourselves, the avowal of belonging to "something," is an error that you thank yourselves for.

Our companionship (by the way, one in which we all respect each other) dissolved in the acid of a tender or grey desperation . . . but, nevertheless, up-standing attitude—lies beyond any group, movement or Dada magazine. A juggling act with one's own bones, including the intestines, on the backstage of the concept of a lost world is, by far, the best method of communication.

Those men da, got going da . . . Dada . . . That is our curse, to conjure the UNPREDICTABLE.

We are riding on the concept of a melody and swing with the super-tune and over-swing, wide, long, rhymed, bong, or else in politics (oh, beautiful earnestness—your playfulness, incomparable, admirable).

Umst, Umst (?) never existed, and it is even impossible that it ever did; but it is Dada. That is astrology and I realize it as I fall asleep. When associations escape through the bars, no business can be concluded. (Apotheosis of Dada)

Let's take the miracle! Dada?—Dada! . . . Jumping into FORM over any possible backside, let's compose it of an easily digestible salad of railroad tickets and the instantaneous reflex of a melody mixed with the occasional beat of all the accidents crossing and recrossing our soul.

Do you want to have happiness?

Voilà, but this time, really without stealing it from anyone? Just take this mixture (salad, railroad-ticket, reflex—you understand, don't you!!)

If you want, instead, the real miracle—do you want to see it? We rent the miracle. Only (pardon me) we need pre-conditions to show it other than your "seriousness" (applause). No misunderstanding! You make good business out of seriousness, war, children, cruelty, what else? Tzara—Dada, he trains the miracle (nothing special, we all do), but he cannot make any guarantee of its obedience or delivery. Because miracles are miracles only on their own terms—But he throws so much dirt and shit—manufactured from his honestly-acquired-belief in the miracle, that it could not prevent a certain, personal attachment to him (oh, clear, good-old, cloud-pump fellow).

Curse upon Dada. (We transmit to you this formula), it prevents our direct contract with the miracle. Our whistle's length disbelief—in the future and the already born. Serner's head appears as the bud of a flower in the ripe lap of his brain, a balloon of pus, which he himself has milked from his desperation, kept at the post office box.—Take out an insurance policy with your agent for philosophic and moral depression—on your word of honor, of course—against fakery, against pus. Otherwise everything will seep out of you, secretly but <u>incessantly</u>.

Let me detach myself from you with a misshapen gesture, in a prepared accident.

Don't worry! Nothing will take place that you would accept or cherish, that would facilitate your understanding or improve your attitude to something which you, in your cheap ways, could ever accept.

Cheap! Destiny has bought us cheaply, it didn't pay a cent, that we may count on the divine right of interest. (Hollah!) You will have to pay dearly for us.

9.20 JACQUES VACHÉ
Manifesto of UMORE
1917

LETTER OF AUGUST 18 TO ANDRÉ BRETON

However . . . and then, almost the whole TONE of our gestures still remains to be decided—I want it to be dry, with no literature to it, especially not in the sense of "ART."

Moreover,

ART, doubtless, does not exist—So it is useless to sing on about it—and yet! people make art—because that is the way it is and not any other way—Well—What can we do about it?

So we love neither ART, nor artists (down with Apollinaire) AND how RIGHT TOGRATH IS TO ASSASSINATE THE POET!—However since on account of that we have to spill out a bit of acid or old lyricism, quick, let it be jerky—because locomotives go in a hurry.

So too modernity, constant and killed every night again—We have nothing to do with MALLARMÉ, no hatred—but he's dead—But we no longer know either Apollinaire, nor Cocteau—For—We suspect them of making art too consciously, of patching up some romanticism with telephone wire and not knowing the engines. THE Constellations unhooked again!—how boring—and then sometimes don't they speak seriously! Someone believing something is a very peculiar being.

BUT SINCE SOME ARE BORN HAM ACTORS . . . .

Well—I see two ways to let that take place—To form personal sensation with a flamboyant collision of rare words—say, not too often!—or then to draw angles, or squares of feelings—the latter, naturally, at the moment—We will let logical Honesty—the responsibility of contradicting us—like everyone.

—OH ABSURD GOD!—for everything is a contradiction—isn't that so?—and the person who will not let himself be caught up in the hidden and shady life of everything will be UMORE.—O My alarm clock—eyes—and hypocritical—who detests me so frightfully! . . . and will be UMORE the person who will feel the pitiful trompe-l'oeil of the universal simili-symbols.

—It's in their nature to be symbolical.

—UMORE should not produce—but what can you do?—I grant a little UMOUR to LAFCADIO—for he doesn't read and only produces amusing experiments—like assassinations—and without any satanic lyricism —my old rotted Baudelaire!!!—He needed our dry art a bit; machinery —rotating things with stinking oils—vibrate—vibrate—vibrate—whistle! —Reverdy—amusing the poet, and boring in prose, Max Jacob, my old faker—MARIONETTES—MARIONETTES—MARIONETTES—do you want some nice marionettes of colored wood?—Two eyes—dead-flame and the crystal round of a monocle—with an octopus typewriter—that's better.

9.21 MARCEL DUCHAMP

Kind of Sub-Title

1934

DELAY IN GLASS

Use "delay" instead of "picture" or
"painting"; "picture on glass" becomes
"delay in glass"—but "delay in
glass" does not mean "picture
on glass"—
    It's merely a way
of succeeding in no longer thinking
that the thing in question is
a picture—to make a "delay" of it
in the most general way possible,
not so much in the different meanings
in which "delay" can be taken, but
rather in their indecisive reunion
"delay"—a "delay in glass"
    as you would say a "poem in prose"
        or a spittoon in silver

9.22 THE BARONESS ELSE VON FREYTAG-LORINGHOVEN

The Modest Woman

1921

Artists are aristocrats.
    Artists who call themselves artists—not aristocrats—are plain working people, mixing up art with craft, in vulgar untrained brain.
    Who wants us to hide our joys (Joyce?)
    If I can eat I can eliminate—it is logic—it is why I eat! My machinery is built that way. Yours also—though you do not like to think of—mention it—because you are not aristocrat.
    Your skirts are too long—out of "modesty," not decoration—when you lift them you do not do it elegantly—proudly.

Why should I—proud engineer—be ashamed of my machinery—part of it?

Joyce is engineer! one of boldest—most adventurous—globetrotter—! to talk shop is his sacred business—we want him to—to love engine that carries him through flashing glades to his grave—his glorious estate.

If your ears are too vulgar—put white cotton into—in tufts—bunches! fitting decoration! Afflicted people should stay home — with family — friends. You are immodest—because you are not healthy.

America's comfort: — sanitation — outside machinery — has made American forget own machinery—body! He thinks of himself less than of what should be his servant—steel machinery.

He has mixed things! For: he has no poise—no tradition. Parvenu—ashamed of his hide—as he well might.

That is American! it is truly disgusting to imagine him in any "physical functions"—eating not excluded.

Eats stupidly also.

Has reason to hide—feels that—and:—because newly rich—in vast acquisition—feels also he has something to say—everything—everybody.

Smart aleck—countrylout—in sunday attire—strutting!

Yawning—all teeth—into space—sipping his coffee with thunder noise—elbow on table—little finger outspread stiffly—he knows how to behave in society!

Why—America—can you not be modest? stay back—attentive—as wellbred child? You have so much to learn—just out of bushes!

But—you are no wellbred child—you are noisy—nosey—bad-mannered—assumptive.

. . . Goethe was grandly obscene—what do you know about it? Flaubert—Swift—Rabelais—Arabian Nights—Bible if you please! only difference—Bible is without humour—great stupidity! So: how dare you strut—step out—show yourself with your cotton-tuft in ear?

In Europe—when inferiors do not understand superiors—they retire modestly—mayhap baffled—but in good manner. By that fact—that they do not understand—they know their place. They are not invited—of class inferior—the dance is not theirs.

They can not judge—for: they lack real manners—education—class.

If they are desirous of judging—sometime—they must think—study—rise—*slowly!* So society is made—in Europe—slowly—! so: culture—so: aristocratic public.

That attitude of the learner—the inferior—you should feel in regard to James Joyce.

That you do not—shows you have less inherent culture than European washer-lady.

Here—madame—every bank clerk meddles.

Ancient Romans had proverb—one of few great principles of world-structure—culture: *Quod licit Jovi, non licit Bovi.*

To show hidden beauty of things—there are no limitations! Only artist can do that—that is his holy office. Stronger—braver he is—more he will explore into depths.

Do not eat the *Little Review.*

Therein all strong angels are!

I have not read "Ulysses." As story it seems impossible—to James Joyce's style I am not yet quite developed enough—makes me difficulty—too intent on my own creation—no time now.

Sometime I will read him—have no doubt—time of screams—delights—dances—soul and body—as with Shakespeare.

From snatches I have had shown me it is more worth while than many a smooth coherent story by author of real genuine prominence.

The way he slings "obscenities"—handles them—never forced—never obscene—vulgar! (thank Europe for such people—world will advance.)

Shows him one of highest intellects—with creative power abundant—soaring!

Such one you dare approach—little runt?

Whatever made you read him—*Little Review*—anyway?

Back to my astonishment!

You see how ridiculous you are?

Well—if not—others will.

That is why I wrote this—!

9.23 MINA LOY
Aphorisms on Futurism
1914–1919

DIE in the Past
Live in the Future.

THE velocity of velocities arrives in starting.

IN pressing the material to derive its essence, matter becomes deformed.

AND form hurtling against itself is thrown beyond the synopsis of vision.

THE straight line and the circle are the parents of design, form the basis of art; there is no limit to their coherent variability.

LOVE the hideous in order to find the sublime core of it.

OPEN your arms to the delapidated; rehabilitate them.

YOU prefer to observe the past on which your eyes are already opened.

BUT the Future is only dark from outside.
Leap into it—and it EXPLODES with *Light.*

FORGET that you live in houses, that you may live in yourself—

FOR the smallest people live in the greatest houses.

BUT the smallest person, potentially, is as great as the Universe.

WHAT can you know of expansion, who limit yourselves to compromise?

HITHERTO the great man has achieved greatness by keeping the people small.

BUT in the Future, by inspiring the people to expand to their fullest capacity, the great man proportionately must be tremendous—a God.

LOVE of others is the appreciation of oneself.

MAY your egotism be so gigantic that you comprise mankind in your self-sympathy.

THE Future is limitless—the past a trail of insidious reactions.

LIFE is only limited by our prejudices. Destroy them, and you cease to be at the mercy of yourself.

TIME is the dispersion of intensiveness.

THE Futurist can live a thousand years in one poem.

HE can compress every aesthetic principle in one line.

THE mind is a magician bound by assimilations; let him loose and the smallest idea conceived in freedom will suffice to negate the wisdom of all forefathers.

LOOKING on the past you arrive at "Yes," but before you can act upon it you have already arrived at "No."

THE Futurist must leap from affirmative to affirmative, ignoring intermittent negations—must spring from stepping-stone to stone of creative exploration; without slipping back into the turbid stream of accepted facts.

THERE are no excrescences on the absolute, to which man may pin his faith.

TODAY is the crisis in consciousness.

CONSCIOUSNESS cannot spontaneously accept or reject new forms, as offered by creative genius; it is the new form, for however great a period of time it may remain a mere irritant—that molds consciousness to the necessary amplitude for holding it.

CONSCIOUSNESS has no climax.

LET the Universe flow into your consciousness, there is no limit to its capacity, nothing that it shall not re-create.

UNSCREW your capability of absorption and grasp the elements of Life— *Whole.*

MISERY is in the disintegration of Joy;
Intellect, of Intuition;
Acceptance, of Inspiration.

CEASE to build up your personality with the ejections of irrelevant minds.

NOT to be a cipher in your ambient,
But to color your ambient with your preferences.

NOT to accept experience at its face value.

BUT to readjust activity to the peculiarity of your own will.

THESE are the primary tentatives towards independence.

MAN is a slave only to his own mental lethargy.

YOU cannot restrict the mind's capacity.

THEREFORE you stand not only in abject servitude to your perceptive consciousness—

BUT also to the mechanical re-actions of the subconsciousness, that rubbish heap of race-tradition—

AND believing yourself to be free—your least conception is colored by the pigment of retrograde superstitions.

HERE are the fallow-lands of mental spatiality that Futurism will clear—

MAKING place for whatever you are brave enough, beautiful enough to draw out of the realized self.

TO your blushing we shout the obscenities, we scream the blasphemies, that you, being weak, whisper alone in the dark.

THEY are empty except of your shame.

AND so these sounds shall dissolve back to their innate senselessness.

THUS shall evolve the language of the Future.

THROUGH derision of Humanity as it appears—

TO arrive at respect for man as he shall be—

ACCEPT the tremendous truth of Futurism
Leaving all those
                            Knick-knacks.

9.24 MINA LOY
Aphorisms on Modernism
1914–1919

MODERNISM is a prophet crying in the wilderness that Humanity is wasting its time.

CONSCIOUSNESS originated in the nostalgia of the universe for an audience.

LIVING is projecting reflections of ourselves into the consciousness of our fellows.

THE individual is the inhibition of infinity.

IMPACT with beauty is immortality.

GENIUS is the faculty for outstripping exposure.

EMOTION looks at life through a magnifying glass.

IRONY is the death-rattle of emotion.

ONLY the irresponsible can carry the world on their shoulders.

HUMANITY is raw material for the opportunist.

NEWSPAPERS are printed in hypnotic fluid.

MORALITY was invented as an excuse for murdering the neighbors.

CHRISTIANITY evolved because its doctrines keep failure in countenance.

GOOD FORM is the ideal value of the lie.

MORAL ORDER in society is a system for simplifying bureaucracy.

ANARCHISTS in art are art's instantaneous aristocracy.

ANXIETY is a circus-master exercising the noctambulist.

Notes on Existence

1914–1919

It matters not that in our own location we may have travelled a million miles in that desolate dimension—inwards. Our apparent person, which marks the confines of the ego, though seemingly what we must *be*, is actually where we leave off. Our apparent person remains a changeless mannequin, arranged by accident.

*   *   *

The past is dead as an outgrown superstition, a mummy with a thousand features crumbled into dust of which every now and again a grain blows into the eye of memory.

*   *   *

The devout do often, inserting a finger at random among the pages of the Bible, find the counsel sought for in the verse thus blindly picked; but there for the religious is stored so inexhaustible an ethical provision that they are hardly taking chances. Whereas, amid the exceptional emptiness of my early youth, how should signs and wonders take form from nothingness to appear from nowhere? Or the casual gestures of inattentive people make patterns precise as keys that fitted into what?

*   *   *

Lacking the material for conversation, one can imagine a rudimentary family only aroused to social intercourse by the front door. A face is lifted. A voice inquires "Going out?" or "So you've come in?" almost with animation, for a temporary escape from over-familiar circumstances favors the possibility that an absentee may, like the primitive hunter returning to his cave with a carcass, capture an incident to be shared with those who remained at home.

*   *   *

In my silent somnambulant world, angles play acrobat on a silver screen until the automaton, halted by the heavy bolts on the street door, awakens.

*   *   *

Wisdom effects the transparences of things.

*   *   *

War has not left any mark on us except the disgrace of a few old ladies who publickly wallow in their sons' graves when they ought to have known how to bring them up better.

*   *   *

If sight were a sense that took contact with its object, at too close quarters beauty would not disappear . . . As a voice becomes sonorous after leaving the lips, beauty is given off by the face—or rather, no beauty appears until brought to that focus where the elements of beauty rush together in combinative grace; beauty being ever a surreality that perturbs our response with the indefinite extravagance of a dream.

*   *   *

Youth is expectancy—age, regret. For nothing.

*   *   *

Once having been over-alive, the rest of life is a hang-over. For we are but a ramshackle edifice around an eternal exaltation; a building in which the moralities are a flight of stairs whose bases dissolve in the wake of our ascension; and at last our foundations sag heavier into earth; the whole of Nature withdraws to an impersonal distance. Left unrecognizable and alone in the undying conviction of our perfection, we wonder if Life is fleeting and escaped us while we essayed to reason it out, or whether Life is static while we absent-mindedly shamble past it. Being alive is a long time while so little comes within reaching-distance. But, more than all, being alive is a queer coincidence.

*   *   *

Falling in love is the trick of magnifying one human being to such proportions that all comparisons vanish.

*   *   *

Looking for love, with all its catastrophes, is a less risky experience than finding it. The longer it lasts, so much less can the habit of felicity when turned adrift withstand the onslaught of memory.

*   *   *

Looking back on my life I can observe one absolute law of physics—that energy is always wasted.

The Artist and the Public

1917

The only trouble with *The Public* is education.

The Artist is uneducated, is seeing IT for the first time; he can never see the same thing twice.

Education is the putting of spectacles on wholesome eyes. *The Public* does not naturally care about these spectacles, the cause of its quarrels with art. *The Public* likes to be jolly; *The Artist* is jolly and quite irresponsible. Art is *The Divine Joke,* and any *Public,* and any *Artist,* can see a nice, easy simple joke, such as the sun. But only *Artists* and *Serious Critics* can look at a greyish stickiness on smooth canvas.

Education, recognizing something that has been seen before, demands an art that is only acknowledgeable by way of diluted comparisons. It is significant that the demand is half-hearted.

"Let us forget the democratically simple beginnings of an art," is the cry of the educator — so that we may talk of those things that have only middle and no end, and together wallow in grey stickiness.

The Public knows better than this, knowing such values as the under-inner curve of women's footgear, one factor of the art of our epoch. It is unconcerned with curved Faun's legs and maline-twirled scarves of artistic imagining or with allegories of life with thorn-skewered eyes. It knew before the Futurists that life is a jolly noise and a rush and sequence of ample reactions.

The Artist then says to *The Public:* "Poor pal — what has happened to you? . . . We were born similar — and *now* look!" But *The Public* will not look; that is, look at *The Artist.* It has unnaturally acquired prejudice.

So, *The Public* and *The Artist* can meet at every point except the — for *The Artist* — vital one, that of pure, uneducated seeing. They like the same drinks, can fight in the same trenches, pretend to the same women — but never see the same thing ONCE.

You might, at least, keep quiet while I am talking.

Auto-Facial-Construction

1919

The face is our most potent symbol of personality. The adolescent has facial contours in harmony with the condition of his soul. Day by day the new interests and activities of modern life are prolonging the youth of our souls, and day by day we are becoming more aware of the necessity for our faces to express that youthfulness, for the sake of psychic logic. Different systems of beauty culture have compromised our inherent right not only to *be* ourselves but to *look like* ourselves by producing a facial contour in middle age which does duty as a "well-preserved appearance." This preservation of partially distorted muscles is, at best, merely a pleasing parody of youth. That subtle element of the ludicrous inherent in facial transformation by time is the signpost of discouragement pointing along the path of the evolution of personality. For to what end is our experience of life if deprived of a fitting esthetic revelation in our faces? One distorted muscle causes a fundamental disharmony in self-expression, for no matter how well gowned or groomed men or women may be, how exquisitely the complexion is cared for, or how beautiful the expression of the eyes, if the original form of the face (intrinsic symbol of personality) has been effaced in muscular transformation, they have lost the power to communicate their true personalities to others and all expression of sentiment is veiled in pathos. Years of specialized interest in physiognomy as an artist have brought me to an understanding of the human face which has made it possible for me to find the basic principle of facial integrity, its conservation, and, when necessary, its reconstruction.

I will instruct men or women who are intelligent—and for the briefest period, patient—to become masters of their facial destiny. I understand the skull with its muscular sheath as a sphere whose superficies can be voluntarily energized. And the foundations of beauty as embedded in the three interconnected zones of energy encircling this sphere: the centers of control being at the base of the skull and highest point of the cranium. Control, through the identity of your Conscious Will with these centers and zones, can be perfectly attained through my system, which does not include any form of cutaneous hygiene (the care of the skin being left to the skin specialists) except insofar as the stimulus to circulation it induces is of primary importance in the conservation of all the tissues. Through *Auto-Facial-Construction* the attachments of the muscles to the bones are revitalized, as also the gums, and the original facial contours are permanently preserved as a structure which can be relied upon without anxiety as to the ravages of time—a structure which Complexion Culture enhances in beauty instead of attempting to disguise.

This means renascence for the society woman, the actor, the actress, the man of public career, for everybody who desires it. The initiation to this esoteric anatomical science is expensive but economical in result, for it places at the disposal of individuals a permanent principle for the independent conservation of beauty to which, once it is mastered, they have constant and natural resource.

9.28 MAN RAY
L'Inquiétude

1921

L'Inquiétude

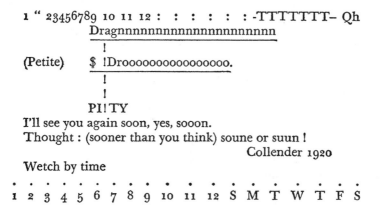

I'll see you again soon, yes, sooon.
Thought : (sooner than you think) soune or suun !
Collender 1920

Wetch by time

PART 10

Vorticism

When Wyndham Lewis, the feisty founder of Vorticism, reformulated Imagism in 1914 to put the accent on a greater forcefulness, he aimed at the "radiant node or cluster . . . a VORTEXT, from which, and through which, and into which, ideas are constantly rushing." This was a matter of pure process: not an idle aesthetic image, but rather "Form, and not the form of anything" (Nicholls, *Modernisms*, 174). Art was completely autonomous, for G. E. Moore, for Wyndham Lewis, as it had been for Whistler, with his arrangements of lines and colors independent of personality. But the Vorticist work of art is closely allied with Machinism and the fascination with straight lines, perpendiculars, and efficient energy.

Lewis was setting himself and Vorticism up against Filippo Tommaso Marinetti's Futurism, imported into England. As Futurism *receives* perception, says Lewis, Vorticism *conceives* it, in terms taken over from Wilhelm Worringer's influential *Abstraction and Empathy*. The movement is allied to Futurism by its fascination with the dynamism of the mechanical but wants its own character independent of that of Marinetti and his "automobilism." "Automobilism (Marinettism) bores us. We don't want to go about making a hullobuloo about motorcars, anymore than about knives and forks, elephants or gas-pipes. Elephants are VERY big. Motorcars go quickly" ("Long Live the Vortex," BLAST, 8). Vorticism foresaw the 1916 movements in France and Germany grouped around PREsentism and Simultaneism. "The new vortex plunges to the heart of the Present," said Lewis. "We stand for the Reality of the Present," said BLAST, and "not for the sentimental Future ("Long Live the Vortex," 9, 147). Certainly not for the past. Just like Dada, Vorticism's ally in the realm of thought.

Manifestos have, of course, to down the foe—that is, any other than the partisans of the movement. So Ezra Pound, in *Poetry* (1914), calls out from the page: "Impressionism, Futurism, which is only an accelerated sort of impression, DENY the vortext. They are the CORPSES OF VORTICES." Lewis's movement, with which Pound, Christopher Nevinson, and Henri Gaudier-Brzeska were associated, stood for dynamic power and energy against a lackadaisical sensibility it compared with the effeminate and with which it aligned the sensibilities of Bloomsbury (see Lewis's novel *The Apes of God* for his virulent parodies). The outlandish typographical brilliance of the journal *BLAST* extends to its cover, upon which the title is printed in the dynamic diagonal that gives the modernist Russian photographer Aleksandr Rodchenko's pictures their energy. The "Vorticist Manifesto," with its pages of invective BLASTing this and that and its opposite pages of BLESSings, is a perfect example of a manifest and noisy appearance.

In fact, Vorticism was, underneath its highly combative pose, closely allied to Symbolist aesthetics, and the term itself may come from the use of "vortical" and the "Great Vortext" applied to the energetic center of the universe (*The Great Vortext of Infinite Perfection*) in Andrew Jackson Davis's celebrated study of Swedenborgian millenarianism, *The Principles of Nature* (1847).

The black-caped and forceful artist and writer Lewis, designating himself as The Enemy, The Outsider, shouting his way through the art world, BLESSING some ideas and nations and BLASTING others, eventually allied himself, like Marinetti, with Fascism, and came down on the side of the least liberal doctrines: war appealed to the New Egos, as he called the "civilized savages," of which he was one ("The New Egos," *BLAST*, 141). As for real battle, the Vorticist and sculptor Gaudier-Brzeska, after writing his manifesto from the trenches, died in one.

England

10.1

The Egoist

An Individualist Review

1914

THE EGOIST

An Individualist Review.

Recognises no taboos.

Editor, H. S. Weaver; Assistant Editor, Richard Aldington; Contributors, Allen Upward, Ford Madox Hueffer, Ezra Pound, Remy de Gourmont, Robert Frost, Muriel Ciolkowska, Wyndham Lewis, John Cournos, Reginald W. Kauffman, Huntley Carter, J. G. Fletcher, Carlos Williams, "M. de V-M.," J. Rodker, James Joyce, etc., etc.

Subscriptions should be sent to Miss Harriet Shaw Weaver, Oakley House, Bloomsbury Street, London, W.C.

Terms of subscription: Yearly, U. S. A., 3 dollars 50 cents, six months 1 dollar 75 cents. Single copies 7d. post free to any address in the Postal Union.

The only fortnightly in England that an intelligent man can read for three months running.

10.2 R. ALDINGTON *and others*

Beyond Action and Reaction

1914

MANIFESTO.

I.

1 Beyond Action and Reaction we would establish ourselves.

2 We start from opposite statements of a chosen world. Set up violent structure of adolescent clearness between two extremes.

3 We discharge ourselves on both sides.

4 We fight first on one side, then on the other, but always for the SAME cause, which is neither side or both sides and ours.

5 Mercenaries were always the best troops.

6 We are Primitive Mercenaries in the Modern World.

7 Our Cause is NO-MAN'S.

8 We set Humour at Humour's throat. Stir up Civil War among peaceful apes.

9 We only want Humour if it has fought like Tragedy.

10 We only want Tragedy if it can clench its side-muscles like hands on its belly, and bring to the surface a laugh like a bomb.

II.

1 We hear from America and the Continent all sorts of disagreeable things about England: "the unmusical, anti-artistic, unphilosophic country."

2 We quite agree.

3 Luxury, sport, the famous English "Humour," the thrilling ascendancy and idée fixe of Class, producing the most intense snobbery in the World; heavy stagnant pools of Saxon blood, incapable of anything but the song of a frog, in home-counties:—these phenomena give England a peculiar distinction in the wrong sense, among the nations.

4 This is why England produces such good artists from time to time.

5 This is also the reason why a movement towards art and imagination could burst up here, from this lump of compressed life, with more force than anywhere else.

6 To believe that it is necessary for or conducive to art, to "Improve" life, for instance—make architecture, dress, ornament, in "better taste," is absurd.

7 The Art-instinct is permanently primitive.

8 In a chaos of imperfection, discord, etc., it finds the same stimulus as in Nature.

9 The artist of the modern movement is a savage (in no sense an "advanced," perfected, democratic, Futurist individual of Mr. Marinetti's limited imagination): this enormous, jangling, journalistic, fairy desert of modern life serves him as Nature did more technically primitive man.

10 As the steppes and the rigours of the Russian winter, when the peasant has to lie for weeks in his hut, produces that extraordinary acuity of feeling and intelligence we associate with the Slav; so England is just now the most favourable country for the appearance of a great art.

R. ALDINGTON, GAUDIER-BRZESKA, E. POUND,

W. ROBERTS, E. WADSWORTH, WYNDHAM LEWIS

Our Vortex

1914

I.

Our vortex is not afraid of the Past: it has forgotten its existence.

Our vortex regards the Future as as sentimental as the Past.

The Future is distant, like the Past, and therefore sentimental.

The mere element "Past" must be retained to sponge up and absorb our melancholy.

Everything absent, remote, requiring projection in the veiled weakness of the mind, is sentimental.

The Present can be intensely sentimental—especially if you exclude the mere element "Past."

Our vortex does not deal in reactive Action only, nor identify the Present with numbing displays of vitality.

The new vortex plunges to the heart of the Present.

The chemistry of the Present is different to that of the Past. With this different chemistry we produce a New Living Abstraction.

The Rembrandt Vortex swamped the Netherlands with a flood of dreaming.

The Turner Vortex rushed at Europe with a wave of light.

We wish the Past and Future with us, the Past to mop up our melancholy, the Future to absorb our troublesome optimism.

With our Vortex the Present is the only active thing.

Life is the Past and the Future.

The Present is Art.

II.

Our Vortex insists on water-tight compartments.

There is no Present—there is Past and Future, and there is Art.

Any moment not weakly relaxed and slipped back, or, on the other hand, dreaming optimistically, is Art.

"Just Life" or soi-disant "Reality" is a fourth quantity, made up of the Past, the Future and Art.

This impure Present our Vortex despises and ignores.

For our Vortex is uncompromising.

We must have the Past and the Future, Life simple, that is, to discharge ourselves in, and keep us pure for non-life, that is Art.

The Past and Future are the prostitutes Nature has provided.

Art is periodic escapes from this Brothel.

Artists put as much vitality and delight into this saintliness, and escape out, as most men do their escapes into similar places from respectable existence.

The Vorticist is at his maximum point of energy when stillest.

The Vorticist is not the Slave of Commotion, but its Master.

The Vorticist does not suck up to Life.

He lets Life know its place in a Vorticist Universe!

III.

In a Vorticist Universe we don't get excited at what we have invented.

If we did it would look as though it had been a fluke.

It is not a fluke.

We have no Verbotens.

There is one Truth, ourselves, and everything is permitted.

But we are not Templars.

We are proud, handsome and predatory.

We hunt machines, they are our favourite game.

We invent them and then hunt them down.

This is a great Vorticist age, a great still age of artists.

IV.

As to the lean belated Impressionism at present attempting to eke out a little life in these islands:

Our Vortex is fed up with your dispersals, reasonable chicken-men.

Our Vortex is proud of its polished sides.

Our Vortex will not hear of anything but its disastrous polished dance.

Our Vortex desires the immobile rhythm of its swiftness.

Our Vortex rushes out like an angry dog at your Impressionistic fuss.

Our Vortex is white and abstract with its red-hot swiftness.

R. ALDINGTON, GAUDIER-BRZESKA, E. POUND,

W. ROBERTS, E. WADSWORTH, WYNDHAM LEWIS

BLESS ENGLAND !

BLESS ENGLAND

FOR ITS SHIPS

which switchback on Blue, Green and Red SEAS all around the PINK EARTH-BALL,

BIG BETS ON EACH.

BLESS ALL SEAFARERS.

THEY exchange not one LAND for another, but one ELEMENT for ANOTHER. The MORE against the LESS ABSTRACT.

BLESS the vast planetary abstraction of the OCEAN.

BLESS THE ARABS OF THE ATLANTIC.

THIS ISLAND MUST BE CONTRASTED WITH THE BLEAK WAVES.

BLESS ALL PORTS.

PORTS, RESTLESS MACHINES of | scooped out basins
heavy insect dredgers
monotonous cranes
stations
lighthouses, blazing
through the frosty
starlight, cutting the
storm like a cake
beaks of infant boats,
side by side,
heavy chaos of
wharves,
steep walls of
factories
womanly town

BLESS these **MACHINES** that work the little boats across clean liquid space, in beelines.

BLESS the great **PORTS** | HULL
LIVERPOOL
LONDON
NEWCASTLE-ON-TYNE
BRISTOL
GLASGOW

BLESS ENGLAND,

Industrial island machine, pyramidal workshop, its apex at Shetland, discharging itself on the sea.

BLESS | cold
magnanimous
delicate
gauche
fanciful
stupid

ENGLISHMEN.

**Curse with Expletive of Whirlwind
the Britannic Aesthete**

1914–1915

CURSE

WITH EXPLETIVE OF WHIRLWIND

THE BRITANNIC ÆSTHETE

CREAM OF THE SNOBBISH EARTH
ROSE OF SHARON OF GOD-PRIG
OF SIMIAN VANITY
SNEAK AND SWOT OF THE SCHOOL-
ROOM

IMBERB (or Berbed when in Belsize)-**PEDANT**

PRACTICAL JOKER
DANDY
CURATE

BLAST all products of phlegmatic cold
Life of **LOOKER-ON.**

CURSE

SNOBBERY
(disease of femininity)
FEAR OF RIDICULE
(arch vice of inactive, sleepy)
PLAY
STYLISM
SINS AND PLAGUES
of this LYMPHATIC finished
(we admit in every sense
finished)
VEGETABLE HUMANITY.

Oh Blast France

1914–1915

OH BLAST FRANCE
pig plagiarism
BELLY
SLIPPERS
POODLE TEMPER
BAD MUSIC
SENTIMENTAL GALLIC GUSH
SENSATIONALISM
FUSSINESS.

PARISIAN PAROCHIALISM. Complacent young man,
so much respect for Papa
and his son !—Oh !—Papa
is wonderful : but all papas
are !

BLAST

APERITIFS (Pernots, Amers picon)
Bad change
Naively seductive Houri salon-
picture Cocottes
Slouching blue porters (can
carry a pantechnicon)
Stupidly rapacious people at
every step
Economy maniacs
Bouillon Kub (for being a bad
pun)

PARIS.   Clap-trap Heaven of amative German
             professor.
         Ubiquitous lines of silly little trees.
         Arcs de Triomphe.
         Imperturbable, endless prettiness.
         Large empty cliques, higher up.
         Bad air for the individual.

BLAST

MECCA OF THE AMERICAN

because it is not other side of Suez Canal, instead of an
afternoon's ride from London.

PART 11

Imagism

In England and America, roughly between 1912 and 1914, the spirit of the 1908 writings of T. E. Hulme was revived, mostly by Ezra Pound. Other Imagists included the brilliant Hilda Doolittle (H. D.)—termed by Pound "H. D. Imagiste"—Richard Aldington, F. R. Flint, and the cigar-smoking, self-propangandizing Amy Lowell. The characteristics Pound stated as "imagiste" were a direct treatment of the subjective or objective thing, the rejection of anything unessential, and the rhythm of the musical phrase. What took preeminence was Pound's definition of the image, given here in "A Few Don'ts by an Imagiste" (11.4), as presenting "an intellectual and emotional complex in an instant of time." To Symbolist "evocation," Imagism as Pound conceives of it opposes precision, hardness, clarity of outline; to Symbolist transcendence, the natural world. There was a reformulation of Imagism in 1914, into the Vorticist movement led by Wyndham Lewis, which put the accent on energy and movement. Art is autonomous, for Lewis as it was for Whistler, with the arrangements of lines and colors independent of personality, with objects in process as form independent of reference.

Pound wrote to Harriet Monroe in America: "My problem is to keep alive a certain group of advancing poets, to set the arts in their rightful place as the acknowledged guide and lamp of civilization." Contrasting, in 1918, "the Hard and the Soft in French Poetry," Pound railed against mushy technique and sentimentalism or "emotional slither" in favor of a hard precisionism, reminiscent of the emphasis among the French Parnassians on the hard profile and lastingness of bronze. In this, too, as with his political leanings and his detestation of the "mob" visible in his 1918 statement for the journal *Poetry*, he remains allied with the Vorticist movement.

Imagism favors the dense, the terse, the definite, the energy of vision held in a moment. Writing also in *Poetry*, the painter-poet Marsden Hartley means the same kind of hard-edged poetic business. This density will carry over into the essays of such major figures as Marianne Moore, with her emphasis on "compacity" and precision, and Cynthia Ozick, in her thinking about *particularism* as the defining characteristic of what makes literature last.

11.1 PIERRE REVERDY

The Image

1918

The image is a pure creation of the mind.

It cannot be born from a comparison but only from bringing together two more or less distant realities.

The more the relations of the two realities brought together are distant and fitting, the stronger the image—the more emotive power and poetic reality it will have.

Two realities without any relation can't be usefully brought together. There is no creation of the image.

Two contrary realities do not come together. They are opposed.

Rarely do you obtain any strength from this opposition.

An image is not strong because it is BRUTAL or FANTASTIC—but because the association of ideas is distant and fitting.

The result obtained takes immediate control.

The mind must seize and taste a created image without any admixture.

*   *   *

The creation of the image is thus a powerful poetic means and you shouldn't be astonished by the major role it plays in a *poetry of creation.*

To remain pure this poetry requires that all the means come together to create a *poetic reality.*

You can't have direct means of observation interfere which only destroy the whole by not fitting in. These means have another source and another goal.

Means of different aesthetics cannot strive together toward one same work.

Only the purity of means commands the purity of works.

The purity of aesthetics comes from that.

11.2 F. S. FLINT

Imagisme

1913

Some curiosity has been aroused concerning *Imagisme,* and as I was unable to find anything definite about it in print, I sought out an *imagiste,* with intent to discover whether the group itself knew anything about the "movement." I gleaned these facts.

The *imagistes* admitted that they were contemporaries of the Post Impressionists and the Futurists; but they had nothing in common with these schools. They had not published a manifesto. They were not a revolutionary school; their only endeavor was to write in accordance with the best tradition, as they found it in the best writers of all time,—in Sappho, Catullus, Villon. They seemed to be absolutely intolerant of all poetry that was not written in such endeavor, ignorance of the best tradition forming no excuse. They had a few rules, drawn up for their own satisfaction only, and they had not published them. They were:

1. Direct treatment of the "thing," whether subjective or objective.
2. To use absolutely no word that did not contribute to the presentation.
3. As regarding rhythm: to compose in sequence of the musical phrase, not in sequence of a metronome.

By these standards they judged all poetry, and found most of it wanting. They held also a certain "Doctrine of the Image," which they had not committed to writing; they said that it did not concern the public, and would provoke useless discussion.

The devices whereby they persuaded approaching poetasters to attend their instruction were:

1. They showed him his own thought already splendidly expressed in some classic (and the school musters altogether a most formidable erudition).
2. They re-wrote his verses before his eyes, using about ten words to his fifty.

Even their opponents admit of them—ruefully—"At least they do keep bad poets from writing!"

I found among them an earnestness that is amazing to one accustomed to the usual London air of poetic dilettantism. They consider that Art is all science, all religion, philosophy and metaphysic. It is true that *snobisme* may be urged against them; but it is at least *snobisme* in its most dynamic form, with a great deal of sound sense and energy behind it; and they are stricter with themselves than with any outsider.

11.3 MARSDEN HARTLEY
The Business of Poetry
1919

I am riding through Arizona in the Pullman. I am thinking of the business of poetry. Every other man attends to the details of business, if he is a good business man. A train is mostly business men. . . .

Poets must, it seems to me, learn how to use a great many words before they can know how to use a few skillfully. Journalistic verbiage is not fluency. Alfred Kreymborg agrees with me that poets do not write prose often enough. I speak mostly of the poets who do not write with the sense of volume in their brevities. Brevity of all things demands intensity, or better say tensity. Tensity comes from experience. The poet must see the space for the word, and then see to it the word occupies it. It is almost mechanical science these days, it would seem—the fitting of parts together so the whole produces a consistent continuity. Subjects never matter, excepting when they are too conspicuously autobiographical. "Moi-même, quand même" is attractive enough, but there are so many attractive ways of presenting it. Personal handling counts for more than personal confessions. We can even learn to use hackneyed words, like "rose" and "lily," relieving them of Swinburnian encrustations. We can relieve imagery from this banality.

Poets cannot, as aspiring poets, depend, it seems to me, ever upon the possible natural "flow" that exists in themselves. Poets have work to do for the precision of simplicity, and for the gift of volume in simplicity. It is the business of good poetry to show natural skill as well as natural impetus. Some poets would like to say the former is more important. It surprises one a deal how much even the better poets effuse, or rely upon their momentary theories. The subject calls for handling, not for enthusiasms. Painters of this time have learned this; or ought to have learned it by now, with the excellent examples of the time. Personality is a state, it is not the consummate virtue. It begins, but it does not finish anything. We have eventually to insert in the middle spaces all we can of real ability. What is much needed is solidity, even of sentiment, combined with efficacy of form. This might be served as an injunction to some of the "girl" poets. Poets have not so much to invent themselves as to create themselves, and creation is of course a process of development.

We are to remember that Ingres, with his impeccable line, was otherwise almost nothing else but silhouette. We cannot subsist merely upon silhouette in poetry, nor upon the pantomimic gesture only. For every lightness there must be a conscious structure. Watteau was the genius of lightness in gesture. No one will accuse him, or even his pupils, Lancret or Pater, of emptiness. A fan has structure by which it exists, a structure that calls for delicate artistry in mechanics. The aeroplane is propelled by motors weighing tons, made of solid metals; and is directed by a master mechanic. Its own notion of lightness would never get it off the ground. Poetry will never "fly" on the notion of its mere lightness, for lightness is not triviality. Francis Thompson had a wing in his brain, but he had feet also. Those men were not mere personalities. They were master mechanics in the business of poetry. A bird could never rely upon the single strong feather. Poetry might rather well take up the mania of Flaubert, if only as a stimulus to exactitude of feeling and idea. You find the best poets doing all they can of that, or else intending that.

The fierce or fiery spaciousness is the quality we look for in a real poem, and coupled with that the requisite iron work according to the personal tastes of the poet. The mere gliding of musical sequences is not sufficient. Poetry is not essentially or necessarily just vocalism. It may have plot or it may be plotless—that is for the poet to decide: what is wanted is some show of mechanistic precision such as the poet can devise. He must know his motive as well as himself, and to invent the process of self-creation is no little task. That is the first principle to be learned by the versifiers. Poetry is not only a tool for the graving of the emotions; nor is it an ivory trinket. It calls for an arm. We need not be afraid of muscularity or even of "brutality."

It is a refreshing omen that big poets write but little poetized autobiography. We find it so much in small poetry, poetry written behind moral arras, where the writer looks out upon a clear space with longing. Anyone would best set it aside, and get outside himself and among the greater trivialities. Preoccupation, blocked introspection, are old-fashioned stimuli for modern poetry. Painting has become definitely masculine at last, in its substance, mechanistic in its purport. Delicacy and frankness are not necessarily feminine. Nor are strength and vigor necessarily muscular qualities.

What Mr. Untermeyer pleases to call the "cult of brutality" does not apply to the poets he names, unless he regards all poetry as delicate and "good." You may find the most infinite tenderness in Masters, in Wallace Gould, and in the others whom he names. He chooses to call picturing brutality. Brutality exists only in the preferential attitude. No one finds Whitman brutal. One finds him presenting the picture. Yet the effect of Whitman on the "sick soul," as William James calls it, is essentially a brutal one. His simple frankness hurts. He removes the loin-cloth because it always hints at secrecy and cheap morality. He undresses the body we are forever dressing. He thinks it handsomest so. He is right. It is a poor body that doesn't look best without clothes. Nature is naked, and, not to speak tritely, quite unashamed. It has no moralistic attitude. It has no attitude at all. It is therefore natural.

Frost writes of New England, and the natives say they know nothing of that New England. The native who looks in from the outside with a world vision says, "How familiar!" He doesn't say, "How cold, how forbidding!" Masters would probably not wish to live by his *Spoon River,* yet his later books are just other shades of the same powerful grey. Wallace Gould will not want to live by his "so dreadful" *Out of Season,* in *Children of the Sun;* yet his books will probably always be tense and severe. Wallace Stevens thinks, or at least says, he isn't interested in producing a book at all. Well, that is superbly encouraging. It is not therefore what the poet thinks of, that is the "delicacy" of his subject. He is looking for the mechanism by which to render "subject" with the precision called for by his feelings and attitudes toward it.

I personally would call for more humor in poetry. If it is true with poetry as with the play, that almost anyone can write a drama or a tragedy, while the comedy man is rare, this would at least account for the lack of charming humor in verse. Satire is delectable, as Henry James has shown. Even the so serious-minded Emily Dickinson had her inimitable gift of humor. She did the best kind of fooling with "God." An intellectual playfulness with great issues she certainly had to an irresistible degree.

A quotation from someone, apropos of Rainer Maria Rilke, stating that "The poet, in order to depict life, must take no part in it," offers a fine truism. He is of necessity the looker-on. How else? He must see first and feel afterward, or perhaps not feel at all. Modern expression teaches that most noticeably. Real art comes from the brain, as we know, not from the soul. We have the excellent examples of this in Mary Garden and Mrs. Fiske — fine refutations of the attitude toward femininity. It is a geometric of self-invention art purposes to create. The poet, it seems, must learn this along with the other artists of the time. Art of the time is the art of the mechanism of the time. We must make poetry of today according to the theme of radio-telephony, and of commutation over oceans by the plane. We cannot feel as we do and attempt Keats' simplicities, or Keats' lyricism even. We have other virtues and defects. We are not melodists. Cacophonists, then? We do not concentrate on the assonant major alone. We find the entire range of dissonance valuable as well as attractive. Or is it all a fierce original harmonic we are trying to achieve?

There is no less need of organization even if we do not employ the established metre and rhyme. Likewise, if a poet must state his or her personal history, he or she may be asked to be as brief as possible. It is easier to read epigrams than to read the diary, no matter how short the latter may be. The age of confession perished with the Parnassians. We are a vastly other type of soul—if we are soul at all, which I keenly doubt. The poet's attitude then, for today, is toward the outside. This does not necessarily imply surface. We present ourselves in spite of ourselves. We are most original when we are most like life. Life is the natural thing. Interpretation is the factitious. Nature is always variable. To have an eye with brain in it—that is, or rather would be, the poetic millennium. We are not moonlit strummers now: we are gun-pointers and sky-climbers.

11.4 EZRA POUND

A Few Don'ts by an Imagiste

1913

An "Image" is that which presents an intellectual and emotional complex in an instant of time. I use the term "complex" rather in the technical sense employed by the newer psychologists, such as Hart, though we might not agree absolutely in our application.

It is the presentation of such a "complex" instantaneously which gives that sense of sudden liberation; that sense of freedom from time limits and space limits; that sense of sudden growth, which we experience in the presence of the greatest works of art.

It is better to present one Image in a lifetime than to produce voluminous works.

All this, however, some may consider open to debate. The immediate necessity is to tabulate A LIST OF DONT's for those beginning to write verses. But I can not put all of them into Mosaic negative.

To begin with, consider the three rules recorded by Mr. Flint, not as dogma—never consider anything as dogma—but as the result of long contemplation, which, even if it is some one else's contemplation, may be worth consideration.

Pay no attention to the criticism of men who have never themselves written a notable work. Consider the discrepancies between the actual writing of the Greek poets and dramatists, and the theories of the Graeco-Roman grammarians, concocted to explain their metres.

LANGUAGE

Use no superflous word, no adjective, which does not reveal something.

Don't use such an expression as "dim lands *of peace*." It dulls the image. It mixes an abstraction with the concrete. It comes from the writer's not realizing that the natural object is always the *adequate* symbol.

Go in fear of abstractions. Don't retell in mediocre verse what has already been done in good prose. Don't think any intelligent person is going to be deceived when you try to shirk all the difficulties of the unspeakably difficult art of good prose by chopping your composition into line lengths.

What the expert is tired of today the public will be tired of tomorrow.

Don't imagine that the art of poetry is any simpler than the art of music, or that you can please the expert before you have spent at least as much effort on the art of verse as the average piano teacher spends on the art of music.

Be influenced by as many great artists as you can, but have the decency either to acknowledge the debt outright, or to try to conceal it.

Don't allow "influence" to mean merely that you mop up the particular decorative vocabulary of some one or two poets whom you happen to admire. A Turkish war correspondent was recently caught red-handed babbling in his dispatches of "dove-gray" hills, or else it was "pearl-pale," I can not remember.

Use either no ornament or good ornament.

RHYTHM AND RHYME

Let the candidate fill his mind with the finest cadences he can discover, preferably in a foreign language so that the meaning of the words may be less likely to divert his attention from the movement; e.g., Saxon charms, Hebridean Folk Songs, the verse of Dante, and the lyrics of Shakespeare—if he can dissociate the vocabulary from the cadence. Let him dissect the lyrics of

Goethe coldly into their component sound values, syllables long and short, stressed and unstressed, into vowels and consonants.

It is not necessary that a poem should rely on its music, but if it does rely on its music that music must be such as will delight the expert.

Let the neophyte know assonance and alliteration, rhyme immediate and delayed, simple and polyphonic, as a musician would expect to know harmony and counterpoint and all the minutiae of his craft. No time is too great to give to these matters or to any one of them, even if the artist seldom have need of them.

Don't imagine that a thing will "go" in verse just because it's too dull to go in prose.

Don't be "viewy"—leave that to the writers of pretty little philosophic essays. Don't be descriptive; remember that the painter can describe a landscape much better than you can, and that he has to know a deal more about it.

When Shakespeare talks of the "Dawn in russet mantle clad" he presents something which the painter does not present. There is in this line of his nothing that one can call description; he presents.

Consider the way of the scientists rather than the way of an advertising agent for a new soap.

The scientist does not expect to be acclaimed as a great scientist until he has *discovered* something. He begins by learning what has been discovered already. He goes from that point onward. He does not bank on being a charming fellow personally. He does not expect his friends to applaud the results of his freshman class work. Freshmen in poetry are unfortunately not confined to a definite and recognizable class room. They are "all over the shop." Is it any wonder "the public is indifferent to poetry?"

Don't chop your stuff into separate *iambs*. Don't make each line stop dead at the end, and then begin every next line with a heave. Let the beginning of the next line catch the rise of the rhythm wave, unless you want a definite longish pause.

In short, behave as a musician, a good musician, when dealing with that phase of your art which has exact parallels in music. The same laws govern, and you are bound by no others.

Naturally, your rhythmic structure should not destroy the shape of your words, or their natural sound, or their meaning. It is improbable that, at the start, you will be able to get a rhythm-structure strong enough to affect them very much, though you may fall a victim to all sorts of false stopping due to line ends and caesurae.

The musician can rely on pitch and the volume of the orchestra. You cannot. The term harmony is misapplied to poetry; it refers to simultaneous sounds of different pitch. There is, however, in the best verse a sort of residue of sound which remains in the ear of the hearer and acts more or less as an organ-base. A rhyme must have in it some slight element of surprise if it is to give pleasure; it need not be bizarre or curious, but it must be well used if used at all.

Vide further Vildrac and Duhamel's notes on rhyme in *"Technique Poétique."*

That part of your poetry which strikes upon the imaginative *eye* of the reader will lose nothing by translation into a foreign tongue; that which appeals to the ear can reach only those who take it in the original.

Consider the definiteness of Dante's presentation, as compared with Milton's rhetoric. Read as much of Wordsworth as does not seem too unutterably dull.

If you want the gist of the matter go to Sappho, Catullus, Villon, Heine when he is in the vein, Gautier when he is not too frigid; or, if you have not the tongues, seek out the leisurely Chaucer. Good prose will do you no harm, and there is good discipline to be had by trying to write it.

Translation is likewise good training, if you find that your original matter "wobbles" when you try to rewrite it. The meaning of the poem to be translated cannot "wobble."

If you are using a symmetrical form, don't put in what you want to say and then fill up the remaining vacuums with slush.

Don't mess up the perception of one sense by trying to define it in terms of another. This is usually only the result of being too lazy to find the exact word. To this clause there are possibly exceptions.

The first three simple proscriptions will throw out nine-tenths of all the bad poetry now accepted as standard and classic; and will prevent you from many a crime of production.

"... *Mais d'abord il faut être un poète,*" as MM. Duhamel and Vildrac have said at the end of their little book, *Notes sur la Technique Poétique;* but in an American one takes that at least for granted, otherwise why does one get born upon that august continent!

Axiomata

1921

I

(1) The intimate essence of the universe is *not* of the same nature as our own consciousness.

(2) Our own consciousness is incapable of having produced the universe.

(3) God, therefore, exists. That is to say, there is no reason for not applying the term God, *Theos,* to the intimate essence.

(4) The universe exists. By exists we mean normally: is perceptible to our consciousness or deducible by human reason from data perceptible to our consciousness.

(5) Concerning the intimate essence of the universe we are utterly ignorant. We have no proof that this God, Theos, is one, or is many, or is divisible or indivisible, or is an ordered hierarchy culminating, or not culminating, in a unity.

(6) Not only is our consciousness, or any concentration or coagulation of such consciousness or consciousnesses, incapable of having produced the universe, it is incapable of accounting for how said universe has been and is.

(7) Dogma is bluff based upon ignorance.

(8) There is benevolent and malevolent dogma. Benevolent dogma is an attempt to "save the world" by instigating it to accept certain propositions. Malevolent dogma is an attempt to gain control over others by persuading them to accept certain propositions.

There is also *nolent,* un-volent dogma, a sort of automatic reaction in the mind of the dogmatiser, who may have come to disaster by following certain propositions, and who, from this, becomes crampedly convinced that contrary propositions are true.

(9) Belief is a cramp, a paralysis, an atrophy of the mind in certain positions.

II

(1) It is as foolish to try to contain the *theos* in consciousness as to try to manage electricity according to the physics of water. It is as non-workable as to think not only of our consciousness managing electricity according to the physics of water, but as to think of the water understanding the physics of electricity.

(2) All systems of philosophy fail when they attempt to set down axioms of the *theos* in terms of consciousness and of logic; similiter by the same figure that electricity escapes the physics of water.

(3) The selection of monotheism, polytheism, pluralism, dual, trinitarian god or gods, or hierarchies, is pure matter of individual temperament (in free minds), and of tradition in environment of discipular, bound minds.

(4) Historically the organisation of religions has usually been for some ulterior purpose, exploitation, control of the masses, etc.

III

(1) This is not to deny that the consciousness may be affected by the theos (remembering that we ascribe to this *theos* neither singular nor plural number).

(2) The theos may affect and may have affected the consciousness of individuals, but the consciousness is incapable of knowing why this occurs, or even in what manner it occurs, or whether it be the *theos;* though the consciousness may experience pleasant and possibly unpleasant sensations, or sensations partaking neither of pleasure or its opposite. Hence mysticism. If the consciousness receives or has received such effects from the theos, or from something not the theos yet which the consciousness has been incapable of understanding or classifying either as theos or a-theos, it is incapable of reducing these sensations to coherent sequence of cause and effect. The effects remain, so far as the consciousness is concerned, in the domain of experience, not differing intellectually from the taste of a lemon or the fragrance of violets or the aroma of dung-hills, or the feel of a stone or of tree-bark, or any other direct perception. As the consciousness observes the results of the senses, it observes also the mirage of the senses, or what may be a mirage of the senses, or an affect from the theos, the non-comprehensible.

(3) This is not to deny any of the visions or auditions or sensations of the mystics, Dante's rose or Theresa's walnut; but it is to affirm the propositions in Section I.

IV

(1) The consciousness may be aware of the effects of the unknown and of the non-knowable on the consciousness, but this does not affect the proposition that our consciousness is utterly ignorant of the nature of the intimate essence. For instance: a man may be hit by a bullet and not know its composition, nor the cause of its having been fired, nor its direction, nor that

it is a bullet. He may die almost instantly, knowing only the sensation of shock. Thus consciousness may perfectly well register certain results, as sensation, without comprehending their nature. (I, (1).) He may even die of a long-considered disease without comprehending its bacillus.

(2) The thought here becomes clouded, and we see the tendency of logic to move in a circle. Confusion between a possibly discoverable bacillus and a non-knowable *theos*. Concerning the ultimate nature of the bacillus, however, no knowledge exists; but the consciousness may learn to deal with superficial effects of the bacillus, as with the directing of bullets. Confusion enters argument the moment one calls in analogy. We return to clarity of Section I (1–9).

(3) The introduction of analogy has not affected our proposition that the "intimate essence" exists. It has muddied our conception of the non-knowability of the intimate essence.

[Speculation.—Religions have introduced analogy? Philosophies have attempted sometimes to do without it. This does not prove that religions have muddied all our concepts. There is no end to the variants one may draw out of the logical trick-hat.]

V

(1) It is, however, impossible to prove whether the theos be one or many.

(2) The greatest tyrannies have arisen from the dogma that the *theos* is one, or that there is a unity above various strata of theos which imposes its will upon the sub-strata, and thence upon human individuals.

(3) Certain beauties of fancy and of concept have arisen both from the proposition of many gods and from that of one god, or of an orderly arrangement of the theos.

(4) A choice of these fancies of the *theos* is a matter of taste; as the preference of Durer or Velasquez, or the Moscophorus, or Amen Hotep's effigy, or the marbles of Phidias.

(5) Religion usually holds that the theos can be, by its patent system, exploited.

(6) It is not known whether the theos may be or may not be exploited.

(7) Most religions offer a system or a few tips for exploiting the theos.

(8) Men often enjoy the feeling that they are performing this exploitation, or that they are on good terms with the theos.

(9) There is no harm in this, so long as they do not incommode anyone else.

(10) The reason why they should not incommode anyone else is not de-

monstrable; it belongs to that part of the concepts of consciousness which we call common decency.

(11) We do not quite know how we have come by these concepts of common decency, but one supposes it is our heritage from superior individuals of the past; that it is the treasure of tradition. Savages and professed believers in religion do not possess this concept of common decency. They usually wish to interfere with us, and to get us to believe something "for our good."

(12) A belief is, as we have said, a cramp, and thence progressively a paralysis or atrophy of the mind in a given position.

PART 12

Spanish, Catalan, and Latin American Avant-Gardes

French avant-garde art and thought was to have an enormous influence in the Spanish-speaking world, through such journals as *Troços*, which carried the work of Albert Gleizes alongside that of Joan Miró and Joaquin Torres-Garcia, and through interpreters of Futurism, Nunism, Cubism, and Surrealism. In 1911 José Ortega y Gasset saluted Futurism. In 1917 an exhibition of French art in Barcelona showed Roger de La Fresnaye, Henri Matisse, and Pierre Bonnard and many Impressionists. Nineteen eighteen was a good year in Spain for the avant-garde, with exhibitions of Miró and Torres-Garcia and, in the fall, the publication of the "Ultraist Manifesto" by Jorge Luis Borges and others (12.8). There was an international exhibition in Bilbao, with Pablo Picasso, and elsewhere a "Vibrationist" exhibition. In 1920 Dada Number 5 had, among other Spanish names, that of Guillermo de Torre, one of the principal intermediaries between the arts of France and Spain. Avant-garde art had its most important exhibition to date in Dalmau in 1920, including the work of Raoul Dufy, André Derain, Dunoyer de Segonzac, Albert Gleizes, Juan Gris, Fernand Léger, Marie Laurencin, Matisse, Picasso, Gino Severini, Paul Signac, Félix Vallotton, Kees van Dongen and Maurice de Vlaminck. The single issue of the *Reflector* appeared, edited by Torre, featuring work by the Surrealist Philippe Soupault, the Futurists Filippo Tommaso Marinetti and Ardengo Soffici, and the Constructivist Theo van Doesburg. In 1921 the journal *Alfar* was illustrated by Gris and Sonia Delaunay, while the Japanese prints of Hokusai and Utamaro were presented by Maurice Utrillo in Dalmau; in 1922 Rafael Alberti had his first exhibition, in Madrid, where Salvador Dali installed himself. Manifestos of Catalan art appeared, Cubism was interpreted to the Spanish public. Blaise Cendrars came to Madrid to give a lecture on "Black Literature," and the first text about Surrealism appeared in Spanish, followed shortly after by the translation of André Breton's "First Manifesto," in 1925 and lectures in Spain by the Surrealist Louis Aragon and the Cubist Max Jacob.

Two epoch-marking books about the avant-garde appeared: Ortega y Gasset's *The Dehumanization of Art* and Torre's *Avant-Garde European Literature*. From 1926 to 1928 the journal *L'Amic de les arts* (Friend of the arts) published the most important texts of the second waves of the Catalan avant-garde. In Dalmau again, the European avant-garde was shown side by side with that of Spain, and there was exhibition of contemporary German engravings, with Emil Nolde, Oskar Kokoshka, Otto Dix, and George Grosz.

The Latin-American movements, of which the Brazilian Jorge Luis Borges and the Chilean Vicente Huidobro are the best-known exponents, along with Oswaldo and Mario de Andrade and the concrete poet Haroldo de

Campos, all aimed at freeing the creative spirit from the bonds of the past, the corsets of rationality and convention by which past literature and thought had been shackled, or, in another metaphor, the prisons in which their products had been closed off from what is free and ongoing. In keeping with that aim, they themselves are not closed off but remain in sustained contact with the revolutionary aesthetics of European modernism.

From this heady mixture come the following manifestos, proclaiming freedom from the requirements of "good art," violence and moral subversion, and above all, the pure uninhibited imagination: "Photography," cries Salvador Dalí, "pure creation of the mind!" (Dalí, *Salvador Dalí*, 216).

12.1 SALVADOR DALÍ

Yellow Manifesto

1928

We have eliminated from this MANIFESTO all courtesy in our attitude. It is useless to attempt any discussion with the representatives of present-day Catalan culture, which is artistically negative although efficient in other respects. Compromise and correctness lead to deliquescent and lamentable states of confusion of all values, to the most unbreatheable spiritual atmospheres, to the most pernicious of influences. An example: *La Nova Revista*. Violent hostility, in contrast, clearly locates values and positions and creates a hygienic state of mind.

WE HAVE ELIMINATED	all reasoning	There exists an enor-
WE HAVE ELIMINATED	all literature	mous bibliography and
WE HAVE ELIMINATED	all poetry	all the effort of artists of
WE HAVE ELIMINATED	all philosophy in favour of our ideas	today to replace all this.

WE CONFINE OURSELVES	to the most objective listing of facts.
WE CONFINE OURSELVES	to pointing out the grotesque and extremely sad spectacle of the Catalan intelligentsia of today, shut in a blocked and putrefied atmosphere.

WE WARN those still uncontaminated of the risk of infection. A matter of strict spiritual asepsis.

WE KNOW that we are not going to say anything new. We are certain, however, that it is the basis of everything new that now exists and everything new that could possibly be created.

WE LIVE in a new era, of unforeseen poetic intensity.

MECHANIZATION has revolutionized the world.
MECHANIZATION —the antithesis of circumstantially indispensable futurism—has established the most profound change humanity has known.

A MULTITUDE anonymous—and anti-artistic—is collaborating with its daily endeavours towards the affirmation of the new era, while still living in accordance with its own period.

A POST-MACHINIST STATE OF MIND HAS BEEN FORMED

ARTISTS of today have created a new art in accordance with this state of mind. In accordance with their era.

HERE, HOWEVER, PEOPLE GO ON VEGETATING IDYLLICALLY

THE CULTURE of present-day Catalonia is useless for the joy of our era. Nothing is more dangerous, more false or more adulterating.

WE ASK CATALAN INTELLECTUALS:

'What use has the Bernat Metge Foundation been to you, if you end up confusing Ancient Greece with pseudo-classical ballerinas?'

WE DECLARE	that sportsmen are nearer the spirit of Greece than our intellectuals.
WE GO ON TO ADD	that a sportsman, free from artistic notions and all erudition is nearer and more suited to experience the art of today and the poetry of today than myopic intellectuals, burdened by negative training.
FOR US	Greece continues in the numerical precision of an aeroplane engine, in the anti-artistic, anonymously manufactured English fabric meant for golf, in the naked performer of the American music-hall.
WE NOTE	that the theatre has ceased to exist for some people and almost for everybody.
WE NOTE	that everyday concerts, lectures and shows taking place among us now, tend to be synonymous with unbreathable, crushingly boring places.
IN CONTRAST	new events, of intense joy and cheerfulness, demand the attention of the youth of today.
THERE IS	the cinema
THERE ARE	stadia, boxing, rugby, tennis and a thousand other sports
THERE IS	the popular music of today: jazz and modern dance
THERE ARE	motor and aeronautics shows
THERE ARE	beach games
THERE ARE	beauty competitions in the open air
THERE IS	the fashion show
THERE IS	the naked performer under the electric lights of the music-hall

THERE IS	modern music
THERE IS	the motor-racing track
THERE ARE	art exhibitions of modern artists
THERE ARE	moreover, great engineering and some magnificent ocean liners
THERE IS	an architecture of today
THERE ARE	implements, objects and furniture of the present era
THERE IS	modern literature
THERE ARE	modern poets
THERE IS	modern theatre
THERE IS	the gramophone, which is a little machine
THERE IS	the camera, which is another little machine
THERE ARE	newspapers with extremely quick and vast information
THERE ARE	encyclopaedias of extraordinary erudition
THERE IS	science in great action
THERE IS	well-documented, guiding criticism
THERE ARE	etc., etc., etc.,
THERE IS	finally, an immobile ear over a small puff of smoke.
WE DENOUNCE	the sentimental influence of Guimerà's racial clichés
WE DENOUNCE	the sickly sentimentality served up by the Orfeó Català, with its shabby repertoire of popular songs adapted and adulterated by people with no capacity whatsoever for music, and even, of original compositions. (We think optimistically of the choir of American Revelers.)
WE DENOUNCE	the total lack of youth in our youth
WE DENOUNCE	the total lack of decision and audacity
WE DENOUNCE	the fear of new events, of words, of the risk of the ridiculous
WE DENOUNCE	the torpor of the putrid atmosphere of clubs and egos mingled with art

WE DENOUNCE	the total unawareness of critics with regard to the art of the present and the past
WE DENOUNCE	young people who seek to repeat painting of the past
WE DENOUNCE	young people who seek to imitate literature of the past
WE DENOUNCE	old, authentic architecture
WE DENOUNCE	decorative art, unless it is standardized
WE DENOUNCE	painters of crooked trees
WE DENOUNCE	present-day Catalan poetry, made with stale Maragallian clichés
WE DENOUNCE	artistic poisons for the use of children. like: *Jordi.* (For the joy and understanding of children, nothing is more suitable than Rousseau, Picasso, Chagall . . .)
WE DENOUNCE	the psychology of little girls who sing: "Rosó, Rosó . . ."
WE DENOUNCE	the psychology of little boys who sing: "Rosó, Rosó . . ."

FINALLY WE DEDICATE OURSELVES TO THE GREAT ARTISTS OF TO-DAY, within the most diverse tendencies and categories:

PICASSO, GRIS, OZENFANT, CHIRICO, JOAN MIRO, LIPCHITZ, BRANCUSI, ARP, LE CORBUSIER, REVERDY, TRISTAN TZARA, PAUL ELUARD, LOUIS ARAGON, ROBERT DESNOS, JEAN COCTEAU, GARCÍA LORCA, STRAVINSKY, MARITAIN, RAYNAL, ZERVOS, ANDRÉ BRETON, ETC., ETC.

12.2 Ramón Gómez de la Serna [Tristán]
Futurist Proclamation to the Spaniards
1910

Futurism! Insurrection! Clamor! Feast with Wagnerian music! Modernism! Sidereal violence! Whirling about amid the poisonous pomp and circumstance of life! Antiuniversityism! Cypress bark! Iconoclasm! A stone cast in the nick of time at the moon! Earthquake renewing, invigorating! Ploughs changed into swords! Secularizing of graveyards! Discaring your wife free into her moment without all this toomuchness of idylls and weddings! Conspiracy in the open air, conspiracy of aviators and drivers! Debauchery like a shaft of high timber felled by a lightning rod with a hundred electric snakes and a rain of stars flaming in its curtain of space! A youthful voice its enough to hear without taking any account of the words: this puerile graffito of the voice! Voice, force, volt, more than a word! Voice uniting all the young without any question, like the hearth the Arabs light when they are separated before arguments! Intersection, spark, exhalation, text like a telegraph or something still more subtle flying over seas and mountains! Winging north, winging south, winging east and winging ever faster! Healthy spectacle of areodrome and of a track out of orbit! Masonic and rebellious camaraderie! Lyricism with its branches stripped off into a bullet and projected in extraordinary headlights! Happiness like a triumph after struggle, in the Thermopylos passage! The birth of a few men alone faced with the nonchalance and the horrendous apathy of the multitudes! Delighting in attack, in sceptical sarcastic regret, seeing yourself finally with a face free of lust, envy, and any greedy desires of complacencies—for luncheons and larders! Going at a great gallop over the old cities and the wise men, over all the canopies and all the garrulous grotesque processions! Primitive nuptials joyous and enthusiastic amid all the pessimism, darkness, and seriousness! Simulacrum of the conquest of the land, give us the land!

The Point of View in the Arts (*excerpt*)

1924

Cézanne, in the middle of his impressionistic tradition, discovers volume. In his surfaces there start appearing cubes, cylinders, cones. Somone a bit distracted might have thought that, once his pictorial peregrination had finished, he had returned to the beginning and taken up once more Giotto's point of view. What a mistake! There have always been lateral tendencies in the history of art, gravitating toward archaism. Nevertheless, the central current of evolution leaps over them in a magnificent rush and follows its inevitable course.

Cézanne's cubism and that of the artists who were in fact cubists, that is to say sterometers, is only one further step toward the internationalism of painting. Sensations, the theme of impressionism, are subjective states, for all that they are realities, effective alternations in the subject. But even here, are ideas. Ideas are also realities that happen in the individual soul but distinct from sensations in that their content—the ideated—is unreal and sometimes near to impossible. When I think about the strictly geometrical cylinder, my *thought* is an effective event produced in me; on the other hand, the geometrical cylinder *about which* I think is an unreal object. Ideas are, then, subjective realities that contain virtual objects, a whole world of new species, distinct from what our eyes transmit to us, marvelously emerging from the physical senses.

Then, the volumes that Cézanne evokes have nothing to do with those that Giotto discovers; they are rather antagonistic. Giotto looks for the proper volume of each thing, its realistic and tangible corporeality. Before him, only the Byzantime image of two dimensions was known. Cézanne, on the other hand, substitutes for the bodies of things unreal volumes of pure invention that have only a metaphoric connection with them. After him, painting only paints ideas—which, certainly, are objects also, but ideal objects, immanent to the subject or intersubjective.

This explains the melancholia that, in spite of erroneous explanations, appears in the disturbed lap of so-called *cubism*. Face to face with volumes in which the rotundity of bodies seems to be superbly obvious, Picasso, in his most scandalous and typical paintings, annhilates the closed form of the object and in pure Euclidean planes notes parts of one: an eyebrow, a mustache, a nostril—without any other use than as the symbolic cipher of the idea.

Cubist ambiguity is nothing else than a particular style within contemporary expressionism. It has reached the minimum of exterior objectivity. A new displacement of the point of view will only be possible if, reaching back behind the retina—the subtle border between the external and the internal—it could completely invert the function of painting and, instead of putting inside what is outside for us, it tried to tilt onto the canvas what is within: the invented ideal objects. Notice how, by a simple advance of the point of view in the same and unique trajectory that we were following from the beginning, we have arrived at the opposite result. The eyes, instead of absorbing things, are changed into projectors of landscapes and intimate faunas. Before they were the sewers of the real world; now they are the purveyors of unreality.

It is possible that the art of the present has little aesthetic value, but whoever doesn't see anything in it but a caprice can be sure not to have understood either new or old art. Evolution has led painting—and art in general—inexorably, fatally, to what it is today.

12.4 Joaquin Torres-Garcia
Art-Evolution (In Manifesto-Style)
1917

Art has to concur with the course of life. So we have to be evolutionists. We can't admit anything that doesn't in itself evolve. In each of our works this evolutionary process should be realized. We cannot do this in one single inalterable way, nor can we admit the formation of any school. Nor can we have any criteria, if they would imply something stable used as a point or the base of comparison. In any case, our criteria have to evolve constantly.— As we are in the middle of that natural evolution, our role must consist only in signaling, like a sensitive receiving apparatus that we could call the plasticity of time. But without belonging to one land rather than another. We want to be international.—Nothing that has already come to pass can be useful to us; not even our own works. For us, nothing is definitive. We have to ignore anything we'll be doing tomorrow. We must find those who have the right temperament to choose and select, spontaneously.—Intuitive and sympathetic connections compose our reality. I have to identify myself, so as truly to connect things.—The day is the only interesting phenomenon. We must not paint or speak of anything else, remaining in this state of sympathy with things. — Being an evolutionist or not is not belonging to a school; it is being independent; it is being an anarchist opposed to all schools. It is being someone in time. Because we don't have to believe that we can connect everything. Our motto should be to exist: individualism, presentism, internationalism.

Creationism

This movement wants to be, like the others, international: Vicente Huidobro, its Chilean founder, delighted in the idea that languages were transgressing national boundaries and flying above them, and above any referent. His preface to *Square Horizon* (1917) calls for "Nothing descriptive or anecdotal. Emotion must be born from the creative strengths alone" (qtd. in Nicholls, *Modernisms*, 245). His aim was to restructure language and thought by various forms of osmosis and combinations of phonetic, linguistic, even letteral techniques—thus his precursorship of the Créatique of the Romanian-French lettrist Isidore Isou and of the combinatorial and constraint-work of the Paris-based Oulipo. So, in his epic poem *Altazor* (1919–30), Huidobro inserted musical and metaphoric references that, along with his other experimentations, anticipate concrete poetry.

In the Creationist case, as often, dates are problematic in relation to effects. Huidobro dated his movement from 1914, when he used the word in a lecture, "Non serviam" (12.5)—and when, in one of his articles for his collection *Pasando y pasando* (roughly translatable as "Just passing through"), he called Futurism Chilean, created by Armando Vasseur's "languralism"! In 1916 he lectured on Creationism in Buenos Aires, published his ars poetica in his *Espejo de agua* (Water mirror), with the basic ideas to be developed in his 1925 *Manifestos*, and arrived in Paris, where he was associated with Pierre Albert-Birot's journal *sic* and the Nunist group. In 1917 he published his first book in French, *Horizons carrés* (Square horizons). He would later refer to this "heroic period" in Paris and to himself as having been part of the Cubist group, the only important group in the history of contemporary art. His major quarrel with Pierre Reverdy over the dating of Creationism came about because the latter was quoted in a Madrid newspaper as saying, about the avant-garde movement in Spanish (in a Madrid stay of 1918 Huidobro had been associated with the future members of the Ultraist group), that Huidobro had predated *Espejo de agua* to make it look as if the Paris group had imitated him instead of the other way around. . . . So much for inter-nationalism.

In any case, in Madrid on April 1, 1921, Huidobro founded the journal *Creación*, in which we read the names of Georges Braque, Albert Gleizes, Juan Gris, Jacques Lipchitz, Pablo Picasso, and so on, and in the next year the journal appeared in Paris. "The wind is turning my flute towards the future," he claimed in his manifesto "Creationism" (Huidobro, *Manifestes, Altazor*, 158). His *Manifestes* of 1925 includes the following.

12.5 VICENTE HUIDOBRO

Non Serviam

(Manifesto read at the Ateneo in Santiago, Chile, 1914)

1914

And it happens that one lovely morning, after a night of charming dreams and delicious nightmares, the poet rises and cries to Mother Nature: *Non serviam.*

At the top of his lungs, an echoing translator optimistically repeats: "I won't serve you."

Mother Nature was already going to strike down the young rebellious poet when, taking off his hat and making a gracious gesture, he exclaims: "You are an old charmer."

This *non serviam* remained engraved on a morning of the world's history. It was neither a capricious cry nor a superficial act of rebellion. It was the result of a whole revolution, the sum of multiple experiences.

The poet, fully conscious of his past and his future, cast against the world the declaration of his independence from Nature.

He no longer wanted to serve it like a slave.

The poet says to his brothers: "Until now we haven't done anything other than imitate the world in its appearances, we haven't created anything. What might have come from us which wasn't already here in front of us, in front of our eyes, surrounding them, defying our feet or our hands?

"We have sung Nature (which didn't concern her). Never have we cre-ated any proper realities, as she does and used to do when she was young and heavy with creative impulses.

"We have accepted, without reflecting further, the fact that there can be no other realities than those that surround us, and we haven't thought that we also could create realities in a world that would be ours, in a world awaiting its own flora and fauna. Fauna and flora that only the poet can create, through this particular gift that this same NATURE gave him and him alone."

Non serviam. I don't have to be your slave, Mother Nature: I shall be your master. You will use me; that's fine. I don't want it and cannot understand it: but I will use you too. I'll have my trees, too, which won't be like yours, I'll have my mountains, I'll have my rivers and my oceans, I'll have my sky and my stars.

And you'll never be able to say to me: "This tree is not lovely, this heaven doesn't please me. . . . I prefer mine."

I will answer you that my heavens and my trees are mine and not yours and that they don't have to look alike. Then you can no longer crush us with your exaggerated claims of being old, sensual, and senile. Now we are fleeing your traps.

Farewell, old charmer: farewell mother and stepmother, I will not deny you or curse you for all these years of slavery serving you. They were the most precious of teachings. The only thing I desire is never to forget your lessons, but I know I am old enough to go alone throughout the world, yours and mine.

A new era is beginning. Opening its jasper doors, I bend one knee to the ground and salute you respectfully.

Avis aux touristes (Warning to tourists)

1914–1917

Je suis arrivé en retard pour prendre le train que j'avais mis en marche.

AVIS
AUX
TOURISTES

J'ai eu le temps de prendre en mouvement le dernier wagon et chaque fois que le train allait dérailler je faisais des signes au conducteur lui montrant de loin la manœuvre. Dans les wagons de troisième, de seconde et même de première classe, s'étaient faufilé plusieurs commis voyageurs de grandes maisons. En arrivant à la gare je m'aperçus que le train avait changé d'itinéraire et de chemin. Je descendis et je pris tout seul la route des rêves polaires.

Le motor-man me ressemblait vaguement mais ce n'était pas moi-même.

I came too late to catch the train I had started.

I just had time to catch in motion the last car on the train and each time the train was going to derail I signaled the conductor to show him. In the third, second, and even first class there were many traveling salesmen from the large stores. Arriving in the station I perceived that the train had changed itinerary and its route. I got out and took alone the route of polar dreams.

The motorman looked vaguely like me but he wasn't me.

We Must Create

1922

We must create.

Man no longer imitates. He invents, he adds to the facts of the world, born in Nature's breast, new facts born in his head: a poem, a painting, a statue, a steamer, a car, a plane. . . .

We must create.

That's the sign of our times.

Today's man has shattered the bark of appearances and surprised what there was underneath.

Poetry must not imitate the aspects of things but rather follow the constructive laws that are their essence, guaranteeing the real independence of everything.

*Inventing is making things that are parallel in space meet in time or vice-versa, so that they present a new fact in their conjunction.**

The totality of the diverse new facts united by a single spirit constitutes the created work.

If they are not united by a single spirit, the result will be an impure work with an amorphous look, resulting from a fantasy with no laws.

The study of art throughout history shows us very clearly this tendency of imitation to move toward creation in all human productions. We can establish a law of Scientific and Mechanical Selection equivalent to the law of Natural Selection.

In art the power of the creator interests us more than that of the observer, and besides the former contains in itself the second, to a higher degree.

---

* Saltpeter, coal, and sulfur have existed in parallel since the beginning of the world; it took a superior man, an inventor who, by bringing them together, created the tinderpowder able to blow up your brain like a lovely image.

Ultraism

Ultraism is the first avant-garde grouping in Spain and Latin America of purely Spanish origin. (Ramón Gómez de la Serna's "Futurist Proclamation to the Spaniards" [12.2], published in 1910 in Madrid in the journal *Prometeo*, had simply brought Filippo Tammaso Marinetti's Italian Futurism to Spain, with all its "Sidereal Violence.")

"We have cut the umbilical cord," claimed the new group called Ultraists in 1918, composed of Jorge Luis Borges, de la Serna, Federico Garcia Lorca, and José Ortega y Gasset. El Greco was an Ultraist, they claimed, as were many others: "our audacious and conscious creed is not to have a creed." Ultraism claims creation for creation's sake. It is PRISMATIC, it says in capital letters, and shines like a REFLECTOR. The latter gives its name to one of the movement's journals.

The next year, 1919, Ultraism brought forth new journals: *Perseo* in Madrid (one issue only) and *Ultra* in Ovidedo. The group organized Ultraist soirées, as scandalous as those of the Surrealists. In 1922 other Ultraists appeared in the short-lived journal *Horizonte*, including the influential writer Damaso Alonso. In 1925 the last issue of the Ultraist journal *Plural* appeared.

Although it had no one particular point of view of its own, Ultraism was always a Modernist salute to the avant-garde work of others. In this it exemplified the enthusiam characteristic of the manifesto at its best. So Guillermo de la Torre proclaimed that Vladimir Tatlins's "New Eiffel Tower" in Russia reached a summit that had not been attained even with the other one in France. This is Modernism at its most international.

Ultraist Manifesto

1921

There are two aesthetics: the passive aesthetic of mirrors and the active aesthetic of prisms. When guided by the first, art transforms itself into an objective copy of its surroundings or of the physical history of the individual. When guided by the second, art frees itself, uses the world as its own instrument, and creates—beyond any spatial and temporal prison—its own personal vision.

This is the aesthetics of Ultra. It wants to create: that is, to impose so far unsuspected ways of seeing on the universe. It demands from each poet a fresh view of things, clear of any ancestral stigmas; a fragrant vision, as if the world were arising like dawn in front of our eyes. And to conquer this vision, it is essential to cast away every aspect of the past. Everything: right-angled classical architecture, romantic exaltation, the microscopic observations of the naturalists, the blue twilights that were the lyrical banners of the nineteenth-century poets. That whole absurd vast cell where the ritualists would imprison the marvelous bird of beauty. Everything, until each one of us can make an architectural construction of our own subjective creation.

From that exposition, the reader will have seen that the ultraist direction is not and never could be weighed down with a difficult set of arbitrary rules—as some would have it. The ultraists have always existed: they are those who, prescient for their times, have brought to the world new aspects of vision and expression. To them we owe evolution itself, the vitality of things. Without them, we would have kept on turning in a circle, around one single light, like moths. El Greco, in relation to his contemporaries, came out an ultraist also, like so many others. Our audacious and conscious creed is not to have a creed. That is to say, we reject all the recipes and corsets so absurdly proper, leaving them for ordinary minds. Our motto is creation for creation. Ultraist poetry has as much cadence and musicality as any other. It has just as much tenderness. As much visuality and more imagination. What is changed is the structure. Each of its most essential innovations has its root in this: the sensitivity and the feeling will always be the same. We make no claim to modify the soul or nature. What we are renovating is the means of expression.

Our iconoclastic ideology, what sets the philistines against us, is precisely what enobles us. Every great affirmation takes a negation, as our companion Nietzsche said or forgot to say. . . . Our poems have the freewheeling and decisive structure of telegrams.

By this superactive work we are reinforcing the strength of the ultraist magazines *Grecia, Cervantes, Reflector,* and *Ultra.*

JACOBO SUREDA, FORTUNIO BONANOVA,

JUAN ALOMAR, JORGE LUIS BORGES

Hallucinism

Brazil

12.9 MARIO DE ANDRADE
Extremely Interesting Preface (*excerpt*)
1922

Dans mon pays de fiel et d'or
j'en suis la loi.
E. VERHAEREN

Reader:

Hallucinism has been launched.

This preface—although interesting—useless.

A few facts. Not all of them. No conclusions. For those who accept me, both facts and conclusions are useless. The curious will have the pleasure of discovering my conclusions, by comparing the work with the facts. As for those who reject me, it is wasted effort to explain to them what they have rejected even before they have read it.

When I feel the lyric impulse upon me, I write without thinking all that my unconscious shouts out to me. I think afterward: not only to correct but also to justify what I have written. Hence the reason for this Extremely Interesting Preface.

Furthermore, in this kind of chit-chat it is very difficult to know where the *blague* leaves off and the serious begins. I do not even know myself.

And forgive me for being so behind the times regarding present-day artistic movements. I am old-fashioned, I confess. No one can liberate himself once and for all from the grandaddy-theories he has imbibed, and the author of this book would be a hypocrite if he pretended to represent a modern orientation which as yet he himself does not totally comprehend.

.   .   .

Every writer believes in the worth of what he writes. If he shows it, it is out of vanity. If he does not show it, it is also out of vanity.

I do not flee from the ridiculous. I have illustrious companions.

The ridiculous is often subjective. It does not depend on the greater or lesser goal of the one who suffers it. We create it in order to garb in it the person who wounds our pride, ignorance, or sterility.

A little theory?

I believe that lyricism, born in the subconscious, purified into a clear or confused thought, creates phrases which are entire verses, without the necessity of counting so many syllables with predetermined accentuation. Run-on lines are a welcome respite to those poets who are trapped in the Alexandrine prison. There are only rare examples of that in this book. As the twig is bent. . . .

Inspiration is short-lived, violent. Any obstacle whatever upsets it and even silences it. When Art is added to Lyricism to create Poetry, this process does not consist of halting the mad dash of the lyric state in order to warn it of the stones and barbed-wire fences along the road. Let it stumble, fall, and wound itself. Art is a subsequent weeding out of all irksome repetitions, romantic sentimentalities, and useless or unexpressive details.

Let Art, therefore, not consist of ridding verses of colorful exaggerations. Exaggeration: ever-new symbol of life as well as of the dream. Through exaggeration, life and dreams are linked. And, employed consciously, it is not a defect, rather a legitimate means of expression.

"The wind sits in the shoulder of your sail!" Shakespeare. Homer had long ago written that the earth groaned beneath the feet of men and horses. But you must know that there are millions of exaggerations in the works of the masters.

.　.　.

Marinetti was wonderful when he rediscovered the suggestive, associative, symbolic, universal, and musical power of the liberated word. Beyond that: it is as old as Adam. Marinetti was wrong: he made a system out of the liberated word. It is merely an extremely powerful auxiliary. I employ liberated words. I feel that my cup is too large for me, and yet I drink from the cups of others.

I am capable of constructing ingenious theories. Do you want to see one? Poetics is far more backward than music. Maybe even before the eighth century, music abandoned the regimen of melody, which at most dared to use octaves, in order to enrich itself with the infinite resources of harmony. Poetics, with rare exception down to the middle of the nineteenth century in

France, was essentially melodic. I consider melodic verse the same as musical melody: a horizontal arabasque of consecutive tones (sounds) which
contain intelligible thought. Now, if instead of using only verses which are
horizontally melodic, such as:

> Mnesarete, the divine, the pale Phryne
> Appears before the austere and stern assembly
> of the supreme Areopagus . . .

we have words follow each other without any immediate connection among
themselves, these words, for the very reason that they do not follow intellectually and grammatically, overlie one another for the gratification of our
senses, and no longer form melodies but rather harmonies. I shall explain
more fully. Harmony: combination of sounds. Example:

> Ravishments . . . Struggles . . . Arrows . . .
> Songs . . . Populate!

These words have no connection. They do not form a series. Each one is
a phrase, an elliptical period, reduced to the telegraphic minimum. If I
pronounce "Ravishments," since it does not belong to a phrase (melody),
the word calls our attention to its detachment and it continues to vibrate,
waiting for a phrase which will give it meaning, a phrase which DOES NOT
FOLLOW. "Struggles" gives no conclusion whatever to "Ravishments"; and,
under the same conditions, as we are not made to forget the first word,
it continues to vibrate along with the other word. The other voices do the
same. Thus: instead of melody (grammatical phrase) we have an arpeg-
giated chord, harmony—the harmonic verse. But, if instead of using only
disconnected words, I use disconnected phrases, I get the same sensation of
overlay, not now of words (notes) alone but of phrases (melodies). Hence:
poetic polyphony. . . .

Sir Lyricism, when he disembarked from the El Dorado of the Unconscious at the pier of the Land of the Conscious, is inspected by the ship's
doctor, Intelligence, who cleanses him of quirks and of all sickness whatever
that might spread confusion and obscurity in this progressive little land.
Sir Lyricism undergoes one more visit from the customs officials, a visit discovered by Freud who called it Censure. I am a smuggler! I am against the
vaccination laws.

It appears that I am all instinct. That is not true. There is in my book—
and it does not displease me—a pronounced intellectualist tendency. What
do you expect? I smuggle my silk in without paying the duties. But it is

psychologically impossible for me to liberate myself from vaccinations and tonics.

Grammar appeared after languages were organized. It so happens that my unconscious knows nothing of the existence of grammars or of organized languages. And my unconscious, like Sir Lyricism, is a smuggler. . . .

You will easily note that if grammar is sometimes scorned in my poetry, it does not suffer serious insults in this extremely interesting preface. Preface: skyrocket of my higher self. The poems: landscape of my deeper self.

Pronouns? I write Brazilian. If I use Portuguese orthography, it is because it furnishes me an orthography without altering the result.

In my opinion, to write modern art never means to represent modern life through its externals: automobiles, movies, asphalt. If these words frequent my book, it is not because I think that I write "modern" with them; but since my book is modern, these things have their reason for being in it.

Besides, I know that there may be a modern artist who seeks inspiration in the Greece of Orpheus or in the Lusitania of Nun' Alvares. I recognize furthermore the existence of eternal themes, open to adoption because of their modernity: universe, homeland, love and the presence-of-the-absent, ex-bitter-pleasure-of-wretches.

Neither did I seek to attempt insincere and cross-eyed primitivism. We are actually the primitives of a new epoch. Esthetically: I sought an expression more human and freer from art among the hypotheses of psychologists, naturalists, and critics of the primitives of past ages.

The past is a lesson to be meditated, not to be imitated.

E tu che sé costí, anima viva,
Pártiti da cotesti che son morti.

For many years I sought myself. I have found myself. Do not tell me now that I seek originality because I have already discovered where it was: it belongs to me, it is mine.

When one of the poems in this book was published, many people told me: "I did not understand it." There were some, however, who confessed: "I understood it, but I did not feel it." As for my dear friends . . . I saw more than once that they felt it, but they did not understand it. Evidently my book is good.

A famous writer said about me and my friends that we were either geniuses or jackasses. I think that he is right. We feel, I as well as my friends, the desire to be showoffs. If we were sheep to the point of forming a collective school, this would surely be "Showoffism." Our desire: to illuminate.

The extreme left in which we have stationed ourselves will not permit half-way solutions. If we are geniuses: we will point the road to follow; if we are jackasses: shipwrecks to avoid.

I sing in my own way. What do I care if no one understands me? You say that I do not have enough strength to universalize myself? What do I care! Singing to the accompaniment of the complex lute that I have constructed, I strike out through the wild jungle of the city. Like primitive man, at first I shall sing alone. But song is an engaging fellow: it gives rebirth in the soul of another man — predisposed or merely sincerely curious and free — to the same lyric state provoked in us by joys, sufferings, ideals. I shall always find some man or some woman who will be rocked in the hammock of the libertarian cadence of my verses. At that moment: a new, dark and bespectacled Amphion, I shall make the very stones rise up like a wall at the magic of my song. And within those walls we shall sequester our tribe.

My hand has written about this book that: "I neither had nor do I now have the slightest intention of publishing it." *Jornal do Comércio*, June 6. Read the words of Gourmont concerning contradiction: first volume of the *Promenades Littéraires*. Rui Barbosa has a lovely page on contradiction, I do not remember where. There are a few words also in Jean Cocteau, *La Noce Massacrée*.

But this whole preface, with all the nonsensical theories which it contains, is not worth a damn. When I wrote *Hallucinated City* I did not think about any of this. I guarantee, however, that I wept, sang, laughed, and bellowed . . . I am alive!

Besides, verses are not written to be read by mute eyes. Verses are meant to be sung, bellowed, wept. If you cannot sing, do not read "Landscape I." If you cannot bellow, do not read "Ode to the Bourgeois Gentleman." If you cannot pray, do not read "Religion." Scorn: "The Escalade." Suffer: "Colloque Sentimental." Forgive: the lullaby, one of the solos of My Madness from "The Moral Fibrature." I will not go on. It disgusts me to hand over the key to my book. If you are like me, you already have the key.

So the poetic school of "Hallucinism" is finished.

In the next book I will found another school.

PART 13

Merz, Verbophonics, Optophonics

Created by Kurt Schwitters, Merz (as in *Kommerz*) is the Hanoverian Succession of Dada: the town Hanover becomes Revon, for Revonah, in Schwitters's inversion and deformation of its name. Merz, as Schwitters defines it, "stands for freedom from all letters . . . the product of strict artistic discipline. . . . From the interaction of letters, syllables, words, sentences, poetry arises . . . meaning is important only if it is employed as one such factor" (qtd. in Chipp, *Theories*, 384). For Merz, as for Dada, any form remains forever unfinished, in progress. Schwitters's *Merzbau*, or Merz building, an ironic Dada parody of the Weimar Bauhaus and yet also a neoplastic Constructivist statement after his discovery of Theo van Doesburg's Dutch work, was made entirely of found objects. It climbed through the roof of its room in Hanover, Germany, and started into the next story, until it was destroyed in the war.

It was Schwitters who wrote the "Manifesto of Proletarian Art," signed by van Doesburg, Jean Arp, and Tristan Tzara and dated March 6, 1923. He himself, his publications having been burned by the Nazis, fled first to Norway and then to Ambleside, England, where he died, leaving his last Merzbau construction behind, incomplete. He also left his thirty-five-minute *Ursonata* of 1924, whose score was printed in 1932 as the twenty-fourth and last number of his journal *Merz*, which had lasted for ten years. This groundbreaking piece of verbal music, based partly on Raoul Hausmann's sound poetry, is made of bird sounds and other picked-up auditory bits, Merz in music, as his collages are Merz in art.

In 1921 Hausmann organized an Antidada series with the Constructivists before a reconciliation in 1922 in Weimar. In later years Hausmann, fleeing from Austria, ended in Limoges, with his eyesight nearly gone, bitterly aware that much of his initiatory work in verbophonics and optophonics had been appropriated by others. He always wanted to be at the origin of everything, as indeed he often had been. This was the origin of his quarrel with Schwitters, whom he accused of appropriating his ideas, such as sound poetry. Reconciled in 1946 by the intermediary of László Moholy-Nagy, they began developing a review together.

Jasia Reichardt writes, "One of the most moving modernist manifestoes was compiled by Raoul Hausmann and Kurt Schwitters in 1946. A year after the end of World War II, each discovered that the other was still alive: Schwitters in Ambleside in England and Raoul Hausmann in Limoges in France. In their correspondence they tried to bridge the distance between them and to recapture the adventure of experiment that had fired their spirits before the war. They planned, in Hausmann's words: 'a little review' that would keep the spirit of Dada and Merz alive. It was to be published in Paris in 4 languages. At first it was to be called *Schwittmail*, then *PinholeMail* and finally *PIN* [Poetry Is Now]. Its theme could be described, in Schwitters' words, as 'play with serious problems.' *PIN* was to include some 30 texts: poems, menus, nonsense songs, stories, as well as images. In 1959, Hausmann sent the material to Stefan Themerson, author of *Kurt Schwitters in England* (1958) and director of Gaberbocchus Press, who published it in 1962" (personal communication, 1999). Kurt Schwitters died in 1948.

13.1 RAOUL HAUSMANN
B.T.B
1946

Some two dozen french and foreign upstarts have founded the "dictature lettriste" in Paris. They claim to be the inventors of the sort of phonetic poems we created between 1918 and 1921. But we have had an interview with them by the medium of telebrain (B.T.B.) and we reproduce it here for our readers.

Qu: h gf egh. mjh ert gguhnjjj mn. Uz egb effgehejtrzebsg gdgebtimé ebth bkj ugf dbgndmab j k d e z g b wEtrgeh Axq g uhnf vo ge ljhn trgfd vh defghu jznh. ä. mn bbgbbvf fdcdsc xyax cfgt n pol dgfbr?
A: D ghtn djt gjh mnnebgdvdfdsce fg hgnbefdvfr etrffämhngj BG evfr drevri e ingtfjuhb fjhtb drebglkjh nmgungefrt Der fgrtre er Getrefre Quande vgg grbefrdant gbrnedfznbegfs g r b d e v z g n dW ggrbevf Kmnbghe dveu t gbengfvdt Hbehrgbec d eugrfe dtegz f r e bnghrgrfede svfr sgfefrvde.
Qu: D gtrh nefrbecedexse Gefrdevsjanbfe vdeega ö bnfbevrf Detrfrv Geugrgebn G eurnfebvf Dajed bmdnbrve Ftfgb xcsh veced Sagfevecnemiebeced Feda thrg?
A: D gr n drefevchgbbn alfhegb negte fff ecd Gm cefcbevcedc s Atdegb Wo p fferd virgbefe Gafrde bhj diatjrgfed Mangebvrfe Ci vgabh ne oft F gedar gfbvt decevbeve Cjabgefevbsedaittunvefr Tjanfdect Was W ghe nebefev nidencerv fadserw nquanderat gefancedebev Nimmentebgt da gegeben Gedanken favebtert, gerfrgiateggunbegft Anderder der gerdaberd gjert Bw ehbnedgat fnhein de ten defet g Gehiffugzbmengefen Lamderbattunbfev.

Qu: D gbnehefrt Fassss fjeffüte fez gttree D eht b dhT cerde jeiend aider? F bau n cerd brtz sdfe bgFer aW fer cfer Hö ver dfutiof erat Qn abder

A: Mmann der hder unfer gad wtz vvofrneder A ge datoind Fore eg abttunf Iger abfer da hert m andgztzh n Kangert Hazbedert Mabgebdft, ber dir? amder behnmvefr ger dierr ger a bfert hnabfdert mgert Hmfer habfder.

Qu: D ve er hgert fadscebvcffotnht Gkander henvedrt Gab dert giw der Hamvder?

A: H cdfet ha menv k k derr hhhhg trfeb dej fedret Am der Heandbvert-zuibfd Nbafertw ituzogert ngert mjhgfrt fdabcdvfdert La mbedret bag-vedert jancfg.

Conclusion:

(b Baderg bdftgbevefrd Danveddfft Hbam vedert a qgdert kanvder-bgfdvan A bfert Hancedert ghanvedertf ahv dertb z a d f fgrt!)

13.2 KURT SCHWITTERS
Cow Manifesto
1922

First, I find it very unnatural to milk different cows into a single pail. You should milk different cows into different pails. Even like that it isn't really ideal, because I think it completely contrary to general human morale for different people to drink milk from the same pail. You could remedy this by milking the same cow into different pails meant for different people. But then it's still very unnatural to milk a cow into a pail, or even (as it happens frequently these days) to bottle the milk. By its nature, milk should be either in the cow or in the veal's or human's stomach, but never in a bottle. On the other hand, given the rhythm of present life, it isn't easy for people living in big cities to run off to the country when they want to drink milk, so that each of them can drink from the udder of his personal cow. On the other hand, because of space, it would be rather difficult to raise enough cows in cities. Consequently, there is only one solution hygenically irreproachable for the modern man, adapted to modern times and worthy of a cow:

Let the cows graze tranquilly and peacefully in their pastures, with flex-ible rubber tubes attached to their udders and connected at the other end to subterranean conduits leading to the big cities, like those used for gas. It is essential that the conduits never communicate and that they be parallel. These conduits can be placed right in the buildings and come out into the room at some practical height. You can put a tasteful faucet there to close off the tube. You can place a nipple on this faucet whenever necessary. That way, whenever an owner of a cow is thirsty, he can milk his nipple. As you see, this is hygenically irreproachable, healthy, worthy of a cow, and harmless for general morals.

13.3 KURT SCHWITTERS

i (a manifesto)

1922

Today every child knows about Merz. But what's i? i is the middle vowel, it designates the coherence and the intensity of Merz in the way it apprehends artistic form. To make a work of art, Merz uses as a basic material those great wholes already formed, so as to shorten the distance between intuition and visualisation of the artistic concept, avoiding waste through friction. i supposes this distance as equal to zero, = o. Concept, material, and work of art are the same thing. i considers the work of art in nature. Here artistic creation means the recognition of rhythm and expression in one part of nature. Here there is no reason to fear any waste through friction: there is no perturbation during creation. I demand i, not as the only artistic form but as a particular form.

The first i drawings were shown to the public when I had my exhibit at *Sturm* on May 22 of this year. For the art critics I will add that, of course, it takes much more knowledge to cut out a work of art within nature, unformed from an artistic point of view, than to construct a work of art starting with its own artistic rules, and that with an unimportant material. In art the material isn't important, you just have to give it form to make it a work of art. For i however, the material is far from unimportant, to the extent that a world of nature doesn't necessarily become a work of art. That is why i is a particular form. But at least this time it's a matter of coherence. Do you think an art critic can grasp that?

PIN Manifesto

Present Inter Noumenal/Poetry Intervenes Now

1946

Poetry does not serve any more for needs
Since four thousand years it has served feudal archetypes
Since Homer, Aeschylos, Sophocles, Vergil, till Racine, Molière,
Shakespeare, Goethe and Hugo, it has served to revive the great
EMPTINESS by a heroic IMAGINARY, in a metaphoric language
Poetry of the PRESENT has given up the asiano-mediterranian archetypes
It has given up the HEROES
Poetry of the PRESENT has found the new objectivity of things in the
living space
It does not seek any more to explicate phenomena, be they social or false
philosophical
Poetry of the PRESENT does not spring out of fear, it has liberated itself of
the world-agony and the ridiculously tragic keeping up of the cunning of
struggle for eating
Poetry of the PRESENT understands its objects, the words, as agents of
our living space
It gives back to the words and by the words the correspondances of the
things before and outside their social and eugenic needs
The poetical (non-musical) sound creates complex dimensions:
functional, temporal and numerical, it shows by these inter-relations the
"coincidentia oppositorum" of the things by their own value
These values are no ware of social classes, nor of historical aspect
Poetry of the PRESENT is outside the restrained history, outside the
coward anthropophagous and anthropomorphous utilisations
PRESENT poetry aims at the relative life of untamed and non-classified
functions, avoiding the false semblances
PRESENT Poetry is neither FOR nor AGAINST, neither classic, nor
romantic, nor surrealistic
It integrates BEING and it IS

Poetry Intervenes Now

Presence Is New

PIN

A Fancy

1962

A fancy
A thing of fan
The right thing of phan
World needs new tendencies in poeting and paintry
Old stuff is not able to lead further on
Muses ought to be whisked, when mankind will survive
In the very war creative whisky is fallen very dry
We will develop whisky spirit, because we see with our ears and hear with
    our eyes
Our phantic drsls and rlquars are full of whisked away formal life
They overwhelm "modern poetry" by their new taste
Their phantic contents are so direct, that they are placed above the
    meanings of language at all
Language is only a medium to understand and not to understand
You prefer the language, when you understand by it things, which
    everybody knows by heart already. We prefer the language, which
    provides you a new feeling for new whiskers to come
Give up your human feelings and please go through our fan pin and you
    will know, that it was worth while.

PIN

The thing of phan—fan

13.6 EL LISSITZKY

Topography of Typography

1923

1. The words on the printed page are seen, not heard.
2. Through conventional words you get concepts across. The concepts are embodied in letters.
3. The economy of expression: optics instead of phonetics.
4. The organization of the space of the book through the material of the sentence according to the laws of typographical technique must correspond to the tensions and the pressures of the content.
5. The organization of the space of the book by the illustrations that realize the new optics. The supernaturalist reality of the perfect eye.
6. The continual sequence of pages—the bioscopic book.
7. The new book requires a new *writer*. Inkwells and goosequills are dead.
8. The printed page goes past space and time. Printed notebooks, this immensity of print, must give way. THE ELECTRICLIBRARY.

PART 14

Constructivism/Realism

Constructivism is the final movement of the Russian avant-garde that began with the *world of art*. This wide-ranging term includes much, starting with conceptions from the early teens in Paris and in Russia. Pablo Picasso's early constructions in Paris inspired Vladimir Tatlin, who saw them in 1913, to make his "Counter-reliefs," the assemblages of wire and metal and wood that he hung in "real space." And when, in the same year, Mikhail Larionov and Natalya Goncharova, in "Rayonists and Futurists: A Manifesto" (5.25), advanced the idea of building or constructing a painting according to the intersection of rays, they too influenced Tatlin, who would eventually build a famous Constructivist Tower.

If the celebrated "Realistic Manifesto" (14.1) of Naum Gabo and Antoine Pevsner predates the term "Constructivism," it was nevertheless taken as speaking for the movement. Insisting on realism as "truth to materials," it included the experimental photography of Aleksandr Rodchenko, so successful that it was finally called, in the 1920s, "Rodchenko perspective" and "Rodchenko foreshortening." Rodchenko was accused of presenting reality "upside down and downside up"—and of plagiarizing from László Moholy-Nagy. His radical experimentation profoundly influenced Sergei Eisenstein.

After the Revolution of 1917, the Constructivist movement split into the personal Constructivists, or Utopians, and the more utilitarian ones, called Productivists; some of the artists moved to the Bauhaus, thus spreading the influence of Constructivism to Germany.

14.1 NAUM GABO AND ANTOINE PEVSNER

The Realistic Manifesto

1920

Above the tempests of our weekdays.
  Across the ashes and cindered homes of the past,
  Before the gates of the vacant future,
  We proclaim today to you artists, painters, sculptors, musicians, actors, poets . . . to you people to whom Art is no mere ground for conversation but the source of real exaltation, our word and deed.

The impasse into which Art has come to in the last twenty years must be broken.

The growth of human knowledge with its powerful penetration into the mysterious laws of the world which started at the dawn of this century,

The blossoming of a new culture and a new civilization with their unprecedented-in-history surge of the masses towards the possession of the riches of Nature, a surge which binds the people into one union, and last, not least, the war and the revolution (those purifying torrents of the coming epoch), have made us face the fact of new forms of life, already born and active.

What does Art carry into this unfolding epoch of human history?

Does it possess the means necessary for the construction of the new Great Style?

Or does it suppose that the new epoch may not have a new style?

Or does it suppose that the new life can accept a new creation which is constructed on the foundations of the old?

In spite of the demand of the renascent spirit of our time, Art is still nourished by impression, external appearance, and wanders helplessly back and forth from Naturalism to Symbolism, from Romanticism to Mysticism.

The attempts of the Cubists and the Futurists to lift the visual arts from the bogs of the past have led only to new delusions.

Cubism, having started with simplification of the representative technique, ended with its analysis and stuck there.

The distracted world of the Cubists, broken in shreds by their logical anarchy, cannot satisfy us who have already accomplished the Revolution or who are already constructing and building up anew.

One could heed with interest the experiments of the Cubists, but one cannot follow them, being convinced that their experiments are being made on the surface of Art and do not touch on the bases of it, seeing plainly that the end result amounts to the same old graphic, to the same old volume and to the same decorative surface as of old.

One could have hailed Futurism in its time for the refreshing sweep of its announced Revolution in Art, for its devastating criticism of the past, as in no other way could one have assailed those artistic barricades of "good taste" . . . powder was needed for that and a lot of it . . . but one cannot construct a system of art on one revolutionary phrase alone.

One had to examine Futurism beneath its appearance to realize that one faced a very ordinary chatterer, a very agile and prevaricating guy, clad in the tatters of worn-out words like "patriotism," "militarism," "contempt for the female," and all the rest of such provincial tags.

In the domain of purely pictorial problems, Futurism has not gone further than the renovated effort to fix on the canvas a purely optical reflex which has already shown its bankruptcy with the Impressionists. It is obvious now to every one of us that by the simple graphic registration of a row of momentarily arrested movements, one cannot recreate movement itself. It makes one think of the pulse of a dead body.

The pompous slogan of "Speed" was played from the hands of the Futurists as a great trump. We concede the sonority of that slogan and we quite see how it can sweep the strongest of the provincials off their feet. But ask any Futurist how does he imagine "speed" and there will emerge a whole arsenal of frenzied automobiles, rattling railway depots, snarled wires, the clank and the noise and the clang of carouselling streets . . . does one really need to convince them that all that is not necessary for speed and for its rhythms?

Look at a ray of sun . . . the stillest of the still forces, it speeds more than 300 kilometres in a second . . . behold our starry firmament . . . who hears it . . . and yet what are our depots to those depots of the Universe? What are our earthly trains to those hurrying trains of the galaxies?

Indeed, the whole Futurist noise about speed is too obvious an anecdote, and from the moment that Futurism proclaimed that "Space and Time are yesterday's dead," it sunk into the obscurity of abstractions.

Neither Futurism nor Cubism has brought us what our time has expected of them.

Besides those two artistic schools our recent past has had nothing of importance or deserving attention.

But Life does not wait and the growth of generations does not stop and we who go to relieve those who have passed into history, having in our hands the results of their experiments, with their mistakes and their achievements, after years of experience equal to centuries . . . we say . . .

No new artistic system will withstand the pressure of a growing new culture until the very foundation of Art will be erected on the real laws of Life.

Until all artists will say with us . . .

All is a fiction . . . only life and its laws are authentic and in life only the active is beautiful and wise and strong and right, for life does not know beauty as an aesthetic measure . . . efficacious existence is the highest beauty.

Life knows neither good nor bad nor justice as a measure of morals . . . need is the highest and most just of all morals.

Life does not know rationally abstracted truths as a measure of cognizance, deed is the highest and surest of truths.

Those are the laws of life. Can art withstand these laws if it is built on abstraction, on mirage, and fiction?

We say . . .

Space and time are re-born to us today.

Space and time are the only forms on which life is built and hence art must be constructed.

States, political and economic systems perish, ideas crumble, under the strain of ages . . . but life is strong and grows and time goes on in its real continuity.

Who will show us forms more efficacious than this . . . who is the great one who will give us foundations stronger than this?

Who is the genius who will tell us a legend more ravishing than this prosaic tale which is called life?

The realization of our perceptions of the world in the forms of space and time is the only aim of our pictorial and plastic art.

In them we do not measure our works with the yardstick of beauty, we do not weigh them with pounds of tenderness and sentiments.

The plumb-line in our hand, eyes as precise as a ruler, in a spirit as taut as a compass . . . we construct our work as the universe constructs its own, as the engineer constructs his bridges, as the mathematician his formula of the orbits.

We know that everything has its own essential image; chair, table, lamp, telephone, book, house, man . . . they are all entire worlds with their own rhythms, their own orbits.

That is why we in creating things take away from them the labels of their owners . . . all accidental and local, leaving only the reality of the constant rhythm of the forces in them.

1. *Thence in painting we renounce colour as a pictorial element, colour is the idealized optical surface of objects; an exterior and superficial impression of them; colour is accidental and it has nothing in common with the innermost essence of a thing.*

We affirm *that the tone of a substance, i.e. its light-absorbing material body is its only pictorial reality.*

2. We renounce *in a line, its descriptive value; in real life there are no descriptive lines, description is an accidental trace of a man on things, it is not bound up with the essential life and constant structure of the body. Descriptiveness is an element of graphic illustration and decoration.*

We affirm *the line only as a direction of the static forces and their rhythm in objects.*

3. We renounce *volume as a pictorial and plastic form of space; one cannot measure space in volumes as one cannot measure liquid in yards: look at our space . . . what is it if not one continuous depth?*

We affirm *depth as the only pictorial and plastic form of space.*

4. We renounce *in sculpture, the mass as a sculptural element.*

It is known to every engineer that the static forces of a solid body and its material strength do not depend on the quantity of the mass . . . example a rail, a T-beam, etc.

But you sculptors of all shades and directions, you still adhere to the age-old prejudice that you cannot free the volume of mass. Here (in this exhibition) we take four planes and we construct with them the same volume as of four tons of mass.

Thus we bring back to sculpture the line as a direction and in it we affirm depth as the one form of space.

5. We renounce *the thousand-year-old delusion in art that held the static rhythms as the only elements of the plastic and pictorial arts.*

We affirm *in these arts a new element the kinetic rhythms as the basic forms of our perception of real time.*

These are the five fundamental principles of our work and our constructive technique.

Today we proclaim our words to you people. In the squares and on the streets we are placing our work convinced that art must not remain a sanctuary for the idle, a consolation for the weary, and a justification for the lazy. Art should attend us everywhere that life flows and acts . . . at the bench, at the table, at work, at rest, at play; on working days and holidays . . . at home and on the road . . . in order that the flame to live should not extinguish in mankind.

We do not look for justification, neither in the past nor in the future.

Nobody can tell us what the future is and what utensils does one eat it with.

Not to lie about the future is impossible and one can lie about it at will.

We assert that the shouts about the future are for us the same as the tears about the past: a renovated day-dream of the romantics.

A monkish delirium of the heavenly kingdom of the old attired in contemporary clothes.

He who is busy today with the morrow is busy doing nothing.

And he who tomorrow will bring us nothing of what he has done today is of no use for the future.

Today is the deed.

We will account for it tomorrow.

The past we are leaving behind as carrion.

The future we leave to the fortune-tellers.

We take the present day.

The Initiative Individual Artist
in the Creativity of the Collective

1919

THESES

1   The initiative individual is the collector of the *energy* of the collective, directed towards knowledge and invention.

2   The initiative individual serves as a contact between the invention and the creativity of the collective.

3   The viability of the collective is confirmed by the number of initiative units distinguished by it.

4   The initiative individual is the refraction point of the collective's creativity and brings realization to the idea.

5   Art, always being connected with life at the moment of change in the political system (change of the Collective-consumer), and being cut off from the collective in the person of the artist, goes through an acute revolution. A revolution strengthens the impulse of invention. That is why there is a flourishing of art following a revolution, when the interrelationship between the initiative individual and the collective is clearly defined.

6   Invention is always the working out of impulses and desires of the collective and not of the individual.

7   The world of numbers, as the nearest to the architectonics of art, gives us: (1) confirmation of the existence of the inventor; (2) a complete organic connection of the individual with the collective numeral. There is no error in Khlebnikov's example. (1) "In a series of natural numbers, prime numbers, indivisible and non-recurring, are scattered. Each of these numbers carries with it its new numerical world. From this it follows that among numbers too there are inventors." (2) "If we take the principle of addition, and add one more to a thousand individuals, the arrival and departure of this individual will be unnoticed. If we take the principle of multiplication, then a positive singular multiplied by a thousand makes the entire thousand positive. A negative singular multiplied by a thousand makes the whole thousand negative. From this it follows that there exists a complete organic connection between the individual and the collective numeral."

PART 15

Suprematism, Bauhaus, and Elementarism

With a flourish, the Russian school of Suprematism—including Lyubov Popova and Alexandr Rodchenko—announced its supreme importance by its title. Kasimir Malevich called his paintings in "The Last Exhibition of Futurist Pictures" in Petrograd, 1915, Suprematist compositions. His celebrated *Black Rectangle* of 1914 and his *Suprematist Composition: White on White* of 1918 were the outstanding examples of this totally abstract movement. Through the Hungarian László Moholy-Nagy and through El Lissitzky, Suprematist ideas filtered into the Bauhaus (the arts and crafts school of "building house" founded by Walter Gropius in Weimar, Germany, in 1919, including Paul Klee, Lionel Feininger, Oskar Schlemmer, and Joseph Albers) and, through Vladimir Tatlin, into Constructivism.

Russia

15.1 KASIMIR MALEVICH

Suprematism

1927

Under Suprematism I understand the supremacy of pure feeling in creative art.

To the Suprematist the visual phenomena of the objective world are, in themselves, meaningless; the significant thing is feeling, as such, quite apart from the environment in which it is called forth.

The so-called "materialization" of a feeling in the conscious mind really means a materialization of the *reflection* of that feeling through the medium of some realistic conception. Such a realistic conception is without value in suprematist art. . . . And not only in suprematist art but in art generally, because the enduring, true value of a work of art (to whatever school it may belong) resides solely in the feeling expressed.

Academic naturalism, the naturalism of the Impressionists, Cézanne-ism, Cubism, etc.—all these, in a way, are nothing more than dialectic methods which, as such, in no sense determine the true value of an art work.

An objective representation, having objectivity as its aim, is something which, as such, has nothing to do with art, and yet the use of objective forms in an art work does not preclude the possibility of its being of high artistic value.

Hence, to the Suprematist, the appropriate means of representation is always the one which gives fullest possible expression to feeling as such and which ignores the familiar appearance of objects.

Objectivity, in itself, is meaningless to him; the concepts of the conscious mind are worthless.

Feeling is the determining factor . . . and thus art arrives at non-objective representation—at Suprematism.

It reaches a "desert" in which nothing can be perceived but feeling.

Everything which determined the objective-ideal structure of life and of "art"—ideas, concepts, and images—all this the artist has cast aside in order to heed pure feeling.

The art of the past which stood, at least ostensibly, in the service of religion and the state, will take on new life in the pure (unapplied) art of *Suprematism*, which will build up a new world—the world of feeling. . . .

When, in the year 1913, in my desperate attempt to free art from the ballast of objectivity, I took refuge in the square form and exhibited a picture which consisted of nothing more than a black square on a white field, the critics and, along with them, the public sighed, "Everything which we loved is lost. We are in a desert. . . . Before us is nothing but a black square on a white background!"

"Withering" words were sought to drive off the symbol of the "desert" so that one might behold on the "dead square" the beloved likeness of "reality" ("true objectivity" and a spiritual feeling).

The square seemed incomprehensible and dangerous to the critics and the public . . . and this, of course, was to be expected.

The ascent to the heights of non-objective art is arduous and painful . . . but it is nevertheless rewarding. The familiar recedes ever further and further into the background. . . . The contours of the objective world fade more and more and so it goes, step by step, until finally the world—"everything we loved and by which we have lived"—becomes lost to sight.

No more "likeness of reality," no idealistic images—nothing but a desert!

But this desert is filled with the spirit of non-objective sensation which pervades everything.

Even I was gripped by a kind of timidity bordering on fear when it came to leaving "the world of will and idea," in which I had lived and worked and in the reality of which I had believed.

But a blissful sense of liberating non-objectivity drew me forth into the "desert," where nothing is real except feeling . . . and so feeling became the substance of my life.

This was no "empty square" which I had exhibited but rather the feeling of non-objectivity.

I realized that the "thing" and the "concept" were substituted for feeling and understood the falsity of the world of will and idea.

Is a milk bottle, then, the symbol of milk?

Suprematism is the rediscovery of pure art which, in the course of time, had become obscured by the accumulation of "things."

It appears to me that, for the critics and the public, the painting of Raphael, Rubens, Rembrandt, etc., has become nothing more than a *conglomeration* of countless "things," which conceal its true value—the feeling which gave rise to it. The virtuosity of the objective representation is the only thing admired.

If it were possible to extract from the works of the great masters the feeling expressed in them—the actual artistic value, that is—and to hide this away, the public, along with the critics and the art scholars, would never even miss it.

So it is not at all strange that my square seemed empty to the public.

If one insists on judging an art work on the basis of the virtuosity of the objective representation—the verisimilitude of the illusion—and thinks he sees in the objective representation itself a symbol of the inducing emotion, he will never partake of the gladdening content of a work of art.

The general public is still convinced today that art is bound to perish if it gives up the imitation of "dearly-loved reality" and so it observes with dismay how the hated element of pure feeling—abstraction—makes more and more headway. . . .

Art no longer cares to serve the state and religion, it no longer wishes to illustrate the history of manners, it wants to have nothing further to do with the object, as such, and believes that it can exist in and for itself, without "things" (that is, the "time-tested wellspring of life").

But the nature and meaning of artistic creation continue to be misunderstood, as does the nature of creative work in general, because feeling, after all, is always and everywhere the one and only source of every creation.

The emotions which are kindled in the human being are stronger than the human being himself . . . they must at all costs find an outlet—they must take on overt form—they must be communicated or put to work.

It was nothing other than a yearning for speed . . . for flight . . . which, seeking an outward shape, brought about the birth of the airplane. For the airplane was not contrived in order to carry business letters from Berlin to Moscow, but in obedience to the irresistible drive of this yearning for speed to take on external form.

The "hungry stomach" and the intellect which serves this must always have the last word, of course, when it comes to determining the origin and purpose of *existing* values . . . but that is a subject in itself.

And the state of affairs is exactly the same in art as in creative technology. . . . In painting (I mean here, naturally, the accepted "artistic" painting) one can discover behind a technically correct portrait of Mr. Miller or an ingenious representation of the flower girl at Potsdamer Platz not a trace of the true essence of art — no evidence whatever of feeling. Painting is the dictatorship of a method of representation, the purpose of which is to depict Mr. Miller, his environment and his ideas.

The black square on the white field was the first form in which non-objective feeling came to be expressed. The square = feeling, the white field = the void beyond this feeling.

Yet the general public saw in the non-objectivity of the representation the demise of art and failed to grasp the evident fact that feeling had here assumed external form.

The suprematist square and the forms proceeding out of it can be likened to the primitive marks (symbols) of aboriginal man which represented, in their combinations, *not ornament but a feeling of rhythm.*

Suprematism did not bring into being a new world of feeling but rather, an altogether new and direct form of representation of the world of feeling.

The square changes and creates new forms, the elements of which can be classified in one way or another depending upon the feeling which gave rise to them.

When we examine an antique column, we are no longer interested in the fitness of its construction to perform its technical task in the building but recognize in it the material expression of a pure feeling. We no longer see in it a structural necessity but view it as a work of art in its own right.

"Practical life," like a homeless vagabond, forces its way into every artistic form and believes itself to be the genesis and reason for existence of this form. But the vagabond doesn't tarry long in one place and once he is gone (when to make an art work serve "practical purposes" no longer seems practical) the work recovers its full value.

Antique works of art are kept in museums and carefully guarded, not to preserve them for practical use but in order that their eternal artistry may be enjoyed.

The difference between the new, non-objective ("useless") art and the art of the past lies in the fact that the full artistic value of the latter comes to

light (becomes recognized) only after life, in search of some new expedi-
ent, has forsaken it, whereas the unapplied artistic element of the new art
outstrips life and shuts the door on "practical utility."

And so there the new non-objective art stands—the expression of pure
feeling, seeking no practical values, no ideas, no "promised land."

An antique temple is not beautiful because it once served as the haven
of a certain social order or of the religion associated with this, but rather
because its form sprang from a pure feeling for plastic relationships. The
artistic feeling which was given material expression in the building of the
temple is for us eternally valid and vital but as for the social order which
once encompassed it—this is dead.

Life and its manifestations have hitherto been considered from two different standpoints—the material and the religious. It would seem that a
consideration of life from the standpoint of art ought to become a third and
equally valid point of view. But in practice, art (as a second-rate power) is
relegated to the service of those who view the world and life from one or
the other of the first two standpoints. This state of affairs is curiously incon-
sistent with the fact that art always and under all circumstances plays the
decisive role in the creative life and that art values alone are absolute and
endure forever. With the most primitive of means (charcoal, hog bristles,
modeling sticks, catgut, and steel strings) the artist creates something which
the most ingenious and efficient technology will never be able to create.

The adherents of "utility" think they have the right to regard art as the
apotheosis of life (the utilitarian life, that is).

In the midst of this apotheosis stands "Mr. Miller"—or rather, the portrait of Mr. Miller (that is, a copy of a "copy" of life).

The mask of life hides the true countenance of art. Art is not to us what
it could be.

And moreover, the efficiently mechanized world could truly serve a purpose if only it would see to it that we (every one of us) gained the greatest
possible amount of "free time" to enable us to meet the only obligation to
nature which mankind has taken upon itself—namely to create art.

Those who promote the construction of useful things, things which serve
a purpose, and who combat art or seek to enslave it, should bear in mind
the fact that there is no such thing as a constructed object which is useful.
Has the experience of centuries not demonstrated that "useful" things don't
long remain useful?

Every object which we see in the museums clearly supports the fact that
not one single, solitary thing is really useful, that is, convenient, for other-

wise it would not be in a museum! And if it once seemed useful this is only because nothing more useful was then known. . . .

Do we have the slightest reason to assume that the things which appear useful and convenient to us today will not be obsolete tomorrow . . . ? And shouldn't it give us pause that the oldest works of art are as impressive today in their beauty and spontaneity as they were many thousands of years ago?

The Suprematists have deliberately given up objective representation of their surroundings in order to reach the summit of the true "unmasked" art and from this vantage point to view life through the prism of pure artistic feeling.

Nothing in the objective world is as "secure and unshakeable" as it appears to our conscious minds. We should accept nothing as predetermined —as constituted for eternity. Every "firmly established," familiar thing can be shifted about and brought under a new and, primarily, unfamiliar order. Why then should it not be possible to bring about an artistic order?

The various complementary and conflicting feelings—or rather, images and ideas—which, as reflections of these feelings, take shape in our imaginations, struggle incessantly with each other: the awareness of God against that of the Devil; the sensation of hunger versus a feeling for the beautiful.

The awareness of God strives to vanquish the awareness of the Devil— and the flesh at the same time. It tries to "make credible" the evanescence of earthly goods and the everlasting glory of God.

And art, too, is condemned, except when it serves the worship of God— the Church. . . .

—Out of the awareness of God arose religion—and out of religion the Church.

—Out of the sensation of hunger developed concepts of utility—and out of these concepts trade and industry.

Both the Church and industry tried to monopolize those artistic abilities which, being creative, are constantly finding expression, in order to provide effective bait for their products (for the ideal-material as well as for the purely material). In this way, as the saying goes, "the pill of utility is sugar-coated."

The aggregated reflections of feelings in the individual's consciousness— feelings of the most varied kinds—determine his "view of life." Since the feelings affecting him change, the most remarkable alterations in this "view of life" can be observed; the atheist becomes pious, the God-fearing, godless, etc. . . . The human being can be likened, in a way, to a radio receiver which picks up and converts a whole series of different waves of feeling, the sum-total of which determines the above-mentioned view of life.

Judgments concerning the values of life therefore fluctuate widely. Only art values defy the shifting drift of opinion, so that, for example, pictures of God or the saints, insofar as the artistic feeling incorporated in them is apparent, can be placed by atheists in their collections without compunction (and, in fact, actually are collected by them). Thus do we have, again and again, the opportunity of convincing ourselves that the guidance of our conscious minds—"creation" with a purpose—always calls into being relative values (which is to say, valueless "values") and that nothing but the expression of the pure feeling of the subconscious or superconscious (nothing, that is, other than artistic creation) can give tangible form to absolute values. Actual utility (in the higher sense of the term) could therefore be achieved only if the subconscious or superconscious were accorded the privilege of directing creation.

Our life is a theater piece, in which non-objective feeling is portrayed by objective imagery.

A bishop is nothing but an actor who seeks with words and gestures, on an appropriately "dressed" stage, to convey a religious feeling, or rather the reflection of a feeling in religious form. The office clerk, the blacksmith, the soldier, the accountant, the general . . . these are all characters out of one stage play or another, portrayed by various people, who become so carried away that they confuse the play and their parts in it with life itself. We almost never get to see the *actual human face* and if we ask someone who he is, he answers, "an engineer," "a farmer," etc., or, in other words, he gives the title of the role played by him in one or another affective drama.

The title of the role is also set down next to his full name, and certified in his passport, thus removing any doubt concerning the surprising fact that the owner of the passport is the engineer Ivan and not the painter Kasimir.

In the last analysis, what each individual knows about himself is precious little, because the "actual human face" cannot be discerned behind the mask, which is mistaken for the "actual face."

The philosophy of Suprematism has every reason to view both the mask and the "actual face" with skepticism, since it disputes the reality of human faces (human forms) altogether.

Artists have always been partial to the use of the human face in their representations, for they have seen in it (the versatile, mobile, expressive mimic) the best vehicle with which to convey their feelings. The Suprematists have nevertheless abandoned the representation of the human face (and of natural objects in general) and have found new symbols with which to render direct feelings (rather than externalized reflections of feelings), for *the Suprematist does not observe and does not touch—he feels.*

We have seen how art, at the turn of the century, divested itself of the ballast of religious and political ideas which had been imposed upon it and came into its own—attained, that is, the form suited to its intrinsic nature and became, along with the two already mentioned, a third independent and equally valid "point of view." The public is still, indeed, as much convinced as ever that the artist creates superfluous, impractical things. It never considers that these superfluous things endure and retain their vitality for thousands of years, whereas necessary, practical things survive only briefly.

It does not dawn on the public that it fails to recognize the real, true value of things. This is also the reason for the chronic failure of everything utilitarian. A true, absolute order in human society could only be achieved if mankind were willing to base this order on lasting values. Obviously, then, the artistic factor would have to be accepted in every respect as the decisive one. As long as this is not the case, the uncertainty of a "provisional order" will obtain, instead of the longed-for tranquillity of an absolute order, because the provisional order is gauged by current utilitarian understanding and this measuring-stick is variable in the highest degree.

In the light of this, all art works which, at present, are a part of "practical life" or to which practical life has laid claim, are in some sense devaluated. Only when they are freed from the encumbrance of practical utility (that is, when they are placed in museums) will their truly artistic, absolute value be recognized.

The sensations of sitting, standing, or running are, first and foremost, plastic sensations and they are responsible for the development of corresponding "objects of use" and largely determine their form.

A chair, bed, and table are not matters of utility but rather, the forms taken by plastic sensations, so the generally held view that all objects of daily use result from practical considerations is based upon false premises.

We have ample opportunity to become convinced that we are never in a position for recognizing any real utility in things and that we shall never succeed in constructing a really practical object. We can evidently only *feel* the essence of absolute utility but, since a feeling is always non-objective, any attempt to grasp the utility of the objective is Utopian. The endeavor to confine feeling within concepts of the conscious mind or, indeed, to replace it with conscious concepts and to give it concrete, utilitarian form, has resulted in the development of all those useless, "practical things" which become ridiculous in no time at all.

It cannot be stressed too often that absolute, true values arise only from artistic, subconscious, or superconscious creation.

The new art of Suprematism, which has produced new forms and form relationships by giving external expression to pictorial feeling, will become a new architecture: it will transfer these forms from the surface of canvas to space.

The suprematist element, whether in painting or in architecture, is free of every tendency which is social or otherwise materialistic.

Every social idea, however great and important it may be, stems from the sensation of hunger; every art work, regardless of how small and insignificant it may seem, originates in pictorial or plastic feeling. It is high time for us to realize that the problems of art lie far apart from those of the stomach or the intellect.

Now that art, thanks to Suprematism, has come into its own—that is, attained its pure, unapplied form—and has recognized the infallibility of non-objective feeling, it is attempting to set up a genuine world order, a new philosophy of life. It recognizes the non-objectivity of the world and is no longer concerned with providing illustrations of the history of manners.

Non-objective feeling has, in fact, always been the only possible source of art, so that in this respect Suprematism is contributing nothing new but nevertheless the art of the past, because of its use of objective subject matter, harbored unintentionally a whole series of feelings which were alien to it.

But a tree remains a tree even when an owl builds a nest in a hollow of it.

Suprematism has opened up new possibilities to creative art, since *by virtue of the abandonment of so-called practical considerations, a plastic feeling rendered on canvas can be carried over into space.* The artist (the painter) is no longer bound to the canvas (the picture plane) and can transfer his compositions from canvas to space.

Dynamics of a Metropolis

A Film Sketch

1921–1922

Building construction with an iron crane (Use of special trick effects — line drawings — melting slowly into the filming of nature)
Crane for construction:

     shot from below

               diagonally

      from above
      elevator for bricks
      revolving crane

This movement is continued by an automobile racing

      to the left. The same house is always seen
      in the center of the picture.

(The house should always be re-photographed to place it in the center.)

      Another automobile appears which tears along at the same speed, but in the opposite direction.

      Tempo, tempo!

One row of houses rushes by in the same direction, always allowing the house in the middle to be seen. The row of houses runs past and comes back.

      Rows of houses race transparently in opposite directions, and so do the automobiles. Faster and faster, so that the spectators are made dizzy.

        A tiger, TIGER walks about in his cage
        walks back and forth angrily.

High up, clearly visible traffic signals.

    Moving automatically
    a-u-t-o-m-a-t-i-c-a-l-l-y

        (Close up)

  up   up
      down   down
  up up up down down
  1   2   3   4   5

Goods-station.
Shunting yard.
Warehouses and cellars   Dark   Dark
                    DARKNESS

Railway

Highway with vehicles. Bridge. Viaduct. Ships passing below.

Above an overhead railway. (Elberfeld)

View of a train from a high embankment, shot diagonally.

A track-watchman salutes standing at attention.

Eyes become fixed. (Close up)

Train seen from a bridge, from above.

From below: from the ditch between the rails the belly of the train as it rushes along. The turning wheels—so fast as to be an indistinct vibration.

<pre>
          TEMPO

            TEMPO

              TEM

              TEM   PO

              TEM   TEEEM

                       M

                     M POOOOO

                                    DOWN
</pre>

In a department store glass-enclosed lift with Negro children.

<pre>
Obliquely.   UP

                                           UP
</pre>

Distorted perspective.

Longshot.   A CROWD

At the entrance tethered dogs

Beside the glass lifts glass telephone boxes with callers

Filming from the ground floor through the glass

The FACE of a caller, painted with phosphorescent paint (so as to produce no shadow) turns slowly to the right, directly beside the lift.

Over his head a distant airplane spirals in the air.

View from a slight altitude: a square where

many streets converge.

Masses of vehicles. Tramways, motor-cars, lorries, carts, bicycles, buses drive fast from the square.

Suddenly all of them go backwards.

They pile up in the center of the square.

The square opens in the middle and swallows them up.

(The camera is at an angle to create the impression of falling.)

underground
cables

TEMPO

Gas-tank
Sewers. (deep beneath the town)

Light reflected on water.
Arc lamp.
Sparks *spraying.*
Highway at night, gleaming city streets.
Gliding automobiles from above, diagonally.

For five seconds only a black screen
Electric advertising with flashing letters:
     MOHOLY   MOHOLY
Fireworks in the amusement park.
Riding on the roller-coaster.
SPEEDing.
Ferris-wheel.
Fun-house.
Distorting mirrors.
Other jokes.
Picture of exhibition in a railway station.
The camera moves in a horizontal circle,
then in a vertical circle

Taut
telephone wires and telegraph cables between houses.
     Towers of porcelain insulators.
     Radio-aerials on roofs.

Factory.
   Wheels turning.
   An acrobat twirls and turns somersaults.

   Pole-vaulting. A fall shown 10 times in succession.

Variety show. Frantic activity.
Football match. Rough. Fast tempo.

Women wrestling. Kitsch!
Jazz-band instruments. (in Close-up.)

POINTED AT THE PUBLIC

A hollow, shining metal funnel is fixed on the lens of the camera.
Immediately:
a man jerks away his head in a flash. (Close-up)

A glass of WATER.
(only the surface of the water, in Close-up.)
Gushing like a fountain.
Jazz-band, *with its sound.*

            FORTISSIMOOOO

Wild dance caricature.
Prostitutes.
Boxing, Close-up.
          ONLY gloves.
          With slow-motion (Zeitlupe) camera
A cloud of smoke. (Coming through a bridge, as a train runs under it)
Chimney-stack, aslant.
A diver plunges down into water.
Propeller turning under the water.
Opening of drain above and under water.
Filming from motor boat along the canal to

RUBBISH dump.
Utilization of rubbish.
            Hills of scrap iron.
            Mounds of old shoes.
            Stacks of tin cans.
Perpetual motion lift, with view. All around.
        From here the whole section, back to the JAZZ BAND
        (also reversed), should go from
        fortissimo to PIANISSIMO
Mortuary. From above.
Military parade.

March-march.

Women riding horses
The two shots are superimposed, so that both are visible.

Slaughter-house. Oxen.
Machinery of a cold-storage plant.
Sausage machine. Thousands of sausages.
A LION'S HEAD snarling (Close-up.)
Audience.
A LION'S HEAD snarling (Close-up.)
Policeman with a rubber truncheon in the middle of a crowded square.
The TRUNCHEON (Close-up.)
Audience in a theater.
Snarling LION'S HEAD (Close-up.)
    For a few seconds total darkness.

        CIRCLE
Circus.
           TEMPO
Trapeze.
           LION,   Lion
        CLOWN.
           LION,   Lion
Clowns
clowns   LION
clowns
Slowly. WATERFALL: with sound.
A body floats on the water.
Soldiers.
March—march.
A glass of WATER
with moving surface.
a brief,
rapid jet of water upwards.
        THE END

Remarks for Those Who Refuse
to Understand the Film Immediately

1921–1922

This film mostly flowed from the possibilities offered by the camera.

My aim was for a film to produce an effect by its own action, its own tempo and rhythm, instead of the still fashionable plots that force cinema to ape literature or theater.

The speeding autos are necessary for a shocking introduction. To show the breathless rush, the turmoil of a city. The tiger is used for contrast. And so that the audience would get used to such surprises and inconsistency from the start.

The purpose of this film is not to teach, nor to moralize, nor to tell a story. Its acting is purely visual.

Bridges, trains, ships, etc. are here to illustrate the services and conveniences of an urban civilization.

The belly of the train: this is a visual experience that we would not normally encounter.

The phosphorescent face that slowly turns away: reminding us of fatiguing telephone conversations. A dream-like state. (Glass, glass, glass)—the direction of the movement prepares us for the spiral course of the pilot.

The rushing of a roller-coaster: many things escape your attention. Many things pass unnoticed, because the senses are unable to perceive everything, rapid motion, moments of danger, etc. On the roller-coaster almost all passengers close their eyes at the great downward drop. But the camera does not close its eye. We rarely watch objectively babies or animals because our attention is taken by the apprehension of numerous other circumstances.

The metal funnel: is to frighten so terribly that it should almost hurt.

The surface of the glass of water: should be brilliant.

The frequent recurrence of the lion's head is a nightmare. (Again, again, again.)

The audience of the theater is gay, but we are still conscious of the lion's head.

In general one should understand more from a rapid reading of the manuscript than can ever be expressed by explanations.

Statement in Catalogue of Tenth State Exhibition

1919

(+)	(−)
Painting	Not painting but the depiction of reality
I. *Architectonics*	I. *Aconstructiveness*
(a) Painterly space (cubism)	(a) Illusionism
(b) Line	(b) Literariness
(c) Color (suprematism)	(c) Emotions
(d) Energetics (futurism)	(d) Recognition
(e) Texture	
II. The necessity for transformation by means of the omission of parts of form (began in cubism)	

Construction in painting = the sum of the energy of its parts.

Surface is fixed but forms are volumetrical.

Line as color and as the vestige of a transverse plane participates in, and directs the forces of, construction.

Color participates in energetics by its weight.

Energetics = direction of volumes + planes and lines or their vestiges + all colors.

Texture is the content of painterly surfaces.

* * *

Form is not of equal value throughout its whole sequence. The artistic consciousness must select those elements indispensable to a painterly context, in which case all that is superfluous and of no artistic value must be omitted.

Hence depiction of the concrete—artistically neither deformed nor transformed—cannot be a subject of painting.

Images of "painterly," and not "figurative," values are the aim of the present painting.

PART 16

De Stijl, Plasticism, and Neoplasticism

Theo van Doesburg and Piet Mondrian were greatly influenced by Georg Wilhelm Friedrich Hegel's theories of art showing forth spirit and his celebrated oppositional forms arranged in a dialectical join: horizontal and vertical lines, abstract and concrete forms, spirit and nature, are a great influence here. Mondrian liked putting these oppositions on the mental stage: so his "Trialogues," featuring a naturalistic painter, an abstract-real painter, and a lay nonpainter are, like the dialogues of the Nowists, one of the best ways to see these oppositions at work, in what he called "the harmony of their relationships."

Against the tragedy of the past, Mondrian celebrates the intensity of the new. The "superrealism" he claimed as a possibility of art in its perception of something beyond ordinary reality was a reply to "Surrealism." What he was least fond of was nature: lunching with Jean Arp in Meudon, France, he turned his back to the window so as not to have to look at the landscape.

The De Stijl group was closely allied to other contemporary modernist currents: van Doesburg's visual and sound poems, the *letterklankbeelden* published in *De Stijl*, make him a natural ally of the Dadas. There was a famous Dada-Constructivism encounter in Weimar in the fall of 1922 between Kurt Schwitters and van Doesburg, which van Doesburg tried to persuade Tristan Tzara to attend, but the latter remained in Paris, so that there were two currents of Dada at that point.

16.1 THEO VAN DOESBURG [I. K. BONSET]

Towards a Constructive Poetry

1923

Destruction is part of the rebuilding of poetry.
Destruction of syntax is the first necessary preamble to the new poetry.
Destruction has expressed itself in the following ways:

1. In the use of words (according to their meaning).
2. In atrocity (psychic disturbance).
3. In typography (synoptic poetry).

In (1) were instrumental: Mallarmé, Rimbaud, Ghil, Gorter, Apollinaire, Birot, Arp, Schwitters, etc. . . .

In (2) de Sade, Lautréamont, Masoch, Péladan, all religious writings, Schwitters etc. . . .

In (3) Apollinaire, Birot, Marinetti, Beauduin, Salvat Papaseït, Kurt Schwitters, etc.

POETRY IS UNTHINKABLE WITHOUT AN AESTHETIC FOUNDATION

To take the purely utilitarian as the only general basis of a new artistic expression = nonsense.

$$
\left.\begin{array}{l}
\text{Utilitarian poetry} \\
\text{Utilitarian music} \\
\text{Utilitarian painting} \\
\text{Utilitarian sculpture}
\end{array}\right\} = \text{nonsense}
$$

nonsense — nonsense — nonsense etc.

We are living in a provisional period. We suppose: that there is no difference between the soul and the spinal marrow, between coitus and art.

But when we make art we use no soap (perhaps the painters do if they have inclinations to cleanliness) and one cannot rise up to heaven on a tomato.

One cannot brush one's teeth with art.

Each thing contains its own usefulness

SYPHILIS IS NOT THE OBJECT OF MAKING LOVE

But: the sailors of the new constructivist art insist that:

A piece of iron nailed to weed;		A house without a groundplan;
A chair without a back;	OR	A sword without a blade;
A car which does not drive;		A (red) poem without content;
A gramophone without a voice;		

all that is utilitarian art.

In other words, art rooted in reality!

No, all that is just art-syphilis.

Is there any poetry on which one can sit, as on a chair? Or in which one can drive as in a car? No. Perhaps there only exists a poetry on which one can spit: the utilitarian revolutionary poetry. (I beg the gentlemen to replace the pig's bladders on their head and the tubes in their nose.)

Thus, it does not matter to the reconstruction of Art whether the product has any practical application. In so far as a statue or a painting has a purpose — say to sit on — it is not a statue or a painting but a "chair":

And: in any case, usefulness does not limit itself to the organs of our sensual being. And even if this were so, what we call our spirit belongs equally to our bodily organs.

Let us try to make a poem without feet which would be as good as a shoe.

Do you know, gentlemen, what a city is? A city is a tension in breadth and a tension in height, nothing else. Two straight connecting wires depict a city. Each individual tries by means of: legs, the train, a trolley, or explosives (the transportation of the future) to find the meeting point of these two tensions.

And a poem is just like a city. Everyone tries, as immediately as possible, to represent the square of the two outer tensions. Immediately, that is to say:

The constructivist poet makes himself a new language with the alphabet: the language of great distances, of depth and height, and by means of this creative language he conquers the space-time movement.

The new poet depicts only by conquering, by abolishing, by destroying (like our politicians) through unhumanist abstraction. In the new poetry, to construct means to reduce. In short: the new poet constructs his language with the ruins of the past, and since everything exists only through language, he forms, in spite of "disinterested abstraction," the new man and the world with him.

THAT IS HIS FUNCTION.

16.2 THEO VAN DOESBURG *and others*

Manifesto I of De Stijl *(excerpt)*

1918

1 There is an old and a new consciousness of time.
   The old is connected with the individual.
   The new is connected with the universal.
   The struggle of the individual against the universal is revealing itself in the world war as well as in the art of the present day.

2 The war is destroying the old world and its contents: individual domination in every state.

3 The new art has brought forward what the new consciousness of time contains: a balance between the universal and the individual.

4 The new consciousness is prepared to realize the internal life as well as the external life.

5 Traditions, dogmas, and the domination of the individual are opposed to this realization.

6 The founders of the new plastic art, therefore, call upon all who believe in the reformation of art and culture to eradicate these obstacles to development, as in the new plastic art (by excluding natural form) they have eradicated that which blocks pure artistic expression, the ultimate consequence of all concepts of art.

7 The artists of today have been driven the whole world over by the same consciousness, and therefore have taken part from an intellectual point of view in this war against the domination of individual despotism. They therefore sympathize with all who work to establish international unity in life, art, culture, either intellectually or materially.

. . .

Signatures of the collaborators:

THEO VAN DOESBURG, PAINTER   ANTONY KOK, POET

ROBT. VAN 'T HOFF, ARCHITECT   PIET MONDRIAN, PAINTER

VILMOS HUSZÁR, PAINTER   G. VANTONGERLOO, SCULPTOR

JAN WILS, ARCHITECT

16.3 PIET MONDRIAN

Neoplasticism in Painting

1917–1918

1 INTRODUCTION

The life of modern cultured man is gradually turning away from the natural: it is becoming more and more *abstract.* As the natural (the external) becomes more and more "automatic," we see life's interest centering more and more around the inward. The life of *truly modern* man is directed neither toward the material for its own sake, nor toward the predominantly emotional: it is rather the autonomous life of the human spirit becoming conscious. Modern man—although a unity of body, soul and mind—*shows* a changed consciousness: all expressions of life assume a different appearance, a more *determinately abstract* appearance.

Art too, as the product of a new duality in man, is now expressed as the product of cultivated outwardness and of a deeper, more conscious inwardness. As pure creation of the human *mind*, art is expressed as pure aesthetic creation, manifested in abstract form.

The truly modern artist *consciously* perceives the abstractness of the emotion of beauty: he *consciously* recognizes aesthetic emotion as cosmic, universal. This conscious recognition results in an abstract creation, directs him toward the purely universal.

That is why the new art cannot be manifested as (naturalistic) concrete representation, which—even where universal vision is present—always points more or less to the particular, or in any case conceals the universal within it.

The new plastic cannot be cloaked by what is characteristic of the particular, natural form and colour, but must be expressed by the abstraction of form and colour—by means of the straight line and determinate primary colour.

These universal plastic means were discovered in modern painting by the process of consistent abstraction of form and colour: once these were discovered there emerged, almost of its own accord *an exact plastic of pure relationship*, the essential of all emotion of plastic beauty.

Thus the new art is the determinate plastic expression of aesthetic relationships.

The contemporary artist constructs the new plastic expression in painting as a consequence of all previous creation—in painting, precisely because it is least restricted. The growing profundity of the whole of modern life can be purely reflected in *painting*. In painting—in *pictorial* not *decorative* painting—naturalistic expression and naturalistic means become more inward, are intensified into the abstract.

Decorative art did no more than to *generalize natural* form and colour.

Thus the feeling for the aesthetic expression of relationship was brought to *clarity* in and by pictorial painting. In painting—which incorporates existing decorative art, or rather, becomes "true" decorative art—the *free* construction of pure relationships can nevertheless remain somewhat limited; for although the essence of all art is *one*—and the feeling for aesthetic relationships increasingly seeks more determinate expression in all the arts—not every art can express *determinate relationships* with equal consistency.

Although the content of all art is one, the possibilities of plastic expression are different for each art. These possibilities must be discovered by each art and remain limited by its bounds.

Therefore the possibilities of one art cannot be viewed from those of another, but must be considered independently, and only in relation to the art concerned. Every art has its own emphasis, its particular expression: this justifies the existence of the various arts. We can now define the emphasis of the art of painting as the *most consistent* expression of pure relationships. For it is painting's unique privilege to express relationships *freely* — in other words, its means of expression (when consistently intensified) allow extreme opposites to be expressed as the pure relationships of *position* — without resulting in forms, or even in the appearance of closed forms (as in architecture).

In painting, the duality of relationships can be shown in juxtaposition (on one plane), which is impossible in architecture or sculpture. Thus painting is the most purely "plastic." The free plastic expression of position is unique to painting. The sister arts, sculpture and architecture, are less free in this respect.

The other arts are even less free in *transforming their plastic means:* music is always tied to sound, however much sound may be tensed into "tone"; dramatic art employs natural form as well as sound, and necessarily the word; literary art is expressed through the word, which strongly stresses the particular.

Painting is capable of *consistent* intensification and interiorization of its plastic means *without overstepping their limits.* Neoplastic painting remains pure *painting:* the plastic means remain form and colour — interiorized to the extreme; straight line and plane colour remain the pure pictorial means.

With the advancing culture of the spirit, all the arts, despite their different expressions, become more and more the *plastic creation of equilibrated, determinate relationship:* for equilibrated relationship most purely expresses the universality, the harmony, the inherent unity of the spirit.

Through equilibrated relationship, unity, harmony, universality are plastically expressed amid separateness, multiplicity, individuality — the natural. When we concentrate upon equilibrated relationship, we can *see* unity in the natural. In the natural, however, unity is manifested only in a veiled way. Although inexactly expressed in the natural, all appearance can nevertheless be reduced to this manifestation [of unity]. Therefore the exact plastic expression of unity *can be created, must be created,* because it is not directly apparent in visible reality.

Whereas in nature equilibrated relationship is expressed by *position, dimension and value* of natural form and colour, in the "abstract" it is expressed through *position, dimension and value* of the straight line and rectangular (colour) plane.

In nature, we perceive that all relationship is governed by one relationship above all others: that of extreme opposites.

The abstract plastic of relationship expresses this basic relationship determinately—by duality of position, the perpendicular. This relationship of position is the most equilibrated because it expresses the relationship of extreme opposition in complete harmony and includes all other relationships. If we see these two extremes as manifestations of the inward and the outward, we find that in Neoplastic the bond between spirit and life is unbroken—we see Neoplastic not as denying the full life, but as the *reconciliation* of the matter-mind duality.

If through contemplation we recognize that the existence of all things is aesthetically determined for us by equilibrated relationships, then the idea of this manifestation of unity already had its seed in our consciousness: unity.

When man's consciousness grows from vagueness to determination his understanding of unity will become more and more determinate. The advanced consciousness of an age that has become determinate (the consciousness to which the time has arrived—the spirit of the age) *must necessarily express itself determinately.* Thus art must *necessarily* express itself *determinately.*

If unity is seen "determinately," if attention is focussed purely on the universal, then particularity, individuality will disappear from the expression as painting as shown. Only when the individual no longer stands in the way can universality be purely manifested. Only then can universal consciousness (intuition)—wellspring of all the arts—express itself directly; a purer art arises. However, it does not arise before its time. The consciousness of an age determines the art expression: the art expression reflects the age's awareness. Only that art is truly alive which gives expression to the contemporary—the future—consciousness.

If we see man's consciousness—in time—*growing* toward determination, if we see it—in time—*developing* from individual to universal, then logically the new art can never return to form—or to natural colour. Then, logically, the consistent growth and development of abstract plastic *must* progress to its culmination.

While one-sided development, lack of aesthetic culture, or tradition may oppose it temporarily—an *abstract,* a *truly* new plastic is necessary for the new man.

Only when the new consciousness becomes more general will the new plastic become a universal need: only then will all factors be present for its culmination.

However, the *need* for a new plastic exists because it has come into being through the contemporary artist: the essentials for the new plastic of the future are already there.

If the essential of all art, that which is characteristic in each art expression, lies in the *intensification of the plastic means,* then we clearly see this essential in Neoplasticism's intensification of the means of expression. The new means testify to a new vision. If the aim of all *art* is to *establish relationships* only a more conscious vision can bring this aim to clear expression — precisely through the *plastic means.*

If the proper intensification and use of the plastic means — composition — is the only *pure plastic* expression of art, then the plastic means must be in complete consonance with what they express. If they are to be a *direct* expression of the universal then they *cannot* be other than universal — abstract.

Composition leaves the artist the greatest possible freedom to be subjective — as long and insofar as this is necessary. The *rhythm* of relationship of colour and dimension (in determinate *proportion* and *equilibrium*) permits the absolute to appear within the relativity of time and space.

Thus the new plastic is dualistic through its composition. Through its exact plastic of cosmic relationship it is a direct expression of the universal; through its rhythm, through its material reality, it is an expression of the subjective, of the individual.

In this way it unfolds a world of *universal* beauty without relinquishing the "universally human."

16.4 PIET MONDRIAN

Natural Reality and Abstract Reality

1919

The cultivated man of today is gradually turning away from natural things, and his life is becoming more and more abstract.

Natural (external) things become more and more automatic, and we observe that our vital attention fastens more and more on internal things. The life of the truly modern man is neither purely materialistic nor purely emotional. It manifests itself rather as a more autonomous life of the human mind becoming conscious of itself.

Modern man—although a unity of body, mind, and soul—exhibits a changed consciousness: every expression of his life has today a different aspect, that is, an aspect more positively abstract.

It is the same with art. Art will become the product of another duality in man: the product of a cultivated externality and of an inwardness deepened and more conscious. As a pure representation of the human mind, art will express itself in an aesthetically purified, that is to say, abstract form.

The truly modern artist is aware of abstraction in an emotion of beauty; he is conscious of the fact that the emotion of beauty is cosmic, universal. This conscious recognition has for its corollary an abstract plasticism, for man adheres only to what is universal.

The new plastic idea cannot, therefore, take the form of a natural or concrete representation, although the latter does always indicate the universal to a degree, or at least conceals it within. This new plastic idea will ignore the particulars of appearance, that is to say, natural form and color. On the contrary, it should find its expression in the abstraction of form and color, that is to say, in the straight line and the clearly defined primary color.

These universal means of expression were discovered in modern painting by a logical and gradual progress toward ever more abstract form and color. Once the solution was discovered, there followed the exact representation of relations alone, that is to say, of the essential and fundamental element in any plastic emotion of the beautiful.

The new plastic idea thus correctly represents actual aesthetic relationships. To the modern artist, it is a natural consequence of all the plastic ideas of the past. This is particularly true of painting, which is the art least bound to contingencies. The picture can be a pure reflection of life in its deepest essence.

However, new plasticism is pure painting: the means of expression still are form and color, though these are completely interiorized; the straight line and flat color remain purely pictorial means of expression.

Although each art uses its own means of expression, all of them as a result of the progressive cultivation of the mind, tend to represent balanced relations with ever greater exactness. The balanced relation is the purest representation of universality, of the harmony and unity which are inherent characteristics of the mind.

If, then, we focus our attention on the balanced relation, we shall be able to see unity in natural things. However, there it appears under a veil. But even though we never find unity expressed exactly, we can unify every representation, in other words, the exact representation of unity can be expressed; it must be expressed, for it is not visible in concrete reality.

We find that in nature all relations are dominated by a single primordial relation, which is defined by the opposition of two extremes. Abstract plasticism represents this primordial relation in a precise manner by means of the two positions which form the right angle. This positional relation is the most balanced of all, since it expresses in a perfect harmony the relation between two extremes, and contains all other relations.

If we conceive these two extremes as manifestations of interiority and exteriority, we will find that in the new plasticism the tie uniting mind and life is not broken; thus, far from considering it a negation of truly living life we shall see a reconciliation of the matter-mind dualism.

If we realize through contemplation that the existence of anything is defined for us aesthetically by relations of equivalence, this is possible because the idea of this manifestation of unity is potential in our consciousness. For the latter is a particular instance of the universal consciousness, which is one.

If human consciousness is growing from the indeterminate towards the positive and the determinate, unity in man will also grow towards the positive and determinate.

If unity is contemplated in a precise and definite way, attention will be directed solely towards the universal, and as a consequence, the particular will disappear from art—as painting has already shown. For the universal cannot be expressed purely so long as the particular obstructs the path. Only when this is no longer the case can the universal consciousness (intuition, that is) which is at the origin of all art, be rendered directly, giving birth to a purified art expression.

This, however, cannot appear before its proper time. For it is the spirit of the times that determines artistic expression, which, in turn, reflects the spirit of the times. But at the present moment, that form of art alone is truly alive which expresses our present—or future—consciousness.

Composition allows the artist the greatest possible freedom, so that his subjectivity can express itself, to a certain degree, for as long as needed.

The rhythm of relations of color and size makes the absolute appear in the relativity of time and space.

In terms of composition the new plasticism is dualistic. Through the exact reconstruction of cosmic relations it is a direct expression of the universal; by its rhythm, by the material reality of its plastic form, it expresses the artist's individual subjectivity.

It thus unfolds before us a whole world of universal beauty without thereby renouncing the human element.

The Plastic Means

1927

1 The plastic means must be the plane or the rectangular prism in primary colour (red, blue, yellow) and non-colour (white, black, grey). In architecture, empty space acts as non-colour, and volume acts as colour.
2 The equivalence of the plastic means is necessary. Although differing in dimension and colour, they must nevertheless have the same value. Equilibrium generally requires a large area of non-colour and a smaller area of colour or volume.
3 The duality of opposition in the plastic means is equally required in the composition.
4 Constant equilibrium is achieved through the relationship of position and is expressed by the straight line (the limit of the plastic means) in its principal opposition.
5 Equilibrium neutralizes and annihilates the plastic means and is achieved through the relationships of proportion in which they are placed and which creates the living rhythm.

Here are five Neoplastic laws which determine the pure plastic means and their use.

Towards a New World Plasticism

1927

A new world plasticism has now begun.

The capitalists are deceivers, but the socialists are equally deceivers. The former want to possess, so also do the latter. The former want to swallow up much money, many people and much rump steak, but the latter wish to swallow up the former. Which is worse? Will they be successful?

We are completely unconcerned.

We know only this one thing: only the bearers of the (new) spirit are upright, they want only to *give*. Disinterestedly. They are emerging from among all people, in every land. They are free of deceitful phrases: they do not address each other as "brother," "master" or "Comrade." A spiritual language is again being spoken and in this language they understand one another.

The bearers of the new spirit of the age do not form a sect, church or school.

In the old world spiritual concentration (Christ) and material concentration (capitalism) were the possession, the axis around which the whole nation developed. *Now the spirit has been dispersed.* In spite of that, the bearers of the spirit are joined together. Internally.

There is no longer any help for Europe. Concentration and possession, spiritual and material individualism were the foundations of the old Europe. It imprisoned itself in them. It can no longer escape from them. It is going to ruin. We look on calmly. Even if we were able to do so, we should not wish to help. We do not wish to prolong this old prostitute's life.

Already a new Europe has begun in us. The ludicrous socialist -1-2-3 Internationals were only external; they consisted only of words. The international of the spirit is *internal,* unexpressed. It does not consist of words, but of creative deeds and internal force. Spiritual force. With this, a new world order is being formed.

We do not call to the nations "Unite" or "Join with us." *We do not proclaim anything to the nations. We know that those who join us belong from the beginning to the new spirit. With them alone does the spiritual body of the new world permit itself to be formed. Work!*

PART 17

Purism

The Swiss Le Corbusier (Charles Édouard Jeanneret) and the Frenchman Amédée Ozenfant, writing of the degeneration of Cubism into fantasy, declared a return to a simplified, abstracted, functional art, which would have the clarity and precision of machinery. From 1920 to 1925 they published the journal *L'Esprit nouveau*, with which the proponents of De Stijl (Theo van Doesburg) and Constructivism (Naum Gabo) were associated. Its first preface and that of the revised edition, and its manifesto "Create!" make an optimistic return to the sources of human art as we see them in cave paintings, relating creative energy to cultures as yet unspoiled.

"Man is a geometric animal, animated by a geometric spirit," says Purism. The Purists, says John Golding, admired the geometric spirit of the Cubist Juan Gris and thought of painting as a "machine à émouvoir" (Golding, *Visions*, 144, 145). The combination of emotion and motion reminds us of Guillaume Apollinaire's train: "Fear that some day the sight of a train might not move you" ("La Victoire," in Apollinaire, *Oeuvres poétiques*, 309).

17.1 LE CORBUSIER [CHARLES ÉDOUARD JEANNERET] AND AMÉDÉE OZENFANT

Purism

1920

THE WORK OF ART

The work of art is an artificial object which permits the creator to place the spectator in the state he wishes; later we will study the means the creator has at his disposal to attain this result.

With regard to man, esthetic sensations are not all of the same degree of intensity or quality; we might say that there is a hierarchy.

The highest level of this hierarchy seems to us to be that special state of a mathematical sort to which we are raised, for example, by the clear perception of a great general law (the state of mathematical lyricism, one might say); it is superior to the brute pleasure of the senses; the senses are involved, however, because every being in this state is as if in a state of beatitude.

The goal of art is not simple pleasure, rather it partakes of *the nature of happiness*.

It is true that plastic art has to address itself more directly to the senses than pure mathematics which only acts by symbols, these symbols sufficing to trigger in the mind consequences of a superior order; in plastic art, the senses should be strongly moved in order to predispose the mind to the release into play of subjective reactions without which there is no work of art. But there is no art worth having without this excitement of an intellectual order, of a mathematical order; architecture is the art which up until now has most strongly induced the states of this category. The reason is that everything in architecture is expressed by order and economy.

The means of executing a work of art is a transmittable and universal language.

One of the highest delights of the human mind is to perceive the order of nature and to measure its own participation in the scheme of things; the work of art seems to us to be a labor of putting into order, a masterpiece of human order.

Now the world only appears to man from the human vantage point, that is, the world seems to obey the laws man has been able to assign to it; when man creates a work of art, he has the feeling of acting as a "god."

Now a law is nothing other than the verification of an order.

In summary, a work of art should induce a sensation of a mathematical order, and the means of inducing this mathematical order should be sought among universal means.

SYSTEM

One cannot, therefore, hope to obtain these results by the empirical and infinitely impure means that are used habitually.

Plastic art, modern architecture, modern painting, modern sculpture, use a language encumbered by terms that are confused, poorly defined, undefinable. This language is a heterogeneous mixture of means used by different and successive schools of esthetics, nearly all of which considered only the release of the sensations of immediate feeling; it does not suit the creation of works which shall have what we demand.

We established in our article "On the Plastic" that there are two quite distinct orders of sensation:

1. Primary sensations determined in all human beings by the simple play of forms and primary colors. *Example:* If I show to everyone on Earth — a Frenchman, a Negro, a Laplander — a sphere in the form of a billiard ball (one of the most perfect human materializations of the sphere), I release in each of these individuals an identical sensation inherent in the spherical form: *this is the constant primary sensation.*

The Frenchman will associate with it ideas of sport, billiards, the pleasures or displeasures of playing, etc. — variables. The Laplander or the Negro
may not associate any idea with it at all or, on the other hand, they might
associate with it an idea of divinity: *there is thus a constant, fixed sensation
released by the primary form.*

[2.] There are secondary sensations, varying with the individual because
they depend upon his cultural or hereditary capital. *Example:* If I hold up
a primary cubic form, I release in each individual the same primary sensation of the cube; but if I place some black geometric spots on the cube, I
immediately release in a civilized man an idea of dice to play with, and the
whole series of associations which would follow.

A Papuan would only see an ornament.

*There are, therefore, besides the primary sensation, infinitely numerous and
variable secondary sensations.* The primary sensation is constant for every
individual, it is universal, it can be differentiated by quantity, but it is *constant in quality:* there are some people who have thick skins. This is a capital
point, a fixed point.

What we have said for the cube and the sphere is true for all the other
primary forms, for all the primary colors, for all the primary lines; it is just
as true for the cube, the sphere, the cylinder, the cone and the pyramid as
for the constituent elements of these bodies, the triangle, the square, the
circle, as for straight, broken or curved lines, as for obtuse, right, or acute
angles, etc. — all the primary elements which react unthinkingly, uniformly,
in the same way, on all individuals.

The sensations of a secondary order graft themselves on these primary
sensations, producing the intervention of the subject's hereditary or cultural contribution. If brute sensations are of a universal, intrinsic order, secondary sensations are of an individual, extrinsic order. Primary sensations
constitute the bases of the plastic language; these are the *fixed words* of the
plastic language; it is a fixed, formal, explicit, universal language determining subjective reactions of an individual order which permit the erection on
these raw foundations of a sensitive work, rich in emotion.

It does not seem necessary to expatiate at length on this elementary truth
that anything of universal value is worth more than anything of merely individual value. It is the condemnation of "individualistic" art to the benefit of
"universal" art.

It then becomes clear that to realize this proposed goal it is necessary
right now to make an inventory of the plastic vocabulary and to purify it in
order to create a transmittable language.

An art that would be based only upon primary sensations, using uniquely primary elements, would be only a primary art, rich, it is true, in geometric aspects, but denuded of all sufficient human resonance: it would be an ornamental art.

An art that would be based only upon the use of secondary sensations (an art of allusions) would be an art without a plastic base. The mind of some individuals—only those in intimate resonance with the creator—could be satisfied with it: an art of the initiated, an art requiring knowledge of a key, an art of symbols. This is the critique of most contemporary art; it is this art which, stripped of universal primary elements, has provoked the creation of an immense literature around these works and these schools, a literature whose goal is to explain, to give the key, to reveal the secret language, to permit comprehension.

The great works of the past are those based on primary elements, and this is the only reason why they endure.

Superior sensations of a mathematical order can be born only of a choice of primary elements with secondary resonance.

Having shown that the use of primary elements by themselves can lead only to an ornamental art, we think that to paint means to create constructions: formal and colored organizations based on the theme-objects endowed with elementary properties rich in subjective trigger actions. Thus it will be well to chose those theme-objects whose secondary trigger actions are the most universal. The list of these objects would have at its head: man, the beings organized by and the objects fabricated by man, particularly those which one might consider as complements of the human organism.

Man and organized beings are products of *natural selection.* In every evolution on earth, the organs of beings are more and more adapted and purified, and the entire forward march of evolution is a function of purification. The human body seems to be the highest product of natural selection.

When examining these selected forms, one finds a tendency toward certain identical aspects, corresponding to constant functions, functions which are of maximum efficiency, maximum strength, maximum capacity, etc., that is, maximum economy. ECONOMY is the law of natural selection.

It is easy to calculate that it is also the great law which governs what we will call "mechanical selection."

Mechanical selection began with the earliest times and from those times provided objects whose general laws have endured; only the means of making them changed, the rules endured.

In all ages and with all people, man has created for his use objects of prime necessity which responded to his imperative needs; these objects were associated with his organism and helped complete it. In all ages, for example, man has created containers: vases, glasses, bottles, plates, which were built to suit the needs of maximum capacity, maximum strength, maximum economy of materials, maximum economy of effort. In all ages, man has created objects of transport: boats, cars; objects of defense: arms; objects of pleasure: musical instruments, etc., all of which have always obeyed the law of selection: economy.

One discovers that all these objects are true extensions of human limbs and are, for this reason, of human scale, harmonizing both among themselves and with man.

The machine was born in the last century. The problem of selection was posed more imperatively than ever (commercial rivalry, cost price); one might say that the machine has led fatally to the strictest respect for, and application of, the laws of economy.

M. Jacques-Emile Blanche will think that these considerations lead us far from painting. On the contrary! It is by the phenomenon of mechanical selection that the forms are established which can almost be called permanent, all interrelated, associated with human scale, containing curves of a mathematical order, curves of the greatest capacity, curves of the greatest strength, curves of the greatest elasticity, etc. These curves obey the laws which govern matter. They lead us quite naturally to satisfactions of a mathematical order.

Modern mechanization would appear to have created objects decidedly remote from what man had hitherto known and practiced. It was believed that he had thus retreated from natural products and entered into an arbitrary order; our epoch decries the misdeeds of mechanization. We must not be mistaken, this is a complete error: the machine has applied with a rigor greater than ever the physical laws of the world's structure. To tell the truth, contemporary poets have only lamented one thing, the peasants' embroidered shirts and the Papuans' tattoos. If blind nature, who produces eggs, were also to make bottles, they would certainly be like those made by the machine born of man's intelligence.

From all this comes a fundamental conclusion: that respect for the laws of physics and of economy has in every age created highly selected objects; that these objects contain analogous mathematical curves with deep resonances; that these artificial objects obey the same laws as the products of natural selection and that, consequently, there thus reigns a total harmony, bringing together the only two things that interest the human being: himself and what he makes.

Both natural selection and mechanical selection are manifestations of purification.

From this it would be easy to conclude that the artist will again find elitist themes in the objects of natural and mechanical selection. As it happens, artists of our period have taken pleasure in ornamental art and have chosen ornamented objects.

A work of art is an association, a symphony of consonant and architectured forms, in architecture and sculpture as well as in painting.

To use as theme anything other than the objects of selection, for example, objects of decorative art, is to introduce a second symphony into the first; it would be redundant, surcharged, it would diminish the intensity and adulterate the quality of the emotion.

Of all recent schools of painting, only Cubism foresaw the advantages of choosing selected objects, and of their inevitable associations. But, by a paradoxical error, instead of sifting out the general laws of these objects, Cubism only showed their accidental aspects, to such an extent that on the basis of this erroneous idea it even re-created arbitrary and fantastic forms. Cubism made square pipes to associate with matchboxes, and triangular bottles to associate with conical glasses.

From this critique and all the foregoing analyses, one comes logically to the necessity of a reform, the necessity of a logical choice of themes, and the necessity of their association not by deformation, but *by formation.*

If the Cubists were mistaken, it is because they did not seek out the invariable constituents of their chosen themes, which could have formed a universal, transmittable language.

Between the chosen theme-object and the plastic organism which the creator's imagination derives from it, there intervenes the necessary labor of total plastic re-creation.

Our concept of the object comes from total knowledge of it, a knowledge acquired by the experience of our senses, tactile knowledge, knowledge of its materials, its volume, its profile, of all its properties. And the usual perspective view only acts as the shutter-release for the memory of these experiences.

Ordinary perspective with its theoretical rigor only gives an accidental view of objects: the one which an eye, having never before seen the object, would see if placed in the precise visual angle of this perspective, always a particular and hence an incomplete angle.

A painting constructed with exact perspective appeals nearly exclusively to sensations of a secondary order and is consequently deprived of what could be universal and durable.

There are, then, good grounds for creating images, organizations of form and color which bear the invariable, fundamental properties of the object-themes. It is by a skillful, synthesizing figuration of these invariable elements that the painter will, upon bases of primary sensations, make his disposition of secondary sensations that are transmittable and universal: the *"Purist"* quest.

The Purist element is like a plastic word duly formed, complete, with precise and universal reactions.

Of course it must not be assumed that Purist elements are like so many stencils that one could juxtapose on the surface of a painting; but we do wish to say that the Purist element, a bottle-element for example, ought always to embody the characteristic and invariant constants of the object-theme, subject to the modifications demanded by the composition.

Purism would never permit a bottle of triangular shape, because a triangular bottle, which eventually could be produced by a glass-blower, is only an exceptional object, a fantasy, like the idea behind it.

17.2 AMÉDÉE OZENFANT

The Art of Living (*excerpt*)

1927–1928

It is often imagined that freedom, in art as in life, is identical with trusting to luck. But the best work does not spring from the endowments of that all too friendly purveyor which absolves us from the need to live at our highest; it is a product determined by our own attitudes as inevitably as a bunch of grapes is the result of the vine it springs from. I shall show that we create our own determinism and in what manner we are responsible for it. And for that reason I have formulated a system of ethics.

The one aim an artist could confess to should be that of producing great art. But this postulates a nobility of spirit that at no period has been so difficult to attain. Has man ever found himself in so tragic a moral situation? Every belief has been bled white or abolished, and we are left stewing in our own skins. Yet heroes and saints do exist, but they are civilians and wear hard hats. Scientists devote their lives, and do not in return expect either fortune or paradise; there is something fine in the stoicism of today, only it is rather rare. But the ordinary run of artists cannot be taken seriously, because it is so hard for them to dispense with acclamation.

The wretched attitude towards art that is general today wobbles on a foundation of Turkish Delight. This is a gifted age, yet think of the gifts that have been ruined by the need for distraction. We demand that the painter shall lead us from surprise to surprise; it is not the matured egg we demand, but Easter eggs in the latest fashion. The result is that the miserable artist, harried by the bored rapacity of his patron, goes on pretending to lay new sensational wonders. Frivolities merely. Or again. Nowadays the word "new" is the highest praise, even when applied to the worst trash. It is easy enough to seem "new" by perpetrating something the masters would never have permitted themselves, had they even thought of it. What imbecility, this prejudice of the hideous called beautiful is, merely because it is new: as if every novelty necessarily meant something!

I have completely finished with what is pleasurable and with pleasure. Europe is just cram-full of art, the result of the ferocious existence led by its inhabitants, for which some antidote must be found; but no race has ever invented worse sauces for it. Enough of this art for up-to-date messieurs, mesdames, and mesdemoiselles, who know everything, but to whom a mere trifle passes for art, a flirtation for love, Jean Jacques Rousseau for the Douanier Rousseau, the Meistersingers for singing masters, Monet for Manet, Pissarro for a Cubist, Henri Poincaré for a President of the Republic, Chateaubriand for a way of cooking beef.*

That sort of person I am not writing for, but for artists who seek to scale the summits, and for such men as seek in art grandeur and the breath of inspiration. I write for the elect whose ideal it is to be the repository of grandeur, and who, because of the jeers they meet with, hide it as a blemish. The object of this book is to aid those whose desire is the reconciliation of the heart and reason, and to prove themselves according to that most generous interpretation.

---

* *Am I exaggerating? Larousse's "Universel," the well-known Dictionary, gives "*CUBIST*, relating to Cubism.* CUBIST PAINTER, *expert at Cubism. Pissarro* (sic) *is a Cubist* (sic)."

My desire is to provide them with arguments in favour of an active optimism, and to indicate a technic capable of leading them to some sort of fulfilment, the only happiness permitted us: that which results from the realising of some magnificent concept elaborated from the fundamental "constants" of humanity.

Shut out from that splendid highway traced by Faith, which allowed us to traverse life without too much anguish, Art still remains on which to drift a while. Yet for that, too, we need a certain depth.

This book is in favour of "constants" and against the conventions dictated by circumstance: in favour of an Art based on our categorical and eternal feelings.

Being French, I should have preferred to demonstrate the time on a dial most scrupulously marked; but consider my difficulty, when so many people seem to have mislaid noon and to be looking for it round two p.m.

Yet so that my readers may find their way in the mazes of this book, I offer them the thread which will guide them through its elaborations (as electricians colour their wires variously in order to distinguish them).

The first is black and green inextricably commingled, and is the dramatic soliloquy which treats of the problem of the universe, our lives, our destiny, our death. This thread ends in an oasis. THE UNCERTAINTY OF UNCERTAINTY. Consequence: the right to believe.

The second is red. Familiarity with certain "constants." ART BASED ON THEIR EVERLASTINGNESS.

The third is a singing blue like the gusty expanses of a summer's day: GREAT ART. Distractions scorned.

The fourth is of crystal most difficult of apprehension. Love of underlying laws, of interrelations, cadences, and fine STRUCTURES.

The fifth acts as a spring-board to fling us to the heights of ELEVATION.

A Prehistoric Hand

17.3 AMÉDÉE OZENFANT

The Life of the Artist Today (excerpt)

1928

How will art manage in the present state of drift? We are machines which demand attention and also special "instructions for use."

Talent is certainly less something inborn than the acquired capacity of knowing how to use oneself and perfect oneself.

Turn your day into a time-table, unvarying, implacable. However impulses may tempt, they must be sternly denied except in the time allowed for them. The artist too often believes that he must sit about in readiness for the kind attentions of the "Muse," but that amiable creature quickly learns to be in time for her appointments (as easily, in fact, as learning to miss them altogether). A discipline must be imposed on her. Inspiration is not a flame, like the Holy Ghost, but a potency gleaming in us like a night-light, which should glow brightly in working hours. We must train our inspiration, for it is ourselves always. The romantic conception of will-o'-the-wisp inspiration must be done away with; inspiration must obey. It does not care for processes of slow digestion nor little sleep; it likes best method, regularity, a jockey's regimen.

Inspiration has a just right to week-ends off. On holidays the eyes, the heart, the head, must be bathed in the light of plains, and the world contemplated. Our mother the sea, the blue of heaven like the scarves of miraculous virgins, the sombre green of oaks, earth's foundations. Return only when the sun's last ardours fade. That should be good for a week.

Realise that this age is a difficult one to please: it demands from art products potent to overcome and stabilise the feverishness of today. Production results from convergence. The focal point of convergence must be our ideal, placed so high that nothing can ever reach it or put a bound to our climbing. Some find attempts at breaking records stupid. If speed had a limit, it would interest us little: but speed has no limit other than that of light, and from us to that. . . . Ideal speed will never be attained, but the impulse towards that infinite constitutes a lever that can never exert its full power. Men, like civilisations, enter on Decadence not when they have lost but GAINED their ideal.

When I sometimes begin to feel lassitude creep over me, I say to myself: "If one form of Asiatic wisdom is to teach that all is vain, and that one should be inert enough to make no effort, our Western wisdom is that knowing all to be vanity we must act to the best of our human capacity."

PART 18

Surrealism

Taking its origins in the Dada movement, Surrealism was developed in the years 1923–24 by a group of writers including Paul Eluard, Louis Aragon, and particularly André Breton, the undisputed pope of the movement as Robert Desnos was to call him a few years later, in his "Third Manifesto." A negative rendering of what was, in its origin, a movement of energy and high hopes, Dada had become, said Desnos, a kind of chapel. The point was to liberate the human mind from the rational ordering that would tie it down, by means of automatic processes of writing, drawing, and speaking in a hypnotized state, the latter experiment undertaken at its best by Desnos. It is to this experimentation that the first "Surrealist Manifesto" bears witness.

Among the other Surrealists were Benjamin Péret, Breton's most faithful friend and Surrealist companion, and Antonin Artaud, the theoretician of a Theater of Cruelty, who presided for a while over the Office of Dreams. Artaud and Desnos were expelled from the movement, Eluard and Aragon ended up with a more purely political involvement, whereas Breton — whose revolutionary longings (*The Surrealist Revolution*, the first review was called) attracted him for a while to the Communist Party (the time of *Surrealism at the Service of the Revolution*) — went from a Trotskyite position to a more mystical attitude at the end of his life.

No movement in French Modernism has had a greater impact on cultural life: from the slick appropriations of Salvador Dali (Salvador Dollars, as he was called) to the adaptation of Surrealist (or then Dada) methods of analogy and creation, the heritage is long in literature and in art. Breton's celebrated advocacy of taking two elements from fields as opposed as possible and confronting them ("a sewing machine and an umbrella on a dissection table," in his expression borrowed from Lautréamont) was originally a theory of the Cubist poet Pierre Reverdy, who headed the review ironically called *Littérature* (lis-tes-ratures, read your erasures).

Surrealism is allied with Magic Realism in the Spanish-speaking world and has followers, in fact, all over the world at present. It put an official end to itself in Paris in 1969, three years after the death of Breton, as Dada officially ended itself in 1923. These were graceful exits.

Besides the value of the texts left behind, the major significance of Surrealism remains its bringing to consciousness of the ways in which the artistic imagination can be fruitfully tapped by the techniques of dream writing and speaking and drawing. Roberto Matta's use of the doodle or the scribble in painting, like Desnos's scribbles a few years earlier, was at the origin of much of the painting of the Abstract Expressionists or the New York School, such as that of Robert Motherwell, closest to the Surrealists exiled in New York during World War II. What might formerly have seemed the triviality of game (wordplays, "the game of truth," the "exquisite corpse," and other forms of collective experimentation) became an all-important work, for the freeing effect it had on the individual spirit.

18.1

DECLARATION OF JANUARY 27, 1925

With regard to a false interpretation of our enterprise, stupidly circulated among the public,

We declare as follows to the entire braying literary, dramatic, philosophical, exegetical and even theological body of contemporary criticism:

1) We have nothing to do with literature;
   But we are quite capable, when necessary, of making use of it like anyone else.
2) *Surrealism* is not a new means or expression, or an easier one, nor even a metaphysic of poetry.
   It is a means of total liberation of the mind *and of all that resembles it.*
3) We are determined to make a Revolution.
4) We have joined the word *surrealism* to the word *revolution* solely to show the disinterested, detached, and even entirely desperate character of this revolution.
5) We make no claim to change the *mores* of mankind, but we intend to show the fragility of thought, and on what shifting foundations, what caverns we have built our trembling houses.
6) We hurl this formal warning to Society: Beware of your deviations and *faux-pas*, we shall not miss a single one.
7) At each turn of its thought, Society will find us waiting.
8) We are specialists in Revolt.
   There is no means of action which we are not capable, when necessary, of employing.
9) We say in particular to the Western world: *surrealism* exists. And what is this new ism that is fastened to us? Surrealism is not a poetic form. It is a cry of the mind turning back on itself, and it is determined to break apart its fetters, even if it must be by material hammers!

LOUIS ARAGON	MICHEL LEIRIS
ANTONIN ARTAUD	GEORGES LIMBOUR
JACQUES BARON	MATHIAS LÜBECK
JOË BOUSQUET	GEORGES MALKINE
J.-A. BOIFFARD	ANDRÉ MASSON
ANDRÉ BRETON	MAX MORISE
JEAN CARRIVE	PIERRE NAVILLE

RENÉ CREVEL	MARCEL NOLL
ROBERT DESNOS	BENJAMIN PÉRET
PAUL ÉLUARD	RAYMOND QUENEAU
MAX ERNST	PHILIPPE SOUPAULT
T. FRAENKEL	DÉDÉ SUNBEAM
FRANCIS GÉRARD	ROLAND TUAL

18.2 ANTONIN ARTAUD
The Theater of Cruelty
First Manifesto

1932

We cannot go on prostituting the idea of the theater, whose only value lies in its excruciating, magical connection with reality and with danger.

Stated this way, the question of the theater must arouse general attention, since theater, because of its physical aspect and because it requires *expression in space* (the only real expression, in fact), allows the magical means of art and speech to be practiced organically and as a whole, like renewed exorcisms. From all this it follows that we shall not restore to the theater its specific powers of action until we have restored its language.

That is to say: instead of relying on texts that are regarded as definitive and as sacred we must first of all put an end to the subjugation of the theater to the text, and rediscover the notion of a kind of unique language halfway between gesture and thought.

This language can only be defined in terms of the possibilities of dynamic expression in space as opposed to the expressive possibilities of dialogue. And what theater can still wrest from speech is its potential for expansion beyond words, for development in space, for a dissociative and vibratory effect on our sensibilities. This is the function of intonations, the particular way a word is uttered. And beyond the auditory language of sounds, this is the function of the visual language of objects, movements, attitudes, gestures, but provided their meaning, their physiognomy, their combinations, are extended until they become signs and these signs become a kind of alphabet. Once the theater has become aware of this language in space, which is a language of sounds, cries, lights, onomatopoeia, it must organize it by making the characters and the objects true hieroglyphs, and by utiliz-ing their symbolism and their correspondences in relation to all organs and on all levels.

The question for the theater, then, is to create a metaphysics of speech, gesture, and expression, in order to rescue it from its psychological and human stagnation. But all this can be of use only if there is behind such an effort a kind of real metaphysical temptation, an appeal to certain unusual ideas which by their very nature cannot be limited, or even formally defined. These ideas, which have to do with Creation, with Becoming, with Chaos, and are all of a cosmic order, provide an elementary notion of a realm from which the theater has become totally estranged. These ideas can create a kind of passionate equation between Man, Society, Nature, and Objects.

It is not a question, however, of putting metaphysical ideas directly on the stage, but of creating various kinds of temptations, of indrafts of air around these ideas. And humor with its anarchy, poetry with its symbolism and its images, provide a kind of elementary notion of how to channel the temptation of these ideas.

We must now consider the purely material aspect of this language. That is, of all the ways and means it has of acting on the sensibility.

It would be meaningless to say that this language relies on music, dance, pantomime, or mimicry. Obviously it utilizes movements, harmonies, and rhythms, but only insofar as they can converge in a kind of central expres-sion, without favoring any particular art. This does not mean, either, that it does not make use of ordinary events, ordinary passions, but it uses them only as a springboard, just as HUMOR-AS-DESTRUCTION, through laughter, can serve to win over to its side the habits of reason.

It is with an altogether Oriental sense of expression that this objective and concrete language of the theater serves to corner and surround the organs. It flows into the sensibility. Abandoning Western uses of speech, it turns words into incantations. It extends the voice. It utilizes vibrations and qualities of the voice. It wildly stamps in rhythms. It pile-drives sounds. It seeks to exalt, to benumb, to charm, to arrest the sensibility. It releases the sense of a new lyricism of gesture which, by its rapidity or its spatial ampli-tude, ultimately surpasses the lyricism of words. In short, it ends the intel-lectual subjugation to language by conveying the sense of a new and more profound intellectuality which hides itself under the gestures and signs, ele-vated to the dignity of particular exorcisms.

For all this magnetism and all this poetry and these direct means of seduction would be nothing if they were not designed to put the mind physically on the track of something, if the true theater could not give us the sense of a creation of which we possess only one face, but whose completion exists on other levels.

And it does not matter whether these other levels are really conquered by the mind, that is, by the intelligence; this is to diminish them and that has no interest or meaning. What matters is that by reliable means the sensibility be put in a state of subtler and more profound perception, and this is the very purpose of that magic and those rites, of which the theater is only a reflection.

TECHNIQUE

It is a question, therefore, of making the theater, in the proper sense of the word, a function; something as localized and as precise as the circulation of the blood in the arteries, or the apparently chaotic development of dream images in the brain, and this by a powerful linkage, a true enslavement of the attention.

The theater cannot become itself again—that is, it cannot constitute a means of true illusion—until it provides the spectator with the truthful precipitates of dreams, in which his taste for crime, his erotic obsessions, his savagery, his fantasies, his utopian sense of life and of things, even his cannibalism, pour out on a level that is not counterfeit and illusory but internal.

In other words, the theater must seek by every possible means to call into question not only the objective and descriptive external world but the internal world, that is, man from a metaphysical point of view. It is only thus, we believe, that we may once again be able to speak in connection with the theater about the rights of the imagination. Neither Humor, nor Poetry, nor Imagination means anything unless, by an anarchic destruction generating a fantastic flight of forms which will constitute the whole spectacle, they succeed in organically calling into question man, his ideas about reality, and his poetic place in reality.

But to regard theater as a second-hand psychological or moral function, and to believe that dreams themselves have only a replacement function, is to diminish the profound poetic bearing of both dreams and theater. If the theater, like dreams, is bloody and inhuman, it is in order to manifest and to root unforgettably in us the idea of a perpetual conflict and a spasm in which life is constantly being cut short, in which everything in creation rises up and struggles against our condition as already formed creatures, it is to perpetuate in a concrete and immediate way the metaphysical ideas of certain Fables whose very atrociousness and energy are enough to demonstrate their origin and their content of essential principles.

This being so, one sees that, by its proximity to the principles that transfuse it poetically with their energy, this naked language of the theater, a language that is not virtual but real, must make it possible, by utilizing the nervous magnetism of man, to transgress the ordinary limits of art and speech, in order to realize actively, that is magically, *in real terms*, a kind of total creation in which man can only resume his place between dreams and events.

THEMES

We have no intention of boring the audience to death with transcendent cosmic preoccupations. That there may be profound keys to thought and action with which to read the spectacle as a whole, does not generally concern the spectator, who is not interested in such things. But they must be there all the same; and this concerns us.

The Spectacle
Every spectacle will contain a physical and objective element, perceptible to all. Cries, groans, apparitions, surprises, theatrical tricks of all kinds, the magical beauty of costumes taken from certain ritual models, dazzling lighting effects, the incantatory beauty of voices, the charm of harmony, rare notes of music, the colors of objects, the physical rhythm of movements whose crescendo and decrescendo will blend with the rhythm of movements familiar to everyone, concrete apparitions of new and surprising objects, masks, puppets larger than life, sudden changes of lighting, physical action of light which arouses sensations of heat and cold, etc.

Mise en Scène
It is in terms of *mise en scène*, regarded not merely as the degree of refraction of a text on the stage but as the point of departure of all theatrical creation, that the ideal language of the theater will evolve. And it is in the utilization and handling of this language that the old duality between author and director will disappear, to be replaced by a kind of unique Creator who will bear the double responsibility for the spectacle and the plot.

The Language of the Stage
It is not a question of eliminating spoken language but of giving words something of the importance they have in dreams.

Also, one must find new methods of transcribing this language, which might be related to the methods of musical notation, or might make use of some sort of code.

As for ordinary objects, or even the human body, elevated to the dignity of signs, it is obvious that one can derive inspiration from hieroglyphic characters, not only in order to transcribe these signs in a legible way that enables one to reproduce them at will, but also in order to compose on the stage symbols that are precise and immediately legible.

This code language and this musical notation will also be invaluable as a means of transcribing voices.

Since it is fundamental to this language to make a specialized use of intonations, these intonations must constitute a kind of harmonic balance, a kind of secondary distortion of speech that must be reproducible at will.

Similarly, the ten thousand and one facial expressions captured in the form of masks will be labeled and catalogued, so that they can participate directly and symbolically in this concrete language of the stage; and this independently of their particular psychological utilization.

Furthermore, these symbolic gestures, these masks, these attitudes, these individual or group movements whose innumerable meanings constitute an important part of the concrete language of the theater—evocative gestures, emotive or arbitrary attitudes, frenzied pounding out of rhythms and sounds—will be reinforced and multiplied by a kind of reflection of gestures and attitudes that consists of the mass of all the impulsive gestures, all the failed attitudes, all the slips of the mind and the tongue which reveal what might be called the impotences of speech, and in which there is a prodigious wealth of expressions, to which we shall not fail to have recourse on occasion.

There is, besides, a concrete idea of music in which sounds make entrances like characters, in which harmonies are cut in two and are lost in the precise entrances of words.

From one means of expression to another, correspondences and levels are created; and even the lighting can have a specific intellectual meaning.

Musical Instruments
They will be used for their qualities as objects and as part of the set.

Also, the need to act directly and profoundly upon the sensibility through the sense organs invites research, from the point of view of sound, into qualities and vibrations of sounds to which we are absolutely unaccustomed, qualities which contemporary musical instruments do not possess and which compel us to revive ancient and forgotten instruments or to create new ones. They also compel research, beyond the domain of music, into instruments and devices which, because they are made from special combinations or new alloys of metals, can achieve a new diapason of the octave and produce intolerable or ear-shattering sounds or noises.

Light—Lighting

The lighting equipment currently in use in theaters is no longer adequate. In view of the peculiar action of light on the mind, the effects of luminous vibrations must be investigated, along with new ways of diffusing light in waves, or sheets, or in fusillades of fiery arrows. The color range of the equipment currently in use must be completely revised. In order to produce particular tone qualities, one must reintroduce into light an element of thinness, density, opacity, with a view to producing heat, cold, anger, fear, etc.

Costumes

As for costumes, and without suggesting that there can be any such thing as a standard theatrical costume that is the same for all plays, we shall insofar as possible avoid modern dress—not because of any fetishistic and superstitious taste for the old, but because it seems absolutely obvious that certain age-old costumes intended for ritual use, although they were once of their time, retain a beauty and appearance that are revelatory, by virtue of their closeness to the traditions that gave them birth.

The Stage—The Auditorium

We are eliminating the stage and the auditorium and replacing them with a kind of single site, without partition or barrier of any kind, which will itself become the theater of the action. A direct communication will be reestablished between the spectator and the spectacle, between the actor and the spectator, because the spectator, by being placed in the middle of the action, is enveloped by it and caught in its cross-fire. This envelopment is the result of the very shape of the room.

For this reason we shall abandon existing theater buildings and use some kind of hangar or barn, which we shall have reconstructed according to techniques that have resulted in the architecture of certain churches or certain sacred buildings, and certain Tibetan temples.

In the interior of this construction, special proportions of height and depth will prevail. The room will be enclosed by four walls, without any kind of ornament, and the audience will be seated in the middle of the room, below, on movable chairs, to allow them to follow the spectacle that will go on all around them. In effect, the absence of a stage in the ordinary sense of the word will allow the action to spread out to the four corners of the room. Special areas will be set aside, for the actors and the action, at the four cardinal points of the room. The scenes will be played in front of whitewashed walls designed to absorb the light. In addition, overhead galleries will run around the entire periphery of the hall, as in certain Primitive paintings. These galleries will enable the actors to pursue each other from one part of the room to another whenever the action requires, and will permit the action to spread out on all levels and in all perspectives of height and depth. A cry uttered at one end of the room can be transmitted from mouth to mouth, with successive amplifications and modulations, to the other end of the room. The action will unfold, will extend its trajectory from level to level, from point to point; paroxysms will suddenly break out, flaring up like fires in different places; and the quality of true illusion of the spectacle, like the direct and immediate hold of the action on the spectator, will not be an empty phrase. For this diffusion of the action over an immense space will mean that the lighting of a scene and the various lighting effects of a performance will seize the audience as well as the characters;—and several simultaneous actions, several phases of an identical action in which the characters, clinging together in swarms, will withstand all the assaults of the situations, and the external assaults of the elements and the storm, will have their counterpart in physical means of lighting, thunder, or wind, whose repercussions the spectator will undergo.

Nevertheless, a central area will be set aside which, without serving as a stage properly speaking, will enable the main part of the action to be concentrated and brought to a climax whenever necessary.

Objects—Masks—Props

Puppets, enormous masks, objects of unusual proportions will appear by the same right as verbal images to emphasize the concrete aspect of every image and every expression—and the counterpart of this will be that things which usually require their objective representation will be treated summarily or disguised.

Sets

There will be no sets. This function will be adequately served by hieroglyphic characters, ritual costumes, puppets thirty feet high representing the beard of King Lear in the storm, musical instruments as tall as men, objects of strange shape and unknown purpose.

Immediacy

But, people will say, a theater so removed from life, from facts, from current preoccupations . . . From the present and events, yes! From profound preoccupations which are the prerogative of the few, no! In the *Zohar*, the Story of Rabbi Simeon, who burns like fire, is as immediate as fire.

Works

We shall not perform any written plays, but shall attempt to create productions directly on stage around subjects, events, or known works. The very nature and arrangement of the room require spectacle and there is no subject, however vast, that can be denied us.

Spectacle

There is an idea of total spectacle that must be revived. The problem is to make space speak, to enrich and furnish it; like mines laid in a wall of flat rocks which suddenly give birth to geysers and bouquets.

The Actor

The actor is at once an element of prime importance, since it is on the effectiveness of his performance that the success of the spectacle depends, and a kind of passive and neutral element, since all personal initiative is strictly denied him. It is an area in which there are no precise rules; and between the actor from whom one requires the mere quality of a sob and the actor who must deliver a speech with his own personal qualities of persuasion, there is the whole margin that separates a man from an instrument.

Interpretation

The spectacle will be calculated from beginning to end, like a language. In this way there will be no wasted movement and all the movements will follow a rhythm; and since each character will be an extreme example of a type, his gesticulation, his physiognomy, his costume will appear as so many rays of light.

The Cinema

To the crude visualization of what is, the theater through poetry opposes images of what is not. From the point of view of action, moreover, one cannot compare a cinematic image which, however poetic, is limited by the properties of celluloid, to a theatrical image, which obeys all the exigencies of life.

Cruelty

Without an element of cruelty at the foundation of every spectacle, the theater is not possible. In the state of degeneracy, in which we live, it is through the skin that metaphysics will be made to reenter our minds.

The Public

First of all this theater must exist.

The Program

We shall stage, without taking account of the text:

1. An adaptation of a work from the period of Shakespeare that is entirely relevant to our present state of mental confusion, whether it be one of Shakespeare's apocryphal plays, like *Arden of Feversham*, or an altogether different play from the same period.
2. A play of extreme poetic freedom by Léon-Paul Fargue.
3. An excerpt from the *Zohar:* The Story of Rabbi Simeon, which has the violence and the ever present force of a conflagration.
4. The story of Bluebeard reconstructed from historical documents, with a new idea of eroticism and cruelty.
5. The Fall of Jerusalem, according to the Bible and History; with the blood-red color that trickles from it, and with the feeling of despair and panic in people's minds visible even in the light; and on the other hand, the metaphysical disputes of the prophets, with the frightful intellectual agitation they create, whose repercussions fall physically on the King, the Temple, the Populace, and Historical Events.
6. A Tale by the Marquis de Sade in which the eroticism will be transposed, represented allegorically and clothed, resulting in a violent externalization of cruelty and a concealment of the rest.
7. One or more romantic melodramas in which improbability will become an active and concrete element of poetry.
8. Büchner's *Woyzeck*, in a spirit of reaction against our principles, and to illustrate what can be derived theatrically from a formal text.
9. Works of the Elizabethan theater stripped of their texts, of which we shall retain only trappings of the period, situations, characters, and plots.

18.3 ANTONIN ARTAUD
All Writing Is Pigshit
1965

All writing is pigshit.

People who leave the obscure and try to define whatever it is that goes on in their heads, are pigs.

The whole literary scene is a pigpen, especially this one.

All those who have vantage points in their spirit, I mean, on some side or other of their heads and in a few strictly localized brain areas; all those who are masters of their language; all those for whom words have a meaning; all those for whom there exist sublimities in the soul and currents of thought; all those who are the spirit of the times, and have named these currents of thought—and I am thinking of their precise works, of that automatic grinding that delivers their spirit to the winds—

are pigs.

Those for whom certain words have a meaning, and certain manners of being; those who are so fussy; those for whom emotions are classifiable, and who quibble over some degree or other of their hilarious classifications; those who still believe in "terms"; those who brandish whatever ideologies belong to the hierarchy of the times; those about whom women talk so well, and also those women who talk so well, who talk of the contemporary currents of thought; those who still believe in some orientation of the spirit; those who follow paths, who drop names, who fill books with screaming headlines

are the worst kind of pigs.

And you are quite aimless, young man!

No, I am thinking of bearded critics.

And I told you so: no works of art, no language, no word, no thought, nothing.

Nothing; unless maybe a fine Brain-Storm.

A sort of incomprehensible and totally erect stance in the midst of everything in the mind.

And don't expect me to tell you what all this is called, and how many parts it can be divided into; don't expect me to tell you its weight; or to get back in step and start discussing all this so that by discussing I may get lost myself and even, without even realizing it, start THINKING. And don't expect this thing to be illuminated and live and deck itself out in a multitude of words, all neatly polished as to meaning, very diverse, and capable of throwing light on all the attitudes and all the nuances of a very sensitive and penetrating mind.

Ah, these states which have no name, these sublime situations of the soul, ah these intervals of wit, these minuscule failures which are the daily bread of my hours, these people swarming with data . . . they are always the same old words I'm using, and really I don't seem to make much headway in my thoughts, but I am really making more headway than you, you beard-asses, you pertinent pigs, you masters of fake verbiage, confectioners of portraits, pamphleteers, ground-floor lace-curtain herb collectors, entomologists, plague of my tongue.

I told you so, I no longer have the gift of tongue. But this is no reason you should persist and stubbornly insist on opening your mouths.

Look, I will be understood ten years from now by the people who then will do what you are doing now. Then my geysers will be recognized, my glaciers will be seen, the secret of diluting my poisons will have been learnt, the plays of my soul will be deciphered.

Then all my hair, all my mental veins will have been drained in quicklime; then my bestiary will have been noticed, and my mystique become a hat. Then the joints of stones will be seen smoking, arborescent bouquets of mind's eyes will crystallize in glossaries, stone aeroliths will fall, lines will be seen and the geometry of the void understood: people will learn what the configuration of the mind is, and they will understand how I lost my mind.

They will then understand why my mind is not all here; then they will see all languages go dry, all minds parched, all tongues shrivelled up, the human face flattened out, deflated as if sucked up by shriveling leeches. And this lubricating membrane will go on floating in the air, this caustic lubricating membrane, this double membrane of multiple degrees and a million little fissures, this melancholic and vitreous membrane, but so sensitive and also pertinent, so capable of multiplying, splitting apart, turning inside out with its glistening little cracks, its dimensions, its narcotic highs, its penetrating and toxic injections, and

all this then will be found to be all right,

and I will have no further need to speak.

18.4 ANTONIN ARTAUD

Here Where Others . . .

1965

Here where others offer up their works I pretend to nothing more than showing my mind.

Life is a burning up of questions.

I can't conceive of a work detached from life.

I don't love detached creation. I can no longer conceive of the mind as detached from itself. Each of my works, every one of my maps, every one of the glacial blooms of my inner soul dribbles all over me.

I recognize myself as much in a letter written to explain the intimate shrinkage of my being and the insane castration of my life, as in an essay exterior to myself that seems to me like an indifferent pregnancy of my mind.

I suffer because the Spirit is not in life and life not in the Spirit. I suffer from Spirit as organ, Spirit as translation, Spirit as intimidation-with-things, in order to make them enter into the Spirit.

I suspend this book in life, I'd like it to be bitten by external things, and first of all by all the fits and starts, all the twitching *of my future self.*

All these pages are leftover icicles of the mind. Excuse my absolute freedom. I refuse to make distinctions between any of the minutes of myself. And I don't recognize the existence of any map of the mind.

You have to do away with the mind, as with literature. I say the mind and life communicate at all levels. I want to make a Book that will derange men, that will be like an open door leading them where they would never have consented to go. A door simply ajar on reality.

And this is no more a preface to a book than the poems, for example, that stake it out, or the enumeration of all the furies of a torn soul.

This is merely an icicle stuck in my throat.

18.5 ANTONIN ARTAUD

Revolt against Poetry

1965

We have never written anything except against a backdrop of the incarnation of the soul, but the soul already is made (and not by ourselves) when we enter into poetry. The poet, who writes, addresses himself to the Word, and the Word to its laws. It is in the unconscious of the poet to believe automatically in these laws. He believes himself free thereby, but he is not. There is something back of his head and over the ears of his thought. Something budding in the nape of his neck, rooted there from even before his beginning. He is the son of his works, perhaps, but his works are not of him; for whatever is of himself in his poetry has not been expressed by him but rather by that unconscious producer of life, who has pointed life out to him in order that he not be his own poet, in order that he not designate life himself; and who obviously has never been well-disposed toward him. Well, I don't want to be the poet of my poet, of that self which fancied it'd choose me to be a poet; but rather a poet-creator, in rebellion against the ego and the self. And I call to mind the old rebellion against the forms that came over me. It is by revolt against the ego and the self that I disemburden myself from all the evil incarnations of the Word, which have never been anything more for man than a compromise between cowardice and illusion, and I only know abject fornication when it comes to cowardice and illusion. And I don't want a word of mine coming from I don't know what astral libido completely aware of the formations of, say, a desire that is mine and mine alone. There is in the forms of the human Word I don't know what operation of rapaciousness, what self-devouring greed going on; whereby the poet, binding himself to the object, sees himself eaten by it. That is a crime weighing heavy on the idea of the Word-made-flesh, but the real crime is in having allowed the idea in the first place. Libido is animal-thought, and it was these same animals which one day were changed into men. The word produced through these men is the idea of an invert buried by his animal response to things, who has forgotten (through the martyrdom of time and things) that the word has been invented. The invert is he who eats his self, and desires that his self nourish him, seeking his mother in it and wanting to possess her for himself. The primitive crime of incest is the enemy of poetry and the killer of poetry's immaculacy. I don't want to eat my poem but I want to give my heart to my poem. And what is my heart to my poem? My heart is what isn't my ego. To give one's self to one's poem is also to risk being violated by it. And if I am Virgin for my poem, it ought to be virgin for my ego. I am that forgotten poet who one day saw himself hurtle to matter, and matter never will devour me, my ego. I don't want those old reflexes, results of an ancient incest come from an animal ignorance of the Virgin law of life. The ego and the self are those catastrophic states of being in which the Living Man allows himself to be imprisoned by the forms that he perceived by himself. To love his ego is to love death, and the law of the Virgin is infinite. The unconscious producer of our selves is that of an ancient copulator who frees himself to commit more vulgar magicks, and who has pulled off the most infamous wizardry by having brought himself back to his self-same self over and above his very self, eternally, so that he was able even to pull a word out of a cadaver. The libido is the definition of that cadaverous desire, and the falling man an invert criminal. I am such a primitive, discontented with the inexpiable horror of things. I don't want to reproduce myself in things but I want things to happen through my self. I don't want an idea of my ego in my poem and I don't want to meet my self again there, either. My heart is that eternal Rose come from the magic power of the initial Cross. He who crucified Himself never returned to himself. Never. For he also surrendered to Life the self by which he sacrificed Himself, after having forced it within himself to become the being of his own life. I want only to be such a poet forever, who sacrificed himself in the Kabbala of self for the immaculate conception of things.

18.6 ANTONIN ARTAUD

Shit to the Spirit

1965

> After romanticism,
>> symbolism,
>> dadaism,
>> surrealism,
>> lettrism,
> and marxism,

i.e., a hundred "schools" of political, philosophical or literary subversion, there is one word, one thing that remains standing, one value that hasn't budged,

that's kept its ancient pre-eminence through thick and thin,

and that word and thing is spirit,

the value attached to spirit,

the value of the spiritual thing;

as if it sufficed by statement

to make that magnetic word stand out on a corner of the page, so that everything truly were said.

As if it were understood in fact and as principle and essence

that spirit is the innate term,

the model value,

     the apex word

by which the old atavistic automatism of the beast named man might get going without jamming at the start.

For the universal shaft would be well greased.

It has been understood everywhere, for I don't know how many centuries of Kabbala, hermeticism, mystagogy, platonism and psycho-surgery,

that the body is the son of the spirit,

that it belongs to it like a density, a conglomeration

     or a magic mass,

and that one cannot conceive of body as ever being, in terms of its in-born way, the materialization of some somber marriage between the spirit and its own power, the terminus of an elite journey of the spirit along its own road,

lo kundam

a papa

da mama

la mamama

a papa

dama

lokin

a kata

repara

o leptura

o ema

lema

o ersti

o popo

erstura

o erstura
o popo
dima

as if it were impossible to have body without having had some part spirit;
as if the state called body, the bodily thing, were in essence and by nature
inferior to the spiritual state,
    and came from the spiritual state.
    As if the body were the carriage and the spirit the mind, which was led
by another spirit, called the coachman.
    As if the body were the millworkers and the spirit the boss who'd con-
trived how to keep them in chains.
    As if the body were the body of all the soldiers who get themselves killed
at the command of that great spirit, the general who makes them kill.
    As if it were understood for life that the body is this filthy stuff the spirit
takes its footbaths in
    when there aren't bloodbaths enough for jackbooted capucine monks to
kick around in.
    And the body can do nothing but buckle up.
    And I'd like to see the body of a spirit in the midst of putting its future
piles of flesh in order.
    But before that I'd like to speak of nightmares.
    Screwy jumping from one thing to another, no?
    To go suddenly and brutally like that from the spirit to nightmares.
    Nightmares come from all the bastards, all the body-born who are at the
same time bloated with spirit, and who make magic in order to live, and
who've only lived off the spirit, i.e., of magic.
    Without partisans of pure spirit, of pure spirit as the origin of things,
and of god as pure spirit, there never would have been any nightmares.
    And everyone, of course, somewhere in the earth, blames the nightmare,
accuses it of being the torturer of his last night (upon waking up), but without attaching other significance to it, without noting the gravity of the fact.
    He doesn't know that the nightmare is the introduction of unreason by
way of the void, is the anarchy in the inherent and normal logic of the brain,
is the poison put into its well-being, is an intervention from top to bottom,
    a drop of a hatred of others flowing into the breath of the night,
    the instilling of a grub of spirit, a tear of pure spirit,
    insinuately into the body without a sound,
    by everything that is impotence, emptiness, void, hatred, frailty, envy.
    Now for most sleepers on earth the nightmare is only a pretty story to

tell as you jump out of bed. Something like a tale by Edgar Poe or Herman Melville or Hoffman or La Motte-Fouquet or Nathaniel Hawthorne or Lewis or Chamisso; wherein the dream furnishes the contents for the illustration of life, so to speak. But what they didn't suspect, what they don't think of telling themselves is that some people look to a nightmare

as a way of stopping life,

as a way of *their*

procuring
life

at the expense of the agony of the sleeper attacked by them.
How?

By profitting from man's sleep, from that release that sleep gives to man, in order to root out from the normal course of the molecular states of man's life a little slice of that life, a small bloody network of atoms that might serve to nourish *their* life.

A nightmare never is an accident, but an evil fastened on to us by a whore, by the mouth of a ghoul of a whore who finds us too rich with life, and so creates by very exact slurps some interferences in our thought, some catastrophic voids in the passage of the breath of our sleeping body, which believes itself free from care.

Now those who create these nightmares are men, but they are likewise spirits, spirits that wanted to stay . . . in that spiritual state, without going deeper into life.

And just what is spirit?

Spirit *in fact.*

I mean, outside philosophy.

And why would the body come from the spirit, and not vice-versa?

Why should the spirit hold all the values, while the body is only the vestment, a miserable shambles, the stuff of incarnation?

As if there had ever been a mystery called incarnation.

What connection is there between body and spirit?

Think about it awhile. There isn't any.

For we know what the body is,

but who says

that the spirit is the principle from which all that is living gushes?

It is the spirit that holds the data; it is in the spirit you see ideas.

Those womby udders bloating everything that shows energy.

But, Plato, you make us shit; and so do you, Socrates, Epictetes, Epicurus; and you, Kant, and you, Descartes, too.

For one can very well invert the problem and say that the spirit and its values and data might never have existed if the body, which at least sweated them out, had not been there,

when the spirit, which never moves, was contented just to sit around and look at them,

waiting for the best one to blow;

for without the principle of sodomy there was nothing left for the spirit but to vacate the earth as well as the vast emptiness of the spheres that Plato, sad old beginner that he was, believed one day he'd furnish with ideas.

Only nobody bumped into them.

So it's all a bravado and a bluff.

A kind of smoky grub that lives only on what it has pulled from the body that was struggling to make some gesture

and not some idea or proposition.

For what, after all, are these ideas, data, values, qualities?

Terms without life that take on substance only when the body has sweated them out, going through a dead sweat in order to help them decide to let themselves go.

For the body doesn't ever need us to define what it's done.

Without the labor-pain of the body one day, an idea never would have been born,

and it isn't from the body that it was born, but against it,

when the idea of a gesture,

i.e., the shadow of it,

chose to live its own life.

Under the action already called: spirit.

That grub of expulsed wind that wanted to give itself substance without taking the trouble to earn it.

When one has no body, and therefore is nothing; when one hasn't even begun breathing, there has to be a terrible will at work in order to manufacture oneself into a something, and earn the place where breathing can go on freely.

And it isn't a matter involving an idea but rather of surmounting terrifying pangs.

And it was right there that the big bully, the big coward, that buggerer of the tide of pure essences, was knocked out; the same one who, in so far as principles and essences are concerned, and without the body to resist such notions, is only a hole for the eternal passage of every idea or datum of existence, god, pure spirit, shadow and virtuality.

Too cowardly to try making it to a body, the spirits, those volatile farts more frivolous than any suffering body, roam around in the empyrean where their emptiness, their nuls and voids, their downright laziness keeps them spiritual.

By virtue of having seen the body of man underneath them, they came to the conclusion that they were going to be superior to the body of man.

By virtue of being held contemptible and repulsive by man, they've sought to give that void which is known as the spiritual state—that castration of the body of the fathermother, that impotence in slicing through anything that has life or energy—a kind of risky dignity which they've propped up by the most filthy kind of magic.

The spirit was never anything but the parasite of man, the ringworm of his worthy body when the body was no more than an animalcule swimming around and having no desire about having to be worthy of existing.

But how, by what filthy trickery, did it one day decide to be god?

That is the never-revealed story.

And I say: shit to the spirit.

I know too well by the effect of what grubby orgies, the spirit has ended up by grabbing the place before the body that actually preceded it.

I know too well that what one calls spirit is only a grinding shortage of existence, which was disgusted at the idea of becoming a body itself, and counted on what the body would lose in life in order to insure its seizure and its own subsistence

via the body that it vampirized.

The body that works has no time for thinking or, as they say, making up ideas.

Ideas are only the voids of the body. Those interferences of absence and want between two movements of a brilliant reality that the body, by its singular presence, has never stopped thrusting forward.

It isn't merely that matter is animated prior to thought;

it's simply that matter did not animate itself at all,

that it never went in the direction where animate perception trips along,

where either dialectic or discursive life has been able to be expressed; where culture has been able to get started;

but rather it's that body has always existed, I say body, and its manner of life or existence never had anything to do with

not only what is called spirit or idea,

but what we call the soul.

The body is a fact which dispenses with idea and all feeling emotion, but which, from the depths of its dark cavern, throws up a look so that even the heart hasn't time quick enough to register its own existence.

Which means that when I see Claudel calling upon the spirits at the outset of the century for help, I am still able to get up a chuckle,

but when I see the word spirit in Karl Marx or Lenin,

like an old invariable value, a reminder of that eternal entity back to which all things are brought,

I tell myself that there's scum and crud abroad and god's sucked Lenin's ass:

and that's the way it's always been,

and it isn't worth talking about anymore,

it doesn't matter, it's just another fucking bill to pay.

18.7 ANDRÉ BRETON

Declaration VVV

1942

> vvv: that is to say v+v+v. We say . . . — . . . — . . . —

that is to say not only v as the vow—and the energy—to return to a conceivable and habitable world, Victory over the forces of regression and death presently unloosed on the world,

but also v beyond this initial Victory, for this world can no longer, should no longer be the same, v over that which aims at perpetuating the enslavement of man by man,

and beyond this vv, beyond the double Victory, v again over all that is opposed to the emancipation of the mind, of which the first indispensable condition is the liberation of man.

vvv: toward the emancipation of the mind through all its necessary stages. It is only in *this* that our mind can identify its purpose

> or vvv again because:

to the v that stands for viewing what is all around us, eyes turned outward, toward the conscious surface of things,

surrealism has relentlessly opposed W, the view within, eyes turned inward toward the inner world and the depths of the unconscious, whence vvv toward a synthesis, in a third term, of these two Views, the first v centered on the *Ego* and the reality principle, the second vv on the *Id* and the pleasure principle, the resolution of their contradiction aiming solely, of course, at the continuous and systematic expansion of the field of consciousness.

Toward a total view vvv that conveys all the reactions of the eternal upon the actual, of the mental upon the physical, and accounts for the myth evolving beneath the *veil* of events.

*   *   *

vvv, without any sectarian bias, is open to all writers and artists who will agree with our purpose. vvv will not limit itself to being an anthological journal but will set above all else the spirit of free exploration as well as that of *adventure*. The only tradition to which vvv holds is that of such war magazines as *Les Soirées de Paris, Maintenant, Nord-Sud, La Révolution Surréaliste* in Paris, *Lacerba* in Rome, *291* in New York, *Cabaret Voltaire* in Zurich. Whatever the background of its contributors, vvv must by no means be either a station of arrival or a marshaling yard but rather a place to start out. In vvv the freest of poetic, artistic, and scientific views, no matter how daring they might be, will be brought together; through them vvv intends to bring out the spirit that will not fail to spring forth from the new human conditioning bred of this war and to draw tomorrow's main generating lines.

18.8 André Breton and Paul Eluard

Notes on Poetry (*excerpt*)

1929

A poem must be a debacle of the intellect. It cannot be anything but.

Debacle: a panic stampede, but a solemn, coherent one; the image of what one should be, of the state in which efforts no longer count.

In the poet:
the ear laughs,
the mouth swears;
It is intelligence, alertness that kills;
It is sleep that dreams and sees clearly;
It is the image and the hallucination that close their eyes:
It is lack and the lacuna that are *created*.

Poetry is the opposite of literature. It rules over idols of every kind and over realistic illusions; it happily sustains the ambiguity between the language of "truth" and the language of "creation."

Poetry is a pipe.

Lyricism is the development of a protest.

How proud a thing it is to write, without knowing what language, words, comparisons, changes of ideas, of tone are; neither to conceive the *structure* of the work's duration, nor the conditions of its ends; no *why*, no *how!* To turn green, blue, white from being the parrot . . .

We are always, even in prose, led and willing to write what we have not sought and what perhaps does not even seek what we sought.

Perfection

is *laziness.*

18.9 ANDRÉ BRETON AND DIEGO RIVERA [LÉON TROTSKY]*

Manifesto for an Independent Revolutionary Art

1938

Without any exaggeration one can say that human civilization has never before been exposed to so many dangers. The Vandals, with means that were barbaric and relatively ineffective, destroyed the civilization of antiquity in one corner of Europe. Today, we see the whole of civilization being threatened in the integrity of its historical destiny by reactionary forces armed with the entire arsenal of modern technology. We are not only thinking of the impending war: already, while we are still at peace, art and science have been placed in an impossible situation.

Inasmuch as it comes about through the agency of an individual, inasmuch as it makes use of certain subjective skills to bring out something that will constitute an objective enrichment, any philosophical, sociological, scien-

* Instead of Diego Rivera, Léon Trotsky actually wrote this manifesto with André Breton on July 25, 1938. Breton had formulated the aims of the International Federation of Independent Revolutionary Art as an organized "resistance against all the forces of domestication of the spirit." Although this well-intentioned federation was short-lived, its manifesto, widely circulated in pamphlet form, became celebrated.

tific, or artistic discovery appears as the result of a lucky *chance*, that is to say a more or less spontaneous manifestation of *necessity*. Such contributions cannot be minimized, whether from the standpoint of general knowledge (which aims at furthering the interpretation of the world) or from the revolutionary standpoint (which, to achieve the transformation of the world, requires a careful analysis of the laws governing its movement). We especially cannot afford to remain indifferent to the mental conditions in which those contributions are made nor can we fail to ensure that those specific laws that govern intellectual creation are respected.

In the contemporary world, we have to acknowledge the ever more widespread transgression of those laws, a transgression that inevitably entails an increasingly evident degradation not only of the work of art but also of the "artistic" personality. Now that it has rid itself of all the artists whose work showed the slightest evidence of a love for freedom, even on the level of form, Hitlerian fascism has forced those who could still consent to holding a pen or a brush to become lackeys of the regime and to celebrate it by command, within the limits of the worst kind of convention. Though it has not been publicized, the same thing has been happening in the USSR during the period of violent reaction that has now reached its peak.

It goes without saying that we do not for a moment stand by the currently fashionable slogan "Neither fascism nor communism!" that perfectly suits the conservative and frightened philistine clinging to the remnants of the "democratic" past. True art—art that does not merely produce variations on ready-made models but strives to express the inner needs of man and of mankind as they are today—cannot be anything other than revolutionary: it must aspire to a complete and radical reconstruction of society, if only to free intellectual creation from the chains that bind it and to allow all mankind to climb those heights that only isolated geniuses have reached in the past. At the same time, we recognize that only social revolution can clear the way for a new culture. If, however, we reject all solidarity with the caste that is currently ruling the USSR, it is precisely because, in our eyes, it represents not communism but its most treacherous and dangerous enemy. The totalitarian regime of the USSR, through the so-called cultural organizations it controls in other countries, has spread over the entire world a heavy twilight inimical to the emergence of any sort of spiritual values. In this twilight of filth and blood, we see men disguised as intellectuals and artists who have turned servility into a stepping stone, renunciation of their own principles into a perverse game, lying-for-pay into a custom, and glorification of crime into a source of pleasure. The official art of the Stalinist era mirrors with unprecedented harshness their pathetic attempts at deception and their efforts to disguise their true mercenary role.

The muted reprobation inspired in the artistic world by this brazen negation of the principles that have always governed art and that even states built on slavery have not dared to contest must give way to a sweeping condemnation. Artistic *opposition* is right now one of the forces that can effectively help to discredit and overthrow the regimes that are stifling the right of the exploited class to aspire to a better world along with all sense of human greatness or even dignity.

The communist revolution is not afraid of art. It has learned from the study of the development of the artistic calling in the collapsing capitalist society that this calling can only be the result of a clash between the individual and various social forms that are inimical to him. This situation alone, even if he has not become fully aware of it, makes the artist the natural ally of the revolution. The process of *sublimation,* which comes into play in this instance, as psychoanalysis has shown, aims at restoring the balance between the integral "ego" and the repressed elements. This restoration works to the advantage of the "superego," which sets the forces of the inner world, of the "id," *common to all men* and constantly evolving toward self-fulfillment, against the unbearable present reality. The need for the emancipation of the mind has but to follow its natural course to be brought to reimmerse itself into this primordial necessity: the need for the emancipation of man.

Art cannot, therefore, without demeaning itself, willingly submit to any outside directive and ensconce itself obediently within the limits that some people, with extremely shortsighted pragmatic ends in view, think they can set on its activities. It is far better to rely on the gift of prefiguration with which any true artist is endowed: this is what opens the way to a (virtual) resolution of the major contradictions of his time and focuses the attention of his contemporaries on the urgent need for establishing a new order.

It is imperative, at this point in time, to go back to the idea of the role of the writer developed by Marx in his youth. Clearly this idea should be extended to cover the various categories of producers and researchers in the artistic and scientific fields. "The writer," he said, "must naturally make money in order to live and write, but he should under no circumstances live and write in order to make money. . . . The writer does not in any way look on his work as a *means.* It is an *end in itself* and represents so little a means in his own eyes and those of others that if necessary he sacrifices his existence to the existence of his work. . . . *The first condition of freedom of the press is that it should not be a money-making occupation.*" It is more than ever appropriate to set that statement against those who would force intellectual activity to pursue objectives that are foreign to its nature and who would, in defiance of all the historical determinants peculiar to it, prescribe the themes of art in accordance with alleged reasons of state. The freedom to choose those themes and the absence of all restrictions on the range of his exploration represent for the artist prerogatives that he is entitled to claim as inalienable. As regards artistic creation, what is of paramount importance is that imagination should be free of all constraints and should under no pretext let itself be channeled toward prescribed goals. To those who would urge us, whether it be today or tomorrow, to agree that art should conform to a discipline that we regard as radically incompatible with its nature, we give an absolute refusal and we reassert our deliberate intention of standing by the formula: *complete freedom for art.*

We acknowledge, of course, that the revolutionary state has a right to defend itself against the aggressive reaction of the bourgeoisie, even when it drapes itself in the flag of science or art. But there is a huge difference between these necessary and temporary measures of revolutionary self-defense and the presumption to exercise command over intellectual creation within society. Granted that, in order to develop the material forces of production, the revolution has no other choice but to build a *socialist* regime with centralized control; however, it must from the very beginning, when it comes to intellectual creativity, establish an *anarchist* system based on individual freedom. No authority, no constraint, not the slightest trace of orders from above! Only on the basis of free creative friendship, without the least constraint from outside, will it be possible to form various associations of scientists and collectives of artists who will be able to work fruitfully together and to undertake tasks that will be more far-reaching than ever before.

It should be clear by now that, in defending freedom of creation, we have no intention of justifying political indifferentism, nor do we wish to resurrect a so-called pure art that generally serves the thoroughly impure ends of the forces of reaction. No, we have too high an idea of the role of art to deny it an influence on the fate of society. We believe that the supreme task of art in this day and age is consciously to take an active part in preparing the revolution. However, the artist cannot serve the struggle for emancipation unless he has internalized its social and individual content, unless he feels its meaning and its drama in his very nerves and unless he freely seeks to give his inner world an artistic incarnation.

In the present period, characterized by the death throes of capitalism—democratic as well as fascist—the artist, even if he does not overtly display his social dissidence, is threatened with the loss of his right to make a living and to go on with his work because he is denied all means of promoting his creations. It is natural that he should then turn to the Stalinist organizations that hold out the possibility of escaping from his isolation. But, in exchange for some material advantages, he is required to renounce everything that might constitute his own message and to display a terribly degrading servility. Hence, he has no alternative but to withdraw from such organizations, provided that demoralization has not gotten the better of his *character*. From that very moment, he must understand that his place is elsewhere, not among those who betray the cause of the revolution at the same time, necessarily, as that of mankind, but among those who demonstrate their unshakable loyalty to the principles of this revolution, those who, for this reason, are the only ones who can bring it to fruition and who can subsequently ensure the free expression of the human genius in all its manifestations.

Our purpose in issuing this call is to find a ground on which all revolutionary supporters of art can come together to serve the revolution with the specific methods of art and to defend freedom of art itself against the usurpers of the revolution. We are firmly convinced that it is possible for representatives of fairly divergent aesthetic, philosophical, and political orientations to meet on this ground. Marxists can walk hand in hand with anarchists here, provided both groups uncompromisingly break away from the reactionary police mentality, whether it be represented by Joseph Stalin or by his henchman Garcia Oliver.

Thousands upon thousands of isolated artists and thinkers, whose voices are drowned out by the odious clamor of well-drilled fakers, are presently scattered throughout the world. Many small local magazines are trying to gather about them youthful forces, seeking new paths, not subsidies. Every progressive trend in art is branded by fascism as degenerate. Every free creation is labeled fascist by the Stalinists. Independent revolutionary art must gather its forces to fight against reactionary persecution and to assert out loud its right to exist. Such a union of forces is the goal of the International Federation of Independent Revolutionary Art (known as FIARI), which we deem necessary to form.

We have no intention of imposing every single idea put forth in this manifesto, which we ourselves consider only as a first step in the new direction. We urge all representatives, all friends and defenders of art, who cannot fail to realize the need for this rallying cry, to make themselves heard at once. We address the same appeal to all independent leftist publications that are prepared to join in creating the International Federation and in working out its tasks and methods of action.

When a preliminary international contact has been established through the press and by correspondence, we will proceed to the organization of local and national congresses on a modest scale. The next step will be to convene a world congress that will officially mark the foundation of the International Federation.

Our goals:

the independence of art—for the revolution;
the revolution—for the liberation of art once and for all.

18.10 CLAUDE CAHUN

The Invisible Adventure

1930

The invisible adventure.

The lens follows the eyes, the mouth, the wrinkles on the surface of the skin. . . . The face's expression is violent, sometimes tragic. And finally calm —the lucid, elaborate calm of acrobats. A professional smile—and *voilà!*

Then in the hand mirror the rouge and the eyeshadow reappear. A pause. A period. A new paragraph.

I start all over again.

But what a ridiculous game this is for those who have not seen—and I have shown nothing—obstacles, abysses, and steps, all cleared.

Shall I then load myself down with all the gear of facts, stones, tenderly cut ropes, precipices . . . ? This is not interesting. Guess, restore. Vertigo is understood, in the climb or the fall.

To please them must we follow the unknown woman step by step, to illuminate her up to the ankle? The worn-down heels, the mud, the bleeding foot—humble and precise evidence—would touch someone. While . . .

No. I shall follow the wake in the air, the trail in the water, the mirage in the pupils.

I try in vain to relax. The abstract, the world of dreams, are as limited for me as the concrete, the real. What can I do? Choose a narrow mirror and reflect only a part for the whole? Confuse a halo with some mud splatters? Refusing to smash myself against the walls, I instead banged myself against the windowpanes? All in the black night.

While waiting for clarity of sight, I want to track myself down, to wrestle. Sensing oneself armed against oneself, even if only with the most useless words, who would not make an effort, if only to fling oneself precisely into the void?

This is false. It is not much. But it exercises the eye.

I want to sew, to sting, to kill, and only with the sharpest point. The rest of the body, the continuation, what a waste of time! To sail ahead only in the direction of my own prow.

18.11 MAX MORISE

Enchanted Eyes

1924

The only exact representation we have these days of the idea of *surrealism* is more or less limited to the writing procedure inaugurated by *The Magnetic Fields,* so much so that for us, the same word designates both this easily definable technique and at the same time, far beyond it, one of the modalities of the mind now appearing in domains totally ignored up to now, whose existence and importance this technique seems to have revealed for the first time ever. But just let that be missing—that determining material criterion that we have provisionally decided to be crucial—and we will be unable to locate any surrealism in inspiration except by intuition, almost by chance. This universe, on which a window has suddenly opened, might and must belong to us from now on, and it would be impossible now for us not to try to break down the wall separating us from it: every mode we can find to exteriorize our thought may offer us some weapon to use for this. What surrealist writing is to literature, a surrealist artistic practice must be to painting, photography, everything that is made to be seen.

But what touchstone should we use?

Most probably, the rapid succession of images, the flight of ideas, is a fundamental condition of every surrealist manifestation. The course of thought cannot be considered static. But if it is within time that we take cognizance of a written text, then a painting, a sculpture are only perceived in space, and their different regions appear simultaneously. It seems that no painter has yet managed to give an account of a series of images, for we cannot stop with the procedures of the primitive painters who represented on differing places of their picture the successive scenes they imagined. The cinema—a perfected cinema which would let us bypass technical formalities—opens a path towards the solution of this problem. Let us suppose that the figuration of time is not indispensable in a surrealist production (a painting, after all, concretizes a whole of intellectual representations and not just one—you can attribute to it a curve comparable to the curve of thought), it is still the case that in order to paint a canvas you have to begin by one end, to continue elsewhere, then again somewhere else, a procedure leaving a great deal of room for the arbitrary, for mere taste, and that tends to divert the dictation of thought.

The confrontation of surrealism with dream does not yield very satisfying results. Painting and writing are apt to recount some dream. A simple effort of memory will suffice to stamp it out. The same is true of all apparitions: strange landscapes appeared to de Chirico; he only had to reproduce them, relying on the interpretation that his memory supplied him. But this effort of second intention which necessarily deforms images by bringing them to the surface of consciousness demonstrates the illusion of any hope that we have found the key to surrealist painting. Certainly just as much but no more than the recounting of a dream, a painting of de Chirico cannot be taken as typical of surrealism; the images are surrealistic, the expression is not.

Just as the vulture and the leopard, rushing after a succulent prey in flight, fly or bound—according to their particular faculties—over streams and civilizations, mountain and forests, leaving all the paths already beaten in order to catch the object of their desire, the body, deformed by speed and by the irregularities along the way, now taking on the form of a polished spindle sending out a beam of light to each point of the horizon, an accredited ambassador to the infinite, so the elongated and impalpable appearance that you sometimes see in the marshmallow paste hanging from a stick and molded by the expert hands of the kid selling the damp stick for two cents, but which you see more often in the far reaches of the heavens when the clouds foreseeing divine anger try out the suppleness of their muscles in a geometrical and harsh exercise; so does the painter's brush move in the search of his thought.

In this kind of waking dream that characterizes the surrealist state, our thought is revealed to us, among other appearances, by those of words and plastic images. A word is soon written, and there is no great distance from the idea of the star to the word "star," to the symbolic sign that is attributed to it with the writing s t a r. I am thinking about this set of Picasso's for *Mercury* which represented night; in the sky, no stars; just the written word hung sparkling there over and over. The properly pictorial expression is not as privileged as that, if one admits that, while vocabulary is an instrument with the double advantage of being almost unlimited and constantly available, words identifying themselves so to speak with thought, brush strokes, on the contrary, only translate by mediation intellectual images and do not carry in themselves their representation. The painter would then be obliged to elaborate by means of conscious and learned faculties the elements that the writer finds ready-made in his memory.

But in truth we have every possible reason to believe that the direct and simple elements that constitute the touch of the brush on the canvas carry its meaning intrinsically, that a pencil stroke is the equivalent of a word. The first cubist paintings: no preconceived idea came to impose any concern for representation of any kind; the lines organized themselves as they appeared and, so to speak, *by chance;* pure inspiration, it seems, presided over this way of painting, before it found in itself a model and reintegrated taste within its former purview. In any second, the painter could take a cinematographic snapshot of his thought and, as his thought was sometimes applied to the objects that surrounded him, he invented the collage which made it easy for him to use ready-made figures instantly available to his imagination. Whether in brush strokes or tobacco packages, painting has never been of a more fiery temper.

Let's admire the mad, the mediums who find some way to fix their most fugitive visions, as the man given to surrealism tends to do, with a slightly different motive.

We can consider, in this particular case, the plastic works of those we ordinarily called *mad* and *mediums* as perfectly comparable; they are presented schematically under two aspects:

— either the plastic elements are presented to the mind as complex and indivisible wholes and are reproduced as summarily as possible — a tree, a man. These elements are so to speak jotted down just as they rise to consciousness: a house, the horse with a crab mounted on top comes in, and the sun comes into the crab. That could just as well be written as seen; in any case, a rapid and rudimentary drawing can be perfectly appropriate for that kind of expression.

— or then, and this is where we are getting to a truly surrealist activity — the forms and the colors dispense with any object whatsoever, organizing themselves according to a law which escapes any premeditation, establishing and unestablishing itself just as it comes into sight. A good number of paintings by madmen or mediums show the strangest appearances and bear witness to the most imperceptible mental currents. You could put into an algebraic equation that such a painting is to x what the tale of a medium is to a surrealist text. Heavens!

But who will give us the marvelous drug that will permit us to realize x? Just imagine the jealousy of the painter who gets a glimpse of the shadows surrealist writing can bring forth! For the whole difficulty is not starting, but also *forgetting what has just been done,* or better, *ignoring it.* Closing your eyes, blindfolding them, forcing yourself just to look at one part of the canvas, all these ways of upsetting the usual orientation of sight are irrelevant and childish procedures. It is not a matter of mutilating a technique but of rendering it as inefficacious as possible.

Today, we cannot possibly imagine what a surrealist art would be without taking into account certain relations that look fortuitous but that we presume to be due to the omnipotence of a superior intellectual law, the very law of surrealism.

Who exactly is this man we see lazily making his way up the steps of a staircase that isn't going anywhere? Who is this Man Ray, our friend, who is making with sensitized paper things of the most incredible elegance from the most ordinary things? Who is this chalk-white woman who is passing by in a car among those men in top hats?

18.12 SALVADOR DALÍ

Photography, Pure Creation of the Mind

1927

Painting is not photography, the painters say.
But photography is not photography either.
RENÉ CREVEL

Clear objectivity of the little camera. Objective crystal. Glass of real poetry.

The hand ceases to intervene. Subtle physico-chemical harmonies. Plate sensitive to the softest adjustments.

The perfect, exact mechanism demonstrates, by its economical structure, the joy of its poetic functioning.

A nimble ease, an imperceptible tilt, a wise translation in the spatial sense, so that—under the pressure of tepid fingertips and the nickel-plated spring—the spiritual bird of the thirty-six greys and forty new means of inspiration can emerge from the pure, crystalline objectivity of the glass.

When hands cease to intervene, the mind starts to know the absence of murky digital flowerings; inspiration is extricated from the technical process, which is entrusted solely to the unconscious calculations of the machine.

The new method of spiritual creation which is photography, puts all the stages of the production of the poetic act in their right place.

Let's trust in the new imaginative means, born from simple objective transpositions. Only the things we are capable of dreaming lack originality. The miracle is produced with the same precision needed for banking and commercial operations. Spiritualism is another thing altogether . . .

Let's be satisfied with the immediate miracle of opening our eyes and being skilful in the apprenticeship of looking properly. Shutting your eyes is an anti-poetic way of perceiving resonances. Henri Rousseau knew how to look better than the Impressionists. Remember that they looked only with their eyes almost shut, and merely grasped the music of objectivity, which was the only kind that could filter through their half-closed eyelids.

Vermeer of Delft was another thing altogether. His eyes are, in the history of looking, the case of maximum probity. With all the temptations, however, of light. Van der Meer, a new St. Antony, conserves the object intact with a totally photographic inspiration, the product of his humble and passionate sense of touch.

Knowing how to look is a completely new system of spiritual surveying. Knowing how to look is a way of inventing. And no invention has been as pure as that created by the anaesthetic stare of the extremely clear eye, free from eyelashes and the Zeiss: distilled and attentive, immune to the rosy flowering of conjunctivitis.

The camera has immediate practical possibilities, for new themes where painting necessarily remains only in the experience and understanding. Photography glides with continual imagination over new events, which in the pictorial realm have only possibilities for being signs.

The photographic crystal can caress the cold delicacy of white lavatories; follow the sleepy slowness of aquaria, analyse the most subtle articulations of electrical equipment with the unreal precision of its own magic. In painting, on the other hand, if you want to paint a medusa, it is absolutely necessary to depict a guitar or a harlequin playing the clarinet.

The new organic possibilities of photography!

Let us recall that photo by Man Ray—the portrait of the late Juan Gris put in rhythm with a banjo—and think about this new organic method, a pure result of the limpid mechanical process, undiscoverable through paths which are not those of the clearest photographic creation.

Photographic imagination! More agile and faster in discoveries than the murky subconscious processes!

A simple change of scale causes unusual similarities, and existing—although undreamt of—analogies.

A clear portrait of an orchid poetically merges with the photographed inside of a tiger's mouth, where the sun plays in a thousand shadows with the physiological architecture of the larynx.

Photography, grasping the most subtle and uncontrollable poetry!

In the big, limpid eye of a cow we can see deformed, in the spherical sense, a miniature, very white post-machinist landscape, precise enough to define a sky where diminutive, luminous little clouds sail by.

New objects, photographed amidst the agile typography of advertisements!

All recently manufactured machines, as fresh as roses, offer their unknown metallic temperatures to the ethereal spring air of photography.

Photography, pure creation of the mind!

18.13 AIMÉ CÉSAIRE

In the Guise of a Literary Manifesto

1942

No use stiffening up when we go by, those faces of yours like pale treponema, more buttery than the moon,

No use wasting your pity on us, those indecent smiles like cysts full of pus.

Cops and coppers
Verbalize the great half-baked treason, the great crackpot challenge and the satanic impulse, the insolent nostalgic flow of April moons, green lights, yellow fever . . .

Because we hate you, you and your reasonableness, we stick to our precocious dementia, our flaming folly, our stubborn cannibalism.

Let's count:
madness with memory
madness shouting
madness seeing
madness on the make.

Enough of this taste of tasteless corpse!

Not shipwreckers. Not ditch diggers. Not hyenas. Not chacals.
And you know the rest:

That 2 and 2 make 5
That the forest is mewing
That the tree is taking its chestnuts from the fire
That the sky is smoothing down its beard.
Etc., etc. . . .

Who and what are we? What a fine question!
Haters. Builders. Traitors. Voodoo priests. Especially. For we want all the devils
Yesterday's, today's

The iron-collared, the ones with a hoe
Indicted, prohibited, escaped like slaves

not to forget the ones from the slave ship . . .
So we're singing.

We're singing the poisonous flowers springing up in the crazed prairies; the
skies of love streaked with embolisms; the epileptic mornings; the white
blaze of the abysmal sands, the wreckage floating down the nights stricken
with the lightning of savage smells.

What can I do about it?

You have to begin.
Begin what?

The only thing in the world worth beginning.
The *End of the World*, of course!

Tart
oh tart of the frightful fall
when the new steel and the living asphalt grow
tart oh tart
where the air rusts in great plaques of bad delight
when the sanious water sweeps the great solar cheeks

I hate you.

The slow mill crushes the cane
the tardy ox doesn't swallow the mill

Is that absurd enough for you?

The bare feet are stuck in the asphalt
the soft asphalt can't set fire to
a pine forest of bare feet.

In truth, it doesn't make sense.

You still see madras cloths around the women's loins, rings in their ears, smiles on their mouths, children on their breasts, and all the rest: ENOUGH OF THIS SCANDAL!

So there are the horsemen of the Apocalypse

So there are the funeral directors without funerals

the men of the last judgment without judgment.

Uselessly, you keep chewing over the same pitiful consolation in your tepid throat, that we are murmurers of words.

Uselessly: when the fulgurant poetic sentence
crosses the flossy sky,
oh, you simpleton
your feverish apoplexy and your blindness, and your paralysis
and your contractions
and your racing pulse

have given you the luminous lie!

Words! when we arrange sections of this world, when we wed whole continents in delirium, when we force our way through smoking doors, words! ah yes, words, but words of fresh blood, words that are tidal waves and erysipelae and paludisms, and lavae, and brush fires, and flesh aflame, and towns torched . . .

Know this:

I never play except in the year one thousand

I never play except in the Great Fear

Adapt yourself to me. I will never adapt myself to you.

Sometimes you see me with a great mental gesture snap at a cloud too red, or a caress of the rain, or a prelude of the wind, don't get too calm:

I force the yolk sack separating me from myself.
I force the great waters which belt me about with blood

It's me, nothing but myself choosing my seat on the last train of the last
surge of the last tidal wave,

It's me, nothing but me

coming to speech in the final anguish

It's me, oh! nothing but me

assuring myself in my gourd
of the first drops of virginal milk!

You have met, gaunt under the moon sometimes, a great baying of the ma-
rauding dog.
Came no warning of the ions of ashen light, but simply a great sniffing and
a great snarling hardened in the thickness of air. And you were suddenly
taken in a liquid net of summary resayings, of rocketrisings without light,
the fires of the herd, the laurels pouring out benzoin. . . . And you will have
trembled unspeakably.

So our hell will grab you by the collar.
Our hell will set your thin bones to bending.
Your black grouse graces won't exorcise anything.

That's enough. I won't have forgotten you.

I am a corpse with closed eyes, tapping our a frenetic morse code on the thin
roof of Death

I am a corpse exuberating from the sleppy riverbank of its members a steel
cry not to be confused.

You
oh you covering up your ears

It's to you, it's for you I am speaking, for you who will spread apart tomorrow weeping the peacethick peace of your smiles,
for you who one morning will stick all my words in your knapsack and set off, in the hour when the children of fear are still asleep,

along the oblique path of fleeing and monsters.

18.14 SUZANNE CÉSAIRE

The Domain of the Marvelous

1941

No longer is it a matter of the narrow roads where traditional beauty is offered in its clarity and obviousness to the admiration of the crowds. The crowds were taught the victory of intelligence over the world and the submission of the forces of nature to man.

Now it is a question of seizing and admiring a new art which leaves humankind in its true condition, fragile and dependent, and which nevertheless, in the very spectacle of things ignored or silenced, opens unsuspected possibilities to the artist.

And this is the domain of the strange, the Marvelous, and the fantastic, a domain scorned by people of certain inclinations. Here is the freed image, dazzling and beautiful, with a beauty that could not be more unexpected and overwhelming. Here are the poet, the painter, and the artist, presiding over the metamorphoses and the inversions of the world under the sign of hallucination and madness. . . . Here at last the world of nature and things makes direct contact with the human being who is again in the fullest sense spontaneous and natural. Here at last is the true communion and the true knowledge, chance mastered and recognized, the mystery now a friend and helpful.

18.15 SUZANNE CÉSAIRE
Surrealism and Us

1943

Many believe that surrealism is dead. Many have declared it so in writing. What childishness! Surrealism's activity today extends throughout the entire world, and it remains livelier and bolder than ever. André Breton may regard the period between the two wars with pride, and he can affirm that an increasingly immense, indeed boundless, "beyond" has opened up to the mode of expression he created more than twenty years ago.

If the entire world is struck by the radiance of French poetry just as the most terrible disaster in French history crushes France, it is in part because André Breton's powerful voice has not been silenced; it is also because everywhere—in New York, Brazil, Mexico, Argentina, Cuba, Canada, and Algiers—other voices also resound: voices that would not be what they are (either in timbre or resonance) without surrealism. In reality, today as twenty years ago, surrealism can claim the glory of being at the extreme point of life's super-taut bow.

Surrealism lives! And it is young, ardent, and revolutionary. In 1943 surrealism surely remains, as always, an activity whose aim is to explore and express systematically—and thus, neutralize—the forbidden zones of the human mind, an activity which desperately tries to give humankind the means of reducing the old antinomies, those "true alembics of suffering," and the only force enabling us to recover "this unique, original faculty, traces of which are retained by the primitive and the child, and which lifts the curse of the insurmountable barrier between inner and outer worlds."

But surrealism, further proving its vitality, has evolved—or, rather, *blossomed*. When Breton created surrealism, the most urgent task was to free the mind from the shackles of absurd logic and of so-called reason. But in 1943, when freedom herself is threatened throughout the world, surrealism, which has never for one instant ceased to remain in the service of the largest and most thoroughgoing human emancipation, can now be summed up completely in one single, magic word: *freedom.*

> The surrealist cause, in art as in life, is the cause of freedom itself. Today more than ever to speak abstractly in the name of freedom or to praise it in conventional terms is to serve it poorly. To light the world freedom must become flesh, and to this end must always be reflected and recreated in the *word.*

Thus speaks Breton. The demand for freedom. The necessity of total purity: that is the Saint-Just aspect of Breton—hence his "no thanks" refusals, so brutally condemned by those who side with compromise.

To those who periodically ask why certain schisms have arisen in the Surrealist Movement, why certain interdictions have been brusquely issued, I believe I can reply in all honesty that those who were weeded out in the process had, in some more or less manifest way, broken faith with freedom. Since freedom is revered in its pure state by surrealists—that is to say, extolled in all its forms—there are, of course, many ways to break faith with it. In my opinion, it was for example breaking faith to return, as did certain former surrealists, to *fixed* forms in poetry, when it has been demonstrated, especially in the French language—the exceptional radiance of French poetry since romanticism permits a generalization of this viewpoint—that the quality of lyric expression has benefited from nothing so much as the will to be liberated from outmoded rules: Rimbaud, Lautréamont, the Mallarmé of *Un Coup de dés* [A Throw of the Dice], the most important symbolists (Maeterlinck, Saint-Pol-Roux), Apollinaire's "conversation-poems."

And this would be just as true in the same epoch, true for painting. In place of the preceding names, it would suffice to cite those of Van Gogh, Seurat, Rousseau, Matisse, Picasso, Duchamp. It was also breaking faith with freedom to give up expressing oneself personally (and by that very fact dangerously, always) outside the strict framework in which a "party" wishes to contain you, even if it is thought to be the party of freedom (loss of the feeling of uniqueness). It was equally erroneous for some to believe that they would always be so much themselves that they could with impunity throw in their lot with anyone at all (loss of the feeling of dependency). Freedom is at once madly desirable and quite fragile, which gives her the right to be jealous.

Surrealism is thus as intransigent, as uncompromising as freedom itself, and this, moreover, is the very condition of its fruitfulness. And we see Breton, in his latest and most moving research, not hesitating to venture into the vast fields of the unknown that surrealism has presented to human audacity. What does Breton ask of the most clear-sighted spirits of our time? Nothing less than the courage to embark on an adventure which—who knows?—may well prove fatal, but from which one can hope—and that is what is essential—to attain the total conquest of the mind.

An epoch such as ours justifies all journeys for the sake of the journey itself, after the fashion of Bergerac and Gulliver, particularly if these journeys constitute a challenge to conventional modes of thinking, the failure of which is only too obvious. And the journey to which I invite you today does not exclude every chance, after certain detours, of arriving somewhere, perhaps even in lands more reasonable than the one we leave behind.

Surrealism lives, intensely and magnificently, having found and perfected an effective method of knowledge. Therein lies surrealism's dynamism. And it is precisely this sense of movement that has always kept it in the forefront of cultural and intellectual life, infinitely sensitive to the upheavals and disruptions of an epoch which is the "scourge of balance."

"With all due respect to some impatient gravediggers," writes Breton,

> I think I understand a little better than they do what the demise of surrealism would mean. It would mean the birth of a new movement with an even greater power of emancipation. Moreover, because of that same dynamic force that we continue to place above all, my best friends and I would make it a point of honor to rally around such a movement immediately.

Such is surrealist activity, a total activity: the only one capable of liberating humankind by revealing the unconscious, an activity that will help free the peoples of the world as it illuminates the blind myths that have led them up till now.

* * *

And now let's return to us.

We know how things stand, here in Martinique. Dizzyingly, the arrow of history points to our human task. A society corrupted by crime at its foundations, currently propped up by injustice and hypocrisy, and, in consequence of its unhappy consciousness, terrified of its own becoming: such a society must perish morally, historically, and necessarily. And from the powerful bombs and other weaponry of war the modern world has placed at our disposal, our boldness has chosen surrealism, which in our times offers the surest chance of success.

One result is already evident. Not for one instant during these hard years of Vichy domination has the image of freedom been completely obliterated here—and this we owe to surrealism. We are glad to have sustained this image in the face of those who believed they had rubbed it out forever.

Blinded by their ignorance, they could not see freedom laughing insolently, aggressively across our pages. When they did realize it, they succumbed to cowardice, timidity, and shame.

Thus, far from contradicting, diluting, or diverting our revolutionary attitude toward life, surrealism strengthens it. It nourishes an impatient strength within us, endlessly reinforcing the massive army of refusals.

And I am also thinking of tomorrow.

Millions of black hands will hoist their terror across the furious skies of world war. Freed from a long benumbing slumber, the most disinherited of all peoples will rise up from plains of ashes.

Our surrealism will supply this rising people with a punch from its very depths. Our surrealism will enable us to finally transcend the sordid antinomies of the present: whites/Blacks, Europeans/Africans, civilized/savages —at last rediscovering the magic power of the mahoulis, drawn directly from living sources. Colonial idiocy will be purified in the welder's blue flame. We shall recover our value as metal, our cutting edge of steel, our unprecedented communions.

*   *   *

Surrealism, tightrope of our hope.

18.16 Matta [Matta Echaurren]

On Emotion

1954

Art serves to arouse one's intuition to the emotion latent in everything around one, and to show up the emotional architecture which people need in order to be and to live together.

Important emotion is a menace to those who live for their own selfish interest; so they have invented the philanthropic lie, and with that philanthropic lie have reduced the artist to the condition of a hostage. They have instituted an "Art Police," a police which operates against deep-rooted human emotion.

I identified myself with this hostage. The philanthropist-masters' comfort is menaced and they "shoot" the hostage.

This new poet-hostage is always conspiring against their selfishness.

To be this hostage one must put poetry at the center of one's life.

True poetry is deeply human. And the true poet is stubborn about not forgetting that "man" is at the center of everything and that all deviation towards anti-human action should be denounced.

To revive the kind of man that a poet always was. (Byron died for the liberty of the Greeks.)

I know that an artist will only be actual if his work enters the two-way traffic of receiving from his people the consciousness of needs they have detected in themselves, and, as an artist, charges this consciousness with an intuition of important emotion, thus sending it back to widen their picture of reality.

For the conscious painter the "subject" is the same as for Cimabue—to make the man of his time think with sentiment.

18.17 LÉOPOLD SÉDAR SENGHOR

Speech and Image

An African Tradition of the Surreal

1965

Speech seems to us the main instrument of thought, emotion and action. There is no thought or emotion without a verbal image, no free action without first a project in thought. This is even more true among peoples who disdained the written word. This explains the power of speech in Africa. The word, the spoken word is the expression *par excellence* of the life-force, of being in its fullness. God created the world through the Word. We shall see how later. For the human being, speech is the living and life-giving breath of man at prayer. It possesses a magical virtue, realizing the law of participation and, by its intrinsic power, creating the thing named. So that all the other arts are only specialized aspects of the great art of speech. In front of a picture made up of a tracery of geometrical forms in white and red representing a chorus of birds or a tree at sunrise, the artist explained: "These are wings, these are songs. These are birds."

The African languages are characterized first of all by the richness of their vocabulary. There are sometimes twenty different words for an object according to its form, weight, volume and colour, and as many for an action according to whether it is single or repeated, weakly or intensely performed, just beginning or coming to an end. In Fulani, nouns are divided into twenty-one genders which are not related to sex. The classification is based sometimes on the meaning of the words or the phonetic qualities and sometimes on the grammatical category to which they belong. Most significant in this respect is the verb. On the same root in Wolof can be constructed more than twenty verbs expressing different shades of meaning, and at least as many derivative nouns. While modern Indo-European languages emphasize the abstract notion of time, African languages emphasize the *aspect*, the concrete way in which the action of the verb takes place. These are essentially *concrete* languages. In them words are always pregnant with images. Under their value as signs, their sense value shows through.

The African image is not then an image by equation but an image by *analogy*, a surrealist image. Africans do not like straight lines and false *mots justes*. Two and two do not make four, but five, as Aimé Césaire has told us. The object does not mean what it represents but what it suggests, what it creates. The Elephant is Strength, the Spider is Prudence; Horns are the

Moon and the Moon is Fecundity. Every representation is an image, and the image, I repeat, is not an equation but a *symbol,* an ideogramme. Not only the figuration of the image but also its material . . . stone, earth, copper, gold, fibre—and also its line and colour. All language which does not tell a story bores them, or rather, Africans do not understand such language. The astonishment of the first Europeans when they found that the "natives" did not understand their pictures or even the logic of their arguments!

I have spoken of the surrealist image. But as you would suppose, African surrealism is different from European surrealism. European surrealism is empirical. African surrealism is mystical and metaphysical. André Breton writes in *Signe Ascendant:* "The poetic analogy (meaning the European surrealist analogy) differs functionally from the mystical analogy in that it does not presuppose, beyond the visible world, an invisible world which is striving to manifest itself. It proceeds in a completely empirical way." In contrast, the African surrealist analogy presupposes and manifests the hierarchized universe of life-forces.

PART 19

Thingism and Machinism

An impulse rather than a school, the concentration upon the object itself, seen as having an aesthetic value regardless of what it is used for or celebrated in, can be seen as Thingism. Edgar Allan Poe is perhaps its best spokesman, with his "Philosophy of Furniture" (19.1), only a partial spoof. Seemingly situated at the opposite pole, Giorgio de Chirico's Scuola Metafisica is clearly haunted by the poetry of objects: his trains and towers, his city squares and plazas, his gloves serving to cover no hand, his measuring instruments doing no measuring—all these speak as loudly of his obsessions with these objects as of any construction in which to place them.

In a sense, the Futurist obsession with trains as the conveyors of speed became, in the work of Umberto Boccioni for example, an obsession with the train itself. Just so, with the metaphysical adoration of the Modernist object, the thing itself takes on the aura of the metaphysical. *Das Ding an sich:* a whole branch of philosophy deals with this circling of the spirit around the thing—not for what it symbolizes or is used for, but in itself.

19.1 EDGAR ALLAN POE

The Philosophy of Furniture

1840

In the internal decoration, if not in the external architecture of their residences, the English are supreme. The Italians have but little sentiment beyond marbles and colours. In France, *meliora probant, deteriora sequuntur*— the people are too much a race of gadabouts to maintain those household proprieties of which, indeed, they have a delicate appreciation, or at least the elements of a proper sense. The Chinese and most of the eastern races have a warm but inappropriate fancy. The Scotch are *poor* decorists. The Dutch have, perhaps, an indeterminate idea that a curtain is not a cabbage. In Spain they are *all* curtains—a nation of hangmen. The Russians do not furnish. The Hottentots and Kickapoos are very well in their way. The Yankees alone are preposterous.

How this happens, it is not difficult to see. We have no aristocracy of blood, and having therefore as a natural, and indeed as an inevitable thing, fashioned for ourselves an aristocracy of dollars, the *display of wealth* has here to take the place and perform the office of the heraldic display in monarchical countries. By a transition readily understood, and which might have been as readily foreseen, we have been brought to merge in simple *show* our notions of taste itself.

To speak less abstractly. In England, for example, no mere parade of costly appurtenances would be so likely as with us, to create an impression of the beautiful in respect to the appurtenances themselves—or of taste as regards the proprietor:—this for the reason, first, that wealth is not, in England, the loftiest object of ambition as constituting a nobility; and secondly, that there, the true nobility of blood, confining itself within the strict limits of legitimate taste, rather avoids than affects that mere costliness in which a *parvenu* rivalry may at any time be successfully attempted.

The people *will* imitate the nobles, and the result is a thorough diffusion of the proper feeling. But in America, the coins current being the sole arms of the aristocracy, their display may be said, in general, to be the sole means of the aristocratic distinction; and the populace, looking always upward for models, are insensibly led to confound the two entirely separate ideas of magnificence and beauty. In short, the cost of an article of furniture has at length come to be, with us, nearly the sole test of its merit in a decorative point of view—and this test, once established, has led the way to many analogous errors, readily traceable to the one primitive folly.

There could be nothing more directly offensive to the eye of an artist than the interior of what is termed in the United States—that is to say, in Appalachia—a well-furnished apartment. Its most usual defect is a want of keeping. We speak of the keeping of a room as we would of the keeping of a picture—for both the picture and the room are amenable to those undeviating principles which regulate all varieties of art; and very nearly the same laws by which we decide on the higher merits of a painting, suffice for decision on the adjustment of a chamber.

A want of keeping is observable sometimes in the character of the several pieces of furniture, but generally in their colours or modes of adaptation to use. *Very* often the eye is offended by their inartistic arrangement. Straight lines are too prevalent—too uninterruptedly continued—or clumsily interrupted at right angles. If curved lines occur, they are repeated into unpleasant uniformity. By undue precision, the appearance of many a fine apartment is utterly spoiled.

Curtains are rarely well disposed, or well chosen in respect to other decorations. With formal furniture, curtains are out of place; and an extensive volume of drapery of any kind is, under any circumstance, irreconcilable with good taste—the proper quantum, as well as the proper adjustment, depending upon the character of the general effect.

Carpets are better understood of late than of ancient days, but we still very frequently err in their patterns and colours. The soul of the apartment is the carpet. From it are deduced not only the hues but the forms of all objects incumbent. A judge at common law may be an ordinary man; a good judge of a carpet *must be* a genius. Yet we have heard discoursing of carpets, with the air "*d'un mouton qui rêve,*" fellows who should not and who could not be entrusted with the management of their own *moustaches.* Every one knows that a large floor *may* have a covering of large figures, and that a small one *must* have a covering of small—yet this is not all the knowledge in the world. As regards texture, the Saxony is alone admissible. Brussels is the preterpluperfect tense of fashion, and Turkey is taste in its dying agonies. Touching pattern—a carpet should *not* be bedizzened out like a Riccaree Indian—all red chalk, yellow ochre, and cock's feathers. In brief—distinct grounds, and vivid circular or cycloid figures, *of no meaning,* are here Median laws. The abomination of flowers, or representations of well-known objects of any kind, should not be endured within the limits of Christendom. Indeed, whether on carpets, or curtains, or tapestry, or ottoman coverings, all upholstery of this nature should be rigidly Arabesque. As for those antique floor-cloths still occasionally seen in the dwellings of the rabble—cloths of huge, sprawling, and radiating devises, stripe-interspersed, and glorious with all hues, among which no ground is intelligible—these are but the wicked invention of a race of time-servers and money-lovers—children of Baal and worshippers of Mammon—Benthams, who, to spare thought and economize fancy, first cruelly invented the Kaleidoscope, and then established joint-stock companies to twirl it by steam.

Glare is a leading error in the philosophy of American household decoration—an error easily recognised as deduced from the perversion of taste just specified. We are violently enamoured of gas and of glass. The former is totally inadmissible within doors. Its harsh and unsteady light offends. No one having both brains and eyes will use it. A mild, or what artists term a cool light, with its consequent warm shadows, will do wonders for even an ill-furnished apartment. Never was a more lovely thought than that of the astral lamp. We mean, of course, the astral lamp proper—the lamp of Argand, with its original plain ground-glass shade, and its tempered and uniform moonlight rays. The cut-glass shade is a weak invention of the enemy. The eagerness with which we have adopted it, partly on account of its *flashiness,* but principally on account of its *greater cost,* is a good commentary on the proposition with which we began. It is not too much to say, that the deliberate employer of a cut-glass shade, is either radically deficient in taste, or blindly subservient to the caprices of fashion. The light proceeding from one of these gaudy abominations is unequal, broken, and painful. It alone is sufficient to mar a world of good effect in the furniture subjected to its influence. Female loveliness, in especial, is more than one-half disenchanted beneath its evil eye.

In the matter of glass, generally, we proceed upon false principles. Its leading feature is *glitter*—and in that one word how much of all that is detestable do we express! Flickering, unquiet lights, are *sometimes* pleasing—to children and idiots always so—but in the embellishment of a room they should be scrupulously avoided. In truth, even strong *steady* lights are inadmissible. The huge and unmeaning glass chandeliers, prism-cut, gas-lighted, and without shade, which dangle in our most fashionable drawing-rooms, may be cited as the quintessence of all that is false in taste or preposterous in folly.

The rage for *glitter*—because its idea has become, as we before observed, confounded with that of magnificence in the abstract—has led us, also, to the exaggerated employment of mirrors. We line our dwellings with great British plates, and then imagine we have done a fine thing. Now the slightest thought will be sufficient to convince any one who has an eye at all, of the ill effect of numerous looking-glasses, and especially of large ones. Regarded apart from its reflection, the mirror presents a continuous, flat, colourless, unrelieved surface,—a thing always and obviously unpleasant. Considered as a reflector, it is potent in producing a monstrous and odious uniformity: and the evil is here aggravated, not in merely direct proportion with the augmentation of its sources, but in a ratio constantly increasing. In fact, a room with four or five mirrors arranged at random, is, for all purposes of artistic show, a room of no shape at all. If we add to this evil, the attendant glitter upon glitter, we have a perfect farrago of discordant and displeasing effects. The veriest bumpkin, on entering an apartment so bedizzened, would be instantly aware of something wrong, although he might be altogether unable to assign a cause for his dissatisfaction. But let the same person be led into a room tastefully furnished, and he would be startled into an exclamation of pleasure and surprise.

It is an evil growing out of our republican institutions, that here a man of large purse has usually a very little soul which he keeps in it. The corruption of taste is a portion or a pendant of the dollar-manufacture. As we grow rich, our ideas grow rusty. It is, therefore, not among *our* aristocracy that we must look (if at all, in Appalachia), for the spirituality of a British *boudoir*. But we have seen apartments in the tenure of Americans of modern means, which, in negative merit at least, might vie with any of the *or-molu'd* cabinets of our friends across the water. Even *now,* there is present to our mind's eye a small and not ostentatious chamber with whose decorations no fault can be found. The proprietor lies asleep on a sofa—the weather is cool—the time is near midnight: we will make a sketch of the room during his slumber.

It is oblong—some thirty feet in length and twenty-five in breadth— a shape affording the best (ordinary) opportunities for the adjustment of furniture. It has but one door—by no means a wide one—which is at one end of the parallelogram, and but two windows, which are at the other. These latter are large, reaching down to the floor—have deep recesses— and open on an Italian *veranda.* Their panes are of a crimson-tinted glass, set in rose-wood framings, more massive than usual. They are curtained within the recess, by a thick silver tissue adapted to the shape of the window, and hanging loosely in small volumes. Without the recess are curtains of an exceedingly rich crimson silk, fringed with a deep net-work of gold, and lined with silver tissue, which is the material of the exterior blind. There are no cornices; but the folds of the whole fabric (which are sharp rather than massive, and have an airy appearance), issue from beneath a broad entablature of rich giltwork, which encircles the room at the junction of the ceiling and walls. The drapery is thrown open also, or closed, by means of a thick rope of gold loosely enveloping it, and resolving itself readily into a knot; no pins or other such devices are apparent. The colours of the curtains and their fringe—the tints of crimson and gold—appear everywhere in profusion, and determine the *character* of the room. The carpet—of Saxony material—is quite half an inch thick, and is of the same crimson ground, relieved simply by the appearance of a gold cord (like that festooning the curtains) slightly relieved above the surface of the *ground,* and thrown upon it in such a manner as to form a succession of short irregular curves—one occasionally overlaying the other. The walls are prepared with a glossy paper of a silver gray tint, spotted with small Arabesque devices of a fainter hue of the prevalent crimson. Many paintings relieve the expanse of the paper. These are chiefly landscapes of an imaginative cast—such as the fairy grottoes of Stanfield, or the lake of the Dismal Swamp of Chapman. There are, nevertheless, three or four female heads, of an ethereal beauty—portraits in the manner of Sully. The tone of each picture is warm, but dark. There are no "brilliant effects." *Repose* speaks in all. Not one is of small size. Diminutive paintings give that *spotty* look to a room, which is the blemish of so many a fine work of Art overtouched. The frames are broad but not deep, and richly carved, without being *dulled* or filagreed. They have the whole lustre of burnished gold. They lie flat on the walls, and do not hang off with cords. The designs themselves are often seen to better advantage in this latter position, but the general appearance of the chamber is injured. But one mirror—and this not a very large one—is visible. In shape it is nearly circular—and it is hung so that a reflection of the person can be obtained from it in none of the ordinary sitting-places of the room. Two large low sofas of rosewood and crimson silk, gold-flowered, form the only seats, with the exception of two light conversation chairs, also of rose-wood. There is a pianoforte (rose-wood, also), without cover, and thrown open. An octagonal table, formed altogether of the richest gold-threaded marble, is placed near one of the sofas. This is also without cover—the drapery of the curtains has been thought sufficient. Four large and gorgeous Sèvres vases, in which bloom a profusion of sweet and vivid flowers, occupy the slightly rounded angles of the room. A tall candelabrum, bearing a small antique lamp with highly perfumed oil, is standing near the head of my sleeping friend. Some light and graceful hanging shelves, with golden edges and crimson silk cords with gold tassels, sustain two or three hundred magnificently bound books. Beyond these things, there is no furniture, if we except an Argand lamp, with a plain crimson-tinted ground-glass shade, which depends from the lofty vaulted ceiling by a single slender gold chain, and throws a tranquil but magical radiance over all.

19.2 SONIA DELAUNAY

The Future of Fashion

1931

Contemporary fashion does not reflect the direction of the art of this century.

Contemporary art has the courage to make a complete revolution and to start again on a new construction.

The art of our time is visual and constructive.

The craft of fashion is not yet constructive, but rather multiplies details and refinements. Instead of adapting the dress to the necessities of daily life, to the movements which it dictates, it complicates them, believing that it thereby satisfies the taste of the buyer or the exporter. For this reason skirts must be too narrow or too short or too long, and the skirt is not adapted to walking but walking to the skirt, which is nonsense.

Contemporary fashion ought to start from two principles: vital, unconscious, visual sensuality on the one hand, and the craft of fabrication on the other. Not inspiration derived from the past, but grappling with the subject as if everything begins anew each day. The future of fashion is very clear to me—there will be centers of creativity, laboratories of research dealing with the practical design of clothing in constant development parallel to the necessities of life. The investigation of the materials used and the simplification of their aesthetic conception will assume an ever-increasing importance. On these considered and executed foundations visuality and sensibility will have free play and engender their own fantasy.

The price of these perfected creations will reflect the value of the research of the product. They will be sold by industries which will themselves study lowering the costs of production by mass production and concern themselves with the expansion of sales.

In this way, fashion will democratize itself and this democratization can only be beneficial since it will raise the general standards of the industry.

It will also accomplish the abolition of the copy which is the real plague of fashion.

19.3 SONIA DELAUNAY
The Issue
1966

1. The issue is learning again how to paint and finding new means of doing it. Technical and plastic means.
2. Color liberated from descriptive, literary use; color grasped in all the richness of its own life.
3. A vision of infinite richness awaits the person who knows how to see the relations of colors, their contrasts and dissonances, and the impact of one color on another.
4. Add to this the essential element—Rhythm—which is its structure, movement based on number.
5. As in written poetry, it is not the aggregation of words which counts, but the mystery of creation which yields or does not yield feeling.

6. As in poetry, so with colors. It is the mystery of interior life which liberates, radiates, and communicates. Beginning there, a new language can be freely created.

19.4 FERNAND LÉGER

The Aesthetic of the Machine (*excerpt*)

1924

Modern man lives more and more in a preponderantly geometric order.

All human creation mechanical or industrial is dependent upon geometric intentions.

I wish especially to speak about the *prejudice* which blinds three-fourths of mankind and absolutely prevents them from ever attaining a free judgment of the ugly or beautiful phenomena by which they are surrounded. I believe that plastic beauty in general is totally independent of sentimental, descriptive, or imitative values. Every object, picture, piece of architecture, or ornamental organization has a value in itself; it is strictly absolute and independent of anything it may happen to represent.

Many individuals would be sensitive to the beauty of common objects, *without artistic intention,* if the preconceived notion of the *objet d'art* were not a bandage over their eyes. Bad visual education is the cause of this tendency, as is the modern mania for classification at all costs which categorizes individuals as well as tools. Men are *afraid of free consideration,* which, however, is the only possible spiritual state which permits reception of the beautiful. Victims of a critical, skeptical, and intellectual epoch, they strain themselves in the attempt to understand instead of relying upon their sensibility. "They have faith in the *fabricators of the arts*" because they are professionals. Titles and distinctions dazzle them and block their view. My aim here is to attempt to prove: that there is no such thing as Beauty that is catalogued, *hiérarchisée;* this is the worst possible error. Beauty is everywhere, in the arrangement of your pots and pans, on the white wall of your kitchen, more perhaps than in your eighteenth-century salon or in the official museum.

I would like therefore to speak about a new architectural order: *the architecture of the mechanical.* All of ancient and modern architecture, too, proceeds from geometric intentions.

In Greek art horizontal lines were made to dominate. It influenced the entire French seventeenth century. The Romanesque: vertical lines. The Gothic realized an equilibrium that was often perfect between the play of curves and of straight lines; it even arrived at that astonishing thing—a mobile architecture. There are Gothic façades that vibrate like a dynamic painting; this is the result of an interplay of complementary and contrasting lines.

One can assert this: a machine or a manufactured object may be beautiful when the relation of the lines which define its volume are balanced in an order corresponding to those of preceding architectures. We are not, then, in the presence of an intrinsically new phenomenon, but simply of an architectural manifestation like those of the past.

Where the question becomes more delicate is when we envisage all the consequences, that is, the *purposes* of mechanical creation. If the objectives of preceding architectural monuments were the predominance of the Beautiful over the useful, it is undeniable that, in the mechanical order, the dominant aim is *utility*, strictly utility. Everything is directed toward utility with the greatest possible severity. *The tendency toward utility does not, however, impede the accession to a state of beauty.*

The case of the evolution of the automobile form is a striking example of my point; it is even a curious fact that the more the machine perfects its utilitarian functions, the more beautiful it becomes.

That is to say, when vertical lines predominated in the beginning, contrary to its purpose, it was ugly—one looked for the horse. It was called a horseless carriage. But when, with the need for swiftness, it became lower and longer, when, in consequence, horizontal lines balanced by curves became dominant, it became a perfect whole logically organized for its end. It was beautiful.

But we must not conclude from this example of the relationship between beauty and utility in the auto that perfection of utility necessarily implies the perfection of beauty. I cannot deny that it may even be the contrary. I have laid eyes upon, but not remembered, frequent examples of the destruction of beauty by emphasis on the utilitarian.

Chance alone presides over the appearance of beauty in the manufactured object.

The Object Is Poetics

1962

The relationship between man and object is not at all limited to possession or use. No, that would be too simple. It's much worse.

Objects are outside the soul, of course; and yet, they are also ballast in our heads.

The relationship is thus in the accusative.

*   *   *

Man is a curious body whose center of gravity is not in himself.

Our soul is transitive. It needs an object that affects it, immediately, like a direct complement.

It is a matter of the most serious relationship (not at all with the verb *to have* but with the verb *to be*).

The artist, more than any other man, bears the burden, reacts.

*   *   *

But what, luckily, is *being*, after all? Only a succession of ways of being. There are as many objects. As many as blinkings of an eyelid.

Furthermore, becoming our object, an object concerns us, we have also embraced it, discovered it. Thank God, it's a matter of reciprocal "judgment"; and just as soon, the artist's goal is in sight.

Yes, only the artist, then, knows how to handle it.

He stops looking, reaches his goal.

The object also reacts.

Truth takes off again, undamaged.

The metamorphosis has occurred.

*   *   *

Were we only a body, we would undoubtedly be in a state of equilibrium with nature.

But our soul is on the same side of the scale as we are.

Heavy or light, I cannot tell.

Memory, imagination, sudden reactions, a growing heaviness; still, we have speech (or some other means of expression); each word that we pronounce relieves us. In *writing*, it even reaches the other side.

Whether heavy or light, I cannot say, but we need a counterweight.

*   *   *

Man is just a heavy ship, a heavy bird, on the edge of an abyss.

We feel it.

Each "battibaleno" confirms it. Our eyelids beat like the wings of a bird, to keep us steady.

Sometimes at the crest of a wave, sometimes ready to sink.

Eternal vagabonds, at least as long as we're alive.

But the world is peopled with objects. On its shores, we see their infinite crowd, their gathering, even though they are indistinct and vague.

Nevertheless, that is enough to reassure us. Because we also feel that all of them, according to our fancy, one after the other, may become our point of docking, the bollard upon which we rest.

It needs only be the proper weight.

Then, rather than our looking at it, it is up to our hands—let them spin out the line.

*   *   *

As I said, it needs only the proper weight.

Most of them do not make the weight.

Most often, man only grasps his emanations, his ghosts. Such are subjective objects.

He only waltzes with them, and they all sing the same song; then he flies away with them or sinks.

Therefore, we must choose true objects, constantly objecting to our own desires. Objects that we would select again and again, and not as a matter of decor or milieu; rather like our spectators, our judges; without our being, of course, either dancers or clowns.

Finally to have our secret council.

And thus decorate our domestic temple:

I suppose that each one of us, as long as we exist, recognizes his own Beauty.

It keeps to the center, untouched.

Everything is in order around it.

It remains intact.

Fountain in our patio.

19.6 GIORGIO DE CHIRICO

Statues, Furniture, and Generals

1968

The world is full of daemons.
HERACLITUS OF EPHESUS

When walking through a museum of antique sculpture and coming across a
deserted room we often receive the impression that the statues take on a new
appearance. A statue on the façade of a palace, or in a temple, as opposed
to a garden or a public place, reveals different metaphysical characteristics;
on top of a palace against the southern sky it acquires a Homeric quality, a
sort of severe and distant joy, mingled with melancholy. In public places its
appearance comes as a surprise, especially if its pedestal is low, for then it
seems to merge into the swirling of the crowd and of everyday town life.

In a museum a statue looks different, and then it is its phantomatic appearance that strikes us, an appearance like that of people suddenly noticed
in a room we had at first thought to be empty.

The lines of the walls, floor and ceiling separate the statue from the exterior world: it is no longer a figure destined to mingle with nature, or with
the beauty of a landscape or to complete the aesthetic harmony of an architectural construction. It appears in its most solitary aspect and becomes a
ghost that appears before us and surprises us.

And yet a statue is not destined always to stand in a place enclosed by
well-defined lines. In ancient times statues were to be seen everywhere: in
and outside palaces and temples, in gardens and towns, in harbours and
the courtyards of houses.

We have long been accustomed to seeing statues in museums, and the appearances of statues standing in the above-mentioned places has long been
known and often exploited by poets as well as painters. To discover newer
and more mysterious aspects we must have access to new combinations.
For example: a statue in a room, whether it be alone or in the company of
living people, could give us a new emotion if it were made in such a way that
its feet rested on the floor and not on a base. The same impression could
be produced by a statue sitting in a *real* armchair or leaning against a *real*
window.

The furniture to which we have been accustomed since our childhood awakens in us feelings with which many of us are familiar. And yet as far as I

know furniture is not credited with the power of being able to awaken ideas of any particular strangeness within us. For some time I have known from experience that this is often possible.

The reader may have noticed the singular appearance of beds, mirror-fronted wardrobes, armchairs, divans, and tables when one comes across them unexpectedly in a street in the midst of unaccustomed surroundings, as happens when people are moving house, or in areas where dealers show their merchandise on the pavement. The pieces of furniture then appear in a new light; they are reclothed in a strange solitude, a great intimacy grows between them, and one could say that a strange happiness hovers in the narrow space they occupy on the pavement in the midst of the fevered life of the town and the hasty comings and going of men. An immense and strange happiness is radiated by this blessed and mysterious little island against which the thundering waves of the raging sea crash in vain. One can imagine that if a passer-by somewhere down there in the crowd in the town, where people mill in ever greater numbers and the roar of man's activity and obsessive work is even more intense, if such a passer-by were suddenly to be seized by an indescribable terror and panic, like Orestes pursued by the Furies, or a deposed tyrant fleeing from the unleashed anger of his rebelling people, and were to seek refuge in the little island formed by the furniture displayed on the pavement and let himself sink into an armchair in their midst, then he would suddenly find himself sheltered from all the persecutions of gods and men, and could contemplate the thundering of the clouds or the wrath of an unleashed mob, as a Sunday stroller in the zoo contemplates the cruel tiger gnawing angrily and in vain at the bars of his cage.

Furniture, removed from the atmosphere of our rooms and shown outside, awakens in us an emotion that also reveals a new aspect of the street in which it stands.

The effect of furniture placed in deserted countryside, in the midst of infinite Nature, is also very profound: like an armchair, a divan and chairs grouped together on a Greek plain, or on the traditionless prairies of distant America.

And by contrast the countryside surrounding the furniture reveals to us an aspect of itself that we did not know.

Furniture abandoned in the midst of great Nature: this is innocence, tenderness, and sweetness in the midst of blind and destructive forces, children and pure virgins in a circus full of famished lions; protected by their innocence they are there, distant and solitary. And in the same way we see great armchairs and large divans on the shore of the roaring sea, or at the bottom of valleys surrounded by high mountains.

But these are only a few of the impressions and emotions that such things can impart. There are others even more solitary and mysterious. The furniture in the street is, as I said, the temple into which Orestes flings himself. On the threshold of these temples the Furies come impotent to a halt, and in the boredom of the wait they finally fall asleep and snore.

For some time now I have been obsessed by the appearance of such furniture left standing outside houses, and in some of my recent paintings I have tried to express the emotion I feel.

I find a reflection of all these emotions in this strange image expressed by the poet Jean Cocteau: "In this landscape we saw two screens and a chair. It was the opposite of a ruin. Fragments of a palace of the future."

The funerals of senior officers, generals, field-marshals, etc., have always made a very strange impression on me. . . . Above all at the moment when the body of the dead man is still in the house, whilst below, in the street, the cortège is being formed amidst the manœuvres of a military or marine detachment; the arrival of the civil servants and dignitaries, the movement of the crowd, etc., all this has always made a very deep and mysterious impression upon me. I imagine that the burial of a king, or a prince, or a pope would have the same effect on me.

I think the origin of this must reside in the fact that all these characters are basically phantoms. This phantomlike nature appears even more when they mingle with the life of the crowd, for they seem to belong to another element, and to find themselves there due only to a strange combination of enigmatic circumstances. And so, when we are present at their funerals what strikes us above all is the idea of the *death of a phantom*. We think: a phantom is dead, and men—who did not know him—come to honour and mourn him!

And yet painting concerns us as much for its material and craft side as for its enigmatic and disturbing aspects.

The one side enriches the other and makes painting worthy of existence. Painting demonstrates not only the enigmatic and the disturbing, but also the lyrical and consoling, and it is good that it should be so, otherwise we would be forced to leave our studios and dedicate ourselves to pure meditation, as did Socrates Deliomachos on the memorable night that preceded the battle.

The Futurist Manifesto of the Italian Hat

1933

The indispensable and longed for revolution in Italian men's attire was initiated on September 11, 1914, with the celebrated manifesto *The Antineutral Suit* penned by the great Futurist painter Giacomo Balla.

This synthetic, dynamic, agile suit with white, red, and green sections was worn by the free-word Futurist Francesco Cangiullo in the patriotic demonstrations that were followed by violent scuffles in the squares and related arrests, instigated by the Roman Futurists, and led by Marinetti, against the neutralist professors of the University of Rome (December 11–12, 1914).

We Futurists once again take up the lead in the clothing revolution, secure in our victory, guaranteed by the ever proven creative power of our race. While a comprehensive manifesto is being prepared by Futurists specially chosen for the task, today we launch one devoted to the Italian hat.

The world preeminence of the Italian hat was absolute for a long time. Recently, for love of foreign things and misunderstood hygiene, many Italians have taken up the American and German way of the bare head. The decline of the hat, which impoverished its market and prevented any possible improvements, has damaged the masculine look, amputating the profile and substituting for the severed part, the stupidest savagery of mops of hair, which are hardly aggressive, virile, or smart.

The combatants of Vittorio Veneto, of the squad activities in the Italian squares and of the March on Rome, whose heroism has surpassed that of the Romans, must not copy the cultural fashions of centuries ago and in a climate that has certainly changed. The young athletic Italians, victorious in Los Angeles, must now also overcome this barbaric habit that derives from a foolish sentimentality toward history.

Affirming, therefore the aesthetic necessity of the hat

1. We condemn the Nordic use of black and of neutral colors that give the wet, snowy, foggy streets of the city the appearance of a stagnant muddy melancholy, as if it were raining tortoises and chunks of stone swept along by torrents of brown.
2. We condemn the types of traditional headgear that jar with the speed and utilitarian aesthetic of our great mechanical civilization, as for ex-

ample, the pretentious top hat that hinders swiftness of foot, and attracts funerals like a magnet.

In August, in the Italian squares flooded by dazzling light and torrid silence, the black or gray hat of the passerby floats along sadly, like dung.

Color! We need color to compete with the Italian sun.

3. We propose the Futurist functionality of the hat, which until now has done little or nothing for man. From now on it must illuminate him, signal to him, take care of him, defend him, speed him up, slow him down, etc.

We will create the following types of hat, which through aesthetic, hygienic, and functional perfection, will serve, complete, or correct the ideal Italian masculine figure with emphases on variety, ferocity, dynamic momentum, and lyricism indebted to the new style of Mussolini: (1) speed hat (for everyday use); (2) night hat (for evening); (3) sumptuous hat (for parading); (4) aerial-sportive hat; (5) sun hat; (6) rain hat; (7) mountaineering hat; (8) marine hat; (9) defense hat; (10) poetic hat; (11) publicity hat; (12) simultaneous hat; (13) plastic hat; (14) tactile hat; (15) illuminated-signal hat; (16) gramophone hat; (17) radiotelephonic hat; (18) therapeutic hat (resin, camphor, menthol, with a screen that moderates the cosmic waves); (19) automatic greeting hat (through a system of infrared rays); (20) an intelligence imparting hat for the idiots who criticize this manifesto.

They will be made in felt, velvet, straw, cork, light metals, glass, celluloid, agglomerations, fur, sponge, fiber, neon tubes, etc., alone or combined.

The polychromy of these hats will give to the sunlit squares the flavor of immense fruit dishes and the luxury of huge jewelry stores. The night streets will be perfumed and illuminated by melodious currents, which will finally kill off the age-old fondness for moonlight.

So will emerge the ideal hat—a work of Italian art, both uplifting and multipurpose, which, while intensifying and propagating the beauty of the race, will impose one of our most important national industries once again upon the world.

Given that our beautiful peninsula is the byway for tourists of every nation—they even come to visit bareheaded, if that is their pleasure—we will welcome them with our customary gentility. But we will yank the new Italian hat over their heads, to show them that there is nothing in common anymore between the servility of the ciceroni a hundred years ago and the fierce inventive originality of the fascist Futurists of today.

F. T. MARINETTI, FRANCESCO MONARCHI,

ENRICO PRAMPOLINI, MINO SOMENZI

19.8 VOLT [VINCENZO FANI]
Futurist Manifesto of Women's Fashion
1920

Women's fashion has always been more or less Futurist. Fashion: the female equivalent of Futurism. Speed, novelty, courage of creation. Greenish yellow bile of professors against Futurism, old bags against style. For the moment, they can rejoice! Fashion is going through a period of stagnation and boredom. Mediocrity and wretchedness weave gray spider webs upon the colored flower beds of fashion and art.

Current styles (the blouse and chemise) try in vain to hide their basic poverty of conception under the false labels of distinction and sobriety. There is a complete lack of originality, a withering of fantasy. The imagination of the artist is relegated to details and nuances. The sickening litany of "saintly simplicity" "divine symmetry" and so-called good taste. Silly dreams of exhuming the past: "Let's revive the classics." Exhaustion, mollification, feeble-mindedness.

We Futurists intend to react against this state of things with extreme brutality. We don't need to start a revolution. It's enough to multiply a hundredfold the dynamic virtues of fashion, unleashing the bridles that hinder them from surging forth, leaping over the vertiginous jaws of the Absurd.

A. INGENUITY

One must absolutely claim the dictatorship of artistic ingenuity in female fashion against the parliamentary meddling of foolhardy speculation and the routine. A great poet or painter must take over the directorship of all the great women's fashion houses. Fashion is an art, like architecture and music. A dress that is ingeniously conceived and carried well has the same value as a fresco by Michelangelo or a Titian Madonna.

B. DARING

The Futurist woman must have the same courage in donning the new styles of clothing as we did in declaiming our words-in-freedom against the asinine rebelliousness of Italian and foreign audiences. *Women's fashion can never be extravagant enough.* And here too we will begin by *abolishing symmetry.* We will fashion zigzag decolletés, sleeves that differ from one another, shoes of varying shapes, colors, and heights. We will create illusionistic, sarcastic, sonorous, loud, deadly, and explosive attire: gowns that trigger surprises and transformations, outfitted with springs, stingers, camera lenses, electric currents, reflectors, perfumed sprays, fireworks, chemical preparations, and thousands of gadgets fit to play the most wicked tricks and disconcerting pranks on maladroit suitors and sentimental fools. *In woman we can idealize the most fascinating conquests of modern life.* And so we will have the machine-gun woman, the thanks-de-Somme woman [*sic*], the radiotelegraph antenna woman, the airplane woman, the submarine woman, the motorboat woman. We will transform the elegant lady into a real, living three-dimensional complex. There is no need to fear that in so doing the female silhouette will lose its capricious and provocative grace. The new forms will not hide but accentuate, develop, and exaggerate the gulfs and promontories of the female peninsula. Art exaggeration. Upon the feminine profile we will graft the most aggressive lines and garish colors of our Futurist pictures. We will exalt the female flesh in a frenzy of spirals and triangles. We will succeed in sculpting the astral body of woman with the chisel of an exasperated geometry!

C. ECONOMY

The new fashions will be affordable for all the beautiful women, who are legion in Italy. The relative cost of precious material makes a garb expensive, not the form or color, which we will offer, free, to all Italians. After three years of war and shortages of raw material, it is ridiculous to continue manufacturing leather shoes and silk gowns. *The reign of silk in the history of female fashion must come to an end,* just as the reign of marble is now finished in architectural constructions. One hundred new revolutionary materials riot in the piazza, demanding to be admitted into the making of womanly clothes. We fling open wide the doors of the fashion ateliers to paper, cardboard, glass, tinfoil, aluminum, ceramic, rubber, fish skin, burlap, oakum, hemp, gas, growing plants, and living animals.

Every woman will be a walking synthesis of the universe.

You have the high honor of being loved by us, sapper-soldiers at the avant-garde of an army of lightning.

Concretism

Theo van Doesburg's "Manifesto of Concrete Art," published in his journal *Art concret* of 1930, relies on geometry and color and form. The all-important term *concrete* is thus related to abstract art. Pierre Albert-Birot, the French Nunist, Dada's Swiss Jean Arp, and the Russian Constructivist El Lissitsky had used it in the same way, if with a more lyrical bent.

Concrete poetry is visually based, relying on slippages and ambiguities of language and on the spatial configurations of letters. In this way it is as closly linked to Spatialism, as it is conceived by France's Ilse and Pierre Garnier and Henri Chopin of the journal *Ou*, as to Lettrism and the shapes and sounds of the letter as discussed in "La Créatique," the system of Isidore Isou and Maurice Lemaître. Concretism and Spatialism are based on the dynamics of language seen as a thing in itself, independent of any content. Everything "anecdotal" is discarded, together with all vestiges of sentiment and of the romanticism or lyrical longings often attributed to the Surrealist movement by its detractors.

This is formal Modernism and, as such, significant far beyond any of its precise terms or particular movements. Concretism *abstracts* the object from all attachment to reference, seeing it as obliged only by its own rules and order. In Wilhelm Worringer's 1908 tract *Abstraction and Empathy* we find the statement that "Aesthetic enjoyment is objectified self-enjoyment. To enjoy aesthetically means to enjoy myself in a sensous object diverse from myself, to empathize myself into it." Aligning itself against Naturalism as the product of a "happy pantheistic relationship of confidence between man and phenomena of the outside world," abstraction considers the art object as distinct from both that confidence and from any human sentiment (Worringer, *Abstraction*, 5). As Augusto de Campos of the Noigandres group of Brazil puts it, "the concrete poem is an object in itself and for itself" (Campos, *Poesure*, 527). Indeed, one of the leading concrete poets, George Oppen, wanted to treat the poem like a Cubist work of art.

This dissociative mode of Concretism ranges widely, including Lettrism (Isou, Lemaître, François Dufrêne, Raymond Hains) and international concrete poetry (Ian Hamilton Finlay of little Sparta, Scotland, with his politically oriented garden constructions; Haroldo and Augusto de Campos of the Noigandres group in Brazil; the Swede Oyvind Fahlstrom; and Japan's Seichii Niikuni and Kitasono Katué, the creator of "plastic poems" who was associated with the journal *Vou*, which tried to go beyond "the fetishism" of Japanese characters and of Latinate letters). Other adherents include Eugen Gomringer of Switzerland, whose mother was Bolivian, Diter Rot of Germany, and Brion Gysin of England, France, and the United States. More recently, Julien Blaine and Jean-François Bory of France have been linked to concrete or "lisual" poetry—a pun on "visual" and "readerly" or "lettered"—to optophonic declamation, and to semieotic spatalism. (The latter term has an "e" to distinguish it from the simple semiotic sign as Roland Barthes analyzed it.)

According to Gomringer, concrete poetry should not be considered apart from other genres of poetry. Postmodernist, yes, but it is part of a long tradition, from the Greeks through to the present. The concrete artists and writers explicity refer back to their precedents: the Lettrist Isou back to Marcel Proust and James Joyce and the Lettrist Lemaître back to Luigi Russolo's "Art of Noises" and Tristan Tzara's "Seven Dada Manifestoes" as well as to Breton, Philippe Soupault, Robert Desnos, and Antonin Artaud among the Surrealists and to Erik Satie, paying homage to the other avant-garde movements of his century and to their creators. So, too, the Brazilian Concretists refer back to Dada, Julien Blaine refers back to ee cummings and the Simultaneist Pierre Albert-Birot of *Sic,* and other contemporary workers in concrete refer back to the former ones.

And Concretism leads on, to the contemporary L=A=N=G=U=A=G=E poets.

20.1 THEO VAN DOESBURG

Basis of Concrete Painting

1930

We declare:

1. Art is universal.
2. The work of art must be entirely conceived and formed by the mind before its execution. It must receive nothing from nature's given forms, or from sensuality, or sentimentality.

   We wish to exclude lyricism, dramaticism, symbolism, etc.
3. The picture must be entirely constructed from purely plastic elements, that is, planes and colors. A pictorial element has no other meaning than "itself" and thus the picture has no other meaning than "itself."
4. The construction of the picture, as well as its elements, must be simple and visually controllable.
5. Technique must be mechanical, that is, exact, anti-impressionistic.
6. Effort for absolute clarity.

EXISTE-T-IL UNE POÉSIE CONSTRUCTIVE?

[IS THERE A CONSTRUCTIVE POETRY?]

20.2 WASSILY KANDINSKY

Concrete Art

1938

All the arts derive from the same and unique root.

Consequently, all the arts are identical.

But the mysterious and precious fact is that the "fruits" produced by the same trunk are different.

The difference manifests itself by the means of each particular art—by the means of expression.

It is very simple at first thought. Music expresses itself by sounds, painting by colors, etc., facts that are generally recognized.

But the difference does not end here. Music, for example, organizes its means (sounds) within time, and painting its means (colors) upon a plane.

Time and plane must be exactly "measured" and sound and color must be exactly "limited." These "limits" are the preconditions of "balance" and hence of composition.

Since the enigmatic but precise laws of composition are the same in all the arts, they obliterate differences.

I should like in passing to emphasize that the organic difference between time and plane is generally exaggerated. The composer takes the listener by the hand, makes him enter into his musical work, guides him step by step, and abandons him once the "piece" is finished. Exactitude is perfect. It is imperfect in painting. But—the painter does not possess this power to "guide." He can if he wishes force the spectator to commence here, to follow an exact path in the pictorial work, and to "leave" it there. These are questions that are excessively complicated, still very little known, and above all very seldom resolved.

I wish only to say that the affinity between painting and music is evident. But it manifests itself still more profoundly. You are well acquainted with the question of "associations" provoked by means of the different arts? Some scientists (especially physicists), some artists (especially musicians) have noticed long ago that a musical sound, for example, provokes an association of a precise color. (Note for example the correspondences established by Scriabin.) Stated otherwise, you "hear" the color and you "see" the sound.

Almost 30 years ago I published a small book which dealt with this question. YELLOW, for example, possesses the special capacity to "ascend" higher and higher and to attain heights unbearable to the eye and the spirit; the sound of a trumpet played higher and higher becoming more and more "pointed," giving pain to the ear and to the spirit. BLUE, with the completely opposite power to "descend" into infinite depths, develops the sounds of the flute (when it is light blue), of the cello (when it has descended farther), of the double bass with its magnificent deep sounds; and in the depths of the organ you "see" the depths of blue. GREEN is well balanced and corresponds to the medium and the attenuated sounds of the violin. When skillfully applied, RED (vermillion) can give the impression of strong drum beats, etc. (*Über das Geistige in der Kunst* [Munich, 1912,] pp. 64–71, English and American editions: *The Art of Spiritual Harmony*—W. K.)

The vibrations of the air (sound) and of light (color) surely form the foundation of this physical affinity.

But it is not the only foundation. There is yet another: the psychological foundation. A problem of "spirit."

Have you heard or have you yourself used the expressions: "Oh, such cold music!" or "Oh, such frigid painting!"? You have the impression of frigid air entering through an open window in winter. And your entire body is uncomfortable.

But a skillful application of warm "tones" and "sounds" gives the painter and the composer an excellent possibility of creating warm works. They burn you directly.

Forgive me, but painting and music are able to make you (rather rarely, however) sick to the stomach.

You are also familiar with the case that, when you have the feeling of running your finger over several combinations of sounds or colors, you feel that your finger has been "pricked." As if by spines. But at other times your "finger" runs over painting or music as if over silk or velvet.

Finally, is not VIOLET less odoriferous than YELLOW, for example? And ORANGE? Light BLUE-GREEN?

And as "taste," are not these colors different? Such savory painting! Even the tongue of the spectator or the auditor commences to participate in the work of art.

These are the five known senses of man.

Do not deceive yourself; do not think that you "receive" painting by the eye alone. No, unknown to you, you receive it by your five senses.

Do you think that it could be otherwise?

What we understand by the word "form" in painting is not color alone. What we call "drawing" is inevitably another part of the means of pictorial expression.

To begin with a "point," which is the origin of all other forms, and of which the number is unlimited, the little point is a living being possessed of many influences upon the spirit of man. If the artist places it properly on his canvas, the little point is satisfied, and it pleases the spectator. He says, "Yes, that's me. Do you understand my little necessary sound in the great 'chorus' of the work?"

And how painful it is to see the little point where it should not be! You have the sensation of eating a meringue and tasting pepper on the tongue. A flower with the odor of rot.

Rot—that's the word! Composition transforms itself into decomposition. It is death.

Have you noted that in speaking so long of painting and its means of expression I have said not a single word about the "object"? The explanation of this fact is very simple: I have spoken of the essential pictorial means, that is, of inevitables.

One will never find the possibility to make painting without "colors" and "line," but painting without objects has existed in our time for more than 25 years.

As for the object, it can be *introduced* into a painting, or it cannot.

When I think of all the *disputes* about this "not," those disputes which began almost 30 years ago and which today have not yet completely ended, I see the immense force of "habit." At the same time I see the immense force of the painting called "abstract" or "nonfigurative." I prefer to call this painting "concrete."

This art is a "problem" which some wanted to "bury" too often, which they said is definitely resolved (naturally, in the negative sense), but which will not let itself be buried.

It is too much alive.

There no longer exists a problem, neither of Impressionism, nor Expressionism (the Fauves!), nor of Cubism. All these "isms" are distributed into the different compartments of the history of art.

The compartments are numbered and bear labels corresponding to their contents. And, thus, the arguments are concluded.

It is the past.

But the arguments around "concrete art" do not yet allow an anticipation of their end. In good time! "Concrete art" is in full development, above all in the free countries, and the number of young artists participating in the "movement" increases in these countries.

The future!

20.3 Jean (Hans) Arp

Concrete Art

1944

We don't want to copy nature. We don't want to reproduce, we want to produce. We want to produce like a plant that produces a fruit, and not reproduce. We want to produce directly and not by way of any intermediary.

Since this art doesn't have the slightest trace of abstraction, we name it: concrete art.

Works of concrete art should not be signed by the artists. These paintings, sculptures—these objects—should remain anonymous in the huge studio of nature, like clouds, mountains, seas, animals, men. Yes! Men should go back to nature! Artists should work in communities as they did in the Middle Ages. In 1915, O. van Rees, C. van Rees, Freundlich, S. Taeuber, and myself made an attempt of that sort.

That year I wrote: "These works are constructed with lines, surfaces, forms, and colors that try to go beyond the human and attain the infinite and the eternal. They reject our egotism. . . . The hands of our brothers, instead of being interchangeable with our own hands, have become enemy hands. Instead of anonymity, we have renown and masterpieces; wisdom is dead. . . . Reproduction is imitation, play acting, tightrope walking."

The Renaissance bumptiously exalted human reason. Modern times with their science and technology have turned man into a megalomaniac. The atrocious chaos of our era is the consequence of that overrating of reason.

The evolution of traditional painting toward concrete art, from Cézanne by way of the cubists, has been frequently explained, and these historical explanations have merely confused the issue. All at once, "according to the laws of chance," around 1914, the human mind underwent a transformation: it was confronted with an ethical problem.

Concrete art wants to transform the world. It wants to make life more bearable. It wants to save man from the most dangerous of follies: vanity. It wants to simplify the life of man. It wants to identify him with nature. Reason uproots man and makes him lead a tragic life. Concrete art is a basic art, a sane and natural art that grows the stars of peace, love, and poetry in the head and in the heart. Wherever concrete art appears, melancholy leaves, dragging along its gray suitcases full of black sighs.

Kandinsky, Sonia Delaunay, Robert Delaunay, Magnelli, and Léger were among the first masters of concrete art. Without having met, we were all working toward the same goal. Most of these works were not exhibited until 1920. This marked a blossoming of all the colors and all the shapes in the world. These paintings, these sculptures—these objects—were stripped of any conventional element whatsoever. Partisans of this new art cropped up in all countries. Concrete art influenced architecture, furniture, film making, and typography.

Aside from their exhibited works, certain works by Duchamp, Man Ray, Masson, Miró, and Ernst, and a number of "surrealist objects," are also concrete art. Devoid of any descriptive, dreamlike, literary, or polemical content, the works of these artists are, it seems to me, highly important in the evolution of concrete art, for, by allusion, they manage to introduce into that art the psychic emotion that makes it live.

PART 21

Verticalism and The Revolution of the Word

Eugène Jolas, the charismatic multilingual Swiss poet and founder of the journal *transition*, was a catalyst for many Modernist discoveries and a one-man exchange program among countries in Western Europe. He created in 1928 a movement he called Verticalism or, later, Vertigralism, a term that combined the ideas of vertigo, upward movement, and integrality and suggested the quest for the Grail. The movement has many of the impulses of Surrealism, being a late version of Romanticism.

A Jungian, Jolas was aiming at what was lasting and eternal, a positive, upward movement of preconscious experience. To Jolas's "Poetry Is Vertical" manifesto (21.1), Jean (Hans) Arp contributed his ideas, and others were asked to append their signatures, as they had been for the manifesto called "The Revolution of the Word" (21.2). This widely admired manifesto, funny and serious and optimistic all at once, caused James Laughlin to dedicate an entire series of his *New Directions* publications to Jolas. Jolas's *transition* published much of the Dada and Surrealist material we now know, as well as an impressive roster of well- and less-well-known writers and thinkers, from Gertrude Stein to those whose names have been long since forgotten, except in these pages and in the signatures to this manifesto, to which the additions from William Blake give a particular edge.

The close contacts of the Jolas family with James Joyce and Samuel Beckett, Maria Jolas's remarkable skills as a translator of French texts, and the general energy level of the whole enterprise were crucial to a whole period of Modernist excitement. As James Johnson Sweeney cracked about Jolas, "the word was his oyster."

In exile in the New York area in the 1930s, Jolas continued to manifest his belief in a real "community of spirits," as the vertical manifesto would have it: down with the mind sunk in classical ideals, a new poetic and collective mythology is on the rise. This time Icarus won't fall.

The impulse to a verticalizing structure in the early twentieth century was the counterpart to Baudelaire's horizontal "correspondances" and then the domination of the square. And then came the vertical. Of course, Stéphane Mallarmé, the predecessor of much, was already haunted by the azure, but Symbolism takes on another form. "Skyscraper primitives," Dickran Tashijian called this double will to the modern and the recapturing of the primitive. From the return to the earth, the land, the rooted life, to the perception of the Eiffel Tower, style rises up like a shout. It can be compared to Blaise Cendrars's novelistic meditation on the patron saint of levitation, then to Ramón Gómez de la Serna's declaration of 1922 in *Espana* on "The New Eiffel Tower," and then to the *transition* group in its fascination with Verticalism.

21.1 HANS (JEAN) ARP *and others*
Poetry Is Vertical
1941

On a été trop horizontal, j'ai envie d'être vertical.
LÉON PAUL FARGUE

In a world ruled by the hypnosis of positivism, we proclaim the autonomy of the poetic vision, the hegemony of the inner life over the outer life.

We reject the postulate that the creative personality is a mere factor in the pragmatic conception of progress, and that its function is the delineation of a vitalistic world.

We are against the renewal of the classical ideal, because it inevitably leads to a decorative reactionary conformity, to a factitious sense of harmony, to the sterilisation of the living imagination.

We believe that the orphic forces should be guarded from deterioration, no matter what social system ultimately is triumphant.

Esthetic will is not the first law. It is in the immediacy of the ecstatic revelation, in the a-logical movement of the psyche, in the organic rhythm of the vision that the creative act occurs.

The reality of depth can be conquered by a voluntary mediumistic conjuration, by a stupor which proceeds from the irrational to a world beyond a world.

The transcendental "I" with its multiple stratifications reaching back millions of years is related to the entire history of mankind, past and present, and is brought to the surface with the hallucinatory irruption of images in the dream, the daydream, the mystic-gnostic trance, and even the psychiatric condition.

The final disintegration of the "I" in the creative act is made possible by the use of a language which is a mantic instrument, and which does not hesitate to adopt a revolutionary attitude toward word and syntax, going even so far as to invent a hermetic language, if necessary.

Poetry builds a nexus between the "I" and the "you" by leading the emotions of the sunken, telluric depths upward toward the illumination of a collective reality and a totalistic universe.

The synthesis of a true collectivism is made possible by a community of spirits who aim at the construction of a new mythological reality.

> HANS ARP, SAMUEL BECKETT, CARL EINSTEIN,
> EUGÈNE JOLAS, THOMAS MCGREEVY, GEORGES PELORSON,
> THEO RUTRA, JAMES J. SWEENEY, RONALD SYMOND

The Revolution of the Word

1928

PROCLAMATION

TIRED OF THE SPECTACLE OF SHORT STORIES, NOVELS, POEMS AND PLAYS STILL UNDER THE HEGEMONY OF THE BANAL WORD, MONOTONOUS SYNTAX, STATIC PSYCHOLOGY, DESCRIPTIVE NATURALISM, AND DESIROUS OF CRYSTALLIZING A VIEWPOINT . . .

WE HEREBY DECLARE THAT:

1. THE REVOLUTION IN THE ENGLISH LANGUAGE IS AN ACCOMPLISHED FACT.

2. THE IMAGINATION IN SEARCH OF A FABULOUS WORLD IS AUTONOMOUS AND UNCONFINED.

> (*Prudence is a rich, ugly old maid courted by Incapacity* . . . Blake)

3. PURE POETRY IS A LYRICAL ABSOLUTE THAT SEEKS AN A PRIORI REALITY WITHIN OURSELVES ALONE.

> (*Bring out number, weight and measure in a year of dearth* . . . Blake)

4. NARRATIVE IS NOT MERE ANECDOTE, BUT THE PROJECTION OF A METAMORPHOSIS OF REALITY.

> (*Enough! Or Too Much!* . . . Blake)

5. THE EXPRESSION OF THESE CONCEPTS CAN BE ACHIEVED ONLY THROUGH THE RHYTHMIC "HALLUCINATION OF THE WORD."

> (Rimbaud)

6. THE LITERARY CREATOR HAS THE RIGHT TO DISINTEGRATE THE PRIMAL MATTER OF WORDS IMPOSED ON HIM BY TEXT-BOOKS AND DICTIONARIES.

> (*The road of excess leads to the palace of Wisdom* . . . Blake)

7. HE HAS THE RIGHT TO USE WORDS OF HIS OWN FASHIONING AND TO DISREGARD EXISTING GRAMMATICAL AND SYNTACTICAL LAWS.

> (*The tigers of wrath are wiser than the horses of instruction* . . . Blake)

8. THE "LITANY OF WORDS" IS ADMITTED AS AN INDEPENDENT UNIT.

9. WE ARE NOT CONCERNED WITH THE PROPAGATION OF SOCIO-
LOGICAL IDEAS, EXCEPT TO EMANCIPATE THE CREATIVE ELE-
MENTS FROM THE PRESENT IDEOLOGY.

10. TIME IS A TYRANNY TO BE ABOLISHED.

11. THE WRITER EXPRESSES. HE DOES NOT COMMUNICATE.

12. THE PLAIN READER BE DAMNED.

(Damn braces! Bless relaxes! . . . Blake)

Signed: KAY BOYLE, WHIT BURNETT, HART CRANE,
CARESSE CROSBY, HARRY CROSBY, MARTHA FOLEY,
STUART GILBERT, A. L. GILLESPIE, LEIGH HOFFMAN,
EUGÈNE JOLAS, ELLIOT PAUL, DOUGLAS RIGBY, THEO RUTRA,
ROBERT SAGE, HAROLD J. SALEMSON, LAURENCE VAIL

PART 22

Dimensionalism and Spatialism

The early twentieth century's obsession with size and shape marked many of its experiments, to lasting effect. The very Dada Francis Picabia, in New York in 1913, deliberately made his *Udnie: (An American Girl: Dance)* very large, to capture "in its plenitude" his idea of America and the "evocations from there which . . . become representative of an idea, of a nostalgia, of a fugitive impression." To Alfred Stieglitz he announced his original conception of it as "a purer painting of a dimension having no title" (Canfield, *Francis Picabia*, 60).

From the painters to the poets to the theoreticians of the cinema, first the large square and the rectangle began to occupy the imagination, as in Kasimir Malevich's *Black Square* of 1915 and the allied work of the other Russian Suprematists. "The *'dynamic' square screen* . . . providing in its dimensions the opportunity of impressing, in projection, with absolute grandeur every geometrically conceivable form of the picture limit": so Sergei Eisenstein "chants the hymn of the male, the strong, the virile, active, *vertical* composition" of his screen (Eisenstein, *Film Essays*, 51–52). The ways in which energy is allied to size, to the massive projection of an idea, is akin to the later workings of Abstract Expressionism and its push toward hugeness.

From 1936 on into the 1940s there was a great deal of talk, influenced by current scientific controversies and experiments, about the number of dimensions one could perceive, imagine, or paint. The "Manifesto of Spatialist Art" (22.4), signed by such a large quantity of well-known people, is the major witness to the excitement.

22.1 PIERRE AND ILSE GARNIER
Spatial Eroticism
1966

Is eroticism now just a part of history? If we consider the eroticism of preceding generations, inversely proportional to the social and religious taboos, repression-expression, a corporeal and intellectual striptease, the revendication of a sexual freedom ceaselessly refused (today because of the interdictions in certain countries about the usage of contraceptives in certain countries, which would grant women the same freedom as men) but nevertheless ineluctable—or if we are talking about the mythology of the male and the female (as out-of-date as the Greek myths) or of the apotheosis of woman (as the object of adoration and possession) (see the linguistic ravings of certain surrealist poets on this subject) — then yes, this kind of eroticism is out-of-date and belongs to history.

Spatialists don't have to worry with this kind of eroticism. They discard this ballast, abandoning it to its pathetic fate, as they also abandon to that fate countries, parties, churches, the unconscious and all its represeed treasure, all the weathercocks, and man and woman such as the most conformist social or religious imaginations have conceived them.

Spatialists remain haughtily unaware of the world — already abolished in their eyes — for it could slow down the development of new structures; they think it is by disengaging themselves to the greatest possible extent from all rotten frameworks that they can create (that does not mean that these poets, as integral members of society, do not act, or will not act socially and politically).

But since spatialist eroticism exists, what is it anyway?

It is desire, a universal energy, impelling beings toward each other, separating them, causing them to touch each other, to gravitate, structure themselves, self-destruct, reproduce, to be always the same and always different. The spatialisation of language corresponds to that eroticism. The fact that in spatial texts there is no longer subject or verb or object means a love without a male-as-master and a female-as-object, without myth or taboo.

That is to say the negation of eroticism as it has been understood until our time.

Nonetheless love continues, esthetic and ethical, as it were lightened, purified, as the relations of universal esthetic structures. It is conceived by Spatialism as the mutation of sentimental and vague desire into its transcendant other: movement.

So erotico-spatialist works are above all kinetic works; our desire is no longer enclosed in an unconscious dream but disengaged, it is radiance and movement.

Linguistic particles are placed in tension.

The reader is no longer cast by the linear and evocative phrase into a feverish imagination centered on the object to conquer and violate (generally the woman-object) but rather guided, by the esthetic vision of words (the crudest words are washed clear of any vulgarity by spatialisation), toward an erotically pure vision (esthetic information), and the impulses received provoke more of a cosmic desire than the disquiet based for so long on the ideas of violation and possession.

Spatialism creates an eroticism of situation and no longer of domination:

the woman (or any other being) is no longer an object to be adored or possessed but a person. She is no longer the symbol of everything in this world (see André Breton's "Free Union," a summit-poem of all romanticisms), but she quite simply is.

The end of religions and of myths.

For how to speak of love in the same terms as we still could a few years ago, with all the sentimental ornament and the lovely vagueness of language, when you know about the hormonal mechanism or the fact that a few shots of folliculine are enough to inspire or reinspire maternal feeling.

All that is chemistry—and not metaphysics.

Spatialism takes account of these scientific discoveries and does not claim to continue living in a washed-out dream like those who keep saying that "the sun rises," whereas for centuries we have known that it does not.

Our eroticism is energy and structures, that is, physical and aesthetic; it is whirlwinds, impulses, particular exchanges, waves, radiations spatialized throughout the body: it's man and woman coextensive with the universe— man and woman in their gravitational fields.

It's language itself, coextensive with the universe; itself in its gravitational fields.

22.2 FRANCIS PICABIA *and others*

Dimensionist Manifesto

1936

ANTONIO PEDRO, CAMILLE BRYEN, CESAR DOMELA, CHARLES SIRATO, ENRICO PRAMPOLINI, ERVAND KOTCHAR, FRANCIS PICABIA, FREDERICK KANN, HANS ARP, KAKABADZE, LADISLAS MOHOLY-NAGY, MARCEL DU-CHAMP, MARIO MISSIM, NINA NEGRI, PIERRE ALBERT-BIROT, PRINNER, ROBERT DELAUNAY, SONIA DELAUNAY, SIRI RATHSMAN, SOPHIE TAUBER-ARP, VINCENT HUIDOBRO, WASSILY KANDINSKY.

Dimensionism is a general movement in the arts, begun unconsciously by cubism and futurism—continuously elaborated and developed afterward by every people in Western civilization.

Today the essence and the theory of this great movement explode in an absolute conviction.

At the origin of dimensionism are the new ideas of space-time present in the European way of thinking, promulgated in particular by Einstein's theories as well as the recent techniques of our age.

The absolute need to evolve—an irreducible instinct—leaves dead forms and exhausted contents as the prey for dilettantes, forcing the avant-gardes to move toward the unknown.

We are obliged to admit—contrary to the classical thesis—that Space and Time are no longer different categories but according to the non-Euclidian conception are coherent dimensions, putting an end to all the old limits and boundaries of the arts.

This new ideology has provoked a real earthquake and a subsequent slippage in the conventional systems of the arts. We designate all of these phenomena taken as a whole by the term "DIMENSIONISM."

Tendency or Principle of Dimensionism. Formula "N + I."

(Formula found in the theory of Planism and then generalized, reducing to a common law the most apparently chaotic and inexplicable manifestations of the art of our time.)

ANIMATED BY A CONCEPTION OF THE WORLD, THE ARTS, IN A COLLECTIVE FERMENTATION (Interpenetration of the Arts)

HAVE STARTED MOVING

AND EACH OF THEM HAS EVOLVED WITH A NEW DIMENSION

EACH OF THEM HAS FOUND A FORM OF EXPRESSION INHERENT TO THE SUPPLEMENTARY DIMENSION OBJECTIFYING THE GRAVE MENTAL CONSEQUENCES OF THIS FUNDAMENTAL CHANGE

So the dimensionist tendency has constrained:

I. . . . Literature to come forth from the line and

pass   into   the   plane.
Calligrams   Typograms   Planism
(preplanism)   Electric poems

II. . . . Painting to leave the plane and occupy space.
Painting in space   "Konstructivism"
                                                      Spatial Constructions
                                                      Ploy-Material Constructions.

III. . . . Sculpture to abandon closed space unmoving and dead, that is, Euclidian space in three dimensions, in order to use Minkovsky's four-dimensional space for artistic expression.

First, "full" sculpture (Classical Sculpture), will disembowel itself, and by introducing in its own body the sculpted and calculated "lack" of interior space—then movement—is transformed into:

Hollow Sculpture.

Open Sculpture.

Mobile Sculpture.

Motorized Objects.

Then must come the creation of an absolutely new art: Cosmic Art Vaporisation of Sculpture, Synos-Sense Theater, provisional denominations. Total conquest by art of four-dimensional space

until now a "Vacuum Artis"

Rigid matter is abolished and replaced by gazefied materials. Instead of looking at objects of art, the person becomes the center and the subject of creation; creation consists of sersorial effects taking place in a closed cosmic space.

That is the most concise statement of the principle of dimensionism. Deductive toward the past. Inductive toward the future. Living for the present.

22.3 Paul de Vree

Declaration

1966

TOUTE
PREDICATION EST UN ATTENTAT A
LA LIBERTE DE L'HOMME. - LA POESIE, COMME
JE LA CONÇOIS, N'EST PLUS LA FEMME DE CHAMBRE
DES PRINCES, PRELATS, POLITICIENS, PARTIS, OU ENCO-
RE DU PEUPLE. - ELLE EST ENFIN ELLE-MEME : UN PHENOME-
NE PHONETIQUE VOCAL EN SOI DE SOURCE PSYCHO-PHYSIQUE ET
OBJECTIVEMENT STRUCTURE A L'AIDE DE MOTS, DE SONS ET DE MO-
YENS MECHANIQUES ET GRAPHIQUES (ENREGISTEMENTS ET ECRITURES).
- LE VISUEL VERBAL PUR N'EXISTE PAS. - IL SUSCITE TOUJOURS LE SON OU
LE BRUIT D'OU IL PROVIENT ET DONT IL EST LE SIGNE. - LE POEME EST UNE
EMISSION DE RESPIRATION AUDIBLE (AUDITION) OU SILENCIEUSE (LECTURE).
CREATIVEMENT MODULEE, PRO- VOQUEE PAR LA NECESSITE DE DI-
RE, NE SE REFERANT A RIEN D' AUTRE QU'A LA SENSIBILITE D'
ETRE (PRESENT ET PLANE- TAIRE). - C'EST CE QUE JE COM-
PRENDS PAR L'INTENTION OB- JECTIVE DES SONORITES VO-
CALES : UNE COMMUNICATION CONCERTEE DE VIBRATIONS
CREATRICES SPONTANEES. LA POESIE PHONETIQUE NE
PEUT EXSISTER SANS UNE REINVENTION DE LA RECITA-
TION, C'EST-A-DIRE LA SONO- RISATION OU LA REGIE DU SON
- TOUT DEPEND EN EFFET DES NOUVELLES POSSIBILITES D'EX-
PRESSION MECANIQUE POUR RE- ALISER LA TRANSMISSION DE LA
SENSIBILITE TOTALE DU POEME, LUI-MEME AU FOND UNE PARTIE DU
SPECTACLE CINETIQUE TOTAL QU'HENRI CHOPIN PREVOIT PAR L'UTILISATION
INEVITABLE DE LA MACHINE MUE PAR LES ONDES. - L'ŒUVRE SONORE EST
LE RESULTAT D'UN TRAVAIL D'EQUIPE SOUS LA REGIE DU POETE ET LA
REPRODUCTION IDEALE EST CELLE REALISEE SUR DISQUE H.F. - LA EN-
CORE LA MACHINE EST INDISPENSABLE. - CELA VA DE SOI QUE LE
RECITANT (SI CE N'EST PAS LE POETE) ET L'INGENIEUR DE
DE SONS (EN CE QUI CONCERNE MES ENREGISTREMENTS)
CONTRIBUENT PERSONNELLEMENT A L'ORIGINAL-
ITE DE LA REALISATION. - A L'AUBE DE
L'ERE ELECTRONIQUE LA POESIE
NE PEUT PLUS ETRE UN
FABLIAU.

Every Preachment is an attack on human liberty.—Poetry, as I conceive it, is no longer the chambermaid of princes, prelates, politicians, parties, or again the people. It is finally Itself: a vocal phonetic phenomenon in itself, a psycho-physical source objectively structured with the aid of words, sounds, and mechanical and graphic means (recordings and writings). The pure visual-verbal exists no more.—It always arouses the sound or noise from which it comes and whose sign it is. The poem is an emission of audible respiration (audition) or silent (reading), creatively modulated, provoked by the necessity of saying, not referring to anything else than the sensitivity of being (present and planetary). That's what I understand by the objective intention of vocal sonorites: a concerted communication of spontaneous creative vibrations. Phonetic poetry cannot exist without a reinvention of recitation, that is, sonorisation or the rule of sound. Everything depends in fact on the new possibilities of mechanical expression to realise the transmission of the total sensitivity of the poem, itself at bottom a part of the kinetic spectacle as a whole that Henri Chopin foresees by the inevitable utilization of the machine moved by the sound waves. The sounded creation is the result of a teamwork under the rule of the poet and the ideal reproduction is that realized on a hi fi record. There again the machine is indispensable. It is obvious that the reciter (if it isn't the poet) and the sound engineer (when it is a matter of my recordings) personally contribute to the originality of the realization. At the dawn of the electronic era poetry can no longer be a fable.

22.4 LUCIO FONTANA *and others*
Manifesto of Spatialist Art
1951

Five years after the first manifesto of spatial art, many "facts" have emerged in the field of art. We are not about to examine them one by one, but one precise "fact" we can report: the elimination of those currents that preferred to continue closed in the same old grasp of the "contingent and terrestrial reality in all senses," denying or then evading anything real by some abstract fantasy henceforth recognized as sterile, empty, and desperately abstruse. These five years have permitted artists to shift to our own direction: to consider reality that space, that vision of universal matter, about which science, philosophy, and art based on knowledge and intuition have nourished the human spirit. And we have seen a series of manifestations devoted to enhancing the new vision of the universe of the microcosms of that space, trying to represent figuratively that energy, today shown to be "rigorous matter," and that space seen as "plastic matter." We reaffirm today the priority of art as an intuitional force of creation and proceed upon the same streets to intuit practically the aspects of the mind which will be joined by knowledge.

ANTON GUILIO AMBROSINI	VIRGILIO GIUDI
GIANCARLO CAROZZI	BENIAMINO JOPPOLO
ROBERTO CRIPPA	MILENA MILANI
MARIO DELUIGI	BERTO MORUCCHIO
GIANNI DOVA	CESARE PEVERELLI
LUCIO FONTANA	VINCIO VIANELLO

Position 3 of Spatialism

For a Supranational Poetry

1966

Civilization today exists in the heart of a civilization in decline.

Nations are no more than folklore; the poet must "expatriate" the national tongues.

That is why spatialism has as its goal making people aware of anachronisms

— making evident in poetry today's culture (helped in this by the evolution of humanity; we are all heading toward the same technical and spatial age).
— and defining the linguistic supranational, even universal fact.

Why spatialism?

1. The poet is now working *objectively* with a tongue considered as matter and creating (or fabricating) texts with all the elements of this tongue: phrases, words, letters, syllables, accents, articulations, breaths, and with the semantic and aesthetic information furnished by these elements. The poet considers each tongue as an autonomous universe and utilizes all the technical means of creation, multiplication, diffusion. So it is a matter of a considerable enlargement of the poetic field, that is, a spatializing of the multiplication of creative possibilities.
2. Spatialism has as its goal the passage from national tongues to a supranational one and to works no longer translatable but *transmissible* over a linguistic surface always larger.
3. This spatialization is indicated by poetry's own extension; now it fills up its full volume: on one side it touches music (phonetic poetry), on the other the figurative arts (visual poetry), but it remains poetry because it is only made of linguistic elements. Spatialism does not present itself as a negation of traditional-type poetry but as their extension and expansion. The passage from national tongues to a supranational one happens in several moments: The poet creates in each tongue—through an appropriate choice—linguistic crystals, with the aesthetic information that the tongue under consideration can furnish in the most vast of linguistic domains.

Through this creation of linguistic objects, through the objective work of tongues considered as matter, the poet strips these tongues of any sentimental or historical, expressionist, or psychic content. There only remain structures, that is, an aesthetics.

So it is that poets "demythify" language.

In the conditions of objective creation appropriate to spatialism, all national tongues — and even all languages — are at the disposition of poets: an author whose maternal tongue is English can create, even with a limited knowledge of these tongues, concrete poems in Spanish, Russian Arabic, Japanese. He will take from each of these tongues what seems to him the purest.

At the same time there is a continuing exploration of infratongues, signs, articulations, breaths, gestures, often common to all of humanity.

Through this exploration, through this exploitation, through this creation:

— Tongues taken as matter will cease to fog up the thought processes.
— A poetic art is created (apart from objectified national tongues) that is valuable for all.
— Each tongue, reduced to its crystals, sees itself radiating toward a supranational level, for it furnishes prototypes.
— A supranational tongue begins to be discovered on the aesthetic level in the space of the new civilization.
— The activity of the poet joins that of the scientist in the discovery of a linguistic aesthetics and of a language common to all humanity.
— Doing this, the poet takes part in the genesis of a humanity that has just burst out from its terrestrial envelope.

PART 23

Lettrism

Lettrism, a movement originally conceived by Isidore Isou, in which he remained involved along with Maurice Lemaître, François Dufrêne, and Raymond Hains, is allied with concrete art and poetry of all sorts. It aims at giving prevalence to the materiality of the letter itself, calling its systematization "La Créatique," a kind of Creationism. Added to or replacing all poetic and musical elements, the letter in its exact form makes from all it adjoins or holds together a coherent work.

The Lettrist movement, says its founder, Isou, has nothing to do with either the nihilism of Dada or the dreaminess of Surrealism. André Breton had first praised the Lettrist work, but when Isou's pamphlet "The Revolution of Youth" appeared, Breton is said to have exclaimed to Isou: "Youth? I hadn't given it a thought," occasioning an angry response by Isou.

Lettrism also terms itself hypergraphy or infinitesimal or supertemporal art and had among its disciples at the outset of the fifties Guy Debord the Situationist, among others who later grouped themselves around the Lettrist International in defense of Charlie Chaplin (thus the divergence with Isou). They then proclaimed an end to art. In Debord's words: "All the arts are just mediocre games that change nothing."

23.1 ISIDORE ISOU

Manifesto of Lettrist Poetry

1942

COMMONPLACES ABOUT WORDS

Pathetic I.	The explosions burst beyond us.
	Every delirium is expansive.
	Every impulse *escapes* stereotype.
Always I.	An intimate experience keeps a singular specificity.
Pathetic II.	Discharges are transmitted by notions.
	What a difference between our fluctuations and the brutality of the word.
	There are always transitions between feeling and saying.[1]
Always II.	The first stereotype is the word.
Pathetic III.	What a difference between the organism and the sources.
	Notions—what an inherited dictionary of them!
	Tarzan learns in his father's book to call tigers cats.
	To name the Unknown with the Always.
Always III.	*The translated word is not expressed.*
Pathetic IV.	The rigidities of forms get in the way of transmissibility.
	Words are so heavy that effusions cannot carry them.
	Temperaments die before reaching their point (blank shots).
	No word can contain the impulses that we want to send with it.

* * *

THE ORDER OF LETTERS

It isn't a matter of	destroying words for others.
	Or of making up notions to specify their nuances.
	Or of mixing terms together to make them hold more meaning.
But rather of	ALWAYS TAKING ALL THE LETTERS TOGETHER;
	UNFOLDING BEFORE THE DAZZLED SPECTATORS THE MARVELS BROUGHT ABOUT BY LETTERS (DEBRIS OF DESTRUCTIONS);

1 *A report can register the beatings about the bush of Feeling, taking from Saying its equivalent. A parakeet always pulls out the same tickets.*

CREATING AN ARCHITECTURE OF LETTRIC
RHYTHMS;
ACCUMULATING IN A PRECISE FRAMEWORK THE
FLUCTUATING LETTERS;
ELABORATING SPLENDIDLY THE HABITUAL
MURMUR;
COAGULATING THE CRUMBS OF LETTERS FOR A
REAL MEAL;[2]
RESUSCITATE THE CONFUSED IN A DENSER ORDER;
RENDERING UNDERSTANDABLE AND PALPABLE
EVERYTHING INCOMPREHENSIBLE AND VAGUE;
CONCRETISING SILENCE; WRITING NOTHINGS.

2 The miracle of Jesus and of Sisyphus.

23.2 ISIDORE ISOU
DADALETTRIE Meca-Esthetically Destructive 1 and 2
1970

DADALETTRIE MECA-ESTHETICALLY DESTRUCTIVE 1

Recording all the utilitary "preparations": washing the face, brushing the teeth (spitting, gargling . . .), peeing, shitting, hairbrushing, nailcutting, etc.

Each operation is reproduced (actually or on tape) according to its own rhythm, one on top of the other, with the following durations and concentrations:

1) very slow;
2) maximal concentration;
3) very slow
4) progressive concentration;
5) maximum concentration ad libitum.

DADALETTRIE MECA-ESTHETICALLY DESTRUCTIVE 2

Amplified recording of a tooth event.

You can interrupt the detailed recording by short violent sound bites of diverse effective mastications from soup (slurping between the teeth) and mashed potatoes to the whole nut and the stone.

PART 24

Projectivism and Open Field

Charles Olson's 1950 manifesto "Projective Verse" (24.1) initiates, with its "open field" technique, precisely a whole open field of body language and orality as they determine the poem, unleashing the primitive forces that rationality and traditional methods would stifle. The poem is recited rather than read, and its rhythmic declamation calls on all the available powers of breath and muscle of each individual "chanter." One could see this as an extension of Expressionism and as closely related to the kind of extreme individualism or personalism that Frank O'Hara's manifesto "Personism" (26.4) would later celebrate, however ironically.

Olson's followers are many, among the poets of a younger generation who read his "Maximus" poems and their confessional warmth as the high point of the fifties, situated at the exact opposite pole from the concrete poets and leading to the very personal and yet universalizing and primitive gestural poetry of the beats like Allen Ginsberg and Jack Kerouac.

Open field poetics is the sometimes invisible ground upon which a great deal of contemporary work and thought are inscribed. Closure stops here.

24.1 CHARLES OLSON

PROJECTIVE   VERSE

1950

> (projectile   (percussive   (prospective
>
>   *vs.*
>
>   The NON-Projective

(or what a French critic calls "closed" verse, that verse which print bred and which is pretty much what we have had, in English & American, and have still got, despite the work of Pound & Williams:

it led Keats, already a hundred years ago, to see it (Wordsworth's, Milton's) in the light of "the Egotistical Sublime"; and it persists, at this latter day, as what you might call the private-soul-at-any-public-wall)

Verse now, 1950, if it is to go ahead, if it is to be of *essential* use, must, I take it, catch up and put into itself certain laws and possibilities of the breath, of the breathing of the man who writes as well as of his listenings. (The revolution of the ear, 1910, the trochee's heave, asks it of the younger poets.)

*   *   *

I want to do two things: first, try to show what projective or OPEN verse is, what it involves, in its act of composition, how, in distinction from the non-projective, it is accomplished; and II, suggest a few ideas about what stance toward reality brings such verse into being, what that stance does, both to the poet and to his reader. (The stance involves, for example, a change beyond, and larger than, the technical, and may, the way things look, lead to new poetics and to new concepts from which some sort of drama, say, or of epic, perhaps, may emerge.)

I

First, some simplicities that a man learns, if he works in OPEN, or what can also be called COMPOSITION BY FIELD, as opposed to inherited line, stanza, over-all form, what is the "old" base of the non-projective.

(1) the *kinetics* of the thing. A poem is energy transferred from where the poet got it (he will have some several causations), by way of the poem itself to, all the way over to, the reader. Okay. Then the poem itself must, at all points, be a high energy-construct and, at all points, an energy-discharge. So: how is the poet to accomplish same energy, how is he, what is the process by which a poet gets in, at all points energy at least the equivalent of the energy which propelled him in the first place, yet an energy which is peculiar to verse alone and which will be, obviously, also different from the energy which the reader, because he is a third term, will take away?

This is the problem which any poet who departs from closed form is specially confronted by. And it involves a whole series of new recognitions. From the moment he ventures into FIELD COMPOSITION—put himself in the open—he can go by no track other than the one the poem under hand declares, for itself. Thus he has to behave, and be, instant by instant, aware of some several forces just now beginning to be examined. (It is much more, for example, this push, than simply such a one as Pound put, so wisely, to get us started: "the musical phrase," go by it, boys, rather than by, the metronome.)

(2) is the *principle*, the law which presides conspicuously over such composition, and, when obeyed, is the reason why a projective poem can come into being. It is this: FORM IS NEVER MORE THAN AN EXTENSION OF CONTENT. (Or so it got phrased by one, R. Creeley, and it makes absolute sense to me, with this possible corollary, that right form, in any given poem, is the only and exclusively possible extension of content under hand.) There it is, brothers, sitting there, for USE.

Now (3) the *process* of the thing, how the principle can be made so to shape the energies that the form is accomplished. And I think it can be boiled down to one statement (first pounded into my head by Edward Dahlberg): ONE PERCEPTION MUST IMMEDIATELY AND DIRECTLY LEAD TO A FURTHER PERCEPTION. It means exactly what it says, is a matter of, at *all* points (even, I should say, of our management of daily reality as of the daily work) get on with it, keep moving, keep in, speed, the nerves, their speed, the perceptions, theirs, the acts, the split second acts, the whole business, keep it moving as fast as you can, citizen. And if you also set up as a poet, USE USE USE the process at all points, in any given poem always, always one perception must must must MOVE, INSTANTER, ON ANOTHER!

So there we are, fast, there's the dogma. And its excuse, its usableness, in practice. Which gets us, it ought to get us, inside the machinery, now, 1950, of how projective verse is made.

If I hammer, if I recall in, and keep calling in, the breath, the breathing as distinguished from the hearing, it is for cause, it is to insist upon a part that breath plays in verse which has not (due, I think, to the smothering of the power of the line by too set a concept of foot) has not been sufficiently observed or practiced, but which has to be if verse is to advance to its proper force and place in the day, now, and ahead. I take it that PROJECTIVE VERSE teaches, is, this lesson, that that verse will only do in which a poet manages to register both the acquisitions of his ear *and* the pressures of his breath.

Let's start from the smallest particle of all, the syllable. It is the king and pin of versification, what rules and holds together the lines, the larger forms, of a poem. I would suggest that verse here and in England dropped this secret from the late Elizabethans to Ezra Pound, lost it, in the sweetness of meter and rime, in a honey-head. (The syllable is one way to distinguish the original success of blank verse, and its falling off, with Milton.)

It is by their syllables that words juxtapose in beauty, by these particles of sound as clearly as by the sense of the words which they compose. In any given instance, because there is a choice of words, the choice, if a man is in there, will be, spontaneously, the obedience of his ear to the syllables. The fineness, and the practice, lie here, at the minimum and source of speech.

> O western wynd, when wilt thou blow
> And the small rain down shall rain
> O Christ that my love were in my arms
> And I in my bed again

It would do no harm, as an act of correction to both prose and verse as now written, if both rime and meter, and, in the quantity words, both sense and sound, were less in the forefront of the mind than the syllable, if the syllable, that fine creature, were more allowed to lead the harmony on. With this warning, to those who would try: to step back here to this place of the elements and minims of language, is to engage speech where it is least careless—and least logical. Listening for the syllables must be so constant and so scrupulous, the exaction must be so complete, that the assurance of the ear is purchased at the highest—40 hours a day—price. For from the root out, from all over the place, the syllable comes, the figures of, the dance:

> "Is" comes from the Aryan root, *as*, to breathe. The English "not" equals the Sanscrit *na*, which may come from the root *na*, to be lost, to perish. "Be" is from *bhu*, to grow.

I say the syllable, king, and that it is spontaneous, this way: the ear, the ear which has collected, which has listened, the ear, which is so close to the mind that it is the mind's, that it has the mind's speed . . .

it is close, another way: the mind is brother to this sister and is, because it is so close, is the drying force, the incest, the sharpener . . .

it is from the union of the mind and the ear that the syllable is born.

But the syllable is only the first child of the incest of verse (always, that Egyptian thing, it produces twins!). The other child is the LINE. And together, these two, the syllable *and* the line, they make a poem, they make that thing, the—what shall we call it, the Boss of all, the "Single Intelligence." And the line comes (I swear it) from the breath, from the breathing of the man who writes, at the moment that he writes, and thus is, it is here that, the daily work, the WORK, gets in, for only he, the man who writes, can declare, at every moment, the line its metric and its ending—where its breathing, shall come to, termination.

The trouble with most work, to my taking, since the breaking away from traditional lines and stanzas, and from such wholes as, say, Chaucer's *Troilus* or S's *Lear*, is: contemporary workers go lazy RIGHT HERE WHERE THE LINE IS BORN.

Let me put it baldly. The two halves are:
>   the HEAD, by way of the EAR, to the SYLLABLE
>   the HEART, by way of the BREATH, to the LINE

And the joker? that it is in the 1st half of the proposition that, in composing, one lets-it-rip; and that it is in the 2nd half, surprise, it is the LINE that's the baby that gets, as the poem is getting made, the attention, the control, that it is right here, in the line, that the shaping takes place, each moment of the going.

I am dogmatic, that the head shows in the syllable. The dance of the intellect is there, among them, prose or verse. Consider the best minds you know in this here business: where does the head show, is it not, precise, here, in the swift currents of the syllable? can't you tell a brain when you see what it does, just there? It is true, what the master says he picked up from Confusion: all the thots men are capable of can be entered on the back of a postage stamp. So, is it not the PLAY of a mind we are after, is not that that shows whether a mind is there at all?

And the threshing floor for the dance? Is it anything but the LINE? And when the line has, is, a deadness, is it not a heart which has gone lazy, is it not, suddenly, slow things, similes, say, adjectives, or such, that we are bored by?

For there is a whole flock of rhetorical devices which have now to be brought under a new bead, now that we sight with the line. Simile is only one bird who comes down, too easily. The descriptive functions generally have to be watched, every second, in projective verse, because of their easiness, and thus their drain on the energy which composition by field allows into a poem. *Any* slackness takes off attention, that crucial thing, from the job in hand, from the *push* of the line under hand at the moment, under the reader's eye, in his moment. Observation of any kind is, like argument in prose, properly previous to the act of the poem, and, if allowed in, must be so juxtaposed, apposed, set in, that it does not, for an instant, sap the going energy of the content toward its form.

It comes to this, this whole aspect of the newer problems. (We now enter, actually, the large area of the whole poem, into the FIELD, if you like, where all the syllables and all the lines must be managed in their relations to each other.) It is a matter, finally, of OBJECTS, what they are, what they are inside a poem, how they got there, and, once there, how they are to be used. This is something I want to get to in another way in Part II, but, for the moment, let me indicate this, that every element in an open poem (the syllable, the line, as well as the image, the sound, the sense) must be taken up as participants in the kinetic of the poem just as solidly as we are accustomed to take what we call the objects of reality; and that these elements are to be seen as creating the tensions of a poem just as totally as do those other objects create what we know as the world.

The objects which occur at every given moment of composition (of recognition, we can call it) are, can be, must be treated exactly as they do occur therein and not by any ideas or preconceptions from outside the poem, must be handled as a series of objects in field in such a way that a series of tensions (which they also are) are made to *hold*, and to hold exactly inside the content and the context of the poem which has forced itself, through the poet and them, into being.

Because breath allows *all* the speech-force of language back in (speech is the "solid" of verse, is the secret of a poem's energy), because, now, a poem has, by speech, solidity, everything in it can now be treated as solids, objects, things; and, though insisting upon the absolute difference of the reality of verse from that other dispersed and distributed thing, yet each of these elements of a poem can be allowed to have the play of their separate energies and can be allowed, once the poem is well composed, to keep, as those other objects do, their proper confusions.

Which brings us up, immediately, bang, against tenses, in fact against syntax, in fact against grammar generally, that is, as we have inherited it. Do not tenses, must they not also be kicked around anew, in order that time, that other governing absolute, may be kept, as must the space-tensions of a poem, immediate, contemporary to the acting-on-you of the poem? I would argue that here, too, the LAW OF THE LINE, which projective verse creates, must be hewn to, obeyed, and that the conventions which logic has forced on syntax must be broken open as quietly as must the too set feet of the old line. But an analysis of how far a new poet can stretch the very conventions on which communication by language rests, is too big for these notes, which are meant, I hope it is obvious, merely to get things started.

Let me just throw in this. It is my impression that *all* parts of speech suddenly, in composition by field, are fresh for both sound and percussive use, spring up like unknown, unnamed vegetables in the patch, when you work it, come spring. Now take Hart Crane. What strikes me in him is the singleness of the push to the nominative, his push along that one arc of freshness, the attempt to get back to word as handle. (If logos is word as thought, what is word as noun, as, pass me that, as Newman Shea used to ask, at the galley table, put a jib on the blood, will ya.) But there is a loss in Crane of what Fenollosa is so right about, in syntax, the sentence as first act of nature, as lightning, as passage of force from subject to object, quick, in this case, from Hart to me, in every case, from me to you, the VERB, between two nouns. Does not Hart miss the advantages, by such an isolated push, miss the point of the whole front of syllable, line, field, and what happened to all language, and to the poem, as a result?

I return you now to London, to beginnings, to the syllable, for the pleasures of it, to intermit:

> If music be the food of love, play on,
> give me excess of it, that, surfeiting,
> the appetite may sicken, and so die.
> That strain again. It had a dying fall,
> o, it came over my ear like the sweet sound
> that breathes upon a bank of violets,
> stealing and giving odour.

What we have suffered from, is manuscript, press, the removal of verse from its producer and its reproducer, the voice, a removal by one, by two removes from its place of origin *and* its destination. For the breath has a double meaning which latin had not yet lost.

The irony is, from the machine has come one gain not yet sufficiently observed or used, but which leads directly on toward projective verse and its consequences. It is the advantage of the typewriter that, due to its rigidity and its space precisions, it can, for a poet, indicate exactly the breath, the pauses, the suspensions even of syllables, the juxtapositions even of parts of phrases, which he intends. For the first time the poet has the stave and the bar a musician has had. For the first time he can, without the convention of rime and meter, record the listening he has done to his own speech and by that one act indicate how he would want any reader, silently or otherwise, to voice his work.

It is time we picked the fruits of the experiments of Cummings, Pound, Williams, each of whom has, after his way, already used the machine as a scoring to his composing, as a script to its vocalization. It is now only a matter of the recognition of the conventions of composition by field for us to bring into being an open verse as formal as the closed, with all its traditional advantages.

If a contemporary poet leaves a space as long as the phrase before it, he means that space to be held, by the breath, an equal length of time. If he suspends a word or syllable at the end of a line (this was most Cummings' addition) he means that time to pass that it takes the eye—that hair of time suspended—to pick up the next line. If he wishes a pause so light it hardly separates the words, yet does not want a comma—which is an interruption of the meaning rather than the sounding of the line—follow him when he uses a symbol the typewriter has ready to hand:

"What does not change / is the will to change"

Observe him, when he takes advantage of the machine's multiple margins, to juxtapose:

> "Sd he:
>> to dream takes no effort
>>> to think is easy
>>>> to act is more difficult
>
>> but for a man to act after he has taken thought, this!
> is the most difficult thing of all"

Each of these lines is a progressing of both the meaning and the breathing forward, and then a backing up, without a progress or any kind of movement outside the unit of time local to the idea.

There is more to be said in order that this convention be recognized, especially in order that the revolution out of which it came may be so forwarded that work will get published to offset the reaction now afoot to return verse to inherited forms of cadence and rime. But what I want to emphasize here, by this emphasis on the typewriter as the personal and instantaneous recorder of the poet's work, is the already projective nature of verse as the sons of Pound and Williams are practicing it. Already they are composing as though verse was to have the reading its writing involved, as though not the eye but the ear was to be its measurer, as though the intervals of its composition could be so carefully put down as to be precisely the intervals of its registration. For the ear, which once had the burden of memory to quicken it (rime & regular cadence were its aids and have merely lived on in print after the oral necessities were ended) can now again, that the poet has his means, be the threshold of projective verse.

II

Which gets us to what I promised, the degree to which the projective involves a stance toward reality outside a poem as well as a new stance towards the reality of a poem itself. It is a matter of content, the content of Homer or of Euripides or of Seami as distinct from that which I might call the more "literary" masters. From the moment the projective purpose of the act of verse is recognized, the content does — it will — change. If the beginning and the end is breath, voice in its largest sense, then the material of verse shifts. It has to. It starts with the composer. The dimension of his line itself changes, not to speak of the change in his conceiving, of the matter he will turn to, of the scale in which he imagines that matter's use. I myself would pose the difference by a physical image. It is no accident that Pound and Williams both were involved variously in a movement which got called "objectivism." But that word was then used in some sort of a necessary quarrel, I take it, with "subjectivism." It is now too late to be bothered with the latter. It has excellently done itself to death, even though we are all caught in its dying. What seems to me a more valid formulation for present use is "objectism," a word to be taken to stand for the kind of relation of man to experience which a poet might state as the necessity of a line or a work to be as wood is, to be as clean as wood is as it issues from the hand of nature, to be shaped as wood can be when a man has had his hand to it. Objectism is the getting rid of the lyrical interference of the individual as ego, of the "subject" and his soul, that peculiar presumption by which western man has interposed himself between what he is as a creature of nature (with certain instructions to carry out) and those other creations of nature which we may, with no derogation, call objects. For a man is himself an object, whatever he may take to be his advantages, the more likely to recognize himself as such the greater his advantages, particularly at that moment that he achieves an humilitas sufficient to make him of use.

It comes to this: the use of a man, by himself and thus by others, lies in how he conceives his relation to nature, that force to which he owes his somewhat small existence. If he sprawl, he shall find little to sing but himself, and shall sing, nature has such paradoxical ways, by way of artificial forms outside himself. But if he stays inside himself, if he is contained within his nature as he is participant in the larger force, he will be able to listen, and his hearing through himself will give him secrets objects share. And by an inverse law his shapes will make their own way. It is in this sense that the projective act, which is the artist's act in the larger field of objects, leads to dimensions larger than the man. For a man's problem, the moment he takes speech up in all its fullness, is to give his work his seriousness, a seriousness sufficient to cause the thing he makes to try to take its place alongside the things of nature. This is not easy. Nature works from reverence, even in her destructions (species go down with a crash). But breath is man's special qualification as animal. Sound is a dimension he has extended. Language is one of his proudest acts. And when a poet rests in these as they are in himself (in his physiology, if you like, but the life in him, for all that) then he, if he chooses to speak from these roots, works in that area where nature has given him size, projective size.

It is projective size that the play *The Trojan Women* possesses, for it is able to stand, is it not, as its people do, beside the Aegean—and neither Andromache or the sea suffer diminution. In a less "heroic" but equally "natural" dimension Seami causes the Fisherman and the Angel to stand clear in *Hagoromo*. And Homer, who is such an unexamined cliche that I do not think I need to press home in what scale Nausicaa's girls wash their clothes.

Such works, I should argue — and I use them simply because their equivalents are yet to be done — could not issue from men who conceived verse without the full relevance of human voice, without reference to where lines come from, in the individual who writes. Nor do I think it accident that, at this end point of the argument, I should use, for examples, two dramatists and an epic poet. For I would hazard the guess that, if projective verse is practiced long enough, is driven ahead hard enough along the course I think it dictates, verse again can carry much larger material than it has carried in our language since the Elizabethans. But it can't be jumped. We are only at its beginnings, and if I think that the *Cantos* make more "dramatic" sense than do the plays of Mr. Eliot, it is not because I think they have solved the problem but because the methodology of the verse in them points a way by which, one day, the problem of larger content and of larger forms may be solved. Eliot is, in fact, a proof of a present danger, of "too easy" a going on the practice of verse as it has been, rather than as it must be, practiced. There is no question, for example, that Eliot's line, from "Prufrock" on down, has speech-force, is "dramatic," is, in fact, one of the most notable lines since Dryden. I suppose it stemmed immediately to him from Browning, as did so many of Pound's early things. In any case Eliot's line has obvious relations backward to the Elizabethans, especially to the soliloquy. Yet O. M. Eliot is *not* projective. It could even be argued (and I say this carefully, as I have said all things about the non-projective, having considered how each of us must save himself after his own fashion and how much, for that matter, each of us owes to the non-projective, and will continue to owe, as both go alongside each other) but it could be argued that it is because Eliot has stayed inside the non-projective that he fails as a dramatist — that his root is the mind alone, and a scholastic mind at that (no high *intelletto* despite his apparent clarities) — and that, in his listenings he has stayed there where the ear and the mind are, has only gone from his fine ear outward rather than, as I say a projective poet will, down through the workings of his own throat to that place where breath comes from, where breath has its beginnings, where drama has to come from, where, the coincidence is, all act springs.

PART 25

Nativism

Individualism is often, at its strongest, attached to the notion of place. Each page written by the most particular of writers, in the sense of individuality, seems to spring from some special land. So we identify Willa Cather with the Midwest, sense that Yoknapataupha County is part of Mississippi, invented as it might be and belonging to the world as it does. So we feel that the New York of Edith Wharton and Henry James is the real one, that Flannery O'Connor's peacocks are strictly Southern, and that *The Country of the Pointed Firs* could exist only in New England.

Among the writers bound up with and speaking for their brand of regionalism or Nativism, the poet and painter Marsden Hartley and the writer Eudora Welty are two of the most convincing.

25.1 D. H. LAWRENCE

The Spirit of Place

1923

We like to think of the old-fashioned American classics as children's books. Just childishness, on our part. The old American art-speech contains an alien quality, which belongs to the American continent and to nowhere else. But, of course, so long as we insist on reading the books as children's tales, we miss all that.

One wonders what the proper high-brow Romans of the third and fourth or later centuries read into the strange utterances of Lucretius or Apuleius or Tertullian, Augustine or Athanasius. The uncanny voice of Iberian Spain, the weirdness of old Carthage, the passion of Libya and North Africa; you may bet the proper old Romans never heard these at all. They read old Latin inference over the top of it, as we read old European inference over the top of Poe or Hawthorne.

It is hard to hear a new voice, as hard as it is to listen to an unknown language. We just don't listen. There is a new voice in the old American classics. The world has declined to hear it, and has babbled about children's stories.

Why? — Out of fear. The world fears a new experience more than it fears anything. Because a new experience displaces so many old experiences. And it is like trying to use muscles that have perhaps never been used, or that have been going stiff for ages. It hurts horribly.

The world doesn't fear a new idea. It can pigeon-hole any idea. But it can't pigeon-hole a real new experience. It can only dodge. The world is a great dodger, and the Americans the greatest. Because they dodge their own very selves.

There is a new feeling in the old American books, far more than there is in the modern American books, which are pretty empty of any feeling, and proud of it. There is a "different" feeling in the old American classics. It is the shifting over from the old psyche to something new, a displacement. And displacements hurt. This hurts. So we try to tie it up, like a cut finger. Put a rag round it.

It is a cut too. Cutting away the old emotions and consciousness. Don't ask what is left.

Art-speech is the only truth. An artist is usually a damned liar, but his art, if it be art, will tell you the truth of his day. And that is all that matters. Away with eternal truth. Truth lives from day to day, and the marvellous Plato of yesterday is chiefly bosh to-day.

The old American artists were hopeless liars. But they were artists, in spite of themselves. Which is more than you can say of most living practitioners.

And you can please yourself, when you read *The Scarlet Letter*, whether you accept what that sugary, blue-eyed little darling of a Hawthorne has to say for himself, false as all darlings are, or whether you read the impeccable truth of his art-speech.

The curious thing about art-speech is that it prevaricates so terribly, I mean it tells such lies. I suppose because we always all the time tell ourselves lies. And out of a pattern of lies art weaves the truth. Like Dostoevsky posing as a sort of Jesus, but most truthfully revealing himself all the while as a little horror.

Truly art is a sort of subterfuge. But thank God for it, we can see through the subterfuge if we choose. Art has two great functions. First, it provides an emotional experience. And then, if we have the courage of our own feelings, it becomes a mine of practical truth. We have had the feelings *ad nauseam*. But we've never dared dig the actual truth out of them, the truth that concerns us, whether it concerns our grandchildren or not.

The artist usually sets out—or used to—to point a moral and adorn a tale. The tale, however, points the other way, as a rule. Two blankly opposing morals, the artist's and the tale's. Never trust the artist. Trust the tale. The proper function of a critic is to save the tale from the artist who created it.

Now we know our business in these studies; saving the American tale from the American artist.

Let us look at this American artist first. How did he ever get to America, to start with? Why isn't he a European still, like his father before him?

Now listen to me, don't listen to him. He'll tell you the lie you expect. Which is partly your fault for expecting it.

He didn't come in search of freedom of worship. England had more freedom of worship in the year 1700 than America had. Won by Englishmen who wanted freedom, and so stopped at home and fought for it. And got it. Freedom of worship? Read the history of New England during the first century of its existence.

Freedom anyhow? The land of the free! This the land of the free! Why, if I say anything that displeases them, the free mob will lynch me, and that's my freedom. Free? Why, I have never been in any country where the individual has such an abject fear of his fellow countrymen. Because, as I say, they are free to lynch him the moment he shows he is not one of them.

No, no, if you're so fond of the truth about Queen Victoria, try a little about yourself.

Those Pilgrim Fathers and their successors never came here for freedom of worship. What did they set up when they got here? Freedom, would you call it?

They didn't come for freedom. Or if they did, they sadly went back on themselves.

All right then, what did they come for? For lots of reasons. Perhaps least of all in search of freedom of any sort: positive freedom, that is.

They came largely to get *away*—that most simple of motives. To get away. Away from what? In the long run, away from themselves. Away from everything. That's why most people have come to America, and still do come. To get away from everything they are and have been.

"Henceforth be masterless."

Which is all very well, but it isn't freedom. Rather the reverse. A hopeless sort of constraint. It is never freedom till you find something you really *positively want to be.* And people in America have always been shouting about the things they are *not.* Unless, of course, they are millionaires, made or in the making.

And after all there is a positive side to the movement. All that vast flood of human life that has flowed over the Atlantic in ships from Europe to America has not flowed over simply on a tide of revulsion from Europe and from the confinements of the European ways of life. This revulsion was, and still is, I believe, the prime motive in emigration. But there was some cause, even for the revulsion.

It seems as if at times man had a frenzy for getting away from any control of any sort. In Europe the old Christianity was the real master. The Church and the true aristocracy bore the responsibility for the working out of the Christian ideals: a little irregularly, maybe, but responsible nevertheless.

Mastery, kingship, fatherhood had their power destroyed at the time of the Renaissance.

And it was precisely at this moment that the great drift over the Atlantic started. What were men drifting away from? The old authority of Europe? Were they breaking the bonds of authority, and escaping to a new more absolute unrestrainedness? Maybe. But there was more to it.

Liberty is all very well, but men cannot live without masters. There is always a master. And men either live in glad obedience to the master they believe in, or they live in a frictional opposition to the master they wish to undermine. In America this frictional opposition has been the vital factor. It has given the Yankee his kick. Only the continual influx of more servile Europeans has provided America with an obedient labouring class. The true obedience never outlasting the first generation.

But there sits the old master, over in Europe. Like a parent. Somewhere deep in every American heart lies a rebellion against the old parenthood of Europe. Yet no American feels he has completely escaped its mastery. Hence the slow, smouldering patience of American opposition. The slow, smouldering, corrosive obedience to the old master Europe, the unwilling subject, the unremitting opposition.

Whatever else you are, be masterless.

"Ca Ca Caliban
Get a new master, be a new man."

Escaped slaves, we might say, people the republics of Liberia or Haiti. Liberia enough! Are we to look at America in the same way? A vast republic of escaped slaves. When you consider the hordes from eastern Europe, you might well say it: a vast republic of escaped slaves. But one dare not say this of the Pilgrim Fathers, and the great old body of idealist Americans, the modern Americans tortured with thought. A vast republic of escaped slaves. Look out, America! And a minority of earnest, self-tortured people.

The masterless.

"Ca Ca Caliban
Get a new master, be a new man."

What did the Pilgrim Fathers come for, then, when they came so gruesomely over the black sea? Oh, it was in a black spirit. A black revulsion from Europe, from the old authority of Europe, from kings and bishops and popes. And more. When you look into it, more. They were black, masterful men, they wanted something else. No kings, no bishops maybe. Even no God Almighty. But also, no more of this new "humanity" which followed the Renaissance. None of this new liberty which was to be so pretty in Europe. Something grimmer, by no means free-and-easy.

America has never been easy, and is not easy to-day. Americans have always been at a certain tension. Their liberty is a thing of sheer will, sheer tension: a liberty of THOU SHALT NOT. And it has been so from the first. The land of THOU SHALT NOT. Only the first commandment is: THOU SHALT NOT PRESUME TO BE A MASTER. Hence democracy.

"We are the masterless." That is what the American Eagle shrieks. It's a Hen-Eagle.

The Spaniards refused the post-Renaissance liberty of Europe. And the Spaniards filled most of America. The Yankees, too, refused, refused the post-Renaissance humanism of Europe. First and foremost, they hated masters. But under that, they hated the flowing ease of humour in Europe. At the bottom of the American soul was always a dark suspense, at the bottom of the Spanish-American soul the same. And this dark suspense hated and hates the old European spontaneity, watches it collapse with satisfaction.

Every continent has its own great spirit of place. Every people is polarized in some particular locality, which is home, the homeland. Different places on the face of the earth have different vital effluence, different vibration, different chemical exhalation, different polarity with different stars: call it what you like. But the spirit of place is a great reality. The Nile valley produced not only the corn, but the terrific religions of Egypt. China produces the Chinese, and will go on doing so. The Chinese in San Francisco will in time cease to be Chinese, for America is a great melting-pot.

There was a tremendous polarity in Italy, in the city of Rome. And this seems to have died. For even places die. The Island of Great Britain had a wonderful terrestrial magnetism or polarity of its own, which made the British people. For the moment, this polarity seems to be breaking. Can England die? And what if England dies?

Men are less free than they imagine; ah, far less free. The freest are perhaps least free.

Men are free when they are in a living homeland, not when they are straying and breaking away. Men are free when they are obeying some deep, inward voice of religious belief. Obeying from within. Men are free when they belong to a living, organic, *believing* community, active in fulfilling some unfulfilled, perhaps unrealized purpose. Not when they are escaping to some wild west. The most unfree souls go west, and shout of freedom. Men are freest when they are most unconscious of freedom. The shout is a rattling of chains, always was.

Men are not free when they are doing just what they like. The moment you can do just what you like, there is nothing you care about doing. Men are only free when they are doing what the deepest self likes.

And there is getting down to the deepest self! It takes some diving.

Because the deepest self is way down, and the conscious self is an obstinate monkey. But of one thing we may be sure. If one wants to be free, one has to give up the illusion of doing what one likes, and seek what IT wishes done.

But before you can do what IT likes, you must first break the spell of the old mastery, the old IT.

Perhaps at the Renaissance, when kingship and fatherhood fell, Europe drifted into a very dangerous half-truth: of liberty and equality. Perhaps the men who went to America felt this, and so repudiated the old world together. Went one better than Europe. Liberty in America has meant so far the breaking away from *all* dominion. The true liberty will only begin when Americans discover IT, and proceed possibly to fulfil IT. IT being the deepest *whole* self of man, the self in its wholeness, not idealistic halfness.

That's why the Pilgrim Fathers came to America, then; and that's why we come. Driven by IT. We cannot see that invisible winds carry us, as they carry swarms of locusts, that invisible magnetism brings us as it brings the migrating birds to their unforeknown goal. But it is so. We are not the marvellous choosers and deciders we think we are. IT chooses for us, and decides for us. Unless, of course, we are just escaped slaves, vulgarly cocksure of our ready-made destiny. But if we are living people, in touch with the source, IT drives us and decides us. We are free only so long as we obey. When we run counter, and think we will do as we like, we just flee around like Orestes pursued by the Eumenides.

And still, when the great day begins, when Americans have at last discovered America and their own wholeness, still there will be the vast number of escaped slaves to reckon with, those who have no cocksure, ready-made destinies.

Which will win in America, the escaped slaves, or the new whole men?

The real American day hasn't begun yet. Or at least, not yet sunrise. So far it has been the false dawn. That is, in the progressive American consciousness there has been the one dominant desire, to do away with the old thing. Do away with masters, exalt the will of the people. The will of the people being nothing but a figment, the exalting doesn't count for much. So, in the name of the will of the people, get rid of masters. When you have got rid of masters, you are left with this mere phrase of the will of the people. Then you pause and bethink yourself, and try to recover your own wholeness.

So much for the conscious American motive, and for democracy over here. Democracy in America is just the tool with which the old master of Europe, the European spirit, is undermined. Europe destroyed, potentially, American democracy will evaporate. America will begin.

American consciousness has so far been a false dawn. The negative ideal of democracy. But underneath, and contrary to this open ideal, the first hints and revelations of IT. IT, the American whole soul.

You have got to pull the democratic and idealistic clothes off American utterance, and see what you can of the dusky body of IT underneath.

"Henceforth be masterless."

Henceforth be mastered.

25.2 MARSDEN HARTLEY

On the Subject of Nativeness—A Tribute to Maine

1937

The subject matter of the pictures in this present exhibition [at An American Place, January 7–February 27, 1936] is derived from my own native country—New England—and the country beyond to the north—geologically much the same thing, with, if possible, an added tang because it is if anything wilder still, and the people that inhabit it, fine types of hard boned sturdy beings, have the direct simplicity of these unique and original places, this country being of course, Nova Scotia. These people, the kind one expects to encounter in the forests where the moose and caribou range, and who, sauntering toward the nearer south in search of food which deep snows deny them, are on perilous ground, doomed to decrease in numbers. As a boy in Maine, one read the news items in the paper after October, and the casual daily report was—So-and-So lost in the woods, perished of hunger and cold, and often never found until the thaws of spring, and it is exactly the same today.

The opulent rigidity of this north country, which is a kind of cousin to Labrador and the further ice-fields, produces a simple, unaffected conduct and with it a kind of stark poetry exudes from their behaviours, that hardiness of gaze and frank earnestness of approach which is typical of all northerners which is sometimes as refreshing to the eye as cool spring water is to the throat, because there is the quality of direct companionship in it, and—if you are seen, you are seen "through," there is no mystery you can offer, quite like the encounter with the Indians in the southwest, for whom silent contact is the sure means of a declaration of friendship, and since you cannot deceive them, they make no attempt to deceive you, so that, generally speaking, how do you do is much the same thing as how do you do my friend, which is exactly the Indian method.

Those great sea faces up there in the north are wonderful with directness and trust, and since silence is the bond, silence is the enriching channel by which you make social contact, or at least to say, brief speech and much meat in it.

Husbands and sons are drowned at sea, and this is just as natural to hear as if they died of the measles or of a fever, and these men who are pretty much as children always, go to their death without murmur and without reproach.

Maine is likewise a strong, simple, stately and perhaps brutal country, you get directness of demeanor, and you know where you stand, for lying is a detestation, as it is not in the cities.

To the outsider New England is New England, no matter what route he takes, he takes out his gasoline road map, and it is much the same thing to him because he thinks of routes and of how much ground he can cover, but tell this to the secular New Englander and you get into trouble, and for a Vermonter—New England is never anything but Vermont—New Hampshire, being pretty much sold out to the rich invader, has without doubt its sense of pure locality when the said invader has left.

To the Maine-"iac" New England is never anything but Maine, he never says he comes from New England, he comes from Maine, and Maine is his country and his place of origins, bounded on every side by its people, its place, and its ideas, just as a Boston one would never dream of saying he is from Massachusetts, and how could he?

This quality of abstract yet definite reality appears in the realm of art in its strongest and most powerful degree in the paintings of Albert Ryder, who has said once and for all—all that will ever be known about that country, and it is given further local significance in the work of George Fuller and of Winslow Homer, who though having been born in Boston, spent the most expressive part of his life at Prout's Neck, Maine.

A fierce Yankee was Homer, keeping a shotgun behind his door for years against the local invader of his property, so the story goes, who must at that time have harrassed him.

In the field of music, Maine has come to the front with such names as Emma Eames of Bath, Lillian (Norton) Nordica of Skowhegan, Annie Louise Cary of Durham, as in the field of literature there are the names of Edwin Arlington Robinson of Gardiner, Edna St. Vincent Millay of Rockland, Wallace Gould and Holman Day of Lewiston, and as a native Maine artist, myself from Lewiston, and we are not forgetting Longfellow.

There is a new school of literature of Maine coming to the front such as the names of Rachel Field, Mary Ellen Chase, Gerald Warner Brace, William Haynes, Frederick Nebel, I. H. Carter, E. Myers, B. A. Williams, and Robert Tristram Coffin, whose latest volume of local flavour verse surprises one with the vivid localism of its characterization, proving that when localism is true, it is bound to survive and recreate itself.

"The Country of the Pointed Firs" and the other attractive stories of Maine of Sara Orne Jewett did much to produce the local sense of literature, and the tradition has been carried on by the now well known others, Robert Frost added his sharp values to the west in New Hampshire.

If you will probably find never a mention of Maine in the stark poetry of Edwin Arlington Robinson, no one could be more representative in his type of speech, no one more typical of the bitter behaviours of place, but we must correct the New York art critic who says, "why do Vermont and Maine always weep" by remarking that they never weep, they grit their teeth and face the gale.

It is the habit of middle westerner regional rooters to speak of New England as the fag end of Europe, but that is because, knowing little or nothing about it, they dispatch it at once with a derogation of Harvard, which of course is not a place but a school.

The essential nativeness of Maine remains as it was, and the best Maine-iacs are devout with purposes of defense.

The Androscoggin, the Kennebec, and the Penobscot flow down to the sea as solemnly as ever, and the numberless inland lakes harbour the loon, and give rest to the angles of geese making south or north according to season, and the black bears roam over the mountain tops as usual.

If the Zeppelin rides the sky at night, and aeroplanes set flocks of sea gulls flying, the gulls remain the same and the rocks, pines, and thrashing seas never lose their power and their native tang.

Nativeness is built of such primitive things, and whatever is one's nativeness, one holds and never loses no matter how far afield the traveling may be.

Henry Adams' Boston is in every line of the "Education" and the great Jameses never shook the soil of their native heath from their traveling feet, not even Henry the European, who pled inwardly at the last for return, and if Edith Wharton spends a deal of her time at Hyères in the South of France, she writes just as bitterly of her native New England, William James always discouraging the family habit of traversing Europe, came home finally and planted himself under his own loved Chocorua.

If there are no pictures of Maine in this present exhibition, it is due entirely to forward circumstance and never in any sense to lack of interest, my own education having begun in my native hills, going with me—these hills wherever I went, looking never more wonderful than they did to me in Paris, Berlin, or Provence.

Dogtown and Nova Scotia then, being the recent hunting ground of my art endeavors, are as much my native land as if I had been born in them, for they are of the same stout substance and texture, and bear the same steely integrity.

Those pictures which are not scenes, are in their way portraits of objects which relieves them from being still-lives, objects thrown up with the tides on the shores of the island where I have been living of late, the marine vistas to express the seas of the north, the objects at my feet everywhere which the tides washed up representing the visible life of place, such as fragments of rope thrown overboard out on the Grand Banks by the fishermen, or shells and other crustaces driven in from their moorings among the matted seaweed and the rocks, given up even as the lost at sea are sometimes given up.

This quality of nativeness is coloured by heritage, birth, and environment, and it is therefore for this reason that I wish to declare myself the painter from Maine.

We are subjects of our nativeness, and are at all times happily subject to it, only the mollusc, the chameleon, or the sponge being able to affect dissolution of this aspect.

When the picture makers with nature as their subject get closer than they have for some time been, there will naturally be better pictures of nature, and who more than Nature will be surprised, and perhaps more delighted?

And so I say to my native continent of Maine, be patient and forgiving, I will soon put my cheek to your cheek, expecting the welcome of the prodigal, and be glad of it, listening all the while to the slow, rich, solemn music of the Androscoggin, as it flows along.

25.3 Eudora Welty
Place in Fiction
1956

Place is one of the lesser angels that watch over the racing hand of fiction, perhaps the one that gazes benignly enough from off to one side, while others, like character, plot, symbolic meaning, and so on, are doing a good deal of wing-beating about her chair, and feeling, who in my eyes carries the crown, soars highest of them all and rightly relegates place into the shade. Nevertheless, it is this lowlier angel that concerns us here. There have been signs that she has been rather neglected of late; maybe she could do with a little petitioning.

What place has place in fiction? It might be thought so modest a one that it can be taken for granted: the location of a novel; to use a term of the day, it may make the novel "regional." The term, like most terms used to pin down a novel, means little; and Henry James said there isn't any difference between "the English novel" and "the American novel," since there are only two kinds of novels at all, the good and the bad. Of course Henry James didn't stop there, and we all hate generalities, and so does place. Yet as soon as we step down from the general view to the close and particular, as writers must and readers may and teachers well know how to, and consider, what good writing may be, place can be seen, in her own way, to have a great deal to do with that goodness, if not to be responsible for it. How so?

First, with the goodness—validity—in the raw material of writing. Second, with the goodness in the writing itself—the achieved world of appearance, through which the novelist has his whole say and puts his whole case. There will still be the lady, always, who dismissed *The Ancient Mariner* on grounds of implausibility. Third, with the goodness—the worth—in the writer himself: place is where he has his roots, place is where he stands; in his experience out of which he writes, it provides the base of reference; in his work, the point of view. Let us consider place in fiction in these three wide aspects.

Wide, but of course connected—vitally so. And if in some present-day novels the connection has apparently slipped, that makes a fresh reason for us to ponder the subject of place. For novels, besides being the pleasantest things imaginable, are powerful forces on the side. Mutual understanding in the world being nearly always, as now, at low ebb, it is comforting to remember that it is through art that one country can nearly always speak reliably to another, if the other can hear at all. Art, though, is never the voice of a country; it is an even more precious thing, the voice of the individual, doing its best to speak, not comfort of any sort, indeed, but truth. And the art that speaks it most unmistakably, most directly, most variously, most fully, is fiction; in particular, the novel.

Why? Because the novel from the start has been bound up in the local, the "real," the present, the ordinary day-to-day of human experience. Where the imagination comes in is in directing the use of all this. That use is endless, and there are only four words, of all the millions we've hatched, that a novel rules out: "Once upon a time." They make a story a fairy tale by the simple sweep of the remove—by abolishing the present and the place where we are instead of conveying them to us. Of course we shall have some sort of fairy tale with us always—just now it is the historical novel. Fiction is properly at work on the here and now, or the past made here and now; for in novels *we* have to be there. Fiction provides the ideal texture through which the feeling and meaning that permeate our own personal, present lives will best show through. For in his theme—the most vital and important part of the work at hand—the novelist has the blessing of the inexhaustible subject: you and me. You and me, here. Inside that generous scope and circumference—who could ask for anything more?—the novel can accommodate practically anything on earth; and has abundantly done so. The novel so long as it be *alive* gives pleasure, and must always give pleasure, enough to stave off the departure of the Wedding Guest forever, except for that one lady.

It is by the nature of itself that fiction is all bound up in the local. The internal reason for that is surely that *feelings* are bound up in place. The human mind is a mass of associations—associations more poetic even than actual. I say, "The Yorkshire Moors," and you will say, "*Wuthering Heights,*" and I have only to murmur, "If Father were only alive—" for you to come back with "We could go to Moscow," which certainly is not even so. The truth is, fiction depends for its life on place. Location is the crossroads of circumstance, the proving ground of "What happened? Who's here? Who's coming?"—and that is the heart's field.

Unpredictable as the future of any art must be, one condition we may hazard about writing: of all the arts, it is the one least likely to cut the cord that binds it to its source. Music and dancing, while originating out of place—groves!—and perhaps invoking it still to minds pure or childlike, are no longer bound to dwell there. Sculpture exists out in empty space: that is what it commands and replies to. Toward painting, place, to be so highly visible, has had a curious and changing relationship. Indeed, wasn't it when landscape invaded painting, and painting was given, with the profane content, a narrative content, that this worked to bring on a revolution to the art? Impressionism brought not the likeness-to-life but the mystery of place onto canvas; it was the method, not the subject, that told this. Painting and writing, always the closest two of the sister arts (and in ancient Chinese days only the blink of an eye seems to have separated them), have each a still closer connection with place than they have with each other; but a difference lies in their respective requirements of it, and even further in the way they use it—the written word being ultimately as different from the pigment as the note of the scale is from the chisel.

One element, which has just been mentioned, is surely the underlying bond that connects all the arts with place. All of them celebrate its mystery. Where does this mystery lie? Is it in the fact that place has a more lasting identity than we have, and we unswervingly tend to attach ourselves to identity? Might the magic lie partly, too, in the *name* of the place—since that is what *we* gave it? Surely, once we have it named, we have put a kind of poetic claim on its existence; the claim works even out of sight—may work forever sight unseen. The Seven Wonders of the World still give us this poetic kind of gratification. And notice we do not say simply "The Hanging Gardens"— that would leave them dangling out of reach and dubious in nature; we say "The Hanging Gardens of Babylon," and there they are, before our eyes, shimmering and garlanded and exactly elevated to the Babylonian measurement.

Edward Lear tapped his unerring finger on the magic of place in the limerick. There's something unutterably convincing about that Old Person of Sparta who had twenty-five sons and one darta, and it is surely beyond question that he fed them on snails and weighed them in scales, because we know where that Old Person is *from*—Sparta! We certainly do not need further to be told his *name*. "Consider the source." Experience has ever advised us to base validity on point of origin.

Being shown how to locate, to place, any account is what does most toward *making* us believe it, not merely allowing us to, may the account be the facts or a lie; and that is where place in fiction comes in. Fiction is a lie. Never in its inside thoughts, always in its outside dress.

Some of us grew up with the china night-light, the little lamp whose lighting showed its secret and with that spread enchantment. The outside is painted with a scene, which is one thing; then, when the lamp is lighted, through the porcelain sides a new picture comes out through the old, and they are seen as one. A lamp I knew of was a view of London till it was lit; but then it was the Great Fire of London, and you could go beautifully to sleep by it. The lamp alight is the combination of internal and external, glowing at the imagination as one; and so is the good novel. Seeing that these inner and outer surfaces do lie so close together and so implicit in each other, the wonder is that human life so often separates them, or appears to, and it takes a good novel to put them back together.

The good novel should be steadily alight, revealing. Before it can hope to be that, it must of course be steadily visible from its outside, presenting a continuous, shapely, pleasing and finished surface to the eye.

The sense of a story when the visibility is only partial or intermittent is as endangered as Eliza crossing the ice. Forty hounds of confusion are after it, the black waters of disbelief open up between its steps, and no matter which way it jumps it is bound to slip. Even if it has a little baby moral in its arms, it is more than likely a goner.

The novel must get Eliza across the ice; what it means—the way it proceeds—is always in jeopardy. It must be given a surface that is continuous and unbroken, never too thin to trust, always in touch with the senses. Its world of experience must be at every step, through every moment, within reach as the world of appearance.

This makes it the business of writing, and the responsibility of the writer, to disentangle the significant—in character, incident, setting, mood, every-thing—from the random and meaningless and irrelevant that in real life surround and beset it. It is a matter of his selecting and, by all that implies, of changing "real" life as he goes. With each word he writes, he acts—as lit-erally and methodically as if he hacked his way through a forest and blazed it for the word that follows. He makes choices at the explicit demand of this one present story; each choice implies, explains, limits the next, and illu-minates the one before. No two stories ever go the same way, although in different hands one story might possibly go any one of a thousand ways; and though the woods may look the same from outside, it is a new and dif-ferent labyrinth every time. What tells the author his way? Nothing at all but what he knows inside himself: the same thing that hints to him after-ward how far he has missed it, how near he may have come to the heart of it. In a working sense, the novel and its place have become one: work has made them, for the time being, the same thing, like the explorer's tentative map of the known world.

The reason why every word you write in a good novel is a lie, then, is that it is written expressly to serve the purpose; if it does not apply, it is fancy and frivolous, however specially dear to the writer's heart. Actuality, it is true, is an even bigger risk to the novel than fancy writing is, being fre-quently even more confusing, irrelevant, diluted and generally far-fetched than ill-chosen words can make it. Yet somehow, the world of appearance in the novel has got to *seem* actuality. Is there a reliable solution to the prob-lem? Place being brought to life in the round before the reader's eye is the readiest and gentlest and most honest and natural way this can be brought about, I think; every instinct advises it. The moment the place in which the novel happens is accepted as true, through it will begin to glow, in a kind of recognizable glory, the feeling and thought that inhabited the novel in the author's head and animated the whole of his work.

Besides furnishing a plausible abode for the novel's world of feeling, place has a good deal to do with making the characters real, that is, themselves, and keeping them so. The reason is simply that, as Tristram Shandy ob-served, "We are not made of glass, as characters on Mercury might be." Place *can* be transparent, or translucent: not people. In real life we have to express the things plainest and closest to our minds by the clumsy word and the half-finished gesture; the chances are our most usual behavior makes sense only in a kind of daily way, because it has become familiar to our nearest and dearest, and still demands their constant indulgence and under-standing. It is our describable outside that defines us, willy-nilly, to others, that may save us, or destroy us, in the world; it may be our shield against chaos, our mask against exposure; but whatever it is, the move we make in the place we live has to signify our intent and meaning.

Then think how unprotected the poor character in a novel is, into whose mind the author is inviting us to look—unprotected and hence surely un-believable! But no, the author has expressly seen to believability. Though he must know all, again he works with illusion. Just as the world of a novel is more highly selective than that of real life, so character in a novel is much more definite, less shadowy than our own, in order that we may believe in it. This is not to say that the character's scope must be limited; it is our vision of it that is guided. It is a kind of phenomenon of writing that the likeliest char-acter has first to be enclosed inside the bounds of even greater likelihood, or he will fly to pieces. Paradoxically, the more narrowly we can examine a fictional character, the greater he is likely to loom up. We must see him set to scale in his proper world to know his size. Place, then, has the most delicate control over character too: by confining character, it defines it.

Place in fiction is the named, identified, concrete, exact and exacting, and therefore credible, gathering spot of all that has been felt, is about to be experienced, in the novel's progress. Location pertains to feeling; feeling profoundly pertains to place; place in history partakes of feeling, as feeling about history partakes of place. Every story would be another story, and un-recognizable as art, if it took up its characters and plot and happened some-where else. Imagine *Swann's Way* laid in London, or *The Magic Mountain* in Spain, or *Green Mansions* in the Black Forest. The very notion of moving a novel brings ruder havoc to the mind and affections than would a century's alteration in its time. It is only too easy to conceive that a bomb that could destroy all trace of places as we know them, in life and through books, could also destroy all feelings as we know them, so irretrievably and so happily are recognition, memory, history, valor, love, all the instincts of poetry and praise, worship and endeavor, bound up in place. From the dawn of man's imagination, place has enshrined the spirit; as soon as man stopped wan-dering and stood still and looked about him, he found a god in that place; and from then on, that was where the god abided and spoke from if ever he spoke.

Feelings are bound up in place, and in art, from time to time, place undoubtedly works upon genius. Can anyone well explain otherwise what makes a given dot on the map come passionately alive, for good and all, in a novel—like one of those novae that suddenly blaze with inexplicable fire in the heavens? What brought a *Wuthering Heights* out of Yorkshire, or a *Sound and the Fury* out of Mississippi?

If place does work upon genius, how does it? It may be that place can focus the gigantic, voracious eye of genius and bring its gaze to point. Focus then means awareness, discernment, order, clarity, insight—they are like the attributes of love. The act of focusing itself has beauty and meaning; it is the act that, continued in, turns into mediation, into poetry. Indeed, as soon as the least of us stands still, that is the moment something extraordinary is seen to be going on in the world. The drama, old beyond count as it is, is no older than the first stage. Without the amphitheatre around it to persuade the ear and bend the eye upon a point, how could poetry ever have been spoken, how have been heard? Man is articulate and intelligible only when he begins to communicate inside the strict terms of poetry and reason. Symbols in the end, both are permanent forms of the act of focusing.

Surely place induces poetry, and when the poet is extremely attentive to what is there, a meaning may even attach to his poem out of the spot on earth where it is spoken, and the poem signify the more because it does spring so wholly out of its place, and the sap has run up into it as into a tree.

But we had better confine ourselves here to prose. And then, to take the most absolutely unfanciful novelist of them all, it is to hear him saying, "*Madame Bovary—c'est moi.*" And we see focusing become so intent and aware and conscious in this most "realistic" novel of them all as to amount to fusion. Flaubert's work is indeed of the kind that is embedded immovably as rock in the country of its birth. If, with the slicers of any old (or new) criticism at all, you were to cut down through *Madame Bovary*, its cross section would still be the same as the cross section of that living earth, in texture, color, composition, all; which would be no surprise to Flaubert. For such fusion always means accomplishment no less conscious than it is gigantic— effort that must exist entirely as its own reward. We all know the letter Flaubert wrote when he had just found, in the morning paper, in an account of a minister's visit to Rouen, a phrase in the Mayor's speech of welcome

which I had written the day before, textually, in my *Bovary* . . . Not only were the idea and the words the same, but even the rhythm of the style. It's things like this that give me pleasure . . . Everything one invents is true, you may be perfectly sure of that! Poetry is as precise as geometry . . . And besides, after reaching a certain point, one no longer makes any mistakes about the things of the soul. My poor Bovary, without a doubt, is suffering and weeping this very instant in twenty villages of France.

And now that we have come to the writer himself, the question of place resolves itself into the point of view. In this changeover from the objective to the subjective, wonderful and unexpected variations may occur.

Place, to the writer at work, is seen in a frame. Not an empty frame, a brimming one. Point of view is a sort of burning-glass, a product of personal experience and time; it is burnished with feelings and sensibilities, charged from moment to moment with the sun-points of imagination. It is an instrument—one of intensification; it acts, it behaves, it is temperamental. We have seen that the writer must accurately choose, combine, superimpose upon, blot out, shake up, alter the outside world for one absolute purpose, the good of his story. To do this, he is always seeing double, two pictures at once in his frame, his and the world's, a fact that he constantly comprehends; and he works best in a state of constant and subtle and unfooled reference between the two. It is his clear intention—his passion, I should say—to make the reader see only one of the pictures—the author's—under the pleasing illusion that it is the world's; this enormity is the accomplishment of a good story. I think it likely that at the moment of the writer's highest awareness of, and responsiveness to, the "real" world, his imagination's choice (and miles away it may be from actuality) comes closest to being infallible for his purpose. For the spirit of things is what is sought. No blur of inexactness, no cloud of vagueness, is allowable in good writing; from the first seeing to the last putting down, there must be steady lucidity and uncompromise of purpose. I speak, of course, of the ideal.

One of the most important things the young writer comes to see for himself is that point of view *is* an instrument, not an end in itself, that is useful as a glass, and not as a mirror to reflect a dear and pensive face. Conscientiously used, point of view will discover, explore, see through—it may sometimes divine and prophesy. Misused, it turns opaque almost at once and gets in the way of the book. And when the good novel is finished, its cooled outside shape, what Sean O'Faolàin has called "the veil of reality," has all the burden of communicating that initial, spontaneous, overwhelming, driving charge of personal inner feeling that was the novel's reason for being. The measure of this representation of life corresponds most tellingly with the novel's life expectancy: whenever its world of outside appearance grows dim or false to the eye, the novel has expired.

Establishing a chink-proof world of appearance is not only the first responsibility of the writer; it is the primary step in the technique of every sort of fiction: lyric and romantic, of course; the "realistic," it goes without saying; and other sorts as well. Fantasy itself must touch ground with at least one toe, and ghost stories must have one foot, so to speak, in the grave. The black, squat, hairy ghosts of M. R. James come right out of Cambridge. Only fantasy's stepchild, poor science-fiction, does not touch earth anywhere; and it is doubtful already if happenings entirely confined to outer space are ever going to move us, or even divert us for long. Satire, engaged in its most intellectual of exercises, must first of all establish an impeccable *locus operandi;* its premise is the kingdom where certain rules apply. The countries Gulliver visits are the systems of thought and learning Swift satirizes made visible one after the other and set in operation. But while place in satire is a purely artificial construction, set up to be knocked down, in humor place becomes its most revealing and at the same time is itself the most revealed. This is because humor, it seems to me, of all forms of fiction, entirely accepts place for what it is.

"Spotted Horses," by William Faulkner, is a good case in point. At the same time that this is just about Mr. Faulkner's funniest story, it is the most thorough and faithful picture of a Mississippi crossroads hamlet that you could ever hope to see. True in spirit, it is also true to everyday fact. Faulkner's art, which often lets him shoot the moon, tells him when to be literal too. In all its specification of detail, both mundane and poetic, in its complete adherence to social fact (which nobody knows better than Faulkner, surely, in writing today), by its unerring aim of observation as true as the sights of a gun would give, but Faulkner has no malice, only compassion; and even and also in the joy of those elements of harlequinade-fantasy that the spotted horses of the title bring in—in all that shining fidelity to place lies the heart and secret of this tale's comic glory.

Faulkner is, of course, the triumphant example in America today of the mastery of place in fiction. Yoknapatawpha County, so supremely and exclusively and majestically and totally itself, is an everywhere, but only because Faulkner's first concern is for what comes first—Yoknapatawpha, his own created world. I am not sure, as a Mississippian myself, how widely it is realized and appreciated that these works of such marvelous imaginative power can also stand as works of the carefulest and purest representation. Heightened, of course: their specialty is they are twice as true as life, and that is why it takes a genius to write them. "Spotted Horses" may not have happened yet; if it had, some others might have tried to make a story of it;

but "Spotted Horses" could happen tomorrow—that is one of its glories. It could happen today or tomorrow at any little crossroads hamlet in Mississippi; the whole combination of irresistibility is there. We have the Snopses ready, the Mrs. Littlejohns ready, nice Ratliff and the Judge ready and sighing, the clowns, sober and merry, settled for the evening retrospection of it in the cool dusk of the porch; and the Henry Armstids armed with their obsessions, the little periwinkle-eyed boys armed with their indestructibility; the beautiful, overweening spring, too, the moonlight on the pear trees from which the mockingbird's song keeps returning; and the little store and the fat boy to steal and steal away at its candy. There are undoubtedly spotted horses too, in the offing—somewhere in Texas this minute, straining toward the day. After Faulkner has told it, it is easy for one and all to look back and see it.

Faulkner, simply, knew it already; it is a different kind of knowledge from Flaubert's, and proof could not add much to it. He was born knowing, or rather learning, or rather prophesying, all that and more; and having it all together at one time available while he writes is one of the marks of his mind. If there *is* any more in Mississippi than is engaged and dilated upon, and made twice as real as it used to be and applies now to the world, in the one story "Spotted Horses," then we would almost rather not know it—but I don't bet a piece of store candy that there is. In Faulkner's humor, even more measurably than in his tragedy, it is all there.

It may be going too far to say that the exactness and concreteness and solidity of the real world achieved in a story correspond to the intensity of feeling in the author's mind and to the very turn of his heart; but there lies the secret of our confidence in him.

Making reality real is art's responsibility. It is a practical assignment, then, a self-assignment: to achieve, by a cultivated sensitivity for observing life, a capacity for receiving its impressions, a lonely, unremitting, unaided, unaidable vision, and transferring this vision without distortion to it onto the pages of a novel, where, if the reader is so persuaded, it will turn into the reader's illusion. How bent on this peculiar joy we are, reader and writer, willingly to practice, willingly to undergo, this alchemy for it!

What is there, then, about place that is transferable to the pages of a novel? The best things—the explicit things: physical texture. And as place has functioned between the writer and his material, so it functions between the writer and reader. Location is the ground conductor of all the currents of emotion and belief and moral conviction that charge out from the story in its course. These charges need the warm hard earth underfoot, the light and lift of air, the stir and play of mood, the softening bath of atmosphere that give the likeness-to-life that life needs. Through the story's translation and ordering of life, the unconvincing raw material becomes the very heart's familiar. Life *is* strange. Stories hardly make it more so; with all they are able to tell and surmise, they make it more believably, more inevitably so.

I think the sense of place is as essential to good and honest writing as a logical mind; surely they are somewhere related. It is by knowing where you stand that you grow able to judge where you are. Place absorbs our earliest notice and attention, it bestows on us our original awareness; and our critical powers spring up from the study of it and the growth of experience inside it. It perseveres in bringing us back to earth when we fly too high. It never really stops informing us, for it is forever astir, alive, changing, reflecting, like the mind of man itself. One place comprehended can make us understand other places better. Sense of place gives equilibrium; extended, it is sense of direction too. Carried off we might be in spirit, and should be, when we are reading or writing something good; but it is the sense of place going with us still that is the ball of golden thread to carry us there and back and in every sense of the word to bring us home.

What can place *not* give? Theme. It can present theme, show it to the last detail—but place is forever illustrative: it is a picture of what man has done and imagined, it is his visible past, result. Human life is fiction's only theme.

Should the writer, then, write about home? It is both natural and sensible that the place where we have our roots should become the setting, the first and primary proving ground, of our fiction. Location, however, is not simply to be used by the writer—it is to be discovered, as each novel itself, in the act of writing, is discovery. Discovery does not imply that the place is new, only that we are. Place is as old as the hills. Kilroy at least has been there, and left his name. Discovery, not being a matter of writing our name on a wall, but of seeing what that wall is, and what is over it, is a matter of vision.

One can no more say, "To write stay home," than one can say, "To write leave home." It is the writing that makes its own rules and conditions for each person. And though place is home, it is for the writer writing simply *locus*. It is where the particular story he writes can be pinned down, the circle it can spin through and keep the state of grace, so that for the story's duration the rest of the world suspends its claim upon it and lies low as the story in peaceful extension, the *locus* fading off into the blue.

Naturally, it is the very breath of life, whether one writes a word of fiction or not, to go out and see what is to be seen of the world. For the artist to be unwilling to move, mentally or spiritually or physically, out of the familiar is a sign that spiritual timidity or poverty or decay has come upon him; for what is familiar will then have turned into all that is tyrannical.

One can only say: writers must always write best of what they know, and sometimes they do it by staying where they know it. But not for safety's sake. Although it is in the words of a witch—or all the more because of that—a comment of Hecate's in *Macbeth* is worth our heed: "Security / Is mortal's chiefest enemy." In fact, when we think in terms of the spirit, which are the terms of writing, is there a conception more stupefying than that of security? Yet writing of what you know has nothing to do with security: what is more dangerous? How can you go out on a limb if you do not know your own tree? No art ever came out of not risking your neck. And risk—experiment—is a considerable part of the joy of doing, which is the lone, simple reason all writers of serious fiction are willing to work as hard as they do.

The open mind and the receptive heart—which are at last and with fortune's smile the informed mind and the experienced heart—are to be gained anywhere, any time, without necessarily moving an inch from any present address. There must surely be as many ways of seeing a place as there are pairs of eyes to see it. The impact happens in so many different ways.

It may be the stranger within the gates whose eye is smitten by the crucial thing, the essence of life, the moment or act in our long-familiar midst that will forever define it. The inhabitant who has taken his fill of a place and gone away may look back and see it for good, from afar, still there in his mind's eye like a city over the hill. It was in the New Zealand stories, written eleven thousand miles from home and out of homesickness, that Katherine Mansfield came into her own. Joyce transplanted not his subject but himself while writing about it, and it was as though he had never left it at all: there it was, still in his eye, exactly the way he had last seen it. From the Continent he wrote the life of Dublin as it was then into a book of the future, for he went translating his own language of it on and on into a country of its own, where it set up a kingdom as renowned as Prester John's. Sometimes two places, two countries, are brought to bear on each other, as in E. M. Forster's work, and the heart of the novel is heard beating most plainly, most passionately, most personally when two places are at meeting point.

There may come to be new places in our lives that are second spiritual homes—closer to us in some ways, perhaps, than our original homes. But the home tie is the blood tie. And had it meant nothing to us, any other place thereafter would have meant less, and we would carry no compass inside ourselves to find home ever, anywhere at all. We would not even guess what we had missed.

It is noticeable that those writers who for their own good reasons push out against their backgrounds nearly always passionately adopt the new one in their work. Revolt itself is a reference and tribute to the potency of what is left behind. The substitute place, the adopted country, is sometimes a very much stricter, bolder, or harsher one than the original, seldom more lax or undemanding—showing that what was wanted was structure, definition, rigidity—perhaps these were wanted, and understanding was not.

Hemingway in our time has sought out the formal and ruthless territories of the world, archaic ones often, where there are bullfight arenas, theatres of hunting and war, places with a primitive, or formidable, stripped-down character, with implacable codes, with inscrutable justices and inevitable retributions. But whatever the scene of his work, it is the *places* that never are hostile. People give pain, are callous and insensitive, empty and cruel, carrying with them no pasts as they promise no futures. But place heals the hurt, soothes the outrage, fills the terrible vacuum that these human beings make. It heals actively, and the response is given consciously, with the ardent care and explicitness, respect and delight of a lover, when fishing streams or naming over streets becomes almost something of the lover's secret language—as the careful conversations between characters in Hemingway bear hints of the secret language of hate. The response to place has the added intensity that comes with the place's not being native or taken for granted, but found, chosen; thereby is the rest more heavily repudiated. It is the response of the aficionado; the response, too, is adopted. The title "A Clean Well Lighted Place" is just what the human being is not, for Hemingway, and perhaps it is the epitome of what man would like to find in his fellowman but never has yet, says the author, and never is going to.

We see that point of view is hardly a single, unalterable vision, but a profound and developing one of great complexity. The vision itself may move in and out of its material, shuttle-fashion, instead of being simply turned on it, like a telescope on the moon. Writing is an expression of the writer's own peculiar personality, could not help being so. Yet in reading great works one feels that the finished piece transcends the personal. All writers great and small must sometimes have felt that they have become part of what they wrote even more than it still remains a part of them.

When I speak of writing from where you have put down roots, it may be said that what I urge is "regional" writing. "Regional," I think, is a careless term, as well as a condescending one, because what it does is fail to differentiate between the localized raw material of life and its outcome as art. "Regional" is an outsider's term; it has no meaning for the insider who is doing the writing, because as far as he knows he is simply writing about life. Jane Austen, Emily Brontë, Thomas Hardy, Cervantes, Turgenev, the authors of the books of the Old Testament, all confined themselves to regions, great or small—but are they regional? Then who from the start of time has not been so?

It may well be said that all work springing out of such vital impulse from its native soil has certain things in common. But what signifies is that these are not the little things that it takes a fine-tooth critic to search out, but the great things, that could not be missed or mistaken, for they are the beacon lights of literature.

It seems plain that the art that speaks most clearly, explicitly, directly and passionately from its place of origin will remain the longest understood. It is through place that we put out roots, wherever birth, chance, fate or our traveling selves set us down; but where those roots reach toward—whether in America, England or Timbuktu—is the deep and running vein, eternal and consistent and everywhere purely itself, that feeds and is fed by the human understanding. The challenge to writers today, I think, is not to disown any part of our heritage. Whatever our theme in writing, it is old and tried. Whatever our place, it has been visited by the stranger, it will never be new again. It is only the vision that can be new; but that is enough.

PART 26

Individualism and Personism

Needless to say, the project of Individualism has a long history, as does Egoism. Writing in *The Ego and His Own*—Steven T. Byington's translation of which was published in London in 1907—Max Stirner claimed: "I am unique. Hence my wants too are unique, and my deed: in short, everything about me is unique. And it is only as this unique I that I take everything for my own, as I set myself to work, and develop myself, only as this." Augustus John and Ezra Pound, through John Quinn, knew of this book, which is remarkably close to Wyndham Lewis's Vorticist writings.

It was Harriet Shaw Weaver's *New Freewoman* of 1913 that was to become the influential journal *The Egoist* and Weaver who was to publish James Joyce's *Portrait of the Artist as a Young Man* and *Ulysses*. In the same current, and totally opposed to the impersonalism of T. S. Eliot on one hand and the philosopher Ludwig Feuerbach's altruistic humanism on the other, are Wyndham Lewis's *Tarr,* as well as the writings of the American poet H. D. (Hilda Doolittle).

In his celebration of the solitary chamber, Walter Pater was the ur-individualist, as was D. H. Lawrence in his celebration of the individual impulse. It is of this impulse that Francis Picabia's "Egoisme" is a partial spoof:

Thinking Alone

You don't have anything else to look for
because you've found everything
except your stupidity
that others will find
(CANFIELD, *Francis Picabia,* 70)

Personism is just one manifestation, humorous in kind, of the poetics of the particular protest against the general and impersonal. Frank O'Hara's manifesto "Personism" (26.4), a spoof of much else, can be seen as part of this impulse—the impulse is serious, if the text is funny. Confining its subject deliberately to only one person, it has no need to shout and no claim to any group allegiance. Given O'Hara's importance to a whole circle of New York painters and poets, his modest declaration, taken seriously by much of the art community at the time, has an importance out of all proportion to its modest size.

Like O'Hara's lunch poems, and unlike many manifestos written in terms of an ideology, this manifesto has a style uniquely the poet's own.

26.1 MARSDEN HARTLEY

A Word

1916

Personal quality, separate, related to nothing so much as to itself, is a something coming to us with real freshness, not traversing a variety of fashionable formulas, but relying only upon itself. The artist adds something minor or major more by understanding his own medium to expression, than by his understanding of the medium or methods of those utterly divergent from him. Characteristics are readily imitable; substances never; likeness cannot be actuality. Pictural notions have been supplanted by problem, expression by research. Artistry is valued only by intellectualism with which it has not much in common. A fixed loathing of the imaginative has taken place: a continual searching for, or hatred of, subject-matter is habitual, as if presence or absence of subject were a criterion, or, from the technical point of view, as if the Cézannesque touch, for instance, were the key to the esthetic of our time, or the method of Picasso the clew to modernity.

I am wondering why the autographic is so negligible, why the individual has ceased to register himself—what relates to him, what the problematic for itself counts. I wonder if the individual psychology of El Greco, Giotto and the bushmen had nothing to do with their idea of life, of nature, of that which is essential—whether the struggle in El Greco and Cézanne, for example, had not more to do in creating their peculiar individual esthetic than any ideas they may have had as to the pictural problem. It is this specialized personal signature which certainly attracts us to a picture—the autographic aspect or the dictographic. That which is expressed in a drawing or a painting is certain to tell who is its creator. Who will not, or cannot, find that quality in those extraordinary and unexcelled watercolors of Cézanne, will find nothing whatsoever anywhere. There is not a trace anywhere in them of struggle to problem: they are expression itself. He has expressed, as he himself has said, what was his one ambition—that which exists between him and his subject. Every painter must traverse for himself that distance from Paris to Aix or from Venice to Toledo. Expression is for one knowing its own pivot. Every expressor relates solely to himself—that is the concern of the individualist.

It will be seen that my personal wishes lie in the strictly pictural notion, having observed much to this idea in the kinetic and the kaleidoscopic principles. Objects are incidents: an apple does not for long remain an apple if one has the concept. Anything is therefore pictural; it remains only to be observed and considered. All expression is illustration — of something.

26.2 MARSDEN HARTLEY
Art and the Personal Life
1928

As soon as a real artist finds out what art is, the more is he likely to feel the need of keeping silent about it, and about himself in connection with it. There is almost, these days, a kind of *petit scandale* in the thought of allying oneself with anything of a professional nature. And it is at this point that I shrink a little from asserting myself with regard to professional aspects of art. And here the quality of confession must break through. I have joined, once and for all, the ranks of the intellectual experimentalists. I can hardly bear the sound of the words "expressionism," "emotionalism," "personality," and such, because they imply the wish to express personal life, and I prefer to have no personal life. Personal art for me is a matter of spiritual indelicacy. Persons of refined feeling should keep themselves out of their painting, and this means, of course, that the accusation made in the form of a querulous statement to me recently "that you are a perfectionist," is in the main true.

I am interested then only in the problem of painting, of how to make a better painting according to certain laws that are inherent in the making of a good picture — and not at all in private extraversions or introversions of specific individuals. That is for me the inherent error in a work of art. I learned this bit of wisdom from a principle of William Blake's which I discovered early and followed far too assiduously the first half of my esthetic life, and from which I have happily released myself — and this axiom was: "Put off intellect and put on imagination; the imagination is the man." From this doctrinal assertion evolved the theoretical axiom that you don't see a thing until you look away from it — which was an excellent truism as long as the principles of the imaginative life were believed in and followed. I no longer believe in the imagination. I rose one certain day — and the whole thing had become changed. I had changed old clothes for new ones, and I couldn't bear the sight of the old garments. And when a painting is evolved from imaginative principles I am strongly inclined to turn away because I have greater faith that intellectual clarity is better and more entertaining than imaginative wisdom or emotional richness. I believe in the theoretical aspects of painting because I believe it produces better painting, and I think I can say I have been a fair exponent of the imaginative idea.

I have come to the conclusion that it is better to have two colors in right relation to each other than to have a vast confusion of emotional exuberance in the guise of ecstatic fullness or poetical revelation—both of which qualities have, generally speaking, long since become second rate experience. I had rather be intellectually right than emotionally exuberant, and I could say this of any other aspect of my personal experience.

I have lived the life of the imagination, but at too great an expense. I do not admire the irrationality of the imaginative life. I have, if I may say so, made the intellectual grade. I have made the complete return to nature, and nature is as we all know, primarily an intellectual idea. I am satisfied that painting also is like nature, an intellectual idea, and that the laws of nature as presented to the mind through the eye—and the eye is the painter's first and last vehicle—are the means of transport to the real mode of thought: the only legitimate source of esthetic experience for the intelligent painter.

All the isms from impressionism down to the present moment have had their inestimable value and have clarified the mind and the scene of all superfluous emotionalism; and the eye that turns toward nature today receives far finer and more significant reactions than previously when romanticism and the imaginative or poetic principles were the means and ways of expression.

I am not at all sure that the time isn't entirely out of joint for the so-called art of painting, and I am certain that very few persons, comparatively speaking, have achieved the real experience of the eye either as spectator or performer. Modern art must of necessity remain in the state of experimental research if it is to have any significance at all. Painters must paint for their own edification and pleasure, and what they have to say, not what they are impelled to feel, is what will interest those who are interested in them. The thought of the time is the emotion of the time.

I personally am indebted to Segantini the impressionist, not Segantini the symbolist, for what I have learned in times past of the mountain and a given way to express it—just as it was Ryder who accentuated my already tormented imagination. Cubism taught me much and the principle of Pissarro, furthered by Seurat, taught me more. These with Cézanne are the great logicians of color. No one will ever paint like Cézanne, for example —because no one will ever have his peculiar visual gifts; or to put it less dogmatically, will any one ever appear again with so peculiar and almost unbelievable a faculty for dividing color sensations and making logical realizations of them? Has any one ever placed his color more reasonably with more of a sense of time and measure than he? I think not, and he furnishes for the enthusiast of today, new reasons for research into the realm of color for itself.

It is not the idiosyncrasy of an artist that creates the working formula, it is the rational reasoning in him that furnishes the material to build on. Red, for example, is a color that almost any ordinary eye is familiar with—but in general when an ordinary painter sees it he sees it as isolated experience— with the result that his presentation of red lives its life alone, where it is placed, because it has not been modified to the tones around it—and modification is as good a name as any for the true art of painting color as we think of it today. Even Cézanne was not always sure of pure red, and there are two pictures of his I think of, where something could have been done to put the single hue in its place—the art for which he was otherwise so gifted. Real color is in a condition of neglect at the present time because monochrome has been the fashion for the last fifteen or twenty years—even the superb colorist Matisse was for a time affected by it. Cubism is largely responsible for this because it is primarily derived from sculptural concepts and found little need for color in itself. When a group feeling is revived once again, such as held sway among the impressionists, color will come into its logical own. And it is timely enough to see that for purposes of outdoor painting, impressionism is in need of revival.

Yet I cannot but return to the previous theme which represents my conversion from emotional to intellectual notions; and my feeling is: of what use is a painting which does not realize its esthetical problem? Underlying all sensible works of art, there must be somewhere in evidence the particular problem understood. It was so with those artists of the great past who had the intellectual knowledge of structure upon which to place their emotions. It is this structural beauty that makes the old painting valuable. And so it becomes to me—a problem. I would rather be sure that I had placed two colors in true relationship to each other than to have exposed a wealth of emotionalism gone wrong in the name of richness of personal expression. For this reason I believe that it is more significant to keep one's painting in a condition of severe experimentalism than to become a quick success by means of cheap repetition.

The real artists have always been interested in this problem, and you felt it strongly in the work of da Vinci, Piero della Francesca, Courbet, Pissarro, Seurat and Cézanne. Art is not a matter of slavery to the emotions—or even a matter of slavery to nature—or to the esthetic principles. It is a tempered and happy union of them all.

Personism

1959

Everything is in the poems, but at the risk of sounding like the poor wealthy man's Allen Ginsberg I will write to you because I just heard that one of my fellow poets thinks that a poem of mine that can't be got at one reading is because I was confused too. Now, come on. I don't believe in god, so I don't have to make elaborately sounded structures. I hate Vachel Lindsay, always have, I don't even like rhythm, assonance, all that stuff. You just go on your nerve. If someone's chasing you down the street with a knife you just run, you don't turn around and shout, "Give it up! I was a track star for Mineola Prep."

That's for the writing poems part. As for their reception, suppose you're in love and someone's mistreating (*mal aimé*) you, you don't say, "Hey, you can't hurt me this way, I *care!*" you just let all the different bodies fall where they may, and they always do may after a few months. But that's not why you fell in love in the first place, just to hang onto life, so you have to take your chances and try to avoid being logical. Pain always produces logic, which is very bad for you.

I'm not saying that I don't have practically the most lofty ideas of anyone writing today, but what difference does that make? they're just ideas. The only good thing about it is that when I get lofty enough I've stopped thinking and that's when refreshment arrives.

But how can you really care if anybody gets it, or gets what it means, or if it improves them. Improves them for what? for death? Why hurry them along? Too many poets act like a middle-aged mother trying to get her kids to eat too much cooked meat, and potatoes with drippings (tears). I don't give a damn whether they eat or not. Forced feeding leads to excessive thinness (effete). Nobody should experience anything they don't need to, if they don't need poetry bully for them, I like the movies too. And after all, only Whitman and Crane and Williams, of the American poets, are better than the movies. As for measure and other technical apparatus, that's just common sense: if you're going to buy a pair of pants you want them to be tight enough so everyone will want to go to bed with you. There's nothing metaphysical about it. Unless, of course, you flatter yourself into thinking that what you're experiencing is "yearning."

Abstraction in poetry, which Allen recently commented on in *It is*, is intriguing. I think it appears mostly in the minute particulars where decision is necessary. Abstraction (in poetry, not in painting) involves personal removal by the poet. For instance, the decision involved in the choice between "the nostalgia of the infinite" and "the nostalgia *for* the infinite" defines an attitude towards degree of abstraction. The nostalgia *of* the infinite representing the greater degree of abstraction, removal, and negative capability (as in Keats and Mallarmé). Personism, a movement which I recently founded and which nobody yet knows about, interests me a great deal, being so totally opposed to this kind of abstract removal that it is verging on a true abstraction for the first time, really, in the history of poetry. Personism is to Wallace Stevens what *la poésie pure* was to Béranger. Personism has nothing to do with philosophy, it's all art. It does not have to do with personality or intimacy, far from it! But to give you a vague idea, one of its minimal aspects is to address itself to one person (other than the poet himself), thus evoking overtones of love without destroying love's life-giving vulgarity, and sustaining the poet's feelings towards the poem while preventing love from distracting him into feeling about the person. That's part of personism. It was founded by me after lunch with LeRoi Jones on August 27, 1959, a day in which I was in love with someone (not Roi, by the way, a blond). I went back to work and wrote a poem for this person. While I was writing it I was realizing that if I wanted to I could use the telephone instead of writing the poem, and so Personism was born. It's a very exciting movement which will undoubtedly have lots of adherents. It puts the poem squarely between the poet and the person, Lucky Pierre style, and the poem is correspondingly gratified. The poem is at last between two persons instead of two pages. In all modesty, I confess that it may be the death of literature as we know it. While I have certain regrets, I am still glad I got there before Alain Robbe-Grillet did. Poetry being quicker and surer than prose, it is only just that poetry finish literature off. For a time people thought that Artaud was going to accomplish this, but actually, for all its magnificence, his polemical writings are not more outside literature than Bear Mountain is outside New York State. His relation is no more astounding than Dubuffet's to painting.

What can we expect of Personism? (This is getting good, isn't it?) Everything, but we won't get it. It is too new, too vital a movement to promise anything. But it, like Africa, is on the way. The recent propagandists for technique on the one hand, and for content on the other, had better watch out.

26.4 WALT WHITMAN

Song of Myself (*excerpt*)

1855

1

I celebrate myself, and sing myself,
And what I assume you shall assume,
For every atom belonging to me as good belongs to you.

I loafe and invite my soul,
I lean and loafe at my ease observing a spear of summer grass.

My tongue, every atom of my blood, form'd from this soil, this air,
Born here of parents born here from parents the same, and their parents
    the same,
I, now thirty-seven years old in perfect health begin,
Hoping to cease not till death.

Creeds and schools in abeyance,
Retiring back a while sufficed at what they are, but never forgotten,
I harbor for good or bad, I permit to speak at every hazard,
Nature without check with original energy.

2

Houses and rooms are full of perfumes, the shelves are crowded with
    perfumes,
I breathe the fragrance myself and know it and like it,
The distillation would intoxicate me also, but I shall not let it.

The atmosphere is not a perfume, it has no taste of the distillation, it is
    odorless,
It is for my mouth forever, I am in love with it,
I will go to the bank by the wood and become undisguised and naked,
I am mad for it to be in contact with me.

The smoke of my own breath,
Echoes, ripples, buzz'd whispers, love-root, silk-thread, crotch and vine,
My respiration and inspiration, the beating of my heart, the passing of
    blood and air through my lungs,

The sniff of green leaves and dry leaves, and of the shore and dark-color'd
    sea-rocks, and of hay in the barn,
The sound of the belch'd words of my voice loos'd to the eddies of the wind,
A few light kisses, a few embraces, a reaching around of arms,
The play of shine and shade on the trees as the supple boughs wag,
The delight alone or in the rush of the streets, or along the fields and
    hill-sides,
The feeling of health, the full-noon trill, the song of me rising from bed
    and meeting the sun.

Have you reckon'd a thousand acres much? have you reckon'd the earth
    much?
Have you practis'd so long to learn to read?
Have you felt so proud to get at the meaning of poems?

Stop this day and night with me and you shall possess the origin of all
    poems,
You shall possess the good of the earth and sun, (there are millions of suns
    left,)
You shall no longer take things at second or third hand, nor look through
    the eyes of the dead, nor feed on the spectres in books,
You shall not look through my eyes either, nor take things from me,
You shall listen to all sides and filter them from your self.

3
I have heard what the talkers were talking, the talk of the beginning and
    the end,
But I do not talk of the beginning or the end.

There was never any more inception than there is now,
Nor any more youth or age than there is now,
And will never be any more perfection than there is now,
Nor any more heaven or hell than there is now.

Urge and urge and urge,
Always the procreant urge of the world.
Out of the dimness opposite equals advance, always substance and
    increase, always sex,
Always a knit of identity, always distinction, always a breed of life.

To elaborate is no avail, learn'd and unlearn'd feel that it is so.

Sure as the most certain sure, plumb in the uprights, well entretied,
    braced in the beams,
Stout as a horse, affectionate, haughty, electrical,
I and this mystery here we stand.

Clear and sweet is my soul, and clear and sweet is all that is not my soul.

Lack one lacks both, and the unseen is proved by the seen,
Till that becomes unseen and receives proof in its turn.

Showing the best and dividing it from the worst age vexes age,
Knowing the perfect fitness and equanimity of things, while they discuss I
    am silent, and go bathe and admire myself.
Welcome is every organ and attribute of me, and of any man hearty and
    clean,
Not an inch nor a particle of an inch is vile, and none shall be less familiar
    than the rest.

I am satisfied—I see, dance, laugh, sing;
As the hugging and loving bed-fellow sleeps at my side through the night,
    and withdraws at the peep of the day with stealthy tread,
Leaving me baskets cover'd with white towels swelling the house with
    their plenty,
Shall I postpone my acceptation and realization and scream at my eyes,
That they turn from gazing after and down the road,
And forthwith cipher and show me to a cent,
Exactly the value of one and exactly the value of two, and which is ahead?

4
Trippers and askers surround me,
People I meet, the effect upon me of my early life or the ward and city I
    live in, or the nation,
The latest dates, discoveries, inventions, societies, authors old and new,
My dinner, dress, associates, looks, compliments, dues,
The real or fancied indifference of some man or woman I love,
The sickness of one of my folks or of myself, or ill-doing or loss or lack of
    money, or depressions or exaltations,

Battles, the horrors of fratricidal war, the fever of doubtful news, the fitful
    events;
These come to me days and nights and go from me again,
But they are not the Me myself.
Apart from the pulling and hauling stands what I am,
Stands amused, complacent, compassionating, idle, unitary,
Looks down, is erect, or bends an arm on an impalpable certain rest,
Looking with side-curved head curious what will come next,
Both in and out of the game and watching and wondering at it.

Backward I see in my own days where I sweated through fog with linguists
    and contenders,
I have no mockings or arguments, I witness and wait.

    5
I believe in you my soul, the other I am must not abase itself to you,
And you must not be abased to the other.

Loafe with me on the grass, loose the stop from your throat,
Not words, not music or rhyme I want, not custom or lecture, not even the
    best,
Only the lull I like, the hum of your valvèd voice.

I mind how once we lay such a transparent summer morning,
How you settled your head athwart my hips and gently turn'd over
    upon me,
And parted the shirt from my bosom-bone, and plunged your tongue to
    my bare-stript heart,
And reach'd till you felt my beard, and reach'd till you held my feet.

Swiftly arose and spread around me the peace and knowledge that pass all
    the argument of the earth,
And I know that the hand of God is the promise of my own,
And I know that the spirit of God is the brother of my own,
And that all the men ever born are also my brothers, and the women my
    sisters and lovers,

And that a kelson of the creation is love,
And limitless are leaves stiff or drooping in the fields,

And brown ants in the little wells beneath them,
And mossy scabs of the worm fence, heap'd stones, elder, mullein and
     poke-weed.

     6
A child said *What is the grass?* fetching it to me with full hands,
How could I answer the child? I do not know what it is any more than he.

I guess it must be the flag of my disposition, out of hopeful green stuff woven.

Or I guess it is the handkerchief of the Lord,
A scented gift and remembrancer designedly dropt,
Bearing the owner's name someway in the corners, that we may see and
     remark, and say *Whose?*

Or I guess the grass is itself a child, the produced babe of the vegetation.

Or I guess it is a uniform hieroglyphic,
And it means, Sprouting alike in broad zones and narrow zones,
Growing among black folks as among white,
Kanuck, Tuckahoe, Congressman, Cuff, I give them the same, I receive
     them the same.

And now it seems to me the beautiful uncut hair of graves.

Tenderly will I use you curling grass,
It may be you transpire from the breasts of young men,
It may be if I had known them I would have loved them,
It may be you are from old people, or from offspring taken soon out of
     their mothers' laps,
And here you are the mothers' laps.

This grass is very dark to be from the white heads of old mothers,
Darker than the colourless beards of old men,
Dark to come from under the faint red roofs of mouths.

O I perceive after all so many uttering tongues,
And I perceive they do not come from the roofs of mouths for nothing.
I wish I could translate the hints about the dead young men and women,

And the hints about old men and mothers, and the offspring taken soon
    out of their laps.

What do you think has become of the young and old men?
And what do you think has become of the women and children?

They are alive and well somewhere,
The smallest sprout shows there is really no death,
And if ever there was it led forward life, and does not wait at the end to
    arrest it,
And ceas'd the moment life appear'd.

All goes onward and outward, nothing collapses,
And to die is different from what any one supposed, and luckier.

7
Has any one supposed it lucky to be born?
I hasten to inform him or her it is just as lucky to die, and I know it.

I pass death with the dying and birth with the new-wash'd babe, and am
    not contain'd between my hat and boots,
And peruse manifold objects, no two alike and every one good,
The earth good and the stars good, and their adjuncts all good.

I am not an earth nor an adjunct of an earth,
I am the mate and companion of people, all just as immortal and
    fathomless as myself,
(They do not know how immortal, but I know.)

Every kind for itself and its own, for me mine male and female,
For me those that have been boys and that love women,
For me the man that is proud and feels how it stings to be slighted,
For me the sweet-heart and the old maid, for me mothers and the mothers
    of mothers,
For me lips that have smiled, eyes that have shed tears,
For me children and the begetters of children.

Undrape! you are not guilty to me, nor stale nor discarded,
I see through the broadcloth and gingham whether or no,

And am around, tenacious, acquisitive, tireless, and cannot be shaken
    away.

8
The little one sleeps in its cradle,
I lift the gauze and look a long time, and silently brush away flies with my
    hand.

The youngster and the red-faced girl turn aside up the bushy hill,
I peeringly view them from the top.

The suicide sprawls on the bloody floor of the bedroom,
I witness the corpse with its dabbled hair, I note where the pistol has
    fallen.

The blab of the pave, tires of carts, sluff of boot-soles, talk of the
    promenaders,
The heavy omnibus, the driver with his interrogating thumb, the clank of
    the shod horses on the granite floor,
The snow-sleighs, clinking, shouted jokes, pelts of snow-balls,
The hurrahs for popular favorites, the fury of rous'd mobs,
The flap of the curtain'd litter, a sick man inside borne to the hospital,
The meeting of enemies, the sudden oath, the blows and fall,
The excited crowd, the policeman with his star quickly working his
    passage to the centre of the crowd,
The impassive stones that receive and return so many echoes,
What groans of over-fed or half-starv'd who fall sunstruck or in fits,
What exclamations of women taken suddenly who hurry home and give
    birth to babes,
What living and buried speech is always vibrating here, what howls
    restrain'd by decorum,
Arrests of criminals, slights, adulterous offers made, acceptances,
    rejections with convex lips,
I mind them or the show or resonance of them—I come and I depart.

26.5 William Carlos Williams
The Pluralism of Experience
1974

Everything rests, so far as I can see, on a condition, obvious to the eye, which may be called, if one care to, the pluralism of experience. And, obviously, no "law" or abstract summary can include this since in itself it stands outside a generalization, it is plural concretely and in fact.

This has not been sufficiently realized in thought: it is crudely stated in the multiples of Pagan mythology, in the politics of "Democracy" and in such inborn feelings as nationalism, "states' rights," etc. etc.

Its present use to me—

It offers this release—life, continued productivity not only in fish eggs but thought.

It is opposed by the pinching academy which tries to relegate it to paleontology, to the "crude beginnings," to an earlier condition. But it is as new—so new, that it will shortly be the newest, most pregnant motivation of thought and life in the world.

It is decentralizing in effect as opposed to the merely opportunistic tendencies (due to the surrounding barbarism of the world) of centralization—in the sciences, arts, etc.

Quickly, it is this: that every individual, every place, every opportunity of thought is both favored and limited by its emplacement in time and place. Chinese 8th cent., Italian 12th, English 15th, French 18th, African, etc. All sorts of complicated conditions and circumstances of land, climate, blood, surround every deed that is done.

Due to certain conditions there flourishes a "school" of thought, Western, Eastern. It is one. It brings to a certain perfection that which it can do—and then can do no more—without destruction first. It has flowered.

Now, America is such a place. The old cultures *cannot*, can never without our history, our blood or climate, our time of flowering in history—can never be the same as we. They cannot.

We all work side by side for the same things (tho' we don't know what these things are) but the impasses of older cultures are not ours. And these impasses are intrinsic in their work, their beginnings enforce them, to destroy their history would be just to destroy themselves. We may and surely will find impasses but they will be different from theirs.

Thus we are to work in our own "locality": not piggishly, not narrowly.

We must see, steal, beg, borrow—but we borrow only that *which we want*. What we feel, think, conclude that we need. Not what is imposed on us (unless we can't help it, then we use that too: Negro American music).

And the justice of this is that by such pluralism of effort in each several locality a "reality" is kept; in plural—and so verified.

By success in many places on different planes our efforts are confirmed, not driven to defeat and pessimism as in the case of mere central supremacy —which is in effect a denial of reality, not its consummation. Each school enhances the perfection of some other. But all strongly sanction—all. And enrich. But a later "school" must have as great leeway—and it will—it is insured to thought in the limitations of each "perfection."

PART 27

Thresholds

From the beginning there have been borders. Living—or imagining—on the boundary between this and that, between one sort of appearance or origin or happenstance and another, a great number of writers and creators have spent much time, or indeed their lives, thinking of or past the boundaries.

These manifestos, selected from many of the same kind, take various genres for their shape and sight, yet all concern the testing of boundaries and try to work out the crossing of borders. They state, they claim, they fight, but above all, they speak for something. They represent. Their tone marks out both a political position and a personal one. If, as has been said for a number of years, the personal is political, these crossings are public as well as private.

The examples here include W. E. B. DuBois, whose "Souls of Black Folk" (27.1) is a touchstone for all the subsequent manifestos of blackness, and four feminists: the Swiss painter and poet Méret Oppenheim, the French writers Hélène Cixous and Catherine Clément, the American-British Mina Loy, and the Chicana Gloria Anzaldua, all of whom represent different ways of making their "sorties" or waging their wars and exits from the imprisonments of binary thinking—white/black, man/woman, straight/queer, imported American/Native American, domestic/foreign. These manifestos, like the others in this volume, were chosen for their differing styles and not for the contingents of which they might be seen as token texts.

27.1 W. E. B. DuBois

The Souls of Black Folk (excerpt)

1903

O water, voice of my heart, crying in the sand,
  All night long crying with a mournful cry,
As I lie and listen, and cannot understand
  The voice of my heart in my side or the voice of the sea,
  O water, crying for rest, is it I, is it I?
    All night long the water is crying to me.

Unresting water, there shall never be rest
  Till the last moon droop and the last tide fail,
And the fire of the end begin to burn in the west;
      And the heart shall be weary and wonder and cry like the sea,
  All life long crying without avail,
    As the water all night long is crying to me.

ARTHUR SYMONS

Between me and the other world there is ever an unasked question: unasked by some through feelings of delicacy; by others through the difficulty of rightly framing it. All, nevertheless, flutter round it. They approach me in a half-hesitant sort of way, eye me curiously or compassionately, and then, instead of saying directly, How does it feel to be a problem? they say, I know an excellent colored man in my town; or, I fought at Mechanicsville; or, Do not these Southern outrages make your blood boil? At these I smile, or am interested, or reduce the boiling to a simmer, as the occasion may require. To the real question, How does it feel to be a problem? I answer seldom a word.

And yet, being a problem is a strange experience, — peculiar even for one who has never been anything else, save perhaps in babyhood and in Europe. It is in the early days of rollicking boyhood that the revelation first bursts upon one, all in a day, as it were. I remember well when the shadow swept across me. I was a little thing, away up in the hills of New England, where the dark Housatonic winds between Hoosac and Taghkanic to the sea. In a wee wooden schoolhouse something put it into the boys' and girls' heads to buy gorgeous visiting-cards—ten cents a package—and exchange. The exchange was merry, till one girl, a tall newcomer, refused my card,—refused it peremptorily, with a glance. Then it dawned upon me with a certain suddenness that I was different from the others; or like, mayhap, in heart and life and longing, but shut out from their world by a vast veil. I had thereafter no desire to tear down that veil, to creep through; I held all beyond it in common contempt, and lived above it in a region of blue sky and great wandering shadows. That sky was bluest when I could beat my mates at examination time, or beat them at a foot-race, or even beat their stringy heads. Alas, with the years all this fine contempt began to fade; for the worlds I longed for, and all their dazzling opportunities, were theirs, not mine. But they should not keep these prizes, I said; some, all, I would wrest from them. Just how I would do it I could never decide: by reading law, by healing the sick, by telling the wonderful tales that swam in my head,—some way. With other black boys the strife was not so fiercely sunny: their youth shrunk into tasteless sycophancy, or into silent hatred of the pale world about them and mocking distrust of everything white; or wasted itself in a bitter cry, Why did God make me an outcast and a stranger in mine own house? The shades of the prison-house closed round about us all: walls strait and stubborn to the whitest, but relentlessly narrow, tall, and unscalable to sons of night who must plod darkly on in resignation, or beat unavailing palms against the stone, or steadily, half hopelessly, watch the streak of blue above.

After the Egyptian and Indian, the Greek and Roman, the Teuton and Mongolian, the Negro is a sort of seventh son, born with a veil, and gifted with second-sight in this American world,—a world which yields him no true self-consciousness, but only lets him see himself through the revelation of the other world. It is a peculiar sensation, this double-consciousness, this sense of always looking at one's self through the eyes of others, of measuring one's soul by the tape of a world that looks on in amused contempt and pity. One ever feels his two-ness—an American, a Negro; two souls, two thoughts, two unreconciled strivings; two warring ideals in one dark body, whose dogged strength alone keeps it from being torn asunder. . . .

Throughout history, the powers of single black men flash here and there like falling stars, and die sometimes before the world has rightly gauged their brightness. Here in America, in the few days since Emancipation, the black man's turning hither and thither in hesitant and doubtful striving has

often made his very strength to lose effectiveness, to seem like absence of
power, like weakness. And yet it is not weakness, —it is the contradiction of
double aims. The double-aimed struggle of the black artisan—on the one
hand to escape white contempt for a nation of mere hewers of wood and
drawers of water, and on the other hand to plough and nail and dig for a
poverty-stricken horde—could only result in making him a poor craftsman,
for he had but half a heart in either cause. By the poverty and ignorance of
his people, the Negro minister or doctor was tempted toward quackery and
demagogy; and by the criticism of the other world, toward ideals that made
him ashamed of his lowly tasks. The would-be black *savant* was confronted
by the paradox that the knowledge his people needed was a twice-told tale
to his white neighbors while the knowledge which would teach the white
world was Greek to his own flesh and blood. The innate love of harmony
and beauty that set the ruder souls of his people a-dancing and a-singing
raised but confusion and doubt in the soul of the black artist; for the beauty
revealed to him was the soul-beauty of a race which his larger audience
despised, and he could not articulate the message of another people. This
waste of double aims, this seeking to satisfy two unreconciled ideals, has
wrought sad havoc with the courage and faith and deeds of ten thousand
thousand people, —has sent them often wooing false gods and invoking
false means of salvation, and at times has even seemed about to make them
ashamed of themselves.

  . . . Whatever of good may have come in these years of change [since
Emancipation from slavery], the shadow of a deep disappointment rests
upon the Negro people, —a disappointment all the more bitter because the
unattained ideal was unbounded save by the simple ignorance of a lowly
people.

  The first decade was merely a prolongation of the vain search for freedom, the boon that seemed ever barely to elude their grasp, —like a tan-
talizing will-o'-the-wisp, maddening and misleading the headless host. The
holocaust of war, the terrors of the Ku Klux Klan, the lies of carpet-baggers,
the disorganization of industry, and the contradictory advice of friends and
foes, left the bewildered serf with no new watchword beyond the old cry for
freedom. As the time flew, however, he began to grasp a new idea. The ideal
of liberty demanded for its attainment powerful means, and these the Fifteenth Amendment gave him. The ballot, which before he had looked upon
as a visible sign of freedom, he now regarded as the chief means of gaining
and perfecting the liberty with which war had partially endowed him. And
why not? Had not votes made war and emancipated millions? Had not votes

enfranchised the freedmen? Was anything impossible to a power that had done all this? A million black men started with renewed zeal to vote themselves into the kingdom. So the decade flew away, the revolution of 1876 came, and left the half-free serf weary, wondering, but still inspired. Slowly but steadily, in the following years, a new vision began gradually to replace the dream of political power,—a powerful movement, the rise of another ideal to guide the unguided, another pillar of fire by night after a clouded day. It was the ideal of "book-learning"; the curiosity, born of compulsory ignorance, to know and test the power of the cabalistic letters of the white man, the longing to know. Here at last seemed to have been discovered the mountain path to Canaan; longer than the highway of Emancipation and law, steep and rugged, but straight, leading to heights high enough to over-look life.

Up the new path the advance guard toiled, slowly, heavily, doggedly; only those who have watched and guided the faltering feet, the misty minds, the dull understandings, of the dark pupils of these schools know how faith-fully, how piteously, this people strove to learn. It was weary work. The cold statistician wrote down the indices of progress here and there, noted also where here and there a foot had slipped or some one had fallen. To the tired climbers, the horizon was ever dark, the mists were often cold, the Canaan was always dim and far away. If, however, the vistas disclosed as yet no goal, no resting-place, little but flattery and criticism, the journey at least gave leisure for reflection and self-examination; it changed the child of Emanci-pation to the youth with dawning self-consciousness, self-realization, self-respect. In those sombre forests of his striving his own soul rose before him, and he saw himself,—darkly as through a veil; and yet he saw in himself some faint revelation of his power, of his mission. He began to have a dim feeling that, to attain his place in the world, he must be himself, and not another. For the first time he sought to analyze the burden he bore upon his back, that dead-weight of social degradation partially masked behind a half-named Negro problem. He felt his poverty; without a cent, without a home, without land, tools, or savings, he had entered into competition with rich, landed, skilled neighbors. To be a poor man is hard, but to be a poor race in a land of dollars is the very bottom of hardships. He felt the weight of his ignorance,—not simply of letters, but of life, of business, of the humanities; the accumulated sloth and shirking and awkwardness of decades and centuries shackled his hands and feet. Nor was his burden all poverty and ignorance. The red stain of bastardy, which two centuries of systematic legal defilement of Negro women had stamped upon his race, meant not only the loss of ancient African chastity, but also the hereditary weight of a mass of corruption from white adulterers, threatening almost the obliteration of the Negro home.

A people thus handicapped ought not to be asked to race with the world, but rather allowed to give all its time and thought to its own social problems. But alas! while sociologists gleefully count his bastards and his prostitutes, the very soul of the toiling, sweating black man is darkened by the shadow of a vast despair. Men call the shadow prejudice, and learnedly explain it as the natural defense of culture against barbarism, learning against ignorance, purity against crime, the "higher" against the "lower" races. To which the Negro cries Amen! and swears that to so much of this strange prejudice as is founded on just homage to civilization, culture, righteousness, and progress, he humbly bows and meekly does obeisance. But before that nameless prejudice that leaps beyond all this he stands helpless, dismayed, and well-nigh speechless; before that personal disrespect and mockery, the ridicule and systematic humiliation, the distortion of fact and wanton license of fancy, the cynical ignoring of the better and the boisterous welcoming of the worse, the all-pervading desire to inculcate disdain for everything black, from Toussaint to the devil,—before this there rises a sickening despair that would disarm and discourage any nation save that black host to whom "discouragement" is an unwritten word.

But the facing of so vast a prejudice could not but bring the inevitable self-questioning, self-disparagement, and lowering of ideals which ever accompany repression and breed in an atmosphere of contempt and hate. Whisperings and portents came borne upon the four winds: Lo! we are diseased and dying, cried the dark hosts; we cannot write, our voting is vain; what need of education, since we must always cook and serve? And the Nation echoed and enforced this self-criticism, saying: Be content to be servants, and nothing more; what need of higher culture for half-men? Away with the black man's ballot, by force or fraud,—and behold the suicide of a race! Nevertheless, out of the evil came something of good,—the more careful adjustment of education to real life, the clearer perception of the Negroes' social responsibilities, and the sobering realization of the meaning of progress.

So dawned the time of *Sturm und Drang:* storm and stress to-day rocks our little boat on the mad waters of the world sea; there is within and without the sound of conflict, the burning of body and rending of soul; inspiration strives with doubt, and faith with vain questionings. The bright ideals of the past,—physical freedom, political power, the training of brains and the training of hands,—all these in turn have waxed and waned, until even the last grows dim and overcast. Are they all wrong,—all false? No, not that, but each alone was over-simple and incomplete,—the dreams of a credulous race-childhood, or the fond imaginings of the other world which does not know and does not want to know our power. To be really true, all these ideals must be melted and welded into one. The training of the schools we need to-day more than ever,—the training of deft hands, quick eyes and ears, and above all the broader, deeper, higher culture of gifted minds and pure hearts. The power of the ballot we need in sheer self-defense,—else what shall save us from a second slavery? Freedom, too, the long-sought, we still seek,—the freedom of life and limb, the freedom to work and think,— the freedom to love and aspire. Work, culture, liberty,—all these we need, not singly but together, not successively but together, each growing and aiding each, and all striving toward that vaster ideal that swims before the Negro people, the ideal of human brotherhood, gained through the unifying ideal of Race; the ideal of fostering and developing the traits and talents of the Negro, not in opposition to or contempt for other races, but rather in large conformity to the greater ideals of the American Republic, in order that some day on American soil two world-races may give each to each those characteristics both so sadly lack. We the darker ones come even now not altogether empty-handed: there are to-day no truer exponents of the pure human spirit of the Declaration of Independence than the American Negroes; there is no true American music but the wild sweet melodies of the Negro slave; the American fairy tales and folk-lore are Indian and African; and, all in all, we black men seem the sole oasis of simple faith and reverence in a dusty desert of dollars and smartness. Will America be poorer if she replace her brutal dyspeptic blundering with light-hearted but determined Negro humility? or her coarse and cruel wit with loving jovial good-humor? or her vulgar music with the soul of the Sorrow Songs?

Merely a concrete test of the underlying principles of the great republic is the Negro Problem, and the spiritual striving of the freedmen's sons is the travail of souls whose burden is almost beyond the measure of their strength, but who bear it in the name of an historic race, in the name of this the land of their fathers' fathers, and in the name of human opportunity.

Feminist Manifesto

1914

The feminist movement as at present instituted is
Inadequate

Women if you want to realise yourselves—you are on the eve of a devastating psychological upheaval—all your pet illusions must be unmasked—
the lies of centuries have got to go—are you prepared for the Wrench—?
There is no half-measure—NO scratching on the surface of the rubbish
heap of tradition, will bring about Reform, the only method is Absolute
Demolition

Cease to place your confidence in economic legislation, vice-crusades & uniform education—you are glossing over Reality.
Professional & commercial careers are opening up for you—Is that all
you want?

And if you honestly desire to find your level without prejudice—be Brave
& deny at the outset—that pathetic clap-trap war cry Woman is the
equal of man—
                                    for
She is NOT!

The man who lives a life in which his activities conform to a social
code which is a protectorate of the feminine element————is no longer
masculine
The women who adapt themselves to a theoretical valuation of their sex as
a relative impersonality, are not yet Feminine
Leave off looking to men to find out what you are not—seek within yourselves to find out what you are
As conditions are at present constituted—you have the choice between
Parasitism, & Prostitution—or Negation

Men & women are enemies, with the enmity of the exploited for the parasite, the parasite for the exploited—at present they are at the mercy of the

advantage that each can take of the other's sexual dependence—. The only point at which the interests of the sexes merge—is the sexual embrace.

The first illusion it is to your interest to demolish is the division of women into two classes—the mistress, & the mother every well-balanced & developed woman knows that is not true. Nature has endowed the complete woman with a faculty for expressing herself through all her functions— there are no restrictions the woman who is so incompletely evolved as to be un-self-conscious in sex, will prove a restrictive influence on the temperamental expansion of the next generation: the woman who is a poor mistress will be an incompetent mother—an inferior mentality—& will enjoy an inadequate apprehension of Life.

To obtain results you must make sacrifices & the first & greatest sacrifice you have to make is of your "virtue" The fictitious value of woman as identified with her physical purity—is too easy a stand-by—rendering her lethargic in the acquisition of intrinsic merits of character by which she could obtain a concrete value—therefore, the first self-enforced law for the female sex, as a protection against the man made bogey of virtue—which is the principal instrument of her subjection, would be the unconditional surgical destruction of virginity through-out the female population at puberty—.

The value of man is assessed entirely according to his use or interest to the community, the value of woman, depends entirely on chance, her success or insuccess in manoeuvering a man into taking the life-long responsibility of her—The advantages of marriage are too ridiculously ample—compared to all other trades—for under modern conditions a woman can accept preposterously luxurious support from a man (with-out return of any sort— even offspring)—as a thank offering for her virginity
The woman who has not succeeded in striking that advantageous bargain— is prohibited from any but surreptitious re-action to Life-stimuli—& entirely debarred maternity.
Every woman has a right to maternity—
Every woman of superior intelligence should realize her race-responsibility, in producing children in adequate proportion to the unfit or degenerate members of her sex—

Each child of a superior woman should be the result of a definite period of psychic development in her life—& not necessarily of a possibly irksome &

outworn continuance of an alliance—spontaneously adapted for vital creation in the beginning but not necessarily harmoniously balanced as the parties to it—follow their individual lines of personal evolution—

For the harmony of the race, each individual should be the expression of an easy & ample interpenetration of the male & female temperaments—free of stress

Woman must become more responsible for the child than man—

Women must destroy in themselves, the desire to be loved—The feeling that it is a personal insult when a man transfers his attentions from her to another woman

The desire for comfortable protection instead of an intelligent curiosity & courage in meeting & resisting the pressure of life sex or so called love must be reduced to its initial element, honour, grief, sentimentality, pride & consequently jealousy must be detached from it.

Woman for her happiness must retain her deceptive fragility of appearance, combined with indomitable will, irreducible courage, & abundant health the outcome of sound nerves—Another great illusion that woman must use all her introspective clear-sightedness & unbiased bravery to destroy—for the sake of her <u>self respect</u> is the impurity of sex the realisation in defiance of superstition that there is <u>nothing impure in sex</u>—except in the mental attitude to it—will constitute an incalculable & wider social regeneration than it is possible for our generation to imagine.

27.3 Gloria Anzaldúa
Borderlands/La Frontera (excerpt)
1987

MOVIMIENTOS DE REBELDÍA
Y LAS CULTURAS QUE TRAICIONAN

Esos movimientos de rebeldía que tenemos en la sangre nosotros los mexicanos surgen como ríos desbocanados en mis venas. Y como mi raza que cada en cuando deja caer esa esclavitud de obedecer, de callarse y aceptar, en mi está la rebeldía encimita de mi carne. Debajo de mi humillada mirada está una cara insolente lista para explotar. Me costó muy caro mi rebeldía—acalambrada con desvelos y dudas, sintiendome inútil, estúpida, e impotente.

Me entra una rabia cuando alguien—sea mi mamá, la Iglesia, la cultura de los anglos—me dice haz esto, haz eso sin considerar mis deseos.

Repele. Hable pa' 'tras. Fuí muy hocicona. Era indiferente a muchos valores de mi cultura. No me deje de los hombres. No fuí buena ni obediente.

Pero he crecido. Ya no soló paso toda mi vida botando las costumbres y los valores de mi cultura que me traicionan. También recojo las costumbres que por el tiempo se han provado y las costumbres de respeto a las mujeres. But despite my growing tolerance, for this Chicana *la guerra de independencia* is a constant.

THE STRENGTH OF MY REBELLION

I have a vivid memory of an old photograph: I am six years old. I stand between my father and mother, head cocked to the right, the toes of my flat feet gripping the ground. I hold my mother's hand.

To this day I'm not sure where I found the strength to leave the source, the mother, disengage from my family, *mi tierra, mi gente,* and all that picture stood for. I had to leave home so I could find myself, find my own intrinsic nature buried under the personality that had been imposed on me.

I was the first in six generations to leave the Valley, the only one in my family to ever leave home. But I didn't leave all the parts of me: I kept the ground of my own being. On it I walked away, taking with me the land, the Valley, Texas. *Gané mi camino y me largué. Muy andariega mi hija.* Because I left of my own accord *me dicen, "¿Cómo te gusta la mala vida?"*

At a very early age I had a strong sense of who I was and what I was about and what was fair. I had a stubborn will. It tried constantly to mobilize my soul under my own regime, to live life on my own terms no matter how unsuitable to others they were. *Terca.* Even as a child I would not obey. I was "lazy." Instead of ironing my younger brothers' shirts or cleaning the cupboards, I would pass many hours studying, reading, painting, writing. Every bit of self-faith I'd painstakingly gathered took a beating daily. Nothing in my culture approved of me. *Había agarrado malos pasos.* Something was "wrong" with me. *Estaba mas alla de la tradición.*

There is a rebel in me—the Shadow-Beast. It is a part of me that refuses to take orders from outside authorities. It refuses to take orders from my conscious will, it threatens the sovereignty of my rulership. It is that part of me that hates constraints of any kind, even those self-imposed. At the least hint of limitations on my time or space by others, it kicks out with both feet. Bolts.

. . .

INTIMATE TERRORISM: LIFE IN THE BORDERLANDS

The world is not a safe place to live in. We shiver in separate cells in enclosed cities, shoulders hunched, barely keeping the panic below the surface of the skin, daily drinking shock along with our morning coffee, fearing the torches being set to our buildings, the attacks in the streets. Shutting down. Woman does not feel safe when her own culture, and white culture, are critical of her; when the males of all races hunt her as prey.

Alienated from her mother culture, "alien" in the dominant culture, the woman of color does not feel safe within the inner life of her Self. Petrified, she can't respond, her face caught berween *los intersticios,* the spaces between the different worlds she inhabits.

The ability to respond is what is meant by responsibility, yet our cultures take away our ability to act—shackle us in the name of protection. Blocked, immobilized, we can't move forward, can't move backwards. That writhing serpent movement, the very movement of life, swifter than lightning, frozen.

We do not engage fully. We do not make full use of our faculties. We abnegate. And there in front of us is the crossroads and choice: to feel a victim where someone else is in control and therefore responsible and to blame (being a victim and transferring the blame on culture, mother, father, ex-lover, friend, absolves me of responsibility), or to feel strong, and, for the most part, in control.

My Chicana identity is grounded in the Indian woman's history of re-sistance. The Aztec female rites of mourning were rites of defiance protest-ing the cultural changes which disrupted the equality and balance between female and male, and protesting their demotion to a lesser status, their denigration. Like *la Llorona*, the Indian woman's only means of protest was wailing.

So mamá. Raza, how wonderful, *no tener que rendir cuentas a nadie.* I feel perfectly free to rebel and to rail against my culture. I fear no betrayal on my part because, unlike Chicanas and other women of color who grew up white or who have only recently returned to their native cultural roots, I was totally immersed in mine. It wasn't until I went to high school that I "saw" whites. Until I worked on my master's degree I had not gotten within an arm's distance of them. I was totally immersed *en lo mexicano*, a rural, peas-ant, isolated, *mexicanismo.* To separate from my culture (as from my family) I had to feel competent enough on the outside and secure enough inside to live life on my own. Yet in leaving home I did not lose touch with my ori-gins because *lo mexicano* is in my system. I am a turtle, wherever I go I carry "home" on my back.

Not me sold out my people but they me. So yes, though "home" perme-ates every sinew and cartilage in my body, I too am afraid of going home. Though I'll defend my race and culture when they are attacked by *non-mexicanos, conosco el malestar de me cultura.* I abhor some of my culture's ways, how it cripples its women, *como burras,* our strengths used against us, lowly *burras* bearing humility with dignity. The ability to serve, claim the males, is our highest virtue. I abhor how my culture makes *macho* carica-tures of its men. No, I do not buy all the myths of the tribe into which I was born. I can understand why the more tinged with Anglo blood, the more adamantly my colored and colorless sisters glorify their colored culture's values—to offset the extreme devaluation of it by the white culture. It's a legitimate reaction. But I will not glorify those aspects of my culture which have injured me and which have injured me in the name of protecting me.

So, don't give me your tenets and your laws. Don't give me your luke-warm gods. What I want is an accounting with all three cultures—white, Mexican, Indian. I want the freedom to carve and chisel my own face, to staunch the bleeding with ashes, to fashion my own gods out of my entrails. And if going home is denied me then I will have to stand and claim my space, making a new culture—*una cultura mestiza*—with my own lumber, my own bricks and mortar and my own feminist architecture.

.   .   .

SI LE PREGUNTAS A MI MAMÁ, "¿QUÉ ERES?"

Identity is the essential core of who we are as individuals,
the conscious experience of the self inside.
KAUFMAN

Nosotros los Chicanos straddle the borderlands. On one side of us, we are constantly exposed to the Spanish of the Mexicans, on the other side we hear the Anglos' incessant clamoring so that we forget our language. Among ourselves we don't say *nosotros los americanos, o nosotros los españoles, o nosotros los hispanos.* We say *nosotros los mexicanos* (by *mexicanos* we do not mean citizens of Mexico; we do not mean a national identity, but a racial one). We distinguish between *mexicanos del otro lado* and *mexicanos de este lado.* Deep in our hearts we believe that being Mexican has nothing to do with which country one lives in. Being Mexican is a state of soul—not one of mind, not one of citizenship. Neither eagle nor serpent, but both. And like the ocean, neither animal respects borders.

Dime con quien andas y te diré quien eres.
(Tell me who your friends are and I'll tell you who you are.)
MEXICAN SAYING

Si le preguntas a mi mamá, "¿Qué eres?" te dira, "Soy mexicana." My brothers and sister say the same. I sometimes will answer "*soy mexicana*" and at others will say "*soy Chicana*" *o* "*soy tejana.*" But I identified as "*Raza*" before I ever identified as "*mexicana*" or "Chicana."

As a culture we call ourselves Spanish when referring to ourselves as a linguistic group and when copping out. It is then that we forget our predominant Indian genes. We are 70–80 percent Indian. We call ourselves Hispanic or Spanish-American or Latin American or Latin when linking ourselves to other Spanish-speaking peoples of the Western hemisphere and when copping out. We call ourselves Mexican-American to signify we are neither Mexican nor American, but more the noun "American" than the adjective "Mexican" (and when copping out).

Chicanos and other people of color suffer economically for not acculturating. This voluntary (yet forced) alienation makes for psychological conflict, a kind of dual identity—we don't identify with the Anglo-American cultural values and we don't totally identify with the Mexican cultural values. We are a synergy of two cultures with various degrees of Mexicanness or Angloness. I have so internalized the borderland conflict that sometimes I feel like one cancels out the other and we are zero, nothing, no one. *A veces no soy nada ni nadie. Pero hasta cuando no lo soy, lo soy.*

When not copping out, when we know we are more than nothing, we call ourselves Mexican, referring to race and ancestry; *mestizo* when affirming both our Indian and Spanish (but we hardly ever own our Black ancestry); Chicano when referring to a politically aware people born and/or raised in the U.S.; *Raza* when referring to Chicanos; *tejanos* when we are Chicanos from Texas.

Chicanos did not know we were a people until 1965 when Ceasar Chávez and the farmworkers united and *I Am Joaquín* was published and *la Raza Unida* party was formed in Texas. With that recognition, we became a distinct people. Something momentous happened to the Chicano soul—we became aware of our reality and acquired a name and a language (Chicano Spanish) that reflected that reality. Now that we had a name, some of the fragmented pieces began to fall together—who we were, what we were, how we had evolved. We began to get glimpses of what we might eventually become.

Yet the struggle of identities continues, the struggle of borders is our reality still. One day the inner struggle will cease and a true integration take place. In the meantime, *tenémos que hacer la lucha. ¿Quién está protegiendo los ranchos de migente? ¿Quién está tratando de cerrar la fisura entre la india y el blanco en nuestra sangre? El Chicano, si, el Chicano que anda como un ladrón en su propia casa.*

Los Chicanos, how patient we seem, how very patient. There is the quiet of the Indian about us. We know how to survive. When other races have given up their tongue, we've kept ours. We know what it is to live under the hammer blow of the dominant *norteamericano* culture. But more than we count the blows, we count the days, the weeks, the years, the centuries, the eons until the white laws and commerce and customs will rot in the deserts they've created, lie bleached. *Humilides* yet proud, *quietos* yet wild, *nosotros los mexicanos-Chicanos* will walk by the crumbling ashes as we go about our business. Stubborn, persevering, impenetrable as stone, yet possessing a malleability that renders us unbreakable, we, the *mestizas* and *mestizos*, will remain.

27.4 MÉRET OPPENHEIM

It Is Not Easy

1975

NOTE

In my speech of January 1975, I said that we still have no image for the male tendency in women and we still have to camouflage it. Three years later it occurred to me that the allegorical image can simply be reversed. If the female tendency, which is essential to the genius of the male poet or artist, must share in the evolution of a work, then in the case of women writers, artists, thinkers, it is the male tendency within them that shares in the evolution of a work. Women are the "Muses" whom genius has kissed, just as man, the genius, has been "kissed by the Muse."

It is not easy to be a young artist. If you work in the same style as an accepted master, ancient or contemporary, success will not be long in coming, but if you speak a new language of your own that others have yet to learn, you may have to wait a very long time for a positive echo.

It was, and still is even more difficult for a woman artist.

The segregation begins with seemingly external things. Men, as artists, can live as they please without provoking censure, but people look disdainfully at a woman who claims the same privilege. This and much more is a woman's lot. I think it is the duty of a woman to lead a life that expresses her disbelief in the validity of the taboos that have been imposed upon her kind for thousands of years. Nobody will give you freedom, you have to take it.

Why are there still men, even young men, who refuse to concede women a creative spirit?

A great work of literature, art, music, philosophy is always the product of a whole person. And every person is both male and female. In ancient Greece, men were inspired by the Muses, which means that the female tendency within them shared in their creations, and this still applies today. Conversely, the male tendency is contained in the works of women.

We have neither an image nor a name for this. I venture to claim that the male tendency in women is still forced to wear camouflage. But why? As I see it, since the establishment of a patriarchy—in other words, since the devaluation of the female element—men have projected their inherent femininity as a quality of inferior ilk, on to women. For women this entails living not only their own femininity, but also that projected on to them by men. They have to be women to the second power. Now that really is too much. Yet it is what women have been for a long time, and what many still are today.

Of this strange breed Nietzsche says, "Women are still cats. . . ." (Note the 'still'!) "Women are still cats, and birds. Or cows, at best." And he's right. That is why women do not and cannot appreciate each other. You cannot appreciate a non-value. They project their male tendency on to men because they are forced to suppress it in themselves. "Women should not think." Is male self-esteem really so vulnerable? "Intellectual achievements by women are embarrassing." So, they have to be repressed and forgotten as quickly as possible. Ideas? Every genuinely new idea is by nature aggressive, and aggression, as a trait, is diametrically opposed to the image of femininity imprinted in the minds of men and projected on to women.

Men are an equally strange breed and, like women, a distorted version of what they could be.

For some years now, people have been saying that humanity has upset the balance of nature. Doesn't this justified thought embrace the veiled realization that it is the balance of humanity itself that has been upset? It has been upset by being split into two sexes locked in opposition, except that one of them has the undisputed upper hand.

Naturally neither men nor women are to blame for this development.

The great miracle, the "tool-making animal," evolved in different places on earth and, in obeying similar laws the world over, became the human being who *for the very first time* gave expression to an all-pervasive penetrating spirit—in rhythm, dance, picture and myth.

Much later, this great miracle took another step and developed its intellect. I think, I fear, that all the peoples of the earth will have to pass through the stage we are in today, with its appalling concretion, its brutality, its consuming greed for commodities—all side-effects of the fascinating finds of scientific scholarship.

To permit the development of the sharp instrument of the intellect, other traits had to be ignored. So much so that I think we are now suffering the dire consequences of having neglected these other qualities. I am talking about feelings, intuition, wisdom.

If we look at life on this planet since prehistoric times, we see nothing but steadily increasing complexity.

Since life means change, and since nature apparently tends to become more complex, there is no reason why nature shouldn't impel life in another direction again.

After all we mustn't forget that it was Eve who took the first bite of the apple from the Tree of Knowledge, or rather, the tree of conscious thought.

There were a few voices in the wilderness as early as the 18th century. Now women from all corners of the earth are raising their voices and rebelling against their despised position, an indication perhaps that feelings, which have been suppressed for so long, are coming to the surface again to take their rightful place in our hearts—on equal footing with reason!

And who knows . . . maybe wisdom will also be released from its dungeon someday.

27.5 Hélène Cixous and Catherine Clément
Sorties
1975

SORTIES: OUT AND OUT: ATTACKS/WAYS OUT/FORAYS

Where is she?
Activity/passivity
Sun/Moon
Culture/Nature
Day/Night
Father/Mother
Head/Heart
Intelligible/Palpable
Logos/Pathos
Form, convex, step, advance, semen, progress
Matter, concave, ground—where steps are taken, holding- and dumping-ground
<u>Man</u>
Woman

Always the same metaphor: we follow it, it carries us, beneath all its figures, wherever discourse is organized. If we read or speak, the same thread or double braid is leading us throughout literature, philosophy, criticism, centuries of representation and reflection. Thought has always worked through opposition, Speaking/Writing, Parole/Écriture, High/Low.

Through dual, hierarchical oppositions. Superior/Inferior. Myths, leg-

ends, books. Philosophical systems. Everywhere (where) ordering intervenes, where a law organizes what is thinkable by oppositions (dual, irreconcilable; or sublatable, dialectical). And all these pairs of oppositions are
couples. Does that mean something? Is the fact that Logocentrism subjects
thought—all concepts, codes and values—to a binary system, related to
"the" couple, man/woman?

Nature/History
Nature/Art
Nature/Mind
Passion/Action

Theory of culture, theory of society, symbolic systems in general—art, religion, family, language—it is all developed while bringing the same schemes
to light. And the movement whereby each opposition is set up to make sense
is the movement through which the couple is destroyed. A universal battlefield. Each time, a war is let loose. Death is always at work.

Father/son
Relations of authority, privilege, force.
The Word/Writing Relations: opposition, conflict, sublation, return.
Master/slave
Violence.
Repression.

We see that "victory" always comes down to the same thing: things get
hierarchical. Organization by hierarchy makes all conceptual organization
subject to man. Male privilege, shown in the opposition between *activity*
and *passivity*, which he uses to sustain himself. Traditionally, the question
of sexual difference is treated by coupling it with the opposition: activity/
passivity.

There are repercussions. Consulting the history of philosophy—since
philosophical discourse both orders and reproduces all thought—one no-
tices that it is marked by an absolute *constant* which orders values and which
is precisely this opposition, activity/passivity.

Moreover, woman is always associated with passivity in philosophy.
Whenever it is a question of woman, when one examines kinship structures,
when a family model is brought into play. In fact, as soon as the question
of ontology raises its head, as soon as one asks oneself "what is it?," as soon
as there is intended meaning. Intention: desire, authority—examine them
and you are led right back . . . to the father. It is even possible not to notice
that there is no place whatsoever for woman in the calculations. Ultimately

the world of being can function while precluding the mother. No need for a mother, as long as there is some motherliness: and it is the father, then, who acts the part, who is the mother. Either woman is passive or she does not exist. What is left of her is unthinkable, unthought. Which certainly means that she is not thought, that she does not enter into the oppositions, that she does not make a couple with the father (who makes a couple with the son).

There is Mallarmé's tragic dream, that father's lamentation on the mystery of paternity, that wrenches from the poet the mourning, the mourning of mournings, the death of the cherished son: this dream of marriage between father and son. — And there's no mother then. A man's dream when faced with death. Which always threatens him differently than it threatens a woman.

"a union
a marriage, splendid   And dreams of filiation
—and with life   that is masculine, dreams
still in me   of God the father
I shall use it   issuing from himself
for . . .   in his son—and
so not mother then?"   no mother then

She does not exist, she cannot be; but there has to be something of her. He keeps, then, of the woman on whom he is no longer dependent, only this space, always virginal, as matter to be subjected to the desire he wishes to impart.

And if we consult literary history, it is the same story. It all comes back to man—to *his* torment, his desire to be (at) the origin. Back to the father. There is an intrinsic connection between the philosophical and the literary (to the extent that it conveys meaning, literature is under the command of the philosophical) and the phallocentric. Philosophy is constructed on the premise of woman's abasement. Subordination of the feminine to the masculine order, which gives the appearance of being the condition for the machinery's functioning.

Now it has become rather urgent to question this solidarity between logocentrism and phallocentrism—bringing to light the fate dealt to woman, her burial—to threaten the stability of the masculine structure that passed itself off as eternal-natural, by conjuring up from femininity the reflections and hypotheses that are necessarily ruinous for the stronghold still in possession of authority. What would happen to logocentrism, to the great philosophical systems, to the order of the world in general if the rock upon which they founded this church should crumble?

If some fine day it suddenly came out that the logocentric plan had always, inadmissibly, been to create a foundation for (to found and fund) phallocentrism, to guarantee the masculine order a rationale equal to history itself.

So all the history, all the stories would be there to retell differently; the future would be incalculable; the historic forces would and will change hands and change body—another thought which is yet unthinkable—will transform the functioning of all society We are living in an age where the conceptual foundation of an ancient culture is in the process of being undermined by millions of a species of mole (Topoi, ground mines) never known before.

When they wake up from among the dead, from among words, from among laws

Once upon a time . . . [. . .]

It is impossible to predict what will become of sexual difference—in another time (in two or three hundred years?). But we must make no mistake: men and women are caught up in a web of age-old cultural determinations that are almost unanalyzable in their complexity. One can no more speak of "woman" than of "man" without being trapped within an ideological theater where the proliferation of representations, images, reflections, myths, identifications, transform, deform, constantly change everyone's Imaginary and invalidate in advance any conceptualization.

Nothing allows us to rule out the possibility of radical transformation of behaviors, mentalities, roles, political economy—whose effects on libidinal economy are unthinkable—today. Let us simultaneously imagine a general change in all the structures of training, education, supervision—hence in the structures of reproduction of ideological results. And let us imagine a real liberation of sexuality, that is to say, a transformation of each one's relationship to his or her body (and to the other body), an approximation to the vast, material, organic, sensuous universe that we are. This cannot be accomplished, of course, without political transformations that are equally radical. (Imagine!) Then "femininity" and "masculinity" would inscribe quite differently their effects of difference, their economy, their relationship to expenditure, to lack, to the gift. What today appears to be "feminine" or "masculine" would no longer amount to the same thing. No longer would the common logic of difference be organized with the opposition that remains dominant. Difference would be a bunch of new differences.

But we are still floundering—with few exceptions—in Ancient History.

THE MASCULINE FUTURE

There are some exceptions. There have always been those uncertain, poetic persons who have not let themselves be reduced to dummies programmed by pitiless repression of the homosexual element. Men or women: beings who are complex, mobile, open. Accepting the other sex as a component makes them much richer, more various, stronger, and—to the extent that they are mobile—very fragile. It is only in this condition that we invent. Thinkers, artists, those who create new values, "philosophers" in the mad Nietzschean manner, inventors and wreckers of concepts and forms, those who change life cannot help but be stirred by anomalies—complementary or contradictory. That doesn't mean that you have to be homosexual to create. But it does mean that there is no *invention* possible, whether it be philosophical or poetic, without there being in the inventing subject an abundance of the other, of variety: separate-people, thought-/people, whole populations issuing from the unconscious, and in each suddenly animated desert, the springing up of selves one didn't know—our women, our monsters, our jackals, our Arabs, our aliases, our frights. That there is no invention of any other I, no poetry, no fiction without a certain homosexuality (the I/play of bisexuality) acting as a crystallization of my ultrasubjectivities. I is this exuberant, gay, personal matter, masculine, feminine or other where I enchants, I agonizes me. And in the concert of personalizations called I, at the same time that a certain homosexuality is repressed, symbolically, substitutively, it comes through by various signs, conduct-character, behavior-acts. And it is even more clearly seen in writing.

Thus, what is inscribed under Jean Genêt's name, in the movement of a text that divides itself, pulls itself to pieces, dismembers itself, regroups, re-members itself, is a proliferating, maternal femininity. A phantasmic meld of men, males, gentlemen, monarchs, princes, orphans, flowers, mothers, breasts gravitates about a wonderful "sun of energy"—love,—that bombards and disintegrates these ephemeral amorous anomalies so that they can be recomposed in other bodies for new passions.

She is bisexual:

What I propose here leads directly to a reconsideration of *bisexuality*. To reassert the value of bisexuality; hence to snatch it from the fate classically reserved for it in which it is conceptualized as "neuter" because, as such, it would aim at warding off castration. Therefore, I shall distinguish between two bisexualities, two opposite ways of imagining the possibility and practice of bisexuality.

1. Bisexuality as a fantasy of a complete being, which replaces the fear of castration and veils sexual difference insofar as this is perceived as the mark of a mythical separation—the trace, therefore, of a dangerous and painful ability to be cut. Ovid's Hermaphrodite, less bisexual than asexual, not made up of two genders but of two halves. Hence, a fantasy of unity. Two within one, and not even two wholes.

2. To this bisexuality that melts together and effaces, wishing to avert castration I oppose the *other bisexuality*, the one with which every subject, who is not shut up inside the spurious Phallocentric Performing Theater, sets up his or her erotic universe. Bisexuality—that is to say the location within oneself of the presence of both sexes, evident and insistent in different ways according to the individual, the nonexclusion of difference or of a sex, and starting with this "permission" one gives oneself, the multiplication of the effects of desire's inscription on every part of the body and the other body.

For historical reasons, at the present time it is woman who benefits from and opens up within this bisexuality beside itself, which does not annihilate differences but cheers them on, pursues them, adds more: in a certain way *woman is bisexual*—man having been trained to aim for glorious phallic monosexuality. By insisting on the primacy of the phallus and implementing it, phallocratic ideology has produced more than one victim. As a woman, I could be obsessed by the scepter's great shadow, and they told me: adore it, that thing you don't wield.

But at the same time, man has been given the grotesque and unenviable fate of being reduced to a single idol with clay balls. And terrified of homosexuality, as Freud and his followers remark. Why does man fear *being* a woman? Why this refusal (*Ablehnung*) of femininity? The question that stumps Freud. The "bare rock" of castration. For Freud, the repressed is not the other sex defeated by the dominant sex, as his friend Fliess (to whom Freud owes the theory of bisexuality) believed; what is repressed is leaning toward one's own sex.

Psychoanalysis is formed on the basis of woman and has repressed (not all that successfully) the femininity of masculine sexuality, and now the account it gives is hard to disprove.

We women, the derangers, know it only too well. But nothing compels us to deposit our lives in these lack-banks; to think that the subject is constituted as the last stage in a drama of bruising rehearsals; to endlessly bail out the father's religion. Because we don't desire it. We don't go round and round the supreme hole. We have no *woman's* reason to pay allegiance to the negative. What is feminine (the poets suspected it) affirms: . . . and yes I said yes I will Yes, says Molly (in her rapture), carrying *Ulysses* with her in the direction of a new writing; I said yes, I will Yes.

To say that woman is somehow bisexual is an apparently paradoxical way of displacing and reviving the question of difference. And therefore of writing as "feminine" or "masculine."

I will say: today writing is woman's. That is not a provocation, it means that woman admits there is an other. In her becoming-woman she has not erased the bisexuality latent in the girl as in the boy. Femininity and bisexuality go together in a combination that varies according to the individual, spreading the intensity of its force differently and (depending on the moments of their history) privileging one component or another. It is much harder for man to let the other come through him. Writing is the passageway, the entrance, the exit, the dwelling place of the other in me—the other that I am and am not, that I don't know how to be, but that I feel passing, that makes me live—that tears me apart, disturbs me, changes me, who?— a feminine one, a masculine one, some?—several, some unknown, which is indeed what gives me the desire to know and from which all life soars. This peopling gives neither rest nor security, always disturbs the relationship to "reality," produces an uncertainty that gets in the way of the subject's socialization. It is distressing, it wears you out; and for men this permeability, this nonexclusion is a threat, something intolerable.

In the past, when carried to a rather spectacular degree, it was called "possession." Being possessed is not desirable for a masculine Imaginary, which would interpret it as passivity—a dangerous feminine position. It is true that a certain receptivity is "feminine." One can, of course, as History has always done, exploit feminine reception through alienation. A woman, by her opening up, is open to being "possessed," which is to say, dispossessed of herself.

But I am speaking here of femininity as keeping alive the other that is confided to her, that visits her, that she can love as other. The loving to be other, another, without its necessarily going the route of abasing what is same, herself.

As for passivity, in excess, it is partly bound up with death. But there is a nonclosure that is not submission but confidence and comprehension; that is not an opportunity for destruction but for wonderful expansion.

Through the same opening that is her danger, she comes out of herself to go to the other, a traveler in unexplored places; she does not refuse, she approaches, not to do away with the space between, but to see it, to experience what she is not, what she is, what she can be.

Writing is working; being worked; questioning (in) the between (letting oneself be questioned) of same *and of* other without which nothing lives; undoing death's work by willing the togetherness of one-another, infinitely charged with a ceaseless exchange of one with another—not knowing one another and beginning again only from what is most distant, from self, from other, from the other within. A course that multiplies transformations by the thousands . . .

If there is a self proper to woman, paradoxically it is her capacity to de-propriate herself without self-interest: endless body, without "end," without principle "parts"; if she is a whole, it is a whole made up of parts that are wholes, not simple, partial objects but varied entirety, moving and boundless change, a cosmos where eros never stops traveling, vast astral space. She doesn't revolve around a sun that is more star than the stars.

That doesn't mean that she is undifferentiated magma; it means that she doesn't create a monarchy of her body or her desire. Let masculine sexuality gravitate around the penis, engendering this centralized body (political anatomy) under the party dictatorship. Woman does not perform on herself this regionalization that profits the couple head-sex, that only inscribes itself within frontiers. Her libido is cosmic, just as her unconscious is worldwide: her writing also can only go on and on, without ever inscribing or distinguishing contours, daring these dizzying passages in other, fleeting and passionate dwellings within him, within the hims and hers whom she inhabits just long enough to watch them, as close as possible to the unconscious from the moment they arise; to love them, as close as possible to instinctual drives, and then, further, all filled with these brief identifying hugs and kisses, she goes and goes on infinitely. She alone dares and wants to know from within where she, the one excluded, has never ceased to hear what-comes-before-language reverberating. She lets the other tongue of a thousand tongues speak—the tongue, sound without barrier or death. She refuses life nothing. Her tongue doesn't hold back but holds forth, doesn't keep in but keeps on enabling. Where the wonder of being several and turmoil is expressed, she does not protect herself against these unknown feminines; she surprises herself at seeing, being, pleasuring in her gift of changeability. I am spacious singing Flesh: onto which is grafted no one knows which I—which masculine or feminine, more or less human but above all living, because changing I.

PART 28

Oulipo

Following in the footsteps of Alfred Jarry and Marcel Duchamp, Raymond Queneau, Harry Matthews, Jacques Roubaud, Marcel Benabou, and other related workers in the field of the impossible possible have created a system of poetics that delights in constraints—for example, the elimination of the letter *e*, the most frequent letter in French, from the entire text of Georges Perec's brilliantly conceived *A Void (La Disparition)*. Among other precedents for this kind of rule is the Russian Ferroconcretist Vasily Kamensky's "word columns," in which one letter is omitted in each succeeding word, or words are blended together, replaced by symbols, graphic representations of scenes. These resemble Guillaume Apollinaire's experimental graphic poems and the work of the Italian Futurists as well, in a typical convergence of avant-garde ideas.

Oulipo, or the Ouvroir de Littérature Potentielle, the workplace for potential literature, is devoted to the possibilities of combinatorial research. It is witty, serious, secret, and openly irritating to those not of its stripe.

François Le Lionnais's "The Litpot: The First Manifesto" (28.1), from the Oulipian library, gives the feeling of the thing. Like all successful manifestos, it turns you either off or on.

28.1 FRANÇOIS LE LIONNAIS

The Litpot

The First Manifesto

1962

Let's open a dictionary[1] to the words "Potential Literature." Nothing. A terrible gap. What follows are just some simple tidbits, if not a definition, just to stave off hunger while waiting for the real dish to be served up by those worthier than me.

Do you remember the discussions that accompanied the invention of language? Mystification, childish fantasy, degeneration of the race and dissolution of the State, treason against Nature, attack on the emotions, crime of *lèse-inspiration*, what wasn't language accused of (without using language) at the time?

And the creation of writing, and grammar, do you think that occurred

---

1. Any one at all.

without any protest? The truth is that the quarrel of the Ancients and the Moderns has gone on forever. It began with the Zinjanthropic Age (one million seven hundred and fifty thousand years ago) and won't end until humanity does, unless the Mutants that come after that pick it up, of course. On top of that, it's a very badly named Quarrel. Those we call the Ancients are quite often the ossified descendants of those who were Moderns in their time; and the latter, if they came back to us, would be on the side of the innovators, denouncing their over-faithful imitators.

Potential literature only represents a new running of sap in this debate.[2]

Every literary work is constructed from some initial inspiration (at least, that's what its author suggests), which has to accommodate itself for better or worse to a series of constraints and procedures that fit each into the other like Russian dolls. Constraints of vocabulary and grammar, constraints for the novel and its rules (chapter divisions and so on) or for classical tragedy (the rule of the three unities), constraints for versification, constraints for fixed forms (like the rondeau, the sonnet, etc.).

Should we really stick to the rules we know, buttheadedly refusing to imagine new formulas? The partisans of immobilism will unhesitatingly answer yes. Their convictions don't depend as much on reasoned reflection as on the force of habit and the impressive series of masterpieces (and also, alas, some less masterful pieces) that derived from the present rules and forms. So must the adversaries of the invention of language have argued, so sensitive were they to the beauty of shouts, the expressivity of sighs and furtive looks (and no one is asking lovers to do without them.)

Should humanity rest and content itself with composing old verses on new thoughts? We don't think so. What certain writers have introduced in their style, with talent (even genius), some upon occasion (concocting new words), others deliberately (counterrhymes), others insistently but in a single direction (lettrism), the Workplace for Potential Literature (WOPOLI) [Ouvroir de Littérature Potentielle, OULIPO] means to do systematically and scientifically, using computers if need be. You can see in the research that the Ouvroir is undertaking two principal tendencies, turned respectively toward Analysis and Synthesis. The analytic tendency works on the works of the past to find possibilities that often go far past what the authors had suspected. That's the case, for example, of the cento, which could be revitalized by some considerations taken from the theory of Markov chains.

The synthetic tendency is more ambitious; it constitutes the essential

---

2. How can sap run in a debate? We are totally uninterested in this question, which has nothing to do with poetry, only with vegetal physiology.

vocation of OULIPO. New directions are opening up that were totally unknown to our predecessors. Take, for example, the case of the Hundred
Thousand Thousands of Poems or Boolian haikai. Mathematics—particularly the abstract structures of contemporary mathematics—offers a thousand directions for us to explore, either starting with Algebra (recourse to
new laws of composition) or Topology (considerations of proximity, of the
opening or closure of texts).

We are also thinking about anaglyphic poems, texts that can be transformed by projection, and so on. Other innovations can be imagined, notably in the domain of particular vocabularies (crows, foxes, dolphins; the
language of computers; and so on). It would take a long article just to enumerate the possibilities evident so far, some just being sketched out. You
can't easily detect, just from examining the seed, what the taste of a totally
new fruit will be. Take the case of alphabetic constraint. In literature it can
lead to the acrostic, which hasn't so far produced any very remarkable works
(although Villon, and way before him, the Psalmist and the Lamentations
of Jeremiah . . .); in painting, it gave us Herbin, and that's altogether better;
and in music, the fugue with Bach's name in it, now that's an appreciable
work. How could the inventors of the alphabet have suspected any of that?

To sum it up, anoulipism is devoted to discovery, synthoulipism to invention. From one to the other there are some subtle correspondences.

Finally, just a remark for the particularly serious people who are used
to condemning without further study and without appeal any work where
there is some propensity to humor.

When they are done by poets, light things, farces, and hoaxes still belong
to poetry. Potential literature remains, therefore, the most serious thing in
the world. That is what was was to be proved: QED.

PART 29

L=A=N=G=U=A=G=E

Placing the emphasis on language instead of what it represents, denotes, or connotes began far before Stéphane Mallarmé, but is best known in its origin by his determination "to give a purer sense to the words of the tribe" (*Stéphane Mallarmé*, 51). This purer sense, nonrepresentational and so independent of anything outside itself, an obsession positive in itself, motivates Gertrude Stein's explanation of composition and much else, as well as the poets of the movement called by the name L=A=N=G=U=A=G=E. The visual strangeness of this term puts, and is meant to put, the weight on the nonrepresentational value of the term and the movement. Its manifestos are many, its texts readable and devoid of Stein's weighty solemnity. But all these texts have their own genius, and it is specifically American in its feeling. On the contemporary scene, L=A=N=G=U=A=G=E is one of the leading poetic movements.

In the mid 1970s Charles Bernstein, Bruce Andrews, Ron Silliman, Susan Howe, and Lyn Hejinian began to bring attention, as the Lettrists and the concrete poets had done, to language itself rather than to the personality of the poet. They were implicitly setting themselves up against the Black Mountain school of poets and the New York School and the Abstract Expressionist mode of the personal sublime. They were interested less in what their predecessors had cared about — primitivism, mysticism, and the conveying of the poetic presence — than in Charles Olson's Projectivism and the breathing sequence from which the poet and poem were to derive the energy they were to pass on to the reader.

L=A=N=G=U=A=G=E poetry can be seen as another way of making strange — the celebrated Russian *ostranenie* of Victor Shklovsky — what we might have wanted to see as normal. In unnormalizing language, flattening it out, detonalizing it as it were, they are the most recent examples of a true Postmodernism.

29.1 SUSAN BEE [LAUFER] AND CHARLES BERNSTEIN
Style
1978

It is said that one can tell during a conversation that lasts no longer than a summer shower whether or not a person is cultivated. Often it does not take even so long, for a raucous tone of voice and grossly ungrammatical or vulgar expressions brand a person at once as beyond the pale of polite society. As one goes forth one is weighed in the balance and if found wanting he is quietly dropped by refined and cultured people, and nearly always he is left wondering why with his diamonds and his motors and his money he yet cannot find entree into the inner circles. An honest heart may beat beneath the ragged coat, a brilliant intellect may rise above the bright checkered suit and yellow tie, the man in the shabby suit may be a famous writer, the woman in the untidy blouse may be an artist of great promise, but as a general rule the chances are against it and such people are dull, flat, stale and unprofitable both to themselves and to other people. In the end, coherence is always a quality of thought rather than a manner of expression. The confused mind cannot produce coherent prose. A well-proportioned letter is the product of a well-balanced mind. The utterance of the single word "Charles!" may signify: "Hello, Charles! are you here? I am surprised to see you." Language, however, is not confined to the utterance of single words. To express our thoughts we must put words together in accordance with certain fixed rules. Otherwise we should fail to express ourselves clearly and acceptably, and we may even succeed in saying the opposite of what we mean. Since language is the expression of thought, the rules of grammar agree, in the main, with the laws of thought. Even in matters of divided usage, it is seldom difficult to determine which of two forms is preferred by careful writers. Everything is taken care of in the most orderly fashion: terms are defined, possible ambiguities eliminated, implications and assumptions explained, proofs adduced, and examples provided. On the whole it is safe for the writer to leave semantic theory unexplored. We favor the standards of the more precise stylists if only because we cannot be more permissive without risking their disapproval, whereas those who do

Sources include Follet's *Modern American Usage*, Kittridge's *Advanced English Grammar*, Stein's *How to Write*, the Modern Language Association's *In-House Style Sheet*, Hagar's *The English of Business*, Martin and Ohmann's *Logic and Rhetoric of Exposition*, Raleigh's *Style*, and Eichler's *Book of Etiquette*.

not object to less exacting usage are not likely to be offended by the correct usage. A good expository sentence does not call attention to itself, although Strunk comments that an occasional loose sentence has its virtues. No one who speaks and writes can expect his audience to respond to connotations that arise from his own purely personal experience. Some people associate colors with numbers, but orange is not a connotation of "four." The trouble with Humpty Dumpty's stipulative definitions, if they can be dignified by such a word, is that they are entirely capricious and absurd. For sentences must measure up to standards: it is always fair to ask of a sentence, "How *good* is it?" Among the qualities that contribute to an effective impression, the five most essential are clearness, correctness, conciseness, courtesy, and character. For style is ingratiation; negative ideas, as a rule, should not be developed at length. And constructions to be shunned include those that are vague, abstract, equivocal, slanted, misleading, exaggerated, understated, loose, abbreviated, oversimplified, obvious, irrelevant, oblique, figurative, redundant, empty, impossible, or obscure. It would be a curious state of affairs if only those who seldom think about the words they use, who read little and who "cannot be bothered" with distinctions should be the only ones with full powers over vocabulary and syntax. Even on the grounds of free democratic choice the hands-off attitude about language receives no support. These assumptions further suggest that the desire for correctness, the very idea of better or worse in speech, is a hangover from aristocratic and oppressive times. . . . The young foreigner who apologizes for the fact that the chocolates he has bought as a gift are *molten* is told with a smile that that is not English: the right word is *melted*. — We talk to our fellows in the phrases we learn from them, which seem to mean less and less as they grow worn with use. The quiet cynicism of our everyday demeanor is open and shameless, we callously anticipate objections founded on the well-known vacuity of our seeming emotions, and assure our friends that we are "truly" grieved or "sincerely" rejoiced at their hap—as if joy or grief that really exists were some rare and precious brand of joy or grief. A sentence says you know what I mean, dear do I well I guess I do. Grammar does not mean that they are to limit themselves. More and more grammar is not a thing. Grammar does not make me hesitate about prepositions. I am a grammarian I do not hesitate I rearrange prepositions.

29.2 Charles Bernstein

The Conspiracy of "Us"

1979

I don't believe in group formation, I don't like group formation, but I am constantly finding myself contending with it, living within it, seeing through it. "Okay, break it up boys." First, there is the isolation of the atom, looking for some place to feel housed by, a part of, & every which way the people passing seem to have that—"see it over there"—"look." But every group as well has the same possibility for insularity as each individual: this new "we" having the same possibility for vacancy or satisfaction, a group potentially as atomized in its separation from other groups as a person from other persons. This is the problem of family life. Property, territory, domain. But, "for us now," group (family, aesthetic, social, national) is merely another part of our commoditized lives—for we consume these formations, along with most other things, as commodities, & are ourselves consumed in the process. ((Putting aside here the extent to which political groupings and parties would be different from groups of "artists"; also the place of groupings based on class oppression on the one hand and minority oppression— women, gays, mental patients—on the other.)) So we use groups as badges —shields—as much screening us off from the intrusion of outside, others, as sheltering us from the sheer invasiveness of it, them (& so allowing us a place to occupy, inhabit). I don't so much think that such shelter is a fraud, unnecessary, as much as "let's look at it, call the strictures into question, understand that we *can* reshape": a call against paralysis from a sense of boundaries fixed without, or before, our having had a chance to participate in their making. "The danger is that our demands on each other will trample what we really feel." The danger is that we will hide ourselves amidst the shuffle to proclaim who we are.

We're afraid to say poetry, afraid of the *task*—that's why simply having the goods—"Oh he's gifted as hell"—is never enough. I want to see more than fine sentiments beautifully expressed "in the manner of . . ." "He's really picked up on me" but sadly, not on *us*. One might as well go back to fruit picking. It's hard to talk about content these days, everyone pointing to the trace of their ideas as if *that* was "it" but we don't want mere conceptualizations. "*But*, I mean, that person is really saying something," which is the wrong way of making the point. But: enough of empty vessels for sure. It's necessity which makes the form, which then inheres; not just any "constructs" but the ones we live by, the ones we live in & so the ones we *come upon*—

"Getting it." "Using it." "Pretending." "Imagining." "On the inside track." "In contention." "An authority that genuinely speaks from its heart, letting us know that here . . ." "Great hips." "Thyroid problems." "Oh how come you done that." "Ain't that *Christian* of you." "Grace." "Grave." "Maria of the *fleurs.*" "An open cavity, about three to six inches from the back of tongue, who . . ." "Naturally." "Over-intellectual." "With too much *effort* . . ." "Over-emotional." "Grecian." ". . . which at times one only wishes would give way to some greater sense of necessity, like why bother to write it in the first place." "From up here, the low-lying clouds obscuring the view . . ."

Language-centered writing and other art-historical epithets. For instance, you're right that the need for recognition, given that the work is important, does demand that action be taken. Cuts are made but not without enormous confusion on all sides—what's in common within & different from without both get exaggerated. A kind of blinder's vision begins as we look at the world in terms of the configurations being made. "At a given time we responded to each other's work, were there for each other." "To the permanent removal of everyone else after, simultaneous?" No. These things arise in practice, have a practical value. ((Imagine a world in which people allied along lines of hair color. Or what unified a group of artists was their use of a given shade of blue, or that they live (or grew up in, or went to school in) the same place—the impress of a common environment a constant to facilitate art-historical apprehension. How does Richard Diebenkorn get seen by those who think of non-figuration as the key issue of his generation of painters? & *wasn't* it the key issue?)) But the "final" cuts have not—will not be—made. Only cuts for "here" & "there"—

The identification of "younger" poets "coming up" by a group or community can imply the beginning for these people of inclusion within a paternalistic hierarchy—an initiation into it. — Simply, the walls must be stripped down & new ones constantly built as (re)placements—or rather this is always happening whether we attend to it or not. We see through these structures which we have made ourselves & cannot do even for a moment without them, yet they are not fixed but provisional. (. . . that poetry gets shaped—informed and transformed—by the social relations of publication, readership, correspondence, readings, etc (or, historically seen, the "tradition") and, indeed, that the poetry community(ies) are not a secondary phenomenon to writing but a primary one. So it won't do to just "think about the work." But it still needs to be explored what the relation between "normal" and "extraordinary" poetry is—& why both need to be more valued in some respects and devalued in others (snobbery, elitism, cliquishness, historical over-self-consciousness, self-aggrandizement, &c)—especially at a time in which there is an increase in the number of people and the number of people engaging in art activities—not just a few "men" "out there" doing the "heroic" work. — That poetry, with written language as its medium, is, in fact, the exploration and realization of the human common ground, of "us," in which we are—"that holds our sights within its views.")

Or what we have is a series of banana republics with internecine (ie inner) conflict as to whose to "be the" THE of the court, all that fading with jocular regularity as we paddle our gondolas down the canals of time and look back at the many remnants of period mannerism. You want to name names? I feel very bloated at last & want to take this opportunity to thank everyone. I wish I had a quill pen. I'll take a dime for every time they . . . "I mean some of this stuff really knocks you out." A great place to take you date, &c, I mean it really impresses boys. "You wanna know something—I'm glad what they done to you. . . ." The foundations of a linguistic empire on the coinage of a distinctive and recognizable style—"& that means don't hone in on my territory" "& that means *you*" is about as crucial as the opera of Luca Della Robbia. But not to stop there. "We" ain't about no new social groupings— nobody gotta move over—*this is the deconstruction of team.* This is *looking at language,* which *is* "us," & not creating the latest fashion splash of the "up & coming."

What happens, which is what it is when something happens & you say "oh, look at that ———" — already having arrived in your mind as a ———. But not just to plug in—"oh I got it let me dig some out for you—" The skips on the record which our pounding feet accentuate, making the needle dance out of synch to the rhythm our bodies seem to want to keep . . .—keep us honest. "Honest"? But not to "groove into," it's to make the words that come out *that* way more aware of themselves & so we more responsible to them, not that we "say" them with whatever capacity our "gifts" allow us but that we *mean* them with a twice told intention that puts "mere facility for images & transitions" in its place & puts "poetry"—a guild without members, only occasionally one or another of us finds ourselves there, or not "ourselves" but rather "those syllables so ordered . . ." & *we* mere spectators, out in the public field, watching *that,* now already behind us. . . .

If Written Is Writing

1978

I think of you, in English, so frequent, and deserved, and thereby desired, their common practice and continually think of it, who, since the Elizabethans, save Sterne and Joyce, have so trothed language to the imagination, and Melville, of whose *Mardi* the critics wrote, in 1849, "a tedious, floundering work of uncertain meaning or no meaning at all. A hodgepodge. . . . A story without movement, or proportions, or end . . . or point! An undigested mass of rambling metaphysics."

No-one is less negligent than you, to render the difficulties less whether well-protected, in grammar, in which it has been customary to distinguish *syntax* from *accidence*, the latter tending to the inflections of words—inflections, or towards itself, a bending in. The choices have always been fashioned and executed from within. Knowing is right and knowing is wrong. Nodding is, or could be, to you.

In such are we obsessed with our own lives, which lives being now language, the emphasis has moved. The emphasis is persistently centric, so that where once one sought a vocabulary for ideas, now one seeks ideas for vocabularies. Many are extant. Composition is by. The technique is very cut and the form is very close. Such is surprising even now, if overdue. Now so many years ago Donne wrote, Some that have deeper digg'd Loves Mine than I, Say, where his centrique happinesse doth lie.

The text is anterior to the composition, though the composition be interior to the text. Such candor is occasionally flirtatious, as candor nearly always so. When it is trustworthy, love accompanies the lover, and the centric writers reveal their loyalty, a bodily loyalty. Quite partial is necessity, of any text. Marvelous are the dimensions and therefore marvelling is understandable—and often understanding. Much else isn't, but when that comes, from the definite to an indefinite, having devised excuses for meeting, though we have not yet recognized, a selection, or choice, of what is combed out. The original scale determines the scope, the mood, the feel, the tone, the margin, the degree, the mathematics, the size, the sign, the system, the pursuit, the position, the mark. Of centricities, an interior view, there are two sources, perhaps three. One locates in the interior texture of such language as is of the person composing from it, personal and inclusive but not necessarily self-revelatory—in fact, now, seldom so; through improvisatory techniques building on the suggestions made by language itself—on patterns of language which are ideas and corresponding behavior or relevant quirks; this becomes an addictive motion—but not incorrect, despite such distortion, concentration, condensation, deconstruction and such as association by, for example, pun and etymology provide; an allusive psycholinguism. In the second it is the bibliography that is the text. The writing emerges from within a pre-existent text of one's own devising or another's. The process is composition rather than writing.

There are characteristic, contracting rhythms. The long line, with ramifying clauses, an introductory condition, and other cumulative devices have been fragmented, the rhythm accentuated. You can read. You can write. An unstable condition is given pause. The Elizabethans were given to a long system and we to purchase for pause, though not stop.

A possible third centricity, the perhaps, emerges from the imperatives and prerogatives of grammar. Such might be a work of, say, conjunctions, in which, for example, John Lloyd Stephens writes, "There is no immediate connection between taking Daguerreotype portraits and the practice of surgery, but circumstances bring close together things entirely dissimilar in themselves, and we went from one to the other." Such is a definition of the Elizabethan conceit. And in a blue book of French grammar one reads, "Linking is rare between a plural noun and a verb or between a plural adjective and a verb except in poetry."

All theory is safest ascribed in retrospect. On the line is an occasion to step off the line. The critic is a performer, good or bad. Facility is splendid, however—think of such heroic figures as Dr. Johnson, John Donne. Love was not easy. The cat gets the chair and you get the edge.

Conclusion:
by usual standing under half

29.4 MICHAEL PALMER
The Flower of Capital
1979

(sermon faux - vraie histoire)

. . . and the old dogmatism will no longer be able to end it.

ADOLFO SÁNCHEZ VÁZQUEZ

The flower of capital is small and white large and grey-green in a storm
its petals sing. (This refers to capital with the capital *L*.) Yesterday I borrowed Picabia's Lagonda for a drive through the Bois. A heavy mist enveloped the park so that we could barely discern the outline of a few silent
figures making their way among the sycamores and elms. Emerging at Porte
de Neuilly the air grew suddenly clear and ahead to my right I noticed M
pushing a perambulator before her with a distracted mien. Her hair fell di-
sheveled about her face, her clothes were threadbare, and every few steps
she would pause briefly and look about as if uncertain where she was. I tried
repeatedly to draw her attention with the horn, even slowing down at one
point and crying her name out the car window, all to no apparent effect.
Passing I saw once more (and as it developed, for the last time) the lenticu-
lar mark on her forehead and explained its curious origin to my companion, the Princess von K, who in return favored me with her wan smile. We
drove on directly to the Château de Verre where the Princess lived with her
younger sister and a few aged servants. The château itself was encircled by
the vestiges of a moat now indicated only by a slight depression in the grass
at the base of the walls. Or: we drove for hours through the small towns surrounding Paris, unable to decide among various possible courses of action.
Or: they have unearthed another child's body bringing the current total to
twenty-eight. Or: nine days from now will occur the vernal equinox. Yesterday in the artificial light of a large hall Ron spoke to me of character hovering
unacceptably at several removes above the page. The image of the Princess
and of M who were of course one and the same returned to mind as I con-
gratulated him on the accuracy of his observation. L knitted this shirt I told
him, and carved the sign on my brow, and only yesterday they removed the
tree that for so long had interfered with the ordered flow of language down
our street. Capital is a fever at play and in the world (silent *l*) each thing is
real or must pretend to be. Her tongue swells until it fills my mouth. I have
lived here for a day or part of a day, eyes closed, arms hanging casually at

my sides. Can such a book be read by you or me? Now he lowers the bamboo shade to alter the angle of the light, and now she breaks a fingernail against the railing of the bridge. Can such a text invent its own beginning, as for example one—two—three? And can it curve into closure from there to here?

*   *   *

A FOLLOWING NOTE

The problem is that poetry, at least my poetry and much that interests me, tends to concentrate on primary functions and qualities of language such as naming and the arbitrary structuring of a code—its fragility—the ease with which it empties (nullifies?) itself or contradicts what might simplistically qualify as intention. (And I might add conversely, its tyranny—how it resists amendment.)

Poetry seems to inform politically (this being a poetry that does transmit material of some immediate as well as enduring freshness) beyond its aspect as opinion or stance. Thus a Baudelaire, Pound, Eliot et al may render a societal picture of transcendent accuracy. Note of course the political "intelligence" of Shakespeare's Tudor apologies, of Racine's hierarchical poetics, of Dante's vision. It is clear that political "rectitude" is not necessarily equivalent to political "use" in a larger sense, though we can also find instances where there is a coinciding of poetic and immediate historical impulse, where in fact a poetry transmits its energy from a specifically political moment. Paradoxically I am thinking of a politics that *inheres*, such as Vallejo's, in contrast let's say with the more practical motives of much of Neruda's work.

Politics seems a realm of power and persuasion that would like to subsume poetry (and science, and fashion, and . . .) under its mantle, for whatever noble or base motives. Yet if poetry is to function—politically—with integrity, it must resist such appeals as certainly as it resists others.

The call to language in a poem does not begin or end with its discursive flow and does not give way to qualified priorities. Not to make of poetry a "purer" occasion, simply to give credit to its terms and the range of possibilities it attends. Poetry seems a *making* within discrete temporal conditions, and I would happily dispense with the word "creative." Poetry is profoundly mediational and relative and exists as a form of address singularly difficult to prescribe or define.

A poet's political responsibility is human, like that of a cabinetmaker or machinist, and his or her activity is subject to similar examination. Synchronically the results are predictably various. We treasure and perhaps survive by those moments when the poetic and political intelligence derive from an identical urgency and insight. Recently I came across Terry Eagleton's quotation from an article by Marx in the Rheinische Zeitung, "form is of no value unless it is the form of its content." "Simple," as Zukofsky used to say. And is it if it is?

29.5 NICK PIOMBINO

Writing and Remembering

1993

History is a catalogue of endings, but poetry speaks of being, of beginnings. Through an experience of linguistic recreation by immersion in a semantic continuous present of simultaneities, echoes, symbols, variously shaded fragments of raw and refined perceptions, the text (and its corresponding thought process) is momentarily liberated from its history (memory) and from its history-making function (remembering). This is why poetry is relatively free, compared to related disciplines like philosophy and psychology, from its own history. Its elements, including its formal properties, are subject to aesthetic, but not temporal, critiques. There is no linear historical conceptual development in poetry — only a process of eroding and building.

Poetry tends to have an ambivalent relationship toward any temporal function to which it is assigned. Unlike most other human endeavors, at certain moments, often its best ones, it cloaks itself in obscurity, withdraws from everyday life and takes the form of a static, receptive object. A process made to be acted upon, germinative, wood and oxygen waiting to be ignited by a determinant, though not necessarily parallel, flash of thought. And this is how it transcends history and is not only to be recognized and remembered, but contemplated, like the Sphinx.

Writing as remembering is nominative, ordering, and elicits from its reading a fixed, functional relationship. But poetry can be composed of any number of continuously altered, modulated and interrelated emotional tones, purposes, and intentions. These real, apparent, and illusory intentions are usually consciously parodied, at least at some point in a poem, if not in the form itself, creating still another shifting ground of contexts.

Historicity, that is, the legitimation or authentication of a work or event by establishing its historical relevance, binds language to fixed significances by ordering its syntax into descriptions of familiar or unfamiliar sequences of related perceptions or memories. Language, though bound to time by its passive connection with the process of recall, can be made to listen to itself. Again and again heard differently, through its poetry, language directs attention to its plastic and iconographic qualities by means of a kind of lexical hovering in and around, and subterranean plummeting through, meaning and memory. Familiar connotations, meanings, and connections fade into apparently new ones, ones otherwise too close and familiar to sense and feel.

To read poetry is to enjoy a mimetic gesticulation towards the thought process, to demand from it alternatives to ordinary remembering and comprehension. In this elusive, decorous, and ceremonial absence of significant reportage, history is a minor character in a timeless masque enacted in the evolving theater of language.

PART 30

Miscellaneous Manifestos

The grouping here is meant to symbolize, after the initial impulse of Symbolism, the wide range of significant manifesto-like texts produced after the first great flowering of the manifesto from 1885 to the 1960s. In those fields like poetics and art that had produced a full blooming in what we call high Modernism, and in other fields like music, architecture, and philosophy, all sorts of hybrids sprang up. This is a hybrid group but no less powerful.

The musical examples are taken from the early musings on time and space of George Antheil and the experimental imaginations of the American composer John Cage, whose meditations on silence and on performance have had an unimaginable impact on writers and thinkers of all stripes, and of the French composer Pierre Boulez, known for his writings on music and the explanations and unfoldings of his settings of Stéphane Mallarmé's Symbolist pieces (*Improvisations sur Mallarmé* and *Pli selon pli*) and those of the Surrealist René Char (*Le Marteau sans maître, Le Visage nuptial*). The range of Boulez's multifaceted work is immense: from his influential writings on the arts, such as "The Composer as Critic" of 1954, through his sober reflection "Demythologizing the Conductor" (30.3) in 1960, a model of protest against the star personality by the very personification of a star. In his witty "Experiment, Ostriches and Music" (30.2) of December 1955, he teases and demythologizes Arnold Schoenberg (AS-74), Anton Webern (AW-83), and Igor Stravinsky (IS-82). It is a masterpiece of the genre of musical manifesto.

The architectural examples come from some of the most significant architectural thinkers of recent times: Christopher Alexander, Charles Jencks, and John Hejduk.

Three mock-serious manifestos belong here as antidotes. The "Manifesto of Naples" (30.8) brilliantly harks back and teases to Filippo Tommaso Marinetti's dramatic ur-manifesto of Futurism ("We stayed up all night" [5.5], with its violent wreckage and luminous salvation, in that memorably heightened tone) before breaking into Brooklynese: "get outta here . . ." Tom Phillips, a multifaceted genius as artist and poet and *savant*, is known for his translations of Dante, his television experiment "The Inferno" with Peter Greenaway, his extraordinary lifelong involvement with W. H. Mallock's three-volume *A Human Document*, which he has compacted, "treated," and illustrated in his various editions of *The Humument*, his opera *Irma*, and more. His "Postcard Vision" (30.9) illustrates the virtues of a mock-and-real manifesto: a neat listing of suggestions and aphorisims and a call for action. Its fragmented form testifies to our lack of patience with the would-be organic, and its vision reads as the other side of the philosopher Jacques

Derrida's long meditation on the *Carte postale*, about the exchange between sender and receiver, and Ray Johnson's correspondence art.

Born to the Oulipo mathematician Jacques Roubaud in 1995, and launched in the first issue of the *Revue de littérature générale*, the mimimalist spoof of a manifesto called "Hypothesis of the Compact" (30.10) is linked at once with the ongoing interest in a poetics and an art that does not say too much and with the idea of a new sort of infinite, an "effinite" able to profit from the implosion of process art. This manifesto, to be read on two diagonals at once, takes up the suggestions of Rodolfo Hinostroza about the presentation of "the interior geometry of written poetry." On a surface not immobile but twisted and twisting in an orthogonal motion, in an instant back to its beginning according to two oblique axes—from top left to bottom right, like Mallarmé's "Un coup de Dés," and from top right to bottom left—it is *visualist* and *virtualist* in its performance. Its presentation is inspired by Emmanuel Fournier's *Croire devoir penser* (To believe to have to think), also numbered, its aphorisms set askew, like a takeoff on Ludwig Wittgenstein's numbered thoughts. Given its gaps and reversals, it can only properly end with an "etc.etc.etc.," after which we might want to read, all the same, "3186," which preceded it and yet remains in memory: "3186. Poetry has a contract of compactification with language." It exemplifies these manifestos of the avant-garde, moving about in the fields of condensed or compact thought, its sound and its setting moving from book to building and back.

As the manifesto reflects on writing itself it becomes a meta-text. To call these "meta-manifestos" draws attention to the form of self-reflection that these texts are, as well as to the ideal shape of a text that has only its own substance to consume, having no outside to motivate it. These are not the statements of movements but the individual outcroppings of individual experiments related to the genre of the manifesto.

The examples given here could have been augmented by many others: this sampling of texts is also a sampling of genres and, as it happens, of countries and continents. So Gertrude Stein's Americanist composition and the Americanism of the L=A=N=G=U=A=G=E poets, Tom Phillips's Welsh postcards, the Frenchness of Oulipo, and Edmond Jabès's Egyptian reflection on the Book of Questions meet in a space that is a meta-space, large enough to house such manifest diverseness.

30.1 GEORGE ANTHEIL

Abstraction and Time in Music

n.d.

I

The most important and least experimented-with part of music is TIME.

Music has always been the adventures of TIME with SPACE. Just in-so-far as this space is tightened is the music great music.

No superficial outward antiquity or ultra-modernity can alter this.

Beauty or ugliness which appeals to, or shocks the primary senses has nothing to do with determining a work of art. Art is determined by the voltage of its synthesis.

The ear, like the eye, is merely the outward human organ used for determining the surface and placing the line. The ear in itself can recognise no perfection. The latter quality lies solely within ourselves. When we look at a painting we can see only color and line. The eye sees nothing more than this.

The form we must feel within ourselves. If this does not exist there, it will never exist anywhere. We will then merely find enjoyable canvases with nice colors and little voluptuous lines. In music we have now known for some time that Scriabine was this kind of composer . . . in music.

No music can exist which is based upon such a superficial and primary thing as the ear.

II

I have no doubt that some day in the future vast rhythmic edifices of sound, tightened and stretched a thousand-fold through the evolving of the inner abstraction of music, will radiate a higher voltage than we can imagine to-day. And it may be that these sounds may not at all be what we today call "musical vibration." It may even be made by beating vast pieces of wood and steel, and attain vibrations today unknown. But this will all be by-product, in relation to the abstraction of time-space which is the first problem of musical art of the future . . . and incidentally, in a weak and oftentimes halting way, has been the great problem of musical art of the past . . . perhaps the sole great problem. The only men whom we call masters today are those men who got their work into some kind of form. The melodic and harmonic masters are dying rapidly. Their projections into space might have been nice and novel for the time in which they were written . . . novelty has a certain value.

The more enduring masters, Mozart and Bach, occupied themselves not with superficial beauty . . . or as we are doing today . . . with superficial ugliness, but with form. Form in music *is* TIME.

Therefore, as proved by every single instance in the past, it will be solely through a concentration on time that greater evolution will bring itself about in music.

III

Any musical mathematics which does not concern itself with the stuff of which music is fundamentally made, which is TIME, is emphatically a fraud and an imbecility. And as it is as impossible to work with algebraic and Arabian mathematics even as it is impossible to plot good draughtsmanship in painting by higher geometry . . . all numerical calculation of harmony is apt to be the sheerest futility.

IV

It is about time that we discard all bunkum about "chords" and "harmony." One cannot base criticism of painting upon light-vibration. Let us not talk about how concordant or discordant a composer appears to be. He may orchestrate a work for three thousand strange instruments . . . and still be only a "color" composer.

V

Let us not judge by external newnesses. They are easy to manufacture. Let us, rather, take the case of Brancusi who could work twenty years to make the finest abstract form that lay inert in a piece of stone.

The GREATEST ARTIST should be he who is able to bring out of THIS special and THAT special material, the finest forms that lay inert and potent in that material.

As I said before . . . the stuff of which music is made is not sound-vibration, but TIME. So it is not a question of new chords one may be inventing, or new musical resources one may be trying to glorify by a more elegant harmony (such as jazz!), but what new projections one is making into musical space, and one's own musical strength in the tightness of the abstractions you may or may not succeed in making.

VI

In music the only possible abstraction possible is the sense of TIME-SPACE, and its relation to the human body through the organ of the ear; through the spacing-off and draughtsmanship of TIME-SPACE by the means of various points of sound.

And sound merely means "vibration." Abstraction cannot be accomplished by vibration, but by the draughtsmanship of points of sound, and the musically invisible lines that go between them.

These forms find themselves entirely in TIME. It is impossible to establish any critical or mathematical consideration of music without beginning at this point. And to consider abstraction or any other true modernity in music without this basis would be the purest folly.

30.2 PIERRE BOULEZ
Experiment, Ostriches and Music
1955

What is experimental music? There is a wonderful new definition that makes it possible to restrict to a laboratory, which is tolerated but subject to inspection, all attempts to corrupt musical morals. Once they have set limits to the danger, the good ostriches go to sleep again and wake only to stamp their feet with rage when they are obliged to accept the bitter fact of the periodical ravages caused by experiment.

"Messieurs nos Consciences, et ainsi de suite, dans vos valises!" Your disapproving, masochistic yelps might well discredit you. "What!" they will say to us, "We have just *seen* a great moment come to life, *undergone* a shattering experience. Like true catechumens, we have organized *congresses* to promote the true faith; for years we have eaten locusts and preached to our own reflections in the desert. And now that our breath has at last created a slight mist and doubt has shrunk, you want to rob us of the reward of our penitential exercises?"

Seraphic souls! Be so good as to hook your phantoms on to any portemanteau you like. The time has come for you to do away with the austere ghosts and to exorcize your little devils. We had known for days that you were obsessed by high-water marks and safety railings; there is nothing surprising to us in the fact that you are now raising your voices to assert your possession of these precious attributes. All that irritates us is the shamelessness of your protestations, and above all the cause for which you are fighting.

You pride yourselves on belonging to the race of *Homo discipulus;* you boast of having been pupils of some great master or other, of having enjoyed his unique advice and known his first (or his last) wishes. You feed your collection of polyhedra on vague memories and imagine that you exist in a tradition by your funeral wakes and odours of decay. Is there any tradition but that of the funeral parlour in which you would not choke, you dear transparent people!

By way of conciliating us you will be said to have been useful. Yes, indeed, you have despite yourselves served as necessary stepping stones. But is there anything more ludicrous than an empty staircase, the only evidence of the fact that the plane has taken off?

Why should I not develop further this notorious personification! What a dialogue we could dream up between these staircases against an empty sky! Or even something like snatches of conversation between these two empty (and stinking) shoes the sight of which opens the second act of *Waiting for Godot.* From one personification to another we should probably soon tire of this larval existence that calmly bases its self-assurance on tumuli.

Having played the roles of John Baptists, our admirable empty-shirts now wish to enjoy the prerogatives of Pius, excommunicating as "experimental" all the new music that they no longer pant to decipher. They note as on the right path the class of "journalists" who play the part of the dead dogs of music, going from one concert hall to another—as others go from one commissariat to another—for the daily harvest.

And they decide that the Grand Master of the Order is AS-74, not AW-83; they proclaim that AW-83 himself considered himself inferior to AS-74 and that this humbler path is therefore the right one to take; they declare that AS-74 and his satellite AW-83 have discovered (finally and overwhelmingly) so many possibilities that it is useless, "experimental" to quarter them; and finally they set out on the rocky search for Offenbach and Verdi, if it is not divinely to establish the green lucidity of IS-82.

The most harmless of these common marionettes generally have at least a "presence"; but these transparent barkers are totally without anything of the kind. As long as these shabby-wretched clowns do not make of contemporary music a kind of Versailles with a code of behaviour drawn up by a mad Saint-Simon. As long as they do not forget that they are nothing—"and nothing, as you know, means nothing or very little"—which they have not learned in twenty or thirty years, which means no longer being disciples or epigones—as long as they do not start blaming a new generation for having realized it. Seniority has never been an enviable privilege: all that count are the evidences of activity, actual works. So let these poor shrimps who have achieved nothing but pale plagiarisms (anything, indeed, but "experimental") shut up. For the future, silence is their only salvation—allowing themselves to be forgotten.

There is no such thing as experimental music, which is a fond utopia; but there is a very real distinction between sterility and invention. The ostriches demonstrate to us the existence of *danger*—with their heads tucked under their folded wings.

30.3 PIERRE BOULEZ
Demythologizing the Conductor
1960

neither dictator nor artisan!

it is high time to *demystify* the word "specialist," which provides too convenient a way out for people anxious to escape without too many scruples from today's musical facts, to monopolize history and "the past" and to turn it into a rather mawkish sauce for queasy stomachs!

no less urgent a task is the *demythification* of the personality of the conductor, who plays the *chef* (is it *d'école* or *de cuisine?*) all too often to the detriment of contemporary events, denying (or rather disowning) his essential *raison d'être*—and still more commonly to the detriment of the reputation of works that, by a little shuffling, have become identified with his own personal reputation.

neither oracle nor flunkey!

to be avoided, then, at all costs, both the cleverly disguised amateur and the blinkered professional: two plagues equally formidable and leading to parallel disappointments, identical defeats and similar catastrophes. they distort knowledge; they refuse solidarity; they bring about confusion and provoke misunderstanding; they retard unification, warp vision, drain the vital flow of communication.

in the matter of contemporary development: every new point requires a knowledge, a background, a reserve of expedients.

(present-day works increasingly present problems which are as much acoustical as dramatic. yet the appearance of these difficulties was not sudden, still less surreptitious: they match a number of extended ideas whose origin can be found in the most important of the works written since 1900. if student conductors are not made aware of these early stages of contemporary music, it is small wonder that there are terrible gaps in their understanding of today's music!)

a quick glance at these new points of interest:

non-metrical gestures imply a perfect training in the most complex metrical gestures;

a free acoustic demands a particularly subtle understanding of the traditional acoustic;

the ability to control an "expanding" music can be acquired only by an absolutely accurate hearing of a "fixed" score.

it would be pointless deliberately to neglect the basic strata of investigation and then to ask the composer for his approval, to demand the player's confidence, to claim and require the approbation of the public, while allowing—as often happens at present—none of them any previous awareness of your convictions, your abilities or your powers.

as for the music of the past: to believe that codification is a function of distance in time is an initial contradiction that very few avoid, on the other hand, there is an aesthetic of physical demonstration that overshoots the mark—in other words, the conductor's control of his body is no substitute for intellectual training!

intellectually, the conductor must have a clear conception of a work: of the music itself, its background, its harmonic resonances, which change from one period to another, its constant factors, and the reasons for its durability, a mere exterior dramatization, by means of a more or less appropriate miming will give no account of any style, any emotion, any form; instead of mediating between the work and the listener, such miming simply substitutes a vulgar byproduct, which slurs the work's intelligibility and comprehension, this dialectic of the present in the past, and the past in the present, with an essential implication of the future—this is the fundamental demand that should be satisfied by all interpreters.

when alban berg was asked what he demanded of an opera house he used to say, "give the operas of the classical repertory as if they were contemporary works . . . and vice versa."

this wish was expressed on 12 september 1928 (admittedly in a review called "music and revolution") and we are still a long way from fulfilling it in any branch of musical life.

*   *   *

neither messiah nor sacristan!

might not this dichotomy in the "repertory" be due to a still more dangerous dichotomy between creation and performance? thought on one side of
the line and action on the other, the headless woman and the cripple! an
odd sort of fable.

without feeling nostalgic about a unity that has disappeared, the earthly
paradise said to have been lost by the apple of specialization, we may legiti-
mately consider some dilemmas useless, and even harmful.

there is inevitably a "magic" element in the relationship that must be
established between a work and its performers through the agency of the
conductor/medium; not every creative idea necessarily possesses the power
of transmitting itself independently—or independently enough—of any
performing plan. purely psychological phenomena are involved, and these
have very little to do with the search for "truth" for its own sake; professional
skills, too; in fact, a specific gift directed towards specific ends.

nevertheless, without demanding an impossible ideal in the distribution
of interest, we do come to wish for a stronger current between the two poles
of the magnetic field of musical activity.

to restrict oneself to prophecies of doom / to sail grandly through the
palace of shadows; to pontificate and to dream / to "realize" and to get on
with the job; to exclude / to be excluded—can we not spare ourselves misleading trivialities of this kind, since none of them can obviate the necessity
of choosing?

in the last resort the alternative may be stated—with the indispensable
dash of bitters—as

neither angel nor animal!

30.4 JOHN CAGE
Bang Fist
1937

10″	
	There is no
20″	
	such thing as silence. Something is al- ways happening that makes a sound. No one can have an idea
30″	
	once he starts really listening. It is very simple but extra-urgent The Lord knows whether or not
40″	
	the next
50″	
	(Bang fist)

30.5 CHRISTOPHER ALEXANDER
The Timeless Way of Building (*excerpt*)
1979

THE TIMELESS WAY

A building or a town will only be alive to the extent that it is governed by the timeless way.

1   It is a process which brings order out of nothing but ourselves; it cannot be attained, but it will happen of its own accord, if we will only let it.

The Quality
To seek the timeless way we must first know the quality without a name.

2   There is a central quality which is the root criterion of life and spirit in man, a town, a building, or a wilderness. This quality is objective and precise, but it cannot be named.

3   The search which we make for this quality, in our own lives, is the central
    search of any person, and the crux of any individual person's story. It is
    the search for those moments and situations when we are most alive.

4   In order to define this quality in buildings and in towns, we must begin
    by understanding that every place is given its character by certain pat-
    terns of events that keep happening there.

5   These patterns of events are always interlocked with certain geometric
    patterns in the space. Indeed, as we shall see, each building and each
    town is ultimately made out of these patterns in the space, and out of
    nothing else: they are the atoms and the molecules from which a build-
    ing or a town is made.

6   The specific patterns out of which a building or a town is made may be
    alive or dead. To the extent they are alive, they let our inner forces loose,
    and set us free; but when they are dead, they keep us locked in inner
    conflict.

7   The more living patterns there are in a place—a room, a building, or
    a town—the more it comes to life as an entirety, the more it glows,
    the more it has that self-maintaining fire which is the quality without
    a name.

8   And when a building has this fire, then it becomes a part of nature. Like
    ocean waves, or blades of grass, its parts are governed by the endless
    play of repetition and variety created in the presence of the fact that all
    things pass. This is the quality itself.

THE GATE

To reach the quality without a name we must then build a living pattern
language as a gate.

9   This quality in buildings and in towns cannot be made but only gener-
    ated, indirectly, by the ordinary actions of the people, just as a flower
    cannot be made, but only generated from the seed.

10 The people can shape buildings for themselves, and have done it for
    centuries, by using languages which I call pattern languages. A pattern
    language gives each person who uses it the power to create an infinite
    variety of new and unique buildings, just as his ordinary language gives
    him the power to create an infinite variety of sentences.

11 These pattern languages are not confined to villages and farm society.
    All acts of building are governed by a pattern language of some sort, and

the patterns in the world are there, entirely because they are created by the pattern languages which people use.

12 And, beyond that, it is not just the shape of towns and buildings which comes from pattern languages—it is their quality as well. Even the life and beauty of the most awe-inspiring great religious buildings came from the languages their buildings used.

13 But in our time the languages have broken down. Since they are no longer shared, the processes which keep them deep have broken down; and it is therefore virtually impossible for anybody, in our time, to make a building live.

14 To work our way towards a shared and living language once again, we must first learn to discover patterns which are deep, and capable of generating life.

15 We may then gradually improve these patterns which we share, by testing them against experience: we can determine, very simply, whether these patterns make our surroundings live, or not, by recognizing how they make us feel.

16 Once we have understood how to discover individual patterns which are alive, we may then make a language for ourselves from any building task we face. The structure of the language is created by the network of connections among individual patterns: and the language lives, or not, as a totality, to the degree these patterns form a whole.

17 Then finally, from separate languages for different building tasks, we can create a larger structure still, a structure of structures, evolving constantly, which is the common language for a town. This is the gate.

THE WAY

Once we have built the gate, we can pass through it to the practice of the timeless way.

18 Now we shall begin to see in detail how the rich and complex order of a town can grow from thousands of creative acts. For once we have a common pattern language in our town, we shall all have the power to make our streets and buildings live, through our most ordinary acts. The language, like a seed, is the genetic system which gives our millions of small acts the power to form a whole.

19 Within this process, every individual act of building is a process in which space gets differentiated. It is not a process of addition, in which pre-

formed parts are combined to create a whole, but a process of unfolding, like the evolution of an embryo, in which the whole precedes the parts, and actually gives birth to them, by splitting.

20 The process of unfolding goes step by step, one pattern at a time. Each step brings just one pattern to life; and the intensity of the result depends on the intensity of each one of these individual steps.

21 From a sequence of these individual patterns, whole buildings with the character of nature will form themselves within your thoughts, as easily as sentences.

22 In the same way, groups of people can conceive their larger public buildings, on the ground, by following a common pattern language, almost as if they had a single mind.

23 Once the buildings are conceived like this, they can be built, directly, from a few simple marks made in the ground—again within a common language, but directly, and without the use of drawings.

24 Next several acts of building, each one done to repair and magnify the product of the previous acts, will slowly generate a larger and more complex whole than any single act can generate.

25 Finally, within the framework of a common language, millions of individual acts of building will together generate a town which is alive, and whole, and unpredictable, without control. This is the slow emergence of the quality without a name, as if from nothing.

26 And as the whole emerges, we shall see it take that ageless character which gives the timeless way its name. This character is a specific, morphological character, sharp, precise, which must come into being any time a building or a town becomes alive: it is the physical embodiment, in buildings of the quality without a name.

THE KERNEL OF THE WAY

And yet the timeless way is not complete, and will not fully generate the quality without a name, until we leave the gate behind.

27 Indeed this ageless character has nothing, in the end, to do with languages. The language, and the processes which stem from it, merely release the fundamental order which is native to us. They do not teach us, they only remind us of what we know already, and of what we shall discover time and time again, when we give up our ideas and opinions, and do exactly what emerges from ourselves.

30.6 JOHN HEJDUK
Thoughts of an Architect
1986

1 That architectural tracings are apparitions, outlines, figments.
They are not diagrams but ghosts.

2 Tracings are similar to X-rays, they penetrate internally.

3 Erasures imply former existences.

4 Drawings and tracings are like the hands of the blind
touching the surfaces of the face in
order to understand
a sense of volume, depth and penetration.

5 The lead of an architect's pencil disappears (drawn away)
metamorphoses.

To take a site: present tracings, outlines, figments, apparitions,
X-rays of thoughts. Meditations on the sense of erasures.
To fabricate a construction of time.

To draw out by compacting in. To flood (liquid densification)
the place-site with missing letters and disappeared signatures.
To gelatinize forgetfulness.

30.7 CHARLES JENCKS
13 Propositions of Post-Modern Architecture
1996

GENERAL VALUES

1 Multivalence is preferred to univalence, imagination to fancy.
2 "Complexity and contradiction" are preferred to over-simplicity and
"Minimalism."

3 Complexity and Chaos theories are considered more basic in explaining nature than linear dynamics: that is, "more of nature" is nonlinear in behaviour than linear.
4 Memory and history are inevitable in DNA, language, style and the city and are positive catalysts for invention.

LINGUISTIC AND AESTHETIC

5 All architecture is invented and perceived through codes, hence the languages of architecture and symbolic architecture, hence the double-coding of architecture within the codes of both the professional and populace.
6 All codes are influenced by a semiotic community and various taste cultures, hence the need in a pluralist culture for a design based on Radical Eclecticism.
7 Architecture is a public language, hence the need for a Post-Modern Classicism which is partly based on architectural universals and a changing technology.
8 Architecture necessitates ornament (or patterns) which should be symbolic and symphonic, hence the relevance of information theory.
9 Architecture necessitates metaphor and this should relate us to natural and cultural concerns, hence the explosion of zoomorphic imagery, face houses and scientific iconography instead of "machines for living."

URBAN, POLITICAL, ECOLOGICAL

10 Architecture must form the city, hence Contextualism, Collage City, Neo-Rationalism, small-block planning, and mixed uses and ages of buildings.
11 Architecture must crystallise social reality and in the global city today, the Heteropolis, that very much means the pluralism of ethnic groups; hence participatory design and adhocism.
12 Architecture must confront the ecological reality and that means sustainable development, Green architecture and cosmic symbolism.
13 We live in a surprising, creative, self-organising universe which still gets locked-into various solutions; hence the need for a cosmogenic architecture which celebrates criticism, process and humour.

30.8 NANNI BALESTRINI *and others*

Manifesto of Naples

1959

Abstraction is not art but merely a philosophical and conventional concept. Art is not abstract, although there can be an abstract concept of art.

This neo-neoplatonism has long been surpassed by the events *of modern science;* it therefore no longer has any reason to be considered a vital and current phenomenon.

Having arrived at Naples the morning of 9 January 1959, we climbed to the top of Vesuvius, which, bubbling furiously, immediately spewed out towering clouds of smoke. We sought shelter, throwing ourselves to the ground until silence returned. We then raised our eyes to the sky, and there appeared the writing:

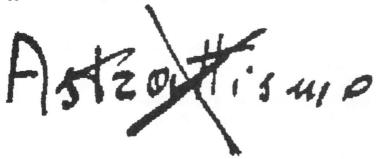

Still trembling, we stood back up and one of us, walking toward the chasm, said: *"May our works be meteors, lava and lapilli, cosmic dust, flaming carbide, orbits of violence, trajectories of senses, radioactive intuitions, sulphur, phosphorus and mercury. . . ."*

Descending from the crater, we dived into the waters of the gulf and landed at Cumae to consult the oracle. The sybil emerged from her cave, and her words further confirmed the fact:

"Get outta here! . . . Abstractionism is old, and stinks worse than me!"

NANNI BALESTRINI, PEOLO REDAELLI, LEO PAOLAZZI, SANDRO
BEJIM, EDOARDO SANGUINETTI, LUCA, BRUNO DI BELLO,
LUCIO DEL POZZO, MARIO PERSICO, GUIDO BIASI, GIUSEPPE
ALFANO, DONATO GRIECO, ENRICO BAJ, ANGELO VERGA,
ETTORE SORDINI, RECALCATI, SERGIO FERGOLA

The Postcard Vision

1971

n.b. I refer throughout to actual and currently available photographically based postcards.

Categories and characteristics to be examined with a view to isolating the elements to be incorporated in the definitive postcard.

GENERAL CATEGORIES OF CARD

1. I had not known death had undone so many.
2. News from another planet.
3. The civic dream.
4. Et in arcadia ego.
5. O châteaux, o saisons.
6. This is the here where I wish you were though it is not the here which is here.
7. A place, a million places.
8. Location chosen by purely aleatoric means; photograph taken in a chance direction at a randomly selected moment in time.
9. Pastoral/historical; carless technicolour tudor with erased telegraph wires.
10. National cliché compendium; kilted bagpiper in the heather seen through thistles with inset of haggis.

CATEGORIES OF EVENT IN POSTCARDS

1. Occlusions (various); "an object leads us to suppose there are other objects behind it"—Bunuel.
2. Bisections. e.g. lamp-post bisections of a. red car, b. flowerbed (in Bournemouth); meanwhile (in Chipping Norton), c. a bench.
3. Time of day (the fixing of the event or absence of event or stage of an event by the presence of a clock, including possible erroneous information of stopped clocks, or cryptic information of clocks without hands).
4. Performances of extant theatre/music compositions, e.g. Water Yam pieces (George Brecht) and Prose Pieces (Christian Wolff), or Scratch Music (inventor—Cornelius Cardew).

5. Performances of unknown pieces thus creating source performances of *Postcard Compositions op. XI* (Tom Phillips) viz.

BUY A POSTCARD. ASSUME THAT IT DEPICTS THE PERFORMANCE OF A PIECE. DEDUCE THE RULES OF THE PIECE. PERFORM IT.

or opus XI no. 2

BUY TWO POSTCARDS. ASSUME THAT THEY DEPICT PERFORMANCES OF THE SAME PIECE. DEDUCE THE RULES OF THE PIECE. PERFORM IT.

6. Secret and minor rites and customs.
7. Sculpture.
8. Psychic phenomena (out of the body experiences).
9. The prelude to, or aftermath of, catastrophe.

CHARACTERISTICS OF THE POSTCARD: AXIOMS

1. *Postcard reality* has a higher incidence of red cars and a higher incidence of people dressed in bright red or bright blue than "real life."
2. *People on postcards* are
   a. possibly dead when the card is purchased.
   b. randomly selected and indulge in unconsidered practises and are not noticed by the *Blind Photographer.*
3. Fixtures and fittings tend to predominate over the avowed subject matter. A litter bin may be the real subject of a card said to be depicting St. Paul's, occupying a larger surface area than that cathedral.
4. The postcard image need not include the subject matter alluded to in the caption.
5. The postcard does not constitute proof that anything happened or that anyone was there or that anything was any colour or that there were or were not clouds in the sky. A card can be bought in both Bulawayo and Leicester Square depicting an elephant superimposed (in Huntingdonshire) upon a view of Wimbledon Common.
6. Life aspires to the condition of the postcard more than the postcard aspires to the imitation of life.
7. The postcard creates the future of the site shown in it. After two or three postcards had appeared, Carnaby Street started to become a *postcard reproduction of itself.*
8. The postcard you bought in Madeira is printed in the Isle of Wight and the postcards of the Isle of Wight are printed in Czechoslovakia, obeying some unwritten international code of fair play. Occasionally there is foul play as in the example of the postcard of Bournemouth, hideously misrepresented by bad registration, printed as propaganda in Scarborough.

9. The great number of daring and taste-defying images that can be found on the postcard racks of stationers and tobacconists, postcards which echo and prefigure the most advanced trends in art, leads one to suspect the existence of a complot in which anonymous artists create cards which are filtered through the normal trade outlets as a way of broadcasting the ideas of new art to the masses who visit no galleries. Occasionally there are clues which support this Borgesian hypothesis; is there for instance a connection between the frequent presence of Dieter Rot at Watford and the impenetrably banal images on postcards of that place?

10. The miracle (levitation, rendering the body transparent, walking upon the waters) is the commonplace of the postcard.

11. There is no caption, be it monosyllabic or verbose, that the imagination could invent, that could not be matched for improbability by the caption of an actual postcard.

12. There is no location so far fetched that its parallel could not be found in a picture postcard.

13. Although the postcard is of its own world (as if it described a distant but related planet) there is no sublunary organisation of forms (in space or on a surface), however extreme in barren featurelessness or enmeshed complexity, unmirrored in the picture postcard.

14. The postcard is to the world as the dream is to the individual (David Rudkin adapted).

15. Everything in the world exists to end up as a postcard (Mallarmé adapted).

16. In the other world that the postcard describes justice prevails: humdrum people are the stars, their going about is the ballet, their groupings the drama, their silence (the harrowed silence of the bench or the raucous silence of the beach) the song, and the vision, in the midst of which they move, the art.

30.10 Jacques Roubaud
Hypothesis of the Compact (excerpt)
1995

PRELIMINARY REMARKS AS A BACKGROUND:
MEMORY, POETRY, ET CETERA ET CETERA:

Poetry doesn't think, doesn't say anything, says what it says saying it, is not to be paraphrased, is "now," is memory, is memory of a language in a language, etc. etc. etc.

.   .   .

CONTRACT OF COMPACT

3186. Poetry has a contract of compactification with language.

224. Poetry, the third memory, the effector of memory, arouses the "effinite" sequences of remembering. If there is any infinite in poetry, it is an effinitude, there, in its interior effects of memory-images.

3161. The memory of poetry seizes a poem instantly, without leaving the present, by a immediatization.

437. The tree and the sphere: two topological modes of poetry's memory.

447. There is no paraphrase of remembering.

448. Ut memoria poesis.

3157. In poetry's memory, words dissolve, unconcentrate, decentrify, bifurcate on their syllables.

1019. A poetic event arouses a memory process. You could compare it to the trajectory of a particle. Just as the particle in the physically very small is only identifiable indirectly, so the poetically infinitely small can be invisible and only consist (for the look of the observer) in trajectories of memory.

.   .   .

3031. A poem the voice proposes, just like a poem the page proposes, is only a line, a surface (at best an object in three dimensions). It is only in entering into the interior memory of the person who receives it and appropriates it that it accedes to a respectable number of dimensions, really becoming a poem, and further a score, a simple performance of a score.

3176. The effect of poetry, in a memory, can be compared to an explosion.

3178. In poetry, you do not control what you say, not because you don't know what you are saying, but because you cannot predict what the effect of memory of a poem in a memory of poetry will be.

3180. Poetry, seen from the side of writing, is an implosion.

3181. The poetic condensation of memory is instantaneous. It isn't a question of a narrative undoing-doing-up.

3182. The image of "cords" of miniscule filaments has many dimensions enclosed in ordinary three-dimensional quasi-points (one of the propositions of physics), is a likely comparison for the exterior reserve of memory that poetry constitutes (this component of poetry put in a poem).

etc.etc.etc.etc.etc.etc.etc.etc.etc.etc.etc.etc.etc.etc.etc.etc.etc.etc.etc.etc.
etc.etc.etc.etc.etc.etc.etc.etc.etc.etc.etc.etc.etc.etc.etc.etc.etc.etc.etc.etc.

PART 31

Writing and the Book

A manifesto like unto no other, and as important as any, Gertrude Stein's "Composition as Explanation" (31.13) claims its own space rather than explaining anything in particular.

The philosophical musing of the Egyptian Jewish poet Edmond Jabès, all of whose works are meditations upon the Book, makes a fitting conclusion to these manifestos of the Modernism whose beginning was so marked by Stephane Mallarmé's experimental textual gesture.

Composition as Explanation

1926

There is singularly nothing that makes a difference a difference in beginning and in the middle and in ending except that each generation has something different at which they are all looking. By this I mean so simply that anybody knows it that composition is the difference which makes each and all of them then different from other generations and this is what makes everything different otherwise they are all alike and everybody knows it because everybody says it.

It is very likely that nearly every one has been very nearly certain that something that is interesting is interesting them. Can they and do they. It is very interesting that nothing inside in them, that is when you consider the very long history of how every one ever acted or has felt, it is very interesting that nothing inside in them in all of them makes it connectedly different. By this I mean this. The only thing that is different from one time to another is what is seen and what is seen depends upon how everybody is doing everything. This makes the thing we are looking at very different and this makes what those who describe it make of it, it makes a composition, it confuses, it shows, it is, it looks, it likes it as it is, and this makes what is seen as it is seen. Nothing changes from generation to generation except the thing seen and that makes a composition. Lord Grey remarked that when the generals before the war talked about the war they talked about it as a nineteenth century war although to be fought with twentieth century weapons. That is because war is a thing that decides how it is to be when it is to be done. It is prepared and to that degree it is like all academies it is not a thing made by being made it is a thing prepared. Writing and painting and all that, is like that, for those who occupy themselves with it and don't make it as it is made. Now the few who make it as it is made, and it is to be remarked that the most decided of them usually are prepared just as the world around them is preparing, do it in this way and so I if you do not mind I will tell you how it happens. Naturally one does not know how it happened until it is well over beginning happening.

To come back to the part that the only thing that is different is what is seen when it seems to be being seen, in other words, composition and time-sense.

No one is ahead of his time, it is only that the particular variety of creating his time is the one that his contemporaries who also are creating their own time refuse to accept. And they refuse to accept it for a very simple reason and that is that they do not have to accept it for any reason. They themselves that is everybody in their entering the modern composition and they do enter it, if they do not enter it they are not so to speak in it they are out of it and so they do enter it; but in as you may say the non-competitive efforts where if you are not in it nothing is lost except nothing at all except what is not had, there are naturally all the refusals, and the things refused are only important if unexpectedly somebody happens to need them. In the case of the arts it is very definite. Those who are creating the modern composition authentically are naturally only of importance when they are dead because by that time the modern composition having become past is classified and the description of it is classical. That is the reason why the creator of the new composition in the arts is an outlaw until he is a classic, there is hardly a moment in between and it is really too bad very much too bad naturally for the creator but also very much too bad for the enjoyer, they all really would enjoy the created so much better just after it has been made than when it is already a classic, but it is perfectly simple that there is no reason why the contemporaries should see, because it would not make any difference as they lead their lives in the new composition anyway, and as every one is naturally indolent why naturally they don't see. For this reason as in quoting Lord Grey it is quite certain that nations not actively threatened are at least several generations behind themselves militarily so æsthetically they are more than several generations behind themselves and it is very much too bad, it is so very much more exciting and satisfactory for everybody if one can have contemporaries, if all one's contemporaries could be one's contemporaries.

There is almost not an interval.

For a very long time everybody refuses and then almost without a pause almost everybody accepts. In the history of the refused in the arts and literature the rapidity of the change is always startling. Now the only difficulty with the *volte-face* concerning the arts is this. When the acceptance comes, by that acceptance the thing created becomes a classic. It is a natural phenomena a rather extraordinary natural phenomena that a thing accepted becomes a classic. And what is the characteristic quality of a classic. The characteristic quality of a classic is that it is beautiful. Now of course it is perfectly true that a more or less first rate work of art is beautiful but the trouble is that when that first rate work of art becomes a classic because it is accepted the only thing that is important from then on to the majority of the acceptors the enormous majority, the most intelligent majority of the acceptors is that it is so wonderfully beautiful. Of course it is wonderfully beautiful, only when it is still a thing irritating annoying stimulating then all quality of beauty is denied to it.

Of course it is beautiful but first all beauty in it is denied and then all the beauty of it is accepted. If every one were not so indolent they would realise that beauty is beauty even when it is irritating and stimulating not only when it is accepted and classic. Of course it is extremely difficult nothing more so than to remember back to its not being beautiful once it has become beautiful. This makes it so much more difficult to realise its beauty when the work is being refused and prevents every one from realising that they were convinced that beauty was denied, once the work is accepted. Automatically with the acceptance of the time-sense comes the recognition of the beauty and once the beauty is accepted the beauty never fails any one.

Beginning again and again is a natural thing even when there is a series.

Beginning again and again and again explaining composition and time is a natural thing.

It is understood by this time that everything is the same except composition and time, composition and the time of the composition and the time in the composition.

Everything is the same except composition and as the composition is different and always going to be different everything is not the same. Everything is not the same as the time when of the composition and the time in the composition is different. The composition is different, that is certain.

The composition is the thing seen by every one living in the living they are doing, they are the composing of the composition that at the time they are living is the composition of the time in which they are living. It is that that makes living a thing they are doing. Nothing else is different, of that almost any one can be certain. The time when and the time of and the time in that composition is the natural phenomena of that composition and of that perhaps every one can be certain.

No one thinks these things when they are making when they are creating what is the composition, naturally no one thinks, that is no one formulates until what is to be formulated has been made.

Composition is not there, it is going to be there and we are here. This is some time ago for us naturally.

The only thing that is different from one time to another is what is seen and what is seen depends upon how everybody is doing everything. This makes the thing we are looking at very different and this makes what those who describe it make of it, it makes a composition, it confuses, it shows, it is, it looks, it likes it as it is, and this makes what is seen as it is seen. Nothing changes from generation to generation except the thing seen and that makes a composition.

Now the few who make writing as it is made and it is to be remarked that the most decided of them are those that are prepared by preparing, are prepared just as the world around them is prepared and is preparing to do it in this way and so if you do not mind I will again tell you how it happens. Naturally one does not know how it happened until it is well over beginning happening.

Each period of living differs from any other period of living not in the way life is but in the way life is conducted and that authentically speaking is composition. After life has been conducted in a certain way everybody knows it but nobody knows it, little by little, nobody knows it as long as nobody knows it. Any one creating the composition in the arts does not know it either, they are conducting life and that makes their composition what it is, it makes their work compose as it does.

Their influence and their influences are the same as that of all of their contemporaries only it must always be remembered that the analogy is not obvious until as I say the composition of a time has become so pronounced that it is past and the artistic composition of it is a classic.

And now to begin as if to begin. Composition is not there, it is going to be there and we are here. This is some time ago for us naturally. There is something to be added afterwards.

Just how much my work is known to you I do not know. I feel that perhaps it would be just as well to tell the whole of it.

In beginning writing I wrote a book called *Three Lives* this was written in 1905. I wrote a negro story called *Melanctha*. In that there was a constant recurring and beginning there was a marked direction in the direction of being in the present although naturally I had been accustomed to past present and future, and why, because the composition forming around me was a prolonged present. A composition of a prolonged present is a natural composition in the world as it has been these thirty years it was more and more a prolonged present. I created then a prolonged present naturally I knew nothing of a continuous present but it came naturally to me to make one, it was simple it was clear to me and nobody knew why it was done like that, I did not myself although naturally to me it was natural.

After that I did a book called *The Making of Americans* it is a long book about a thousand pages.

Here again it was all so natural to me and more and more complicatedly a continuous present. A continuous present is a continuous present. I made almost a thousand pages of a continuous present.

Continuous present is one thing and beginning again and again is another thing. These are both things. And then there is using everything.

This brings us again to composition this the using everything. The using everything brings us to composition and to this composition. A continuous present and using everything and beginning again. In these two books there was elaboration of the complexities of using everything and of a continuous present and of beginning again and again and again.

In the first book there was a groping for a continuous present and for using everything by beginning again and again.

There was a groping for using everything and there was a groping for a continuous present and there was an inevitable beginning of beginning again and again and again.

Having naturally done this I naturally was a little troubled with it when I read it. I became then like the others who read it. One does, you know, excepting that when I reread it myself I lost myself in it again. Then I said to myself this time it will be different and I began. I did not begin again I just began.

In this beginning naturally since I at once went on and on very soon there were pages and pages and pages more and more elaborated creating a more and more continuous present including more and more using of everything and continuing more and more beginning and beginning and beginning.

I went on and on to a thousand pages of it.

In the meantime to naturally begin I commenced making portraits of anybody and anything. In making these portraits I naturally made a continuous present an including everything and a beginning again and again within a very small thing. That started me into composing anything into one thing. So then naturally it was natural that one thing an enormously long thing was not everything an enormously short thing was also not everything nor was it all of it a continuous present thing nor was it always and always beginning again. Naturally I would then begin again. I would begin again I would naturally begin. I did naturally begin. This brings me to a great deal that has been begun.

And after that what changes what changes after that, after that what changes and what changes after that and after that and what changes and after that and what changes after that.

The problem from this time on became more definite.

It was all so nearly alike it must be different and it is different, it is natural that if everything is used and there is a continuous present and a beginning again and again if it is all so alike it must be simply different and everything simply different was the natural way of creating it then.

In this natural way of creating it then that it was simply different everything being alike it was simply different, this kept on leading one to lists. Lists naturally for a while and by lists I mean a series. More and more in going back over what was done at this time I find that I naturally kept simply different as an intention. Whether there was or whether there was not a continuous present did not then any longer trouble me there was or there was not, and using everything no longer troubled me if everything is alike using everything could no longer trouble me and beginning again and again could no longer trouble me because if lists were inevitable if series were inevitable and the whole of it was inevitable beginning again and again could not trouble me so then with nothing to trouble me I very completely began naturally since everything is alike making it as simply different naturally as simply different as possible. I began doing natural phenomena what I call natural phenomena and natural phenomena naturally everything being alike natural phenomena are making things be naturally simply different. This found its culmination later, in the beginning it began in a center confused with lists with series with geography with returning portraits and with particularly often four and three and often with five and four. It is easy to see that in the beginning such a conception as everything being naturally different would be very inarticulate and very slowly it began to emerge and take the form of anything, and then naturally if anything that is simply different is simply different what follows will follow.

So far then the progress of my conceptions was the natural progress entirely in accordance with my epoch as I am sure is to be quite easily realised if you think over the scene that was before us all from year to year.

As I said in the beginning, there is the long history of how every one ever acted or has felt and that nothing inside in them in all of them makes it connectedly different. By this I mean all this.

The only thing that is different from one time to another is what is seen and what is seen depends upon how everybody is doing everything.

It is understood by this time that everything is the same except composition and time, composition and the time of the composition and the time in the composition.

Everything is the same except composition and as the composition is different and always going to be different everything is not the same. So then

I as a contemporary creating the composition in the beginning was groping toward a continuous present, a using everything a beginning again and
again and then everything being alike then everything very simply everything was naturally simply different and so I as a contemporary was creating everything being alike was creating everything naturally being naturally simply different, everything being alike. This then was the period that
brings me to the period of the beginning of 1914. Everything being alike
everything naturally would be simply different and war came and everything being alike and everything being simply different brings everything
being simply different brings it to romanticism.

Romanticism is then when everything being alike everything is naturally
simply different, and romanticism.

Then for four years this was more and more different even though this
was, was everything alike. Everything alike naturally everything was simply
different and this is and was romanticism and this is and was war. Everything being alike everything naturally everything is different simply different naturally simply different.

And so there was the natural phenomena that was war, which had been,
before war came, several generations behind the contemporary composition, because it became war and so completely needed to be contemporary
became completely contemporary and so created the completed recognition of the contemporary composition. Every one but one may say every
one became consciously became aware of the existence of the authenticity
of the modern composition. This then the contemporary recognition, because of the academic thing known as war having been forced to become
contemporary made every one not only contemporary in act not only contemporary in thought but contemporary in self-consciousness made every
one contemporary with the modern composition. And so the art creation of
the contemporary composition which would have been outlawed normally
outlawed several generations more behind even than war, war having been
brought so to speak up to date art so to speak was allowed not completely to
be up to date, but nearly up to date, in other words we who created the expression of the modern composition were to be recognized before we were
dead some of us even quite a long time before we were dead. And so war
may be said to have advanced a general recognition of the expression of the
contemporary composition by almost thirty years.

And now after that there is no more of that in other words there is peace
and something comes then and it follows coming then.

And so now one finds oneself interesting oneself in an equilibration, that of course means words as well as things and distribution as well as between themselves between the words and themselves and the things and themselves, a distribution as distribution. This makes what follows what follows and now there is every reason why there should be an arrangement made. Distribution is interesting and equilibration is interesting when a continuous present and a beginning again and again and using everything and everything alike and everything naturally simply different has been done.

After all this, there is that, there has been that that there is a composition and that nothing changes except composition the composition and the time of and the time in the composition.

The time of the composition is a natural thing and the time in the composition is a natural thing it is a natural thing and it is a contemporary thing.

The time of the composition is the time of the composition. It has been at times a present thing it has been at times a past thing it has been at times a future thing it has been at times an endeavour at parts or all of these things. In my beginning it was a continuous present a beginning again and again and again and again, it was a series it was a list it was a similarity and everything different it was a distribution and an equilibration. That is all of the time some of the time of the composition.

Now there is still something else the time-sense in the composition. This is what is always a fear a doubt and a judgement and a conviction. The quality in the creation of expression the quality in a composition that makes it go dead just after it has been made is very troublesome.

The time in the composition is a thing that is very troublesome. If the time in the composition is very troublesome it is because there must even if there is no time at all in the composition there must be time in the composition which is in its quality of distribution and equilibration. In the beginning there was the time in the composition that naturally was in the composition but time in the composition comes now and this is what is now troubling every one the time in the composition is now a part of distribution and equilibration. In the beginning there was confusion there was a continuous present and later there was romanticism which was not a confusion but an extrication and now there is either succeeding or failing there must be distribution and equilibration there must be time that is distributed and equilibrated. This is the thing that is at present the most troubling and if there is the time that is at present the most troublesome the time-sense that is at present the most troubling is the thing that makes the present the most troubling. There is at present there is distribution, by this I mean expression and time, and in this way at present composition is time that is the reason that at present the time-sense is troubling that is the reason why at present the time-sense in the composition is the composition that is making what there is in composition.

And afterwards.

Now that is all.

31.2 EDMOND JABÈS

To Be in the Book

1963

If we have been created to endure the same suffering, to be doomed to the same prearranged death: why give us lips, why eyes and voices, why souls and languages all different?
REB MIDRASH

To be in the book. To figure in the book of questions, to be part of it. To be responsible for a word or a sentence, a stanza or chapter.

To be able to say: "I am in the book. The book is my world, my country, my roof, and my riddle. The book is my breath and my rest."

I get up with the page that is turned. I lie down with the page put down. To be able to reply: "I belong to the race of words, which homes are built with"—when I know full well that this answer is still another question, that this home is constantly threatened.

I will evoke the book and provoke the questions.

If God is, it is because He is in the book. If sages, saints, and prophets exist, if scholars and poets, men and insects exist, it is because their names are found in the book. The world exists because the book does. For existing means growing with your name.

The book is the work of the book. It is the sun, which gives birth to the sea. It is the sea, which reveals the earth. It is the earth, which shapes man. Otherwise, sun, sea, earth, and man would be focused light without object, water moving without going or coming, wealth of sand without presence, a waiting of flesh and spirit without touch, having nothing that corresponds to it, having neither doubles nor opposites.

Eternity ticks off the instant with the word.

The book multiplies the book.

To Enlarge the Horizons of the Word

1984

I

(Verb. Verbena: gift of moist ground, with green leaves, with leaves of sound.

"The earth speaks to us through every blade of grass, every branch of a tree, every fruit: the sky, through the infinite silence of our scattered words," he said.
"And the pebble?" he was asked.
"The pebble once spoke for the universe before it became a pebble for good," he replied.

Monstrous mouth, forsaken by its first words, O gaping hole, pit of oblivion.)

We get used to pain. Others make us get used to it.
"What charms, cradles, beguiles us in writing is the wall, the obstacle to overcome, much as the splash and gleam of water for the diver," he had noted.

Fascination of the eye. Reverie of the ear.
To see no more, hear no more, wait no more.
Dive down . . .

. . . without, however, boasting of having touched bottom.
The waves teach us.
They tell the pain of bounding forever high above the depths. They tell the depth of pain.

This aloud is not allowed.

Transparent, the walls of time.

In the unsayable, useless words lie hidden which we will claim later.
Stars. Little stars.

Every book has its weight.
Do not try to make it heavier by an image, a silence, a needless thought, or lighten it by a single symbol.

We should be able to determine the weight of a book as we determine that of the atmosphere.

Alas, we lack experience, hence means.

For the desert crushed by the void, the sky is a burden.
Waking and sleeping must bear the whole universe.

"A weighty book is lighter than the sky. Airy thoughts. Writing lets us read their imperceptible unfolding," he said.

To reach the ease of expression words have among themselves: here is the difficulty of speaking, of writing.

No word is banal. All words are insofar as they do not escape wear and tear. So it is not a matter of saving them from banality, but of turning to them as to the common ovens or mills which everybody had to work as rent to the lord of the estate.

Ah, the sums owed to silence. Who can add them up?
We pay in order to go on living.
Could writing, in this sense, mean making sure that we pay regular installments on a debt we know will never be cancelled?

II

> To descend.
> Cinders
> without end.

Death, like the sky, is below. At the bottom of the ladder. At the top: wings, soul, life.

To fall means to gravitate across death.
Gravity. Grave: a cave we are called to fill in.

No stone to perpetuate memory, but an always gaping hole. There, as through a telescope, you shall contemplate the universe, the unbroken day and night of an insatiable infinite.

Tomorrow is the fruit of an expectation our hand is ready to seize.

Birds of darkness inhabit the night.

Stars on their foreheads.

In your dreams, you walk on their spread wings: waking, on ground hardened by their massive desertion.

O solitude of the world.

The blue of the sky is perhaps the opposite of night. But who can reverse words black with ink?

Then every stroke of writing would open a new day which the words take into their keeping.

We will never be done with hope.

Selected Bibliography

Works are grouped under the following sections:

DER BLAUE REITER

The Blaue Reiter Almanac. Ed. Wassily Kandinsky and Franz Marc. 1912. Repr. Da Capo, 1989; London: Thames and Hudson, 1974; ed. and intro. Klaus Lankheit, New York: Viking, 1974.

Hoberg, Annegret, and Armin Zweite. *Der Blaue Reiter in the Lenbachhaus, Munich.* Munich: Prestel, 1989.

Kandinsky, Wassily. *Kandinsky: Complete Writings on Art*. Ed. Kenneth C. Lindsay and Peter Vergo. Documents of Twentieth Century Art. Boston: G. K. Hall, 1982.

Kandinsky, Wassily. *Sounds*. Tr. and intro. Elizabeth R. Napier. New Haven: Yale University Press, 1981.

CONCRETISM/SPATIALISM

Fontana, Lucio, ed. *Manifesti spaziali, 1947-53*. Florence: Galleria Michelucci, 1971.

Garnier, Pierre and Ilse. *Spatialisme et poésie concrète*. Paris: Gallimard, 1968.

Gutai: Japanese Avant-Garde, 1954-1965. Darmstadt: Institut Mathildenhohe, 1991.

Wildman, Eugene, ed. *Anthology of Concretism*. Chicago: Swallow Press, 1967.

CREATIONISM, DIMENSIONALISM

Huidobro, Vicente. *Manifestes, Altazor*. Ed. Gérard Cortanze. Paris: Champ Libre, 1976.

CUBISM

Apollinaire, Guillaume. *Apollinaire on Art: Essays and Reviews 1902-1918*. Ed. Leroy C. Breunig. Tr. Susan Suleiman. New York: Viking, 1960.

Cendrars, Blaise. *Modernities and Other Writings.* Ed. Monique Chefdor. Tr. Monique Chefdor and Esther Allen. Lincoln: University of Nebraska Press, 1992.

Cooper, Douglas. *The Cubist Epoch.* London: Phaidon, 1970.

Paulhan, Jean. *La Peinture cubiste.* Paris: Gallimard (Folio), 1990. (Reprinted in *Tchou: Le Cercle du livre précieux,* 1970.)

DADA

Arp, Jean [Hans]. *Arp on Arp: Poems, Essays, Memories.* Ed. Marcel Jean. Tr. Joachim Neugroschel. New York: Viking, 1972.

Benson, Timothy O. *Raoul Hausmann and Berlin Dada.* Ann Arbor: UMI Research Press, 1986.

Caws, Mary Ann. *The Art of Interference: Stressed Readings in Visual and Verbal Texts.* Princeton: Princeton University Press, 1989.

———. *The Eye in the Text: Essays in Perception from Mannerism to Modernism.* Princeton: Princeton University Press, 1973.

———. *The Poetry of Dada and Surrealism.* Princeton: Princeton University Press, 1974.

Caws, Mary Ann, ed. *About French Poetry from Dada to Tel Quel.* Detroit: Wayne State University Press, 1974.

Duchamp, Marcel. *Duchamp du Signe.* Paris: Flammarion, 1994.

Huelsenbeck, Richard, ed. *The DADA Almanac.* Berlin: E. Reiss, 1920; English edition presented by Malcolm Green, London: Atlas Press, 1993.

Lippard, Lucy R., ed. *Dadas on Art.* Englewood Cliffs NJ: Prentice-Hall, Spectrum Books, 1971.

Motherwell, Robert, ed. *Dada Painters and Poets.* New York: Wittenborn, 1951; rpt. Cambridge: Harvard University Press, Belknap Editions, 1981.

Richter, Hans. *Hans Richter by Hans Richter.* Ed. Cleve Gray. New York: Holt, Rinehart and Winston, 1971.

Tzara, Tristan. *Approximate Man and Other Writings.* Ed. and tr. Mary Ann Caws. Detroit: Wayne State University Press, 1973.

DE STIJL

Bann, Stephen, ed. *The Tradition of Constructivism.* London: Thames and Hudson, 1974.

Mondrian, Piet. *The New Art—the New Life: The Collected Writings of Piet Mondrian.* Ed. and tr. Harry Holtzman and Martin S. James. Boston: G. K. Hall, 1986.

EXPRESSIONISM

Hoffmann, Edith. *Kokoschka: Life and Work.* London: Faber and Faber, 1947.

Klee, Paul. *The Inward Vision: Watercolors, Drawings, and Writings by Paul Klee.* New York: Abrams, 1959.

FUTURISMS

Apollonio, Umbro, ed. and intro. *Futurist Manifestos.* Tr. Robert Brain, R. W. Flint, J. C. Higgitt, and Caroline Tisdall. New York: Thames and Hudson, 1973.

Blumenkranz-Onimus, Naomi. *Les Manifestes futuristes: Théorie et praxis.* Paris: Klincksieck, 1975.

Bowlt, John E., ed. and tr. *Russian Art of the Avant-Garde: Theory and Criticism, 1902–1934*. New York: Viking, 1976.

Caruso, Luciano, ed. *Manifesti, proclami, interventi, e documenti teorici del futurismo 1909–1944*. Florence: Coediton SPES-Saliembeni, 1980.

Folejewski, Zbigniew. *Futurism and Its Place in the Development of Modern Poetry: A Comparative Study and Anthology*. Ottowa: University of Ottawa Press, 1980.

Khlebnikov, Velimir. *The King of Time*. Ed. Charlotte Douglas. Tr. Paul Schmidt. Cambridge: Harvard University Press, 1985.

Lawton, Anna, ed. *Russian Futurism through Its Manifestoes, 1912–1928*. Ithaca: Cornell University Press, 1988.

Lista, Giovanni, ed. *Futurisme: Manifestes, proclamations, documents*. Lausanne: L'Age d'homme, 1974.

Loy, Mina. *The Lost Lunar Baedeker*. Ed. Roger L. Conover. New York: Farrar Straus, 1996.

Mandelstam, Ossip. *Selected Essays*. Ed. Sidney Monas. Austin: University of Texas Press, 1977.

Marinetti, Filippo Tommaso. *Marinetti: Selected Writings*. Ed. R. W. Flint. Tr. R. W. Flint and Arthur A. Coppotelli. New York: Farrar Straus Giroux, 1971.

Markov, Vladimir. *Russian Futurism: A History*. Berkeley: University of California Press, 1968.

Menegazzi, Luigi. *Il manifesto italiano 1882–1925*. Milan: Electra Editrici, 1973.

Parton, Anthony. *Mikhail Larionov and the Russian Avant-Garde*. Princeton: Princeton University Press, 1993.

Perloff, Marjorie. *The Futurist Moment: Avant-Garde, Avant-Guerre, and the Language of Rupture*. Chicago: University of Chicago Press, 1986.

IMAGISM

Pound, Ezra. *Ezra Pound: Selected Prose, 1909–1965*. New York: New Directions, 1978.

INDIVIDUALISM, PERSONISM

Lawrence, D. H. "Surgery for the Novel—Or a Bomb?" In *Selected Literary Criticism*, ed. Anthony Beal. New York: Viking, 1966.

Whitman, Walt. *Leaves of Grass*. 1855. New York: Bantam, 1983.

L=A=N=G=U=A=G=E

Andrews, Bruce, and Charles Bernstein, eds. *The L=A=N=G=U=A=G=E Book*. Carbondale: Southern Illinois University Press, 1984.

Piombino, Nick. *The Boundary of Blur*. New York: Roof Books, 1993.

———. *Theoretical Objects*. Copenhagen: Green Integer, 1999.

LETTRISM

Curtay, Jean-Paul. *La Poésie lettriste*. Paris: Seghers, 1974.

REGIONALISM, NATIVISM

Hartley, Marsden. *On Art*. Ed. Gail R. Scott. New Haven: Yale University Press, 1982.

Welty, Eudora. *The Eye of the Story*. New York: Vintage, 1973.

Williams, William Carlos. *The Embodiment of Knowledge.* New York: New Directions, 1974.

MERZ, VERBOPHONICS, OPTOPHONICS

Schwitters, Kurt. *Kurt Schwitters: Merz, écrits choisis et présentés par Marc Dachy.* Paris: Gérard Lebovici, 1990.

Schwitters, Kurt, and Raoul Hausmann. *Pin and the Story of Pin.* Ed. Jasia Reichardt. London: Gaberbocchus Press, 1962.

MISCELLANEOUS MANIFESTOS

Boulez, Pierre. *Orientations.* Cambridge: Harvard University Press, 1986.

Cage, John. *Silence: Lectures and Writings.* Middletown CT: Wesleyan University Press, 1961; reprint, Cambridge: MIT Press, 1966.

Jabès, Edmond. *The Book of Dialogue.* Tr. Rosmarie Waldrop. Middletown CT: Wesleyan University Press, 1987.

———. *The Book of Questions.* Tr. Rosmarie Waldrop. Middletown CT: Wesleyan University Press, 1976.

Jencks, Charles, and Karl Kropf, eds. *Theories and Manifestoes of Contemporary Architecture.* Chichester, West Sussex: Academy Editions, 1997.

Phillips, Tom. *Works and Texts.* New York: Thames and Hudson, 1992.

Stein, Gertrude. *Selected Writings of Gertrude Stein.* New York: Vintage, 1990.

NEOPLASTICISM

Bois, Yve-Alain. "The Iconoclast." In *Piet Mondrian: 1872–1944.* Boston: Bulfinch, with Leonardo Arte, in collaboration with the National Gallery of Art, 1995.

PRIMITIVISM

Rhodes, Colin. *Primitivism and Modern Art.* New York: Thames and Hudson, 1994.

PURISM

Ozenfant, Amédée. *Foundations of Modern Art.* New York: Dover, 1952.

REVOLUTION OF THE WORD, VERTICALISM

Jolas, Eugène. *The Man from Babel.* Ed. Andreas Kramer and Rainer Rumold. New Haven: Yale University Press.

MacMillan, Dougald. *Transition 1927–38: The History of a Literary Era.* New York: Georges Braziller, 1976.

SCUOLA METAFISICA

Carrà, Massimo. *Metaphysical Art.* New York: Praeger, 1971.

SIMULTANEISM

Bergman, Par. *"Modernolatria" et "Simultaneità."* Stockholm: Uppsala, 1962.

Delaunay, Robert and Sonia. *The New Art of Color: The Writings of Robert and Sonia Delaunay.* Ed. Arthur Cohen. Tr. David Shapiro and Arthur Cohen. New York: Viking, 1978.

Hausmann, Raoul. *Raoul Hausmann, Courrier DADA.* Paris: Le Terrain Vague, 1958.

SPANISH AND LATIN AMERICAN AVANT-GARDES

Andrade, Mário de. *Hallucinated City.* Tr. Jack E. Tomlins. Nashville TN: Vanderbilt University Press, 1968.

Andrade, Oswaldo de. *Seraphim Grosse Pointe.* Tr. Kenneth D. Jackson and Albert Bork. Afterword by Haroldo de Campos. Austin: New Latin Quarter Editions, 1979.

Martins, Wilson. *The Modernist Idea: A Critical Survey of Brazilian Writing in the Twentieth Century.* Tr. Jack E. Tomlins. New York: New York University Press, 1970.

Nist, John. *The Modernist Movement in Brazil: A Literary Study.* Austin: University of Texas Press, 1967.

Pablo, Corbalan. *Poesie surrealista en Espana.* Madrid: Ed. del Centro, 1974.

SUPREMATISM

Moholy-Nagy, Ladislaw. *Moholy-Nagy.* Ed. Richard Kostelanetz. New York: Praeger, 1970.

SURREALISM

Artaud, Antonin. *Artaud Anthology.* Ed. Jack Hirschman. San Francisco: City Lights, 1965.

Breton, André. *Free Rein.* Tr. Michel Parmentier and Jacqueline d'Amboise. Lincoln: University of Nebraska Press, 1995.

Caws, Mary Ann. *The Surrealist Look: An Erotics of Encounter.* Cambridge: MIT Press, 1997.

Caws, Mary Ann, ed. *The Surrealist Painters and Poets.* Cambridge: MIT Press, 2000.

Caws, Mary Ann, Rudolf Kuenzli, and Gwen Raaberg, eds. *Surrealism and Women.* Cambridge: MIT Press, 1992.

Nadeau, Maurice. *Documents of Surrealism.* New York: Macmillan, 1965.

Rosemont, Penelope, ed. *Surrealist Women: An International Anthology.* Austin: University of Texas Press, 1998.

Senghor, Léopold Sédar. *Prose and Poetry.* New York: Oxford, 1965.

Tashijian, Dickran. *A Boatload of Madmen: Surrealism and the American Avant-Garde, 1920-1950.* New York: Thames and Hudson, 1995.

SYMBOLISM

Dorra, Henri, ed. *Symbolist Art Theories: A Critical Anthology.* Berkeley: University of California Press, 1995.

Lucie-Smith, Edward. *Symbolist Art* New York: Thames and Hudson, 1972.

Mallarmé, Stéphane. *Stéphane Mallarmé: Selected Poetry and Prose.* Ed. Mary Ann Caws. New York: New Directions, 1982.

Peterson, Ronald E., ed. and trans. *The Russian Symbolists: An Anthology of Critical and Theoretical Writings.* Ann Arbor: Ardis, 1986.

Whistler, James Abbott McNeill. *The Gentle Art of Making Enemies.* Rpt., New York: Dover, 1967.

Wilde, Oscar. *The Artist as Critic: Critical Writings of Oscar Wilde.* Ed. Richard Ellmann. New York: Random House, 1968

Yeats, William Butler. *Mythologies.* New York: Macmillan, 1959.

THINGISM, MACHINISM

Dalí, Salvador. *Salvador Dalí: The Early Years.* Ed. Michael Raeburn. London: South Bank Centre, 1994; New York: Macmillan, 1965.

Poe, Edgar Allan. *Edgar Allan Poe: Selected Writings.* Harmondsworth U.K.: Penguin, 1967.

Ponge, Francis. *The Sun Placed in Abyss and Other Texts.* Ed. and tr. Serge Gavronsky. New York: Sun, 1977.

THRESHOLDS

Oppenheim, Méret. *Méret Oppenheim: Defiance in the Face of Freedom.* Ed. Bice Curiger. Cambridge: MIT Press, 1989.

Rivkin, Julie, and Michael Ryan, eds. *Literary Theory: An Anthology.* Malden MA: Blackwell, 1998.

VORTICISM

BLAST 3. Ed. Seamus Cooney. Los Angeles: Black Sparrow, 1984.

BLAST: Review of the Great English Vortex. New York: Kraus Reprints, 1967.

Cork, Richard. *Vorticism and Abstract Art in the First Machine Age.* 2 vols. Berkeley: University of California Press, 1976.

Michel, Walter, and C. J. Fox, eds. *Wyndham Lewis on Art: Collected Writings.* London: Thames and Hudson, 1969.

Sieburth, Richard. *Instigations: Ezra Pound and Remy de Gourmont.* Cambridge: Harvard University Press, 1978.

OTHER WORKS CITED OR CONSULTED

Allen, Donald, and Warren Tallman, eds. *The Poetics of the New American Poetry.* New York: Grove, 1973.

Anderson, Margaret, ed. *The Little Review Anthology.* New York: Horizon, 1953.

Apollinaire, Guillaume. *Oeuvres poétiques.* Paris: Gallimard, 1965.

Atkins, Robert. *Artspeak: A Guide to Contemporary Ideas, Movements, and Buzzwords.* New York: Abbeville, 1990.

————. *Artspoke: A Guide to Modern Ideas, Movements, and Buzzwords, 1848–1944.* New York: Abbeville, 1993.

Barron, Stephanie, and Maurice Tuchman, eds. *The Avant-Garde in Russia, 1910–30: New Perspectives.* Cambridge: MIT Press, 1980.

Campos, Augusto de. *Poesure et peintierie.* Marseille: Réunion des musées nationaux.

Canfield, William A. *Francis Picabia: His Art, Life, and Times.* Princeton NJ: Princeton University Press, 1979.

Chipp, Herschell, ed., *Theories of Modern Art: A Source Book by Artists and Critics.* Berkeley: University of California Press, 1968.

Eisenstein, Sergei. *Film Essays and a Lecture.* Ed. Jay Leyda. Princeton: Princeton University Press, 1982.

Golding, John. *Visions of the Modern.* Berkeley: University of California Press, 1994.

Harrison, Charles, and Paul Wood, eds. *Art in Theory 1900–1990: An Anthology of Changing Ideas.* Oxford: Blackwell, 1992.

Harrison, Charles, Paul Wood, and Jason Gaiger, eds. *Art in Theory, 1815–1900.* Oxford: Blackwell, 1997.

Herbert, Robert L., ed. *Modern Artists on Art.* Englewood Cliffs NJ: Prentice-Hall, 1964.

Koolhaas, Rem. *Delirious New York: A Retroactive Manifesto for Manhattan.* New York: Oxford University Press, 1978.

Levenson, Michael H. *A Genealogy of Modernism: A Study of English Literary Doctrine 1908-1922.* New York: Cambridge University Press, 1984.

Lista, Giovanni, Serge Lemoine, and Andrei Nakov. *Les Avant-gardes: Futurisme, dadaisme, art moderne 1900-1945.* Paris: F. Hazan, 1991.

Michel Tapié: Manifeste indirect dans un temps autre. Turin: Edizioni d'arte Fratelli Pozzo, 1961.

Nicholls, Peter. *Modernisms: A Literary Guide.* Berkeley: University of California Press, 1995.

Poésure et peintrie: D'un art l'autre. Marseilles: Musées de Marseilles, 1993.

Rothenberg, Jerome, and Pierre Joris, eds. *Poems for the Millennium: The University of California Book of Modern and Postmodern Poetry.* 2 vols. Berkeley: University of California Press, 1995–98.

Scully, James, ed. *Modern Poetics.* New York: McGraw Hill, 1965.

Stangos, Nikos, ed. *Concepts of Modern Art.* New York: Thames and Hudson, 1981.

Taylor, Joshua C. *Futurism.* New York: Museum of Modern Art, 1961.

Worringer, Wihelm. *Abstraction and Empathy.* Tr. Michael Bullock. New York: International Universities Press, 1953.

Source Acknowledgments

1.1   James Abbott McNeill Whistler, "The Ten O'Clock," 1885, given in London, February 20, 1885, 10:00 P.M., first published as *Mr. Whistler's "Ten O'Clock"* (London: Chatto and Windus, 1885); reprinted in *Art in Theory: 1815-1900*, ed. Charles Harrison and Paul Wood, with Jason Gaigar (Oxford: Blackwell, 1998), 838–47.

1.2   Oscar Wilde, "The Poets and the People: By One of the Latter," 1887, *Pall Mall Gazette* 45 (February 17, 1887); reprinted in Oscar Wilde, *The Artist as Critic*, ed. Richard Ellman (New York: Random House, 1968), 43–45.

1.3   Oscar Wilde, preface to *The Picture of Dorian Gray*, 1891, reprinted in *The Works of Oscar Wilde*, ed. G. F. Maine (London: Collins, 1948).

1.4   Pierre-Louis [Maurice Denis], "Definition of Neo-Traditionism" (excerpt), 1890, first published in *Art et Critique* (Paris), August 23 and 30, 1890; trans. Peter Collier in *Art in Theory: 1815-1900*, ed. Charles Harrison and Paul Wood, with Jason Gaigar (Oxford: Blackwell, 1998), 863–69.

1.5   Stéphane Mallarmé, "Action Restricted," 1886, from "As for the Book/Divagations," trans. Mary Ann Caws in *Stéphane Mallarmé: Selected Poetry and Prose*, ed. Mary Ann Caws (New York: New Directions, 1982).

1.6   Stéphane Mallarmé, "Crisis in Poetry" (excerpt), 1886, from "Variations on a Subject," in *Stéphane Mallarmé: Selected Poetry and Prose*, ed. Mary Ann Caws (New York: New Directions, 1982).

1.7   Stéphane Mallarmé, "A Throw of Dice Not Ever Will Abolish Chance," 1897, ("Un coup de Dés jamais n'abolira le Hasard"), trans. Tom Csaszar, © 1997–98, reprinted with permission from Tom Csaszar.

1.8   Jean Moréas, "The Symbolist Manifesto" (excerpt), 1886, trans. Mary Ann Caws from "Le Manifeste Symboliste," in *Les Manifestes littéraires de la belle époque*, comp. Bonner Mitchell (Paris: Seghers, 1966).

1.9   Odilon Redon, "Suggestive Art" (excerpt), 1922; reprinted in Redon, *A soi-même: Journal, 1867-1915* (Paris: Corti, 1961); trans. Herschell B. Chipp in *Theories of Modern Art: A Source Book by Artists and Critics*, ed. Chipp (Berkeley: University of California Press, 1968), 116–19. Copyright © 1968 The Regents of the University of California.

1.10 Ferdinand Hodler, "Parallelism," c. 1900, trans. Robert Goldwater in *Artists on Art*, ed. Goldwater and Marco Treves (New York: Pantheon, 1945), 392–94. Translation reprinted with permission from Louise Bourgeois.

1.11 V. Bryusov, "Keys to the Mysteries" (parts I and II), 1904, in *The Russian Symbolists: An Anthology of Critical and Theoretical Writings*, ed. and trans. Ronald E. Peterson (Ann Arbor: Ardis, 1986), 52–58. Reprinted with permission from Britt Nicole Peterson.

1.12 Vyacheslav Ivanov, "Thoughts about Symbolism," 1912, in *The Russian Symbolists: An Anthology of Critical and Theoretical Writings*, ed. and trans. Ronald E. Peterson (Ann Arbor: Ardis, 1986), 181–88. Reprinted with permission from Britt Nicole Peterson.

1.13   Fyodor Sologub, "The Theater of One Will," 1908, in *The Russian Symbolists: An Anthology of Critical and Theoretical Writings*, ed. and trans. Ronald E. Peterson (Ann Arbor: Ardis, 1986), 107–21. Reprinted with permission from Britt Nicole Peterson.

1.14   William Butler Yeats, "Anima Hominis" (excerpt), 1917, from *Per Amica Silentia Lunae* (London: Macmillan, 1918), 9–43.

2.1   Tristan Tzara, "Note 6 on Negro Art," 1917, trans. Mary Ann Caws from "Note 6 sur l'art nègre," *sic (Sounds Ideas Colors Forms)*, no. 21–22 (September–October 1917); reprinted in *sic (Sounds Ideas Colors Forms)* (Paris: Éditions Jean-Michel Place, 1980), 158.

2.2   Anatol Stern and Aleksander Wat. "primitivists to the nations of the world and to poland," in *Gga: The First Polish Almanac of Futurist Poetry, a Primitivist Bimonthly* (Warsaw, December 1920), trans. David A. Goldfarb. Reprinted with permission from David A. Goldfarb.

2.3   Gary Snyder, "Poetry and the Primitive: Notes on Poetry as an Ecological Survival Technique," 1967, first published in *Earth House Hold* (New York: New Directions, 1969), 117–30. Copyright © 1969 by Gary Snyder. Reprinted by permission of New Directions Publishing Corp. Reprinted in *The Poetics of the New American Poetry*, ed. Donald Allen and Warren Tallman (New York: Grove Press, 1973), 395–406.

3.1   Pierre Albert-Birot, "The Sun Is in the Staircase," 1916–1924, originally published in French in *La Lune ou le livre de poèmes*, in *Poésie 1916-1924* (Paris: Gallimard, 1967), 406; reprinted from *The Cubist Poets in Paris*, ed. L. C. Breunig (Lincoln: University of Nebraska Press, 1995), 17, by permission of the University of Nebraska Press. Copyright © 1995 by the University of Nebraska Press.

3.2   Guillaume Apollinaire, "Picasso," 1905, from "Les jeunes: Picasso peintre," *La Plume*, May 14, 1905; reprinted in Guillaume Apollinaire, *The Cubist Painters 1913*, trans. Lionel Abel (New York: Wittenborn, 1949), 19–24, and in *Theories of Modern Art: A Source Book by Artists and Critics*, ed. Herschel B. Chipp (Berkeley: University of California Press, 1968), 229–35. Reprinted with permission from Lionel Abel.

3.3   Guillaume Apollinaire, "The New Painting: Art Notes," 1912, originally published in *Les Soirees de Paris*, April 13–14, 1912; reprinted in *Apollinaire on Art*, ed. Leroy C. Breunig, trans. Susan Suleiman (New York: Viking, 1972), 222–25.

3.4   Guillaume Apollinaire, "Cubism Differs," 1913, first published as Guillaume Apollinaire, *Les Peintres Cubistes* (Paris: Eugène Figuière, 1913); reprinted from "On Painting," in *The Cubist Painters*, trans. Lionel Abel (New York: Wittenborn, 1949), 17–18. Reprinted with permission from Lionel Abel.

3.5   Guillaume Apollinaire, "Horse Calligram," 1913–1916, from *Poems for the Millennium*, vol. 1, ed. Jerome Rothenberg and Pierre Joris (Berkeley: University of California Press, 1995), 119.

3.6   Guillaume Apollinaire, "Vase," 1913–1916, reprinted from *The Cubist Poets in Paris*, ed. L. C. Breunig (Lincoln: University of Nebraska Press, 1995), 66, by permission of the University of Nebraska Press. Copyright © 1995 by the University of Nebraska Press.

3.7 Guillaume Apollinaire, "Bleuet," 1917, from *Nord-Sud* (June–July 1917).

3.8 Guillaume Apollinaire, "The Little Car," 1918, first published in
Calligrammes: Poemes de la paix et de la guerre, 1913–1916 (Paris: Mercure de
France, 1918); trans. Ron Padgett in *Poems for the Millennium*, vol. 1, ed.
Jerome Rothenberg and Pierre Joris (Berkeley: University of California
Press, 1995), 129.

3.9 Georges Braque, "Reflections on Painting," 1917, first published in *Nord-Sud*
10 (December 1917): 3–5; trans. Robert Goldwater in *Artists on Art*, ed.
Robert Goldwater and Marco Treves (New York: Pantheon, 1945), 422–23.
Translation reprinted with permission from Louise Bourgeois.

3.10 Blaise Cendrars, "On Projection Powder," May 3–28 and December 1917, in
Modernities and Other Writings, trans. Esther Allen in collaboration with
Monique Chefdor (Lincoln: University of Nebraska Press, 1992), 87–88.
English-language translation reprinted by permission of the University of
Nebraska Press. Copyright © 1992 by the University of Nebraska Press

3.11 Blaise Cendrars, "Profound Today," February 13, 1917, in *Modernities and
Other Writings*, trans. Esther Allen in collaboration with Monique Chefdor
(Lincoln: University of Nebraska Press, 1992), 3–6. English-language
translation reprinted by permission of Éditions Denoël and the University
of Nebraska Press. Copyright © 1992 by the University of Nebraska Press.

3.12 Max Jacob, "Words in Freedom," 1917, trans. Mary Ann Caws from "Les
Mots en liberté," *Nord-Sud* (November 1917): 3–5.

3.13 Pierre Reverdy, "On Cubism," 1917, first published in *Nord-Sud*, no. 1
(March 15, 1917); reprinted in *Nord-Sud*, no. 3 (May 15, 1917); trans. Léonce-
Alexandre Rosenberg in *Nord-Sud 1917–1918* (Paris: Jean-Michel Place, 1980),
12–13.

4.1 Pierre Albert-Birot, "Banality," 1916, trans. Mary Ann Caws from "Banalité,"
SIC (Sounds Ideas Colors Forms), February 1916; reprint, Paris: Éditions
Jean-Michel Place, 1980, 10.

4.2 Pierre Albert-Birot, "Ça ne se fait pas (It isn't done)," 1916, trans. Mary Ann
Caws from *SIC (Sounds Ideas Colors Forms)*, no. 7 (July 1916); reprint, Paris:
Éditions Jean-Michel Place, 1980, 50.

4.3 Pierre Albert-Birot, "L'Esprit moderne (The modern spirit)," 1916, trans.
Mary Ann Caws from *SIC (Sounds Ideas Colors Forms)*, no. 11 (November
1916); reprint, Paris: Éditions Jean-Michel Place, 1980, 90.

4.4 Pierre Albert-Birot, "La Loi (The law)," 1916, trans. Mary Ann Caws from
SIC (Sounds Ideas Colors Forms) (1916); reprint, Paris: Éditions Jean-Michel
Place, 1980, 43.

4.5 Pierre Albert-Birot, "Nunic Dialogue: Z and A in Front of Modern
Paintings," 1916, trans. Mary Ann Caws from "Dialogue nunique: Z et A
Devant des peintures modernes," *SIC (Sounds Ideas Colors Forms)*, no. 5 (May
1916); reprint, Paris: Éditions Jean-Michel Place, 1980, 38–39.

4.6 Pierre Albert-Birot, "Nunism," 1916, trans. Mary Ann Caws from "Le
Nunisme," *SIC (Sounds Ideas Colors Forms)*, no. 6 (June 1916); reprint, Paris:
Éditions Jean-Michel Place, 1980, 42.

4.7   Pierre Albert-Birot, "Pas de corset! (No girdle!)," 1917, trans. Mary Ann
      Caws from *sic (Sounds Ideas Colors Forms)*, no. 16 (April 1917); reprint, Paris:
      Éditions Jean-Michel Place, 1980, 122.

4.8   Blaise Cendrars, "The ABCs of Cinema," 1917–1921, in *Modernities and Other
      Writings*, trans. Esther Allen in collaboration with Monique Chefdor
      (Lincoln: University of Nebraska Press, 1992), 25–29. English-language
      translation reprinted by permission of the University of Nebraska Press.
      Copyright © 1992 by the University of Nebraska Press.

4.9   Blaise Cendrars, "Simultaneous Contrast," 1919, in *Modernities and Other
      Writings*, trans. Esther Allen in collaboration with Monique Chefdor
      (Lincoln: University of Nebraska Press, 1992), 102. English-language
      translation reprinted by permission of the University of Nebraska Press.
      Copyright © 1992 by the University of Nebraska Press.

4.10 Robert Delaunay, "Light," 1912, in *The New Art of Color*, ed. Arthur A.
      Cohen, trans. Arthur A. Cohen and David Shapiro (New York: Viking, 1978).
      Translation copyright © 1978 by Sonia Delaunay. Copyright © 1978 by
      Arthur A. Cohen, introduction and translation. Used by permission of
      Viking Penguin, a division of Penguin Putnam Inc.

4.11 Robert Delaunay, "Historical Notes on Painting: Color and the
      Simultaneous," undated though undoubtedly written during 1913, in *The
      New Art of Color*, ed. Arthur A. Cohen, trans. Arthur A. Cohen and David
      Shapiro (New York: Viking, 1978), 52. Translation copyright © 1978 by Sonia
      Delaunay. Copyright © 1978 by Arthur A. Cohen, introduction and
      translation. Used by permission of Viking Penguin, a division of Penguin
      Putnam Inc.

4.12 Robert Delaunay, "Simultaneism in Contemporary Modern Art, Painting,
      Poetry," 1913, in *The New Art of Color*, ed. Arthur A. Cohen, trans. Arthur A.
      Cohen and David Shapiro (New York: Viking, 1978), 47–51. Translation
      copyright © 1978 by Sonia Delaunay. Copyright © 1978 by Arthur A. Cohen,
      introduction and translation. Used by permission of Viking Penguin, a
      division of Penguin Putnam Inc.

4.13 Robert Delaunay, "Simultaneism: An Ism of Art," 1925, in Hans Arp and El
      Lissitzky, *Die Kunstismen* (Erlenbach-Zurich: Eugen Rentsch Verlag, 1925),
      75; reprinted in *The New Art of Color*, ed. Arthur A. Cohen, trans. Arthur A.
      Cohen and David Shapiro (New York: Viking, 1978). Translation copyright
      © 1978 by Sonia Delaunay. Copyright © 1978 by Arthur A. Cohen,
      introduction and translation. Used by permission of Viking Penguin, a
      division of Penguin Putnam Inc.

4.14 Raoul Hausmann, "Manifesto of PResentism," 1920, originally written in
      German as "PResentistisches Manifest"; trans. Mary Ann Caws from the
      French "Manifeste du PResentisme," *De Stijl*, February 1920; French
      translation reprinted in Raoul Hausmann, *Courrier DADA* (Paris: Editions Le
      Terrain Vague, 1958), 94–102.

4.15 Barnett Newman, "The Sublime Is Now," 1948, from "The Ides of Art: Six
      Opinions on What Is Sublime in Art?" *Tiger's Eye*, December 15, 1948;
      reprinted in *Theories of Modern Art: A Source Book by Artists and Critics*, ed.

Herschel B. Chipp (Berkeley: University of California Press, 1968), 552–53.
Copyright © 1968 The Regents of the University of California.

5.1   "Futurist Synthesis of the War," September 20, 1914, from the Milanese Cell,
       Directory of the Futurist Movement: Corso Venezia, 61-Milan; reprinted in
       F. T. Marinetti, *Selected Writings*, ed. R. W. Flint, trans. R. W. Flint and
       Arthur A. Coppotelli (New York: Farrar, Straus, and Giroux, 1972), 62–63.
       Translation copyright © 1972 by Farrar, Straus, and Giroux, Inc.

5.2   Umberto Boccioni, "Technical Manifesto of Futurist Sculpture," 1912, first
       published as a leaflet by *Poesia* (Milan), April 11, 1912; trans. Robert Brain in
       Futurist Manifestos, ed. Umbro Apollonio, trans. Robert Brain, R. W. Flint,
       J. C. Higgitt, and Caroline Tisdall (New York: Thames and Hudson, 1973),
       51–52, 61–65. English-language translation copyright © 1973 Thames and
       Hudson Ltd., London. All rights reserved.

5.3   Umberto Boccioni, Carlo Carrà, Luigi Russolo, Giacomo Balla, and Gino
       Severini, "Futurist Painting: Technical Manifesto," 1910, first published as a
       leaflet by *Poesia* (Milan), April 11, 1910; from the catalogue *Exhibition of
       Works by the Italian Futurist Painters*, Sackville Gallery, London, March 1912;
       reprinted in *Futurist Manifestos*, ed. Umbro Apollonio, trans. Robert Brain,
       R. W. Flint, J. C. Higgitt, and Caroline Tisdall (New York: Thames and
       Hudson, 1973), 27–31. English-language translation copyright © 1973
       Thames and Hudson Ltd., London. All rights reserved.

5.4   Umberto Boccioni, Carlo Carrà, Luigi Russolo, Giacomo Balla, and Gino
       Severini, "Manifesto of the Futurist Painters," 1910, first published as a
       leaflet by *Poesia* (Milan), February 11, 1910; trans. Robert Brain in *Futurist
       Manifestos*, ed. Umbro Apollonio, trans. Robert Brain, R. W. Flint, J. C.
       Higgitt, and Caroline Tisdall (New York: Thames and Hudson, 1973), 24–27.
       English-language translation copyright © 1973 Thames and Hudson Ltd.,
       London. All rights reserved.

5.5   Filippo Tommaso Marinetti, "The Founding and Manifesto of Futurism,"
       1909, from *Le Figaro* (Paris), February 20, 1909; reprinted in F. T. Marinetti,
       Selected Writings, ed. R. W. Flint, trans. R. W. Flint and Arthur A. Coppotelli
       (New York: Farrar, Straus, and Giroux, 1972), 39–44. Translation copyright
       © 1972 by Farrar, Straus, and Giroux, Inc. Reprinted with permission of
       Farrar, Straus, and Giroux, Inc.

5.6   Filippo Tommaso Marinetti, "After the Marne, Joffre Visited the Front in an
       Automobile," 1915, in *Les Mots en liberté futuristes*, 1919 (Beinecke Rare Book
       and Manuscript Library, Yale University, p. 101); reprinted in Marjorie
       Perloff, *The Futurist Moment: Avant-Garde, Avant-Guerre, and the Language of
       Rupture* (Chicago: University of Chicago Press, 1986), 101.

5.7   Filippo Tomasso Marinetti, Emilio Settimelli, and Bruno Corra, "The
       Futurist Synthetic Theatre," 1915, first published by Istituto Editoriale
       Italiano, Milan, January 11 and February 18, 1915; trans. R. W. Flint in
       Futurist Manifestos, ed. Umbro Apollonio, trans. Robert Brain, R. W. Flint,
       J. C. Higgitt, and Caroline Tisdall (New York: Thames and Hudson, 1973),
       183–96. English-language translation copyright © 1973 Thames and
       Hudson Ltd., London. All rights reserved.

5.8   Filippo Tommaso Marinetti, "Tactilism," 1924, in Marinetti, *Selected Writings*, ed. R. W. Flint, trans. R. W. Flint and Arthur A. Coppotelli (New York: Farrar, Straus, and Giroux, 1972), 109–12. Translation copyright © 1972 by Farrar, Straus, and Giroux, Inc.

5.9   Carlo Carrà, "The Painting of Sounds, Noises, and Smells," August 1913, first published in *Lacerbo* (Florence), September 1, 1913; trans. Robert Brain in *Futurist Manifestos*, ed. Umbro Apollonio, trans. Robert Brain, R. W. Flint, J. C. Higgitt, and Caroline Tisdall (New York: Thames and Hudson, 1973), 111–15. English-language translation copyright © 1973 Thames and Hudson Ltd., London. All rights reserved.

5.10   Luigi Russolo, "The Art of Noises" (excerpt), 1913, first published as a leaflet by Direzione del Movimento Futurista, Milan, July 1, 1913; trans. Caroline Tisdall in *Futurist Manifestos*, ed. Umbro Apollonio, trans. Robert Brain, R. W. Flint, J. C. Higgitt, and Caroline Tisdall (New York: Thames and Hudson, 1973), 74–76, 85–88. English-language translation copyright © 1973 Thames and Hudson Ltd., London. All rights reserved.

5.11   Guillaume Apollinaire, "L'Antitradition futuriste," was originally published in 1913.

5.12   Valentine de Saint-Point, "Manifesto of Futurist Woman (Response to F. T. Marinetti)," (Manifeste de la femme futuriste), read on June 3, 1912, in the Gallery Giroux, Brussels, and June 27, 1912, in the Salle Gaveau, Paris. Published in German in *Der Sturm* (Berlin), no. 108 (May 1912); published simultaneously in Italian and French, January 11, 1913, in Giovanni Lista, *Futurisme: Manifestes—Proclamations—Documents* (Lausanne: L'Âge d'homme, 1913), 329–32; trans. Mary Ann Caws from the French with permission from Éditions L'Âge d'Homme. © 1973 by Éditions L'Âge d'Homme S.A., Lausanne.

5.13   Valentine de Saint-Point, "Futurist Manifesto of Lust," 1913, published simultaneously in Italian and French, with a response by Italo Tavolato, "Commentary on the Futurist Manifesto of Lust," as a leaflet, by Direzione del Movimento Futurista, Milan, January 11, 1913; trans. J. C. Higgitt in *Futurist Manifestos*, ed. Umbro Apollonio, trans. Robert Brain, R. W. Flint, J. C. Higgitt, and Caroline Tisdall (New York: Thames and Hudson, 1973), 70–73. English-language translation copyright © 1973 Thames and Hudson Ltd., London. All rights reserved.

5.14   Ossip Mandelstam, "The Morning of Acmeism (parts I–IV)," 1913, first published in 1919; reprinted in Ossip Mandelstam, *Selected Essays*, ed. and trans. Sidney Monas (Austin: University of Texas Press, 1977), 128–31. Copyright © 1977. By permission of the University of Texas Press.

5.15   Graal-Arelsky [Stepan Stepanovich Petrov], "Egopoetry in Poetry," 1912, in *The Orange Urn* (St. Petersburg, 1912); reprinted in *Russian Futurism through Its Manifestoes, 1912-1918*, ed. Anna Lawton, trans. Anna Lawton and Herbert Eagle (Ithaca: Cornell University Press, 1988), 110–11. Copyright © 1988 Cornell University. Used by permission of the publisher, Cornell University Press.

5.16 Graal-Arelsky [Stepan Stepanovich Petrov], "The Tables," January 1912, manifesto of the Ego-Futurist Group, in *Russian Futurism through Its Manifestoes, 1912-1918*, ed. Anna Lawton, trans. Anna Lawton and Herbert Eagle (Ithaca: Cornell University Press, 1988), 109. Copyright © 1988 Cornell University. Used by permission of the publisher, Cornell University Press.

5.17 Lev Zack, "overture," 1913, anonymous preface to *Vernissage*, the first almanac of the Mezzanine of Poetry, by its editor; reprinted in *Russian Futurism through Its Manifestoes, 1912-1918*, ed. Anna Lawton, trans. Anna Lawton and Herbert Eagle (Ithaca: Cornell University Press, 1988), 133–36. Copyright © 1988 Cornell University. Used by permission of the publisher, Cornell University Press.

5.18 David Burliuk, Alexey Kruchenykh, Vladimir Mayakovsky, and Velimir Khlebnikov, "Slap in the Face of Public Taste," 1912, in *Russian Futurism through Its Manifestoes, 1912-1918*, ed. Anna Lawton, trans. Anna Lawton and Herbert Eagle (Ithaca: Cornell University Press, 1988), 51–52. Copyright © 1988 Cornell University. Used by permission of the publisher, Cornell University Press.

5.19 Vladimir Mayakovsky, "We, Too, Want Meat!" 1914, in *Russian Futurism through Its Manifestoes, 1912-1918*, ed. Anna Lawton, trans. Anna Lawton and Herbert Eagle (Ithaca: Cornell University Press, 1988), 87–89. Copyright © 1988 Cornell University. Used by permission of the publisher, Cornell University Press.

5.20 Vladimir Mayakovsky, "A Drop of Tar," 1915, in *Russian Futurism through Its Manifestoes, 1912-1918*, ed. Anna Lawton, trans. Anna Lawton and Herbert Eagle (Ithaca: Cornell University Press, 1988), 100. Copyright © 1988 Cornell University. Used by permission of the publisher, Cornell University Press.

5.21 Anonymous, "Bald Mountain Zaum-Poem," 1836, in *Skazanija ruskogo naroda* (Legends of the Russian People), ed. I. Sakharov, printed in Saint Petersburg; reprinted in *Poems for the Millennium*, vol. 1, ed. Jerome Rothenberg and Pierre Joris (Berkeley: University of California Press, 1995), 36–37.

5.22 Victor Khlebnikov and Alexey Kruchonykh, "The Letter as Such," 1913, in Victor Khlebnikov, *The King of Time*, ed. Charlotte Douglas, trans. Paul Schmidt (Cambridge: Harvard University Press, 1985), 121–22. Reprinted by permission of the publisher. Copyright © 1985 by the Dia Art Foundation.

5.23 Victor Khlebnikov and Alexey Kruchenykh, "The Word as Such," 1913, in Victor Khlebnikov, *The King of Time*, ed. Charlotte Douglas, trans. Paul Schmidt (Cambridge: Harvard University Press, 1985), 119–20. Reprinted by permission of the publisher. Copyright © 1985 by the Dia Art Foundation.

5.24 Victor Khlebnikov, Maria Siniakova, Bozhidar, Grigory Petnikov, and Nikolai Aseev, "The Trumpet of the Martians," 1916, in Victor Khlebnikov, *The King of Time*, ed. Charlotte Douglas, trans. Paul Schmidt (Cambridge: Harvard University Press, 1985), 126–27. Reprinted by permission of the publisher. Copyright © 1985 by the Dia Art Foundation.

5.25   Mikhail Larionov and Natalya Goncharova, "Rayonists and Futurists: A
        Manifesto," 1913, first published in Moscow, July 1913; reprinted in *Russian
        Art of the Avant-Garde: Theory and Criticism, 1902-1934*, ed. and trans.
        John E. Bowlt (New York: Thames and Hudson, 1988), 87–91. © 1976 and
        1988 John Bowlt.

5.26   Ilya Zdanevich and Mikhail Larionov, "Why We Paint Ourselves: A Futurist
        Manifesto," 1913, first published in *Argus* (Petersbury), December, 1913;
        reprinted in *Russian Art of the Avant-Garde: Theory and Criticism, 1902-1934*,
        ed. and trans. John E. Bowlt (New York: Thames and Hudson, 1988), 79–83.
        © 1976 and 1988 John Bowlt.

6.1   Edvard Munch, "The St. Cloud Manifesto [Impressions from a ballroom,
        New Year's Eve in St. Cloud]," 1889, trans. Ingeborg Owesen from *Art in
        Theory: 1815-1900*, ed. Charles Harrison and Paul Wood with Jason Gaigar
        (Oxford: Blackwell Publishers, 1998), 1040–41.

6.2   Edvard Munch, "The Violet Diary" (excerpt), January 2, 1891, and
        January 22, 1892, trans. Ingeborg Owesen from *Art in Theory: 1815-1900*, ed.
        Charles Harrison and Paul Wood, with Jason Gaigar (Oxford: Blackwell
        Publishers, 1998), 1042–44.

6.3   Edvard Munch, "Art and Nature," 1907–1929, from notebooks at
        Warnemünde, 1907–1908, and Ekely, 1928–1929, in Johan H. Langaard and
        Reidar Revold, *Edvard Munch* (Oslo: Belser, 1963), 62; trans. Herschell Chipp
        in *Theories of Modern Art: A Source Book by Artists and Critics*, ed. Herschel B.
        Chipp (Berkeley: University of California Press, 1968), 114–15. Copyright ©
        1968 The Regents of the University of California.

6.4   Oskar Kokoschka, "On the Nature of Visions," 1912, trans. Hedi Medlinger
        and John Thwaites, in Edith Hoffmann, *Kokoschka: Life and Work* (London:
        Faber and Faber, 1947), 285–87; reprinted in *Theories of Modern Art: A Source
        Book by Artists and Critics*, ed. Herschel B. Chipp (Berkeley: University of
        California Press, 1968), 170–74. Copyright © 1968 The Regents of the
        University of California.

6.5   Paul Klee, "Creative Credo," 1920, in *The Inward Vision: Watercolors,
        Drawings and Writings by Paul Klee*, trans. Norbert Guterman (New York:
        H. N. Abrams, 1959), 5–10. All rights reserved. Reprinted in *Theories of
        Modern Art: A Source Book by Artists and Critics*, ed. Herschel B. Chipp
        (Berkeley: University of California Press, 1968), 182–86. Copyright © 1968
        The Regents of the University of California.

6.6   Paul Klee, "We Construct and Construct," 1929, Bauhaus Prospectus, trans.
        Robert Goldwater in *Artists on Art*, ed. Robert Goldwater and Marco Treves
        (New York: Pantheon, 1945). Translation reprinted with permission from
        Louise Bourgeois.

6.7   James Ensor, Preface to His *Collected Writings* (excerpt), 1921, trans. Robert
        Goldwater in *Artists on Art*, ed. Robert Goldwater and Marco Treves (New
        York: Pantheon, 1945), 387. Translation reprinted with permission from
        Louise Bourgeois.

6.8   James Ensor, "Speech Delivered at a Banquet Given for Him by La Flandre
        Littéraire, Ostende" (excerpt), December 22, 1923, trans. Nancy McCauley

8.2   Giorgio de Chirico, "On Metaphysical Art" (excerpt), 1919, first published in
        Valori Plastici (Rome), April–May 1919; reprinted in *Metaphysical Art*, comp.
        Massimo Carrà, trans. Caroline Tisdall (New York: Praeger, 1971), 88–91.
        English translation and historical foreword © 1971 in London, England, by
        Thames and Hudson Ltd. Original edition © 1968 in Milan, Italy, by
        Gabriele Mazzotta Editore.

9.1   "Dada Excites Everything," 1921, trans. Lucy R. Lippard from a collective
        manifesto dated January 12, 1921, in *Dadas on Art*, ed. Lucy R. Lippard
        (Englewood Cliffs NJ: Prentice Hall, 1971), 162–63.

9.2   Jean (Hans) Arp, "Manifesto of the Dada Crocodarium," 1920, in *Jours
        effeuillés* (Paris: Gallimard, 1966), 3; reprinted in *Arp on Arp: Poems, Essays,
        Memories*, ed. Marcel Jean, trans. Joachim Neugroschel (New York: Viking
        Press, 1972). Translation copyright © 1969, 1972 by the Viking Press, Inc.
        Used by permission of the Viking Penguin, a division of Penguin
        Putnam Inc.

9.3   Jean (Hans) Arp, "The Elephant Style versus the Bidet Style," 1934, first
        published in *Revue 14: Rue du Dragon* (Paris: Éditions Cahiers d'Art, 1934);
        reprinted in Jean Arp, *Jours effeuillés* (Paris: Gallimard, 1966); reprinted in
        Arp on Arp: Poems, Essays, Memories, ed. Marcel Jean, trans. Joachim
        Neugroschel (New York: Viking Press, 1972), 80. Translation copyright ©
        1969, 1972 by the Viking Press, Inc. Used by permission of the Viking
        Penguin, a division of Penguin Putnam Inc.

9.4   Jean (Hans) Arp, "Infinite Millimeter Manifesto," 1938, in *Jours effeuillés*
        (Paris: Gallimard, 1966), 128, © Editions Gallimard, 1966. Reprinted in *Arp
        on Arp: Poems, Essays, Memories*, ed. Marcel Jean, trans. Joachim
        Neugroschel (New York: Viking Press, 1972), 96. Translation copyright ©
        1969, 1972 by the Viking Press, Inc. Used by permission of the Viking
        Penguin, a division of Penguin Putnam Inc.

9.5   Richard Huelsenbeck, Marcel Janko, and Tristan Tzara, "L'Amiral cherche
        une maison à louer," 1916, in *Poems for the Millennium*, vol. 1, ed. Jerome
        Rothenberg and Pierre Joris (Berkeley: University of California Press, 1995),
        308–9. Reprinted with permission from Jerome Rothenberg.

9.6   Tristan Tzara, "Note on Art," 1917, from "Tristan Tzara [Sami Rosenstock],"
        in *Approximate Man and Other Writings*, ed. and trans. Mary Ann Caws
        (Detroit: Wayne State University Press, 1973), 135–36.

9.7   Tristan Tzara, "Dada Manifesto," 1918, from "Tristan Tzara [Sami
        Rosenstock]," in *Approximate Man and Other Writings*, ed. and trans. Mary
        Ann Caws (Detroit: Wayne State University Press, 1973), 149–57.

9.8   Tristan Tzara, "Mr. Antipyrine's Manifesto," 1918, from "Tristan Tzara [Sami
        Rosenstock]," in *Approximate Man and Other Writings*, ed. and trans. Mary
        Ann Caws (Detroit: Wayne State University Press, 1973), 147–48.

9.9   Tristan Tzara, "Note on Poetry," 1919, from "Tristan Tzara [Sami
        Rosenstock]," in *Approximate Man and Other Writings*, ed. and trans. Mary
        Ann Caws (Detroit: Wayne State University Press, 1973), 167–69.

9.10   Tristan Tzara, "Mr. AA the Antiphilosopher Has Sent Us This Manifesto,"
        (Monsieur l'Antiphilosophe nous envoie ce manifeste), read at the Festival

Dada, Salle Gaveau, May 26, 1920; first published in *391* (July 1920): 3; trans. Mary Ann Caws from Tristan Tzara, *Oeuvres Complètes*, vol. 1, *1912-1924*, ed. Henri Behar (Paris: Flammarion, 1975).

9.11   Tristan Tzara, "Proclamation without Pretention," 1920, first published in *Die Schammade (Dadameter)*(Cologne), February 25, 1920; reprinted in "Tristan Tzara [Sami Rosenstock]," in *Approximate Man and Other Writings*, ed. and trans. Mary Ann Caws (Detroit: Wayne State University Press, 1973), 157.

9.12   Richard Huelsenbeck, "Pig's Bladder," 1920, in *The DADA Almanac*, ed. Richard Huelsenbeck (Berlin, 1920); English edition presented by Malcolm Green (London: Atlas Press, 1993), 20; trans. and reprinted with permission from Herbert Kapfer.

9.13   Theo van Doesburg [I. K. Bonset], "Characteristics of Dadaism" (excerpt), 1923, in *Dadas on Art*, ed. Lucy R. Lippard (Englewood Cliffs NJ: Prentice Hall, 1971), 112; trans. Claire Nicholas White from *Mecano* (Leyden), no. 4–5 (1923).

9.14   Marcel Duchamp, "Possible," 1913, trans. Mary Ann Caws from *Duchamp du Signe*, ed. Michel Sanouillet (Paris: Flammarion, 1994).

9.15   Francis Picabia, "Dada Cannibalistic Manifesto," 1920, first published in *Dadaphone* (March 1920); trans. William Camfield and Karen Coffey in *Francis Picabia: His Art, Life and Times*, ed. William A. Camfield (Princeton: Princeton University Press, 1979), 140–41; translation reprinted with permission from William Camfield.

9.16   Francis Picabia, "DADA Manifesto," 1920, in *391*, no. 12 (March 1920); trans. Margaret I. Lippard, in *Dadas on Art*, ed. Lucy R. Lippard (Englewood Cliffs NJ: Prentice Hall, 1971), 166–67.

9.17   "Francis Picabia Is an Imbecile, an Idiot, a Pickpocket!!!" 1921, trans. Lucy R. Lippard from a tract distributed at the Salon d'Automne, Paris, 1921, in *Dadas on Art*, ed. Lucy R. Lippard (Englewood Cliffs NJ: Prentice Hall, 1971), 168.

9.18   Man Ray, "Statement," 1916, in *Catalogue of Dada Dokumente einer Bewegung* (Düsseldorf: Kunsthalle, 1958); reprinted in *Dadas on Art*, ed. Lucy R. Lippard (Englewood Cliffs NJ: Prentice Hall, 1971), 156.

9.19   Hans Richter, "Against Without For Dada," 1919, in *Hans Richter By Hans Richter*, ed. Cleve Gray (New York: Holt, Rinehart and Winston, 1971), 96. © 1969 by Cleve Gray. Reprinted by permission of Henry Holt and Company, Inc., and with permission from Cleve Gray.

9.20   Jacques Vaché, Manifesto of UMORE, 1917, from a letter of August 18, 1917, to André Breton, trans. Mary Ann Caws, from Vaché, *Les Lettres de guerre: Suivies d'une nouvelle* (Paris: K Editeur, 1949).

9.21   Marcel Duchamp, "Kind of Sub-Title," 1934, in *The Green Box*, trans. George Heard Hamilton (New Haven CT: The Readymade Press, 1957); typographic version of *The Green Box*, trans. George Heard Hamilton (New York: Wittenborn, 1960).

9.22   The Baroness Else von Freytag-Loringhoven, "The Modest Woman," 1921, first published in *The Little Review* 7, no.2 (spring 1921): 37–40; reprinted in

The Little Review, ed. Margaret Anderson (New York: Horizon Press, 1953), 299–300.

9.23   Mina Loy, "Aphorisms on Futurism," 1914–1919, in *The Last Lunar Baedeker*, ed. Roger L. Conover (Highlands: The Jargon Society, 1982), 272–75. Reprinted courtesy of Roger L. Conover, Mina Loy's literary executor.

9.24   Mina Loy, "Aphorisms on Modernism," 1914–1919, in *The Last Lunar Baedeker*, ed. Roger L. Conover (Highlands: The Jargon Society, 1982), 311. Reprinted courtesy of Roger L. Conover, Mina Loy's literary executor. The text is a construction of the editor from fragments in the papers of Mina Loy.

9.25   Mina Loy, "Notes on Existence," 1914–1919, in *The Last Lunar Baedeker*, ed. Roger L. Conover (Highlands: The Jargon Society, 1982), 312–13. Reprinted courtesy of Roger L. Conover, Mina Loy's literary executor. The text is a construction of the editor from fragments in the papers of Mina Loy.

9.26   Mina Loy, "The Artist and the Public," 1917, in *The Last Lunar Baedeker*, ed. Roger L. Conover (Highlands: The Jargon Society, 1982), 285. Reprinted courtesy of Roger L. Conover, Mina Loy's literary executor.

9.27   Mina Loy, "Auto-Facial-Construction," 1919, in *The Last Lunar Baedeker*, ed. Roger L. Conover (Highlands: The Jargon Society, 1982), 283–84. Reprinted courtesy of Roger L. Conover, Mina Loy's literary executor.

9.28   Man Ray, "L'Inquiétude," 1921, in *The Catalogue of Salon Dada* (Paris: Galerie Montaigne, 1921); reprinted in *Dadas on Art*, ed. Lucy R. Lippard (Englewood Cliffs NJ: Prentice Hall, 1971), 157.

10.1   "The Egoist: An Individualist Review," 1914, first published in *BLAST: Review of the Great English Vortex*, ed. Wyndham Lewis (London: John Lane, 1914–15); from *BLAST: Review of the Great English Vortex* (New York: Kraus Reprint Corporation, 1967), 160. Copyright © 1981 by the Estate of Mrs. G. A. Wyndham Lewis by permission of the Wyndham Lewis Memorial Trust. Reprinted from *BLAST 1* with the permission of Black Sparrow Press.

10.2   R. Aldington, Gaudier-Brzeska, E. Pound, W. Roberts, E. Wadsworth, Wyndham Lewis, "Beyond Action and Reaction," 1914, first published in *BLAST: Review of the Great English Vortex*, ed. Wyndham Lewis (London: John Lane, 1914–15); from *BLAST: Review of the Great English Vortex* (New York: Kraus Reprint Corporation, 1967), 30–33. Copyright © 1981 by the Estate of Mrs. G. A. Wyndham Lewis by permission of the Wyndham Lewis Memorial Trust. Reprinted from *BLAST 1* with the permission of Black Sparrow Press.

10.3   R. Aldington, Gaudier-Brzeska, E. Pound, W. Roberts, E. Wadsworth, Wyndham Lewis, "Our Vortex," 1914, first published in *BLAST: Review of the Great English Vortex*, ed. Wyndham Lewis (London: John Lane, 1914–15); from *BLAST: Review of the Great English Vortex* (New York: Kraus Reprint Corporation, 1967), 147–49. Copyright © 1981 by the Estate of Mrs. G. A. Wyndham Lewis by permission of the Wyndham Lewis Memorial Trust. Reprinted from *BLAST 1* with the permission of Black Sparrow Press.

10.4   Wyndham Lewis, "Bless England," 1914–1915, first published in *BLAST: Review of the Great English Vortex*, ed. Wyndham Lewis (London: John Lane, 1914–

15); from *BLAST: Review of the Great English Vortex* (New York: Kraus Reprint Corporation, 1967), 22–24. Copyright © 1981 by the Estate of Mrs. G. A. Wyndham Lewis by permission of the Wyndham Lewis Memorial Trust. Reprinted from *BLAST 1* with the permission of Black Sparrow Press.

10.5 Wyndham Lewis, "Curse with Expletive of Whirlwind the Britannic Aesthete," 1914–1915, first published in *BLAST: Review of the Great English Vortex*, ed. Wyndham Lewis (London: John Lane, 1914–15); from *BLAST: Review of the Great English Vortex* (New York: Kraus Reprint Corporation, 1967), 15. Copyright © 1981 by the Estate of Mrs. G. A. Wyndham Lewis by permission of the Wyndham Lewis Memorial Trust. Reprinted from *BLAST 1* with the permission of Black Sparrow Press.

10.6 Wyndham Lewis, "Oh Blast France," 1914–1915, first published in *BLAST: Review of the Great English Vortex*, ed. Wyndham Lewis (London: John Lane, 1914–15); from *BLAST: Review of the Great English Vortex* (New York: Kraus Reprint Corporation, 1967), 13–14. Copyright © 1981 by the Estate of Mrs. G. A. Wyndham Lewis by permission of the Wyndham Lewis Memorial Trust. Reprinted from *BLAST 1* with the permission of Black Sparrow Press.

11.1 Pierre Reverdy, "The Image," 1918, trans. Mary Ann Caws from "L'Image," *Nord-Sud*, no. 13 (March 1918).

11.2 F. S. Flint, "Imagisme," 1913, from *Poetry* (Chicago) 1, no. 6 (1913): 198–200.

11.3 Marsden Hartley, "The Business of Poetry," 1919, from *Poetry* (Chicago) 15, no. 3 (1919): 152–58.

11.4 Ezra Pound, "A Few Don'ts by an Imagiste," 1913, from *Poetry* (Chicago) 1, no. 6 (1913): 200–202.

11.5 Ezra Pound, "Axiomata," 1921, from *The New Age*, January 13, 1921; reprinted in *Ezra Pound: Selected Prose, 1909–1965* (New York: New Directions, 1978), 49–52.

12.1 Salvador Dalí, "Yellow Manifesto," 1928, in *Salvador Dalí: The Early Years*, ed. Michael Raeburn, trans. John London (London: South Bank Centre, 1994), 221–22. Published with permission from Fundació Gala-Salvador Dalí. © Salvador Dalí: Gala–Salvador Dalí Foundation, 2000. All rights to the translation reserved by John London and the Estate of Salvador Dalí.

12.2 Ramón Gómez de la Serna, [Tristán] "Futurist Proclamation to the Spaniards," 1910, first published as "Proclama futurista a los españoles" in *Prometeo* (Madrid), no. 20, (1910); trans. Mary Ann Caws from *Poesia surrealista en España*, ed. Pablo Corbalán (Madrid: Ediciones del Centro, 1974).

12.3 José Ortega y Gasset, "The Point of View in the Arts" (excerpt), 1924, trans. Mary Ann Caws from "El punto de vista en los artes," *Revista de Occidente* (Madrid), no. 3 (February 1924): 153–56.

12.4 Joaquin Torres-Garcia, "Art-Evolution (In Manifesto Style)," 1917, trans. Mary Ann Caws from "Art-evolució," *Un Enemic del Poble* (Barcelona), November 1917.

12.5 Vicente Huidobro, "Non Serviam," read at the Ateneo in Santiago, Chile, 1914, published in *Manifestes* (Paris: Imprimerie Union, éditions de la Revue

Mondiale, 1925); trans. Mary Ann Caws from Vicente Huidobro, *Manifestes Altazor* (Paris: Editions Champ Libre/Ivrea, 1976), 221–22. © 1976 Éditions Champ Libre/Ivrea, Paris.

12.6   Vicente Huidobro, "Avis aux touristes" (Warning to tourists), 1914–1917, trans. Mary Ann Caws from Vicente Huidobro, *Manifestes Altazor* (Paris: Editions Champ Libre/Ivrea, 1976), 191. © 1976 Éditions Champ Libre/Ivrea, Paris.

12.7   Vicente Huidobro, "We Must Create," 1922, trans. Mary Ann Caws from "Il faut créer," in Vicente Huidobro, *Manifestes Altazor* (Paris: Editions Champ Libre/Ivrea, 1976), 188–88. © 1976 Éditions Champ Libre/Ivrea, Paris.

12.8   Jorge Luis Borges, Jacobo Sureda, Fortunio Bonanova, and Juan Almovar, "Ultraist Manifesto," 1921, first published as "Manifiesto del ultra" in *Baleares*, 1921; trans. Mary Ann Caws from *Poesia surrealista en España*, ed. Pablo Corbalán (Madrid: Ediciones del Centro, 1974), 322–23.

12.9   Mario de Andrade, "Extremely Interesting Preface" (excerpt), 1922, in *Hallucinated City*, trans. Jack E. Tomlins ([Nashville]: Vanderbilt University Press, 1968). English text copyright ©1968 Vanderbilt University Press.

13.1   Raoul Hausmann, "B.T.B.," 1946, in Kurt Schwitters and Raoul Hausmann, *Pin and the Story of Pin* (London: Gaberbocchus Press, 1962), 48. Reprinted with permission from Jasia Reichardt.

13.2   Kurt Schwitters, "Cow Manifesto," 1922, first published as "manifeste Vache," *Das Literarische Werk*, II, p. 94, Manuscrit dactylographié, Kurt Schwitters-Archiv, Hanovre (Stadbibliothek); trans. Mary Ann Caws from "Manifest KOE," in Kurt Schwitters, *Merz*, ed. Marc Dachy (Paris: Gérard Lebovici, 1990), 74–75.

13.3   Kurt Schwitters "i (a manifesto)," 1922, first published as "i (ein manifest)," *Der Sturm* 13, no. 5 (May 1922): 80; trans. Mary Ann Caws from "I (un manifeste)" in Kurt Schwitters, *Merz*, ed. Marc Dachy (Paris: Gérard Lebovici, 1990), 71.

13.4   Kurt Schwitters and Raoul Hausmann, "PIN Manifesto: Present Inter Noumenal/Poetry Intervenes Now," 1946, in *Pin and the Story of Pin* (London: Gaberbocchus Press, 1962), 25. Reprinted with permission from Jasia Reichardt.

13.5   Kurt Schwitters and Raoul Hausmann, "A Fancy," 1962, in *Pin and the Story of Pin* (London: Gaberbocchus Press, 1962), 23. Reprinted with permission from Jasia Reichardt.

13.6   El Lissitzky, "Topography of Typography," 1923, from "Topographie der Typographie," trans. Mary Ann Caws from *Merz*, no. 4 (July 1923).

14.1   Naum Gabo and Antoine Pevsner, "The Realistic Manifesto," August 1920, trans. Naum Gabo in *Gabo* (London: Lund Humphries; Cambridge: Harvard University Press, 1957). Published with permission from Florin Press by Nina Williams. The works of Naum Gabo © Nina Williams.

14.2   Vladimir Tatlin, "The Initiative Individual Artist in the Creativity of the Collective," 1919, in *Tatlin*, ed. Larissa Alekseevna Zhadova, trans. Paul Filotas et al., translation revised by Colin Wright, 1988 (New York: Rizzoli, 1988), 237–38.

15.1   Kasimir Malevich, "Suprematism," 1927, translated from Russian into
       German by A. von Riesen Kasimir Malevich, first published as vol. 11 of the
       Bauhaus books (Munich: Albert Langen, 1927). This version is one of two
       essays translated by Howard Dearstyne from the German and published as
       The Non-Objective World (Chicago: Paul Theobald and Co., 1959); reprinted
       in *Modern Artists on Art*, ed. Robert L. Herbert (Englewood Cliffs NJ:
       Prentice Hall, 1964), 93–102. Translation reprinted with permission by
       Marjorie Smolka, executor of the Estate of Howard Dearstyne.

15.2   László Moholy-Nagy, "Dynamics of a Metropolis: A Film Sketch," 1921–
       1922, was originally drafted in Berlin; reprinted in István Nemeskürty, *A
       mozgokeptol a filmmuveszetig* (Budapest: Corvina, 1961); trans. Zsuzsanna
       Horn and Fred Macnicol as *Word and Image* (Budapest: Corvina, 1974),
       62–67. Reprinted with permission from Corvina Books Ltd.

15.3   László Moholy-Nagy, "Remarks for Those Who Refuse to Understand the
       Film Immediately," 1921–1922, was originally drafted in Berlin; reprinted in
       István Nemeskürty, *A mozgokeptol a filmmuveszetig* (Budapest: Corvina,
       1961); trans. Zsuzsanna Horn and Fred Macnicol as *Word and Image*
       (Budapest: Corvina, 1974), 68. Reprinted with permission from Corvina
       Books Ltd.

15.4   Lyubov Popova, "Statement in Catalogue of Tenth State Exhibition," 1919, in
       Russian Art of the Avant-Garde: Theory and Criticism, 1902-1934, ed. and
       trans. John E. Bowlt (New York: Thames and Hudson, 1988), 146–47. © 1976
       and 1988 John Bowlt.

16.1   Theo van Doesburg [I. K. Bonset], "Towards a Constructive Poetry," 1923, in
       Mécano (Leyden), no. 4–5 (1923); reprinted in *Dadas on Art*, ed. Lucy R.
       Lippard, trans. Claire Nicholas White (Englewood Cliffs NJ: Prentice Hall,
       1971), 113–15

16.2   Theo van Doesburg and others, "Manifesto I of De Stijl" (excerpt), 1918, in
       De Stijl (Amsterdam) 5, no. 4 (1922); trans. Nicholas Bullock in *The
       Tradition of Constructivism*, ed. Stephen Bann (London: Thames and
       Hudson, 1974), 65. Reprinted with permission from Nicholas Bullock.

16.3   Piet Mondrian, "Neoplasticism in Painting," 1917–1918, trans. Martin S.
       James and Harry Holtzman in *De Stijl*, comp. Hans L. C. Jaffe (New York:
       H. N. Abrams, 1971), 36–40. Published by Harry N. Abrams, Inc., New York.
       All rights reserved.

16.4   Piet Mondrian, "Natural Reality and Abstract Reality," 1919, first published
       in *De Stijl* (Amsterdam), no. 1 (1919); trans. Michel Seuphor in Michel
       Seuphor, *Piet Mondrian, Life and Work* (New York: H. N. Abrams, 1957),
       142–44. Published by Harry N. Abrams, Inc., New York. All rights reserved.

16.5   Piet Mondrian, "The Plastic Means," 1927, trans. Martin S. James and Harry
       Holtzman in *De Stijl*, comp. Hans L. C. Jaffe (New York: H. N. Abrams,
       1971), 226. Published by Harry N. Abrams, Inc., New York. All rights
       reserved.

16.6   Hans Richter, "Towards a New World Plasticism," 1927, trans. Mary Whitall
       in *De Stijl*, comp. Hans L. C. Jaffe (New York: H. N. Abrams, 1971), 147.
       Published by Harry N. Abrams, Inc., New York. All rights reserved.

17.1   Le Corbusier [Charles Édouard Jeanneret] and Amédée Ozenfant, "Purism,"
       1920, in *L'Esprit nouveau* 1, no. 1 (October 15, 1920): 38–48; reprinted in
       Modern Artists on Art, ed. Robert L. Herbert (Englewood Cliffs NJ:Prentice
       Hall, 1964), 60–66.
17.2   Amédée Ozenfant, "The Art of Living" (excerpt), 1927–1928, from the
       preface to Ozenfant, *Foundations of Modern Art* (New York: Dover, 1952),
       xiv–xvi.
17.3   Amédée Ozenfant, "The Life of the Artist Today" (excerpt), 1928, trans. John
       Rodker in Ozenfant, *Foundations of Modern Art* (New York: Dover, 1952),
       230–31.
18.1   "Declaration of January 27, 1925," Bureau de Recherches Surréalistes, in
       Maurice Nadeau, *History of Surrealism*, trans. Richard Howard (New York:
       Macmillan, 1965), 240–41. Reprinted with permission from Richard
       Howard.
18.2   Antonin Artaud, "The Theater of Cruelty: First Manifesto," 1932, in *Antonin
       Artaud: Selected Writings*, ed. Susan Sontag, trans. Helen Weaver (New York:
       Farrar, Straus, and Giroux, 1976), 242–51. Translation copyright © 1976 by
       Farrar, Straus, and Giroux, Inc. Reprinted with permission of Farrar, Straus,
       and Giroux, Inc.
18.3   Antonin Artaud, "All Writing Is Pigshit," 1965, trans. David Rattray in
       Artaud Anthology, ed. Jack Hirschman (San Francisco: City Lights, 1965), 38–
       40. Copyright © 1965 by City Lights Books. Reprinted by permission of City
       Lights Books.
18.4   Antonin Artaud, "Here Where Others . . . ," 1965, trans. Jack Hirschman in
       Artaud Anthology, ed. Jack Hirschman (San Francisco: City Lights, 1965), 26.
       Copyright © 1965 by City Lights Books. Reprinted by permission of City
       Lights Books.
18.5   Antonin Artaud, "Revolt against Poetry," 1965, trans. Jack Hirschman in
       Artaud Anthology, ed. Jack Hirschman (San Francisco: City Lights, 1965),
       100–101. Copyright © 1965 by City Lights Books. Reprinted by permission
       of City Lights Books.
18.6   Antonin Artaud, "Shit to the Spirit," 1965, trans. Jack Hirschman in *Artaud
       Anthology*, ed. Jack Hirschman (San Francisco: City Lights, 1965), 106–12.
       Copyright © 1965 by City Lights Books. Reprinted by permission of City
       Lights Books.
18.7   André Breton, "Declaration vvv," 1942, first published in *Triple V* (New
       York); reprinted in André Breton, *Free Rein*, trans. Michel Parmentier and
       Jacqueline d'Amboise (Lincoln: University of Nebraska Press, 1995), 68.
       Reprinted by permission of the University of Nebraska Press. © 1953,
       Éditions du Sagittaire, © 1979, Société Nouvelle des Éditions Pauvert.
       Translation © 1995 by the University of Nebraska Press.
18.8   André Breton and Paul Eluard, "Notes on Poetry" (excerpt), 1929, originally
       published in *La Révolution surréaliste*, no. 12 (1929); reprinted in Maurice
       Nadeau, *History of Surrealism*, trans. Richard Howard (New York:
       Macmillan, 1965), 274; reprinted in André Breton, *Oeuvres Completes I*, ed.
       Marguerite Bonnet (Paris: Gallimard, 1988), 1014–20. Reprinted with

permission from Richard Howard and Editions Gallimard. © Editions
Gallimard, 1988.

18.9   André Breton and Diego Rivera [Léon Trotsky], "Manifesto for an
        Independent Revolutionary Art," 1938, in *Free Rein*, trans. Michel
        Parmentier and Jacqueline d'Amboise (Lincoln: University of Nebraska
        Press, 1995), 29–34. Reprinted by permission of the University of Nebraska
        Press. © 1953, Éditions du Sagittaire, © 1979, Société Nouvelle des Éditions
        Pauvert. Translation © 1995 by the University of Nebraska Press.

18.10   Claude Cahun, "The Invisible Adventure," 1930, originally published in
        Aveux non avenus (Paris: Editions du Carrefour, 1930); trans. Erin Gibson in
        Surrealist Women: An International Anthology, ed. Penelope Rosemont.
        (Austin: University of Texas Press, 1998), 53. Translation reprinted with
        permission from Erin Gibson.

18.11   Max Morise, "Enchanted Eyes," 1924, first published as "Les Yeux
        Enchantés," *La Révolution surréaliste*, no. 1 (December 1924): 26–27; trans.
        Mary Ann Caws from *La Révolution surréaliste: Collection complete* (Paris:
        Jean Michel Place, 1975).

18.12   Salvador Dalí, "Photography, Pure Creation of the Mind," 1927, originally
        published in *L'Amic de les artes* (Sitges), no. 18 (September 30, 1927);
        reprinted in *Salvador Dalí: The Early Years*, ed. Michael Raeburn, trans. John
        London (London: South Bank Centre, 1994), 216. Published with permission
        from Fundació Gala-Salvador Dalí. © Salvador Dalí: Gala–Salvador Dalí
        Foundation, 2000. All rights to the translation reserved by John London
        and the Estate of Salvador Dalí.

18.13   Aimé Césaire, "In the Guise of a Literary Manifesto," 1942, originally titled
        "En Guise d'un manifeste littéraire," trans. Mary Ann Caws from
        Tropiques (1942). © Aimé Césaire; with permission of the author.

18.14   Suzanne Césaire, "The Domain of the Marvelous," 1941, trans. Erin Gibson
        from *VIEW Magazine*, special issue on Surrealism, no. 7–8,
        (October/November 1941); reprinted in *Surrealist Women: An International
        Anthology*, ed. Penelope Rosemont (Austin: University of Texas Press, 1998),
        137. Translation reprinted with permission from Erin Gibson.

18.15   Suzanne Césaire, "Surrealism and Us," 1943, in *Tropiques*, no. 8–9; trans.
        Erin Gibson in *Surrealist Women: An International Anthology*, ed. Penelope
        Rosemont (Austin: University of Texas Press, 1998), 133–37. Translation
        reprinted with permission from Erin Gibson.

18.16   Matta [Matta Echaurren], "On Emotion," 1954, in *Reality* (New York), no. 2
        (spring 1954): 12; trans. Herschel B. Chipp in *Theories of Modern Art: A
        Source Book by Artists and Critics*, ed. Herschel B. Chipp (Berkeley: University
        of California Press, 1968), 443–45. Copyright © 1968 The Regents of the
        University of California.

18.17   Léopold Sédar Senghor, "Speech and Image: An African Tradition of the
        Surreal," 1965, in *Léopold Sédar Senghor: Prose and Poetry*, ed. and trans. John
        Reed and Clive Wake (New York: Oxford University Press, 1965); reprinted
        in *Poems for the Millennium*, vol. 1, ed. Jerome Rothenberg and Pierre Joris
        (Berkeley: University of California Press, 1995), 564–65. © Oxford University
        Press 1965. Reprinted by permission of Oxford University Press.

19.1   Edgar Allan Poe, "The Philosophy of Furniture," 1840, first published in
       Burton's Gentleman's Magazine, May 1840; slightly revised for publication in
       the *Broadway Journal*, 1845; reprinted in *Edgar Allan Poe: Selected Writings*
       (Harmondsworth, U.K.: Penguin, 1967), 414–20.

19.2   Sonia Delaunay, "The Future of Fashion," 1931, in *HEIM*, no. 3 (September
       1931); reprinted in *The New Art of Color: The Writings of Robert and Sonia
       Delaunay*, ed. Arthur A. Cohen, trans. Arthur A. Cohen and David Shapiro
       (New York: Viking Press, 1978), 207–8. Translation copyright © 1978 by
       Sonia Delaunay. Copyright © 1978 by Arthur A. Cohen, introduction and
       translation. Used by permission of Viking Penguin, a division of Penguin
       Putnam Inc.

19.3   Sonia Delaunay, "The Issue," 1966, text for *Portfolio of Prints* (Milan:
       Galleria Schwarz, 1966); reprinted in *The New Art of Color: The Writings of
       Robert and Sonia Delaunay*, ed. Arthur A. Cohen, trans. Arthur A. Cohen
       and David Shapiro (New York: Viking Press, 1978), 213–14. Translation
       copyright © 1978 by Sonia Delaunay. Copyright © 1978 by Arthur A. Cohen,
       introduction and translation. Used by permission of Viking Penguin, a
       division of Penguin Putnam Inc.

19.4   Fernand Léger, "The Aesthetic of the Machine" (excerpt), 1924, in *Bulletin de
       l'effort moderne* (Paris), no. 1–2; trans. Herschel B. Chipp in *Theories of
       Modern Art: A Source Book by Artists and Critics*, ed. Herschel B. Chipp
       (Berkeley: University of California Press, 1968), 277–79. Copyright © 1968
       The Regents of the University of California.

19.5   Francis Ponge, "The Object Is Poetics," February 1962, in *Nouveau Recueil*
       (Paris: Editions Gallimard, 1967); reprinted in Francis Ponge, *The Sun Placed
       in Abyss and Other Texts*, trans. Serge Gavronsky (New York: Sun, 1977), 36–
       37. Reprinted with permission from Serge Gavronsky and Editions
       Gallimard. © Editions Gallimard, 1967.

19.6   Giorgio de Chirico, "Statues, Furniture, and Generals," 1968, in Massimo
       Carrà, *Metaphysical Art*, trans. Caroline Tisdall (New York: Praeger, 1971),
       151–53. English translation and historical foreword © 1971 in London,
       England, by Thames and Hudson Ltd. Original edition © 1968 in Milan,
       Italy, by Gabriele Mazzotta editore.

19.7   F. T. Marinetti, Francesco Monarchi, Enrico Prampolini, and Mino
       Somenzi, "The Futurist Manifesto of the Italian Hat," 1933, in *Futurismo*
       (Rome), March 5, 1933; trans. Emily Braun, associate professor, Hunter
       College, City University of New York, in *Art Journal* 54, no. 1 (spring 1995).
       Reprinted with permission from Emily Braun.

19.8   Volt [Vincenzo Fani], "Futurist Manifesto of Women's Fashion," 1920, in
       Roma Futurista (Rome), 1920; trans. Emily Braun, associate professor,
       Hunter College, City University of New York, in *Art Journal* 54, no. 1 (spring
       1995). Reprinted with permission from Emily Braun.

20.1   Theo van Doesburg, "Basis of Concrete Painting," 1930, in *Art Concret*;
       reprinted in *The Tradition of Constructivism*, ed. and trans. Stephen Bann
       (London: Thames and Hudson, 1974), 193. Reprinted with permission from
       Stephen Bann. Van Doesburg's open question "Is There a Constructive

Poetry" provides a wry postscript to the manifesto of seven years earlier. The line is a freestanding line separate from "Basis of Concrete Painting." The text in bold is taken straight from *The Tradition of Constructivism*.

20.2   Wassily Kandinsky, "Concrete Art," 1938, in *XXe Siècle* (Paris), no. 1 (1938); trans. Herschel B. Chipp in *Theories of Modern Art: A Source Book by Artists and Critics*, ed. Herschel B. Chipp (Berkeley: University of California Press, 1968), 346–49. Copyright © 1968 The Regents of the University of California.

20.3   Jean (Hans) Arp, "Concrete Art," 1944, in *Arp on Arp: Poems, Essays, Memories*, ed. Marcel Jean, trans. Joachim Neugroschel (New York: Viking, 1972). Translation copyright © 1969, 1972 by the Viking Press, Inc. Used by permission of the Viking Penguin, a division of Penguin Putnam Inc. Translation based on "Art concret," from the catalogue *Konkrete Kunst*, (Basel, 1944): 139–40; reprinted in Jean Arp, *Jours Effeuillés* (Paris: Gallimard, 1966), 183–84. © Editions Gallimard, 1966.

21.1   Hans (Jean) Arp, Samuel Beckett, Carl Einstein, Eugène Jolas, Thomas McGreevy, Georges Pelorson, Theo Rutra, James J. Sweeney, and Ronald Symond, "Poetry Is Vertical," 1941, in *Transition* 21 (1941): 148–49; reprinted in *Transition: The History of a Literary Era 1927-38*, ed. Dougald MacMillan (New York: Georges Braziller, 1976), 66. Reprinted with permission of Tina Jolas and Betsy Jolas.

21.2   Eugène Jolas and others, "The Revolution of the Word," 1928, in *Transition* 16–17 (June 1929); reprinted in *Transition: A Paris Anthology* (New York: Doubleday, 1990), 19. Reprinted with permission of Tina Jolas and Betsy Jolas.

22.1   Pierre and Ilse Garnier, "Spatial Eroticism," March 1966, originally titled "L'Érotisme spatialiste," trans. Mary Ann Caws from "Approches sur l'érotisme dans la poésie matérielle," in Pierre Garnier, *Spatialisme et poésie concrète* (Paris: Gallimard, 1968), 178–80. © Editions Gallimard, 1968.

22.2   Francis Picabia and others, "Dimensionist Manifesto," 1936, first published as "Manifeste dimensioniste," *N + I* "for noneuclidian arts" (Paris), 1936; trans. Mary Ann Caws from Vicente Huidobro, *Manifestes Altazor*, ed. Gerard de Cortanze (Paris: Editions Champ Libre/Ivrea, 1976), 232–33. © 1976 Éditions Champ Libre/Ivrea, Paris.

22.3   Paul de Vree, "Declaration," 1966, trans. Mary Ann Caws from the catalogue *Poesure/peintrie: D'un art à l'autre*, Centre de la Vieillé Charité, Musée de Marseilles, Marseilles, February 12–March 25, 1993; reprinted in *Ou*, no. 28–29, p. 552.

22.4   Lucio Fontana and others, "Manifesto of Spatialist Art," from a discussion at the Galleria del Naviglio, Milan, November 26, 1951; trans. Mary Ann Caws from *Manifesti spaziali, 1947-53*, ed. Lucio Fontana (Florence: Galleria Michelucci, 1971). Reprinted with permission from the Fondazione Lucio Fontana, Milan.

22.5   Seiichi Niikuni and Pierre Garnier, "Position 3 of Spatialism: For a Supranational Poetry," 1966, trans. Mary Ann Caws from "Position 3 du spatialisme: Pour une poésie supranationale," preface to *Poèmes franco-*

japonais (Paris: A. Silvaire, 1966), with permission from Editions André
Silvaire.

23.1 Isidore Isou, "Manifesto of Lettrist Poetry," 1942, trans. Mary Ann Caws
from "Le Manifeste de la poésie lettriste," *Introduction à une nouvelle poésie*
(Paris: Gallimard, 1947), 11–12, 16–17. © Editions Gallimard, 1947.

23.2 Isidore Isou, "DADALETTRIE Meca-Esthetically Destructive 1 and 2," 1970,
first published as "Dadalettrie méca-esthétique déstructice 1 and 2,"
Lettrisme, no. 15 (1970); trans. Mary Ann Caws from Jean-Paul Curtay, *La
Poésie lettriste*, no. 15 (1970): 246.

24.1 Charles Olson, "Projective Verse," 1950, in *Poetry* (New York), no. 3 (1950):
15–26; reprinted in *Selected Writings of Charles Olson*, ed. Robert Creeley
(New York: New Directions, 1966). Reprinted with permission from
Rutherford W. Witthus, Curator of Literary and Natural History
Collections, Thomas J. Dadd Research Center, University of Connecticut
Libraries.

25.1 D. H. Lawrence, "The Spirit of Place," 1923, in *Studies in Classic American
Literature* (New York: Viking Press, 1923). Copyright 1923 by Thomas Seltzer,
Inc., renewed 1950 by Frieda Lawrence. Copyright © 1961 by the estate of
the late Mrs. Frieda Lawrence. Used by permission of Viking Penguin, a
division of Penguin Putnam. Reprinted with permission by Laurence
Pollinger Limited and the Estate of Frieda Lawrence Ravagli.

25.2 Marsden Hartley, "On the Subject of Nativeness—A Tribute to Maine,"
1937, from the catalogue *Marsden Hartley: Exhibition of Recent Paintings* (New
York: An American Place, 1937); reprinted in Marsden Hartley, *On Art*, ed.
Gail R. Scott (New York: Horizon Press, 1982), 112–15.

25.3 Eudora Welty, "Place in Fiction," 1956, a condensation of lectures prepared
for the Conference on American Studies in Cambridge, England, in 1954, in
The Eye of the Story (New York: Random House, 1978), 116–33. Reprinted by
permission of Russell & Volkening as agents for the author. Copyright ©
1956 by Eudora Welty, renewed 1984 by Eudora Welty. Originally appeared
in *South Atlantic Quarterly* 55, no. 1 (January 1956).

26.1 Marsden Hartley, "A Word," 1916, from the catalogue *The Forum Exhibition
of Modern American Painters* (New York: Anderson Galleries); reprinted in
Marsden Hartley, *On Art*, ed. Gail R. Scott (New York: Horizon Press, 1982),
66–67.

26.2 Marsden Hartley, "Art and the Personal Life," 1928, in *Creative Art*, no. 2
(June 1928): xxxi–xxxvi; reprinted in Marsden Hartley, *On Art*, ed. Gail R.
Scott (New York: Horizon Press, 1982), 70–73.

26.3 Frank O'Hara, "Personism," September 3, 1959, in *The Poetics of the New
American Poetry*, ed. Donald Allen and Warren Tallman (New York: Grove
Press, 1973).

26.4 Walt Whitman, "Song of Myself" (excerpt), 1855, in *Leaves of Grass* (New
York: Signet, New American Library, 1955), 49–55.

26.5 William Carlos Williams, "The Pluralism of Experience," 1974, in *The
Embodiment of Knowledge*, ed. Ron Loewinsohn (New York: New Directions,
1974), 149–50. Copyright © 1974 by Florence H. Williams. Reprinted by
permission of New Directions Publishing Corp., New York.

27.1 W. E. B. DuBois, *The Souls of Black Folk* (excerpt), 1903 (Chicago: A. C.
      McClurg & Company, 1903); reprinted in *Literary Theory, an Anthology*, ed.
      Julie Rivkin (Malden: Blackwell, 1998), 868–72.

27.2 Mina Loy, "Feminist Manifesto," 1914, in *The Last Lunar Baedeker*, ed.
      Roger L. Conover (Highlands: The Jargon Society, 1982). Works of Mina Loy
      copyright © 1996 by the Estate of Mina Loy. Introduction and edition
      copyright © 1996 by Roger L. Conover. Reprinted by permission of Farrar,
      Straus, and Giroux, Inc.

27.3 Gloria Anzaldúa, *Borderlands/La Frontera* (excerpt), 1987 (San Francisco:
      Aunt Lute Books, 1987), 15–22, 62–64. © 1987 Gloria Anzaldúa.

27.4 Méret Oppenheim, "It Is Not Easy," January 16, 1975, acceptance speech for
      the 1974 Art Award of the City of Basel; reprinted in *Méret Oppenheim:
      Defiance in the Face of Freedom*, ed. Bice Curiger, trans. Catherine Schelbert
      (New York: Parkett, 1989), 130–31. Reprinted with permission from
      Dr. Burkhard Wenger.

27.5 Hélène Cixous and Catherine Clément, "Sorties," 1975, in *The Newly Born
      Woman*, trans. Betsy Wing (Minneapolis: University of Minnesota Press,
      1986), 63–66, 83–86, 87–88. Reprinted with permission from the University
      of Minnesota Press. English translation and introduction copyright © 1986
      by the University of Minnesota. Reprinted with permission from the
      University of Minnesota Press and I. B. Taurus & Co. Ltd.

28.1 François Le Lionnais, "The Litpot: The First Manifesto," 1962, originally
      titled "La LiPo: Le premier manifeste," trans. Mary Ann Caws from "La
      Littérature Potentielle" in *La Bibliothèque Oulipienne* (Paris: Gallimard,
      1973), 19–22. © Editions Gallimard, 1973.

29.1 Susan Bee [Laufer] and Charles Bernstein, "Style," 1978, in *The
      L=A=N=G=U=A=G=E Book*, ed. Bruce Andrews and Charles Bernstein
      (Carbondale: Southern Illinois University Press, 1984), 181–82. First
      published in *L=A=N=G=U=A=G=E*, no. 6 (1978) and collected in Charles
      Bernstein, *Content's Dream: Essays 1975-1984* (Los Angeles: Sun & Moon
      Press, 1985). Reprinted with the permission of the authors.

29.2 Charles Bernstein, "The Conspiracy of 'Us,' " 1979, in *The
      L=A=N=G=U=A=G=E Book*, ed. Bruce Andrews and Charles Bernstein
      (Carbondale: Southern Illinois University Press, 1984), 185–88. First
      published in *L=A=N=G=U=A=G=E*, no. 8 (1979) and collected in Charles
      Bernstein, *Content's Dream: Essays 1975-1984* (Los Angeles: Sun & Moon
      Press, 1985). Reprinted with the permission of the author.

29.3 Lyn Hejinian, "If Written Is Writing," 1978, in *The L=A=N=G=U=A=G=E
      Book*, ed. Bruce Andrews and Charles Bernstein (Carbondale: Southern
      Illinois University Press, 1984), 29–30. First published in
      L=A=N=G=U=A=G=E, no. 3 (1978). Reprinted with permission from Lyn
      Hejinian.

29.4 Michael Palmer, "The Flower of Capital," 1979, in *The L=A=N=G=U=A=G=E
      Book*, ed. Bruce Andrews and Charles Bernstein (Carbondale: Southern
      Illinois University Press, 1984), 162–64. First published in
      L=A=N=G=U=A=G=E, no. 9-10 (1979). Reprinted with permission from
      Michael Palmer.

29.5 Nick Piombino, "Writing and Remembering," 1993, in *The Boundary of Blur* (New York: Roof Books, 1993), 17. Reprinted with permission from the Segue Foundation.

30.1 George Antheil, "Abstraction and Time in Music," n.d., in *The Little Review*, ed. Margaret Anderson (New York: Horizon Press, 1953), 336–38.

30.2 Pierre Boulez, "Experiment, Ostriches and Music," 1955, first published in *Nouvelle Revue Française (NFR)*, no. 36 (December 1955): i, 174–76; reprinted by permission of the publisher from Pierre Boulez, *Orientations*, trans. Martin Cooper (Cambridge: Harvard University Press, 1986), 430–31. Translation copyright © 1986 by Faber and Faber and the Presidents and Fellows of Harvard College by the President and Fellows of Harvard College.

30.3 Pierre Boulez, "Demythologizing the Conductor," from "Alternatives," opening statement at the Basle courses, 1960; first published in French by Christian Bourgois, editor, as "Points de repère," 1981; reprinted by permission of the publisher from Pierre Boulez, *Orientations*, trans. Martin Cooper (Cambridge: Harvard University Press, 1986), 113–15. Translation copyright © 1986 by Faber and Faber and the President and Fellows of Harvard College by the President and Fellows of Harvard College.

30.4 John Cage, "Bang Fist," 1937, in *Silence* (Middletown CT: Wesleyan University Press, 1961), 191.

30.5 Christopher Alexander, "The Timeless Way of Building" (excerpt), 1979, from "The Detailed Table of Contents," in *The Timeless Way of Building* (New York: Oxford University Press, 1979). Copyright © 1979 Christopher Alexander. Used by permission of Oxford University Press, Inc. Reprinted in *Theories and Manifestoes of Contemporary Architecture*, ed. Charles Jencks and Karl Kropf (Chichester, West Sussex: Academy Editions, 1997), 80–83.

30.6 John Hejduk, "Thoughts of an Architect," 1986, in *Victims* (London: Architectural Association, 1986). © John Hejduk and the Architectural Association. Reprinted in *Theories and Manifestoes of Contemporary Architecture*, ed. Charles Jencks and Karl Kropf (Chichester, West Sussex: Academy Editions, 1997), 285. Reprinted by permission of Irwin Chanin School of Architecture Archive.

30.7 Charles Jencks, "13 Propositions of Post-Modern Architecture," 1996, in *Theories and Manifestoes of Contemporary Architecture*, ed. Charles Jencks and Karl Kropf (Chichester, West Sussex: Academy Editions, 1997), 131–32. Copyright John Wiley & Sons Limited. Reproduced with permission.

30.8 Nanni Balestrini and others, "Manifesto of Naples," 1959. Original publication information and English-language publication information unknown.

30.9 Tom Phillips, "The Postcard Vision," 1971, first published by the Arnolfini Gallery in 1971, reprinted with extensive revisions in *Works and Texts*, ed. Huston Paschal (London: Thames and Hudson, 1992), 76–77. © by Tom Phillips, London, England.

30.10 Jacques Roubaud, "Hypothesis of the Compact," (excerpt), 1995, trans. Mary Ann Caws from *Revue de littérature générale*, no. 1 (1995).

31.1 Gertrude Stein, "Composition as Explanation," 1926, first published by
Leonard and Virginia Woolf at the Hogarth Press, London, 1926; reprinted
in *Selected Writings of Gertrude Stein*, ed. Carl Van Vechten (New York:
Vintage, 1990), 513–23. Copyright © 1946 by Random House, Inc. Reprinted
by permission of Random House, Inc. Reprinted by permission of the
Estate of Gertrude Stein.

31.2 Edmond Jabès, "To Be in the Book," 1963, in *Le Livre des questions* (Paris:
Gallimard, 1963); reprinted in Edmond Jabès, *The Book of Questions*, vol. 1,
trans. Rosmarie Waldrop (Middletown CT: Wesleyan University Press,
1976), 31–32. © 1991 by Rosmarie Waldrop, translator, Wesleyan University
Press by permission of University Press of New England.

31.3 Edmond Jabès, "To Enlarge the Horizons of the Word," 1984, in *Le Livre de
Dialogue* (Paris: Gallimard, 1987); reprinted in Edmond Jabès, *The Book of
Dialogue* (Middletown CT: Wesleyan University Press, 1987), 48–50. © 1987
by Rosmarie Waldrop, translator, Wesleyan University Press by permission
of University Press of New England.